ENVIRONMENTAL LAW HANDBOOK

Eighth Edition

J. Gordon Arbuckle, Michael A. Brown, Nancy S. Bryson,
G. William Frick, Ridgway M. Hall, Jr., Jeffrey G. Miller,
Marshall L. Miller, Thomas F.P. Sullivan,
Timothy A. Vanderver, Jr., and Lydia N. Wegman

Government Institutes, Inc.
Rockville, MD
1985

PUBLISHER'S NOTE

This publication is designed to provide accurate and authoritative information with regard to the subject matter covered. It is sold with the understanding that the publisher is not engaged in rendering legal, accounting or other professional service. If legal advice or other expert assistance is required, the services of a competent professional person should be sought. — From a Declaration of Principles jointly adopted by a Committee of the American Bar Association and a Committee of Publishers.

Publication of this book does not signify that the contents necessarily reflect the views and policies of Government Institutes, Inc.

Eighth Edition

June 1985

Published by
Government Institutes, Inc.
966 Hungerford Drive #24
Rockville, Maryland 20850
U.S.A.

PREFACE

A complex body of environmental laws, regulations, and decisions is now established in the United States. Environmental law, which evolved quickly, now ranks with labor, tax, banking, communications, and several other fields as an accepted part of our legal system.

As the environmental law field has matured so have our publishing efforts. We at Government Institutes are extremely proud that our Environmental Law Handbook, the first such comprehensive text in the field and now in its eighth edition, has become a standard reference. As the environmental law field has evolved, so have our publishing activities. Although this Handbook is the "flagship" of our environmental publishing efforts, we also offer a wide range of other environmental books. Inquiries about our books and suggestions for new publications are invited because our job is to satisfy the informational needs of our clients.

I sincerely hope that our efforts help bring about a better understanding of the environmental laws, regulations and decisions. More importantly, we wish to encourage compliance with the spirit of the law, so that public health and the environment are protected, now and for future generations.

> Thomas F. P. Sullivan
> President
> Government Institutes, Inc.

CONTENTS

Chapter 1 ENVIRONMENTAL LAW FUNDAMENTALS AND THE COMMON LAW

CONTENTS

CONTENTS

Chapter 2 RESOURCE CONSERVATION AND RECOVERY ACT

Chapter 3 COMPREHENSIVE ENVIRONMENTAL RESPONSE, COMPENSATION AND LIABILITY ACT (SUPERFUND)

Chapter 4 TOXIC SUBSTANCES

Chapter 5 SAFE DRINKING WATER ACT

Chapter 6 AIR POLLUTION CONTROL

CONTENTS

Chapter 7 WATER POLLUTION CONTROL

Chapter 8 THE OCCUPATIONAL SAFETY AND HEALTH ACT

Chapter 9 NATIONAL ENVIRONMENTAL POLICY ACT

Chapter 10 FEDERAL REGULATION OF PESTICIDES

CONTENTS

Chapter 11 MARINE PROTECTION, RESEARCH AND SANCTUARIES ACT

Chapter 12 NOISE CONTROL

CONTENTS

Chapter 13 LAND USE: MAJOR ISSUES IN THE CONTROL OF INDUSTRIAL DEVELOPMENT

Chapter 14 ENFORCEMENT AND LIABILITIES

ABOUT THE AUTHORS

J. Gordon Arbuckle

Mr. Arbuckle is a member of the Washington law firm, Patton, Boggs, & Blow. His experience includes representing trade associations, and industrial concerns in connection with the Congressional deliberations which led to adoption of the Federal Water Pollution Control Act, the Ports and Waterways Safety Act and other legislation. He has also been involved in administrative proceedings and litigation under the Water Pollution Control Act, the National Environmental Policy Act, RCRA, TSCA, the Clean Air Act and other state and federal environmental statutes.

Michael A. Brown

Mr. Brown is a partner in the Washington, D.C. law firm of Schmeltzer, Aptaker & Sheppard, P.C. and specializes in product safety and environmental issues. He is a magna cum laude graduate of St. Mary's University and has a Masters in Law from Georgetown University Law Center. He has been General Counsel and later Executive Director of the U.S. Consumer Product Safety Commission and Deputy General Counsel and later Enforcement Counsel of the EPA. An author of many articles on environmental law, he is also a lecturer at numerous environmental and product safety conferences and seminars.

Nancy S. Bryson

Mrs. Bryson is an associate with the Washington, D.C. law firm of Crowell & Moring. She was formerly Assistant Chief of the Environmental Defense Section, Land and Natural Resources Division at the U.S. Department of Justice, where she handled environmental litigation for five years. Prior to that she was Assistant Counsel for appellate litigation at OSHA. She graduated summa cum laude and Phi Beta Kappa from Boston University in 1972, and received a law degree from Georgetown in 1975.

G. William Frick

Mr. Frick is a partner in the Kansas City, Missouri office of the law firm, Lathrop, Koontz, Righter, Clagett & Norquist where he specializes in environmental matters. His background includes service in the U.S. Environmental Protection Agency Headquarters as Associate General Counsel for Water Quality, Deputy General Counsel and during 1976-77, he was General Counsel of the U.S. EPA. He received his undergraduate and law degrees from Kansas University.

Ridgway M. Hall, Jr.

Mr. Hall is a partner in the Washington, D.C. law firm of Crowell & Moring. Formerly Associate General Counsel of the U.S. Environmental Protection Agency, he now practices environmental law and litigation. He has authored numerous articles on environmental law and is a prominent speaker at seminars and symposia on environmental law and regulatory programs. A magna cum laude graduate of Yale University, Mr. Hall received his law degree from Harvard Law School.

Jeffrey G. Miller

Mr. Miller is a partner in the Washington, D.C. law firm of Bergson, Borkland, Margolis & Adler. He was an enforcement and permitting official in the U.S. Environmental Protection Agency for ten years and ended his government career as head of EPA's enforcement program. He practices before federal and state courts and administrative agencies on a variety of pollution control matters. Mr. Miller is the author of numerous articles and a frequent speaker on environmental issues. He is a graduate of Princeton University and Harvard Law School.

Marshall Lee Miller

Mr. Miller, a partner in the Washington, D.C. office of the law firm of Reid & Priest, is the former Deputy Administrator of the U.S. Occupational Safety and Health Administration, Department of Labor. His experience includes service as the Special Assistant to the first Administrator of the U.S. Environmental Protection Agency, Chief EPA Judicial Officer and Associate Deputy Attorney General in the U.S. Department of Justice. He has been educated at Harvard, Oxford, Heidelberg, and Yale.

ABOUT THE AUTHORS

Thomas F. P. Sullivan

Mr. Sullivan has undergraduate degrees from Kenrick Seminary and St. Louis University, and his law degree from Catholic University. He is an attorney in Washington, D.C., who has been in the forefront of the environmental field since the 1960's. Mr. Sullivan has served as editor and author of many books plus being a regular contributing author for "Pollution Engineering" magazine. His lecture credits include numerous environmental engineering conferences and seminars. He also serves as president of Government Institutes, Inc.

Timothy A. Vanderver, Jr.

Mr. Vanderver is a partner in the Washington, D.C. law firm of Patton, Boggs & Blow, and specializes in environmental issues. He is a graduate of Washington & Lee University and Harvard Law School. Mr. Vanderver was awarded the coveted Rhodes Scholarship and as a result achieved his graduate degree in law from Oxford University in England. He has practiced law with the Department of the Interior and the Department of Housing & Urban Development where he specialized in natural resources and land development law.

Lydia N. Wegman

Ms. Wegman is an associate with the firm of Swidler, Berlin & Strelow. In 1977 she joined the Office of the General Counsel of the U.S. Environmental Protection Agency as a staff attorney in the Air, Noise and Radiation Division. She was Acting Assistant General Counsel in that Division from 1981 to 1982. Ms. Wegman worked on a variety of Clean Air Act issues and proposals to amend the Clean Air Act. She has been educated at Wellesley College and Yale College, and attended the Cooperstown Graduate Program and Columbia Law School from which she received her J.D. and was a Harlan Fiske Stone Scholar.

Chapter 1

ENVIRONMENTAL LAW FUNDAMENTALS
AND THE COMMON LAW

Thomas F. P. Sullivan
Attorney & President
Government Institutes, Inc.
Rockville, Maryland

1.0 Objective of this Book

The objective of this book is to satisfy the need for comprehensive and authoritative information on the major environmental
laws and regulations. It is written for those concerned with protecting public health and the environment.

The attainment of this objective is a very difficult and challenging task, because our reading audience includes a broad
spectrum of educational backgrounds and years of experience. Some
readers will have little exposure to environmental law, while others
will be experienced practitioners of the law. This first chapter is
designed primarily for readers without legal training; however,
lawyers may find it to be an interesting review. This chapter will
provide the major fundamentals underlying and complementing the
environmental laws and regulations and some basics about the common law.

2.0 Lawyers and Laymen

Attorneys are professionally trained to provide advice on
"legal matters." However, some knowledge of environmental laws
and regulations is necessary for those non-lawyers who control the
operations and installations that are involved in environmental and
health protection.

1

A basic understanding of fundamental legal principles is also beneficial to environmental managers when the need arises to work with legal counsel. Non-lawyers who have environmental responsibilities should know something about environmental law to better enable them to understand an environmental attorney's advice regarding prevention of problems. The basic information in this book can help a non-lawyer to know when to seek counsel's advice and to even evaluate counsel's performance.

Violations of the law or the rights of others can mean loss of time and money, personal embarrassment and possible disruption of an on-going business. The information provided in this book will, we hope, help to avoid violations, expedite compliance and save the reader time and money.

This book is not intended to be another erudite tome but a useful text that will help those with responsibilities for environmental protection to comply with both the letter and the spirit of the law.

The reader should always be aware of the old axiom that a "little knowledge is dangerous." So, be careful with the knowledge you gain from reading this and other materials.

This chapter will present the fundamentals of environmental law. From these fundamentals can be derived many legal generalities. Generalities are difficult to sustain because the factual situation determines the actual application and, therefore, the results. It should always be remembered that exceptions are born of generalities. When generalities are applied to specific factual situations, the advice of competent counsel should be obtained. Also, the reader should be alert to the fact that this field is extremely dynamic. What is the "law" today changes with time as new laws and regulations are promulgated. In addition, the courts are regularly re-interpreting the application of the laws, regulations and legal principles in their decisions.

The majority of those who will read this book are not lawyers but have their training in the sciences or engineering. These readers should remember that scientists and lawyers deal with different kinds of laws. The laws of nature which the scientist tries to discover are inviolable. The law of gravitation, for example, or Newton's three laws of motion, cannot be disobeyed.

Human laws do not share this characteristic. The moral obligation imposed by man-made laws results precisely from the fact that it is possible to break them.

3.0 What Is Environmental Law?

Environmental law encompasses all the protections for our environment that emanate from the: (1) United States Constitution, (2) state constitutions, (3) federal and state statutes and local ordinances, (4) regulations promulgated by federal, state and local regulatory agencies, (5) court decisions interpreting these laws and regulations and, (6) the common law. This chapter covers (1), (5) and (6) namely, environmental protection derived from the Constitution, the common law and court decisions. In subsequent chapters, we will cover the areas that have been pre-empted by legislation and regulation.

4.0 Environmental Law and the Courts

In order to gain the proper understanding of court decisions, a basic knowledge of the United States court system is needed. As the courts interpret the environmental laws and regulations and apply them to specific factual situations, they are continually determining what the law means in actual cases.

The authority of the U.S. courts is limited to those powers (1) enumerated in Article III of the U.S. Constitution, and (2) not designated in the Constitution as responsibilities of the legislative or executive branches of the federal government.

4.1 States and United States Court Systems

Throughout the United States there are two sets of judicial systems: (1) the state and local courts, established in each state under the authority of the state government, and (2) U.S. courts, set up under the authority of the Constitution by the Congress of the United States.

The state courts have general, unlimited power to decide almost every type of case, subject only to the limitations of state law. State and local courts are located in every town and county and are the tribunals with which citizens most often have contact. The great bulk of legal business such as divorce, probate of estates, traffic accidents and all other matters except those assigned to the U.S. courts is handled by these state and local courts.

The U.S. courts, on the other hand, have the authority to hear and decide only selected types of cases which are specifically enumerated in the Constitution. The U.S. courts are located principally in the larger cities while state and local courts are found throughout the country.

4.2 Cases Which the United States Courts Can Decide

The controversies which can be decided in the U.S. courts are set forth in Section 2 of Article III of the United States Constitution.

These are first "Controversies to which the United States shall be a party." That is, cases in which the U.S. government itself or one of its officers is either suing someone else or is being sued by another party. Obviously, it would be inappropriate for the U.S. government to depend upon the state governments to provide courts in which to decide controversies to which it is a party.

Secondly, the U.S. courts have power to decide cases when state courts are inappropriate or might be suspected of partiality. Thus, federal judicial power extends "to Controversies between two or more States; between a State and Citizens of another State; between Citizens of different States; between Citizens of the same State claiming Lands under Grants of different States . . . " If the State of Missouri sues the State of Illinois for pollution of the Mississippi River, a U.S. court would be a more impartial forum than the courts of either Missouri or Illinois. Foreseeing the possibility of interstate rivalry, the drafters of the Constitution sought to avoid any suspicion of favoritism by vesting power to decide these controversies in the U.S. courts.

State courts are also inappropriate in "Cases affecting Ambassadors, other public Ministers and Consuls" and in cases "between a State, or the Citizens thereof, and foreign States, Citizens, or Subjects." The United States government has responsibility for diplomatic relations with other nations. Since cases involving representatives or citizens of other countries may affect our foreign relations, such cases are decided in the U.S. courts.

And, thirdly, the Constitution provides that the judicial power extends "to all Cases, in Law and Equity, arising under this Constitution, the Laws of the United States, and Treaties made, or which shall be made, under their Authority" and "to all Cases of admiralty and maritime jurisdiction." Under these provisions, the U.S. courts decide cases involving the Constitution, laws enacted by Congress, treaties, and laws relating to navigable waters. For example, in cases brought under provisions of the Clean Air Act, Clean Water Act, or other federal statutes generally the appropriate forum is the U.S. court system.

The Constitution declares what cases may be decided in the U.S. courts. The Congress can and has determined that some of these cases may also be tried in state courts and that others may only be tried in U.S. courts. Specifically, Congress has provided that, with some exceptions, cases arising under the Constitution or laws of the United States or between citizens of different states may be tried in the U.S. courts only if the amount involved exceeds $10,000 and even then may be tried in either the state or the U.S. courts. The Congress has also provided that maritime cases and suits against consuls can be tried only in the U.S. courts. When a state court decides a case involving federal law, it in a sense acts as a U.S. court, and its decision on federal law may be reviewed by the United States Supreme Court.

It should be clear from this discussion that the U.S. courts cannot decide every case which arises, but only those which the Constitution and the laws enacted by Congress allot to them.

The question of which court has jurisdiction can be a complex issue. Also, the selection of the specific court in which a case is initiated is generally a key move in the overall strategy for winning a lawsuit. The selection of the specific court as a legal strategy is called "forum shopping." When bringing a case a good lawyer will evaluate which court is more inclined toward his client's position. For example the judges of the U.S. courts in the District of Columbia are known for their pro-environmentalist record. So organizations such as the Environmental Defense Fund (EDF) and Sierra Club are inclined to initiate their lawsuits in the U.S. district courts for the District of Columbia. Industrial firms are generally more inclined to file a lawsuit in a district court in Louisiana or other such geographic area with a more conservative judicial record.

4.3 United States Court System

The structure of the U.S. court system has evolved throughout the historical development of our country. The Constitution merely provides: "The Judicial Power of the United States, shall be vested in one Supreme Court, and in such inferior Courts as the Congress may from time to time ordain and establish." Thus, the only court which is constitutionally indispensable is the Supreme Court. The authority to establish and abolish other U.S. courts is vested in and has been exercised by the Congress.

At the present time, the United States court system is pyramidal in structure. At the apex of the pyramid stands the Supreme Court of the United States, the highest court in the land. On the next level are the United States courts of appeals, 11 in all. On the next level down are the United States district courts, 94 in all,

including the United States district courts for the District of
Columbia and Puerto Rico and the district courts in the Canal Zone,
Guam, and the Virgin Islands.

A person involved in a suit in a U.S. court may proceed
through three levels of decision. His case will first be heard and
decided by one of the courts or agencies on the lower level. If
either party is dissatisfied with the decision, he may usually have a
right of review in one of the courts of appeals. Then, if he is still
dissatisfied, he may petition for review in the Supreme Court of the
United States. However, review is granted by the Supreme Court
only in cases involving matters of great national importance.

This pyramidal organization of the courts serves two purposes. First, the Supreme Court and the courts of appeals can correct errors which have been made in the decisions of the trial
courts. Secondly, the higher courts can assure uniformity of decision by reviewing cases in which two or more lower courts have
reached different decisions.

State courts have a similar pyramid structure with a basic court of original jurisdiction, an appellate court and then a supreme court, but often states do not call their highest court a supreme court. So, at the state level the nomenclature can be confusing.

4.4 Courts in Practical Perspective

From a practical viewpoint, when you hear of a judicial decision of interest to you, ask which court decided the case. If the Supreme Court of the U.S. decided the case, it is a very important decision for the entire country. If a local court decided the case, it is generally of little interest nationally but of major interest to that local jurisdiction. However, any decision on a point of law is better than none at all.

Also, be aware that courts do differ in their opinions. There are many examples of two lower courts reaching conflicting opinions on a point of law. This is an extremely difficult concept for many to accept. If you are originally trained in engineering or the sciences, you are probably accustomed to dealing in data and facts. To move into the realm of "ifs" and "yes, but" seems to be like going from the "world of black and white" into a "world of gray." For those who find this troubling, remember that in almost everything, we are talking about degrees of certitude. The field of environmental law may involve a higher degree of uncertitude than most other areas because of its newness and changeability. As a result, you do your best to understand what is the meaning of the laws, regulations and court opinions, and you then take into consideration the degree of certitude involved in a particular legal issue before proceeding to a decision.

Also, keep in mind that our court system, although hailed as one of the fairest systems ever developed by mankind, is subject to human frailties. The judges, lawyers, plaintiffs, defendants and jurors all involve human interactions, another source of uncertainties.

5.0 Common Law

Underlying the development of legal theory in the United States is a body of rules and principles relating to the government and security of persons and property which had its origin, development and formulation in England. Brought to the American colonies by peoples of Anglo-Saxon stock, these basic rules were formally adopted in the states in which they were in force after the American Revolution. Known as the "common law," these principles are derived from the application of natural reason, an innate sense of justice, and the dictates of conscience. The common law is not the result of legislative enactment. Rather, its authority is derived solely from usages and customs which have been recognized, affirmed and enforced by the courts through judicial decisions.

It is important to realize that the "common law" is not a fixed or absolute set of written rules in the same sense as statutory or legislatively enacted law. The unwritten principles of common law are flexible and adaptable to the changes which occur in a growing society. New institutions and public policies; modifications of usage and practice; changes in mores, trade, and commerce; inventions; and increasing knowledge, all generate new factual situations which require application and reinterpretation of the fundamental principles of common law by the courts.

As the courts examine each new set of facts in the light of past precedent, an orderly development of common laws occurs through a slow and natural process. Thus, the basic principles underlying American jurisprudence remain fundamentally constant, evolving slowly and progressively in scope as they absorb the surface ripples produced by the winds of social change.

The common law, so far as it has not been expressly abrogated, is recognized as an organic part of the jurisprudence of most of the states. The major exception is Louisiana jurisprudence, which is based on Roman law—a relic of French rule prior to the Louisiana Purchase. However, since the state court systems have functioned independently of each other, subject only to federal review in cases of national importance, the common law varies slightly from state to state.

There is also a federal common law which forms the basis for deciding cases in which a uniform standard is desirable for dealing with such claims as alleged federal rights. 1/

The common law actions that we will discuss in subsequent sections are civil suits in which the plaintiff (the party bringing the lawsuit) seeks to remedy violation of a private right. Civil actions are distinguished from criminal proceedings in which the state seeks to redress a breach of public or collective rights which are established in codified penal law.

1/   Illinois v. Milwaukee, 406 U.S. 91(1972), and a second opinion, U.S. Supreme Court 79-408, 28 April 1981.

Sections 7.1, 7.2 and 7.3 of this chapter review the three most frequently used types of common law actions that can be the basis of a lawsuit in the pollution control field: nuisance, trespass, and negligence. After these three actions are described, collateral matters are covered which should be of concern to industry and government officials responsible for operating facilities that have the potential of causing injury to human health or our environment.

6.0 Case Law

Because there is no unified codification of common law, we must look to the court records of actual judicial decisions to determine the application of common law rules and principles to a given set of facts.

To discover how the laws governing environmental controls are applied in a specific factual situation, it is necessary to analyze cases which arose from similar circumstances.

Since each case or factual situation is unique, the decisions reached in prior cases involving similar circumstances are valuable as precedents for points of law. A judicial opinion represents a synthesis of many factors such as: a careful examination of the facts, the weight of relevant precedent, the strength of the legal principles involved, the balance of equities in the case, and more.

Case law, then, is the aggregate of points of law derived from reported cases which forms the body of law established through judicial decisions. It is separate and distinct from statutory law, which is promulgated by legislative bodies.

6.1 Obiter Dicta

Obiter dicta is a Latin phrase used in the legal profession to refer to extraneous comments in a court's opinion. All that a court says is not law. A judicial opinion is, like evidence, only binding insofar as it is relevant. When a court's opinion touches upon points not at issue, the extraneous statements are not binding court opinions or precedents.

The obiter dicta in a court's opinion are not a compelling precedent. However, if the judge giving the decision is highly regarded as a legal scholar, his opinion—whether obiter dicta or not —may have some impact on succeeding cases.

7.0 Torts

In modern legal terminology, "tort" is the word used to denote a private wrong or wrongful act for which a civil action can be brought by the injured party. Thus, a tort is clearly distinguished from a criminal act which is an offense against statutorily established public rights and is prosecuted by the state in behalf of the citizenry.

A tort arises from the existence of a generalized legal duty to avoid causing harm to others, through acts of omission, as well as of commission. By virtue of citizenship, every adult person is obliged to fulfill a duty of care for the personal and property rights of others while engaged in daily life. Carelessness in exercising this responsibility may give rise to a cause of action (a lawsuit) by means of which the injured party may seek restitution. This duty is non-contractual; that is, it does not arise from an explicit promissory agreement between the parties to the action. So a tort is also distinguished from a contract right which is dependent upon the contract itself.

Tens of thousands of tort lawsuits have been filed against the major asbestos manufacturers resulting in Johns Manville and several other large corporations filing for bankruptcy. These asbestos cases and other toxic chemical litigation have prompted some writers to allege that the 1980s will be the era of "toxic torts." It is clear that tort law will be of considerable interest to industry in the 1980s as its role expands.

Torts are divided into two general classes: (1) property torts which involve injury or damage to property and (2) personal torts which involve injuries to a person, whether to the body, reputation or feelings.

The three types of torts encountered in the environmental field are: (1) nuisance, (2) trespass, and (3) negligence.

7.1 Nuisance

The most common tort action in the field of environmental law is nuisance. Nuisance is defined as "the class of wrongs that arise from the unreasonable, unwarrantable or unlawful use by a person of his own property either real or personal, or from his own lawful personal conduct working an obstruction of or injury to the right of another or of the public and producing material annoyance, inconvenience, discomfort or hurt." 2/

2/   Black, Law Dictionary (Revised 4th ed. 1968) 1214.

The general rule is that a person may use his land or personal property in any manner he sees fit. However, this rule is subject to limitation: the owner must use his property in a reasonable manner. A nuisance arises whenever a person uses his property to cause material injury or annoyance to his neighbor.

In determining whether a given act constitutes a nuisance, the court considers the nature of the act itself, and the place and the circumstance surrounding the act. To be actionable, the injury or discomfort must amount to a material injury or annoyance. It must tangibly affect the physical comfort of ordinary people under normal circumstances or conditions.

7.1.1 Private or Public Nuisances

Nuisances may be private or public. A private nuisance may be abated by an injunction brought by the individual whose property or health is affected. A public nuisance is one which affects an indefinite number of persons in a community. A public official normally abates a public nuisance.

In the United States today, public nuisances are primarily defined by statute and ordinance. Regulation at the local level has resulted in a great variety of specific provisions; for example, local ordinances generally prohibit making loud noises in the immediate vicinity of a hospital. Nearly all states have adopted broad criminal statutes covering public nuisances without attempting to define the specific acts which are covered by them. These have come to be construed as including anything that would have been a public nuisance at common law.

The distinction between public and private nuisance rests on a determination of whether the nuisance affects the rights of the public or the rights of an individual exclusively. The pollution of a stream which inconveniences one or two persons is considered a private nuisance, and the mere number of persons affected will not make it a public nuisance. 3/ But when the pollution kills the fish in a body of water used by the public, an interference with a public right occurs, and the action becomes a public nuisance. 4/

It is generally held that an individual acting privately cannot initiate a legal action for a purely public nuisance, unless his damage

---

3/   Smith v. City of Sedalia, 152 Mo. 283, 53 S.W. 907 (1800).

4/   State ex rel. Wear v. Springfield Gas and Electric Co., 204 S.W. 942 (Mo. App. 1918).

is in some way distinguished from that sustained by other members of the general public. The modern trend, however, is to eliminate this distinction between private and public nuisance and to allow private individuals to initiate legal actions whether the nuisance is private or public. 5/

A public nuisance is generally a crime. It may also be a tort or private nuisance, if a plaintiff can prove that he has suffered some "special" or "particular" damage. The damage must be of a kind that is individual to the plaintiff as distinguished from that which he shares with the rest of the public.

In an Arkansas case, 6/ nine homeowners in the vicinity of a rendering plant brought suit to abate the odor nuisance created by operation of the plant. They claimed that odors from the rendering plant caused them to feel nausea and to lose sleep at night. On the witness stand, the plant manager admitted that operation of the plant violated existing law. The court found the plant to be a public nuisance, and the homeowners obtained a court order to close the plant unless conditions causing the nuisance were corrected within a time limit established by the court.

On appeal, the plant owner argued that the homeowners were not entitled to abatement of a public nuisance because they failed to show that they incurred damages beyond those sustained by the general public. The appeals court found that although the plant was found to be a public nuisance, this did not preclude it from also being a private nuisance with respect to the homeowners who brought suit. So the plant was declared a private nuisance by the appellate judge.

Some states have statutes which allow private individuals to sue in an attempt to abate a public nuisance.

7.1.2 Noise Nuisance

The most common form of environmental nuisance is noise pollution. Noise produced by human activities is a common environmental problem. In order to constitute a nuisance in the legal sense,

---

5/   Prosser, Private Action for Public Nuisance, 52 Va.L. Rev. 997 (1966).

6/   Ozark Poultry Products, Inc. v. Garmon, 251 Ark. 389, 472 S.W. 2d 714(1971).

generally, noise must be of such magnitude and intensity as to cause actual or psychological discomfort to persons of ordinary sensibilities. Noise from the operation of an industrial plant constitutes an actionable nuisance if it affects injuriously the health or comfort of ordinary people in the plant's vicinity to an unreasonable extent. Neither the courts nor legislatures 7/ have been able to set an absolute standard, so this determination rests on the facts.

O'Neil v. Carolina Freight Carriers Corporation 8/ is an example of a "noise nuisance" case in which a homeowner was awarded both an injunction and damages against the operators of a nearby business. In this case, the plaintiffs showed that they were ordinary people and that the noise from trucks and loading operations at a terminal located immediately adjacent to their home was unreasonable. It caused them loss of sleep and prevented general enjoyment of their home. The court ruled that the truck terminal noises between 11:00 p.m. and 6:00 a.m. were unreasonable and that every property owner must make reasonable use of his land so as not to cause unnecessary annoyance to his neighbors.

An example of noise conditions not held to be a nuisance is the case of Tortorella v. H. Traiser and Company. 9/ In the Tortorella case, the plaintiff owned a home about 80 feet from the defendant's cigar factory. The factory noise, between normal working hours of 7:30 a.m. to 4:30 p.m., five days a week, was shown to be annoying to the plaintiff. However, since there was no proof that the plaintiff had suffered materially in comfort or health as a result of the noise, the court found no nuisance.

In the Tortorella case, the court applied a strict interpretation of the law of nuisance, because the plaintiff's request for an injunction against continued operation of the plant entailed a negative impact on local employment and economic conditions.

In the O'Neil case, the facts lead more readily to a conclusion of injury to health because the noise during the night could logically cause loss of sleep and resulting injury to health.

7/   S. Dak. Comp. Law Ann. § 21-10-9; Wis. State § 280.02; Fla. Stat. § 60.05.

8/   156 Conn. 613, 244 A2d 372 (1968).

9/   284 Mass. 497, 188 N.E. 254 (1933).

There is no fixed standard as to what degree or kind of noise constitutes a nuisance. The circumstances of each case must be considered independently, the key determination being whether or not the noise is unreasonable and causes some physical or psychological harm. This determination varies from one community to another and from one period of time to another depending on local attitudes and customs.

7.1.3 Other Nuisances

Smoke, dust, odors, other airborne pollutants, water pollutants and hazardous substances have also been held to be nuisances.

The Ozark Poultry Products case, previously cited (footnote 6), is an example of an odor being classed as a nuisance.

In a New York case, McCarty v. Natural Carbonic Gas Company, 10/ the plaintiffs owned a home adjacent to the defendant's manufacturing plant. The plaintiffs claimed that under specific wind conditions, black smoke settled about their home causing them discomfort, annoyance and injury. The court determined that the operation of the manufacturing plant resulted in an unreasonable use of the property, because all the damage could be avoided by the use of hard coal or by use of some modern emission control systems. Although either would involve an increase in expenses, the court held that the safety of persons, generally, is superior in right to a particular use of a single piece of property by its owner. So the court awarded the decision to the plaintiffs.

It should be noted that air pollutants only constitute a nuisance under certain circumstances. Normal air is usually considered as that common to a locality and so varies from one area to another. To be a nuisance, the air pollution must cause harm and discomfort to ordinary people to an unreasonable extent.

In the case of Chicago v. Commonwealth Edison 11/ the court refused to issue an injunction against alleged air pollution. The court found that although the public had a right to clean air, the notion of pure air has come to mean clean air consistent with the character of the locality and the attending circumstances. The court ruled that "The City has failed to answer the threshold ques-

---

10/   189 N.Y. 40, 81 N.E. 549(1970).

11/   7 ERC 1480 (Ill. App. Ct. 1974).

tion of whether Commonwealth Edison's Indiana facility causes substantial harm so as to constitute an actionable invasion of a public right. In order to be entitled to injunctive relief a substantial harm or injury must be clearly demonstrated." This case is a strict interpretation of the law of nuisance because it was a request for an injunction to cease operation which would have a broad impact on employment and local economics. If the action had been for damages, the court may have decided it differently by not using a strict interpretation of the law.

In a 1973 case, Harrison v. Indiana Auto Shredders, 12/ the Seventh Circuit Court of Appeals also refused to permanently enjoin operation of an automobile shredding and recycling plant based on a nuisance action. The court held that under the evidence presented and in the absence of an imminent hazard to health or welfare—none of which was established—the defendant could not be prevented from continuing to engage in its operation. In addition, the court believed that the operation should be allowed a reasonable time to correct any defects not posing threats of imminent or substantial harm.

In essence, the courts were not convinced by the evidence presented in these last two cases that the harm caused by the alleged nuisance was so great as to justify forcing them to cease operation. If these facilities were shut down, many families would be injured by the forced unemployment. So the weighing of the equities by the court resulted in a determination based on all the evidence presented in favor of allowing continued operations. This is generally called "balancing the equities."

An unusual type of nuisance case of considerable notoriety and interest involved the construction of the 110-story Sears building in Chicago. 13/ In this case, the plaintiffs requested an injunction to prevent completion of the building which they claimed would constitute a nuisance by distorting television reception in surrounding areas. The court held that Sears had a legal right to use the airspace above its property, at least as much as it can occupy or use in connection with the land, subject only to legislative limitation. One

---

12/ 8 ERC 1569 (7th Cir. 1975).

13/ People ex rel Hoogasian v. Sears, Roebuck and Co., 52 Ill. 2d 301, 287 N.E. 2d 677 (1972).

can readily see the adverse consequences that such a theory could pose for solar energy.

The Earthline Corporation, a subsidiary of SCA Services, Inc., attempted to operate an industrial waste recovery, treatment, storage and disposal site on a 130-acre site in Illinois. Ninety acres are located within the Village of Wilsonville and the remaining acres adjacent to the village. The operation accepted hazardous wastes and toxic substances. The Village sued Earthline to stop the operation and also to require the removal of those hazardous wastes and toxic substances that had been deposited on the site. 14/ The court ruled that the site was a public/private nuisance, issued an injunction against Earthline's further operation of the site and required them to remove all wastes and contaminated soil.

It is most important to note that this case was decided against SCA even though there was no showing that SCA had violated any government regulation. Compliance with government regulations is not a defense against a common law nuisance action. Also, the lower court decision emphasized the distinction between a nuisance and negligence action:

> Nuisance and negligence are distinct torts and except in the cases of nuisances created by negligence, liability for nuisance does not depend upon the existence of negligence. Negligence is not an essential or material element of a cause of action for nuisance and need not be pleaded or proved especially where the thing complained of is a nuisance per se or a public nuisance or results from ultra-hazardous conduct on the part of the defendant. A nuisance is a condition and not an act or a failure to act on the part of the person responsible for the condition.

7.1.4 Some Defenses to Nuisance Actions

Nuisance actions have often come down to a question of balancing the equities (weighing the impact of the injuries to the respective parties involved in the litigation). In any balancing of the equities, the good faith efforts of the polluter, while not absolving him, would certainly be a factor if they exist. 15/

14/   Village of Wilsonville v. SCA Services, Inc., 7 Ill. App. 3d 618, 396 N.E. 2d 522 (1979), aff'd 86 Ill. 2d1, 42 N.E. 2d 824 (1981).

15/   McElwain v. Georgia Pacific, 245 Ore. 247, 421 P. 2d 957.

The availability of pollution control devices is, of course, a significant factor that can be considered by the court. For example, in Renkin v. Harvey Aluminum, 16/ the court noted Harvey Aluminum's failure to keep pace with the technological advances in pollution controls. In that case the court ordered adoption of such controls.

One of the reasons why nuisance actions have been of limited value for private relief is that if the nuisance affects the broad general public, it is considered a public nuisance. Theoretically only the proper public official can bring the action on behalf of the "public interest." The plaintiff cannot get damages unless he can show a special kind (not degree) of injury different from that of the general public. In recent cases, such as the previously cited Ozark Poultry Products case, the distinction between public and private nuisance is being altered so that this distinction will probably be eliminated for practical purposes in the future. (See 7.1.1.)

In general, the courts are moving to strict liability for environmental nuisances so that practically speaking, there are no good defenses. The solution is: do not create nuisances.

7.1.5 Coming to a Nuisance

"Coming to a nuisance" is the phrase used to describe a defense that the complainant or plaintiff affected by the nuisance moved into the area where the "complained about activity" had already been in existence.

An example of "coming to a nuisance" occurs when someone moves onto the property next to an airport or near an industrial complex and then complains of the nuisance that existed prior to his moving there. Generally, the fact that an individual purchases property with the knowledge of the existence of a nuisance or that he came to the nuisance will not defeat his right to the abatement of the nuisance or recovery of damages. 17/

However, some cases have held that if the complainant came to a nuisance, this constitutes a defense to a nuisance lawsuit. This

---

16/   226 F. Supp. 169 (D. Ore. 1963).

17/   Fertilizing Co. v. Hyde Park, 97 U.S. 659; Rentz v. Roach, 154 Ga. 491; Vann v. Bowie, 127 Tex. 97 are a few cases.

minority view is probably a result of an old axiom of law that one who voluntarily places himself in a situation whereby he suffers an injury will not prevail. The test of liability in these cases is often the knowledge of the plaintiff regarding the consequences of his conduct.

The majority rule, however, is that the fact alone that a person moved into the vicinity of a nuisance by purchasing or leasing property in the area does not bar him from complaining in an action against the continued operation or maintenance of the nuisance. 18/ The majority rule is based on the theory that pure air and the comfortable enjoyment of property are as much rights belonging to it as the right of possession and occupancy. If population where there was none before approaches a nuisance, it is the duty of those liable to put an end to it.

7.2 Trespass

In a general sense, an invasion of another's rights is a trespass. Usually, trespass is used in a more limited sense. It is to be understood as designating an injury to the person, property, or rights of another which is the immediate result of some unlawful act.

In order to constitute trespass, unlawful intent is not necessary. Intent or motive with which the act was done is immaterial except as far as it may affect the measure of damages. A person is liable even if he acted in good faith and with reasonable care.

Trespass is commonly divided into three types. These are:

(1) **Trespass to personal property** is an injury to or interference with possession, with or without the exercise of physical force. This includes destruction of personal property as well as the taking from the possession of another, or a refusal to surrender possession.

(2) **Trespass to the person** is an unlawful act committed on the person of another such as a vehicle impact or even an unauthorized operation. Mere words are not actionable trespass to the person.

18/ A comprehensive article on this subject is found in 42 ALR 3d starting at page 344. This article includes a listing of cases by jurisdictions that recognize the majority rule.

(3) **Trespass to realty** is an unlawful, forcible entry on another's possession. An injury to the realty of another or an interference with his possession, above or below ground, is a trespass, regardless of the condition of the land and regardless of negligence.

Trespass to realty is the type of trespass action that is generally used in pollution control cases. In an action for trespass to realty, entry upon another's land need not be in person. It may be made by causing or permitting a thing to cross the boundary of the premises. The trespass may be committed by casting material upon another's land, by discharging water, soot or carbon, by allowing gas or oil to flow underground into someone else's land, but not by mere vibrations or light which are generally classed as nuisances.

In the case of <u>Martin v. Reynolds Metal Company,</u> 19/ the deposit on Martin's property of microscopic fluoride compounds, which were emitted in vapor form from the Reynolds' plant, was held to be an invasion of this property—and so a trespass.

Cases have distinguished between trespass and nuisance and held that encroachment of the space above the land is a nuisance. Generally there must be physical invasion of the property to constitute a trespass.

Some courts have used trespass and private nuisance almost interchangeably. The end result is that the distinction between trespass and nuisance is somewhat clouded.

Negligence and trespass have also been used interchangeably as seen in the case of <u>Stacy v. VEPCO.</u> 20/ In this case, the court ruled that there was "negligence and/or trespass on the part of VEPCO" because of damage caused to Stacy's trees by the emissions from VEPCO's Mount Storm plant. It is interesting to note that the court in this case was convinced by the expert meteorologist's testimony that the emissions could travel the 22-mile distance from the plant to damage the trees. The important point to remember is that courts can and do minimize the concern with the form of the action but endeavor to do substantive justice based on all the evidence presented.

19/   221 Ore. 86, 342 P. 2d 790(1959), cert. denied, 362 U.S. 918 (1960).

20/   7 ERC 1443 (D.C. EVa. 1975).

7.3 Negligence

Negligence is: (a) doing or omitting to do an act, (b) which a person owes to another by virtue of a legal duty imposed upon him by law, (c) thereby causing injury to the plaintiff or to his property. Negligence is that part of the law of torts which deals with acts not intended to inflict injury. If there is intent to inflict injury, then the case becomes one of criminal law. The standard of care required by law is that degree which would be exercised by a person of ordinary prudence under the same circumstances. This is often defined as the "reasonable man" rule, namely what a reasonable person would do under all the circumstances.

In order to render the defendant liable, his act must be the proximate cause of the injury. Proximate cause is that which in the natural and continuous sequence, if unbroken by an efficient inter-vening act, produces injury and without which the result would not have happened.

An example of a negligence action in a pollution case is Burgess v. Tamano. 21/ This case involved the July 1972 spill of more than 100,000 gallons of bunker oil from the tank ship Tamano into Maine's Casco Bay. Fishermen, boat owners, and property owners allegedly damaged by the spill brought suit against the Tamano, while Maine filed suit to recover damages sustained by the state as a result of the spill. Since the federal government has a great deal of money with which to pay damages, plaintiffs contended that the proximate cause of the escape and spread of oil from the Tamano was the Coast Guard's negligent conduct of its containment and cleanup operations. The court ruled that the United States, in undertaking any task such as buoyage or pollution abatement, is liable in tort for the consequences of its negligence to the same extent that a private person would be liable.

The evidence convinced the court that the Coast Guard caused injury, which could be foreseen, by its inadequate contain-ment and cleanup operation. Since this conduct was the proximate cause of injury to the plaintiff, the court held that the Coast Guard was guilty of negligence.

Persons harmed as a result of careless and improper disposal or handling of hazardous waste can recover for their losses under a

---

21/   5 ERC 1914 (D.C. Me. 1973) and 6 ERC 1380 (D.C. Me. 1974).

negligence cause of action. Indeed, state and federal courts have long recognized this common law theory of recovery against defendants who engage in the negligent disposal of pollutants such as hazardous waste. 22/ Where negligence can be established, it is no defense that the negligent action was in full compliance with all government regulations 23/ and permit conditions. 24/ On the other hand, noncompliance with regulations or a permit in some states may be prima facie evidence (that is, proof without any more evidence) of liability. 25/

7.3.1 Res Ipsa Loquitur

As a general rule, the mere fact that an accident occurs does not give rise to a presumption of negligence. Negligence must be proved by a preponderance of the evidence. The doctrine of res ipsa loquitur does not relieve the plaintiff of proving negligence but it does rearrange the method of establishing proof. Res ipsa loquitur means that the party claiming injury has produced sufficient facts to warrant an inference of negligence.

In order to rely on res ipsa loquitur, the plaintiff must show that the instrumentality which caused the injury was, to some extent, under the exclusive control of the defendant, and the injury was such that, in the ordinary course of things, it would not have occurred, if the one having control had used proper care.

The following is a hypothetical example of res ipsa loquitur:

Smith is a passenger in the airplane of TransAm Company, a common carrier. In good flying weather,

---

22/ See, e.g., Knabe v. National Supply Division of Armco Steel Corp., 592 F.2d 841 (5th Cir. 1979).

23/ Greater Westchester Homeowners Association v. City of Los Angeles, 26 Cal. 3d 86, 160 Cal. Rptr. 733, 603 P.2d 1329 (1978), cert. denied, 449 U.S. 820 (1980).

24/ Brown v. Petrolane, Inc., 102 Cal. App. 3d 720, 162 Cal. Rptr. 551 (1980); Belton v. Wateree Power Corp., 123 S.C. 291, 115 S.E. 587 (1922).

25/ See Martin v. Herzog, 126 N.E. 814 (N.Y. 1920).

the plane disappears, and no trace of it is ever found. There is no evidence. Various explanations are possible, including mechanical failure which could not have been prevented by reasonable care, or bombs planted on the plane. In this case, however, it may be inferred by the jury that the most probable explanation for Smith's death is negligence on the part of TransAm Company under res ipsa loquitur because airplanes do not normally disappear and a logical explanation would be mechanical failure. 26/

In negligence cases involving pollution, it is generally difficult to link the activities of an alleged polluter with plaintiff's claimed injury from the pollution. Res ipsa loquitur helps to eliminate this difficulty. The case of California Department of Fish and Game v. SS Bournemouth 27/ presented such a case for use of res ipsa. Officers of the California Fish and Game Department took oil samples from an oil slick in a harbor and from the SS Bournemouth. The court found a scientific probability that the two samples came from the same source. The court also found, on the basis of evidence as to wind, current, and tide, that the slick could have come from the ship. There was no other ship in the general area at the relevant time. Then, the court applied the doctrine of res ipsa; the oil spill probably could not have occurred unless someone was negligent; no other source of the spill was indicated; the plaintiff was not negligent; the ship was under exclusive control of the defendant; therefore, the burden of proof was shifted from the plaintiff to the defendant based on res ipsa loquitur. Damages of the cost of cleaning up the spill were awarded against the vessel by the court.

7.3.2 Violation of a Statute or Ordinance

Generally, the violation of a statute or ordinance which was passed to promote safety is negligence. But the violation of such law does not of itself give rise to civil liability. The plaintiff must show that the violation of the law was the proximate cause of the injury. The violation of a statute or ordinance, which is not designed

---

26/ Restatement (Second) Torts, § 328D.

27/ 318 F. Supp. 839 (C.D. Cal. 1970).

to prevent the sort of harm about which the plaintiff is complaining, is not negligence.

An example of the application of this doctrine in an environmental lawsuit is the 1975 case of Springer v. Schlitz Brewing Company. 28/ Mr. and Mrs. Springer owned a large farm downriver from a newly constructed Winston-Salem, N.C., brewery of Schlitz. They sued Schlitz for overloading the city's sewage treatment, causing it to pollute the Yadkin river, resulting in fish kills and so interfering with their riparian rights. In North Carolina, as in many other states, a riparian landowner has a right to the agricultural, recreational and scenic use and enjoyment of the stream bordering his land. A city sewage ordinance prohibited the discharge of pollutants that interfere with the city's waste treatment process.

In this case the plaintiff did not, according to the court's opinion, prove that Schlitz was negligent in the conventional sense. Instead, the Court looked to the theory that violation of a city sewage ordinance is negligence "per se." The appeals court directed that the jury should decide if Schlitz violated the city's ordinance. If the jury decides that the ordinance was violated, it is negligence per se and if the negligence proximately causes injury, then the industry is liable irrespective of any good faith efforts on the part of the defendant.

So, violations of environmental or pollution control statutes or ordinances which are generally designed to protect the public health or safety could result in a successful negligence lawsuit by the injured party even though there is no factual showing of negligence.

7.3.3 Dangerous Substances—Strict Liability

Courts have ruled that a person who keeps a potentially dangerous substance on his land which, if permitted to escape, is certain to injure others, must make good the damage caused by the escape of the substance, regardless of negligence on the defendant's part.

This strict liability theory is very old. It was used in a 1907 case where oil escaped into the Potomac River in Washington, D.C., and resulted in injury to boats in a downstream boathouse. 29/ In

---

28/ 7 ERC 1516 (4th Cir. 1975).

29/ Brennan Construction Co. v. Cumberland, 29 U.S. App. D.C. 554(1907).

this case, it was determined that a potentially dangerous substance is anything which, if permitted to escape, is certain to injure others. This description of a potentially dangerous substance is so broad as to include oil in the case under discussion plus thousands of other substances in subsequent litigation.

The reasoning for this strict liability standard is that, when persons suffer loss, no good reason can be found to charge the loss against anyone who did not contribute to it. If the defendant is engaged in an ultra-hazardous or dangerous activity for profit, he should bear the burden of compensating others who are harmed by his activities.

In making the determination of whether an activity is ultra-hazardous, courts have traditionally scrutinized six factors: (1) the existence of a high degree of risk, (2) the likelihood that the resultant harm will be great, (3) the ability to eliminate the risk by exercising reasonable care, (4) the extent to which the activity is not common in the community, (5) the appropriateness of the activity to the place where it is carried on, and (6) the activity's value to the community.

Not surprisingly, some courts have applied strict liability theories in cases involving the disposal of hazardous waste.

In spite of its rapid development in some jurisdictions, however, the doctrine of strict liability has not been applied to environmental torts in all states. Even those states which have adopted strict liability have not applied the theory in uniform fashion.

7.3.4 Defenses to an Action for Negligence

7.3.4.1 Contributory Negligence

Contributory negligence is an affirmative defense in some jurisdictions. The theory behind this concept is that a person is not entitled to benefit from his own wrong. Therefore, contributory negligence on the part of the plaintiff generally relieves the defendant of liability, unless he, the defendant, had the "last clear chance" of avoiding the accident.

The "last clear chance" doctrine 30/ presupposes a perilous situation created or existing through the negligence of both the plaintiff and the defendant. It assumes that there was a time, after such negligence had occurred, when the defendant could, and the

---

30/   57 Am. Jur. 2d 796.

plaintiff could not by the use of available means, avoid the accident. This doctrine is not applicable when the emergency is so sudden that there is no time to avoid it. Under the "last clear chance" doctrine, a negligent defendant is liable when he (aware of the plaintiff's peril, or unaware of it only through carelessness) had, in fact, a later opportunity than the plaintiff to avert the accident.

A comparative negligence concept (apportionment of responsibility or damages) is recognized in 12 states. 31/

7.3.4.2 Assumption of Risk

Generally any person who knows of a risk and assumes it is not permitted to recover for any injury sustained. This is based on the theory that a person should not be permitted to benefit from his own wrong. One of several exceptions to this rule is when the risk is assumed to save life.

7.3.4.3 Proving Negligence

Negligence actions in the pollution field are generally hampered by the plaintiff's difficulty in proving the defendant negligent. The plaintiff also must prove that the negligence of the defendant was the proximate cause of the plaintiff's injury. However, the increased availability to the public of plant records, monitoring, inspections and source emission data required under the various statutes and regulations will contribute to easing the evidentiary problems of proving a negligence case.

7.4 Sovereign Immunity and Torts

Theoretically, the law has granted immunity from tort liability to governments. Neither the United States nor any of the several states may be sued by a private citizen without the government's consent. The origin of this idea was the common law notion that "the King can do no wrong." But, it was not until the sixteenth century that this concept was fully established as law. When the individual sovereign was replaced by the broader concept of the modern state, the idea was carried over: that to allow a suit against a ruling government without its consent was inconsistent with the very idea of supreme executive power.

In most state jurisdictions, however, consent has been given, usually in a limited form by statutes, which provide for special procedure or create special courts of claims, or which authorize suits

---

31/   Id. 846.

against the state in its own courts for particular causes of action. There is a good deal of variety to these statutes, and reference must be made to those of the particular jurisdiction.

In 1946, the United States waived its immunity, with certain exceptions, from liability in tort, and provided for litigation of tort claims against it in the federal courts by the Federal Tort Claims Act. 32/

So, for anyone contemplating bringing a pollution lawsuit based on a tort action against a government entity, the first questions are: has sovereign immunity been waived, and what are the consent restrictions?

In regard to any suit against a state brought in a federal court, the Eleventh Amendment to the U.S. Constitution states:

> The Judicial power of the United States shall not be constructed to extend to any suit in law or equity commenced or prosecuted against one of the United States by Citizens of another State or by Citizens or subjects of any Foreign State.

While the Eleventh Amendment, by its own terms, does not bar suits against a state by its own citizens, the U.S. Supreme Court has consistently ruled that an unconsenting state is protected from suits brought in federal courts by her own citizens as well as by citizens of another state. 33/ It is also well–settled law that even though a state is not named as a defendant, any judgment which must be paid from public funds of the state falls within the prohibitions of the Eleventh Amendment.

A successful example of the defense of sovereign immunity on the federal level is found in an environmental case entitled Byram River v. Village of Port Chester. 34/ In this case, the plaintiffs were seeking to halt the depositing of allegedly inadequately treated sewage into the Byram River. The plaintiffs named a number of defendants, including the New York State Department of Environmental Conservation. The Court dismissed the action

---

32/   28 U.S.C.A. §§ 1254 et seq.

33/   Hans v. Louisiana, 134 U.S. 1(1890); Edelman v. Jordan, 415 U.S. 651 (1974).

34/   7 ERC 1970 (S.D.N.Y. 1975).

against New York State based on the defense of sovereign immunity as set forth in the Eleventh Amendment.

8.0 Constitutional Law

8.1 Constitution and Government Authority

The federal government was created to be a government of limited authority. The powers granted to the federal government are those enumerated in the U.S. Constitution. Although the federal government's authority is theoretically limited to only those enumerated, in practice these powers have been so expanded in scope by judicial interpretation that it is hard to conceive of any environmental laws being beyond the federal authority. So this section will not review the general question of the theoretical basis of federal power but, instead, focus on the specific constitutional limits to this authority.

These limits appear to be of more pragmatic interest and concern today because they are the issues raised in lawsuits against the abuse of governmental authority.

8.2 Limits on Governmental Action

8.2.1 Search Warrants and the Fourth Amendment

The Fourth Amendment of the Constitution provides that:

The right of the people to be secure in their persons, houses, papers, and effects, against unreasonable searches and seizures shall not be violated, and no Warrants shall issue, but upon probable cause, supported by oath or affirmation and particularly describing the place to be searched and the persons or things to be seized.

One of the most common abuses of governmental authority is in the collection or obtaining of evidence. Evidence is necessary for any civil or criminal enforcement program. However, federal evidence collection is limited by these Fourth Amendment prohibitions.

The courts have held that the Fourth Amendment applies to the corporate entity as well as to the private citizen. The Supreme Court has held that the requirement for a search warrant even applies to routine administrative inspections. 35/ In the Camara

---

35/ Camara v. Municipal Court, 387 U.S. 523 (1967).

case, the Court held that the warrant requirement applied to a municipal health inspector's search of a private residence. A similar conclusion was reached with respect to a fire inspector's attempted search of a commercial warehouse. 36/ In these cases, the Court indicated that a lesser degree of "probable cause" would be required for an administrative search warrant than for the typical criminal search warrant. So there can be routine periodic searches of all structures in a given area based on an appraisal of conditions in the area as a whole rather than on a knowledge of conditions in a particular building. The reasonableness of such inspections is to be weighed against the invasion of rights that the search entails.

Generally warrants are only sought after entry is refused because there is no need for a search warrant when the owner or operator has given his consent.

To avoid this need for search warrants, the Congress has authorized warrantless searches in some statutes. In the famous Barlow case 37/ the constitutionality of these legislative waivers was reviewed by the Supreme Court. The Court held that Section 8 of the Occupational Safety and Health Act (OSHA) authorizing warrantless inspections violated the Fourth Amendment prohibition against warrantless searches and was unconstitutional. How does this affect you? Probably it doesn't affect you directly, but it does put some restraint on the federal government not to harass businesses with needless inspections. 38/

The Environmental Protection Agency (EPA) has avoided the test of the constitutionality of the warrantless search authorizations given to them by Congress in the Noise Control Act and the Resource Conservation and Recovery Act by not challenging the issue. If an EPA inspector is refused admission, EPA, as standard procedure, will then obtain a search warrant and not even try to use the statutory authority. This avoids the constitutional confrontation.

36/   See v. City of Seattle, 387 U.S. 541 (1967).

37/   Marshall v. Barlow's Inc., 436 U.S. 307 (1978).

38/   For a thorough review of the Barlow Case and its impact, see "The Barlow Case and OSHA Inspections" by Marshall Lee Miller in Occupation Health & Safety Regulations (Government Institutes, Washington, D.C., June 1978), pages 147-154.

It is common, in the field of environmental law, to find exceptions to the general rules. An example of an exception to the search warrant requirement is the so-called "open fields" exception described in the Supreme Court case, Air Pollution Variance Board v. Western Alfalfa. 39/ In this case, an inspector of a Division of the Colorado Department of Health entered the premises of Western Alfalfa Corporation without its knowledge or consent to make a Ringelmann reading of plumes of smoke being emitted from the company's chimneys. The Western Alfalfa Corporation claimed that the inspection violated the Fourth Amendment by entering its property to collect evidence without a search warrant. The U.S. Supreme Court ruled that the inspector was within an exception to the Fourth Amendment and had not violated the rights of the Western Alfalfa Corporation. The Court held the general rule to be that the act of conducting tests on a defendant's premises without either a warrant or the consent of defendant constitutes an unreasonable search within the Fourth Amendment. However, in this case the inspector did not enter the plant or offices. Basically he sighted what anyone in the area near the plant could see in the sky. He was on the defendant's property but there was no showing that he was on premises from which the public was excluded. The Court held that there is an "open fields" exception to the constitutional requirement for a search warrant which was applicable in this case.

In the vast majority of practical situations, consent is given for collection of evidence. The consent may be oral or written, with the latter being more desirable, because it simplifies subsequent problems of proof. The consent is commonly given by employees simply admitting the inspectors to the company premises or giving answers to oral or written questions by government employees.

One method of avoiding the necessity of obtaining a search warrant is to require the owner or operator of the pollution source to get a permit or license to operate. Then, a condition is included in the permit, allowing inspections without warrants. The U.S. Supreme Court has not yet ruled on the constitutionality of this method. Since permit systems are now being used more and more by federal, state and local agencies to control pollution, this method of obtaining desired evidence will be the trend of the future and provides the government with the consent needed.

See Section 11 of this chapter for more on evidence.

39/   6 ERC 1571 (U.S. Sup. Ct. 1974).

8.2.2 Prohibition Against Self-Incrimination: The Fifth Amendment
     The Fifth Amendment to the Constitution prohibits compulsory self-incrimination. It is limited in that it only applies to criminal cases. If the government agency collecting the evidence will use it only for civil actions, such as injunctions, the Fifth Amendment is not applicable. In addition, the Fifth Amendment applies only to persons and not to corporations or partnerships.
     Most environmental statutes provide penalties for both individuals and corporations. Therefore, in a case where the evidence or samples taken might be used in a criminal action, the person in authority at the place where the evidence is to be taken should be advised of his rights to remain silent, to an attorney, and that any evidence taken may be used against him in a subsequent criminal action. If these rights are not formally observed, the evidence so collected may not be admissible in a criminal action.

8.2.3 Due Process, the Fifth and Fourteenth Amendments
     The requirement that government entities not deprive anyone of due process of law is found in the Fifth and Fourteenth Amendments.
     Due process is a very basic principle of our system of laws:

     The Fifth Amendment to the U.S. Constitution says:
     "No person shall. . . , nor be deprived of life, liberty, or property, without due process of law; nor shall private property be taken for public use, without just compensation."

     The Fourteenth Amendment to the U.S. Constitution states: "Section 1... No State shall make or enforce any law which shall abridge the privileges or immunities of citizens of the United States; nor shall any State deprive any person of life, liberty, or property without due process of law; nor deny to any person within it jurisdiction the equal protection of the law."

     The Fifth Amendment prohibition applies to the federal government and the Fourteenth applies to the states. These protections guarantee to a person the right not to be deprived of his life, liberty or property without due process of law. Simply stated due process means the law of the land, that is, according to settled usage and mode of proceeding. As long as the law preserves the fundamental rights of a person according to the law of the land, the novelty of the law does not invalidate it.

An example of the application of the legal concept of due process is found in the case, Construction Industry v. Petaluma. 40/ In this case the Court held that a city ordinance that limits issuance of new building permits to achieve a goal of preserving "small town" character, open spaces and low density population does not violate the due process clause of the Fourteenth Amendment. The Court's opinion explained that zoning regulations must find their justification in some aspect of the police power asserted for the public welfare to satisfy the due process mandate. The Court found that the concept of the public welfare is sufficiently broad to uphold Petaluma's desire to preserve its small town character, open spaces and low density population.

The due process argument was used against the beverage container ordinance of the City of Bowie, Maryland. 41/ The Court ruled that there was not a violation of due process because there was not a showing that the police power was exercised arbitrarily, oppressively or unreasonably. The opinion also reasoned that a law should not be held void, if there are any considerations relating to the public welfare by which it can be supported.

8.2.4 Police Power and Due Process

Police power is the inherent right of a government to pass laws for the protection of the health, welfare, morals, and property of the people within its jurisdiction. In a sense, police power is but another name for the power of the government. Police power may not be bartered away by contract. It extends to all public needs. It may be put forth in the aid of what is sanctioned by usage or held by prevailing opinion to be greatly or immediately necessary for public welfare. By the exercise of reasonable police power, a government may regulate the conduct of individuals and of the use of their property and, in some instances, take property without compensation.

Although the police power of a state is very broad, it is not without limitation. It is always within the power of the court to declare a law void which, although enacted as a police regulation, is

---

40/   8 ERC 1001 (9th Cir. 1975).

41/   Bowie Inn v. City of Bowie, 7 ERC 2083 (1975).

not justified as such. In other words, a law enacted as a police regulation must be reasonable. If the law is unreasonable or exercised in
an arbitrary manner, it is taking life, liberty, or property without
due process of law.

Two examples of the allowable exercise of police powers are
given in Section 8.2.3.

Another example of the valid exercise of police power which
did not violate the due process principle was in the Supreme Court
case, Village of Belle Terre v. Borass. 42/ In this case a New York
village ordinance restricted land use to one-family houses and precluded occupancy by more than two unrelated persons. The Court
held this ordinance to be a valid exercise of the city's police power,
stating:

> A quiet place where yards are wide, people few, and
> motor vehicles restricted are legitimate guidelines in a
> land use project addressed to family needs. The police
> power is not confined to elimination of filth, stench, and
> unhealthy places. It is ample to lay out zones where
> family values, youth values, and the blessings of quiet
> seclusion and clean air make the area a sanctuary for
> people.

8.2.5 Prohibition Against Taking Property Without Compensation

The Fifth Amendment to the Constitution states that ". . .
nor shall private property be taken for public use, without just compensation."

Despite numerous court opinions on this issue, the line between "takings" which require compensation and valid exercise of
the "police power" which do not require compensation has never
been clearly drawn. It is difficult to predict the outcome when the
principles in this area are applied to factual situations.

It may be said that the state takes property by eminent
domain because it is useful to the public. This taking requires compensation. When the state takes property because it is harmful, it is
done under the police power and does not require compensation.
What is useful to one person may be harmful to another. So, the
perspective of all the conditions and circumstances is often the
determining factor in choosing between useful and harmful.

42/   416 U.S. 1 (1974).

The problem often comes down to one of degree. In both circumstances damages result. If the damage is suffered by many similarly situated and is in the nature of a restriction on use and ought to be borne by the individual as a member of society for the good of the public, it is a reasonable exercise of the police power not requiring compensation. However, if the damage is so great to the individual that he ought not to bear it under contemporary standards, then courts are inclined to treat it as a "taking" or unreasonable exercise of police power requiring compensation.

This taking issue has been in the forefront of noteworthy litigation. One important case involved the denial of operational drilling permits in the Santa Barbara Channel and was entitled Union Oil v. Morton. 43/ In this case the court reviewed the question of the degree to which the government may interfere with the enjoyment of private property by exercise of its police power without having to pay compensation and concluded that there was not a simple answer to this question. The courts under a variety of tests have recognized that regulation of private property can become so onerous that it amounts to a taking of that property. The court in this case held that a permanent unconditional suspension of permits to install drilling platforms is a taking that requires compensation or violates the Fifth Amendment.

A series of cases have held that airport noise can constitute a taking of property rights. In the landmark case of United States v. Causby, 44/ the Supreme Court held that frequent low flights over the Causby's land by military aircraft landing at a nearby airport operated by the United States constituted a taking of the Causby's property without compensation in violation of the Fifth Amendment of the Constitution. The noise from the aircraft rendered it impossible to continue the use of the property as a commercial chicken farm. Although the flights did not completely destroy the enjoyment and use of the land, they were held to be so low and frequent as to constitute a direct and immediate interference with the full enjoyment of the land, limiting the utility of the land and causing a diminution in its value, and therefore constituted a taking under the Fifth Amendment.

43/   7 ERC 1587 (9th Cir. 1975).

44/   328 U.S. 256 (1946).

In another major Supreme Court decision on this issue, Griggs
v. Allegheny County, 45/ the Court held that Allegheny County,
which owned and operated the Greater Pittsburgh Airport, was liable
for a taking of property under the Fifth Amendment where the noise
from taking off and landing at the airport on flight paths over the
Griggs' property rendered the property undesirable and unbearable
for residential use.   The Court saw no difference between the
county's responsibility to pay for the land on which the runways were
built and its responsibility for the air easements necessary for operation of the airport. The glide path for the northwest runway is as
necessary for the operation of the airport as is a surface right-of-
way, wrote the Court.

A federal circuit court has narrowly interpreted Causby and
Griggs to mean that there is not taking under the Fifth Amendment
unless the aircraft invade the air space directly over the plaintiff's
property and the property is rendered uninhabitable. 46/ However,
several states have interpreted their own constitutions to require
compensation under less strict circumstances when the noise from
aircraft has diminished the market value of the homeowner's property. The interference must be substantial and sufficiently direct in
the majority of jurisdictions.

8.2.6 Commerce Clause Limitations
The Constitution grants to Congress the authority ". . . to
regulate Commerce with foreign Nations and among the several
States and with the Indian Tribes." So, if state statutes or regulations are found by the courts to be an impermissible burden upon
interstate commerce, then they are unconstitutional and unenforce-
able.

It is well settled that a state regulation validly based on the
police power does not impermissibly burden interstate commerce
where the regulations neither discriminate against interstate commerce nor operate to disrupt its required uniformity. Where there is
a reasonable basis to protect the social, as distinguished from the
economic, welfare of a community, the courts will not deny this
exercise of sovereign power and hold it to violate the Commerce
Clause.

45/   369 U.S. 84 (1962).

46/   7 ERC (9th Cir. 1975).

An example of a Commerce Clause case involved a challenge against New Jersey's Waste Control Act. 47/ This law barred disposal within the state of solid waste originating or collected outside the state's territorial borders. The U.S. Supreme Court opinion held that this statute does violate the Commerce Clause of the Constitution.

The Supreme Court held that all objects of interstate trade merit Commerce Clause protection and none is excluded from the definition of "commerce" including "valueless" out-of-state wastes. The Court ruled that the New Jersey statute was basically an economic protectionist measure, and thus virtually per se invalid, and not a law directed at legitimate local concerns that had only incidental effects on interstate commerce.

Another Commerce Clause case involved the Chicago ordinance banning the sale of detergents containing phosphates. 48/ The Seventh Circuit Court of Appeals held that the ordinance did not violate the Commerce Clause because, although it had some minor effect on interstate commerce, the benefits far outweighed these effects and the ordinance was a reasonable method to achieve a legitimate goal of improving Lake Michigan.

A similar result favorable to the legislators was reached in Oregon when the constitutionality of the Oregon "bottle-bill" which in essence banned the sale of non-returnable beverage containers was upheld. 49/

The trend is definitely one of the courts trying to uphold environmental legislation with the rationale being based on a balancing of the equities, namely weighing the benefits against the detrimental effect.

8.2.7 Equal Protection of the Laws

Section One of the Fourteenth Amendment to the Constitution prohibits the states from denying to any person the equal protection of the laws.

47/   City of Philadelphia v. New Jersey, 437 U.S. 617 (1978).

48/   Procter and Gamble v. Chicago, 7 ERC 1328 (7th Cir. 1975).

49/   American Can Co. v. Oregon Liquor Control Commission, 517 P2d 691, 4 ERC 1584 (1973).

Does a state noise law which exempts construction equipment where there is no exemption for mining equipment deny equal protection? The Illinois Supreme Court held no in a suit entitled <u>Illinois Coal Operators Association v. Illinois Pollution Control Board.</u> 50/

The courts generally hold that for a classification to violate the constitutional guarantee of equal protection, there must be a showing that there is no reasonable basis for the distinction. A law is presumptively valid. Unless clear and convincing proof demonstrates that a law is arbitrary and unreasonable, the law must be upheld. The result is that few laws are ever held to violate the equal protection clause.

8.3 Constitutional Protection of the Environment

Three major claims have been proposed to protect the environment which are based on requirements of the Constitution.

The Ninth Amendment of the Constitution has been alleged to include a right to protect the public from unreasonable environmental degradation. The Ninth Amendment states: "The enumeration in the Constitution of certain rights, shall not be construed to deny or disparage others retained by the people." The theory is that one of these other retained rights is the protection of natural resources or an environment free of pollution.

The other constitutional claims come under the general heading of "due process" and are based on the due process requirements of the Fifth and Fourteenth Amendments.

In the case of <u>Hagedorn v. Union Carbide,</u> 51/ the plaintiffs who were residents of the county in which a Union Carbide plant was located, complained about alleged air pollution from Union Carbide's plant which:

> deprived them of the following rights guaranteed by the Constitution:
> (A) The right to breathe clean air and live in a decent environment including the fundamental human right of survival granted and protected by the Ninth Amendment.

50/   7 ERC 1315 (1974).

51/   5 ERC 1755, 363 F. Supp. 1061 (N.D. W.Va. 1973).

(B) The right to their life, health and property and to full use and enjoyment thereof granted and protected by the Fifth Amendment.

The Court in its opinion held:

These and similar claims have been widely advanced but regularly rejected by the Federal courts. Indeed, the Fourth Circuit in Ely v. Velde, 451 F2d 1130 (3 ERC 1280) (1971), emphatically declined. . .to elevate to a constitutional level the claimed right to be protected from unnecessary and unreasonable environmental degradation and destruction. While a growing number of commentators argue in support of a constitutional protection for the environment, this newly-advanced constitutional doctrine has not yet been accorded judicial sanction. . .

This court considers itself bound by the clear language of Ely v. Velde, which is buttressed by the heavy weight of the emerging case law.

In another case entitled Environmental Defense Fund v. Corps of Engineers of the U.S. Army, 52/ the plaintiffs, in seeking to enjoin the damming of an Arkansas river, relied upon the Fifth, Ninth and Fourteenth Amendments. The Court declared that it was not within the province of a district court to bestow Constitutional protection to the environment.

Those who would attempt to protect the environment through the courts are striving mightily to carve out a mandate from the existing provisions of our Constitution. . .such claims, even under our present Constitution, are not fanciful and may, indeed, some day, in one way or another, obtain judicial recognition. But, as stated by Judge Learned Hand in Spector Motor Service, Inc. v. Walsh, 139 F2d 809 (2 Cir. 1944): 'Nor is it desirable for a lower court to embrace the exhilarating opportunity of anticipating a doctrine which may be in the womb of time, but whose birth is distant.'

The Ninth Amendment may well be as important in the development of constitutional law during the

---

52/ 2 ERC 1260, 325 F. Supp. 726 (E.D. Ark. 1971).

remainder of this century as the Fourteenth Amendment
has been since the begining of the century. But the
Court concludes that the plaintiffs have not stated facts
which would under the present state of the law constitute a violation of their constitutional rights. . .

In Tanner v. Armco Steel Corporation, 53/ the plaintiff-
family alleged specific injuries from air pollutants from defendants'
petroleum refineries and plants. The husband claimed that the
pollution caused him pulmonary damage with consequent medical
expense and loss of income. Damage to plaintiffs' homestead and
lands was also alleged. The plaintiffs, the Tanners, sought relief
under the Fifth, Ninth and Fourteenth Amendments. The courts,
however, rejected the Constitutional claims, holding that:

No legally enforceable right to healthful environment,
giving rise to an action for damages, is guaranteed by
the Fourteenth Amendment or any other provision of
the Federal Constitution. As the United States Supreme
Court recently observed in rejecting a similarly imaginative constitutional claim, 'the Constitution does not
provide judicial remedies for every social and economic
ill.' Lindsey v. Normet, 405 U.S. 56, 92 S. Ct. 862, 31 L.
Ed. 2d 36 (1972).

These opinions clearly document the position of the courts
today that the Fifth, Ninth and Fourteenth Amendments of the U.S.
Constitution do not currently include enforceable environmental
rights.

9.0 Defenses

9.1 Generally
Some of the defenses available against civil lawsuits have
already been considered under the discussions of nuisance and negligence. Others not previously covered are considered in this section.
Generally, it is not a defense to an action for pollution that
the defendant was not negligent; nor that he used due care; nor that
his method of operation was customary.

53/   3 ERC 1968, 340 F. Supp. 532 (S.D. Tex. 1972).

Some courts have taken into consideration the relative importance of the interests of the parties and have refused to abate pollution or to grant an injunction against a plant but have relegated the plaintiff to an action for damages. 54/ This approach is based on the concept that closing a plant could cause more harm than good.

The question of how far individual rights must yield to the public good is a complex issue. Some courts have held that an injunction will be granted to restrain pollution without regard to the magnitude of the interest enjoined.

Stanley W. Schroeder in his article, "Pollution in Perspective" for The Natural Resources Lawyer, 55/ sounds a note of concern regarding defenses when he states:

> Not only in the pollution field, but in other social areas there appears to be an effort to shift the basis of liability away from the traditional concept of the nature of the wrong committed toward a concern for the nature of the harm done. Under the common law, whether one had a cause of action was a question of whether 'duty owed' by the wrong-doer had been established. Today, not only is the duty expanded by strict and far-reaching statutory or regulatory standards, but as the Court said in Westchester Homeowners v. Los Angeles, 'The test of liability is coming to be the reasonable expectation of the person injured by the act of another to be free from such injury. The status and relationship of the parties have become important considerations in determinining liability.'
>
> Carried to their logical conclusion these trends would make futile any hope of a defense. The situation would be tantamount to strict liability, which, although helpful to aggrieved parties will certainly facilitate claims; if monitoring devices remove the questions of wrong from the case the only issues left would be causation and damages.

The current situation is a balancing of the equities involved or comparing the injuries between the parties involved in the lawsuit. The trend is definitely toward the strict liability concept.

54/   61 Am. Jur. 2d 977.

55/   Schroeder, Stanley W. "Pollution in Perspective," The Natural Resources Lawyer, Vol. IV, No. 2, 381 (Apr. 1971).

9.2 Laches

The term "laches" generally describes the defense that is based on the failure of the plaintiff to do something which should have been done or to claim or enforce a right at a proper time. Generally, there are three criteria for the equitable doctrine of laches: (a) the defendant must show a delay in asserting a right or claim, (b) the delay was not excusable and (c) there was undue prejudice to the party against whom the claim is asserted.

The defense of laches was successfully used in the Michigan Supreme Court case Thompson v. Enz. 56/ In that case defendants had obtained formal approval for a lake-front development project from all locally concerned governmental agencies, and at least tacit approval from the state. The defendants made a substantial investment in initiating the project. After all of these efforts and investments by the defendants, the plaintiff initiated a lawsuit to stop the development. The court ruled that the plaintiff would not be allowed to stop the completion of the project because of the defense of laches. The plaintiffs had allowed the defendants to proceed, and in the court's opinion, they should have filed their lawsuit in the very beginning of the project. The court indicated that it might have enjoined the project had it been promptly brought to its attention.

Laches is determined in the light of all existing circumstances and requires, generally, that the delay be unreasonable. The mere lapse of time is not sufficient.

The equitable defense of laches should see increased service to put a reasonable time limit on efforts in environmental cases.

9.3 Contractual Authorization

The right to pollute the air or a stream may be acquired by grant or license as against the grantor or licensor. A case that is an example of this defense involved oil pollution in Texas. It was ruled in this case that a release given to an oil company by a rancher for all claims arising from the operation of the oil wells on his property barred recovery of damages by the rancher for harm caused by crude oil leaking onto his property. 57/

56/   2 ERC 1842, 188 N.W. 2nd 579.

57/   Jackson v. Marathon Oil Co., 2 ERC 1533, 441 F.2d 511 (5th Cir. 1971).

Some contract clauses go too far in waiving rights, and are then generally ruled void, as being against public policy. This rule of voidness would probably be applicable to many pollution cases because it could be shown as against public policy to contract away environmental rights.

9.4 Public Authorization

In some jurisdictions, legislative authorization of the cause of the pollution might be a defense against liability. There is authority that a cause of action for abatement of a public nuisance does not arise, if the plant or establishment causing the pollution has legislative or administrative approval. 58/

A legislative license to create a nuisance by pollution must be given in express terms or by necessary implications. A private nuisance may arise, even though the facility has legislative sanction.

However, authority to build sewers is not authority to pollute a stream. Also, the legislature has no power to authorize the taking of property by pollution without just compensation.

9.5 Vagueness

One defense attempted against new statutory and regulatory prescriptions has been to attack them on the grounds of vagueness. However, the courts have not been responsive to this argument in pollution cases.

In Houston Compressed Steel v. Texas, 59/ the Texas Clean Air Act's broad definition of "air pollution" was upheld by the Texas Court of Civil Appeals as not to be too vague to be employed against a scrap metal company that burned railroad boxcars outdoors. The opinion stated that "since the science of air pollution control is new and inexact, and these standards are difficult to devise, if they are to be effective, they must be broad." The Texas court also felt that an air polluter should not escape the consequences of his act merely because he is able to make his contaminants difficult to measure or control.

58/   61 Am. Jr. 2d 983.

59/   456 S.W. 2d 768 (1970).

In <u>Air Commission v. Coated Materials,</u> <u>60</u>/ the Pennsylvania Air Pollution Control Act's definition of air pollution, as some substance "which unreasonably interferes with the comfortable enjoyment of life and property" was found to be uncertain, and was susceptible to acceptable standards of proof "since the language employed in the statute is equivalent to the definition of nuisance which is certainly established in the law."

Similarly, the Connecticut General Statutes were found not unconstitutionally vague when they required every motor vehicle to be so equipped and adjusted as to prevent excessive fumes or exhaust smoke, since any ordinary and interested person would have no difficulty in determining whether or not a motor vehicle put out offensive or excessive exhaust fumes. <u>61</u>/

Based on a review of the current case law, the argument of vagueness as a potential defense does not appear to offer a probability for success.

9.6 Unreasonableness and Impossibility of Performance

The courts do consider the reasonableness of duties imposed by statutes, regulations, standards and even court orders. An example is found in <u>Pennsylvania v. Pennsylvania Power,</u> <u>62</u>/ where the court ruled that the regulations requiring compliance with Pennsylvania's sulfur dioxide emission standards were unreasonable because the technology adequate to meet the standards did not exist and the company acted in good faith.

The court stated:

> To impose sanctions on PPC in an attempt to force it to perform an impossible act would be both meaningless and unjust.
> It has been held that where the defendant cannot perform the duty ordered, and where that inability is

---

<u>60</u>/   778 C.D. 1969 (Pa. Ct. Com. Pls. 1970).

<u>61</u>/   Connecticut v. Schuster's Express, 6 Conn. Cir. Ct. 108 (1970).

<u>62</u>/   6 ERC 1328. See also previous contempt litigation [5 ERC 1373] 301 A. 2d 280 (1973).

not due to actions of the defendant himself that impossibility is a defense. F.T.C. v. Plaine, 308 F. Supp. 932 (N.D. Ga. 1970).

The courts have held in other cases that rules and regulations must be reasonable before the courts will enforce them.

However, the availability of the defense of economic and technological infeasibility in cases arising under the Clean Air Act resulted in contrary or partially contrary decisions in the federal circuit courts. So, the question was resolved by the Supreme Court. The question in issue was: Is technological or economic feasibility a defense against compliance with a State Implementation Plan (SIP) for air pollution control?

The U.S. Supreme Court, in a landmark decision decided on 25 June 1976, said no on this key issue but provided some additional guidance in this area of the law. In the case of Union Electric Co. v. EPA 63/ Mr. Justice Marshall writing for a unanimous Court said:

> After reviewing the relevant provision of the Clean Air Act Amendments of 1970 and their legislative history, we agree that Congress intended claims of economic and technological infeasibility to be wholly foreign to the Administrator's consideration of a state implementation plan.
>
> These requirements are of a technology-forcing character and are expressly designed to force regulated sources to develop pollution control devices that might at the time appear to be economically or technologically infeasible.
>
> This approach is apparent on the face of §110(a)(2). The provision sets out eight criteria that an implementation plan must satisfy, and provides that if these criteria are met and if the plan was adopted after reasonable notice and hearing, the Administrator 'shall approve' the proposed state plan. The mandatory 'shall' makes it quite clear that the Administrator is not to be concerned with factors other than those specified, and none of the eight factors appears to permit consideration of technological or economic infeasibility.

63/ 8 ERC 2143 (U.S. Sup. Ct. 1976).

However, the opinion continues by setting forth that claims of infeasibility can be relevant. This infeasibility issue should be raised before the particular state agency while formulating the SIP. If the industry is not exempted in the original plan, then a variance may be submitted as a revision to the SIP. An industry denied exemption may take its claims of infeasibility to the state courts. Also, a state governor may request an extension or postponement based on infeasibility grounds. Finally, claims of technological or economic feasibility are relevant to fashioning an appropriate compliance order between EPA and the operator in controversies arising under the Clean Air Act.

10.0 Parties

Parties to a lawsuit are classified as nominal, necessary and indispensable. Nominal parties are those who have some interest in the subject matter of the suit but are not affected by the judgment. Necessary parties are those who may be indirectly affected by the judgment and should be made parties (if they can be served with a subpoena to appear in court) but whose interests are separate from the others. Indispensable parties are those without whom the court cannot enter a valid judgment. Indispensable parties must be joined in the suit and must be served with process.

10.1 Standing, or Who May Sue

One of the most basic questions regarding parties that is normally asked is who may sue or in "lawyerese," the question of which parties have "standing" to file a lawsuit. This question was in the forefront of early environmental litigation.

Standing, strictly speaking, differs from who may sue. Theoretically speaking, anyone who has the fee to pay for filing a lawsuit may initiate a lawsuit. Where a party has a sufficient interest in a controversy to obtain judicial resolution of the controversy is what is traditionally referred to as the question of "standing to sue."

The general rule of law under the Administrative Procedure Act is that standing exists only when a plaintiff can satisfactorily demonstrate that (a) the agency action complained of will result in an injury in fact and that (b) the injury is to an interest "arguably within the zone of interests to be protected" by the statute in question.

The leading cases addressing the "injury in fact" question are cases involving the National Environmental Policy Act and environmental impact statements. The key case is the Supreme Court

decision in Sierra Club v. Morton. 64/ This case involved the recreational development of the Mineral King Valley. The question in
Sierra v. Morton was, what must be alleged by persons who claim
injury of a non-economic nature to widely shared interests to give
them standing. The court recognized that environmental well-being,
like economic well-being, is an important ingredient of our society.
The fact that environmental interests are shared by the many rather
than few does not make them less deserving of legal protection. But
the "injury in fact" test, according to the Court, requires that the
party seeking review be himself among the injured. The Sierra Club
did not allege and show that it or its members would be affected in
any of their activities or pastimes by the development. So, the
Court ruled against them. However, this has since proven to be an
easy matter to remedy, by the plaintiffs alleging that an aesthetic
or other non-economic interest was injured. So, the Sierra Club
established in this decision that environmental interests could be the
basis for standing. This was a major development in the law.

In a subsequent Supreme Court case, SCRAP v. U.S., 65/ the
Supreme Court gave some law students standing to sue the I.C.C. in
a rate increase case involving recyclables. The Supreme Court ruled
that standing to sue was demonstrated by the students, showing that
they used the forest and streams in the Washington, D.C. area for
camping and hiking and that this was disturbed by the adverse environmental impact, caused by the nonuse of recyclable goods, brought
on by the I.C.C. rate increase on recyclable commodities.

The rule appears now that injury to a non-economic interest
such as scenery, natural and historic objects and wildlife is a sufficient injury in fact to be a basis for a suit by a person or group who
will suffer the injury directly. This covers a broad range of potential plaintiffs and cases. As a result the issue regarding standing has
now shifted from the "injury in fact" question to the "zone of interests to be protected" by the statute involved in the litigation.

Citizens are given standing or access to the federal courts
explicitly in the Federal Water Pollution Control Act, the Clean Air
Act, the Noise Act, and many other statutes. This question of
standing is only relevant when statutory authority is not available.

64/   3 ERC 2039, 405 U.S. 345 (1972).

65/   412 U.S. 669 (1974).

In summary, almost anyone who alleges an environmental concern can sue the government and most other parties.

10.2 Class Actions

Since many environmental lawsuits are brought as class actions, the basis for these is set forth in this section.

One or more members of a class may sue or be sued as representative parties on behalf of all, only if, as a general rule:

(1)   The class is so numerous that a uniting in the pleadings of all members is impractical.

(2)   There are questions of law, or fact, common to the class.

(3)   The claims or defenses of the representative parties are typical of the claims or defenses of the class.

(4)   The representative parties will fairly and adequately protect the interests of the class.

In a true class suit, plaintiffs stand in judgment for the class. A judgment for or against the plaintiffs benefits or binds each member of the class personally under the principles of res judicata. The members of the class must, therefore, be capable of definite identification, as being either in or out of the class.

11.0. Evidence

Evidence is the legal means, exclusive of arguments, for proving or disproving any fact, the truth of which is submitted to investigation. Since evidence is so critical to many issues in the environmental field, some key points of interest will be presented in the following sections. Evidence is an extremely complex area of the law. So, this is intended only as a brief review to give non-lawyers some basic concepts.

Please note that the law of evidence is known for its exceptions to general rules.

11.1 Burden of Proof

In the law of evidence, the phrase burden of proof is used to denote the duty of affirmatively proving the facts in dispute on an issue raised between the parties.

This burden of proof rests throughout the trial, upon the party asserting the affirmative of the issue.

The burden of proof is generally distinguished from the burden of proceeding. The duty of proceeding with a case is called the burden of proceeding, and shifts between the plaintiff and defendant during the trial.

11.2 Judicial Notice

As a general rule, a party must prove everything he alleges. The exceptions to this general rule are (1) things admitted in the pleadings, (2) things stipulated by the parties, or (3) judicial notice.

Judicial notice means that the court will take cognizance of certain facts without requiring proof. An example of judicial notice is that 12 January 1986 is a Sunday. Many facts of common indisputable knowledge need not be proven by evidence because the courts take judicial notice of this information so as not to waste time.

11.3 Presumptions

A presumption is a conclusion, which is drawn from other facts already proved. Presumptions are either (1) conclusive—which are rules of law and may not be rebutted or (2) rebuttable—presumptions which can be overcome by evidence.

11.4 Admissions

An admission is a voluntary acknowledgement of the existence of or the truth of certain facts. An admission will be recognized in court, if made by an employee against an employer within the scope of employment. As a general rule, an admission made by a party to a suit is admissible no matter when or where made. One exception to this general rule is when the admission is made in an offer to compromise. As a general rule, offers to compromise a lawsuit are not admissable. An admission made during a telephone conversation may be admissible if there is collaborating testimony or evidence.

An admission of guilt in a criminal case is a confession.

11.5 Questions Of Law and Fact

Questions arising during the course of a trial are either: questions of law or questions of fact. Generally, questions of law are decided by the court. Questions of fact are decided by a jury. One exception to that division of duties is whether a witness is an expert, which is determined by the court.

11.6 Relevant and Material

Two of the most commonly used words in the area of evidence are relevant and material. The facts or testimony presented in court must be relevant and material to the issue in question, or these irrelevant and immaterial facts or testimony are subject to exclusion. Whether the facts or testimony are relevant and material is a question of law, and so these are decided by the judge.

11.7 Res Inter Alios Acta

The Latin phrase res inter alios acta is used to denote the general rule that prior acts of a defendant or subsequent acts of precaution are not admitted in evidence, because they tend to multiply the issues or may be unfairly prejudical. There are a number of exceptions which have severely eroded this general rule.

11.8 Hearsay

Hearsay is that evidence which depends solely for its truth or falsity upon statements of a person other than the witness. Hearsay, in itself, has no evidentiary value. The witness cannot be cross-examined regarding hearsay, because the statements are those of another. Generally, hearsay is inadmissible, but there are numerous exceptions. An interesting example of inadmissible hearsay is found in the case Bebbington v. California Western States Life Insurance Company. 66/ In this case the suit was brought by the beneficiary of a life insurance policy against the insurance company (defendant). The policy provided that it was void, if the insured died in a plane crash. The insurance company in trying to prove that the decedent died in a plane crash, introduced a letter from a friend of the deceased, a telegram of condolence, and a newspaper clipping each telling of the plane accident. The court ruled that these were all written hearsay, and so inadmissible. (The insurance company should have proved the accident by an eyewitness or official records.)

Usually in the case of documents, a statute provides for an official custodian or witness who will certify to their authenticity or validity to overcome the hearsay objection.

66/   30 Cal. 2d 157 (1947).

11.9 Opinion Evidence

Generally, the testimony of a witness is confined to a statement of concrete facts based upon his own observation or knowledge. Expert opinion evidence is admissible when it concerns scientific or technical knowledge. Non-expert witnesses may be asked to express an opinion to help understand what was observed, but conjecture is not admissible. The problem with experts is that you can generally find one on either side of a case. For example the prosecutor will have his psychiatrist testify that the defendant is sane while the defendant's psychiatrist is testfying he is insane. This type of opinion evidence is common in environmental litigation.

11.10 Best Evidence Rule

The "best evidence rule" simply states that unless a sufficient reason is given, proof of the contents of a writing must be made by producing the original evidence, or at least a certified copy of the original. The best evidence possible must be submited to the court, or the evidence is inadmissible.

11.11 Parol Evidence Rule

The general rule is that parol (oral) evidence is not admissible to vary, add to, take away from or contradict the terms of a written instrument. There are exceptions, such as explaining an ambiguity, showing a condition precedent, showing fraud and others.

11.12 Witnesses

Generally, all persons are competent to testify, but their credibility can be attacked. Leading questions (ones which suggest an answer), may generally only be asked of unwilling witnesses or adverse parties. A witness must answer all questions asked, which will provide information on the issue under investigation—unless this testimony may subject the witness to criminal prosecution. The opposing party has a right to cross-examine the witness. If the witness refuses to answer a question on cross-examination, his entire testimony may be expunged from the record. Generally, cross-examinations are limited to facts, on which a witness testified during direct examination.

11.13 Privileged Communications

Privilege is an exception to the rule that the public has the right to know every man's evidence. The reason for the exception is public policy.

At common law there was privilege only between an attorney and client, but by statutes and judicial decisions this has been extended to others such as physician and patient, clergy and laymen.

In environmental lawsuits, the concern is with the attorney-client relationship. It is the duty of a lawyer to preserve his client's confidences. This duty outlasts the lawyer's employment.

The concept of privileged communications can be used not only in lawsuits but also when providing legal advice such as during environmental audits.   Nicholas A. Robinson, a New York City attorney, wrote in an unpublished paper:

> If a company does not know exactly the nature, volume, frequency, and sources of its emissions, it should find out. And since such knowledge may reveal that the company is in violation of different laws, it should be careful how it finds out. A company may wish to use the 'attorney-client privilege' to learn such facts without fear that they will fall into the hands of prosecutors or other plaintiffs.
>
> The attorney-client privilege in law provides such protection. If a company, as client, seeks advice on pollution liability from an attorney, that attorney can hire experts or consultants to run tests and determine the facts about the company's pollution. He can then evaluate the legal consequence of these facts and advise the company. Courts have held such investigative findings and legal analysis must be kept secret from both government and private parties. [See e.g., Radiant Burners, Inc. v. Am. Gas Corp., 320 F 2d 314 (7th Cir. 1963) and D. Simon, 'The Attorney-Client Privileges As Applied to Corporations,' 65 Yale Law Journal, 953 (1956).] If the company hired the experts on its own, there would be usually no way to prevent a prosecutor or a private plaintiff from obtaining the data. Only when the facts are known can a company prepare for and avoid liability.

Timothy A. Vanderver, Jr., a Washington, D.C. attorney who has conducted many environmental audits writes:

> By definition, the purpose of an environmental audit is to discover what may have been previously unknown violations of the law. Thus, it is highly desirable that the audit report be protected from disclosure or discovery to the maximum extent

possible. For this reason, the audit should be designed and carried out so that a claim of attorney-client privilege can be successfully asserted with respect to the audit report and all pertinent information gathered in the course of the audit. Establishing an attorney-client privilege requires close involvement of legal counsel in both the design and performance phases of the audit. This is necessary in order to assure that the elements of the privilege are satisfied:

- All communications are made between the client and its attorney for the purpose of rendering legal advice on the company's compliance status.
- Communications are made for the clearly-stated purpose of seeking legal advice.
- Attorney-client communications are kept confidential during and after the audit process.
- The privilege is not inadvertently waived through disclosure.

Thus, it is important that a lawyer supervise the information-gathering process during the audit, and establish procedures for controlling access to all documents generated during the audit. Of particular importance is the audit report. This should be treated as a confidential document and circulation should be limited to top-level management. 67/

11.14 Your Own Reports as Evidence Against You

Many of the environmental laws and regulations require reports or data to be filed with the government. The laws governing occupational health, waste and air pollution all require reports. Even the reports to the Securities and Exchange Commission require disclosure of information on pollution. Most of these reports are available to the public and to competitors.

The extent to which the results of an investigation or inspection are available in private liability litigation remains uncertain. A corporation is not protected by the self-incrimination provisions of the Fifth Amendment to the U.S. Constitution. So, it may not object to the production of its books to be used as evidence against it. 68/

67/ Environmental Audits (3rd Edition, 1984), Government Institutes: Rockville, Md., p.25.

68/ Essgee Co. v. U.S., 262 U.S. 151.

11.15 Samples or Physical Evidence

One of the common evidentiary problems raised in court cases is that involving physical evidence. In environmental cases the evidence is often a sample or some data. Some of the key issues normally involved with physical evidence are: (1) has the evidence or data been altered or contaminated, (2) was the equipment used in evidence collection properly calibrated, (3) were scientifically acceptable and standard methods of analysis used in evaluation and (4) who has handled the evidence (chain of custody)?

In order to lay a proper foundation for the admission of evidence, an attorney should be able to present the principals in the "chain of custody" to testify as to their involvement and appropriate expertise in the proper handling of the evidence. The courts will frequently require the parties to stipulate as to the authenticity of the evidence to avoid this tedious form of proof. In legal terminology, "to stipulate" is to agree initially on conduct or evidence for the purpose of shortening the legal proceedings.

11.16 Evidence Collection and Constitutional Rights

A problem that may arise in the collection of evidence concerns the Fourth Amendment or Constitutional rights of corporate entities and private persons.

The Fourth Amendment to the U.S. Constitution prohibits all unreasonable searches and requires a search warrant for most investigations. However, no search warrant is needed in three basic situations: (1) when there is an emergency, (2) when the owner or operator gives his consent, or (3) when the samples could be taken from outside of the property (open fields exception). Search warrants are described in detail in Section 8.2.1.

In most states, search warrants are used for searches for the implements or fruits of a crime and not for mere investigation of conditions which may lead to either civil or criminal penalties. A few states authorize a special kind of search warrant, sometimes called an inspection warrant, which may be used to investigate conditions.

The Fifth Amendment prohibition against criminal self-incrimination was described earlier in Section 8.2.2. In evidence collection involving criminal charges against private parties, this Fifth Amendment right must be properly observed or the courts will not allow evidence to be introduced in the case. The Fifth Amendment protections apply only to private persons and not to corporations or partnerships.

12.0 Administrative Law

12.1 Generally

Governments are customarily divided into executive, legislative and judicial branches. The executive branches function through a system of administrative agencies. These are the governmental officials with whom environmental managers are in the most contact on a regular basis. The operations of these administrative agencies are regulated by the field of administrative law. We will briefly identify some major points in administrative law which may be of interest to environmental managers.

12.2 Powers of Governmental Agencies

Rules, regulations and general orders promulgated by an administrative agency, pursuant to its delegated powers, have the force and effect of law. They are binding on all persons subject to them without notice, and the courts take judicial notice of them. However, the power to promulgate regulations is not a power to change the law. The environmental regulations must be in conformance with the authorizing environmental law.

In order for a regulation to be the basis of a crime, it is necessary that sufficient statutory authority exists for declaring any act or omission a criminal offense. A breach of a departmental regulation is not a crime, unless made so by the legislature. Regulations prescribed by the President of the United States and heads of departments, under authority granted by Congress, may be regulations prescribed by law. However, it does not follow that an act or omission constitutes a criminal offense when the statute does not make it so. An administrative agency may not provide for penalties or criminal liability unless specifically provided by statute.

An administrative agency has limited jurisdiction, depending entirely on that given to it by the statute.

12.3 Procedures

The procedures to be followed before an administrative agency are usually prescribed by the statute creating the agency. If the statute fails to prescribe the procedure, then the fundamental principle is that the regulations must preserve the requirements of fair play.

In general, an administrative agency is not bound by the technical or formal rules of procedure which govern trials before a court. While the constitutional guaranty of due process of law applies to an administrative agency as well as a court, due process is not necessarily judicial process. All the formalities of a judicial proceeding are not essential to constitute due process of law in an administrative proceeding. Neither the Fifth Amendment nor the Fourteenth Amendment of the federal Constitution guarantee any particular form of procedure. In administrative proceedings due process signifies a right to be heard before a final order becomes effective.

It is not within the power of any tribunal to make a binding adjudication of the rights of any party not brought before it. Consequently, a party is entitled to notice, when a constitutional right is in question, and sufficient time to enable him to prepare a defense.

As in a judicial proceeding, notice by publication may be prescribed by statute and will sustain the jurisdiction. Consequently, it is generally held that a corporation doing business in a state, even though it has not applied for permission to do business in the state, consents to abide by the state laws, including service of notice in a proceeding before an administrative body.

Generally, the federal government announces its environmental regulations and hearing in the Federal Register which is published daily.

12.4 Evidence in Administrative Law

As a general rule, an administrative agency is not bound by the strict rules of evidence, which must be observed in the trial of cases in courts of law. However, unless a statute provides rules of evidence for the agency, the latter, in the exercise of its quasi-judicial powers, must provide rules of evidence which preserve fair play, such as the right of cross-examination of witnesses and the right to subpoena witnesses and documents. But the mere fact that certain evidence which would be inadmissible in a court of law is admitted at a hearing before an administrative agency does not invalidate such administrative proceedings.

Under the Administrative Procedure Act, 69/ generally hearsay evidence is admissible, but no order can issue, unless it is supported by and in accordance with reliable, probative, and substantive evidence.

69/ 5 U.S.C. §§ 551 et seq.

12.5 Hearings

Not every administrative determination for private individuals requires notice and hearing. In order to comply with due process, notice and hearing are required only when some constitutional right is claimed to have been violated.

When the purpose of an administrative determination is to decide whether a right or privilege, which a person does not have, shall be granted or withheld in the exercise of its discretion, it is not necessary to have a notice and hearing in the absence of a statutory provision.

The constitutional guarantee of a trial by jury does not apply to an administrative hearing. Determination of facts may be left to an administrative tribunal. It is common practice to have testimony taken before an examiner, who reports the facts to the tribunal. Exceptions may be taken to the report, and argument may be had before the deciding body. The recommendation in the report is not binding on the determining body, if it is charged with the duty of making final decisions.

12.6 Judicial Review

What decisions an administrative agency makes depends on the statute. It is common for a federal agency to have the power to issue a cease and desist order, and in many instances an agency has the power to take affirmative action. An administrative order cannot be enforced in a court without an express provision in the statute.

Generally, before a person is able to have a court review an administrative action, he must exhaust all his administrative remedies because courts are normally reluctant to interfere with administrative action before it is completed. Once the administrative remedies have been exhausted, then the matter is considered "ripe" for judicial review.

Theoretically, the courts will not review the facts in the case but limit themselves to questions of law, or whether there has been abuse of authority and disregard of due process.

Recent cases are worthy of examination because basic concepts are being challenged in this area of administrative law as the trend develops for the courts to interject themselves more and more into examining the operation of administrative agencies.

In one case the manufacture of a mercury fungicide (use of which was ordered suspended by the secretary of agriculture, based on a single abnormal incident without a hearing), was reviewed by a federal district court. The review was undertaken by the court based on the argument that the agency order was arbitrary and capricious since there was only one incident and a hearing was not held by the Department of Agriculture. 70/

On the state level in a case before the Pennsylvania Court of Common Pleas of Dauphin County, there was a challenge of the findings of the Pennsylvania Air Pollution Commission that a coil coating plant emitted odorous gases in violation of the state Air Pollution Control Act. The court said that it could not modify the finding on the ground of credibility of evidence. 71/ The court said it only considered whether the Air Pollution Commission was arbitrary, and left credibility of the evidence to the commission. This limited review is the usual approach taken by a court when considering an appeal from an administrative agency.

In the case of the Environmental Defense Fund v. Hardin, 72/ the secretary of agriculture's failure to act promptly on a conservation group's request for interim suspension of the registration of a pesticide to protect the public from an "imminent hazard" was held by the U.S. Court of Appeals for the District of Columbia to be tantamount to an order denying suspension and was, therefore, ripe for judicial review. The court held that even a temporary refusal results in irreparable injury on a massive scale, and is thus a final disposition of such rights as plaintiffs and the public may have to interim relief. In a subsequent court action on the same controversy the court's opinion was critical of the handling of the case by the Department of Agriculture. The court stated that for years courts have "treated administrative policy decisions with great deference," but they no longer will "bow to the mysteries of administrative expertise." One judge disagreed and wrote a dissenting opinion charging that "the Court is undertaking to manage the Department of Agriculture." These majority and dissenting comments show two views on review by the courts of administrative decisions.

70/ Nor-Am Agricultural Products, Inc., v. Hardin, 435 F2d 1133 (7th Cir. 1970).

71/ Air Commission v. Coated Materials, 778 C.D. 1969 (Pa. Ct. Comm. Pls. 1970).

72/ 428 F. 2d 1093 (1970).

As the general rule, if you are involved in a dispute with an administrative agency, usually you must exhaust all available administrative remedies before you can initiate court action.

Generally, in the judicial review process, the courts first determine whether or not the agency acted within the scope of its authority. If this question is answered in the affirmative, then there must be a finding whether the choice made was arbitrary, capricious or not in accordance with law. The standard of review then becomes a determination whether the decision was based on a consideration of the relevant factors and whether there has been a clear error of judgment. The courts are not empowered to substitute their judgment for that of the agency.

13.0 Attorneys' Fees—New Concepts

One of the basic traditions of who pays the lawyers has been significantly modified in recent years. This trend is worthy of description in this book because the award of these fees may be a significant factor in an environmental lawsuit.

Generally, under the so-called "American Rule" the winning party in a lawsuit is awarded costs but these costs do not include attorneys' fees. The result is that each party normally is responsible for their respective attorneys' fees.

Several statutes have created exceptions to this rule by authorizing the award of attorneys' fees. These statutes include the Clean Air Act and the Resource Conservation and Recovery Act (RCRA). Successful plaintiffs were awarded attorneys' fees in several environmental lawsuits during the past few years. The matter was becoming confused with various court interpretations of the law. However, the Supreme Court has spoken on the subject of award of attorneys' fees to clarify the situation. In <u>Alyeska v. Wilderness Society</u>, 73/ the Supreme Court ruled that in the absence of statutory authorization or an enforceable contract, litigants must pay their own attorneys' fees.

Congress while fully recognizing this general rule has made specific and explicit provisions for the allowance of attorneys' fees in some statutes. If a statutory provision is not involved, the courts generally will not order payment of attorney fees.

<u>73</u>/   7 ERC 1849 (U.S. Sup. Ct. 1975).

14.0 Criminal and Civil Liability of Corporate Employees

The environmental laws and regulations provide for a wide range of civil and criminal penalties for failure to comply as described in Chapter 14.

Now, there is a quiet evolution taking place. The courts are no longer holding only a corporation liable under the statutes for a fine but are holding individuals personally liable in their corporate roles.

The U.S. Supreme Court case of U.S. v. Park 74/ is a landmark case in this area. In this case the Court held that a corporate officer could be criminally liable under the Food, Drug and Cosmetic Act if he had the corporate authority and responsibility for preventing violations of the statute but failed to do so.

Park, the president of Acme Markets, was convicted of violating the Federal Food, Drug, and Cosmetic Act. It states that "any person who violates a provision of [the Act] . . . shall be imprisoned for not more than one year or fined not more than $1,000, or both." Park was charged with causing interstate food shipments, being held for sale in an Acme Baltimore warehouse, to become adulterated by exposure to rat poison. Park had received notice that there was a violation in Acme's Baltimore warehouse. He had delegated responsibility for remedying the situation to some employees. The trial court was of the opinion that because he knew of a previous violation in a Philadelphia warehouse that had been ineffectively remedied and he had delegated responsibility to the same people, his delegation in the Baltimore case (which also turned out to be ineffective) was not a sufficient attempt to remedy the problem. He was convicted on five counts.

The trial court judge said that Park could be found guilty "even if he did not consciously do wrong" and even if he had not "personally participated in the situation," if it were proved beyond a reasonable doubt that he "had a responsible relationship" to the situation.

Generally, criminal violation requires some element of conscious wrong-doing or some criminal intent. In this case the Supreme Court upheld Park's conviction based on his being the responsible corporate official. This means that corporate officers can be held legally liable for their subordinates' actions or inactions in a broad range of cases.

74/   421 U.S. 658 (1975).

The Supreme Court noted that a finding of guilt cannot be based solely on the officer's position in the company. There should be some measure of "blameworthiness." The test which the Supreme Court used was that a corporate officer could be held criminally responsible if such officer had, "by reason of his position in the corporation, responsibility and authority either to prevent in the first instance, or promptly to correct, the violation complained of, and that he failed to do so." 75/

Criminal liability under other environmental laws is generally not as broad as under the Food, Drug and Cosmetic Act because the other laws use a term such as "knowing" before the proposed violation to require some willfulness or intent.

Governmental officials are also subject to criminal indictment. The "Watergate Cases," resulting from the Nixon re-election campaign, give a famous example of the highest government officials being convicted of crimes for their actions or inactions.

Civil penalties are a definite deterrent but criminal penalties can literally destroy individuals from both a social and economic viewpoint.

In a speech before a bar association meeting 76/ James W. Moorman, then Assistant Attorney General of the U.S. Department of Justice, stated the government's position on strict criminal enforcement against corporate officials in the environmental field:

> Many failures to comply have simply been the result of bumbling or ignorance. For this category of noncompliance, EPA and Justice have sought, and will continue to seek, civil remedies from the courts in the form of monetary penalties and injunctions.
> There is a second form of resistance, however, which involves more deplorable conduct: willful, substantial violations of the pollution control laws of a criminal nature. For these transgressions, the Department of Justice has begun to invoke grand jury investigations both against corporations and against individuals. The Department will prosecute criminal conduct in this areas.

75/ Ibid. at 672.

76/ Statement of James W. Moorman, Assistant Attorney General, Department of Justice. 10 February 1978 before ALI–ABA in Washington, D.C.

The Congress has signaled its intention that vigorous criminal enforcement occur by providing strict and stringent criminal statutes. Under the Water Act, "any person who wilfully or negligently" violates the conditions of a permit or who discharges without a permit is exposed to criminal liability for fines up to $25,000 per day and imprisonment up to 1 year. That is for a first offense. Further offenses are punishable by fines of $50,000 per day of violation and jail terms of up to 2 years. The making of false applications or reports under the act is punishable by a $10,000 fine and 6 months imprisonment. Under the Air Act, there are similar penalties for knowing violations of the requirements of the Act, for false statements and for tampering with monitoring equipment. Other pollution control laws governing pesticides, toxic substances, and so forth, likewise have criminal provisions.

I also invite your attention to the fact that violations of pollution control laws can often be crimes under the more general provisions of the criminal code found in Title 18, Section 1001, which covers false statements to government agencies, and Section 1341, the mail fraud statutes, are two examples of such provisions.

It should be evident to all here that the price paid for criminal misconduct can be quite high. Many of those who have chosen to violate or who will be tempted to violate the pollution control laws are professional and business people. These are people for whom an indictment alone, not to mention conviction or imprisonment, can be a catastrophe. As a consequence, I believe a policy of vigorous criminal enforcement will be truly effective as a deterrent and will result in a higher degree of pollution control.

These trends toward increased severity in punishment for violation of the law should make everyone more conscious of their legal and social duties.

*   *   *

Author's Note:
I sincerely hope that my efforts and those of my colleagues at Government Institutes in publishing this material along with our educational efforts in the form of continuing education courses help everyone in avoiding civil and criminal liabilities. More importantly, our efforts are intended, in some small way, to aid in voluntary compliance with both the letter and spirit of the law.

Chapter 2

RESOURCE CONSERVATION AND RECOVERY ACT

Ridgway M. Hall, Jr.
Nancy S. Bryson
Attorneys
Crowell & Moring
Washington, D.C.

1.0 Overview

The management of the hazardous waste which is being generated in large quantities by our modern, post-World War II economy has come to be recognized as a major environmental problem over the past ten years. On 21 October 1976, Congress enacted the Resource Conservation and Recovery Act (RCRA), the first comprehensive federal effort to deal with the problem of solid waste generally and hazardous waste specifically. 1/ RCRA is basically a regulatory statute, designed to provide cradle to grave management of hazardous waste by imposing management requirements on generators and transporters of hazardous materials and upon owners and operators of treatment, storage and disposal facilities. It does not address what has come to be recognized as the equally serious problem of abandoned and inactive sites. Legislation establishing remedies and allocating responsibilities for correcting problems at those sites is contained in the Comprehensive Environmental Response, Compensation, and Liability Act of 1980, commonly known as Superfund, 2/ and is discussed in detail in Chapter 3.

1/   42 USC 6901 et seq. (1981). Citations throughout this chapter are to sections of the act, rather than to the U.S. Code.

2/   42 USC Section 9601 et seq.

61

RCRA has been amended several times since its enactment, most recently in 1984. 3/ It is currently divided into nine subtitles, A through I. The most significant of these is Subtitle C, which sets the regulatory requirements for the hazardous waste management program, and governs the conduct of generators and transporters of hazardous waste and owners and operators of treatment, storage and disposal facilities.

Subtitle C, which encompasses Sections 3001-3019, establishes the following parameters for the RCRA hazardous waste management program. Section 3001 requires EPA to promulgate regulations which identify specific hazardous waste, either by listing them or identifying characteristics which render them hazardous. Persons managing such waste are required to identify themselves and their hazardous waste activities to EPA. 4/

Persons who generate or produce these wastes must comply with a set of standards authorized by RCRA Section 3002. These include preparing manifests to track the movement of the waste through ultimate disposal. Persons who transport hazardous waste are required by Section 3003 to comply with another set of regulations dealing with recordkeeping, labeling and the delivery of hazardous waste shipments to designated treatment, storage or disposal (T/S/D) facilities.

Section 3004 requires performance standards for such T/S/D facilities including statutory minimum technology standards, ground-water monitoring systems and a ban on the disposal of liquids in landfills. Section 3005 requires owners and operators of T/S/D facilities to obtain permits, which essentially set forth the conditions under which they may operate. Section 3005(e) establishes the "interim status" provision for existing facilities. This allows existing T/S/D facilities to remain in operation past the effective date of the regulatory program, i.e., 19 November 1980, even though a site-specific permit has not been issued. Owners or operators of interim status facilities, nevertheless, must file a timely application for and

---

3/ PL 96-482, 94 Stat. 2334 (1980); 1984 Hazardous and Solid Waste Amendments signed by President Reagan on November 8, 1984, PL 98-616, 98 Stat. 3221.

4/ Section 3010(a).

eventually qualify for a permit under RCRA Section 3005(a). The 1984 RCRA Amendments set a time table for EPA to process and issue such permits.

Sections 3007 and 3008 authorize site inspections and federal enforcement of RCRA and its implementing regulations. Section 3006 authorizes states to assume responsibility for the RCRA program in lieu of the federal program where the state adopts and agrees to enforce a program which is at least equivalent to the federal program.

Other provisions of Subtitle C include provisions for compiling a hazardous waste site inventory; limited monitoring and enforcement authority against previous owners of T/S/D facilities; EPA issuance of performance standards for the management of recycled oil, and an inventory of federal agency hazardous waste facilities. 5/

The 1984 Amendments to RCRA, which are included in the discussion here, are extensive. They significantly expanded both the scope of coverage and the detailed requirements of RCRA. For example, they require EPA to regulate for the first time an estimated 100,000 companies that produce only small quantities of hazardous waste (less than 1,000 kilograms per month). An entirely new regulatory program is created in Subtitle I ("eye") for underground storage tanks containing hazardous substances or petroleum, which will affect hundreds of thousands of facilities for the first time. 6/ The numerous constraints imposed on those who treat, store or dispose of wastes in landfills, including restrictions on the disposal of liquid wastes and other common hazardous wastes, appear to be technically complex and, in many cases, difficult to meet. For example, companies using existing unlined surface impoundments will be required to retrofit with double liners and leachate collection systems within the next four years.

The Amendments contain many so-called "hammer" provisions that require EPA to implement new requirements by a deadline or a congressionally formulated regulation will automatically go into effect. There are 72 major provisions in the new law, by EPA's

---

5/   Sections 3012, 3013, 3014, 3016.

6/   Sections 9001-9010.

count, and 52 require EPA action by late 1986. This will have a substantial impact on every U.S. business that produces hazardous waste from industrial or commercial operations.

These major provisions of the Subtitle C program and the impact of the 1984 regulations are discussed in detail below, as are the requirements of other important subtitles of the Act, including the newly enacted Subtitle I.

2.0 Policy Goals and Objectives of RCRA, as Amended

Subtitle A of RCRA declares that, as a matter of national policy, the generation of hazardous waste is to be reduced or eliminated as expeditiously as possible. In addition, waste that is generated is to be handled so as to minimize the present and future threat to human health and the environment. 7/

Subtitle A also includes a series of objectives designed to achieve these goals, including first instance proper management of hazardous waste, minimization of the generation and land disposal of hazardous waste, prohibition of open dumping, encouragement of state assumption of RCRA programs, encouragement of research and development activities in the waste management area and promotion of recovery and recycling as alternatives to disposal. 8/

3.0 Definition of Solid and Hazardous Waste

Section 1004(27) states that:

> The term "solid waste" means any garbage, refuse, sludge, from a waste treatment plant, water supply treatment plant or air pollution control facility and other discarded material, including solid, liquid, semi-solid, or contained gaseous materials resulting from industrial, commercial, mining and agriculture activities and from community activities but does not include solid or dissolved material in domestic sewage, or solid or dissolved materials in irrigation return flows or industrial discharges which are point sources subject to permits under section 402 of the Federal Water Pollution Control Act, as amended (86 Stat. 880), or source, special nuclear, or byproduct material as defined by the

---

7/   RCRA, Section 1003(b).

8/   RCRA, Section 1003(a).

Atomic Energy Act of 1954, as amended (68 Stat. 923).
(Emphasis supplied.)

The statute therefore applies to potentially any waste regardless of
its physical form.

The Subtitle C regulatory program of RCRA covers the management of those solid wastes categorized as hazardous. As defined
in Section 1004(5), the term "hazardous waste" means a solid waste,
or combination of solid wastes, which because of its quantity,
concentration, or physical, chemical, or infectious characteristics
may—

"(A) cause, or significantly contribute to an
increase in mortality or an increase in serious irreversible, or incapacitating reversible illness; or

"(B) pose a substantial present or potential hazard
to human health or the environment when improperly
treated, stored, transported, or disposed of, or otherwise managed."

These general statutory definitions have been greatly amplified and
explained by EPA regulations implementing RCRA, the first set of
which was issued on 19 May 1980. 9/ These regulations are discussed
in the following section which describes the Title C program in
detail.

4.0 Subtitle C: The Hazardous Waste Management Program

4.1 Identification of Hazardous Wastes under the Implementing Regulations 10/

New regulations adopted by EPA on 4 January 1985 define
solid waste to include any discarded material that is not excluded by
regulation or by a specific variance granted by EPA or an authorized

---

9/   45 FR 33066.

10/   For a more comprehensive description of the regulatory
       provisions of RCRA, the reader is referred to Hall, Watson,
       Davidson and Case, Hazardous Waste Handbook (Government
       Institutes, 5th ed. 1984).

state. 11/ "Discarded material" is in turn defined as any material that is abandoned, recycled or "inherently waste-like." 12/ A material is abandoned if it is disposed of, burned or incinerated, or accumulated, stored or treated prior to or in lieu of abandonment. A material is a solid waste if it is recycled in a manner constituting disposal, by burning for energy recovery, by reclamation or by speculative accumulation. A material is inherently waste-like if EPA so defines it by regulation. 13/

These interlocking definitions result in EPA regulating a universe of materials which may not be commonly understood to be "wastes" for a particular industry or company. The only types of materials which are not solid wastes when recycled are materials which are directly used or reused as ingredients or feedstocks in product processes or as effective substitutes for commercial products or those which are recycled in a closed-loop product process.

Once a material is found to be a solid waste, the next question is: is it a "hazardous waste"? EPA's regulations automatically exempt certain solid wastes from being considered hazardous wastes. Generally these regulatory exemptions include:

(1)   household waste;

(2)   agricultural wastes which are returned to the ground as fertilizer;

(3)   mining overburden returned to the mine site;

(4)   utility wastes from coal combustion;

(5)   oil and natural gas exploration drilling waste;

(6)   wastes from the extraction, benefaction, and processing of ores and minerals, including coal;

(7)   cement kiln dust wastes;

11/   40 CFR 261.2(a), 50 FR 664 (4 January 1985). The list of regulatory exemptions appears at 261.4(a) and is very limited. See pp. 6-7 infra.

12/   40 CFR 261(a)(2), 50 FR 614 (4 January 1985).

13/   40 CFR 261.2, 50 FR 614 (4 January 1985).

(8)   arsenical-treated wood wastes generated by end users of such wood;

(9)   certain chromium-bearing wastes. 14/

EPA has also provided some limited regulatory exemptions under particularly defined circumstances such as for hazardous waste that is generated in a product or raw material storage tank, transport vehicle, pipeline or manufacturing process unit. EPA has also exempted waste samples and other samples collected for monitoring and testing.

If a solid waste material does not qualify for one of the many exemptions, it will be deemed a hazardous waste if it is listed by EPA in 40 CFR Part 261, Subpart D, exhibits any of the four hazardous waste characteristics identified in 40 CFR Part 261, Subpart C, or is a mixture of a listed waste and a solid waste. 15/

4.1.1 Hazardous Waste Lists

EPA has established three hazardous wastes lists: (1) hazardous wastes from nonspecific sources (e.g., spent nonhalogenated solvents, toluene, methyl ethyl ketone...); 16/ (2) hazardous wastes from specific sources (e.g., bottom sediment sludge from the treatment of waste waters from wood preserving); 17/ and (3) discarded commercial chemical products, and all off-specification species, containers, and spill residues thereof. 18/

The first two hazardous waste lists are largely self-explanatory. A company need only compare its solid waste stream to the lists to determine if it manages a hazardous waste.

14/   40 CFR 261.4(b), 45 FR 33120, 45 FR 72037 (30 October 1980), 45 FR 76620 (19 November 1980), 45 FR 78531 (25 November 1980).

15/   40 CFR 261.3(a).

16/   40 CFR 261.31.

17/   40 CFR 261.32.

18/   40 CFR 261.33, 45 FR 33122-27, 45 FR 47833-36 (16 July 1980); 45 FR 72039 (30 October 1980); 45 FR 74890 (12 November 1980); 45 FR 78541-44 (25 November 1980); 46 FR 27476-77 (20 May 1981).

The third list sets forth commercial chemicals which, if discarded, must be treated as hazardous wastes. This hazardous waste list actually consists of two distinct lists. One list sets forth chemicals deemed toxic and, therefore, hazardous if discarded (40 CFR 261.33(f)). These are regulated like the other listed hazardous wastes. A second list contains wastes which EPA identifies as acutely hazardous (40 CFR 261.33(e)) for which more rigorous management requirements apply.

Hazardous waste regulation under the commercial chemical list is expected to be triggered most often when a company decides to reduce inventory and discards a listed commercial chemical product in its pure form. A common scenario which will trigger the commercial chemical list is an accidental spill situation. 19/ If a listed commercial chemical is spilled, the spilled chemical and any contaminated material, i.e., dirt and other residue, is likely to be discarded and thus becomes a hazardous waste and must be managed as such. Therefore, even companies which generally do not discard or intend to discard any of the commercial chemical products on the list must be prepared to comply with the RCRA hazardous waste regulations in the event of an accidental spill. 20/ This will involve, as discussed below, obtaining an EPA identification number and complying, at a minimum, with applicable generator standards.

Congress has directed EPA to decide by February 1986, or sooner in some instances, whether to list as hazardous certain wastes commonly produced by industry. These wastes include solvents, oil refining wastes, inorganic chemical industry wastes, dioxins, dyes and pigments, and coal slurry pipeline effluent. EPA's listing of such wastes over the next 15 months will substantially expand RCRA's coverage.

Since the RCRA program became effective in 1980, many companies have filed "delisting petitions" with EPA to remove wastes generated at their facilities from coverage under the RCRA hazardous waste lists at 40 CFR Part 261. In many instances, EPA has granted these companies "temporary exclusions" from the

---

19/   40 CFR 261.33(d), 45 FR 78541 (25 November 1980), 46 FR 27477 (20 May 1981).

20/   See 45 FR 76629 (19 November 1980).

hazardous waste list based on a substantial likelihood that their delisting petitions would be granted, pending the public notice and comment required for a final decision on the petitions. The granting of a delisting petition, or a temporary exclusion, exempts the waste generated at a particular facility from the RCRA hazardous waste program requirements, provided the waste is not hazardous by characteristic.

Prior to the 1984 RCRA Amendments, a company seeking a delisting had to demonstrate that the particular waste generated at its facility did not contain the hazardous constituents for which EPA listed the waste. Congress has now directed EPA to restrict delisting petitions by requiring companies to demonstrate that their wastes do not contain any constituents that could cause the wastes to be hazardous, not just the constituents EPA considered in listing the waste.

For example, a company seeking to delist a waste which would otherwise be included under F006 (wastewater treatment sludge from electroplating operations) must show not only that the concentrations of chromium, nickel, and cyanide for which the waste was listed are below levels of regulatory concern, but also that no other heavy metals or other constituents are present that may cause the waste to be hazardous.   This is expected to substantially increase the cost, the EPA processing time, for delisting petitions. As a practical matter, in anticipation of the new law EPA had already begun implementing this requirement.

The 1984 Amendments also force EPA to act on a delisting petition within two years of receiving a complete petition, thus restricting the agency's discretion to grant lengthy temporary exclusions. All of the temporary exclusions granted by EPA to date will lapse automatically on 8 November 1986, whether or not EPA has made a final decision on the underlying delisting petition. Thus only a final delisting will survive that deadline.

4.1.2 Hazardous Waste Characteristics

Non-listed wastes are covered by RCRA if they possess one of four hazardous waste characteristics: ignitability, corrosivity, reactivity and/or extraction procedure toxicity. 21/

21/   40 CFR 261.3, 40 CFR 261.20.

The hazardous waste characteristic of ignitability was established to identify solid wastes capable during routine handling of causing a fire or exacerbating a fire once started. 22/ A solid waste is deemed to exhibit the characteristic of ignitability if it meets with one of the following four descriptions. First, it is a liquid, other than an aqueous solution containing less than 24 percent alcohol by volume, with a flash point of less than 60 degrees centigrade (140° F). Second, it is a nonliquid which under normal conditions can cause fire through friction, absorption of moisture or spontaneous chemical changes and burns so vigorously when ignited that it creates a hazard. Third, it is an ignitable compressed gas as defined by the DOT regulations set forth at 49 CFR 173.300. Finally, it is an oxidizer as defined by the DOT regulations set forth at 49 CFR 173.151.

The hazardous waste characteristic of corrosivity was established because EPA believed that wastes capable of corroding metal could escape their own containers and liberate other wastes. 23/ In addition, wastes with a pH at either the high or low end of the scale can harm human tissue and aquatic life and may react dangerously with other wastes. Therefore, EPA determined that any solid waste is deemed to exhibit the characteristic of corrosivity if it is (1) aqueous and has a pH of less than or equal to 2.0 or greater than or equal to 12.5, or (2) a liquid and corrodes steel at a rate greater than 6.35 millimeters (.250 inches) per year under specified testing procedures.

EPA established the hazardous waste characteristic of reactivity to regulate wastes which are extremely unstable and have a tendency to react violently or explode during stages of its management. 24/ The regulation lists several situations where this may happen which warrant specific consideration (e.g., the behavior of the substance when mixed with water, when heated, etc.). Instead of developing a precise scientific description of this characteristic, EPA has promulgated a descriptive, prose definition of reactivity

---

22/   40 CFR 261.21.

23/   41 CFR 261.22.

24/   41 CFR 261.23.

under the view that suitable test protocols for measuring reactivity are unavailable.

The Extraction Procedure (EP) toxicity characteristic is designed to identify wastes which are likely to leach hazardous concentrations of specific toxic constituents into groundwater under improper management conditions, one of the more significant dangers posed by mismanagement of hazardous waste. 25/ This characteristic is determined based on a mandatory testing procedure which extracts the toxic constituents for a solid waste in a manner which EPA believes will stimulate the leaching action which occurs in landfills. 26/ If the extract obtained by use of the EP toxicity testing protocol exhibits concentrations of a toxic constituent at levels 100 times or more than those set forth in the National Interim Primary Drinking Water Standards, then that waste will be deemed to exhibit the characteristics of EP toxicity.

4.1.3 Mixtures of Hazardous Wastes and Solid Wastes

A mixture including a listed hazardous waste and a solid waste is treated as a hazardous waste unless such a mixture qualifies for the following exemption: (1) the listed hazardous waste in the mixture was listed solely because it exhibits a hazardous characteristic and the mixture does not exhibit that characteristic; or (2) the mixture consists of certain specified hazardous wastes and wastewater the discharge of which is subject to regulation under the Clean Water Act. To qualify for the second exemption, the concentrations must not exceed certain specified concentrations. 27/ A mixture including a non-listed hazardous waste and a solid waste will be deemed hazardous only if the entire mixture exhibits one of the four hazardous waste characteristics. 28/

4.1.4 Used, Reused, Recycled or Reclaimed Hazardous Wastes

On 4 January 1985, EPA issued final regulations redefining the term "solid waste" to extend coverage to many recycling

---

25/   40 CFR 261.24.

26/   40 CFR Part 261, Appendix H.

27/   See 40 CFR 261.3(a)(2), 46 FR 56588–89 (17 November 1981).

28/   See 45 FR 33095 (19 May 1980).

activities which were previously exempted. 29/ This redefinition is complex--in fact, it took EPA forty-four Federal Register pages to explain its inner workings. Conceptually, the analysis required to apply the definition requires knowledge of two things--the secondary material being recycled and the manner in which it is being recycled.

The new regulations define a solid waste as any discarded material which is among other things recycled in certain defined ways. 30/ These recycling activities which are defined to produce solid waste are (1) use in a manner constituting disposal (e.g. land application), (2) burning for energy recovery, (3) reclamation, and (4) speculative accumulation. 31/ Two types of recycling activities are excluded. The first involves direct use or reuse of secondary materials as either ingredients or feedstocks in product processes or as effective substitutes for commercial products. The second is the recycling process known as "closed-loop product processes" which returns secondary materials to the original primary production process in which they were generated without first reclaiming them.

Secondary materials that are solid wastes when recycled include spent materials, listed and characteristic sludges, listed and characteristic by-products, commercial chemical products and scrap metals. These are all solid wastes when recycled with two exceptions. Characteristic sludges and by-products are not solid wastes when they are reclaimed. Commercial chemical products are not solid wastes when they are either reclaimed or speculatively accumulated. Generally speaking, hazardous wastes waiting to be recycled are subject to the Part 262 and 263 regulations for generators and transporters and to the storage facility requirements in Part 264 and 265 until the recycling activity is completed. 32/

Case-by-case variances from classification as solid waste are available in three cases from either the appropriate EPA regional administrator or an authorized state. Materials eligible for these variances are those which are (1) accumulated without sufficient

---

29/   50 FR 614.

30/   40 CFR 261.2(c); 50 FR 664.

31/   Id.

32/   40 CFR 261.6(b)(1).

amounts being recycled; (2) reclaimed and then reused within the original primary production process in which they were generated; or (3) reclaimed but must be reclaimed further before material recovery is completed.

The various permutations and combinations of these regulations bear close scrutiny. The agency has adopted a broad definition to provide regulatory authority over many types of activities but has simultaneously deferred action on several issues, including the extent to which it will actually regulate ultimate users of waste derived products put on land for beneficial use and how to design the program to regulate burning of waste oil as fuel. 33/

4.1.5 1984 Amendments Relevant to Fuel Containing Hazardous Waste

Congress has directed EPA to impose by November 1986, technical standards that are protective of human health and the environment on companies that produce, transport, distribute, market or burn fuel containing hazardous wastes. Such wastes were exempted from RCRA regulation in 1980. Companies must also maintain such records regarding fuel blending, distribution, and use as EPA may require. EPA may exempt from the technical standards those companies that burn as fuel de minimis quantities of hazardous wastes at the facility where the waste is produced, provided the waste has a sufficient heating value and the boiler achieves sufficient destruction of hazardous constituents. Certain exemptions are also provided for fuel produced from petroleum refining wastes. 34/

In the meantime, the new law requires companies that produce, distribute, market or burn hazardous waste fuels to file a

---

33/ A proposal on this program was issued 4 January 1985, 50 FR 1684.

34/ The new law is expected to accelerate EPA's planned rulemaking on burning and blending, which includes standards that will require industrial boilers and kilns to meet a 99.99 percent destruction efficiency for toxic organic compounds. Under the planned regulations, boilers that do not meet specific design and operating conditions would be required to undergo trial burns to establish destruction efficiency. See 1984 Amendments, Section 204.

notification with EPA by 8 February 1986, which gives the location, type of facility, and the hazardous waste that is used as fuel. This provision applies to listed and characteristic hazardous wastes (including commercial chemical products used as fuel), mixtures of such hazardous wastes and other materials, and used oil. The new law makes it unlawful for any person who is required to file a notification to distribute or market any hazardous waste-derived fuel after 7 February 1985, without the following legend on the invoice or bill of sale:

WARNING: THIS FUEL CONTAINS HAZARDOUS WASTE
(followed by a list of the hazardous wastes).

This legend must appear in conspicuous type which is clearly distinguishable from other printed matter on the invoice or bill of sale.

In the 1984 Amendments, Congress also directed EPA to propose a rule within one year, and to make a final determination within two years, on whether to identify as hazardous waste used automobile and truck crankcase oil. If EPA finally decides that such used oil should be a listed or characteristic hazardous waste, companies that generate, transport, store, treat or dispose of used oil will become subject to the current RCRA hazardous waste regulations, as well as any other regulations EPA may promulgate, especially for used oil. 35/

Congress also directed EPA to establish a special regulatory scheme within the next two years for companies that generate and transport used oil which is recycled. The new standards may not include a manifest requirement or any recordkeeping and reporting (except records of agreements for delivery of used oil) for generators that send used oil to qualified recycling facilities. EPA is to promulgate special standards for recycling facilities, which are then deemed to have a RCRA permit if they comply with such standards.

4.2 Notification of Hazardous Waste Management Activities

RCRA Section 3010(a) requires that any person who manages a hazardous waste (i.e., generators, transporters, owners, or operators of T/S/D facilities) must file a notification with EPA within 90

35/   See 1984 Amendments, Section 241.

days after regulations are promulgated identifying the waste as hazardous. EPA published EPA Form 8700-12 as a Section 3010(a) notification form, explained the notification requirements, and included instructions for completing the form. 36/ This form requires only a bare minimum of information. The reporting company must identify itself, its location and the EPA identification number for the listed and non-listed hazardous wastes it manages. It is important to remember that notifications are required to be filed for each site (e.g., plant) at which there is hazardous waste management activity because RCRA is a specific facility or site specific regulatory program.

EPA's first regulations identifying hazardous wastes at 40 CFR Part 261 were promulgated on 19 May 1980. 37/ Persons managing any of those hazardous wastes should have filed the Section 3010(a) notification form not later than 18 August 1980. Failure to file makes the transport, treatment, storage or disposal unlawful. 38/ EPA has developed several policies and interpretations of this provision, however, which ameliorate its impact. Companies which failed to submit a notification by 18 August 1980, will be excused if EPA finds the failure was based on an ambiguity in the regulations. Companies which failed to file for reasons unrelated to the regulations may request that EPA exercise its enforcement discretion and permit continued operation if it is in the public interest. 39/

4.3 Generators of Hazardous Waste

Generators play a crucial role in the overall RCRA hazardous waste regulatory scheme. The failure of a generator to properly identify and initiate the management of a hazardous waste may mean that the waste never enters the "cradle to grave" hazardous waste program. Thus, the requirements imposed on generators under RCRA Section 3002 and EPA's implementing regulations at 40 CFR Part 262 are of key concern.

36/   45 FR 12746 (26 February 1980).

37/   45 FR 33066.

38/   45 FR 76632 (19 November 1980).

39/   Id.

EPA's regulations define the term "generator" as: "Any person, by site, whose act or process produces hazardous waste identified or listed in Part 261 of this Chapter" or whose act first causes hazardous waste to become subject to regulation. 40/ This definition refers explicitly to the particular site of generation. Thus, a corporation with several plants must evaluate and comply with the generator requirements individually for each facility.

A generator is initially required to determine whether any of its solid waste is a "hazardous waste" under the criteria described above. 41/ If it is, the generator must obtain an EPA Identification Number before the waste can be transported, treated, stored or disposed of. 42/ In addition, he is required to have his hazardous waste transported, treated, stored, and disposed of by persons who also have obtained their EPA Identification Numbers. 43/

The generator also has the responsibility of preparing the Uniform Hazardous Waste Manifest, a control and transport document that accompanies the hazardous waste at all times from its point of generation to its point of disposal. 44/ The generator must specify the name and EPA Identification Numbers of each authorized transporter and the permitted T/S/D facility which will accept the waste, describe the waste as required by DOT regulations, certify that it is properly packaged and labeled and sign the manifest certification by hand.

In the new era of RCRA, companies must develop new management strategies and new technologies to reduce the volume, quantity, and toxicity of hazardous wastes. As an action-forcing mechanism, Congress has now required all generators to certify on manifests after 1 September 1985, that:

(1) the generator of the hazardous waste has a program in place to reduce the volume or quantity and

---

40/   40 CFR 260.10(a)(26).

41/   40 CFR 262.11.

42/   40 CFR 262.12.

43/   40 CFR 262.12(c).

44/   40 CFR 262.20 - 262.23.

toxicity of such waste to the degree determined by the generator to be economically practicable; and

(2) the proposed method of treatment, storage or disposal (selected by the generator) is that practicable method currently available to the generator which minimizes the present and future threat to human health and the environment.

A sufficient number of copies of the manifest must be prepared so that all parties listed on the manifest as handling the hazardous waste will be provided with a copy and a copy will be returned to the generator from the T/S/D facility. A copy of each signed manifest must be kept for a period of three years from the date of acceptance of the waste by the initial transporter. 45/

A generator, in addition, must properly prepare the waste for transportation off-site. EPA has adopted the DOT regulations issued under the Hazardous Materials Transportation Act, 49 USC 1802 et seq., with respect to the packaging, labeling, marking, and placarding. 46/ In addition to the DOT regulations, EPA requires that any container of 110 gallons or less must be specifically marked with the generator's name, address, manifest document number, and the words:

Hazardous waste—federal law prohibits improper disposal. If found contact the nearest police or public safety authority or the United States Environmental Protection Agency." 47/

A generator is allowed to store hazardous waste on-site prior to shipment for a period of up to 90 days in tanks or containers without having to obtain a permit for a storage facility. 48/

4.3.1 Small Generators

Until now EPA has not regulated small quantity generators, those who generated or accumulated less than 1,000 kilograms (2,200

45/   40 CFR 262.40.

46/   40 CFR 262.31.

47/   40 CFR 262.32.

48/   40 CFR 262.34.

pounds) of hazardous waste, except to require disposal in state or municipally licensed facilities or RCRA permitted facilities. EPA created this exemption because it lacked the administrative resources to regulate small quantity generators under RCRA.

In the new law, however, Congress has all but eliminated the exemption. By 16 August 1985, small quantity generators must begin using the Uniform Manifest when shipping their waste. EPA is directed to promulgate regulations by 31 March 1986, for generators, transporters, and T/S/D facilities that handle hazardous wastes produced by the generator in a total monthly quantity of more than 100 but less than 1,000 kilograms (220 - 2,200 pounds). The regulations may vary from the standards that currently apply to hazardous wastes of larger quantity generators, but at a minimum they must require that all treatment, storage and disposal occur at an interim status or permitted T/S/D facility. Small quantity generators may still store up to 1,000 kilograms of hazardous waste on site for 180 days without a permit. If the waste must be shipped over 200 miles, the limit is increased to 6,000 kilograms (13,200 pounds) for up to 270 days.

If EPA does not promulgate rules by the 31 March 1986 deadline, a legislative "hammer" will fall. Besides using the Uniform Manifest, small quantity generators will then be required to have their waste treated, stored (except short-term storage on site) and disposed of at an interim status or permitted T/S/D facility, and no longer at a state or municipally licensed landfill. Small quantity generators will also be required to file manifest exception reports semi-annually for waste shipments for which a completed manifest is not returned.

A generator must also file certain reports with EPA, the biennial reports and the exception reports, and maintain copies for three years from the date such report was due. The biennial report must include (1) the name, address and EPA identification number of the generator, (2) the calendar year covered by the report, (3) EPA identification number for each transporter used during the year, (4) name, address and identification number of each T/S/D facility to which wastes were sent, and (5) waste identification information including the DOT hazard class, EPA hazardous waste identification number, and the quantity of the waste. 49/ The 1984 Amendments

---

49/ 40 CFR 262.41.

require that the biennial reports also include information on the efforts undertaken to reduce the volume and toxicity of the hazardous wastes and the results actually achieved in comparison with previous years.

An exception report also is required in the event that a generator does not receive a manifest back in a timely or properly executed manner. The regulations specifically provide that a generator must contact the transporter and/or the T/S/D facility to determine what happened to the manifest and the hazardous waste. If, after the 45th day, the generator has not received a manifest with the proper signature from the T/S/D facility, the generator must submit an exception report to the EPA regional administrator including (1) a copy of the manifest for which the generator does not have confirmation of delivery; and (2) a cover letter which describes the efforts taken to locate the waste and the manifest and the result of those efforts. 50/ Both the biennial reports and the exception reports, like the manifests, are required to be kept for a three-year period. Finally, the records of any test results, waste analyses, or determinations that a waste is hazardous must be kept for three years from the date the waste was last sent to a T/S/D facility. 51/ As a practical matter, in view of the liability imposed by Superfund, discussed in Chapter 3, generators should seriously consider maintaining RCRA reports for substantially longer than the minimum three-year period.

4.4 Transporters of Hazardous Wastes

A transporter is defined as any person engaged in the off-site transportation of hazardous waste by air, rail, highway or water. 52/ Off-site transportation includes both interstate and intrastate commerce. 53/ Thus, the reach of RCRA includes not only shippers and common carriers of hazardous wastes, but also the private company that occasionally transports hazardous wastes on its own trucks solely within its home state.

50/   40 CFR 262.42.

51/   40 CFR 262.40(c).

52/   40 CFR 260.10(a).

53/   Section 3003.

Anyone who moves a hazardous waste that is required to be manifested off the site where it is generated, or the site where it is being treated, stored and disposed of, will be subject to the transporter standards. The only persons not covered are generators or operators of T/S/D facilities who engage in on-site transportation of their hazardous waste. Once a generator or a T/S/D facility operator moves its hazardous waste off-site—which can be just a few hundred feet down a public road—he is then considered a transporter and must comply with the regulations.

EPA promulgated standards for all transporters of hazardous wastes on 19 May 1980, 40 CFR Part 263. These standards are closely coordinated with the standards issued by the Department of Transportation under the Hazardous Materials Transportation Act for the transportation of hazardous materials. 54/ For the most part, EPA's regulations incorporate and require compliance with the DOT provisions on labeling, marking, placarding, using proper containers, and reporting discharges. In addition, all transporters must obtain an EPA Identification Number prior to transporting any hazardous waste and may only accept hazardous waste which is accompanied by a manifest signed by the generator. 55/ The transporter himself must sign and date the manifest acknowledging acceptance of the waste and return one copy to the generator before leaving the generator's property. At all times the transporter must keep the manifest with the hazardous waste. When the transporter delivers the waste to another transporter or to the designated T/S/D facility, he must (1) date the manifest and obtain the signature of the next transporter or the T/S/D facility operator, (2) retain one copy of the manifest for his own records, and (3) give the remaining copies to the person receiving the waste. 56/ If the transporter is unable to deliver the waste in accordance with the manifest, he must contact the generator for further instructions and revise the manifest accordingly. 57/

54/   49 USC §1801, et seq., 49 CFR 171-179.

55/   40 CFR 263.11, 263.20.

56/   40 CFR 263.20. Special requirements apply to rail or water transporters of hazardous waste, and those who transport hazardous waste outside of the United States. 40 CFR 263.20(e), (f) and (g), 263.22(b), (c) and (d).

57   40 CFR 263.21(b).

Finally, the transporter may hold a hazardous waste for up to ten days without being required to obtain a RCRA storage permit. 58/ The transporter must keep the executed copy of the manifest for a period of three years. 59/

Transporters of hazardous wastes may also become subject to the Part 262 requirements for generators if, for example, the transporter mixes hazardous wastes of different DOT descriptions by placing them into a single container. 60/ Also, a hazardous waste which accumulates in a transport vehicle or vessel or a product or raw material pipeline will trigger the generator standards when the waste is removed.

If an accidental or intentional discharge of a hazardous waste occurs during transportation, the transporter is responsible for its clean up and must take immediate action to protect human health and the environment. Such action includes treatment or containment of the spill and notification of local police and fire departments. 61/ DOT's discharge reporting requirements are incorporated into the RCRA regulations. 62/ They identify the situations in which telephone reporting of the discharge to the National Response Center and the filing of a written report are required. That telephone number is 800/424-8802 or 202/426-2675.

Transporters are subject to both DOT and EPA enforcement. Under a memorandum of understanding executed by the two agencies, DOT will conduct an ongoing program of inspections of transporters to monitor their compliance. 63/ DOT will immediately advise EPA of "any possible" violations of the RCRA transporter regulations so that EPA can take enforcement action. In addition, EPA has said that it intends to bring enforcement actions against transporters where the transportation of hazardous wastes is ancillary to treatment, storage or disposal of such wastes.

58/   40 CFR 263.12.

59/   40 CFR 263.22.

60/   40 CFR 263.10(c).

61/   40 CFR 263.30(b).

62/   See 49 CFR 171.15 and 171.16 (1979).

63/   45 FR 51645 (4 August 1980).

The 1984 RCRA Amendments will not result in any material change in the standards applicable to transporters of hazardous waste, although transporters are affected by several of the amendments. For example, EPA is required to establish requirements for the transportation of hazardous waste-derived fuels (as discussed above). In addition, transporters who haul used oil for recycling will be subject to the special standards required by the 1984 Amendments for handlers of used oil and will be obligated to deliver the used oil to a permitted recycling facility. The new law also shields railroads from the RCRA "citizen suit" and "imminent hazard" enforcement provisions (discussed below) if the railroad merely transports the hazardous waste under a sole contractual agreement and exercises due care.

4.5 Statutory and Regulatory Requirements for Treatment, Storage, and Disposal (T/S/D) Facilities

The term "T/S/D" is commonly used to refer to the three different hazardous waste management activities that are regulated under RCRA Section 3004, and which thus require a permit under RCRA Section 3005. These activities are treatment, storage and disposal. Section 3004, prior to the 1984 Amendments, directed EPA to establish a comprehensive set of regulations governing the management of all aspects of operation of these facilities. The regulations adopted include both requirements of general applicability to all T/S/D facilities and specific requirements for particular types of facilities. They apply to any T/S/D facility that was active after the effective date of the Subtitle C regulations, 19 November 1980. 64/

In 1984, Congress added a number of important provisions to Section 3004. These establish, among other things, a ban on the disposal of liquids in landfills, and minimum technological requirements for existing and new surface impoundments and landfills. In addition, Congress directed EPA to make a number of regulatory decisions in short order. The most significant provision sets a rigid timetable under which EPA must decide whether to ban land disposal of all listed hazardous wastes. Failure by EPA to meet the deadline will result in a self-enacting statutory ban. The requirements of the current standards and the impact of the new amendments are discussed below.

64/   See 45 FR 33170.

A facility will be regulated as a "treatment" facility if the operator handles hazardous waste by utilizing any method, technique, or process, including neutralization, designed to change the physical, chemical, or biological character or composition of any hazardous waste so as to neutralize such waste, or so as to recover energy or material resources from the waste, or so as to render such waste nonhazardous, or less hazardous; safer to transport, store or dispose of; or amenable for recovery, amenable for storage, or reduced in volume. 65/ A "storage" facility is defined as one which engages in the holding of hazarous waste for a temporary period, at the end of which the hazardous waste is treated, disposed of, or stored elsewhere. 66/ An operator's activities will be regulated as "disposal" if the facility is used for:

> the discharge, deposit, injection, dumping, spilling, leaking, or placing of any solid waste or hazardous waste into or on any land or water so that such solid waste or hazardous waste or any constituent thereof may enter the environment or be emitted into the air or discharged into any waters, including ground waters. 67/

The term "facility" is separately defined to include "all contiguous land, and structures, other appurtenances, and improvements on the land." 68/ The narrower term "disposal facility" is defined as "a facility or part of a facility at which hazardous waste is intentionally placed into or on any land or water, and at which waste will remain after closure" (emphasis added). The reason for the distinction is to separate facilities subject to permitting requirements from facilities which may have limited RCRA coverage as the result of an unintentional act such as a spill. Clarification of the application of the foregoing definitions can be sought during the permitting process.

65/   40 CFR 260.10(a).

66/   Id.

67/   Id.

68/   Id.

A number of T/S/D facilities or hazardous waste activities are currently exempted from regulation all together. This list may be subject to change as a result of the 1984 Amendments and continued regulatory activity. However, the list presently contains the following exclusions:

(1)   Facilities that dispose of hazardous waste by means of ocean disposal pursuant to a permit issued under the Marine Protection, Research, and Sanctuaries Act.

(2)   The disposal of hazardous waste by underground injection pursuant to a permit issued under the Safe Drinking Water Act.

(3)   A Publicly Owned Treatment Works (POTW) which treats or stores hazardous wastes which are delivered to the POTW by a transport vehicle or vessel or through a pipe.

(4)   T/S/D facilities which operate under a state hazardous waste program authorized pursuant to RCRA Section 3006.

(5)   Facilities authorized by a state to manage industrial or municipal solid waste, if the only hazardous waste handled by such a facility is otherwise excluded from regulation pursuant to the special requirements for small generators.

(6)   A facility which treats or stores hazardous wastes that are subject to the special requirement for hazardous wastes which are used, reused, recycled, or reclaimed.

(7)   On-site accumulation of hazardous waste by generators for 90 days or less.

(8)   Farmers who dispose of waste pesticides from their own use in compliance with 40 CFR 262.51.

(9)   Owners or operators of a "totally enclosed treatment facility."

(10) Owners and operators of elementary neutralization units and wastewater treatment units.

(11) Persons taking immediate action to treat and contain spills.

(12) Transporters storing manifested wastes approved in containers at a transfer facility for 10 days or less.

(13) The act of adding absorbent material to hazardous waste in a container or the inverse, adding hazardous waste to absorbent material in a container, to reduce the amount of free liquids in the container, if the materials are added when wastes are first placed in the container.

4.5.1 Standards of General Applicability

As mentioned briefly in the introduction and discussed more fully in the permits discussion below, two categories of T/S/D facilities currently exist, interim status facilities and permitted facilities.   Interim status facilities are those which are currently operating without final RCRA permits based upon a legislative decision recognizing that issuance of permits would be a time consuming process. These facilities had to meet a three-part statutory test of:

(1)   being in existence on 19 November 1980,

(2)   notifying EPA pursuant to RCRA Section 3010(a) of its hazardous waste management activities, and

(3)   filing a preliminary permit application. 69/

69/ Section 3005(e); 40 CFR 265.1. As discussed below, a permit application consists of Part A (two forms) and Part B (detailed information on the facility filed at a later date). Part A must be filed to obtain interim status.

A facility's interim status will end when the facility receives a permit. This in turn is based upon technical standards issued by EPA, or a State with an approved program, which are incorporated into the permit. As discussed in the next section on permits, the 1984 Amendments specify timetables for issuance of all such permits. All other T/S/D facilities, including new facilities that were not "in existence" on 19 November 1980 and facilities that have otherwise failed to qualify for interim status, must obtain an individual RCRA permit and may not operate until they do.

Separate standards have been issued for interim status facilities 70/ and permitted facilities. 71/ Both the interim and permanent status regulations for T/S/D facilities include standards of general applicability (e.g., personnel training, security, financial responsibility) as well as specific design and operating standards for each different type of T/S/D facility (e.g., storage tanks, landfills, incinerators). These are discussed below.

First, operators are required to have an EPA identification number. 72/ Second, the regulations require the operator to obtain or conduct a detailed chemical and physical analysis of a representative sample of a hazardous waste before the waste is treated, stored, or disposed of at the facility. 73/ This is to ensure that the operator has sufficient knowledge of the particular waste being handled to be able to properly manage it. Third, operators must install a security system to prevent unknowing entry, and to minimize the potential for unauthorized entry of people or livestock to the active portion of a T/S/D facility. 74/ This may be either a 24-hour surveillance system or a barrier around the facility and a means to control entry, and posted "Danger" signs. Fourth, operators are required to prepare and implement an inspection plan specifically tailored to the circumstances at their facility. 75/ Fifth, permitted

---

70/   40 CFR Part 265.

71/   40 CFR Part 264.

72/   40 CFR 265.11, 264.11.

73/   40 CFR 265.13, 264.13.

74/   40 CFR 265.14, 264.14.

75/   40 CFR 265.15, 264.15.

facilities to be sited in areas prone to seismic activity or floodplains are subject to location standards designed to reduce the additional risks posed by these facilities. 76/

T/S/D facility personnel also are required to have expertise in the areas to which they are assigned, thus reducing the chances that a mistake due to lack of training might lead to an environmental accident. The training may be by formal classroom instruction or on-the-job training. The program must be directed by a person trained in hazardous waste management procedures. 77/

Special precautions must be taken to prevent accidental ignition or reaction of ignitable or reactive wastes. While many of the requirements for handling ignitable, reactive, and incompatible wastes are largely common sense practices, specific requirements regarding the mixing of such wastes also are included in the regulations. Compliance with the regulations concerning management of ignitable, reactive or incompatible wastes must be documented. 78/

Regulations for preparedness and prevention have been promulgated to minimize the possibility and effect of an explosion, spill, or fire at a T/S/D facility. 79/ Facilities must have, unless unnecessary due to the nature of the wastes handled, the following equipment:

(1)   an internal alarm or communications system,
(2)   a device capable of summoning emergency
          assistance from local agencies,
(3)   fire and spill control equipment, and
(4)   decontamination equipment.

Operators are required also to have a contingency plan for the facility designed to minimize hazards to human health and the environment in the event of an actual explosion, fire, or unplanned release

---

76/   40 CFR 265.18(b), 264.17(c), 264.18(a).

77/   40 CFR 265.16, 264.16.

78/   40 CFR 265.17, 264.17.

79/   See generally 40 CFR 265.30-.49, 264.30-.49.

of hazardous wastes. 80/ And, they are required to obtain liability insurance to provide coverage during the operating life of a facility for claims arising out of injuries to persons or property which result from hazardous waste management operations. 81/

Numerous recordkeeping requirements also apply to T/S/D facilities. 82/ Upon receipt of a manifested shipment of hazardous waste, the operator of a T/S/D facility must immediately sign, date, and give to the transporter a copy of the manifest prepared by the generator. Within 30 days, the operator must return another copy of the manifest to the generator and retain at the facility a copy of each manifest for at least three years from the date of delivery. All T/S/D facilities also must maintain a complete operating record until closure. 83/ Required information includes, among other things, a description and the quantity of each hazardous waste received and the method and date of its treatment, storage and disposal, the location of each waste within the facility, records and results of waste analysis and trial tests and inspections.

There are also basic reports which the T/S/D facility operator is obligated to file with the EPA regional administrator. These include a biennial report of waste management activities for the previous calendar year, 84/ an "unmanifested waste" report which the operator must file within 15 days of accepting any hazardous waste that is not accompanied by the required manifest 85/ and certain specialized reports that must be filed in specific circumstances. For example, reports must be filed in the event of a hazardous waste release, fire, or explosion.

There are general closure requirements applicable to all T/S/D facilities, and additional requirements for each specific type

---

80/   See generally 40 CFR 265.50-.56, 264.50-.56.

81/   40 CFR 265.143(e), 264.143(f).

82/   See generally 40 CFR 265.71-.72, 264.71-.72.

83/   40 CFR 265.73, 264.73.

84/   40 CFR 265.75, 264.75.

85/   See 40 CFR 261.5.

of facility. 86/ "Closure" is the period after which hazardous wastes are no longer accepted by a T/S/D facility and during which the operator completes treatment, storage or disposal operations. "Post-closure" is the 30-year period after closure when operators of disposal facilities only must perform certain monitoring and maintenance activities. Generally, an owner or operator must have a detailed written closure plan and schedule therefore. It must be approved by EPA or the state and amended when any changes in waste management operations affect its terms. Post-closure care must continue for 30 years after the date of completing closure and include groundwater monitoring and maintenance of monitoring and waste containment systems. Post-closure care is required where hazardous waste will remain at the site after closure.

Financial responsibility requirements have been established to ensure that funds for closure and post-closure are adequate and available. 87/

4.5.2 Standards for Specific Types of T/S/D Facilities

The standards discussed above are generally applicable to all T/S/D facilities, from the simple container storage facility to the most complex landfill. EPA has also promulgated specific design and operating standards for each of ten different types of T/S/D facilities that constitute the universe of facilities regulated under RCRA. These are: (1) containers, (2) tanks, (3) surface impoundments, (4) waste piles, (5) land treatment units, (6) landfills, (7) incinerators, (8) thermal treatment units, (9) chemical, physical, and biological treatment units, and (10) underground injection wells. 88/ In the years ahead, additional classes of facilities may also be addressed by distinct sets of standards such as these.

Discussion of the detailed regulatory requirements for each of these types of facilities is beyond the scope of this chapter. 89/ However, the regulations applicable to four of these types of facilities—surface impoundments, waste piles, land treatment units and

---

86/   See generally 40 CFR 265.110-.120, 264.110-.120.

87/   See generally 40 CFR 265.140-.151, 264.140-.151.

88/   40 CFR 265, Subparts J-R, 264, Subparts J-O.

89/   These requirements are discussed in detail in the Hazardous Waste Handbook, Government Institutes, 5th Edition, Chapter 6 (1984).

landfills—will undergo extensive change as a result of the Congressional decision in the 1984 Amendments that land disposal of hazardous waste should be greatly reduced. While some of these concerns were to some extent foreseen and addressed by EPA by incorporating groundwater monitoring standards for these particular facilities 90/ and restricting the disposal of liquids in landfills, the clear thrust of the amendments is that Congress viewed EPA's regulatory activities in this area to date as too little and too late.

The major amendments affecting these facilities are discussed below.

4.5.3 Impact of the 1984 Amendments

4.5.3.1 Prohibitions on Land Disposal of Certain Wastes

Perhaps the most significant provision of the new law calls for EPA to determine whether to ban, in whole or in part, the disposal of all RCRA listed hazardous wastes in landfills and other land disposal facilities. Congress has set forth a phased program for EPA to implement the ban. First, the land disposal of hazardous wastes containing dioxin or solvents is banned after November 1986. 91/ EPA may list the ban only for those methods of land disposal of particular hazardous wastes which EPA determines will be protective of human health and the environment, based on a reasonable degree of certainty that there will be no migration of hazardous constituents from the land disposal facility, and taking into account the persistence, toxicity, mobility, and propensity to bioaccumulate the hazardous waste and the long-term uncertainties associated with land disposal.

Also by November 1986, EPA must publish a ranking of all listed hazardous wastes based on their intrinsic hazard and volume, with a schedule for determining whether to ban the land disposal of such wastes. To prevent delay caused by litigation, the EPA ranking and schedule will not constitute a rulemaking or be subject to challenge in the courts.

90/ See generally 40 CFR 265.90–.94, 264.90–.101.

91/ The dioxin containing wastes are those chlorinated dioxins, -dibenzofurans, and -phenols proposed by EPA for listing as acutely hazardous wastes. 48 FR 14514 (4 April 1983). The solvents are those listed as F001, F002, F003, F004 and F005 at 40 CFR §261.31. See generally Section 201 of the 1984 Amendments, PL 98-616, 98 Stat. 3221 (8 November 1984).

Second, the land disposal of a list of hazardous wastes which is already banned from land disposal in California is banned under RCRA after July 1987, unless EPA lifts the ban for particular wastes. The "California list" includes: (1) liquid hazardous wastes, including free liquids associated with any sludge, containing free cyanides greater than 100 mg/l; (2) specified concentrations of heavy metals (arsenic, cadmium, chromium, lead, mercury, nickel, selenium and thallium); (3) acids below a pH of 2; (4) PCBs; and (5) halogenated organic compounds. 92/

Third, by August 1988, EPA must decide whether to ban from certain kinds of land disposal some or all of the first one-third of the highest priority hazardous wastes on the ranking list. By June 1990, EPA must decide whether to ban the middle of the ranked hazardous wastes. Then by May 1991, EPA must determine whether to ban all RCRA listed hazardous wastes. At each phase of the schedule, EPA can decide not to impose the ban on a particular method of land disposal for a particular hazardous waste if EPA determines that human health and the environment will be protected, taking into account the relevant factors discussed above.

EPA has limited authority to extend the ban deadlines for specific hazardous wastes to the earliest date on which adequate alternative treatment, recovery, or disposal capacity will be available. EPA can also grant a one-year extension, renewable only once, to a company that demonstrates on a case-by-case basis that a binding contractual commitment has been made to construct or otherwise provide alternative treatment, recovery, or disposal capacity, but due to circumstances beyond its control the alternative capacity cannot reasonably be made available by the ban deadline.

Again Congress has used a "hammer" to compel EPA action by the statutory deadlines. If EPA fails to decide whether to ban the land disposal of the hazardous wastes in accordance with the priority ranking and schedule, the ban will automatically go into effect. The only exception is for generators that certify that the only practicable alternative currently available to them is the disposal of their hazardous waste at a landfill or surface impoundment meeting the "minimum technological requirements" of the 1984 law (discussed below).

92/ Disposal by deep well injection is subject to special provisions and a different schedule for implementing the ban. EPA has until August 1988 to decide the extent of the ban on deep well injection of dioxin-containing and solvent hazardous wastes and the California list.

Congress also wanted to promote treatment of hazardous wastes in lieu of land disposal. Therefore at the same time EPA promulgates the land disposal restrictions discussed above, it must also promulgate regulations specifying the methods of treatment, if any, that substantially reduce the likelihood of migration of the waste from land disposal facilities. A company that treats its hazardous waste in accordance with these pretreatment standards will not have the waste or residue subject to the land disposal ban.

4.5.3.2 Liquids in Landfills

EPA has by regulation already placed substantial restrictions on the disposal of liquid hazardous wastes in landfills. Congress has now gone further and banned the disposal in landfills after May 1985, on bulk or non-containerized liquid hazardous wastes, and hazardous wastes containing free liquids. EPA must also promulgate regulations that minimize disposal of containerized liquid hazardous wastes in landfills by February 1986. In order to discourage the use of absorbent materials (e.g., "kitty litter") to reduce free liquids in containerized wastes, EPA's regulations must also prohibit the landfilling of liquids that have been absorbed in materials that biodegrade or that release liquids when depressed during routine landfill operations.

In addition, Congress has banned the disposal in RCRA landfills after November 1985, of any liquids that are not hazardous wastes, unless the owner can demonstrate that disposal in its landfill will not present a risk of contamination of any underground source of drinking water, and the only reasonably available alternative is disposal at another landfill or unlined surface impoundment which contains hazardous wastes.

4.5.3.3 Existing Surface Impoundments and Minimum Technological Requirements

During Congressional consideration of the 1984 RCRA Amendments, one of the most controversial questions was whether companies that are currently using unlined surface impoundments should be required to retrofit by installing liners to prevent groundwater contamination. According to EPA, there are an estimated 200,000 unlined pits, ponds, and lagoons used for the storage, treatment, and disposal of hazardous waste across the nation. EPA believes these impoundments are a major source of groundwater contamination, but the cost of retrofitting or closing all these impoundments is estimated to be very high.

In the end, Congress decided to require companies to retrofit all interim status surface impoundments with double liners, leachate collection systems, and groundwater monitoring systems within the next four years. EPA can modify these requirements only if the operator can demonstrate that the impoundment is located, designed, and operated so as to ensure that there will be no migration of any hazardous constituents to the groundwater or surface water at any future time. 93/ The retrofit requirements are expected to result in the closing of many surface impoundments.

Congress created two carefully limited exemptions to the retrofit requirement. First, a surface impoundment that has at least one liner, is located more than one-quarter mile from an underground source of drinking water, and is in compliance with groundwater monitoring requirements is exempt. EPA expects, however, that very few surface impoundments are, in fact, located more than one-quarter mile from an underground drinking water source.

The second exemption is for surface impoundments which are part of a wastewater treatment facility regulated under the Clean Water Act and which meet the following criteria. The impoundment must be used to contain treated wastewater during the secondary or subsequent phases of "aggressive biological treatment" prior to discharge authorized by an NPDES permit. An "aggressive biological treatment facility" is defined to mean a system of surface impoundments in which the initial impoundment of the secondary treatment segment of the facility utilizes intense mechanical aeration to enhance biological activity to degrade wastewater pollutants. 94/ The wastewater treatment facility must be in compliance with any applicable BAT effluent limitations for toxic pollutants or, if no such effluent limitations are contained in the facility's NPDES permit, then the facility must be achieving significant degradation of toxic pollutants and hazardous constituents contained in the untreated waste stream.

It is possible to obtain these exemptions only during the next two years. Companies that operate surface impoundments must apply to EPA, or an authorized state, for these exemptions by not

---

93/ See 1984 Amendments, Sections 215, 202 and 203.

94/ The initial impoundment must have a maximum five-day hydraulic retention time, or maximum 30-day retention time if the sludge in the impoundment is not EP Toxic, or activated sludge treatment must be used in the first portion of the secondary treatment.

later than 8 November 1986. After that time, the exemptions are deemed to be waived.

A company must submit with its application for an exemption: (1) a completed Part B permit application (see discussion in Section 5.0 below); (2) evidence of compliance with groundwater monitoring and the resulting analyses; (3) all reasonably ascertainable evidence of whether the impoundment is leaking; and (4) a certification by a registered professional engineer that the impoundment qualifies for the exemption.

4.5.3.4 Expansion During Interim Status

Under EPA's current regulations, the existing portion of a surface impoundment, landfill or waste pile that has qualified for interim status is not subject to the liner requirements. This allowed operators to replace or expand units at existing impoundments, landfills and waste piles without complying with the more stringent requirements for new facilities.

Congress has changed that. For hazardous wastes received after 8 May 1985, each new unit, replacement of an existing unit, or lateral expansion of an existing unit at an interim status surface impoundment, landfill or waste pile must have two or more liners and a leachate collection system both above (for a landfill) and between the liners. Groundwater monitoring is also required. 95/

To facilitate permitting of interim status surface impoundments and landfills, the operator must notify EPA or an authorized state at least 60 days prior to receiving hazardous wastes in a new, replacement, or expansion unit. If the operator has not already submitted a Part B permit application, it must do so within six months to expedite permitting of that facility. If a liner and leachate collection system are installed in good faith under the new requirements, no different liner or leachate collection system may be required as a condition of the first RCRA permit issued to the facility, unless EPA has reason to believe that a liner is leaking.

4.5.3.5 Corrective Action Beyond Facility Boundary

When EPA began implementing the interim status and permit programs, it stated that RCRA did not provide authority to require cleanup of pollution beyond the property boundary which may have

---

95/   See 1984 Amendments, Section 243.

occurred before RCRA was enacted. Except for the emergency relief provisions of Section 7003, RCRA is concerned with active operations at T/S/D facilities, not past activities that may have caused contamination, said EPA officials.

Congress has now given EPA authority to require corrective action regarding past releases. EPA must amend its T/S/D facility standards to require that corrective action be taken beyond the facility boundary where necessary to protect human health and the environment. 96/ The only exception is if the operator can demonstrate that it is unable to obtain the necessary permission from the property owner to undertake corrective action.

These regulations will take effect immediately after they are issued and will apply to all permitted T/S/D facilities, and to all landfill units, surface impoundment units, and waste pile units that have received waste after 26 July 1982. Until such regulations are promulgated, EPA is instructed to issue corrective orders for these facilities on a case-by-case basis. This type of authority for cleanup and remedial action is analogous to that which exists under the Comprehensive Environmental Response, Compensation and Liability Act of 1980 ("CERCLA" or "Superfund"), and could have a very substantial impact on some facilities.

As discussed in Section 4.6, a companion provision requires corrective action of releases at any T/S/D facility holding or seeking a permit. 97/

4.5.3.6 Minimum Technological Requirement for New Landfills and Surface Impoundments

In a significant new provision, Congress has directed that any RCRA permit issued by EPA for a new landfill or surface impoundment, a replacement unit at an existing landfill or surface impoundment, or the lateral expansion of an existing landfill or surface impoundment must require the installation of two or more liners and a leachate collection system both above (for a landfill) and between the liners. 98/ Groundwater monitoring will also be required as a

---

96/   See 1984 Amendments, Section 207.

97/   See 1984 Amendments, Section 206.

98/   See 1984 Amendments, Section 202.

permit condition. EPA must promulgate regulations implementing these "minimum technological requirements" within two years.

A company can use alternative design and operating practices in lieu of liners if it can demonstrate that such practices, together with the location characteristics of its facility, will prevent the migration of any hazardous constituents into groundwater or surface water as effectively as liners and leachate collection systems. The double-liner requirement may also be waived for monofills containing certain types of waste.

Location standards specifying criteria for the acceptable location of new and existing T/S/D facilities must also be established, along with guidance criteria identifying areas of vulnerable hydrogeology, by May 1986. By May 1987, EPA also must promulgate standards requiring that new landfill units and surface impoundments have leak detection systems capable of detecting leaks at the earliest practicable time.

Land disposal facilities currently operating under interim status must certify within twelve months that they are in compliance with all applicable groundwater monitoring requirements. Exemptions from groundwater monitoring requirements are available on a case-by-case basis for any engineered structure which does not receive liquid waste, is designed and operated to exclude liquid from precipitation and other run-off, utilizes multiple leak detection systems, and provides for continuing operation and maintenance of those leak detection systems. 99/

4.6 Permits

RCRA requires every owner or operator of a T/S/D facility to obtain a permit. 100/ Different permit application procedures apply to interim status and new facilities or facilities that failed to qualify for interim status. A T/S/D facility which was in existence on 19 November 1980, notified EPA of its hazardous waste management activities, and filed a Part A application, was authorized to continue operations without having been issued a site-specific permit. 101/ A new facility or an existing facility that failed to

---

99/   See 1984 Amendments, Section 203.

100/ Section 3005.

101/ See the discussion of the interim status standards for T/S/D facilities in 40 CFR Part 265.

qualify for interim status must obtain a permit before commencing operations.

A Part A application is a form application containing certain basic information about the facility, such as name, location, nature of business, regulated activities, and a topographic map of the facility site, 102/ and must be filed as soon as an existing facility becomes subject to the hazardous waste regulatory program. For most existing facilities, this was 19 November 1980. For other existing facilities which subsequently become subject to RCRA because of changes in regulations, the deadline for filing the Part A application will be specified by EPA in the preamble. A T/S/D facility that qualifies because it loses its special status—such as a small generation—must file a Part A application within 30 days of the loss of its exemption. 103/

A Part B application requiring substantially more detailed information must be filed after the effective date of the applicable technical standards for T/S/D facilities, and following request for it by EPA or the state. 104/

The final permit will govern the application of these standards to the particular facility. New facilities must submit Part A and B applications simultaneously. A permit is required to be issued before operation. 105/

Permit applications will be requested and final permits will be issued by states authorized under RCRA to administer their own programs, and by the EPA regional administrator in all other states. Permit issuance must be based on a determination that the T/S/D facility is in compliance with all requirements of RCRA.

After a complete RCRA permit application is filed, the rules in 40 CFR Part 124 establish the procedures for processing the application and issuing the permit. These include preparation of

---

102/   40 CFR 270.13.

103/   See 46 FR 60446 (10 December 1981).

104/   See generally 40 CFR 270.13-270.21.

105/   See 1984 Amendments, Section 211. A narrow exception is provided for facilities constructed under the Toxic Substances Control Act for the incineration of PCBs.

draft permits, public comment and hearing, and the issuance of final decisions.

In the 1984 Amendments, Congress has taken steps to accelerate the permitting of existing interim status facilities, even though EPA asserted at legislative hearings prior to enactment that the wave of additional new requirements will delay this process. Congress has provided that interim status for any existing land disposal facility will terminate on 8 November 1985, unless the owner or operator has submitted a Part B application for a final permit and a certification that the facility is in compliance with groundwater monitoring and financial responsibility requirements. 106/ EPA, or an authorized state, must then process all permit applications for land disposal facilities within four years, all incinerator permit applications within five years, and applications for all other facilities within eight years.

The new law also provides that permits for land disposal facilities, storage facilities, incinerators and other treatment facilities can be issued for a ten-year fixed term. While permits may be reviewed and modified at any time during their terms, permits for land disposal facilities must be reviewed five years after issuance. At such time, the terms of a permit may be modified to ensure that the permit continues to incorporate the standards then applicable to land disposal facilities. 107/

In addition, newly issued permits also must require the owner or operator of a T/S/D facility to take corrective action for all releases of hazardous waste and constituents at the facility regardless of when the waste was placed in the unit, or whether the unit is currently active. 108/

4.7 State Hazardous Waste Programs

States are authorized by RCRA to develop and carry out their own hazardous waste programs in lieu of the federal program administered by EPA. 109/ Congress anticipated that states would gain

---

106/   See 1984 Amendments, Section 213.

107/   See 1984 Amendments, Section 212.

108/   See 1984 Amendments, Section 206.

109/   Section 3006; see generally 40 CFR Part 271.

authorization for their programs in two stages. States with legislative authority for hazardous waste programs on 24 October 1982 may first obtain "interim authorization" from EPA to carry out their programs upon a showing that the state program is "substantially equivalent" to the federal program. Interim authorization was divided by EPA into Phase I and II to correspond to the agency's two-prong approach to regulating T/S/D facilities.

Regardless of whether a state receives interim authorization, any state may apply for "final authorization" to administer the RCRA hazardous waste program. The conditions for approval are intended to ensure uniformity among the states. To support a grant of final authorization, the state program must meet three standards. It must be equivalent to the federal program, it must be consistent with federal and authorized state programs, and must provide adequate enforcement of compliance with the requirements of RCRA Subtitle C. The deadline for receiving final authorization was extended by the 1984 Amendments one year to 31 January 1984. 110/

As of October 1984, five states had received final authorization: Delaware, Georgia, Mississippi, Montana and North Dakota. As of 1 September 1984, 28 states had received Phase I and II interim authorization, 13 had received Phase I interim authorization, and nine states were operating their hazardous waste programs under cooperative agreements with EPA. 111/

The 1984 Amendments take effect in states having final or interim authorization to operate their own programs on the same day that they take effect under the federal program. A state which has already received final or interim authorization may submit evidence to EPA that the existing state program contains a requirement substantially similar to the amendments and may request interim authorization to administer the requirement under the state program in lieu of direct administration by EPA. 112/

110/ See 1984 Amendments, Section 227.

111/ Cooperative agreements are a third type of arrangement whereby states which do not qualify for interim authorization may nonetheless administer portions of their programs. 45 FR 33784-86 (20 May, 1980).

112/ See 1984 Amendments, Section 228.

4.8 Inspection and Enforcement

RCRA provides that any officer, employee or representative of EPA or of a state with an authorized hazardous waste program may inspect the premises and records of any person who generates, stores, treats, transports, disposes of, or otherwise handles hazardous waste. 113/ EPA's inspection authority extends to persons or sites which have handled hazardous wastes in the past but no longer do so. The owner/operator must provide government officials access to records and property relating to the wastes for inspection purposes. Copying and sampling are authorized.

EPA's inspection program commenced 19 November 1980, the effective date of the hazardous waste regulations. By the end of 1982 EPA had already inspected over 1000 generation and disposal facilities. Congress has, however, in the 1984 Amendments, directed EPA and authorized states to improve and regularize RCRA inspections.

Within twelve months, EPA and authorized states must commence programs to conduct inspections of all privately-operated T/S/D facilities at least once every two years. Federally-operated T/S/D facilities must be inspected on an annual basis by EPA, or by an authorized state. Similarly, EPA must conduct annual inspections of T/S/D facilities which are operated by a state or local government to ensure compliance with the requirements of the Act. Within six months, EPA must submit to Congress a report on the feasibility of utilizing a program of private inspections to supplement inspections conducted by federal and state employees. 114/

All organizations should have a company policy and procedure for handling inspections properly and it should include consideration of whether or not a warrant should be required.

There are several types of enforcement actions available to EPA under RCRA. These include administrative orders and civil and

---

113/   Section 3007. EPA's inspection activities under RCRA Section 3007 are subject to the Fourth Amendment's protection against unreasonable searches or seizures, which the Supreme Court has applied in holding that a warrant is generally required for an inspection by an administrative agency. Marshall v. Barlow's, Inc., 436 U.S. 307 (1978) involving the inspection provisions of the Occupational Safety and Health Act.

114/   See 1984 Amendments, Sections 229, 230 and 231.

criminal penalties. Whenever EPA determines that any person is violating Subtitle C of RCRA (including any regulation or permit issued thereunder), it may at its option either issue an order requiring compliance immediately or within a specified time period, or seek injunctive relief against the violator through a civil action filed in a U.S. District Court. Any person who violates any requirement of Subtitle C is liable for a civil penalty of up to $25,000 for each day of violation, regardless of whether the person had been served with a compliance order. A person subject to RCRA can not rely on EPA to tell him when he is in violation, then take the required corrective action, and thus avoid a penalty. Failure to comply with an administrative order may also result in suspension or revocation of a permit.

RCRA also imposes criminal liability of up to $50,000, two years imprisonment, or both for persons who "knowingly" commit certain violations of Title C.

The 1984 Amendments significantly expand the list of these criminal violations. It includes generators who knowingly allow hazardous waste to be transported to an unpermitted facility, knowing violations of federal interim status standards, or counterpart state requirements, material omissions or the failure to file reports required under RCRA by generators, transporters, and T/S/D facility operators which are committed knowingly, and knowing transport of hazardous waste without a manifest. 115/

The statute also creates a crime of "knowing endangerment." The purpose of this sanction is to provide more substantial felony penalties for any person who commits the acts described above and "who knows at that time that he thereby places another person in imminent danger of death or serious bodily injury." Here, an individual faces a fine of up to $250,000 and/or up to fifteen years' imprisonment. An organizational defendant is subject to a maximum fine of $1 million. All of this is part of a message from Congress to EPA and the Justice Department that Congress wants to see more rigorous enforcement of the nation's hazardous wastes laws.

5.0 Regulation of Underground Storage Tanks

A last-minute Senate amendment to the 1984 RCRA Amendments established under a new Subtitle I a comprehensive regulatory

---

115/   See 1984 Amendments, Section 232.

program for underground tanks containing "regulated substances." "Regulated substances" are all "hazardous substances" as defined under Superfund (except RCRA hazardous waste, which would be regulated under Subtitle C) and liquid petroleum substances. 116/ By 8 November 1985, each owner of an underground storage tank containing a regulated substance must notify the interested state, local agency, or department of the existence of the tank. Owners of underground storage tanks no longer in use must file the required notification form by May 1986. No notification is required, however, for underground storage tanks that have been taken out of the ground, or for tanks that were taken out of operation before 1 January 1974. The notification requirement also does not apply to tanks for which notice was given previously pursuant to Superfund. A company that begins using an underground storage tank after the initial notification period must notify the designated state or local agency or department within thirty days.

Effective May 1985, the installation of an underground storage tank for the purpose of storing a regulated substance is prohibited unless certain statutory design and construction standards are met. EPA is also directed to promulgate additional standards applicable to all new underground storage tanks by November 1987. The regulations must require a monitoring system to detect leaks, the maintenance of records on the leak detection system, the reporting of releases, corrective action in response to a release, performance standards for new tanks, and regulations on tank closure which will prevent releases of regulated substances into the environment.

The new law allows states to take over the regulatory program for underground storage tanks by submitting "release detection, prevention, and correction programs" for review and approval by EPA. The state program must include the components of the federal program, provide for adequate enforcement of compliance, and have performance standards for new tanks that are no less stringent than federal standards.

Congress provided little or no guidance on what it expects the regulatory relationship to be between the Subtitle C hazardous

---

116/   See 1984 Amendments, Section 601. In a separate Section 207(w), Congress also directed EPA to promulgate permit rules for underground tanks that contain hazardous wastes as defined under Subtitle C.

waste program and the Subtitle I underground storage tank program. This could pose problems for facilities with tanks containing both types of wastes, whether in the same tank or different tanks. Hopefully, EPA will provide guidance, but probably it will need help from the regulated community to do so.

6.0 State or Regional Solid Waste Plans

Regulation of non-hazardous waste is the responsibility of the states pursuant to Subtitle D of RCRA. The federal involvement is limited to establishing minimum criteria that would prescribe the best practicable controls and monitoring requirements on solid waste disposal facilities.

In the 1984 Amendments, Congress directed EPA to conduct a study to answer whether current guidelines and criteria provide sufficient groundwater protection and to submit that study to Congress within three years. In addition, Congress ordered EPA to revise the criteria for facilities receiving hazardous waste from households or from small generators to enable detection of groundwater contamination, provide for corrective action as necessary and facility siting. 117/ Compliance with the minimum requirements determines whether a facility is classified as an "open dump" or not. Disposal of solid waste in "open dumps", (i.e., those facilities not meeting the criteria) is prohibited. Existing dumps are given five years in order to make modifications that will allow them to meet the requirements, and it is the state's responsibility to ensure that such upgrading occurs or the open dumps are closed.

The basic flaw in this strategy, however, is the absence of any enforcement authority for the ban on open dumps. EPA's enforcement authority only covers hazardous wastes. EPA cannot take any steps against a person disposing of non-hazardous wastes in an open dump or against the state for failing to close open dumping, other than terminating certain grant funds available to the state under RCRA. Recognizing this problem, Congress has asked EPA, as part of its study to make recommendations on the need for additional enforcement authorities. 118/

Because the definition of solid waste includes hazardous as well as non-hazardous waste, a facility which receives both types of

---

117/   See 1984 Amendments, Section 302(a)(1).

118/   Id.

wastes would have to meet the Subtitle C criteria as well as the Subtitle D requirements. This presumably will encourage the development of facilities just for disposal of non-hazardous waste, but the breadth of EPA's proposed designation of hazardous waste may make it difficult for facilities to ensure that hazardous wastes are not in fact being disposed of at the site.

RCRA envisions that the state, with the help of federal grant funds, will develop regional solid waste management plans. The program is patterned on Section 208 of the Clean Water Act and relies upon a comprehensive regional planning approach to solving solid waste problems. The state would be responsible for identifying appropriate management areas, developing regional plans through the use of local and regional authorities, inventorying and closing or upgrading existing open dumps, and generally assessing the need for additional solid waste disposal capacity in the area.

Of particular significance is a requirement that states not have any bans on the importation of waste for storage, treatment or disposal, or have requirements that are substantially dissimilar from other disposal practices that would discourage the free movement of wastes across state lines. Although enforcement of this requirement may be difficult, in light of the limited enforcement authority available to EPA, it does evidence a Congressional policy for a national approach to solid waste disposal and prevents localities from shielding themselves from disposal to the detriment of other jurisdictions.

7.0 Role of the Department of Commerce

Subtitle E gives the Department of Commerce (DOC) some responsibilities: (a) develop standards for substituting secondary materials for virgin materials; (b) develop markets for recovered materials; and (c) for the promotion of resource recovery technology generally.

The authorities given to DOC are similar to those assigned to EPA in other sections of the Act, specifically Subtitle H, Research, Development, Demonstrations and Information. DOC and EPA are supposed to work together but the DOC has not received sufficient funding to support a major role.

8.0 Federal Responsibilities

Subtitle F requires that all federal agencies and instrumentalities comply with all federal, state, interstate, and local requirements stemming from RCRA unless exempted by the president. It also requires the federal government to institute a procurement policy which encourages the purchase of recoverable materials when available at reasonable prices and which, because of their performance, can be substituted for virgin materials.

9.0 Additional Enforcement Provisions: Citizen Suits and Imminent Hazard Actions

In addition to the enforcement provisions specifically included in Subtitle C and discussed above, Subtitle G authorizes, among other things, citizens' suits and suits by the federal government to remedy imminent hazards.

Citizen suits are envisioned by Congress and many others as a key enforcement tool for environmental protection. As originally enacted, the RCRA citizen suit provision provided that any person may bring a civil action against any alleged violator of the Act's requirements or against the administrator for a failure to perform a nondiscretionary duty. Further, any person may petition the EPA administrator for promulgation, amendment or repeal of any regulation. Courts were authorized to award costs including attorneys' fees to any party. 119/

The 1984 Amendments substantially enhance the role accorded to these suits. The provision has been expanded to authorize suits in cases where past or present management or disposal of hazardous wastes has contributed to a situation that may present an imminent or substantial endangerment. Citizen suits are prohibited (1) with respect to the siting and permitting of hazardous waste facilities; (2) where EPA is prosecuting an action under RCRA or Superfund; (3) while EPA or the state is engaged in a removal action under Superfund or has incurred costs to engage in a remedial action; or (4) where the responsible party is conducting a removal action, or remedial action, pursuant to an order obtained from EPA. Affected parties may be allowed to intervene in ongoing suits, however. Plaintiffs must notify EPA, the state, and affected parties ninety days prior to commencement of a citizen suit. Attorneys' fees may be awarded to the prevailing or substantially prevailing party. 120/

119/   Section 7002.

120/   See 1984 Amendments, Section 401.

Subpart B also authorizes EPA to bring suits to restrain an imminent and substantial endangerment to health or the environment. 121/

EPA issued a memorandum on 25 January 1980, defining "imminent and substantial endangerment" as posing a "risk of harm" or "potential harm" but not requiring proof of actual harm. 122/ This interpretation was upheld in United States v. Vertac Chemical Corp., 123/ the first published decision interpreting RCRA Section 7003. In issuing a preliminary injunction to contain the migration of dioxin from landfills and a treatment basin into a creek, the court held that under the endangerment provisions of both RCRA and the Clean Water Act harm need only be threatened rather than actually occurring.

In response to conflicting federal court decisions, Congress reworded the "imminent hazard" provision in 1984 to clarify that actions which took place prior to the enactment of RCRA are covered by this provision. Thus a non-negligent generator whose wastes are no longer being deposited at a particular site may still be ordered to abate the hazard resulting from the leaking of previously deposited wastes. 124/

The 1984 Amendments also require EPA to provide for public notice and comment, and the opportunity for a public meeting in the affected area, prior to entering into a settlement or covenant not to sue in any imminent hazard actions. 125/ This expands on existing Department of Justice practice with respect to consent decrees. The new amendment also provides that EPA's decision whether to settle an action is not subject to judicial review. While on its face the scope of this limitation seems broad, the Senate Report on the

---

121/ Section 7003.

122/ Memorandum, 25 January 1980, from Douglas MacMillan, Acting Director of EPA's Hazardous Waste Enforcement Task Force, to Regional Enforcement Division Directors and others.

123/ 489 F. Supp. 870 (E.D. Ark. 1980).

124/ See 1984 Amendments, Section 402.

125/ See 1984 Amendments, Section 404.

bill indicates that this is meant to negate the creation of any "new" rights to judicial review, but not to preclude review of a settlement agreement to determine its unlawfulness.

10.0 Research, Development, Demonstration, and Information

In cooperation with federal, state, and interstate authorities, private agencies and institutions and individuals, EPA is directed to conduct, encourage and promote the coordination of research, investigations, experiments, training, demonstrations, surveys, public education programs and studies relating to: the protection of health; planning, financing and operation of waste management systems including resource recovery; improvements in methodology of waste disposal and resource recovery; reduction of the amount of waste generated, and methods for remedying damages by earlier or existing landfills; and methods for rendering landfills safe for purposes of construction and other uses.

EPA is directed to carry out a number of special studies including the following subjects: small-scale and low technology approaches to resource recovery; front-end separation for materials recovery; mining waste; sludge; and airport landfills.

A cabinet level committee chaired by the administrator of EPA is mandated to investigate the impact on resource recovery and conservation of: (a) incentives and disincentives, including existing public policies such as tax credits and depletion allowances; (b) restricting the manufacture or use of certain categories of consumer products; (c) application of a charge on consumer products to reflect the cost of solid waste management services.

11.0 National Groundwater Commission

The 1984 RCRA Amendments also established a National Groundwater Commission to study and assess, among other things, the groundwater resource, the extent of its contamination, methods of abatement and improved future management of groundwater. The Commission is required to report their findings and recommendations in two phases. A preliminary report is required to be submitted to Congress and the President by November 1984. The final report is due by 30 October 1986. 126/

126/   See 1984 Amendments, Section 704.

12.0 Conclusion

As the foregoing discussion amply demonstrates the RCRA program is complex. The 1984 Amendments have added many new requirements which represent a challenge to the will and imagination of the regulated community. They will challenge industry to find new ways to treat and dispose of hazardous waste. This may include methods of destruction or detoxification using technologies many of which are only recently developed or not yet even on the drawing boards. Never has the incentive been greater to reuse, recycle, or reclaim wastes, or to search out new products, processes, and raw materials which do not result in the generation of hazardous waste in the first place.

Chapter 3

COMPREHENSIVE ENVIRONMENTAL RESPONSE, COMPENSATION AND LIABILITY ACT (SUPERFUND)

Ridgway M. Hall, Jr.
Nancy S. Bryson
Attorneys
Crowell & Moring
Washington, D.C.

1.0 Overview

The "Comprehensive Environmental Response, Compensation and Liability Act of 1980," 1/ commonly known as the "Superfund" Act or as CERCLA, 2/ was passed by Congress and signed into law on 11 December 1980. This statute, enacted in the last hours of the 96th Congress, created the first comprehensive federal law to respond to releases of hazardous substances to the environment. It is the newest of the major environmental laws.

The basic scheme of the statute is to provide federal funding to respond to the releases of hazardous substances or other pollutants or contaminants released to the air, water, or land.

1/   Public Law 96-510 (11 December 1980), 42 U.S.C. Section 9601 et seq. Complete text is contained in Government Institutes' Environmental Statutes, pp. 504-548 (1985).

2/   Throughout this chapter we will use the term "Superfund" to refer to this statute.

Initially, the parties who are "responsible" for the release are supposed to do the cleanup work—normally the owner or operator of the vessel or facility from which there is a release to the environment. The responsibility for such cleanup action may also extend to generators and transporters whose hazardous waste was shipped to the site from which there is a release. If the responsible parties do not voluntarily take appropriate removal and remedial action, EPA has the authority to order them to do so. If they still do not respond, EPA can use the federal funds and then seek recovery of its expenses from the responsible parties.

The two funds which exist at this time are the Hazardous Response Fund and the Post-Closure Liability Fund, each of which is discussed below. As of this writing, those funding mechanisms are scheduled to be reauthorized by Congress during 1985. Legislation has already been introduced not only to extend the authorization and increase the funding for Superfund but also to make substantive amendments to the law in light of EPA's first four years of experience with it. Consequently, those who are affected by Superfund should watch for amendments in this area.

While many sites which have been the target of cleanup or enforcement actions under Superfund have involved one or a small number of responsible parties, many others have involved literally hundreds of potentially responsible parties. This has raised some complicated legal and practical issues relating to liability, enforcement, and the practical task of getting the sites cleaned up. Significant scientific issues also have arisen in connection with properly evaluating a site, determining what if any environmental contamination may be actually associated with a release from a site, particularly old sites, and in determining the appropriate removal and remedial action and the proper cleanup performance standard. These and other issues will be explored in the discussions below and will undoubtedly be the subject of continuing administrative, legislative, and judicial attention in the years to come.

2.0 Statutory Funds

The key purpose of Superfund is to establish a mechanism of response for the immediate cleanup of hazardous waste contamination from an accidental spill or from chronic environmental damage such as is associated with an abandoned hazardous waste disposal site. To achieve the purposes of this Act, certain requirements are placed on all handlers of hazardous waste.

Owners and operators of vessels or facilities handling hazard-ous wastes are required to show evidence of financial responsi-bility. This provision ensures that if a hazardous waste is released, the responsible owner, operator or transporter can pay the costs of removing the contaminant and restoring damaged natural re-sources. Such a release would require immediate notification to the National Response Center and cleanup and response action by the responsible party.

Persons responsible for the release are liable for all costs incurred from the cleanup and restoration of the environment. Only when a financially responsible defendant cannot be found will the Response Fund absorb the costs of removing the released hazardous waste. The law sets forth procedures for making a claim on the Fund when the responsible party is unavailable.

3.0 Agency Responsibilities

Although the law nominally vests most of the response authority with the President, the President has in turn delegated this to various departments and agencies through Executive Order 12316, issued 14 August 1981. 3/   EPA is given overall lead responsibility for implementing the Act. The Coast Guard is responsible for response actions in the coastal zone, Great Lakes, ports and har-bors. The Department of Defense is responsible for releases from its vessels and facilities. Evacuation and relocation is handled by the Federal Emergency Management Agency. 4/ Virtually all other

---

3/   46 FR 42237, 20 August 1981.

4/   The Federal Emergency Management Agency was established through an executive reorganization to deal with certain national emergencies and disasters. See Reorganization Plan No. 3 of 1978 (43 FR 41943); Executive Order 12127 of 31 March 1979 (44 FR 19367); and Executive Order 12148 of 20 July 1979 (44 FR 43239, 24 July 1979). It has major responsi-bilities for implementing the Federal Disaster Relief Act of 1974, 42 U.S.C. § 5121 et seq., the Earthquake Hazards Reduc-tion Act of 1977, 42 USC. § 7701 et seq., as well as responsi-bilities for the stockpiling of strategic and critical materials, emergency broadcasting, federal fire prevention activities, responding to flood disasters, and other national crises. Its role under Superfund thus far is primarily in the area of provid-ing evacuation and relocation assistance.

response action is vested in EPA. Other administrative functions are assigned to the Departments of Transportation, Health and Human Services, Interior, Treasury, Justice and others.

An Agency for Toxic Substances and Disease Registry is established within the U.S. Public Health Service by the Act. This Agency is to report directly to the Surgeon General of the United States to help carry out the health-related functions of the Act in consultation with EPA, FDA, NIOSH, and other federal and state agencies with an interest in the control of hazardous substances. 5/

It should be apparent that there are overlaps and interrelationships between this law and several others, including (1) the Resource Conservation and Recovery Act (RCRA), and (2) the hazardous substance spill provisions of Section 311 of the Clean Water Act. 6/ One of EPA's continuing challenges in implementing this law has been to try to harmonize these relationships to avoid duplication and inconsistency.

4.0 Toxic Substances and Disease Registry

Section 101(14) of the Superfund legislation defines a "hazardous substance" as any substance designated as hazardous under Section 311 of the Clean Water Act, any hazardous waste which is either listed as hazardous or has hazardous waste characteristics under RCRA, any toxic pollutant listed under Section 307(a) of the Clean Water Act, any hazardous air pollutant listed under Section 112 of the Clean Air Act, any imminently hazardous chemical substance with which the EPA Administrator has taken action under Section 7 of the Toxic Substances Control Act, and any other substance which EPA designates as hazardous under Superfund Section 102. The term specifically does not include oil, natural gas, or synthetic gas.

Section 102 also requires EPA to promulgate regulations "establishing that quantity of any hazardous substance the release of which shall be reported pursuant to Section 103" of the Act. Unless and until superseded by these regulations, reportable quantities for hazardous substances listed under Section 311 of the Clean Water Act are those quantities which EPA established for those substances, and for all other substances the reportable quantity is one pound.

5/　　Superfund, § 104(i).

6/　　33 USC § 1321.

EPA has proceeded slowly to implement this provision. In its initial proposal to revise the reportable quantities in 1983, EPA established 24 hours as the accumulation period for determining when a reportable quantity had been reached. 7/

Section 103 requires any person in charge of a vessel or an offshore or onshore facility to immediately notify the National Response Center of any release of any hazardous substance in a reportable quantity. A toll-free telephone number was established for this purpose (800/424-8802). Exempt from the notification requirement is any "federally permitted release." A federally permitted release is any discharge which is in compliance with a permit issued under the Clean Water Act, the Solid Waste Disposal Act (RCRA), the Marine Protection, Research and Sanctuaries Act of 1972 (commonly known as the "Ocean Dumping Act"), the underground injection control program established under the Safe Drinking Water Act, any Clean Air Act permit or state implementation plan, any discharge to a publicly owned treatment works in compliance with Clean Water Act pretreatment standards, and any discharge authorized under the Atomic Energy Act. This exemption applies whether the permit is issued by a federal, state or local authority. 8/

Failure to notify the National Response Center and any other appropriate government agency of an unpermitted release of a reportable quantity will subject the person in charge of the vessel or facility to a fine of up to $10,000 and imprisonment of up to one year.

A second important one-time reporting provision required every person who owned or operated a facility where hazardous substances had been stored, treated or disposed of and which were not permitted or accorded interim status under RCRA to notify EPA of the existence of the facility, and submit an inventory of hazardous substances known to be there as well as any which are known or suspected to have been released there by 9 June 1981. Knowing failure to comply with this requirement also carries a fine of up to $10,000 and imprisonment of up to one year. On 15 April 1981, EPA published a notice as to persons and facilities which must report, and

---

7/   48 FR 23552, 25 May 1983.

8/   Superfund § 101(10).

a suggested reporting form. 9/ EPA has since used this information
to create a prioritized inventory of potential problem sites.

A third reporting provision requires that if there is a release
which threatens the public, notice must be published in a local newspaper which circulates in the area where the release took place, to
minimize public exposure and potential injury. 10/ EPA may issue
regulations requiring the keeping of records with respect to hazardous substances. These records must be retained for 50 years, subject
to a waiver by EPA, if a lesser period would be consistent with the
purposes of the Act. 11/

5.0 Response and Clean Up Authority

Whenever there is a release of a hazardous substance, the
President is authorized to act, consistent with the National Contingency Plan, to remove the hazardous substance and provide appropriate remedial action for environmental protection. 12/ He is not
to take such action, however, if he determines that the removal or
remedial action will be done properly by the owner or operator of
the vessel or facility from which the substance was released. This
removal authority extends not only to listed hazardous substances,
but to any "pollutant or contaminant which may present an imminent
and substantial danger to the public health or welfare." Because
EPA can decide on a case-by-case basis what a pollutant or contaminant may be, consistent with a health-based statutory definition,
the qualifying "endangerment" language was added as an important
check on agency discretion. As indicated above, nothing in the Act
covers oil or gas releases.

In using the Response Fund for this cleanup, the goverment
may not go above $1 million, or six months beyond the day of initial
response, unless emergency conditions require it. There are also
provisions for the state to participate in the funding of such cleanup
efforts, as well as in the actual carrying out of the cleanup. The
state must pay ten percent of the cleanup cost, and fifty percent if

---

9/   46 FR 22144.

10/   Superfund, § 111(g).

11/   Superfund, § 103.

12/   Superfund, § 104.

the state owns the site. EPA normally enters into a written agreement with the state agency to set forth their working relationship on cleanup and remedial action, including funding responsibilities.

In addition to any other abatement action, the government is authorized to issue abatement orders, or go to the U.S. District Court for the district where any "imminent and substantial endangerment to the public health or welfare or the environment" is occurring or threatened to ask for any appropriate injunctive relief. Willful noncompliance with any such order subjects the violator to a fine of up to $5,000 per day of compliance. 13/

EPA has issued guidelines, in consultation with the Justice Department, for the use of imminent hazard and other enforcement and emergency response authorities for the providing of prompt abatement of hazardous substance incidents. These guidelines explain how the agency intends to coordinate its response actions with the enforcement authorities it has under various statutes. 14/

In general, EPA has proceeded with identification of potentially responsible parties contemporaneously with site hazard evaluation. EPA encourages the use of state authorities and personnel for enforcement, if voluntary cleanup arrangements cannot be negotiated with responsible parties. Federal enforcement is used whenever state enforcement is inadequate, and is used at virtually all the National Priorities List sites (discussed below) when voluntary action proves inadequate.

6.0 National Contingency Plan

The blueprint for cleanup and remedial action is the National Contingency Plan (NCP) which had been developed orginally under Section 311 of the Clean Water Act. Under Superfund, EPA has revised this Plan to broaden its scope to include land based facilities with discharges to air and land as well as to the navigable waters, and to include in the words of the statute, a new "national hazardous substance response plan which shall establish procedures and standards for responding to releases of hazardous substances, pollutants,

---

13/ Superfund, § 106.

14/ 47 FR 20664, 13 May 1982.

and contaminants."15/   Thus essentially all environmental releases of pollutants are at least potentially subject to the NCP unless excluded by law. The NCP includes such matters as:

(1)   methods for discovering, reporting, and evaluating hazardous waste disposal facilities;

(2)   determining appropriate response methods and equipment;

(3)   determining and assigning appropriate roles and responsibilities to various levels of government and government entities in carrying out the plan; and

(4)   determining priorities among releases or threatened releases for the purpose of taking effective remedial action.

6.1 Revised National Contingency Plan

Section 105 of Superfund required EPA to issue the revised National Contingency Plan and emergency response guidelines by 9 June 1981. On 28 July 1981 EPA issued an "Interim Superfund Removal Guidance" document, which provides guidance to on-scene coordinators and others responsible for removal and remedial action following a release of hazardous substances. 16/ EPA missed the statutory deadline for promulgating the NCP and was placed under a court order to publish the proposed revisions by 15 March 1982 and to publish the final plan by 12 May 1982. Environmental Defense Fund v. Gorsuch, No. 81-2083 (D.D.C. 12 February 1982, as modified). The revised Plan, formally known as the National Oil and Hazardous Substances Pollution Contingency Plan, was finally issued on 16 July 1982 and appears at 40 CFR Part 300. 17/

The NCP is divided into eight subparts:

15/   Superfund, § 105. The original national contingency plan was set forth at 40 CFR Part 1510, and related primarily to discharges of oil and hazardous substances which affect or may affect the navigable waters. The new Plan is codified at 40 CFR Part 300.

16/   See notice of availability, 46 FR 40800, 12 August 1981.

17/   47 FR 31180, 16 July 1982.

Subpart A   – Introduction, scope, and definitions
Subpart B   – Responsibilities, including federal, state, local
                and private
Subpart C   – Organization, coordination and
                communications
Subpart D   – Regional and local contingency plans
Subpart E   – Oil spill response
Subpart F   – Hazardous substances response
Subpart G   – Trustees for natural resources
Subpart H   – Use of dispersants and other chemicals

Subpart A sets forth the scope of the NCP and provides definitions. The definitions generally follow those in the two authorizing statutes, but several merit special attention. The term "Lead Agency" refers to the agency which provides the on-scene coordinator. In most cases, this will be either EPA or the U.S. Coast Guard. The On-Scene Coordinator (OSC) is the federal official designated by EPA or the Coast Guard to direct and coordinate federal responses. Where the response is a planned removal or remedial action, the duties of the OSC may be transferred to a "responsible official." All references to the responsibilities and authority of the OSC, therefore, equally apply to the responsible official.

Subpart B assigns responsibilities among the affected federal agencies and departments and identifies roles for state and local governments and the private sector. It is based upon Executive Orders 11735 and 12316 which delegate responsibilities under Section 311 of the Clean Water Act and Superfund, respectively. All federal, state, and local agencies are directed to cooperate in carrying out orders and in assisting the OSC in any removal, cleanup, or other response action. Further, this subpart sets forth a role that private organizations may play in responding to a release of a hazardous substance. In this regard, it is important to note that if a party intends to seek reimbursement from the Fund for its response authorities, those activities must receive prior approval from EPA.

Subpart C explains the administrative organizational structure of the response program and sets forth the authorities and responsibilities of the participants. The organizational components of the NCP are discussed in the context of the three types of activity involved: (1) planning and coordination; (2) communication; and (3) on-scene response actions.

The National Response Team (made up of representatives of at least the 12 federal agencies listed in 40 CFR 300.23[b]) is the overall coordinator. The representative from EPA is the chairman, and the representative from the Coast Guard is the vice chairman. The Team is responsible for assuring national preparedness to respond to significant discharges of oil or hazardous substances. Regional Response Teams supplement the National Response Team and carry out response actions at the regional and local levels. The Regional Response Team works together with the federally-designated OSCs for the development of regional and local contingency plans.

EPA and the Coast Guard designate OSCs for all areas in each region. Basically, the Coast Guard appoints the OSCs for coastal areas, and EPA designates the rest. The OSC directs federally-financed response efforts, and coordinates all other federal efforts at the scene of a discharge.

The National Strike Force consists of strike teams established by the Coast Guard on the east, west and gulf coasts to provide emergency assistance. The strike teams will provide assistance to the OSCs on request. They can be supplemented by "emergency task forces" consisting of personnel trained to evaluate, monitor and supervise pollution responses. In addition, EPA has its own Environmental Response Team to deal with emergencies and lesser problems. These personnel have expertise in biology, chemistry, hydrology, engineering, on-site safety, cleanup techniques, and other skills which may be needed in response actions.

The NCP provides that when an emergency exceeds the response capability of the OSC, transects regional boundaries, or poses a substantial threat to the environment, the Regional Response Team may be activated. In more serious situations, notably those with national or international implications, the National Response Team may be activated.

The National Response Center, located in the offices of the U.S. Coast Guard in Washington, D.C., is the center for all communications. Notice of an oil discharge or a release of a hazardous substance, pollutant, or contaminant should be made immediately to this response center.

Subpart D of the NCP requires a regional contingency plan for each "standard federal region." A federal local plan must be developed in all local areas where the Coast Guard furnishes the OSC, and in any other areas where the OSC deems it necessary. The regional contingency plans are to identify information on all useful facilities and resources in the region, and must follow the format of the NCP.

6.2 Response, Removal and Remedial Action

6.2.1 Oil Spill Response (Clean Water Act)

The oil spill response provisions, which are set forth in Subpart E of the NCP, are part of EPA's implementation of Section 311 of the Clean Water Act. This should be read in conjunction with EPA's regulations concerning the reporting and cleanup of oil spills, 40 CFR Parts 109-114. It is divided into four "phases." Phase I is discovery and notification of a discharge. In Phase II, a preliminary assessment of the oil discharge is made, followed by initiation of action. The OSC must make a reasonable effort to have the responsible party perform removal action voluntarily. If the responsible party does not take such action, or is unavailable, the OSC takes the appropriate response action.

Phase III addresses in more detail the containment, countermeasures, cleanup, and disposal actions to be taken by the OSC. Finally, Phase IV deals with the collection of documentation to support cost recovery in connection with the response action. Detailed information must be kept concerning the nature and levels of response action. Pollution reports must be filed with the national and regional response teams following any major pollution incident.

6.2.2 Hazardous Substance and Pollutant and Contaminant Response (Superfund)

Subpart F of the NCP deals with response actions for releases of hazardous substances, pollutants and contaminants. As noted above, "hazardous substances" are defined in advance by statutory definition (the "list of lists" in Superfund § 101(14)), while "pollutants and contaminants" are not listed in advance but are simply substances which EPA determines, on a case-by-case basis, threaten adverse effects to human health or the environment (Superfund § 104). Subpart F is divided into seven "phases." Although most of this subpart applies to Fund-financed responses, a substantial part of the requirements also apply to cleanup by responsible parties. 18/

18/   See 40 CFR 300.68 (e)-(j) (1984).

These activities apply to both releases of hazardous substances and substantial threats of releases.

Phase I is discovery and notification. This should be read in conjunction with the Superfund Section 103(a) reporting requirements and the exemptions under that section for federally-permitted releases. In Phase II of Subpart F, a preliminary assessment of the hazard is made (including identification of the source and the nature of the release). Also, it is determined whether the responsible party is willing and able to take appropriate response action.

Phase III requires immediate removal action when such action is necessary to mitigate significant risks of harm to human life or health or to the environment. A number of specific actions which may be taken are identified, including removal of substances, providing alternate water supplies, sampling and analysis, evacuation, security fences, barriers to the spread of pollutants, and the use of chemical detoxifying agents. Immediate removal action must be terminated after obligation of $1 million or 6 months has elapsed from the date of the initial response, unless it is found that circumstances warrant continued action.

Phase IV requires an evaluation and determination of an appropriate response where circumstances allow planned removal and remedial action. This can be used in lieu of, or after, immediate removal action. It involves a more detailed assessment of the threat of harm and the risks involved.

6.2.3 Evaluating Sites: The National Priorities List

Section 105(8) of Superfund requires EPA to establish a National Priorities List (NPL) consisting of at least 400 sites which are to be given top priority consideration for possible removal and remedial action. "Removal" in this context involves the physical removal of a hazardous substance, pollutant, or contaminant from the location of release. "Remedial action" involves additional measures which may be deemed necessary to repair environmental damage or to protect public health or the environment from injury.

In order to implement this requirement, EPA hired the Mitre Corporation to develop a mathematical formula, or model (sometimes known as the "Mitre model" after its initial developer) to serve as a Hazard Ranking System (HRS). The Hazard Ranking System which was developed appears as Appendix A to the National Contingency Plan. 19/ The purpose of this model, or ranking system,

---

19/   40 CFR Part 300, Appendix A.

is to enable personnel in EPA regional offices and state organizations to gather some basic data about a site which indicates something about its harm or potential harm to human health and the environment and to give the site a numerical scoring which will provide at least a rough indication as to whether in fact the site is posing harm or threat of harm to the environment, and how serious the threat may be. The principal parameters which are considered are an observed release or a threatened release to groundwater, an observed or a threatened release to surface water, and an observed or threatened release to air. In evaluating the observed or threatened release, consideration is given to the nature of the substances involved, including their toxicity and volume, the pathways of exposure to human beings (such as drinking water supplies) or sensitive environmental areas, the containment which is provided by man-made or natural features, and other relevant factors. Numerical rankings are given to the various factors considered, and these are in turn run through a mathematical formula which gives a numerical score and which provides a rough-cut indication as to degree of hazard.

EPA used this ranking system initially to establish an interim priority list of 115 sites in October 1981, which was expanded to 160 sites in July 1982. The first formal National Priorities List was published on 8 September 1983 and consisted of 406 sites. 20/ EPA added another four sites in May 1984, and another 128 sites on 21 September 1984. 21/ On 15 October 1984, EPA proposed to add another 238 sites, including for the first time federally owned facilities. 22/ Prior to that time, EPA had been reluctant to include federally owned facilities, suggesting that because other federal agencies were part of the same executive branch of the government, it would be unseemly for EPA to bring enforcement actions against sister agencies. However, because some of the more serious hazardous waste problems were found at federally owned facilities, and because failure to list such facilities appeared to place an uneven burden on the private sector, EPA altered this policy, at least to the extent of listing such facilities.

20/   48 FR 40658.

21/   49 FR 37070.

22/   49 FR 40320.

In developing the National Priorities List, EPA in 1981 called upon states to evaluate sites and submit lists of candidate sites which were then reviewed in the EPA regional offices. Under Section 105 of Superfund, the top priority site designated by each state must be included on the NPL, in the top 100 portion of the list. This has necessarily led to skewing of priority, since heavily industrial states like New Jersey have a very large number of contaminated sites, while some of the more rural Western states have very few contaminated sites, and those which are even at the top of that state's list may be far less menacing than many sites located in other states. For this reason, among others, EPA has not necessarily followed a lockstep approach down the priorities list in terms of promptness of response.

Once a site is on the NPL—and in some cases even before a site is proposed for a listing on the NPL—EPA uses its broad investigative authority to send letters to potentially responsible parties inquiring about waste management and disposal practices at that facility which may be causing releases or threat of releases to the environment. Sometimes EPA also sends such letters to generators and transporters of hazardous substances which it believes may have been shipped to the site asking for relevant information concerning nature and quantities of such substances, particularly where the present owner and operator is either defunct or lacks adequate records. Where preliminary evidence indicates an environmental problem, a Field Investigation Team (FIT) site inspection is done and a report placed in the administrative record based on its evaluation. Often these evaluations are quite superficial, consisting of an on-site observation, a review of any available reports or other documents concerning waste disposal practices at the site, and occasionally some surface or groundwater monitoring.

Once a site is actually on the NPL, this initial investigation is followed up by a more formal Remedial Investigation and Feasibility Study (RI/FS). These are two separate studies, but often are done by the same contractor to EPA. Where private parties are willing to perform a remedial investigation and/or a feasibility study, they may submit the protocol for such programs to EPA, and, if approved, the private parties may perform this activity.

Although the major focus of the site evaluations to date has been potential groundwater and surface water contamination, the HRS also provides for the gathering of information on potential fire or explosion threat, or evidence of direct human contact with hazardous substances. That information, however, is then used for immediate response action rather than for a determination on a slower paced schedule as to what if any remedial action may be required.

The Mitre model has a number of flaws, some of which have become the subject of litigation. While not purporting to list these flaws comprehensively, frequently the Mitre model, particularly as used by EPA's regional office personnel, has resulted in the use of assumptions rather than facts even when site-specific facts have been furnished by potentially responsible parties. This is not required by Superfund itself, and common sense would suggest that where factual information is available, it should be used rather than arbitrary assumptions in actually evaluating a site. In addition, the model has been severely criticized for its failure to take into account quantities and concentrations of wastes. Once a waste pile is identified, the Mitre model treats the entire quantity as hazardous, even though a tiny fraction of it may involve substances of concern. The result is that the purported hazard associated with high volume, low concentration wastes, such as mining wastes, may be grossly overstated by the model. 23/ Nothing prevents EPA from modifying its model or using different types of models for different environmental circumstances. As of this writing, there is substantial pressure on EPA to move in a more rational and flexible direction.

Following listing and evaluation of a site, EPA makes a determination as to whether the site is in fact posing a hazard to human health or the environment and, if so, what if any removal or remedial action would be feasible and cost-effective to mitigate the damage. It should be noted that the way that the EPA has currently written the NCP, while removal can take place at any site regardless of whether it is on the NPL, remedial action can only be conducted at a site which is on the NPL. At this point therefore we return to discussion of the NCP procedures for responding once a site has been properly evaluated.

Phase V of the NCP deals with the planned removal of hazardous substances. As with immediate removal action, planned removal must be terminated after $1 million has been obligated or six months has elapsed from the date of initial response, unless there is a continuing emergency. The state involved must request the

---

23/   See criticism of the Mitre model by the Senate Environment and Public Works Committee in S. Rept. 98-631, 98th Cong., 2d Sess. (21 September 1984) at 27.

planned removal. Like remedial action, planned removal action is authorized only if the relevant state agrees to pay ten percent of the response costs, or fifty percent if the state owns the site.

Phase VI involves longer term remedial action. Remedial action may be arranged through voluntary agreement with the responsible parties, or by EPA and the state if the responsible parties are unwilling or unable to take the required response action. Remedial action is normally taken with respect to sites on the National Priority List. The lead agency is to consider the nature of the problem and to develop an appropriate remedy, considering all of the relevant circumstances, including cost-effectiveness and alternate response actions. Finally, Phase VII addresses the collection of documentation to support cost recovery.

In determining the appropriate level of cleanup required the OSC seems to have the final word. 24/ While the NCP gives the responsible party an opportunity to confer with the OSC or the lead agency of which he is the representative to determine the appropriate response measures, there is no mechanism for further administrative review of that determination in the event that the responsible party and the OSC or lead agency disagree. This problem is particularly troublesome in view of Section 107 of Superfund, which provides that a responsible person who fails to respond to the OSC's directive is liable not only for all costs of removal or remedial action incurred by the government, but also for punitive damages in an additional amount of up to three times the actual response costs if his failure to respond is found to be "without sufficient cause." These decisions on "how clean is clean" at a given site have been made largely at the EPA Regional Office level. The relevant cleanup performance standard is stated in the NCP as that which is the most cost-effective alternative which substantially mitigates the damage. 25/

EPA has entered into a Memorandum of Understanding with the Coast Guard on accounting for costs incurred by the Coast Guard in supervising or performing cleanup work, 26/ and signed a

---

24/   See, e.g., 40 CFR 300.52-300.55 and 300.63-300.68 (1984).

25   See 40 CFR 300.68(j) (1984).

26/   47 FR 4631, 1 February 1982.

two-year contract with the Corps of Engineers to manage cleanup contracts issued to private companies.

Subpart G of the NCP identifies the official who is "trustee" of specific natural resources. Natural resource damage liability is discussed in the next section, dealing generally with liability under Superfund. The trustee may recover damages for the destruction of these resources caused by a discharge of oil or release of a hazardous substance. Subpart H authorizes the use of chemical dispersants provided they appear on EPA's list of accepted dispersants. Use of dispersants not on the list will continue on a case-by-case basis.

7.0 Liability and Enforcement

The owner and operator of a vessel or a facility from which there is a release, and any person who generated hazardous substances and sent them to that vessel or facility (or site) or who as a transporter selected that location, is liable for:

(1)   all costs of removal or remedial action incurred by the United States or a state;

(2)   any other necessary response costs incurred by any other person;

(3)   damages for injury to or destruction of or loss of natural resources.

This liability is imposed under Section 107 of Superfund. Where the injury is to natural resources, the President (or his designee) or the authorized representative of any state may act on behalf of the public "as trustee of such natural resources" to recover such damages. The recovered damages are available to restore and rehabilitate the damaged natural resources. In some situations, natural resource damage will be addressed in the context of removal and remedial action, including the decisionmaking process as to what if any response action is appropriate. Under those circumstances, it would be inappropriate to allow a separate natural resource damage claim to be maintained. 27/

27/   As of this writing, EPA has not yet fully addressed the circumstances or procedures for natural resource claims. The Department of the Interior in addition is obliged to issue regulations concerning the assessment of natural resources damages, but the government so far has moved slowly.

Liability for such amounts is "strict" in the sense that no showing of actual fault is required. Three statutory defenses are allowed, however, where the damage resulted solely from:

(1)   an act of God;

(2)   an act of war;

(3)   an act or omission of a third party, if the defendant establishes by a preponderance of the evidence that he exercised due care and took appropriate precautions against foreseeable acts or omissions by any such third party and the consequences which could foreseeably result therefrom. 28/

Maximum liability under these provisions is as follows:

(1)   For any vessel which carries hazardous substance as a cargo, $300 per gross ton, or $5 million, whichever is greater;

(2)   For any other vessel, $300 per gross ton, or $500,000, whichever is greater;

(3)   For any motor vehicle, aircraft, pipeline, or rolling stock, $50 million, or such lesser amount as established by regulation (but the ceiling may not be less than $5 million or, for releases of hazardous substances to the navigable waters, $8 million);

(4)   For any other facility, all response costs plus $50 million.

These liability ceilings do not apply where the violation resulted from willful misconduct, or the discharger fails to cooperate in the cleanup.

The statute is silent on whether liability may be "joint and several," which would allow the government to recover full damages from one, some, or all potentially liable parties. Of course no double recovery of the same damages would be allowed from multiple parties. The legislative history indicates that this was a politically sensitive issue which the sponsors deliberately left to the common law as applied by the courts. 29/

28/   Superfund, § 107(b).

29/   See, e.g., 126 Cong. Rec. S 15004 (daily ed. 24 November 1980), and 127 Cong. Rec. S 9334 (daily ed. 9 September 1981).

A number of federal courts have reviewed the liability provisions and have held that liability under Section 107 may be joint and several where there were multiple contributors of the hazardous waste to a site and where the wastes have effectively combined to produce a single, indivisible harm. Under these circumstances, each of the contributing parties has been held to be jointly and severally liable, unless one or more of them can demonstrate that its wastes could either be separately identified, or could not possibly have contributed to the harm. Thus the courts have held that the Act permits, but does not require, the imposition of joint and several liability. United States v. Chem-Dyne Corp., 572 F. Supp. 802 (S.D. Ohio 1983); United States of America v. Northeastern Pharmaceutical and Chemical Company, Inc., 20 E.R.C. 1401 (W.D.Mo. 1984) ("NEPACCO"); United States v. Wade, 20 E.R.C. 1277 (E.D.Pa. 1983); United States v. A&F Materials Company, 20 E.R.C. 1353 (S.D.Ill. 1984); United States v. Conservation Chemical Co., 20 E.R.C. 1427 (W.D.Mo. 1984); United States v. South Carolina Recycling and Disposal, Inc., 20 E.R.C. 1753 (D.S.C. 1984).

The NEPACCO case was the first of the Missouri dioxin cases to go to trial. It was also the first Superfund decision involving Section 107 liability which followed a full-scale trial. The other cases cited above each involved rulings in response to pretrial motions, such as motions to dismiss or for summary judgment. The facts of that case were not favorable from the viewpoint of the industrial community. The 61-page decision by Chief Judge Russell Clark presents a detailed analysis of a number of liability issues, including a careful review of the legislative history and the doctrine of joint and several liability. The principal holdings of the court may be summarized as follows:

(1) Sections 104, 106(a) [authorizing injunctions and abatement orders], and 107(a) of Superfund apply retroactively to past non-negligent off-site generators and transporters, so as to impose liability for conduct which took place prior to enactment of Superfund.

(2) Sections 104, 106(a) and 107(a) do not apply retroactively to response costs which were incurred prior to the effective date of Superfund, which was 11 December 1980.

(3)   The retroactive application to pre-Superfund
        activity does not violate the due process clause of
        the Fifth Amendment of the United States Con-
        stitution.

(4)   The scope of persons who are liable to an abate-
        ment order or an injunction under Section 106(a) is
        identical to that set forth in Section 107(a).

(5)   Superfund imposes strict liability, and allows (but
        does not require) the imposition of joint and
        several liability, which the court proceeded to
        impose in this case based upon defendants' working
        in concert to produce a "single indivisible harm."

(6)   Superfund liability may be imposed on corporate
        employees individually if they were responsible for
        and arranged for the disposal of hazardous sub-
        stances.

(7)   Recoverable response costs for which the defen-
        dants were liable included:

    (a)   investigations, monitoring, and testing to
            identify the extent of the danger to public
            health or the environment;

    (b)   investigations, monitoring, and testing to
            identify the extent of the release or
            threatened release;

    (c)   planning and carrying out the response and
            cleanup action;

    (d)   recovery of the costs to the government in
            implementing these actions, including costs
            for the staffs of EPA and the Department of
            Justice;

    (e)   attorneys' fees in connection with bringing
            the action; and

    (f)   prejudgment interest from the date of the
            filing of the amended complaint which added
            the Superfund allegations.

This may represent the high water mark of Superfund liability, and
obviously these costs will not be recovered in every case.   Their
recoverability will necessarily turn on the facts of each situation.

        At least one court has held that joint and several liability
may not be imposed under Section 106, the injunctive provision of
Superfund, because Section 106 provides for equitable relief to deal

with current dangers of actual or threatened releases of hazardous substances. 30/

Recently potentially responsible parties have sought declaratory or other relief as to their liability for costs for removal or remedial action at a Superfund site. The initial judicial pronouncements have not been uniform. At least one court has held that a plaintiff is not entitled to a judicial determination in the nature of a declaratory judgment under Sections 106 or 107 as to liability for costs or other relief for removal or remedial action. 31/ The basis for this holding is that the controversy is not ripe for judicial determination until a landowner or other potentially responsible party actually incurs the costs of cleanup, or a proceeding (typically a cost recovery action) has actually been commenced by the government under Superfund. Different factual patterns, including different types or degrees of exposure, could produce different results in this area.

It has also been held that a private party cannot seek a declaratory judgment that other private persons are liable for reimbursement or response costs without first obtaining government approval of a cleanup plant. 32/ However, a private party has been allowed to maintain an action against another private party to recover damages for cleanup activities actually undertaken at a dump site under Section 107(a)(4). 33/

Both Congress and the courts have placed at the government's disposal substantial enforcement tools which, if not used carefully, can be subject to abuse. At the same time, EPA and the Justice Department have recognized that the government simply does not have enough resources to litigate the cleanup of every site on the

---

30/ United States v. Stringfellow, 20 E.R.C. 1905 (C.D. Cal. 1984).

31/ Cadillac Fairview/California, Inc. v. Dow Chemical Co., 21 E.R.C. 1108 (C.D.Cal. 1984); the same court in a later decision also held that a private party may not bring suit against other private parties to compel cleanup. 21 E.R.C. 1584 (C.D.Cal. 1984).

32/ Bulk Distribution Centers, Inc. v. Monsanto Co., 21 E.R.C. 1080 (S.D.Fla. 1984).

33/ Pinole Point Properties, Inc. v. Bethlehem Steel Corp., 21 E.R.C. 1869 (N.D.Cal. 1984).

NPL (which will continue to expand), not to mention the enforcement of emergency and other cases not involving the NPL.

Accordingly, EPA has entered into settlement agreements
and consent decrees with a number of private potentially responsible
parties providing for a cleanup at Superfund sites using funds provided by the private sector. These settlements have in some cases
involved only partial clean-ups and also may be entered into with
less than all of the potentially responsible parties. This approach is
illustrated, for example, at the Chem-Dyne waste facility in Hamil-
ton, Ohio, where 109 companies out of 289 parties identified as
potentially responsible for hazardous waste disposal agreed to
participate in financing the cleanup of that location in August of
1982. At the Enviro-Chem facility in Zionsville, Indiana, a cleanup
settlement was reached with over 200 generators, and the government then sued a few non-settling generators. A partial settlement
was also entered into at the Seymour Recycling Corporation facility
at Seymour, Indiana, which was embodied in a consent decree with
certain large generators funding a surface cleanup. 34/

Consent decrees in those cases provide illustrations of types
of covenants not to sue which the government will give in order to
induce a settlement and minimize the risk of further litigation
exposure of a settling party, and also the assurances which the
government is willing to give in order to avoid potential liability of a
settling party in a cost recovery action which might subsequently be
brought by a non-settling party claiming contribution based upon
joint and several liability. These have been two areas which have
inhibited private settlements absent reasonable protection by the
government. 35/

34/ United States of America v. Seymour Recycling Corporation,
18 E.R.C. 1944 (S.D. Ill. 1982).

35/ EPA's policy concerning negotiation and settlement of Superfund cases has been in a state of evolution since the outset. Its
most recent comprehensive policy memorandum, as of this
writing, was issued on 5 December 1984. Memorandum from
Lee M. Thomas, EPA Assistant Administrator, Office of Solid
Waste and Emergency Response, Courtney M. Price, EPA
Assistant Administrator, Office of Enforcement and Compliance Monitoring, and F. Henry Habricht, II, Assistant Attorney
General for Land and Natural Resources Division, U.S. Department of Justice to EPA Regional Administrators entitled
Interim CERCLA Settlement Policy.

A "good Samaritan" provision exempts one who renders assistance in cleaning up a spill in accordance with the National Contingency Plan or at the direction of an on-scene coordinator from liability, except for gross negligence or willful misconduct. Also, there is no liability under these provisions for damages resulting from pesticide applications, which are handled separately under the Federal Insecticide, Fungicide and Rodenticide Act. 36/

It is also provided that where liability under Superfund would run to the owner or operator of a hazardous waste disposal facility which was permitted under RCRA and which has been closed down, such liability may be assumed by the Post-Closure Liability Fund established by Section 232 of Superfund, discussed below. 37/ It is expected that the first source of funds that will be tapped for liability, however, will be the post-closure funds or security (if any) established by the owner or operator of the facility itself under RCRA or, eventually, under Superfund, unless such liability has been effectively released by the government.

8.0 Inspections, Records and Reporting

As in virtually all federal environmental laws of recent vintage, EPA is given broad authority to conduct inspections at sites and facilities where hazardous substances are or may have been generated, stored, treated, or disposed of, or transported to or from. The agency may inspect and take samples, although any such inspections must be commenced and completed "with reasonable promptness." Where sampling is taken, equal split samples must be given to the person in charge of the facility from which the sample is taken. A copy of the results of the analysis must also be furnished promptly to the owner, operator, or person in charge of the facility. 38/

EPA may request and obtain copies of all records relating to hazardous substances at any given facility "for purposes of assisting in determining the need for response to a release." These records

---

36/   7 USC § 136 et seq.

37/· Superfund, § 107(k).

38/   Superfund, § 104(e).

become public information unless a timely claim of confidentiality is asserted by the owner or person in charge of the documents. 39/

EPA has made extensive use of this authority to request records and information and conduct facility inspections, and it has become standard operating procedure at site investigations. The data-gathering authority extends to off-site generators and transporters who may have shipped waste to the site as well.

9.0 Financial Responsibility

All vessels, facilities (including those regulated by RCRA Subtitle C and other federal laws), and motor carriers must show evidence of financial responsibility, the establishment of which guarantees availability of funds for the removal of hazardous substances in case of their release. 40/ Once financial responsibility is established under Superfund, duplication of financial responsibility under any other state or local law is not required.

Any claim authorized under Superfund may be asserted directly against the guarantor providing evidence of financial responsibility. Persons not complying with the financial responsibility requirements will be liable to the U.S. for a civil penalty, not to exceed $10,000 for each day of violation. 41/

9.1 Vessels

Vessel owners and operators bringing into a U.S. port or navigable waters a vessel (except a non-self-propelled barge) over 300 gross tons must establish evidence of financial responsibility of $300 per gross ton or $5,000,000, if it is carrying hazardous substances as cargo. One or any combination of the following will establish financial responsibility: insurance, guarantee, surety bond, or qualification as a self-insurer. Any vessel which fails to produce such evidence of financial responsibility may be denied entrance to or departure from any U.S. port, and subjected to other sanctions as well.

39/   EPA's procedures for asserting claims of confidential business information are set forth at 40 CFR Part 2.

40/   Superfund, § 108.

41/   Superfund, § 109.

9.2 Facilities

The financial responsibility requirements for facilities are to be promulgated no sooner than 11 December 1985, and are to be phased in over a three- to six-year period thereafter according to the degree and duration of risk, associated with the production, transport, treatment, storage, or disposal of hazardous substances involved. This time lag is to enable the government to coordinate this program with the financial responsibility requirements in effect for treatment, storage and disposal facilities under Part 264 of the RCRA program.

The Secretary of the Treasury in 1982 conducted a study and submitted a report to Congress on the feasibility of establishing an optional system of private insurance for post-closure financial responsibility. This report was entitled "Hazardous Substances Liability Insurance." It contains a final report on Section 107(k)(4) on post closure requirements and an interim report on Section 301(b) on the adequacy of private insurance to support the financial responsibility provisions of Superfund. It concluded the insurance industry could not set premiums with any confidence, and therefore would not write policies for these risks. As of this writing, this continues to be the position of the insurance industry. Thus if Congress wants an environment in which commercial insurance is available for Superfund liability, it will probably have to amend the law so as to take at least some of the uncertainty out of the potential period of exposure.

9.3 Motor Carriers

Evidence of financial responsibility requirements for motor carriers will be determined under Section 30 of the Motor Carrier Act of 1980, Public Law 96-296.

10.0 Hazardous Substances Response Fund

10.1 Establishment of the Response Fund

The Hazardous Substance Response Fund (the "Response Fund") receives 87.5 percent of its revenue from petroleum and chemical feedstock taxes, with the remaining 12.5 percent coming from Treasury appropriations.

Title II of Superfund, "The Hazardous Substance Response Revenue Act of 1980," amended the Internal Revenue Code of 1954 to impose a tax on petroleum and 42 listed chemicals. 42/ The purpose of this tax is to accumulate 87.5 percent of the total amount of $1.6 billion, or $1.38 billion, into the Hazardous Substance Response Fund.

A tax of seventy-nine cents (i.e., less than one cent) per barrel must be paid on any petroleum product or crude oil imported to the United States, exported from the United States, or produced in the U.S. for use or storage.

The tax on chemicals is set forth in a table listed under Section 4661(b) of the Internal Revenue Code giving the tax per ton of chemical produced or imported into the United States. The definition of taxable chemical excludes methane and butane used as a fuel, substances derived from coal or used in the production of fertilizer, and sulfuric acid produced as a byproduct of air pollution control. This tax ranges from twenty-four cents to $4.87 per ton of chemical.

The taxes imposed on petroleum products, crude oil, and taxable chemicals became effective on 1 April 1981, and were initially authorized through 30 September 1985. As noted above, at the time of this writing, a reauthorization of this fund for a longer period, and increased amounts, is expected.

In addition to those taxes imposed, the following amounts are added to the Fund:

(1)   amounts recovered as penalties;

(2)   one-half of the unobligated balance in the Fund established under Section 311 of the Clean Water Act, and the entire amount appropriated under Section 504(b) of the Clean Water Act;

(3)   an authorized appropriation from the Treasury of $44,000,000 per year, for the first five years. 43/

10.2 Fund Uses

Money in the Fund will be used by the government to pay for:

(1)   government response costs including removal and remedial action and related expenses;

42/   Superfund, §§ 201-223.

43/   Superfund, § 221(b).

(2)   claims by any other person for necessary response costs;

(3)   claims resulting from the destruction or loss of natural resources, and the costs of assessing those damages (both short and long-term), including claims originally brought under Section 311 of the Clean Water Act and not yet satisfied;

(4)   costs of federal or state efforts in restoring, replacing or acquiring the equivalent of any natural resources damaged;

(5)   costs of a program preventing the recurrence of such an incident;

(6)   studies on, and registry of persons exposed to hazardous substances;

(7)   purchase and maintenance of response equipment; and

(8)   a program protecting the health and safety of employees involved in response actions. 44/

There are a number of restrictions on uses of the funds, including prohibitions on the following uses:

(1)   natural resources injured or destroyed prior to the enactment of this Act;

(2)   releases from hazardous waste facilities for which liability has been transferred to the Post-Closure Liability Fund;

(3)   certain remedial costs at federally owned facilities;

(4)   expenses associated with injury or loss resulting from long-term exposure to ambient concentrations of air pollutants from multiple or diffuse sources; or

(5)   claims in excess of the total money in the Fund at any one time.

44/   Superfund, §§ 111, 221(c).

Note that there is no provision for compensation for death or personal injuries. Efforts to expand this legislation so as to include some form of compensation scheme for personal injuries resulting from exposure to hazardous substances have thus far failed, although the matter has been studied at Congressional request. 45/ Such efforts are likely to be renewed in the future in response to dissatisfaction in some quarters with the ability of the existing tort law system to deal with toxic exposure delayed manifestation cases. 46/

10.3 Procedures for Claims Against the Response Fund

No claim may be presented to the Fund until it has first been presented to any person responsible for the damage, and left unsatisfied. Owners and operators of a vessel or facility must settle those claims asserted against them within 60 days from the time of the claim. Thereafter the claimant can sue the responsible party or present his claim to the Fund. The President (or his agent), upon receipt of a claim against the Fund, will notify the responsible party or parties and seek to arrange a settlement of the claim. To the extent such a settlement cannot be achieved, or fails to fairly satisfy a just claim, the government can pay the claim from the Fund, and sue the responsible party for the amount so paid. 47/

Providing false information in a claim can result in a fine of up to $5,000, imprisonment for one year, or both.

Claims against the Fund or any other responsible party must be presented within three years from the time of the discovery of damage from the incident. Persons receiving compensation under

---

45/   See the report prepared pursuant to Superfund § 301(e), Injuries and Damages From Hazardous Wastes—Analysis and Improvement of Legal Remedies, Senate Committee on Environment and Public Works, Serial 97-12, 97th Cong., 2d. Sess. (September 1982).

46/   The principal problems involve state statutes of limitations and problems of proof, where many years have elapsed between the time when wastes were disposed of, leaking takes place, exposure occurs (along with exposure to many other things in life), and finally, symptoms appear.

47/   Superfund, § 112.

Superfund cannot make additional claims under other laws duplicative of those made under Superfund. 48/

11.0 Post-Closure Liability Trust Fund
Beginning on 30 September 1983, a tax was imposed on any hazardous waste received at a qualified hazardous waste disposal facility so as to create a Post-Closure Liability Trust Fund. 49/ This is a facility which is either permitted or in interim status under RCRA. Any hazardous waste, defined by reference to wastes which are hazardous under RCRA Section 3001 or subject to reporting and recordkeeping requirements of RCRA Sections 3002 and 3004, are taxed $2.13 per dry weight ton at the time it is received at a qualified hazardous waste disposal facility. The tax is imposed on the owner or operator of the facility. It applies only to those hazardous wastes which will remain at the disposal facility after it is closed. The tax will abate whenever the unobligated balance of this fund exceeds $200,000,000.

This fund can be used for payment of claims for damages similar to those described above for the Response Fund, where the cause of the damage arises after closure of the responsible facility, and a waiting period of up to five years has passed without a leak or release from the facility. 50/

12.0 Studies and Reports
Four years after Superfund was enacted, the President was required by law to submit a comprehensive report to Congress on the experience derived from its implementation. 51/ This report was prepared by EPA and submitted in several parts in December, 1984. It evaluated the adequacy of various provisions of the law, the extent of the hazardous substance release problem, alternative methods of financing Superfund, impacts on the economy and the balance of trade, the liability provisions, the claims process, states'

48/ Superfund, § 112(d).

49/ Superfund, § 231.

50/ Superfund, § 232.

51/ Superfund, § 301(a)(1).

roles, and other aspects of the law. This report, or group of reports, is being reviewed widely as of this writing by public and private entities, and is expected to provide useful information in the context of legislative reauthorization and amendment.

Studies are also required on siting and location of T/S/D facilities and, as noted above, the availability and adequacy of private commercial insurance to help the companies who are impacted by Superfund spread the risks and burdens of potential responsibility. These studies will undoubtedly also be used in the forthcoming legislative debates.

13.0 Regulatory Authority

The President is given broad authority to delegate and assign duties imposed under the Act and to promulgate any regulations necessary to carry out its purposes. 52/ However, Congress added a rather complicated "legislative veto" under which, if both houses of Congress disapprove a regulation within 90 days of continuous session following the date of promulgation of a regulation, the regulation may not take effect. 53/ The constitutionality of this provision is questionable in light of the Supreme Court's decision striking down a legislative veto in Immigration and Naturalization Service v. Chadha. 54/

14.0 Judicial Review

Review of any regulation issued under the Superfund legislation may be obtained only in the U.S. Court of Appeals for the District of Columbia Circuit. Such a petition must be made within 90 days of the date of promulgation of the regulation. All other actions arising under Superfund must be brought in the appropriate U.S. District Court. 55/

52/   Superfund, § 115.

53/   Superfund, § 305.

54/   103 S.Ct. 2764 (1983).

55/   Superfund, § 113(a), (b).

15.0 State Superfund Laws

Superfund does not preempt any state from imposing any additional liability requirements with respect to the release of hazardous substances. It does provide, however, that anyone who receives compensation for any claim under Superfund is precluded from recovering compensation for the same claim under any other state or federal law.

While Section 114 of Superfund provides that states may impose additional liability beyond the liabilities set forth in Superfund regarding the release of hazardous substances, it also provides that:

> Except as provided in this Act, no person may be required to contribute to any fund, the purpose of which is to pay compensation for claims for any costs of response or damages or claims which may be compensated under this title.

The first cases to litigate the scope of this limited preemption clause were brought in New Jersey, where industry petitioners challenged the validity of the New Jersey Spill Compensation and Control Act, alleging that it was preempted by the above-quoted language of Section 114. The state court construed the preemption narrowly and ruled that industry could be taxed under both federal and state laws so long as the double tax was not collected and expended on the same project. 56/

Related litigation was dismissed by the United States District Court after the Justice Department stipulated with the plaintiffs that the state law was not preempted. Lesniak v. United States, No. 81-977, and Merlino v. United States, No. 81-1914 (D.N.J. 22 February 1982). The stipulation provided that New Jersey could use its funds, without Superfund conflict, for the following purposes: (a) response to oil spills; (b) purely state-cost items not covered by Superfund; (c) state-share cleanup costs; (d) purchase and placement of equipment; (e) restoration of natural resources not covered by

---

56/ Exxon Corporation v. Hunt, N.J. Sup. Ct., App. Dir., No. A-3913-81, 22 June 1983, Haz. Waste Lit. Rep. at 4312, 5 July 1983; aff'd, N.J. Sup. Ct., __N.J.__, 21 E.R.C. 1794, 19 September 1984. A dismissal of a previously filed federal court action for lack of jurisdiction was affirmed in Exxon Corporation v. Hunt, 17 E.R.C. 1969 (3rd Cir. 1982).

Superfund; (f) expenses coverable by Superfund and to be reimbursed from Superfund; and (g) damage claims that would be eligible under Superfund but for which funds are not available.

Virtually all states have some kind of hazardous waste management and cleanup laws. Most states, for example, have adopted statutes which are similar to the Resource Conservation and Recovery Act in order to obtain interim authorization or final authorization to manage that regulatory program. In addition, many states have response and cleanup authorities which are similar in nature and purpose to the federal Superfund law. These state laws are sometimes called mini-Superfund laws. They vary in scope and some are less broad and some are considerably broader than the federal Superfund law.

As of September 1984, the following states had enacted some form of a Superfund law:

California	Missouri
Florida	Montana
Illinois	New Hampshire
Kansas	New Jersey
Kentucky	New York
Louisiana	North Carolina
Maine	Ohio
Massachusetts	Tennessee
Minnesota	Washington

Others are likely to follow suit.

Obviously, therefore, a corporate environmental manager must pay attention to any applicable state Superfund laws when he is identifying potential exposure. Similarly, whenever a case involving a release or potential release to the environment is settled, there must be a settlement with the state authorities as well as the federal authorities. Otherwise, a company runs the risk of carrying out a settlement in response to federal demands, only to find that the state may later come in and try to impose additional requirements under state law.

*   *   *

In conclusion, Superfund is having a very high impact on how companies manage and dispose of their wastes, and even their selection of product lines, processes, and raw materials. Together with RCRA, it was intended by Congress to result in a major shift in how U.S. industry handles hazardous waste.

Chapter 4

TOXIC SUBSTANCES

Marshall Lee Miller
Attorney
Reid & Priest
Washington, D.C.

1.0 Introduction
     The problem of toxic chemicals, including pesticides and especially hazardous wastes, is acquiring increasing importance with the public realization that thousands of carcinogenic (cancer-causing), teratogenic (birth defect-causing) and mutagenic (genetic-damaging) substances are present in our environment. Both the World Health Organization and the National Cancer Institute have estimated that between 60 and 90 percent of cancers are environmentally induced. 1/ The Toxic Substances Control Act (TSCA) of 1976 provides EPA with authority to require testing of chemical substances, both new and old, entering the environment and to regulate them where necessary. This authority supplements sections of existing toxic substances laws, such as Section 112 of the Clean Air Act, 2/ Section 307 of the Water Act, 3/ and Section 6 of the

---

1/   See for example, "WHO Reports on Cancer," cited in In Re Shell, 6 ERC 2047, 2051. The term "environment," of course, encompasses a wide range of possible exposures from industrial chemicals to food and cosmic radiation.

2/   Clean Air Act, 42 U.S.C. § 1857 et seq., PL 91-604 (1970).

3/   Federal Water Pollution Control Act, 33 U.S.C. § 1251 et seq., PL 92-500 (1972).

Occupational Safety and Health Act, 4/ which already provide regulatory control over toxic substances. It may also be used to regulate
the development of biotechnology and genetic engineering.

2.0 Problem of Unregulated Chemicals

Prior to the passage of the Toxic Substances Control Act of
1976, there was no general federal requirement that the thousands
of new chemicals developed each year be tested for their potential
environmental or health effects before they were introduced into
commerce.   An estimated two million chemical compounds have
been recognized, with thousands of additional substances being
developed each year. 5/ While most such chemicals never reach the
market, EPA calculates that approximately a thousand of these new
chemicals are produced annually in commercial quantities.   Of
these, only a fraction are subject to mandatory testing requirements
under the Pesticide Act (FIFRA) or the Food, Drug and Cosmetic
Act (FDCA). 6/

Recent tragic experiences illustrate the consequences of this
lack of testing. In the late 1960s, there arose national concern over
the widespread contamination of food, water, and soil by certain
highly toxic compounds of organic mercury. By 1972 the government had authority under the Clean Air Act and the Federal Water
Pollution Control Act to control direct emissions of mercury into
the environment, but there was no federal authority to require testing of the effects of various mercuric compounds or to regulate the
multiple uses of mercury in industrial, commercial, and consumer
products.

Another episode in the early 1970s involved polycholorinated
biphenyls (PCBs), used in such diverse applications as printing inks

---

4/   29 U.S.C. § 651 et seq., PL 91-596, 84 Stat. 1950 (1970).

5/   New York Times, 8 July 1975, estimated as high as 250,000.

6/   Only three federal statutes give the government authority to
        require chemical manufacturers to test their products. They
        are the Federal Insecticide, Fungicide and Rodenticide Act,
        as amended (7 U.S.C. § 135 et seq.), dealing with pesticides;
        the Federal Food, Drug and Cosmetic Act, (21 U.S.C. § 321 et
        seq.) requiring testing of drugs and food additives; and Sec-
        tion 211 of the Clean Air Act (42 U.S.C. § 1857 et seq.),
        providing authority to require testing of fuel additives.

and dielectric fluids. PCBs are similar to DDT, Aldrin-Dieldrin, and other chlorinated hydrocarbons in their pervasiveness and persistence in the environment and in their suspected carcinogenicity.

A host of other chemicals have also received recent public attention. A partial list includes asbestos, lead (including tetraethyl lead), arsenic, fluorocarbons (freon), nitrosamines, methyl butyl ketone, cadmium, and fluorides.

Vinyl chloride was involved in one of the most publicized episodes. In January 1975, a link was confirmed between worker exposure to vinyl chloride monomer (VCM) and a rare form of cancer, angiosarcoma of the liver. Except for the extreme rarity of this disease and the unusual number of workers in whom it was found, the carcinogenic properties of VCM might have remained undetected. Medical experts now fear that it may also result in damage to the brain and other key organs. An OSHA standard in 1975 set a permissible limit at one part per million (1 ppm) but not before three decades of workers had been exposed to levels as high as several hundred parts per million. 7/

The incident which contributed directly to the passage of TSCA was the discovery in mid-1975 that workers in a small Virginia manufacturing plant had sustained severe neurological and reproductive damage from exposure to the chemical Kepone. Federal and state health agencies were widely criticized for failure to prevent this tragedy. The head of one agency responded, "We could accomplish a great deal if we were able to keep track of what toxic chemicals are entering our environment. Toxic substances legislation . . . is therefore an important need." 8/ While Kepone may not actually be a good example of this need (as a pesticide, it had long been screened and registered with EPA), the national attention engendered by such tragedies finally prodded Congress to enact the Toxic Substances Control Act.

7/   OSHA "Vinyl Chloride Standard," 29 CFR 1910, 1017. This was upheld unanimously by the Court of Appeals in Society of Plastics Industry v. U.S. Dept. of Labor, 509 F.2d 131 (2nd Cir. 1975); the Supreme Court denied certiorari, sub. nom. Firestone Plastics Co. v. U.S. Dept. of Labor, 95 S.Ct. 1998 (1975).

8/   Testimony of the Assistant Secretary of Labor for OSHA before a Subcommittee of the Senate Committee on Agriculture and Forestry (2 February 1976).

3.0 The Need for a Toxic Substances Control Act

Prior to the passage of the Toxic Substances Act, significant gaps existed in the federal government's authority to test and regulate problem chemicals. The Clean Air Act, the Federal Water Pollution Control Act, and other laws dealt with chemical substances only when they entered the environment as wastes (emissions to the air or discharges into the water). In many cases controls could not be easily fashioned or required without severe economic consequences. Toxic substances legislation, which theoretically would require testing before a chemical reached the production phase, overcame this difficulty.

Other statutes, such as the Occupational Safety and Health Act and the Consumer Product Safety Act, deal only with one phase of the chemical's existence (worker exposure or direct consumer exposure) and contain no authority to address environmental hazards. While both of these statutes are clearly needed, the life cycle of a chemical, from production to ultimate disposal, provides many opportunities for its escape into the environment and human exposure, and federal authority to deal with the overall cycle is fragmented. The Toxic Substances Control Act was designed to fill these gaps, both in regulatory powers and in authority to require that tests be conducted before the human or environmental exposure occurs.

4.0 Legislative Background

In 1970 the President's Council on Environmental Quality (CEQ) recommended that the Administrator of EPA be empowered "to restrict the use or distribution of any substance which he finds is hazardous to human health or to the environment." 9/ This was incorporated in the President's Message to Congress on the Environment in February 1971. 10/ Both the House and Senate passed toxic substances bills during the 92nd Congress, but the House acted too late in the session to permit a resolution of the differences between the two bills. In the 93rd Congress, both houses approved toxic substances legislation, but were unable to reach a compromise in conference.

9/   See CEQ, Environmental Quality, August 1971, p. 306.

10/   Ibid., Appendix F.

The fundamental disagreement was whether the proposed law would require new chemicals to be <u>registered</u>, as with pesticides or drugs, or simply that EPA be <u>notified</u> of plans to manufacture. Senator William Spong (D-Va.) favored the former view, but more senators were influenced by EPA's desultory pesticide registration record to avoid this time-consuming approach.

The 94th Congress, beginning January 1975, considered a variety of toxic substances legislative proposals. A bill similar to that passed by the Senate in the previous Congress was introduced as S.776 by Senators John V. Tunney (D-Cal.), Philip Hart (D-Mich.), and Warren Magnuson (D-Wash.). After considerable debate, the Senate passed a redrafted but substantively similar bill S.3149, on 26 March 1975, by a vote of 60-13, with only three significant amendments.

Three different bills were introduced in the House. One, H.R.7229, sponsored by Congressman Robert Eckhardt (D-Tex.), was reported with amendments from the Subcommittee on Commerce and Finance to the full House Commerce Committee. The Ford Administration, however, actively supported a more limited bill (H.R.12336) sponsored by Representative John McCollister (R-Neb.) and most of the chemical industry. A third bill, introduced by Rep. William Broadhead (D-Mich.), was supported by organizations such as Ralph Nader's Health Research Group. The bill that emerged, H.R. 14032, was a compromise that the House passed on 23 August 1976. 11/

On 28 September 1976, a House and Senate conference committee agreed on a final version of the Toxic Substances Control Bill, which was enacted on 11 October 1976 and signed into law by the President. It became effective, with one exception, on 1 January 1977. 12/

11/   See H.R. 94-1341, accompanying H.R.14032, and the Conference Report at 94-1679; S.R. 94-698 and the Senate Conference Report, 94-1302.

12/   The exception is Section 4(f), which only took effect two years later. Actually, without implementing regulations, none of the sections had immediate force on 1 January 1977, except for Section 8(e) requiring the reporting of significant adverse effects.

5.0 Toxic Substances Control Act of 1976

The Toxic Substances Control Act (TSCA) has two main regulatory features:

First, acquisition of sufficient information by EPA to identify and evaluate potential hazards from chemical substances;

Second, regulation of the production, use, distribution, and disposal of such substances where necessary. The principal provisions of the Act are described in the following sections.

6.0 Premanufacture Notification—Statutory Provisions

The heart of TSCA is the requirement for premanufacture notification (PMN). Under Section 5(a), a manufacturer must notify EPA ninety days before producing a new chemical substance, defined as any chemical not listed on a specially compiled inventory list (discussed later). Notification is also necessary even for older chemicals, already on that list, if the Administrator concludes that there is a significant new use which increases human or environmental exposure. 13/ In either case, EPA may extend the notification processing period for one additional ninety days, but the reasons for requiring longer consideration may be challenged in court. 14/

Many companies may wish to notify EPA well before the ninety day period in order to forestall last-minute delays in marketing. There are disadvantages to this, however: competitors will thereby be tipped off to the company's marketing plans, and EPA has warned that PMN data submitted too far in advance may be rejected as lacking sufficient certainty of the ultimate intention to manufacture.

Within five days of receiving the notice, EPA must publish in the Federal Register an item identifying the chemical substance, listing its intended uses, and a description of the toxicological tests required to demonstrate that there will be no "unreasonable risk of injury to health or the environment."

13/ TSCA § 5(a). The criteria the Administrator must consider for a new use determination (Significant New Use Regulation—SNUR) include the expected production volume, increased quantity or duration of human and environmental exposure, and hazards of manufacturing and distribution.

14/ TSCA § 5(c). Such a challenge is subject to the confidentiality restrictions of Section 14.

If the Administrator decides that the data submitted is "insufficient to permit a reasoned evaluation" and that the chemical may pose a risk to man or the environment, he may restrict or even prohibit any aspect of the chemical's production or distribution. Such an order, however, must be issued no later than forty-five days before the expiration of the notification period, meaning that the Agency must respond very quickly.   The manufacturer then has thirty days to submit specific objections to the order. 15/

Finally, for those chemicals on the priority list for which special testing is required, the Administrator is required to publish in the Federal Register his reason for not taking action to limit production and use, before the end of notification period. 16/

By statute, Section 5 was to take effect thirty days after the publication of the inventory list, which was due in November 1977. Since this did not occur until the summer of 1979, implementation of the manufacturing notification requirements was delayed for almost three years after passage of the Act.

6.1 PMN Regulations Proposed and Reproposed

In January 1979, EPA proposed voluminous PMN regulations, 17/ which required not only the submission of data specified by Congress in Section 5(d) but also extensive reporting and record-keeping derived presumably from Section 8. The proposed requirements would include complete flow charts of the production process, a risk assessment of production and distribution, certification that processors and consumers have been notified regarding the chemical's properties, detailed information on hourly emissions and effluents, and approximately 110 pages of forms with other requirements. 18/

15/   TSCA § 5(e)(1). This description, although complex, is nevertheless an oversimplification.

16/   TSCA § 5(g). This publication, however, is not a prerequisite for the production or marketing of the product.

17/   44 FR 2242, 10 January 1979.

18/   See also EPA, "Explanatory Appendix: Premanufacture Notice Forms," January 1979; "Support Document: Premanufacture Notification Requirements and Review Procedures," January 1979; and "TSCA: Questions and Answers on the Proposed PMN Regulations," February 1979.

The EPA-commissioned Arthur D. Little, Inc. study on the economic burden of complying with the proposed PMN regulations estimated that the paperwork alone would cost from $2500 to $41,000, depending on the assumptions. Preparation would also require hundreds of hours, exclusive of the still unknown testing costs. The report concluded that at $10,000 per chemical for PMN, half of the new chemicals normally introduced each year would not be released. At $40,000, 90 percent would not be introduced. 19/ The effects on small companies, which are responsible for a disproportionate amount of chemical innovation, 20/ would be disastrous if they were not granted some relief. 21/ The irony is that the original EPA estimates on PMN costs, made before passage of the Act, were negligible. They assumed that companies would be required to submit information which most would have developed anyway. 22/

In October 1979, EPA responded to public criticism of its voluminous notification regulations by issuing a new PMN proposal. 23/ This eliminated or made optional many previous Agency demands for "a considerable amount of information that is not related to EPA's decision-making." EPA claimed this revised rule would reduce mandatory PMN compliance costs to a $1200 - $8900 range per chemical, provided neither health questions nor confidentiality was raised. Despite requests, the October reproposal again did not provide special treatment for low-volume substances of, say, less

---

19/   EPA, "Impact of TSCA Proposed PMN Requirements," December 1978, p. 13.

20/   Ibid, p. III-18.

21/   Statement of Ervin Colton, CERAC Inc. of Milwaukee, at EPA PMN hearing 13 February 1979, p.5. The definition of small business in the proposal was annual sales of one million dollars, compared with five million under Section 8. Also, the one thousand pound presumption for exempt R & D was dropped entirely under the proposed Section 5 regulations.

22/   Letter from Gary H. Baise, Director of EPA's Office of Legislation, to Senator John V. Tunney (D-Calif.), no date but approximately June 1973, reprinted in Senate Commerce Committee Report No. 93-254 on S.426, pp. 50-51.

23/   44 FR 59764, October 1979.

than one metric ton a year, but EPA did specifically request additional comments on this issue. An exemption from supplementary
reporting was provided for small business, defined as companies with
annual sales below one million dollars, 24/ and they were promised
extra latitude in answering many of the PMN information forms with
"not available."

6.2 Interim PMN Policy and Final Regulations

In November 1980, just after the presidential election, the
outgoing Carter Administration published a revised interim policy to
be followed until final rules were promulgated. 25/ With the advent
of the Reagan Administration, a much-simplified PMN procedure
was promised that would minimize the burden on the reporting
industries, but this shorter version did not prove any easier to prepare. Thus, after almost seven years, no final regulation had yet
appeared. Meanwhile companies were complying with Section 5 as
best they could, given EPA's shifting attitudes. That meant submitting a notification and hoping the Agency would not find it inadequate in whole or in part.

The PMN regulations were finally issued in May 1983. 26/

6.3 Proposed Testing Guidelines Under Section 5

In March 1979, EPA issued proposed guidelines for testing
under Section 5. 27/ Although TSCA's testing rules are to be issued
under Section 4, EPA took this additional step because of widespread
industry concern that Section 5(e) might be used to delay production
indefinitely. Under that section, the Administrator is empowered to
seek an injunction to prevent the manufacture or distribution of a
substance for which data is insufficient and from which there might
be an unreasonable risk. Producers therefore wished to know what

----

24/   The figure under Section 8(b) was five times higher, while
        under 8(a) a proposal set the level as thirty million.

25/   45 FR 74378, 7 November 1980.

26/   48 FR 21742, 13 May 1983; codified at 40 CFR § 720.

27/   44 FR 16240, 16 March 1979.

data EPA would regard as sufficient. Their concern was heightened
by a provision in the proposed PMN regulation that the 90-day clock
would stop on a notice found to be deficient in some respect. 28/
Despite Agency denials, many companies feared that this was an
imaginative loophole created to extend the statutory 90/180-day
notice period and thereby to convert the process into a certification
program akin to FIFRA or FDA.

6.4 PMN Exemption: Section 5(h)(4)
The statute provides that the Administrator can exempt a
manufacturer of a new substance from all or part of PMN if he
decides that its production, distribution, use, and disposal "will not
present an unreasonable risk of injury to health or the environment." 29/
In 1980, Polaroid requested EPA for a blanket exemption on
minor changes made from time to time in the formulation of instant
photographic film. 30/ After similar requests from other companies,
prolonged debate, and an initial rejection of the exemption by the
White House's Office of Management and Budget (OMB) as (ironically) too restrictive, 31/ the Agency finally approved the first
Section 5(h)(4) exemption in a rule published in June 1982. 32/
In July 1982, in response to industry petitions, EPA proposed
other rules under Section 5(h)(4) which would exempt about half of
all new chemicals produced in the U.S. 33/ They would provide that
manufacture of certain polymers, chemicals used solely at the plant
site, and low volume chemicals (defined generally by the companies

---

28/   44 FR 2242 at 2272, proposing 40 CFR § 720.34.

29/   TSCA § 5(h)(4).

30/   See BNA, Chemical Reporter, 17 October 1980, p. 913.

31/   Ibid., 23 October 1981, p. 803; 30 October 1981, p. 819.

32/   47 FR 24308, 4 June 1982.

33/   47 FR 32609, 28 July 1982.

as 25 thousand pounds annually). 34/ For chemicals produced in volumes under one thousand kilos a year, only a brief notice need be submitted to EPA under the polymer exemption proposal: namely, manufacturer's name, location, chemical identity, and the polymer's molecular weight. Another category of polymers, those produced in quantities of between one thousand and ten thousand kilograms annually, would have to submit somewhat more information under an abbreviated 14-day PMN. Environmentalists, such as the NRDC, predictably reacted with alarm to the proposals. 35/

6.5 Significant New Use Regulations (SNURs)

Although commonly forgotten, Section 5's PMN requirements apply not only to new chemicals but to significant new uses of existing chemicals or even an appreciable increase in their utilization for an existing purpose. According to Section 5(a)(2), relevant factors include:

(A) the projected volume of manufacturing and processing of a chemical substance,

(B) the extent to which a use changes the type or form of exposure of human beings or the environment to a chemical substance,

(C) the extent to which a use increases the magnitude and duration of exposure of human beings or the environment to a chemical substance, and

(D) the reasonably anticipated manner and methods of manufacturing, processing, distribution in commerce, and disposal of a chemical substance.

34/ Section 26 provides that action taken for a single chemical may also be taken for a group; so, to grant a broad Section 5(h)(4) exemption, EPA must follow the rulemaking procedures of TSCA § 6(c)(2) and (3). Within five days of receipt EPA under Section 5(d)(2) must publish in the Federal Register, subject to Section 14 provisions on confidentiality, information on the new substance and its uses. Section 5(c) allows a 90-day extension period, if necessary for good cause, subject to section 5(e) and (f) regulatory triggers.

35/ BNA, Chemical Reporter, 30 July 1982, p. 555.

Determining when a use is a new one, especially for a chemical already having scores of applications, can be difficult. EPA found that drafting rules concerning a multitude of such situations was even harder than anticipated. After several unsuccessful attempts, the Agency decided to issue SNURs on an ad hoc basis. Then, after a pattern perhaps developed, regulations could be prepared.

EPA therefore examined approximately thirty different chemicals with purported new uses, and on 19 November 1980 proposed its first SNUR on N-methanesulfonyl-p-toluenesulfonamide. Despite evidence of some adverse effects, exposure was considered minimal because annual production for this use was only four hundred pounds a year. The manufacturer was required to give the Agency 90-days notice if it should increase production over one thousand pounds (450 kg) a year or change the use. 36/

The significance of its first SNUR was muted, however, by the accompanying explanation from senior EPA officials, such as Deputy Assistant Administrator Warren Muir, that it was not a good example of what they expected in future SNURs. This uniqueness was reinforced when the incoming Reagan Administration indicated its own misgivings about the program. Referring to the candidates for SNUR, Muir's successor, Don Clay, expressed doubt that most of the hundred then suggested were actually sufficiently hazardous enough to warrant special treatment; perhaps Section 8(a) reporting requirements (discussed below) might be more appropriate. 37/ The Chemical Manufacturers Association (CMA) favored this latter approach. 38/

The first final SNUR, on two potassium phosphate chemicals, was issued only in September 1984. The manufacturer was required to notify EPA if the concentration of these substances in consumer products exceeded 5 percent to avoid eye irritation. 39/ In another case, at the same time, the Agency decided to use the monitoring

---

36/   BNA, Chemical Reporter, 28 November 1980, p. 1105.

37/   E.g., ibid., 18 September 1981, p. 555.

38/   Ibid., 8 January 1982, p. 1045; 26 February 1982, p. 1223.

39/   49 FR 35011, 5 September 1984.

authority of Section 8(a), rather than issue a SNUR on a chlorinated napthalene. 40/

For whatever reason, EPA still has done little to implement Section 5(a), either by general rule or on a substance-by-substance basis.

6.6 Rejection of PMNs

In December 1979, EPA rejected its first PMN because of inadequate information concerning production volume, disposal methods, and other essentials. The company, which EPA declined to identify, responded that it had assumed only the facts set forth in Section 5(d)(2) were needed. 41/ The reply was unconvincing because Section 5(d)(1) specifying the required data referred directly to the information listed in Section 8(a)(2).

EPA officials lamented the scarcity of information provided in the early PMNs but, as already discussed, were obliged to deal with the problem on ad hoc basis. 42/ For example, EPA would review the submitted toxicological data and, after critical remarks, would induce the affected company to withdraw its notification, either permanently or pending further submissions or tests. 43/

A more formalistic procedure is provided in the lengthy Sections 5(e) and (f) of the Act. If the Administrator determines that there could be environmental risk and that the information provided is inadequate to make a "reasoned evaluation," he may prohibit chemical production. 44/ If the Agency decides that there is an actual indication of hazard, rather than simply insufficient evidence to rebut, Section 5(f) provides that it may prohibit, limit, or otherwise restrict production or use, as set forth in various portions of Section 6. 45/

40/   49 FR 33649, 24 August 1984.

41/   BNA, Chemical Reporter, 4 January 1980, p. 1557.

42/   Ibid, 25 January 1980, p. 1636.

43/   See, for example, ibid., 14 November 1980, p. 1057.

44/   TSCA, § 5(e).

45/   TSCA, § 5(f), esp. (f)(2) referring to TSCA §§ 6(a) and 6(d)(2)(B).

The first Section 5(e) notice, announced in April 1980, proposed delaying the manufacture of six new but questionable chemicals. The firm dropped its manufacturing plans shortly thereafter. 46/ In September 1980, EPA issued another order to block production of a new chemical pending development of additional information on its human health rules. 47/ That has been the pattern, and to date no manufacturer, either foreign 48/ or domestic, has contested the determinations in federal district court as permitted in Section 5(f). 49/

It is still not clear under the law what happens next, for the statute is ambiguous; there are as yet no court decisions, and the legislative history offers two inconsistent views. Senator Warren Magnuson (D-Wash.) explained that the House-Senate compromise language here was based on procedure in the FDA law, 50/ whereby the Agency could determine if the objections had merit: "If the Administrator determines that valid objections have been filed, then he is required either to seek an injunction or to dismiss the order. If he decides that the objections are not reasonable, then the proposed order becomes effective upon the expiration of the premarket notification." 51/ Rep. James T. Broyhill (R-N.C.), on the other hand, informed the House that a company objection, no matter how frivolous, blocks the effect of the Administrator's order and forces him to resort to a federal district court for injunctive relief. 52/

When EPA concludes that there is sufficient information to classify a chemical as an unreasonable risk, it may issue a proposed

---

46/   BNA, Chemical Reporter, 25 April 1980, p. 91.

47/   BNA, Chemical Reporter, 5 September 1980, p. 753.

48/   BNA, Chemical Reporter, 16 October 1981, p. 787.

49/   TSCA, § 5(f)(3)(B).

50/   Food, Drug, and Cosmetic Act § 701(e); see also Pfizer v. Richardson, 434 F.2d 536 (2nd Cir. 1970).

51/   122 Congressional Record 16803. 28 September 1976: see TSCA § 5(e)(2). The Senate interpretation seems more consistent with the actual language of the Act and is probably the approach which EPA will adopt.

52/   Ibid., H-11344.

order restricting manufacture, processing, or distribution. It may also directly seek an injunction which, like the above procedure for insufficient data, is also necessary if a company challenges the prospective order. 53/

7.0 Inventory List: Section 8(b)

Because the notification rules apply primarily to new chemical substances, there obviously needs to be a list available of pre-existing chemicals. Under Section 8(b), EPA was therefore required to compile an inventory of chemicals manufactured or processed in the United States. This was not to cover every chemical ever produced but was statutorily limited to those substances produced within the three-year period preceding the promulgation of applicable regulations, namely since 1 January 1975. 54/

The statute required that this list be prepared and published "not later than 315 days after the effective date of this Act." This 11 November 1977 deadline proved far too optimistic, for the inventory reporting regulations were not even published until late December 1977, six weeks afterward. 55/ This gave chemical companies until 1 May 1978 to submit their products for inclusion in the inventory, which was finally scheduled for publication in June 1979. 56/ Processors and importers had an additional 210 days to report any other chemicals, and only after that was a final revised inventory list published. 57/ This process thus turned into a rather lengthy

---

53/   TSCA, § 5(f). See also the section in this chapter on Enforcement, Part 11.0.

54/   TSCA, § 8(b). The regulations according to Section 8(a) were supposed to have appeared 180 days after the effective date or 1 July 1977. However, they were signed on 12 December 1977 effective 1 July 1978.

55/   42 FR 64572, 23 December 1977. Regulations were first proposed on 9 March 1977 (42 FR 13130) and after modification were reproposed on 2 August 1977 (42 FR 39182).

56/   Some manufacturers complained that EPA itself should have compiled the basic inventory list and then asked chemical companies only to fill in any gaps. This proposal was rejected as infeasible. See, e.g. Appendix A, Comment 2, 42 FR 64580.

57/   42 FR 64572, 23 December 1977.

one, which consequently considerably delayed the implementation of other parts of the Act, particularly premarket notification. 58/

Any substance not reported for the Inventory by 30 August 1980, or subsequently added under the PMN process, must undergo premanufacture review before it may be manufactured or imported for a commercial purpose. This applies even if a producer can demonstrate that a substance was, in fact, produced before then. The converse, however, does not hold true: EPA has removed from the list certain substances, notably ones involved in synthetic fuels, which it claims were improperly registered as commercial products, and hence "grandfathered," when in fact they were only in research and development at the time. 59/

58/   EPA published inventory reporting regulations on 23 December 1977 (42 FR 64572) and supplemented them on 6 March 1978 (43 FR 9254) and on 17 April 1978 (43 FR 16178). In October 1978 (43 FR 49688), a policy for revised inventory reporting was published. Then, in May 1979, distribution of the initial inventory list, containing over 44,000 chemical substances, began.

A second inventory reporting period lasting 210 days began on 1 June 1979. During this period, a person who processed or used a chemical substance for a commercial purpose or imported a chemical substance as part of a mixture or article could report a chemical substance that was not included on the published Initial Inventory, if the substance was manufactured, processed, or imported for a commercial purpose since 1 January 1975. The notice of availability of a cumulative supplement and revised inventory was published in the Federal Register on 29 July 1980 (45 FR 5544).

EPA has also engaged in considerable debate, again centered on synfuels, whether the particular production process should affect the definition of a substance on the inventory list. Initially, the Agency said it did. In the case of one substance, EPA ruled that since the chemical on the 8(b) list was produced by a method using other raw materials, an identical chemical with identical properties produced by another method was not on the inventory list and hence was not "grandfathered." In early 1984, however, the Agency reconsidered the logic of this position and reversed this stance. In November 1984, EPA made a similar decision regarding (surprisingly) the very definition of petroleum.

59/   BNA, Chemical Reporter, 7 August 1981, p.428; 18 June 1982, p. 390.

The obligation to report did not extend to all companies dealing with chemical substances. By regulation, EPA limited this to manufacturers and others with (a) over thirty percent (by weight) of their products classified under SIC code categories 28 or 2911; 60/ or (b) the total chemical production or importation exceeding one million pounds; or (c) special reporting for any substances produced in quantities over a hundred thousand pounds at one site in 1977. 61/

Small manufacturers, defined in the regulations under Section 8 as those with total sales less than five million dollars, were given a limited exemption from some of the reporting requirements. 62/ They were required to submit a list of substances produced but did not need to give production volumes, except for chemicals produced in excess of a hundred thousand pounds, nor separate volume figures for each plant site. This rather trivial exemption is not available to small companies owned or controlled by a larger, non-eligible company. 63/

All these "exemptions" were illusory. It was not a benefit for, say, a small company not to report on chemicals it was using; if they were put on the Section 8(b) inventory list, they were "grandfathered" and therefore not subject to burdensome PMN requirements.

Another exemption is for chemical substances produced in "small quantities for purposes of scientific experimentation or analysis or chemical research." The regulation declares a legal

---

60/   40 CFR § 710.3(a). SIC is the abbreviation for "Standard Industrial Classification."

61/   As elsewhere in the Act, production includes manufacturing, processing, or importing.

62/   For Section 5 purposes, however, EPA initially proposed defining small business by total sales of less than one million dollars, 44 FR 2242, 10 January 1979.

63/   40 CFR § 710.2(x). The original Section 8 proposal defined small business as a company having total sales under a hundred thousand dollars. 42 FR 39191 (2 August 1977), EPA officials later confided that this unreasonably low figure was never really serious.

presumption that any chemical produced in a quantity of under a thousand pounds annually is for research and development and may therefore not be reported on the inventory, unless the producer can demonstrate otherwise. 64/ A subsequent EPA regulation attempted to clarify this question by suggesting that a manufacturer request his customers to certify that a chemical is not used for purposes other than R & D. 65/

A third exclusion is for "mixtures" which are not considered to be "chemical substances" under Section 8(b). A mixture is defined as any combination of substances which is not the result of chemical reaction and which does not occur in nature. 66/ Remember, however, that mixtures are only excluded from some of the requirements of TSCA; they may still be subject, for example, to the provisions of Sections 4 and 5. 67/

Also exempt from inventory requirements are naturally occurring substances, tobacco, food and food additives, and other chemicals such as drugs and pesticides which are regulated under other federal environmental acts. 68/

The essential point is, however, that exclusion from the inventory reporting requirements was a mixed blessing. Since placing a substance on the list "grandfathered" it from future PMN require-

---

64/   40 CFR § 710.2(y). Section 8(b) of the statute says, "The Administrator shall not include in such list any chemical substance which is manufactured only in small quantities (as defined by the Administrator by rule) solely for purposes of scientific experimentation or analysis of, such substance or other substance, including such research or analysis for the development of a product."

65/   43 FR 9254, 9255, 6 March 1978.

66/   TSCA, §§ 3 and 8(b). See also 122 Congressional Record H-11020, 23 September 1976.

67/   TSCA, §§ 4(a) and 5(a).

68/   The general exemptions from the definition of "chemical substance" under the Act are set forth in § 3(2)(B). EPA has issued several further clarifications on inventory coverage, such as for natural gas streams (43 FR 16178, 17 April 1978) and natural latex (43 FR 9254, 6 March 1978).

ments, except for significant new uses, it was obviously a benefit for a producer or processor to have everything possible in the inventory.

EPA intends periodically to update the inventory list to include products for which notification forms have been submitted. The most recent compilation, listing 58,000 substances, was released in June 1982. Future manufacturers can therefore consult the revised list and know that no futher notification to EPA is required, unless special testing under Section 4 is necessary.

8.0 Reporting Requirements

8.1 Section 8(a)

Under Section 8(a) of TSCA, the Administrator must promulgate rules under which each person who "manufactures or processes or proposes to manufacture or process a chemical substance" must keep records and make reports to the Administrator as is deemed necessary for the effective enforcement of the Act. The Administrator may require such information as molecular structure, categories of use, amounts produced, description of by-products, disposal methods, and all existing data concerning the environment and health effects of each substance. Manufacturers and processors are persons who manufacture or process chemicals for "commercial purposes."

Section 8 generally exempts small manufacturers or processors from the provisions, although they may be subject under certain circumstances. 69/ In the case of manufacturers or processors of mixtures or of small quantities of research and development chemicals, reports and records may be required to the extent "necessary for the enforcement of this Act."

8.2 Proposed 8(a) Regulation, 1980

Rules governing Section 8(a) were to be promulgated no later than 180 days after TSCA went into effect. However, the proposed rules were not published until 29 February 1980, 70/ more than 2 1/2 years after the deadline for final rules.

The proposal required chemical manufacturers, including miners and importers, and some processors to report production and

---

69/ Section 8(a)(3)(A)(ii).

70/ 45 FR 13646.

exposure-related data on approximately 2300 chemicals, chosen because of toxicity or exposure levels. EPA intended to use this data for preliminary risk assessment and for ranking chemicals.

The proposed rules contained two phases of reporting. First, manufacturers and importers of the chemicals listed had to answer several questions including questions on customer use. Second, if they were unable to report customer use, EPA could require customers to submit information.

Under the Section 8(a) proposal, small manufacturers were defined as having:

(1)   total sales for all products at all sites together of less than $30 million for the reportable year, and

(2)   production volume at each site for the chemical reported less than 100,000 pounds (45,400 kilograms) for the reportable year.

In October 1980, EPA proposed a generic small business reporting exemption under Section 8(a). This eliminated all record-keeping requirements for qualifying companies, unless they planned to manufacture or process (a) a substance subject to a Section 4 testing rule, (discussed below), (b) a substance categorized as an unreasonable risk under Section 5(b)(4), (c) a restricted substance under Section 6, or (d) one subject to a Section 5(e) rule for additional testing information. 71/

In a planned subsequent rulemaking, the Agency wanted to propose Section 8(a) reporting rules for the follow-up of selected new chemicals after they had passed through the PMN process.

8.3 Section 8(a) Final Regulations

The final Section 8(a) regulation, when issued in June 1982 72/, cut the reporting list down drastically from almost 2,300 to only around 245 chemicals. Manufacturers must report production, release and exposure data, which will then be used to determine which chemicals deserve further testing. 73/

71/   45 FR 66180, 6 October 1980.

72/   47 FR 26992, 22 June 1982.

73/   See, e.g., 49 FR 25856, June 1984.

EPA also published concurrently a 3-part proposed rule under Section 8(a), requiring processors to report on the listed 250 chemicals whenever the manufacturers' reports fail to account for use of 80 percent of the substance. The proposal added another fifty chemicals for consideration for inclusion in the final list. 74/

Subsequently, EPA has indicated an intention to use Section 8(a) to monitor suspect chemicals that are not deemed to merit regulation under Sections 4(f), 5(e), 6, or other sections. There are also plans to follow up all PMN chemicals for several years using this procedure. 75/

8.4 Reporting of Health and Safety Studies: Section 8(d)

Section 8(d) requires the Administrator to promulgate rules requiring any person who manufactures, processes, or distributes in commerce any chemical substance or mixture to submit to the Administrator:

(1)   lists of health and safety studies (A) conducted or initiated by or for such person with respect to such substance or mixture at any time, (B) known to such person, or (C) reasonably ascertainable by such person, except that the Administrator may exclude certain types or categories of studies from the requirements of this subsection if the Administration finds that submission of lists of such studies are unnecessary to carry out the purposes of this Act; and

(2)   copies of any study contained on a list submitted pursuant to paragraph (1) or otherwise known by such person. 76/

In July 1978 EPA promulgated rules governing this subsection of TSCA 77/ requiring manufacturers, processors, or persons

---

74/   47 FR 26992, 22 June 1982; BNA Chemical Reporter 25 June 1982, pp. 412 and 423ff; 2 April 1982, p. 3.

75/   See, e.g., ibid., 9 March 1984, p. 1707.

76/   TSCA, § 8(d)(1) and 8(d)(2).

77/   43 FR 30984, 18 July 1978.

distributing in commerce the chemicals on the first Interagency Testing Committee priority list to submit lists and copies of health and safety studies on those chemicals. 78/

The Manufacturing Chemists Association filed a petition requesting EPA to amend or repeal the rule in September 1978. EPA rejected the petition, with minor exceptions. 79/

On 15 September 1978, the Dow Chemical Company filed a petition for review of the rule in the U.S. Court of Appeals for the Third Circuit, questioning EPA's authority to obtain studies on chemicals manufactured or processed for research and development purposes, since it was claimed such chemicals are not manufactured or processed for "commercial purposes," or on chemicals from companies that do not manufacture, process or distribute those chemicals. In addition, Dow asserted that EPA had not provided adequate notice and fair opportunity to comment on some of the provisions of the rule.

Although the Court denied Dow's challenge of EPA's authority on 24 August 1979 80/, and EPA itself had no doubt that the provisions of the rule were within the Agency's statutory authority, EPA decided that Dow had raised substantial questions on whether adequate notice and comment were provided with respect to some provisions of the rule. Therefore the rule was revoked on 31 January 1979. 81/

A new proposed rule was published in the Federal Register on 31 December 1979 82/ requiring reporting of lists and copies of studies on all chemicals included in the 18 July rule, as well as additional chemicals recommended by the ITC and other chemicals separately selected by EPA. The Agency specifically requested comment on whether it should exercise authority to obtain copies of studies on substances from persons in possession of such studies

---

78/   Two minor corrections were made to the rule shortly thereafter (43 FR 36249, 16 August 1978 and 43 FR 41205, 15 September 1978).

79/   43 FR 56724, 4 December 1978.

80/   Dow Chemical Co. v. EPA, 605 F. 2d 673 (3rd Cir. 1979).

81/   44 FR 6099, 31 January 1979.

82/   44 FR 77470, 31 December 1979.

whether or not they manufacture, process, or distribute the substances. The proposal also established an obligation to list on-going
studies for five years after a chemical appears on the Section 8(d)
list.

The final rule, which appeared in September 1982, 83/ after
extensive public comment, somewhat reduced the reporting requirements set forth in the earlier rule.

First, the sweeping definitions of "known to" or in the "possession of" were replaced with a procedural definition that would
better indicate when an extensive search could be considered final,
for purposes of the Act. Companies, henceforth, need only search
"the company files in which they ordinarily keep studies and records
kept by employees whose assigned duty is to advise the company on
health and environmental effects of chemicals." 84/ This search
may be limited to records developed after 31 December 1979, when
the revised rule 8(d) was proposed.

However, companies which manufactured a chemical within
the past ten years, even if they are not currently doing so, are
obliged to submit copies of studies but need not provide lists of
other known studies. This could be helpful where, say, a company's
research uncovered that one of its chemicals was potentially harmful and therefore discontinued it, although other manufacturers
continued production unaware.

Distributors are exempted from Section 8(d) reporting by this
revised regulation. They do not normally conduct studies anyway,
and a review of all submissions under the provisions of the Section
8(d) rule indicated none were from distributors.

Also exempted were seven types of studies that the Agency
had not found useful in assessing risks but which were burdensome to
compile. These exceptions include studies of impurities (which
would presumably exempt reports on hazardous dioxin impurities),
published studies, and studies submitted previously to EPA or on
non-confidential basis to another federal agency.

EPA declined, however, to retreat from its previous position
that research and development studies are nevertheless "for commercial purposes" and therefore reportable. Because the Agency's
contention had already been judicially approved, a subsequent

---

83/   47 FR 38780, 2 September 1982 40 CFR Part 716.

84/   Ibid.

change would have been difficult. The final rule nevertheless relied on a different argument, namely that the purpose of Section 8(d) "is to give the Agency access to information from which it can assess the nature and significance of chemical hazards and risks. TSCA is intended to address these hazards and risks to health or the environment whether or not the chemicals are desired commercial products." 85/

8.5 Reports of Health and Safety Studies

Companies routinely test their chemical products for efficiency and safety. Section 8(d) directs that EPA issue rules requiring any person manufacturing, etc., a chemical to provide the Agency with copies of such health and safety studies. 86/ But the rule is broader than just that. If the company has copies of, knows of, or reasonably could ascertain that other experimental reports or studies exist regardless of who performed or conducted them, it must also provide copies or lists of those reports. 87/

The Administrator is given the statutory authority to exclude certain categories of studies, however, if he determines they are "unnecessary to carry out the purposes of this Act." 88/

This seemingly straightforward section has been the source of considerable controversy. One issue involved a query from a major industry-supported but independent testing lab which had important studies; since it was not a manufacturer, however, it contended it had no obligation under Section 8(d) to report them to EPA. (The information was, of course, provided to EPA in due course.)

A chemical company challenged an obligation to report studies conducted for research and development on substances produced in small quantities and not offered for sale. The company contended that the statutory definition of "manufacture" under Section 8 meant "manufacture or process for commercial purposes" and that this excluded R & D. 89/ The Court of Appeals held, however,

---

85/   Ibid., p. 38781.

86/   TSCA, § 8(d)(1)(A).

87/   TSCA, § 8(d)(1)(B), (C), and 8(d)(2).

88/   TSCA, § 8(d)(1)(C).

89/   TSCA, § 8(f).

that Section 8(d) embraced such limited manufacture and, therefore, EPA was authorized to seek the data. 90/

In September 1982 EPA issued a final rule requiring companies to provide the Agency with unpublished studies. 91/ The specifically requested information on forty chemicals and chemical categories—thirty-nine recommended for Section 4(e) testing by the eight-agency Federal Interagency Testing Committee (ITC) through June 1981 (actually about 175 substances), plus asbestos added by EPA. 92/

At the same time, the Agency proposed adding another sixty-five chemicals more recently recommended by the ITC. 93/

9.0 Hazard Reporting Requirements

9.1 Substantial Risk Notification: Section 8(e)

The sweeping general notification requirements of TSCA have swamped EPA with data that, however inadequate, is still more than it could properly analyze and absorb. For the next few years, until comprehensive screening criteria are established, this could mean that information on potentially hazardous substances could languish unanalyzed in EPA files while some chemical tragedy occurs. Indeed, this suggests that notification—the key feature of the entire statute—may require a scientific sophistication that may not be developed for many years.

If health effects cannot be confidently predicted in advance, then EPA must learn of them as soon as they are discovered. Section 8(e) places upon chemical manufacturers, etc., the responsibility for reporting any indication of adverse effect. In the words of the Act, any person:

> who obtains information which reasonably supports the
> conclusion that such substance or mixture presents a
> substantial risk of injury to health or the environment
> shall immediately inform the Administrator of such
> information unless such person has actual knowledge

90/   Dow Chemical Co. v. EPA, 605 F. 2d 673 (3rd Cir. 1979).

91/   47 FR 38780, 2 September 1982.

92/   See this Chapter, Paragraph 10.3.

93/   47 FR 38800, 2 September 1982.

that the Administrator has been adequately informed of such information. 94/

Such a reporting requirement is not unprecedented. Section 6 of FIFRA has a similar provision for "factual information regarding unreasonable, adverse effects on the environment. 95/ However, FIFRA's use of the word "unreasonable" assumes, perhaps naively, that the manufacturer himself will make an adverse risk-benefit analysis and then report it. TSCA insists that any evidence of "substantial risk" must be reported. Hard and unmistakable evidence is not required; instead any "information which reasonably supports the conclusion" of possible substantial risk must be reported. Failure to report may subject any individual or company to civil penalties and even criminal prosecution. 96/

EPA issued regulations implementing Section 8(e) in March 1978. 97/ This placed upon corporation presidents and other top officials the responsibility for ensuring that adverse information is reported. 98/ The regulations state, however, that:

An employing organization may relieve its individual officers and employees of any responsibility for reporting substantial-risk information directly to EPA by

---

94/   TSCA, § 8(e).

95/   FIFRA, § 6(a)(2). A more formal system of five-year post-market surveillance is suggested in the proposed FDA law revisions submitted to Congress in March 1978. FDA Proposal § 108(g).

96/   TSCA, §§ 15(3), 16, and 17. It is interesting to note that in the first major criminal case against a company (Velsicol) for failure to disclose adverse data on the pesticides chlordane and heptachlor, the Justice Department chose to use the general federal criminal laws rather than FIFRA, § 6(a)(2).

97/   43 FR 11110, 16 March 1978.

98/   This is not an empty threat. The Supreme Court held that a chief executive officer was personally and criminally liable under federal health laws for not preventing rodent contamination of food in one of his warehouses, even though he had delegated responsibility to a corporate vice president. U.S. v. Park, 421 US 658 (1975); see also U.S. v. Dotterweich, 320 US 277 (1943).

establishing, internally publicizing, and affirmatively implementing procedures for employee submission and corporate processing of pertinent information. 99/

In defining substantial risk, the regulation excludes from consideration the "economic or social benefits of use, or cost of restricting use." Moreover the regulation takes a strongly health protectionist view by directing that the extent of exposure is to be given little weight in assessing human health risks, since "the mere fact the implicated chemical is in commerce constitutes sufficient evidence of exposure." 100/

9.2 Significant Adverse Reactions: Section 8(c)

A subsection surprisingly similar to Section 8(e) is Section 8(c). Why are both provisions necessary?

Under Section 8(c) of TSCA, any person who manufactures, etc., any chemical substance or mixture shall maintain records of "significant adverse reactions" alleged to have been caused by the chemical. Those records relating to possible health reactions of employees must be kept for thirty years, during which time they may be inspected by or submitted to anyone he designates. All other recorded allegations need be preserved for only five years.

A comparison of Section 8(c) indicates that both the standard of proof and the required response is appreciably lower than for Section 8(e).

	TSCA § 8(c)	TSCA § 8(e)
Trigger	"Significant adverse reactions"	"Substantial risk of injury"
Evidence	"Alleged"	"Information which reasonably supports the conclusion"
Response	Record and retain for 5 or 30 years	Notify EPA immediately
Regulation	Final 1982	Final 1978

99/   43 FR 11110, supra, Section II.

100/   Ibid., at 11111, Section V.

The proposal, published by EPA in July 1980 101/ defined "significant adverse reactions" as "reactions which may indicate a tendency of a chemical substance or mixture to cause long-lasting irreversible damage to health or the environment." Second, all manufacturers, processors and chemical distributors—except retailers—were included in the rule (an estimated 580,000 firms). And third, oral as well as written allegations were required to be recorded.

The final version in September 1982 102/ reflected the Reagan Administration's desire for less burdensome regulations. First, the definition was changed to place more emphasis on the word "significant":

> Significant adverse reactions are reactions that may indicate a tendency of a chemical substance or mixture to cause long-lasting or irreversible damage to health or the environment.

Moreover, only previously "unknown" effects need be recorded. This borrows a concept from Section 8(e) that may be appropriate there, where the goal is to inform EPA of new hazards, but is not fitting in a section that essentially provides for a log of health problems and complaints.

Second, the requirement to record oral allegations is dropped, although realistically that is the form in which most worker complaints would be made. Third, only processors in certain SIC code industries (namely, SIC categories 28 and 2911) are covered, while manufacturers of "naturally-occurring" substances are exempted entirely. This reduces the number of affected firms by over 98 percent to only 10,000. And fourth, while the statute gave EPA an alternative of record inspection or submission, the final regulation opted for the former, with no automatic reporting requirement.

10.0 Testing Requirements

10.1 General Testing Requirements: Section 4(a)

Section 4(a) of TSCA permits EPA to require the testing of any chemicals, both old and new, if an unreasonable risk to health or

---

101/   45 FR 47008, 11 July 1980.

102/   47 FR 38780, 2 September 1982; see also EPA Concept Paper on Section 8(c), 8 July 1982.

the environment is suspected. 103/ Testing may also be required if a chemical will be produced in such quantities that significant human or environmental exposure could result. 104/

Mixtures are also subject to the above rules, but only when the effects cannot be determined or predicted by testing the individual chemical substances which comprise the mixture. 105/ This should reduce the testing burden, particularly for small producers and formulators.

Note that not all questionable chemicals need be tested—only those for which EPA makes a specific determination that additional data is necessary and issues a formal testing rule. This standard may prescribe the biochemical effects to be investigated, the tests to be conducted, and even the experimental protocols to be followed. 106/ The statute itself, in Section 4(b), details many of the studies that may be required, including carcinogenicity, mutagenicity, teratogenicity, behavioral modification, synergism, and various degrees of toxicity. Moreover, EPA must review each testing standard at least once a year and revise them where warranted. 107/

In setting these testing standards, the EPA Administrator is to consider the relative costs and availability of facilities and personnel, and the period within which they can reasonably be performed. 108/ This little-noticed provision could have considerable future significance, if and when the Agency ever gets serious about issuing testing rules, for the present animal testing capability in this country could be saturated by a sudden increase in demand.

103/ TSCA, § 4(a)(1)(A).

104/ TSCA, § 4(a)(1)(B).

105/ TSCA, § 4(a)(2).

106/ This rulemaking is subject to the Administrative Procedure Act, 5 U.S.C. § 551, including requirements for a transcript.

107/ TSCA, § 4(b)(2). An earlier bill required EPA to propose test protocols within one year of enactment but this was not in the final version. See Senate Committee on Commerce, "Toxic Substance Control Act of 1973, Report on S.426," (D.C: G.P.O., 1973), p. 7.

108/ TSCA § 4(b)(1).

EPA's effort to develop test standards under Section 27 is presently encountering serious technical difficulties. Consequently, publication of these important protocols could be delayed. 109/

A company intending to run tests on a chemical for which EPA has issued no standard under Section 4(a) but may do so in the future, can formally request from EPA testing rules for that product. 110/ This could help avoid later charges that the tests were inadequate or otherwise not in conformity with EPA requirements. It would also help a company in litigation with OSHA or other parties, even if no Section 4(a) rule is ever issued.

In 1981, for example, EPA took 14 test rule actions and decided not to regulate testing on three other chemicals. 111/ This was overshadowed, however, by the Reagan Administration's penchant for voluntary testing over required rules, despite charges from environmental groups that it undermines TSCA. 112/ In August 1984, a federal district court agreed with the environmentalists and held that the voluntary system subverted the mandatory system set forth in the statute.

10.2 Testing Reimbursement

Because toxicological testing is so expansive, TSCA borrowed from the pesticide act a provision for sharing of testing costs. 113/ The reimbursement period is generally five years from date of submission but may be modified by the Administrator to conform to the time that was necessary to develop such data. 114/ If the manufac-

---

109/   TSCA, § 27.

110/   TSCA, § 4(g). EPA has sixty days to grant or deny the petition. Then, if granted, it has only seventy-five days to issue test standards; if denied, the Agency must publish reasons for the denial in the Federal Register.

111/   BNA, Chemical Reporter, 26 March 1982, p. 1323.

112/   Ibid., 9 July 1982, p. 468.

113/   FIFRA, § 3(c)(1)(D), 7 U.S.C. § 136a(C)(1)(D). This issue is discussed later, in the chapter on Pesticides.

114/   TSCA, § 4(c)(3)(B).

turers cannot decide among themselves a proper allocation of costs, the Administrator—as formerly in FIFRA—is required to adjudicate the dispute after consultation with the Attorney General and the Federal Trade Commission. 115/ Sharing such data exempts subsequent producers from having to conduct or submit duplicative test results.

The Agency has proposed a reimbursement rule under Section 4 which will share the cost of testing between producers in proportion to their production volume. The proposal also suggests a mechanism for adjudicating disputes on cost claims. 116/

The equivalent section in the pesticide act has been the source of much controversy, uncertainty, and administrative inconvenience. Except that the testing burden for notification is less than for registration of pesticides, this section of TSCA is unlikely to be a greater success under TSCA than FIFRA.

10.3 Priority List for Chemical Testing

There are tens of thousands of potentially toxic substances. Congress recognized that if EPA tried simultaneously to regulate all of them with its limited resources, it might actually accomplish nothing. 117/ This was important, for an earlier Agency attempt to keep short the first list of regulated toxic substances under Section 307 of the Clean Water Act had failed when challenged by environmentalists in court. 118/

Section 4(e) of the Act therefore provided for a priority list of chemicals for testing and directed that it "may not, at any time, exceed 50." 119/ The "list of 50" may contain groups of chemicals

---

115/   TSCA, § 4(c).

116/   BNA, Chemical Reporter, 11 June 1982, p. 349.

117/   Congressional authorization for the first year of TSCA implementation was originally only ten million dollars, a fraction of the sum allocated for other EPA programs at their inception. This has since been substantially increased. See TSCA, § 29.

118/   N.R.D.C. v. Train, 8 ERC 2120 (D.D.C. 1976).

119/   TSCA, § 4(e)(1)(A).

as well as individual substances. This permits considerable expansion of the list's scope, if the Administrator so desires. The final list will leave a number of vacancies that can be filled if important new chemical hazards are discovered.

The procedure for preparing this list is spelled out in excruciating detail: a committee of eight members, each from a designated government agency, 120/ was given until the end of September 1977 to submit a candidate slate, based on toxicity and exposure, to EPA Administrator for public comment and his final decision. 121/ Within twelve months he must either initiate a rulemaking under Section 4(a) or publish the reasons why not. 122/

The preparation of the inventory priority list began with an initial list of approximately 3650 chemicals compiled from nineteen scientific sources. Next, substances under the jurisdiction of other federal laws, such as pesticides and drugs, were deleted. These and other deletions led to a Master File of 1700, which was then screened for production volume and population exposure to produce a Preliminary List of 330 chemicals which was published in July 1977. This list was in turn reduced to a candidate list of eighty.

In October 1977 the Interagency Testing Committee (ITC) nominated the first group of ten substances (six categories of chemicals and four individual substances) to the Administrator. 123/ A

120/   These include EPA, OSHA, CEQ, NIOSH, NIEHS, NCI, NSF, and the Department of Commerce. Several other agencies overlooked by the statute, such as FDA, have unofficially become a part of the committee. Others include the Consumer Product Safety Commission (CPSC), and the Department of Defense and Interior. Members serve four years, may not have any financial interest, or accept employment for one year from anyone subject to TSCA.

121/   TSCA, § 4(e)(2). The priority list is supposed to be updated every six months.

122/   TSCA, § 4(e)(1)(B). One observer, who believed the nine month period was too long, had earlier described the process as confirmation of Parkinson's law that work expands to fit the time. He was overly optimistic.

123/   42 FR 55026, 12 October 1977. This group included alkyl epoxides and phthalates, chlorinated benzenes and paraffins, chloromethane, cresols, hexachlorobutadiene, nitrobenzene, toluene, and xylenes.

second set of eight recommendations (four categories and four individual substances) was submitted in April 1978. 124/

The third report of the ITC recommended the addition of three substances (two categories of chemicals and one individual substance) in October 1978. 125/ Twelve new substances (one category of chemicals and eleven individual substances) were added in April 1979. 126/

In October 1978, twelve months after the publication of the initial priority list, EPA decided it was not yet prepared to issue rules by the statutory deadline, so it withdrew that first group and declared that it would postpone testing rule-making until appropriate standards were developed. 127/ This action was widely criticized as both illegal and unimaginative. On 8 May 1979, the National Resources Defense Council (NRDC) instituted an eventually successful suit against EPA for failure to develop testing rules on the initial ITC recommendations. 128/

The chairman of the ITC under the Reagan Administration, Elizabeth Weinburger, announced in March 1982 that the committee would no longer examine broad categories of chemicals, but half of the first group listed were categories rather than individual substances. 129/ This group of highest priority testing candidates was as follows:

124/   43 FR 16684, 19 April 1978. This listed acylamide, aryl phospates, chlorinated naphthalenes, dichloromethane, halogenated alkyl epoxides, polychlorinated terphenyls, pyridine, and 1,1,1-trichloroethane.

125/   43 FR 50630, 30 October 1978. This group listed dichloropropane, glycidol and its derivatives, and chlorinated benzenes— tri, tetra, and penta.

126/   3 Chemical Regulation Reporter, 4 May 1979, p. 110. This list includes acetonitrile, aniline and chloro-, bromo-, and nitro-anilines; antimony; antimony sulfide; antimony trioxide; cyclohexanone; hexachlorocyclopentadiene; isophorone; mesityl oxide; 4,4-methylenedianiline; methyl ethyl ketone; and methyl isobutyl ketone.

127/   43 FR 50134, 26 October 1978.

128/   N.R.D.C. v. Costle, 14 ERC 1858 (S.D. N.Y. 1980).

129/   BNA, Chemical Reporter, 26 March 1982, p. 1323.

The Original TSCA Section 4(e) Priority List

	Entry	Date of Designation
1.	Acetonitrile	April 1979
2.	Acrylamide (environmental effects)	April 1978
3.	Alkyl epoxides	October 1979
4.	Aniline and bromo-, chloro-, and/or nitroanilines	April 1978
5.	Antimony (metal)	April 1979
6.	Antimony (sulfide)	April 1979
7.	Antimony trioxide	April 1979
8.	Aryl phosphates	April 1978
9.	Biphenyl	April 1982
10.	Bis(2-ethylhexyl) terephthalate	October 1982
11.	Chlorinated benzenes, mono- and, di- (environmental effects)	October 1977
12.	Chlorinated benzenes, tri-, tetra-, and penta-(environmental effects)	October 1978
13.	Cresols	October 1977
14.	Cyclohexanone	April 1979
15.	Dibutyltin bis(isooctyl maleate)	October 1982
16.	Dibutyltin bis(isooctyl mercaptoacetate)	October 1982
17.	Dibutyltin bis(lauryl mercaptide)	October 1982
18.	Dibutyltin dilaurate	October 1979
19.	1,2-Dichloropropane	October 1978
20.	Dimethyltin bis(isooctyl mercaptoacetate)	October 1982
21.	1,3-Dioxolane	October 1982
22.	Ethyltoluene	April 1982
23.	Formamide	April 1982
24.	Glycidol and its derivatives	October 1978
25.	Halogenated alkyl epoxides	April 1978
26.	Hexachloro- 1,3-butadiene	October 1977
27.	Hexachlorocyclopentadiene	April 1979
28.	Hydroquinone	November 1979
29.	Isophorone	April 1979
30.	Mesityl oxide	April 1979
31.	4,4'-Methylenedianiline	April 1979
32.	Methyl ethyl ketone	April 1979
33.	Methyl isobutyl ketone	April 1979
34.	Monobutyltin tris(isooctyl mercaptoacetate)	October 1982
35.	Monomethyltin tris(isooctyl mercaptoacetate)	October 1982

36.	Pyridine	April 1978
37.	Quinone	November 1979
38.	4-(1,1,3,3,-Tetramethylbutyl) phenol	October 1982
39.	Toluene	October 1977
40.	1,2,4-Trimethylbenzene	April 1982
41.	Tris(2-ethylhexyl) trimellitate	October 1982
42.	Xylenes	October 1977

This list, it should be noted, is not a permanent one. A chemical is placed on it until designated for testing or determined to be inappropriate. There has thus been a parade of substances on and off the 4(e) list. So far there have been over three score substances on and off this list.

11.0 EPA's Regulatory Role

EPA is given broad authority to take whatever regulatory measures are deemed necessary to restrict chemicals suspected of posing harm to man or the environment. The procedures are modeled basically on the pesticide act, although there are several important differences. Like FIFRA, there is a regulatory distinction between substances presenting unreasonable risks (Section 6) and those more severe cases which constitute an imminent hazard (Section 7). 130/

11.1 Section 6

TSCA borrows its definition of hazard for invoking "cancellation" directly from FIFRA: "unreasonable risk of injury to health or the environment." 131/ There is, however, one small change—the phrase is preceded by the words "presents or will present." This was added to avoid the contention that "risk" meant a certainty of harm,

---

130/ Compare FIFRA, §§ 6(b) and 6(c) with TSCA, §§ 6 and 7. Note that while TSCA does not use the terms "cancellation" or "suspension," since there is no registration to cancel or suspend as under FIFRA, these are nevertheless convenient terms to use for the process in Section 6 and 7.

131/ TSCA, § 6(a).

as had been proposed by an appellate court panel (later reversed) in a case under Section 211 of the Clean Air Act. 132/

Section 6 authority is not restricted to removing a chemical from the market. It may also include limiting the amount that can be produced, prohibiting or limiting specific uses considered most hazardous, requiring labels and warnings, mandating extensive manufacturing and monitoring records, controlling disposal, "or otherwise regulating any manner or method of commercial use of such substance or mixture." Restrictions may even be applied in some geographical areas and not in others. Quality controls in manufacturing or processing may be required if there is a potential problem of highly toxic impurities, such as TCDD in the herbicide 2,4,5-T. The manufacturer or processor may be required to replace or repurchase products held to constitute a hazard. 133/

The regulations for implementing Section 6 rulemakings were issued in final in December 1977. 134/ These emphasized flexible procedures, rather than strict adherence to the Administrative Procedure Act, although a limited right of cross examination is provided. Subpoena authority is also available, although to be used sparingly.

EPA's recent enforcement record has been much criticized, due to a dramatic drop in referrals to the Justice Department. PCB fines, however, have been considerable for failing to inspect, label, or maintain leaking equipment.

11.2 PCB Regulation under Section 6(e) and CFC

One of the most controversial chemicals EPA has had to deal with is polychlorinated biphenyls (PCBs). Congress sought to insure that EPA would confront the problem by specifically mandating action and a regulatory timetable in Section 6(e). This unusual step prodded EPA into banning some uses of PCBs in 1977 and most pro-

---

132/ Ethyl Corp. v. EPA, 7 ERC 1353 (CADC 1975): reversed en banc by 541 F. 2d 1, 8 ERC 1785 (CADC 1976); cert. denied 426 U.S. 941, 8 ERC 220 (1976). Section 112 of the Clean Air Act authorizes regulation of potentially harmful fuel additives, especially lead.

133/ TSCA, § 6(a) and (b).

134/ 40 CFR Part 750, 2 December 1977.

duction and use in April 1979. 135/ EPA estimates that the new more stringent standard will bring nearly a million additional pounds of PCBs under control. 136/ PCB regulation and enforcement has become so important under TSCA that the next main heading in this Chapter, 12.0, is devoted exclusively to it.

Another widely publicized chemical group is the chlorofluorocarbons. On 17 March 1978, EPA promulgated final regulations prohibiting almost all of the manufacturing, processing, and distribution of chlorofluorocarbons for those aerosol propellent uses subject to TSCA. 137/ These regulations became effective 15 October 1978.

11.3 Imminent Hazards: Section 7

Although "imminent hazard" determinations have been invoked repeatedly under FIFRA (i.e., suspension), the equivalent provision under TSCA, Section 7, has not once been used. It has rarely even been seriously considered as a regulatory option.

The standard for "suspension" actions under Section 7 of TSCA is, as with pesticides, an "imminent hazard." This is defined more stringently than in FIFRA, however, as "a chemical substance or mixture which presents an imminent and unreasonable risk of serious or widespread injury to health or the environment." 138/

EPA may also take action during premarket notification where there is insufficient information to evaluate health or environmental effects. EPA must go to court in order to halt the manufacture or prohibit a specific use of a substance, if the manufacturer objects to the proposed EPA ban, or where there is adequate evidence that the substance presents an unreasonable risk. 139/

135/   3 Chemical Regulation Reporter, 20 April 1979, p.49. See also Preamble to EPA Final Rules for PCBs Manuf., 17 April 1979.

136/   BNA, Chemical Regulation Reporter, 6 April 1979, p. 3.

137/   43 FR 55241, 27 November 1978.

138/   TSCA, § 7(f).

139/   TSCA, § 5(f).

Unlike FIFRA, enforcement orders under TSCA cannot be issued solely on the Agency's own authority, challengeable only before the court of appeals. Instead, if a proposed restrictive rule is contested, EPA must seek an injunction from a federal district court, which will itself determine whether there is sufficient basis for legal action. EPA may also initiate a civil suit in district court to seize an imminently hazardous chemical. 140/ Judicial review of final EPA orders is limited to the circuit of courts of appeals, which must determine whether the Agency action is supported by substantial evidence on the record as a whole. 141/

The rulemaking procedures assure manufacturers of a full range of due process safeguards, including reasonable hearing procedures, the right of cross-examination during rulemaking, and the right of appeal. EPA's authority to propose an immediately effective rule to ban or limit manufacture of an existing chemical is limited by the requirement that it first obtain a court injunction based on the same legal criteria as applied in cases of imminent hazard. Therefore, a substantial degree of proof is required, procedural safeguards afforded, and assurance provided that EPA cannot act without good cause.

While the Agency has used its Section 6 authority sparingly apart from the specific instance of Section 6(e) PCB regulation, it has not used Section 7 at all yet.

12.0 PCB Regulation

The regulation of polychlorinated biphenyls (PCBs) is an anomaly. Nowhere else in the environmental laws is a substance banned by name, although there have been occasional requirements that EPA examine specific substances—such as asbestos, mercury, beryllium and cadmium under Clean Air Act Section 112—for possible eventual regulation. Because of perennial dissatisfaction with various Agency actions, Congress has discussed utilizing this device further, either to restrict additional chemicals or, especially with FDA on saccharin, to prevent regulators from restricting a chemical. Thus, the PCB issue is interesting not only because of the broad public attention it has received but also as a possible regulatory precedent for future actions.

140/   TSCA, § 7(a), (b); see also § 6(c),(d).

141/   TSCA, § 19.

PCBs have been used as transformer fluids and dielectics, but their darker side was not revealed until a tragic episode in Japan in 1969. Cooking oil somehow became contaminated with PCB leaking from a transformer. Whether from the PCBs themselves or from furans and other contaminants, this resulted in deaths, central nervous system damage, serious stomach and liver disorders, and possibly cancer. Immediate steps were taken in Japan to prevent this problem from recurring. No action was taken in the United States, however, until several more years and several serious incidents later.

PCBs are ubiquitous in the environment. They are stable even at high temperatures, and may not break down into non-toxic compounds for many years. PCBs sealed in a transformer may last 15, 20, or perhaps 25 years before needing replacement because of eventual leaks.

Following a number of episodes in Michigan and elsewhere (actually due largely to the unrelated polybrominated biphenyls) Congressman John Dingell (D-Mich.) and other representatives inserted Section 6(e) into the final version of TSCA. It provided for a schedule which would first stop PCB manufacture and then gradually curtail its use. EPA, as usual, missed most of the deadlines but did finally issue a series of regulations implementing the statute.

Section 6(e) directed EPA to phase-out PCB manufacture and use according to a statutorily-mandated timetable. After one year from the passage of the Act (that is, by October 1977) no one was allowed to manufacture, process, distribute, or use any PCB except in "a totally enclosed manner." 142/ Unless the Administrator finds no unreasonable risk, 143/ no one may manufacture PCBs at all after two years, nor distribute it after 2 1/2 years. 144/ If needed, the Administrator may utilize any other provision of TSCA or of any other federal law to regulate PCBs. 145/

At the time of enactment, these provisions seemed to pose no problem. There was only one remaining PCB manufacturer in the

---

142/ Defined in TSCA, § 6(e)(2)(C).

143/ See TSCA, § 6(e)(3)(B).

144/ TSCA, § 6(e)(3).

145/ TSCA, § 6(e)(5).

United States and it intended to abandon the business. Utilities and other owners of PCB-filled electric transformers and capacitors were permitted to maintain their equipment for its working life, provided it did not leak or require major servicing. Congressmen could therefore vote for tough regulation of unpopular PCBs a month before national elections, without any appreciable political risk.

EPA's initial regulations addressed four categories: PCB transformers (those having over 500 parts per million of PCB in the transformer fluid); PCB-contaminated transformers (having between 50 and 500 parts per million); and a category not specifically defined except by exclusion, which would be non-PCB transformers, defined as those less than 50 parts per million. The fourth category, not discussed here, was railroad transformers.

Such transformers were required to be appropriately labeled, standards were set for transport of PCB, and disposal of techniques were outlined including incineration.

The statute exempted transformers and other uses that were "totally enclosed." If a transformer were not "totally enclosed," it must be banned. But how would EPA know; and did a tiny, well-contained leak of a thimblefull a year constitute a non-enclosed use requiring tens of thousands of dollars for equipment replacement? First of all, there is a problem called "sweating"--a fancy word EPA likes for small leaks, and in March 1980 it requested comments on the extent "weeping" or "sweating" was a problem for PCB transformers. The answers the Agency received were quite varied, ranging from estimates of 80-90 percent sweating to a fraction of that. EPA decided not to issue regulations, hoping the issue would just fade away.

An environmental group, the Environmental Defense Fund (EDF), brought suit against EPA's 1978 and 1979 implementing regulations 146/ and persuaded the court of appeals to strike them down as "unsupported by the record." 147/ Because of the broad nature of the suit, this meant that EDF won not only on the issue that

---

146/   43 FR 7150, 17 February 1978; 44 FR 31542, 31 May 1979.

147/   Environmental Defense Fund v. EPA, 636 F. 2d 1267, 15 ERC 1081 (CADC, 1980).

prompted the suit, namely a desire for stringent inspection and maintenance of electrical equipment, but on most other issues as well. This included the 50 ppm cut off level for regulation, which was admittedly arbitrary but reflected the consensus of authorities. And that led to problem number two.

Many chemical processes involving aromatics and chlorine were found to produce small but measureable traces of PCBs as unintended by products. This could affect up to a quarter of all American chemical operations, most of whom did not (and probably still do not) realize they were vulnerable to EPA enforcement or citizens' suits for "manufacturing" PCBs in violation of the law.

After a series of chemical and electrical industry surveys, EPA proposals, 148/ and public hearings, EPA decided to issue three sets of regulations. 149/ Rule One, published in August 1982, 150/ applied to electric transformers and capacitors. It prohibited PCB-filled equipment near food and feed after October 1985 (the proposed rule allowed indefinite use, subject to weekly self-inspections), authorized most other electrical equipment for the remainder of its useful life, subject to (for large transformers) a quarterly self-inspection, allowed storage for disposal of non-leaking equipment outside of qualified storage facilities, and provided for retaining three years of maintenance records.

Rule Two, issued in October 1982, 151/ exempted byproduct manufacture which took place entirely within closed systems or separated as designated waste for disposal by EPA-approved

---

148/ See 47 FR 24976, 8 June 1982.

149/ Ironically, despite the Reagan Administration's expressed preference for agreements instead of edicts, the Agency rebuffed a negotiated settlement proposed in late 1982 by an unusual coalition of chemical industry and environmentalist groups. The final regulation two years later was insubstantially different.

150/ 47 FR 37342, 25 August 1982.

151/ 47 FR 46980, 21 October 1982.

methods.   Although originally requested by the companies, the lengthy final version was opposed because it promised an "exemption" for which few if any companies could honestly qualify. None did.

Rule Three, applying generally to the incidental by-product problem in the chemical industry, is currently in preparation.

A related question involved in protracted litigation is whether monochlorinated biphenyls are polychlorinated biphenyls. Despite linguistic and persistence arguments, EPA decided they were and brought a major enforcement action against a leading chemical company. The company's challenge to the regulations was dismissed for lack of jurisdiction, 152/ then pursued through a protracted series of hearings and appeals within EPA. The Agency judicial officer, Ron McCallum, ruled in July 1982 that the company had indeed violated the PCB rules and that the courts of appeals, not an enforcement proceeding, was the proper forum for a challenge to the definition of PCB. 153/

Meanwhile, the debate continues. The definition of "totally enclosed" had to be modified, with comments obtained in September 1984. For "inadvertent generation" of PCB by-products, EPA prepared new rules in 1984 which showed an annual average of 25 ppm and a maximum concentration of 50 ppm. PCBs vented into the outside air cannot exceed 10 ppm. 154/

The transformer rule issued in 1982 exempted approximately 140,000 potentially dioxin-containing electrical transformers. But the concern has grown that this did not do enough to prevent transformer fires in heavily populated areas that could emit large quantities of dangerous fumes. Therefore, EPA prepared proposed regulations in 1984 to isolate transformers from ventilation ducts and require the removal of combustibles stored near transformers. 155/

152/   Dow Chemical Co. v. Costle, 484 F.Supp. 101 (D.C. Del., 1980).

153/   BNA, Chemical Reporter, 20 August 1982, p. 645; see also 30 July 1982, p. 558.

154/   Ibid., 7 September 1984, p. 590; Washington Post, 2 July 1984.

155/   Washington Post, 2 April 1984, 17 October 1984.

The once-simple PCB issue remains a troublesome one, because of this lawsuit and its consequences, because the Agency was long unwilling to make decisions on incineration and on other disposal techniques, and because the problem is technically and legally more complex than anyone imagined. Meanwhile, Congress has grown impatient with the delays. As it pointed out rather bitterly to EPA on the eve of the current litigation, even four years after decisive action was ordered, 99 percent of the PCBs in the United States are still in existence.

13.0 Confidentiality

Since a principal function of TSCA is the collection of voluminous information on chemical substances, concern for the protection of genuine trade secrets continues to be a hotly debated topic.

Section 14 provides that EPA may not release any information which is not exempt from mandatory disclosure under the Freedom of Information Act (FOIA). 156/ This excludes "trade secrets and commercial or financial information obtained from a person and privileged or confidential." 157/ TSCA does not prohibit the disclosure of health and safety studies nor, of course, the release of information to federal officials in the performance of their duties. Data may also be disclosed to protect "against an unreasonable risk of injury to health or the environment" in a legal proceeding. There is interestingly no allowance for release of information to state health authorities, despite the lessons of the Kepone tragedy, although perhaps they could qualify by being made "contractors with the United States." 158/

EPA's general regulations for dealing with FOIA requests under its various statutes were issued in September 1976. 159/ Although they tend strongly to favor disclosure, EPA had relatively few business secrets in its files, so industry has had few objections

---

156/   TSCA, § 14(a).

157/   Administrative Procedure Act § 2, 5 U.S.C. § 552(b)(4).

158/   TSCA § 14(b) and (a); see also 40 CFR § 2.301(h), 43 FR 2637, 18 January 1978.

159/   41 FR 36902, 1 September 1976.

so far to these procedures. The exception is pesticides regulation, which for several years has been entangled by litigation over release of data. 160/

Some chemical industry representatives have complained that existing laws are not sufficiently protective of confidential business information. The president of the Manufacturing Chemists Association, for example, has expressed concern that as long as the trade secret exemption under the FOIA remains permissive, "there is no assurance that privately developed information submitted to the government in confidence will not be disclosed." 161/

EPA modified some portions of the original March 1977 inventory reporting proposal 162/ to assuage certain industry fears, such as by deleting the requirement that a toxicological bibliography be submitted. 163/ The Agency has also established a task force to establish computer security precautions to protect information submitted or stored on magnetic tape. 164/

Polaroid Corporation challenged the adequacy of protection provided for chemical trade secrets which the company was required to furnish EPA under the reporting regulations. In June 1978, a U.S. district judge denied the request that Polaroid be excused from reporting the information, but also issued an injunction ordering EPA not to disclose the information outside the Agency. 165/

160/   Mobay Chemical Corp v. Train, F. Supp., 8 ERC 1227 (D.C. W. Mich. 1975); dismissed per curiam U.S., 8 January 1979.

161/   Letter from former MCA President William J. Driver to Sen. James Abzourek (D-S.D.), Chairman of the Administrative Practice and Procedure Subcommittee of the Senate Judiciary Committee, 18 January 1978, quoted in BNA Environment Reporter, 1978, p. 1468.

162/   42 FR 13130, 9 March 1977.

163/   42 FR 39182, 39188, 2 August 1977, reproposing 40 CFR 710.7(e).

164/   See, e.g., 42 FR 53804, 53805, 3 October 1977; 43 FR 1836, 12 January 1978.

165/   Polaroid Corp. v. Costle, No. 78-11335 (D.C. Mass. 1978).

Then on 8 September 1978, EPA issued amendments to its confidential business information regulations 166/ providing substantial protection for TSCA confidential information and providing for notice to affected businesses before confidential information is disclosed outside EPA. 167/ Polaroid withdrew its suit and the Court order was vacated. The problem of confidentiality nevertheless will continue to be a sensitive issue for the foreseeable future.

EPA has consistently insisted that requests for confidentality be accompanied by an explanation to why it is needed. Merely calling something a trade secret does not make it so. Although the first policy issued by the Reagan Administration on Section 5 provided that under PMN a manufacturer could withhold data as confidential without providing a rationale, 168/ Congress is monitoring this area very closely and has threatened to pass legislation restricting the scope of confidentiality if companies abuse the privilege. 169/

14.0 Citizen Enforcement and Legal Fees

Private citizens are allowed, even encouraged, to participate in TSCA administrative and judicial proceedings. 170/ Section 21 provides that any person may petition the Administrator to take

---

166/   40 CFR Part 2, 43 FR 3997, 8 September 1978.

167/   This provision for notification to the company was already set forth in Section 14(c) of the statute.

168/   BNA, Chemical Reporter, 7 February 1982, p. 443.

169/   See, e.g., reports in ibid., 3 August 1984, p. 483. The head of EPA's toxics office, John Moore, requested that companies claim less data as confidential, to ease the evaluation by his staff. Ibid., 6 April 1984, p. 3.

170/   The citizen participation sections were missing in whole or part from earlier versions of TSCA. For example, H.R. 5356 of 1973 had neither section, while the Senate bill (S.426) had a citizens suit provision (§ 19) but only an oblique reference to citizen petitions (§ 24a). See House Report 93-360 (1973) and Senate Report 93-254 (1973).

action on rules under Sections 4-8, excepting imminent hazard determinations under Section 7; the Administrator then has 90 days either to grant or deny the petition. If he denies the petition, a citizen may initiate civil action in a federal district court. 171/

The section has been used by the Service Employees International Union requesting asbestos standards for schools (granted), a company wishing to leave PCB-contaminated soil in a mine shaft (denied), and an association wishing to delete the inventory designation of inorganic glass as mixtures (denied). 172/ Despite its name, it has been little used by ordinary citizens.

Citizens may also file suit under Section 20 to compel the Administrator to perform any non-discretionary duty, or against anyone including the government alleged to be in violation of any rules issued under Sections 4-6. The plaintiff, however, must give EPA the traditional 60 days notice before he may commence his litigation. 173/

The exclusion of Section 7 from both the citizens petition and citizens suit sections of TSCA is particularly striking, considering that under FIFRA the imminent hazard area has been a prime focus of activity by environmental groups.

Attorney and witness fees may be awarded by the courts to persons litigating under TSCA. There is no requirement that the person's legal position has prevailed, or that such an award be limited to so-called public interest groups, although that is surely its main concern. The statutory test is simply that costs and reasonable fees may be granted "if the court determines that such an award is appropriate." 174/

15.0 Relationship of TSCA to Other Federal Laws

TSCA was enacted to fill gaps left by other laws, but Congress was also concerned that it not lead to jurisdictional conflicts

---

171/   TSCA, § 21.

172/   EPA Office of Toxic Substances, Bulletin, March 1984; ibid., May 1984; 49 FR 36844, 20 September 1984.

173/   TSCA, § 20.

174/   TSCA, § 19(d).

with other agenices or even between different divisions of EPA. There was no wish to see a repetition of the bitter OSHA-EPA dispute of 1973 over pesticide re-entry standards. 175/ Consequently, Section 9 sets forth in some detail the coordination procedures to be followed when two health regulatory laws overlap.

If the EPA Administrator determines that another law not administered by EPA would be more appropriate for regulating a given hazard, he must submit a description of the situation to that agency for action. The receiving agency must then take whatever regulatory measures it deems necessary, or reply in the Federal Register with a "detailed statement" why no action is warranted. There the matter rests, whether EPA is in accord with the decision or not. (A citizen suit against the second agency is nevertheless possible.) EPA cannot thereafter bring an enforcement action of its own under Sections 6 or 7 concerning that hazard. 176/

For other laws administered under EPA, the Administrator is given the flexibility to apply them where they would be most useful or to rely on the provisions of TSCA. He is not relieved of the procedural or substantive requirements in those other laws, however, if he chooses to rely on them. 177/

Finally, Congress added a special provision concerning OSHA, stating the Environmental Protection Agency's exercise of authority under TSCA did not constitute a preemption of OSHA jurisdiction under OSH Act Section 4. 178/

175/   Under pressure of lawsuit by a migrant farmworkers' group, OSHA sought in spring 1973 to assert jurisdiction over conditions of fieldworker exposure to pesticides. This account is related in the chapter on Pesticides, Section 9.5.

176/   TSCA, § 9(a). EPA could try to circumvent this bar by first initiating an enforcement action and then sending the notification to the other agency, although this Section 9(a)(3) "loophole" is rather narrow for such a statutory departure.

177/   TSCA, § 9(b). At least theoretically, the application of the doctrine to all laws "administered in whole or in part by the Administration" also includes the Food, Drug, and Cosmetic Act. See the chapter on Pesticides, Section 9.1.

178/   TSCA, § 9(c); OSH Act, § 4(b)(1).

In the past several years, congressional frustration with OSHA has exceeded even that with EPA. This has led to proposals that TSCA be used to regulate some occupational exposure to hazardous substances. Despite the clear intrusion in OSHA's jurisdiction, this now has been endorsed by the Senate Environment and Public Works Committee. According to the bipartisan leadership, Sen. Robert Stafford (R.-Vt.) and Jennings Randolph (D.-W.Va.), the fact that Section 5 is directed at pre-manufacture notification, rather than just pre-market, shows that workers too were to be protected. Section 9 is interpreted as merely for coordination. 179/ This view is exceedingly imaginative but of questionable public policy. If Congress wants OSHA to perform its functions better or differently, it should address that problem, rather than expect another agency with probably similar appointments and philosophy to do the job.

15.1 Existing Toxic Substances Laws

The term "toxic substance" has become so identified with this new Act that one often forgets there is considerable legislation dealing with chemical substances already on the books. In one sense, almost all of the recent environmental laws have in fact been directed at toxic substances.

One generally excludes from the term "toxic substance" the six original air pollutants regulated by EPA under Sections 108-110 of the Clear Air Act; carbon monoxide, hydrocarbons, photochemical oxidant, sulfur dioxide, nitrogen oxides, and particulate matter. In sufficient concentrations most of these substances can be immediately deadly and all have serious long-term effects on health. They tend, however, to be the ubiquitous products of combustion, the waste products of an industrial society, and their control necessitates a general national policy that cuts across many diverse industries. Similarly, a number of the substances controlled under the water pollution laws are usually excluded from the definition, including suspended soil particles and decaying organic products which adversely affect the biological oxygen demand (BOD) of the water.

179/   BNA, Chemical Reporter, 1 June 1984, p. 276.

15.2 Clean Air Act

Section 112 of the Clean Air Act, entitled "National Emission Standards for Hazardous Air Pollutants," is specifically directed toward toxic substances. Although this provision has so far been used only for asbestos, mercury, beryllium, and vinyl chloride, it could develop into one of the most important parts of the Act. Arsenic and benzene are currently under consideration for regulation under this section. One reason for its infrequent use is its deliberate omission of economic or technical feasibility in standard setting; the only relevant factor for the Administrator is "the level which in his judgment provides an ample margin of safety to protect the public health from such hazardous air pollutants." 180/   EPA tacitly ignored this unusual provision in the vinyl chloride deliberations 181/ and this, if deemed successful, could lead to greater use of this section in the future. 182/

Congress has been irritated that Section 112 has been so little used over the past decade and a half. For the last couple of years, therefore, legislation has been debated which would mandate the addition of over three dozen substances to the regulatory list.

15.3 Water Pollution Act

Another key law is Section 307 of the Water Pollution Act entitled "Toxic and Pre-treatment Effluent Standards." 183/   This provides specifically for the listing and setting of standards with an "ample margin of safety" for hazardous chemicals discharged into the nation's waterways. In September 1973, EPA listed nine chem-

---

180/   Clear Air Act, § 112(b)(1)(B).

181/   EPA, "Proposed Standard for Vinyl Chloride," 16 December 1975.

182/   The original Clean Air bill considered by Congress had two toxic substances sections—the present one for extreme hazards and a milder version allowing economic considerations for the less serious toxic pollutants. The House–Senate Conference Committee in 1970 dropped the latter section from the final bill without giving any reason.

183/   Federal Water Pollution Control Act, § 307, 33 U.S.C. § 1317.

icals, mostly pesticides, on this list, including DDT, Aldrin-Dieldrin, PCBs, Toxaphene, and cadmium and mercury compounds. 184/ Effluent standards for these substances do not apply to all industries but only to about two dozen broad categories such as non-ferrous metal smelters, textile manufacturers, and agricultural fertilizer manufacturing. 185/ By the consent decree between EPA and the Natural Resources Defense Council in June 1976, a total of sixty-five substances comprising several hundred individual chemicals was added to the Section 307 list. 186/ This decree was subsequently written into the 1977 Amendments to the Clean Water Act. 187/

Under Section 311 entitled "Oil and Hazardous Substance Liability," EPA is to regulate "spills" of hazardous substances into the nation's waterways and coastal zones. The Administrator is required to list those elements and compounds which should be designated "hazardous substances." Within 180 days of this designation he is to establish a unit of measurement and a monetary penalty for the discharge of a unit into the water. EPA finally proposed such a list in December 1975. It announced that although the Act authorizes the imposition of fines up to five million dollars, the Agency would voluntarily limit penalties to $5000 unless gross negligence by the polluter is demonstrated. 188/

184/   38 FR 24342, 7 September 1975. The rules of practice under § 307 were amended by 41 FR 1765, 12 January 1976.

185/   For more detailed information, see Chapter 7 on Water Pollution Control.

186/   N.R.D.C. v. Train, 8 ERC 2120 (D.D.C. 1976); see also N.R.D.C. v. Train, 510 F.2d 692 (D.C. Cir. 1974).

187/   PL 95-217. There has been some dispute about the degree to which Congress incorporated the consent decree into the amendments. Rep. Ray Roberts (D-Tex.) insisted that it didn't, or at least modified it considerably; Sen. Edmund Muskie (D-Me.) said that it did. The latter view is preferred.

188/   EPA, Notice of Proposed Rulemaking, Designation of Hazardous Substances, 40 FR 59960-60017 (30 December 1975). 40 CFR Parts 116-19.

The Administrator also has emergency authority under Section 504 of the Water Act to seek to enjoin any person from discharging any pollutants which are "presenting an imminent and substantial endangerment to health or welfare." 189/ This section has rarely been invoked by EPA, despite numerous situations for which it would be appropriate.

15.4 Occupational Safety and Health Administration

The Occupational Safety and Health Act, although not usually regarded as a toxic substance act, is potentially the most important statute in the field. 190/ Although limited to occupational situations, the Act covers over 80 million workers, many of whom have much greater exposure to highly toxic chemicals than they are ever likely to encounter in the general environment. Section 6 of the Act 191/ requires OSHA to set strict health standards at a level "which most adequately assures, to the extent feasible, on the basis of the best available evidence, that no employee will suffer material impairment of health or functional capacity even if such employee has regular exposure to the hazard dealt with by such standard for the period of his working life. 192/ This Act, if fully implemented, could have a tremendous effect.

In the decade and a half since the passage of this Act, however, OSHA has put out only seven final health standards—asbestos, vinyl chloride, coke oven, arsenic, benzene, lead, and a group of carcinogens. In late 1975, after a change in OSHA's top management, standards were proposed for a dozen other substances, including ammonia, beryllium, and trichloroethylene, but these still are pending. In addition, OSHA has a list of approximately 400 substances with threshold limits adopted from the recommended lists of private industrial hygiene organizations. 193/

189/   Federal Water Pollution Control Act § 504, 33 U.S.C. § 1364.

190/   29 U.S.C. § 651 et seq., PL 91-596, 84 Stat. 1590.

191/   OSH Act § 6, 29 U.S.C. § 655.

192/   OSH Act, § 6(b)(5).

193/   These have been reviewed as part of the Standards Completion Process to convert the bare threshold numbers into a full standard with monitoring, medical, and other requirements.

15.5 Consumer Product Safety Commission

The Consumer Product Safety Act and related statutes such as the Hazardous Substances Act administered by the Consumer Product Safety Commission (CPSC) also confer jurisdiction over certain forms of toxic substances. One should note, however, that "hazardous substances" as used in this act includes devices and equipment, and thus is much broader than the term toxic substances. Furthermore, the CPSC may address only human safety questions derived from the use of consumer products, and thus it has no authority over environmental problems.

In the past, the CPSC has exhibited little activity in the chemical area, except for limited involvement in cases concerning two spray can propellants, vinyl chloride and freon, and a fumbled effort on asbestos hair dryers. It issued a detailed cancer policy document modeled closely on that proposed by OSHA but was forced to withdraw it in April 1979 because of procedural deficiencies.

Because of budget and staff cuts, this disfavored agency is unlikely to be a more important factor in the next few years.

16.0 The Proposed Federal Cancer Policy

The proposed Federal Cancer Policy, initiated by OSHA in October 1977, considered by all four health regulatory agencies— OSHA, EPA, FDA, and CPSC—and currently on hold by the Reagan Administration—could potentially have more effect on toxic chemical control than the better-known Toxic Substances Control Act. This cancer policy, if effectively applied, could directly impact hundreds or thousands of chemical substances throughout American industry. It is currently undergoing "revision," after the OSHA administrator who suspended it decided such a policy could be useful after all. But he has since left the government and the present staff has neither the will nor the ability, at present, to repropose a more coherent policy. Some modification will be needed, in any case, to ensure that the policy is in accord with the Supreme Court's subsequent decision in the Benzene case. 194/

194/   Industrial Union v. American Petroleum Institute v. Donovan, 100 S. Ct. 2478 (1981).

16.1 Goals of the Federal Cancer Policy

The three goals hoped to be reached through OSHA's Federal Cancer Policy are (1) to avoid repetitious scientific debate at OSHA hearings and ad hoc decisions on health standards involving carcinogens, (2) to streamline OSHA's ponderous standard setting process by "prefabricating" the essential elements of several alternative versions, and (3) ultimately to harmonize the policies of the four health regulatory agencies. The regulatory requirements, derived from the cancer principles, spell out monitoring and medical tests in rigorous detail and set a goal of reducing levels of "confirmed" carcinogens to near zero.

16.2 Background of the Policy

Efforts to develop a cancer policy at both OSHA and EPA date from the Aldrin-Dieldrin pesticide suspension decision at EPA in October 1974. This set forth tentative principles of carcinogenicity which the Agency could apply to future regulatory cases. 195/ EPA subsequently established a task force to analyze this fledgling policy and recommended a final version. The focus shifted to OSHA in 1975 with the transfer of several former EPA officials to that agency. In January 1976, a lengthy OSHA draft proposal was widely circulated, but the change of administrations forestalled its issuance. Finally, the proposal, different in only a few details from the version prepared nine months earlier, was signed by the head of OSHA on 28 September 1977 and subsequently appeared in the Federal Register on 4 October 1977, entitled "Identification, Classification and Regulation of Toxic Substances Posing a Potential Occupational Carcinogenic Risk." 196/ The policy in final form was issued in January 1980. 197/

16.3 Scientific Principles of the Cancer Policy

The policy takes a hardline regulatory approach to carcinogens, namely that exposure should be reduced to zero, or as close to zero as feasible. If safer alternative chemicals are available, they should be substituted.

195/   In Re Shell, 6 ERC 2047 (1974).

196/   42 FR 54148, 4 October 1977.

197/   45 FR 5002, 22 January 1980.

The leading scientific policy conclusions in the proposal are as follows:

(1)   A carcinogen is defined as a substance or condition which increases the incidence of generally irreversible benign or malignant tumors, reduces the latency period, or produces unusual tumors in animals or man.

(2)   The results of cancer tests on animals, particularly rodents and other animals, are relevant to human exposure. ("Any substance which is shown to cause tumors in animals should be considered carcinogenic and, therefore, a potential cancer hazard for man.")

(3)   A threshold or "no effect" level may theoretically exist for carcinogens but this has not been conclusively demonstrated; and, even so, it would have to be determined separately for each substance. Therefore, the only safe level is zero.

(4)   Most carcinogens are neither species-specific nor organ-specific.

(5)   A substance may be termed a confirmed carcinogen after replicated tests in only one species. ("If carcinogens are not species-specific, it logically follows that the demonstration of carcinogenic effect in more than one species is not absolutely necessary for finding of carcinogenicity.") Note that EPA has recently commented that under some circumstances even replication should be waived as unnecessary.

(6)   In evaluating test data, no distinction will be made between benign and malignant tumors. ("The Agency proposes to place as much weight on an experiment in which only benign tumors are observed, as upon experiments in which both malignant and benign tumors are induced.")

(7)   Positive test results, (i.e., indicators that a substance is carcinogenic) outweigh negative findings.

(8)   Chemical structural similarity of a suspect chemical to a known carcinogen may be a guide for testing priority but is itself insufficient to classify the former as a carcinogen.

(9)   Induced tumors appearing in animals at the point of application, or due to physical rather than chemical effect, may be disregarded.

(10)   The administration of high doses is a methodological device necessary for finding gross effects in small test samples. "Consequently, a substance that will induce cancer in experimental animals at any dose level, no matter how high or low, should be treated with great caution."

(11)   The Ames test or other in vitro experiments using non-mammalian species are not an appropriate basis for regulatory action, but positive results plus carcinogenicity in one mammalian species may be.

(12)   Human epidemiological studies are generally an insensitive indicator of carcinogenicity, unless the study is exhaustively controlled or the particular cancer is quite unusual (e.g., angiosarcoma from vinyl chloride).

16.4 Implementation Regulations of the Cancer Policy

The implementation regulations and model standards (Part II) are an attempt to convert the scientific principles discussed above into full OSHA standards through a modular format. There are five such formats:

(1)   Category I—Emergency Temporary Standard for Confirmed Carcinogen

   • Lowest levels feasible within the six-month period of the ETS.

   • Most of the medical surveillance, waste disposal, recordkeeping, and other precautions that are required under a permanent standard, allowing for the short compliance period.

(2)   Category I—Permanent Standard for Confirmed Carcinogen

   • Level set at zero exposure or as low as feasible.

   • Feasibility is not really defined in the entire document, nor is it clear whether it is limited to technological feasibility, as OSHA insists, or can also include economic risk-benefit calculations.

   • A full battery of monitoring, medical and protective equipment requirements designed to safeguard employees from exposure to carcinogens in the workplace.

- This category can be triggered by a finding of carcinogenicity in tests with two animal species, one species if replicated, one species unreplicated if accompanied by a positive in vitro test, or other evidence determined sufficient by the Secretary of Labor.

- These regulations are unusually specific, dealing in detail with everything from the laundering of work clothes to the application of cosmetics by employees in the workplace.

(3)   Category II--Suspected Carcinogens

- This category can be applied to all the toxics substances for which the data is "suggestive" of carcinogenicity but for which the tests for Category I are either not met or partially rebutted.

- The standard level will be set sufficient to prevent acute or chronic non-carcinogenic effects.

- Most of the medical, monitoring, and other requirements applicable to Category I are required.

(4)   Category III--Acquitted Chemicals
       (or "Guilt Unproved")

- This class encompasses substances which have either been cleared of suspicion of carcinogenicity, or which still deserve some additional research.

(5)   Category IV--Foreign Toxic Substances

- This provision was merely an attempt to close the loophole by which a toxic substance for which no federal standard exists could be imported to the U.S. from abroad.

- As in Category III, no special regulations other than publication are provided for this group.

- This section was determined to be superfluous in the final versions.

In July 1980, as the final step in the implementation of the policy, OSHA brought out a long, tentative list of cancer candidates for regulation. 198/ In its final version, the candidate list of the substances numbered 204; half were borrowed from an EPA compilation by its Carcinogen Assessment Group (CAG), while the remaining half were submitted by an outside consulting firm on contract to OSHA. 199/   The plan was to select up to twenty for the development of full health standards, ten for Category I and ten for Category II.

The Reagan Administration, under considerable business pressure, put a hold on the cancer policy within days of its coming to office. In December 1981, OSHA announced that it was subjecting the entire issue to extensive review, 200/ and in July 1983 the Agency published a notice suspending the candidate project pending further review by OSHA and, though not mentioned, the development of a government-wide policy 201/ currently under consideration by a committee headed by White House Science Advisor, George Keyworth. The principal reason for this stay was concern that the process could constitute a blacklist of chemicals and cause undo alarm.

17.0 Conclusion

The Toxic Substances Control Act has gotten off to a slow start, due in part to the delay in filling top EPA positions. 202/ The ponderous pace did not accelerate thereafter, however, so the Act

---

198/   OSHA Press Release, 14 July 1978.

199/   45 FR 53672, 12 August 1980.

200/   OSHA Press Release, 31 December 1981; 47 FR 187, 5 January 1982.

201/   48 FR 241, 4 January 1983. See also Administrative Conference of U.S., Recommendation 82-5, "Federal Regulation of Cancer-Causing Chemicals", 18 June 1982.

202/   See, for example, the story entitled, "Search for Toxic Chemicals in Environment Gets A Slow Start, Is Proving Difficult and Expensive," Wall Street Journal, 9 May 1978, p. 48. Similar criticism, almost a year later, arose from Congressional oversight hearings before the House Subcommittee on Consumer Protection on 8 March 1979.

may require an entire decade to implement fully. We should recognize the considerable administrative burden this cumbersome statute
places on EPA; the Agency needs not only technical expertise but
also extensive managerial and legal resources.

For the immediate future TSCA will be essentially an information-gathering act, although the Administrator has promised soon
to initiate legal proceedings under Section 6 against a number of
particularly hazardous substances. The concurrent slowdowns at
OSHA, FDA, and the CPSC have created a back pressure which
could create an impetus for change in the next few years. Even if
this occurs, however, past experience is not comforting that the new
Administration will be any more proficient than its predecessors.

Nevertheless, in the long run, the importance of TSCA is
likely to expand gradually, much as the requirements of FIFRA and
the FDA Act increased substantially long after their enactment.

Chapter 5

SAFE DRINKING WATER ACT

Jeffrey G. Miller 1/
Attorney
Bergson, Borkland, Margolis & Adler
Washington, D.C.

1.0 Safe Drinking Water Act Status

The Safe Drinking Water Act (SDWA) 2/ was enacted in 1974 to assure safe drinking water supplies, protect especially valuable aquifers, and protect drinking water from contamination by the underground injection of waste. Few programs of the Environmental Protection Agency (EPA) have been less aggressively implemented. The result may be ultimate dissatisfaction with and distrust of regulatory protection and an arbitrary pro-regulatory backlash. Such a backlash is already developing toward the underground injection control program.

2.0 Public Water Supplies

2.1 Drinking Water Standards

The Safe Water Drinking Act requires the Environmental Protection Agency to promulgate a series of drinking water standards to protect public health and welfare and to establish a

---

1/   Mr. Miller was an Environmental Protection Agency enforcement official for ten years, ending his government career in charge of EPA's entire enforcement program.

2/   42 U.S.C. §§ 300f et seq.

heavily, state-oriented implementation mechanism. EPA is charged with promulgating primary drinking water regulations containing either: (1) a maximum contaminant level (MCL) for a material in a public water supply, or (2) a treatment technique to reduce the material to an acceptable level, if the MCL is not economically or technologically attainable. 3/   EPA is to promulgate primary drinking water standards for all contaminants found in public water supplies that may have adverse human health effects. MCLs are to be established for such contaminants at a level having no known or anticipated adverse human health effects, with an adequate margin of safety. 4/ These primary standards are to be based on a study conducted by the National Academy of Sciences. 5/   Prior to establishing primary standards, EPA was to promulgate "interim" primary drinking water standards to protect public health to the extent feasible using technology, treatment and other means available as of the end of 1974. 6/   Finally, EPA is to promulgate secondary standards for drinking water supplies, including provisions for aesthetic values such as odor or appearance. 7/

In the ten years EPA has had to implement SDWA, it has established MCLs only for nine heavy metals, coliform bacteria, six pesticides, trihalomethanes which add disinfectants during the treatment process (but only in systems serving 10,000 or more persons), turbidity, and radiation. 8/ EPA has also promulgated secondary drinking water standards for twelve contaminants such as chloride, color, forming agents, odor, sulfate and solids. 9/   EPA specifies minimum sampling and analytical frequencies for the

---

3/   SDWA §§ 1401(1), 1412(b), 42 U.S.C. § 300f(1), 300g-1(b).

4/   SDWA § 1412(b)(1)(B), 42 U.S.C. § 300g-1(b)(1)(B).

5/   SDWA §§ 1412(b)(1)(B) and (e), 42 U.S.C. §§ 300g-1(b)(1)(B) and (e).

6/   SDWA § 1412(a), 42 U.S.C. § 300g-1(a).

7/   SDWA §§ 1412(1), 1412(c), 42 U.S.C. §§ 300f(2) and 300g-1(c).

8/   40 CFR §§ 141.11-141.16.

9/   40 CFR §§ 143.1-143.4.

various regulated contaminants, depending on the size of the population served by the public water supply, and provides for approval of
less frequent monitoring. 10/   Except for rudimentary analysis,
required analyses must be performed at approved laboratories. 11/

　　　MCLs are sometimes taken out of context and applied in
other environmental contexts, e.g., to establish Superfund cleanup
levels. To do so without careful consideration, however, creates an
inappropriate benchmark.   MCLs are established at a no-effect
level, with a margin of safety, for direct and constant, life long
ingestion, without dilution or treatment.   This situation will be
applicable in few environmental contexts.

2.2 The Regulated Public

　　　Once promulgated, standards apply to "public water systems,"
systems which regularly supply water to fifteen or more connections
or to twenty-five or more individuals at least sixty days a year. 12/
This definition applies to most industrial and commercial establishments which supply water to employees and/or customers. They are
excluded from coverage, however, if they: only store and distribute
water; obtain water from a regulated public water supply; sell no
water; and are not a carrier of persons in interstate commerce. 13/

2.3 The Regulatory Scheme

　　　SDWA provides variances and exemptions for public water
supply systems which cannot meet the primary drinking water standards. If a system cannot meet a MCL despite application of the
best treatment technology, it may receive a variance. Cost considerations and the nature of raw water supplies are taken into
account for issuing such variances. Variances also require eventual
compliance and cannot be granted if it would result in an unreasonable risk to public health. 14/   Eventual compliance is illusory
because EPA may specify "an indefinite time period for compliance"

10/   40 CFR §§ 141.21-141.30.

11/   40 CFR § 141.28.

12/   SDWA § 1401(4), 42 U.S.C. § 300f(4), 40 CFR § 141.1(e).

13/   SDWA § 1411, 42 U.S.C. §§ 300g, 40 CFR § 141.3.

14/   SDWA § 1415, 42 U.S.C. § 300g-4, 40 CFR §§ 142.40-.46.

awaiting the development of new treatment technology. 15/ A variance may also be granted to a system from a treatment technology
specified by a primary standard, if the nature of the system's raw
water supply makes such treatment unnecessary to protect public
health. Such a variance need not require eventual compliance with
the standard.

If a system cannot meet a MCL for reasons other than the
nature of its raw water supply or cannot install a treatment technology specified by a primary standard, it may receive an exemption. Exemptions, however, require compliance within seven years
and cannot be granted if they could result in an unreasonable risk to
public health. Exemptions cannot be granted to new systems unless
there is no reasonably available alternative source of drinking
water. Special flexibility is allowed for systems that elect to comply by entering into enforceable agreements to become part of a
regional public water system. 16/

SDWA provides for state implementation, upon application, if
a state has drinking water standards "no less stringent" than the
federal standards, "adequate" enforcement procedures, and variance
and exemption conditions "no less stringent" than the federal
conditions. 17/   These relatively lax entry requirements led all
states but Pennsylvania, Indiana and Oregon to assume SDWA
primacy. States with primary enforcement authority must notify
EPA upon granting a variance or exemption and must submit an
annual status report on all public water supply systems within the
state. 18/

EPA is to review state granted variances and exemptions. If
it finds that in a substantial number of cases a state failed to
include a schedule of compliance or abused its discretion in granting
variances or exemptions, EPA may, after notice and hearing, rescind
the variances or exemptions or correct their deficiencies. 19/ This

---

15/   40 CFR § 142.43(e).

16/   SDWA § 1416, 42 U.S.C. § 300g-5, 40 CFR §§ 142.50-142.55.

17   SDWA § 1413, 42 U.S.C. §§ 300g-2, 40 CFR §§ 142.10-142.15.

18/   40 CFR § 142.15.

19/   SDWA §§ 1415(d), 1416(d), 42 U.S.C. §§ 300g-4(d) and -5(d).

is a particularly ineffective review mechanism, allowing the correction of deficiencies only if a substantial number of deficiencies
exists and allowing corrective action only if an abuse of discretion is
shown. Abuse of discretion is a tough legal standard and for EPA to
find that a state has abused its discretion presents an almost impossible political hurdle.

Federal enforcement against violations of primary drinking
water standards or violations of variances and exemptions from such
standards is equally ineffective. Civil injunctive relief may be
secured from a court, with up to $5,000 a day civil penalty. But
access to a court in a state with primary enforcement responsibility
can be secured only after notifying the state twice in a sixty-day
period; an offer of advice and technical assistance; and findings that
the violation persists and the state has abused its discretion by not
taking enforcement action. A finding that a state has abused its
discretion is politically, if not legally, impossible for EPA to make.
The few enforcement actions EPA has taken under SDWA, predictably have been in the three non-primacy states, where EPA has
access to a court, for the same remedies, without onerous precondi-
tions. 20/

SDWA is notably lacking in effective administration or criminal remedies. One of EPA's chief concerns in SDWA amendments is
to secure better enforcement tools, particularly administrative
penalty authority.

SDWA may be enforced by private citizens in federal court.
However, they must give sixty days prior notice to EPA, the state
and the alleged violator. 21/ Because citizens may gain access to
courts without finding the state's action or inaction is an abuse of
discretion, private enforcement may be more effective than EPA
enforcement.

An unusual enforcement feature of SDWA is the requirement
that public water supply systems notify customers of violations of
MCLs, failure to install required treatment technology, failure to

---

20/   SDWA § 1414, 42 U.S.C. § 300g-3.

21/   SDWA § 1449, 42 U.S.C. § 300j-8. For a discussion of citizen
      enforcement, see J. Miller, "Private Enforcement of Federal
      Environmental Laws," Part I, 13 Envir. Law Rep. 10309
      (October 1983); Part II, 14 Envir. Law Rep. 10063 (February
      1984); and Part III, 14 Envir. Law Rep. 10407 (November 1984).

conduct required monitoring, the procurement of a variance and exemption and any violations of the compliance schedule in a variance or exemption. Notice must be given both in news media and in customer bills. Failure to give notice is punishable by a $5,000 fine. 22/ EPA's regulations attempt to restrict this requirement somewhat. Among other things they allow a state to waive notice if no longer appropriate. 23/ In order to qualify for primary enforcement responsibility, a state must have authority to require public notification. 24/

3.0 Aquifer Protection

SDWA authorizes EPA, on its own initiative or upon petition, to designate an area as having an aquifer which is the sole source of the area's water supply and which would create a significant hazard to public health if contaminated. Once an area is so designated, no federal assistance may be provided for any project in the area which EPA determines may contaminate the aquifer. 25/ To date EPA has designated only the Edwards Underground Reservoir in the vicinity of San Antonio, Texas. 26/ With the increased public awareness to threats of underground contamination, however, more designations can be expected in the future. Indeed, EPA has several petitions for designations before it now. An aquifer designation can only disrupt, force changes in, or possibly thwart projects which have some form of federal assistance. As the desire for groundwater protection increases, however, statutory authority for use of this device will undoubtedly be expanded to affect a wide range of other projects.

4.0 Underground Injection Control

SDWA's most direct affect on industry is through regulation of underground injection to protect usable aquifers from contamination. Underground injection is the subsurface emplacement of fluid

---

22/ SDWA § 1414(c), 42 U.S.C. § 300g-3(c).

23/ 40 CFR § 141.32(b)(3).

24/ 40 CFR §§ 142.10(b)(6)(v) and 142.16.

25/ SDWA § 1424(e), 42 U.S.C. § 300h-3(e).

26/ 40 CFR Part 149.

through a well or dug-hole whose depth is greater than its width. It can include emplacement through a septic tank or cesspool. 27/ The regulation most directly impacts hazardous waste disposal, the re-injection of brine from oil and gas production, and certain mining processes.

4.1 The Regulatory Scheme

SDWA requires EPA publish both a list of states where under-ground injection control (UIC) programs would be necessary to prevent endangerment of drinking water and to propose regulation for approval of state UIC programs. 28/ EPA listed all states as requiring UIC programs and states were supposed to submit their applications by the end of January 1981. 29/ To be approved, state programs must: prevent underground injection unless authorized by permit or rule; authorize underground injection only where the applicant demonstrates it will not endanger drinking water sources; and maintain records, reports, inspection programs, and other such provisions. 30/ EPA may allow temporary permits, either to author-ize existing injection until state permitting can catch up, or to authorize temporary injection when no other means of disposal is technologically or economically feasible. However, both of these authorizations were to have expired at the end of 1984. 31/ Approved programs must protect aquifers that are or may reason-ably be expected to be sources of drinking water supply. These programs must be designed to protect such aquifers from contamina-tion that violates an MCL or adversely affects human health. 32/

Congress imposed several constraints upon EPA's regulations reflecting deference to state programs and a desire not to disrupt oil and gas production. EPA's regulations are supposed to reflect geo-logical and historical differences between the states. 33/ Unless

---

27/   40 CFR §§ 144.1(g) and .3.

28/   SDWA §§1421(a) and 1422, 42 U.S.C. §§ 300h(a) and 300h-1.

29/   40 CFR § 1441.1(e).

30/   SDWA § 1421(b), 42 U.S.C. § 300h(b).

31/   SDWA § 1421(c), 42 U.S.C. § 300h(c).

32/   SDWA § 1421(d), 42 U.S.C § 300h(d).

33/   SDWA § 1421(b)(3)(A), 42 U.S.C. §§ 300h(b)(3)(A).

absolutely necessary to protect public health, EPA may not issue regulations which would interfere with existing UIC regulation in a substantial number of states. 34/ EPA is also prevented from issuing regulations which interfere with the reinjection of brine from oil and gas production or with secondary or tertiary oil or gas recovery, unless absolutely necessary to protect public health. 35/

If EPA disapproves a state's application for approval of a UIC program or a state does not seek approval of a UIC program, EPA must promulgate a UIC program for the state within ninety days. 36/ Because EPA listed all states as requiring UIC programs and states were supposed to have submitted programs for approval by the end of January 1981, 37/ EPA should have promulgated UIC programs by the middle of 1981 for states not submitting programs for approval. But by the end of 1981, EPA had approved only Oklahoma's program for disposal of oil and gas production wastes. 38/ By the end of 1982, EPA approved UIC programs in only five states and partial programs in five more. 39/ By the end of 1983, EPA approved UIC programs in thirteen states and partial programs in six more. 40/

34/   SDWA § 1421(b)(3), 42 U.S.C. § 300h(b)(3).

35/   SDWA § 1421(b)(2), 42 U.S.C. § 300h(b)(2).

36/   SDWA § 1422(c), 42 U.S.C. 300h-1(c).

37/   40 CFR 144.1(e).

38/   See 40 CFR Part 147.

39/   EPA had approved complete UIC programs by the end of 1982 in Louisiana, Massachusetts, New Hampshire, Oklahoma and Texas. By the same time, it had approved programs associated with oil and gas production in Alabama, New Mexico, Utah and Wyoming and programs for all but oil and gas production related injection in Arkansas. See 40 CFR Part 147.

40/   By the end of 1983, EPA had approved complete UIC programs in Maine, New Jersey, Wisconsin, and Guam and had approved the remainder of the programs in Alabama, New Mexico, Utah and Wyoming. By the same time, it had approved programs associated with oil and gas production in California, North Dakota and Ohio, and programs for all but oil and gas related injection in Arkansas, Florida and Mississippi. See 40 CFR Part 147.

Despite the statutory mandate that EPA promulgate UIC programs in the remaining states, it took no action to do so. If SDWA's various deadlines had been adhered to by EPA, it would have promulgated these programs by the end of 1976. It has little excuse for not having done so by the end of 1983. A lawsuit by the National Wildlife Federation finally brought a rush of regulatory activity in 1984 in which state programs were approved or EPA programs were promulgated in most (but not all) of the remaining states.

4.2 UIC Permits

Once a UIC program is in existence, no underground injection may take place except as authorized by permit or rule. 41/ EPA has authorized most existing injections by rule for a sufficient period of time to obtain a permit, although its legal authority to do so beyond the end of 1984 is questionable. 42/ In the meantime, injection must comply with substantive and reporting requirements that are abbreviated versions of ultimate permit requirements. 43/ Permit application, issuance, and appeal procedures and permit conditions are based on those of the more familiar NPDES permitting program under the Clean Water Act. 44/ There are some noteworthy differences. Substantive permit requirements may be less stringent than established by EPA's regulations if the injection does not result in an increased risk of fluid movement into an underground source of drinking water 45/ and states may classify aquifers as not being underground sources of drinking water if they meet specific criteria. 46/ Permits may be issued on an area basis as well as on an individual well basis, except for hazardous waste injection. 47/ Short term

---

41/   40 CFR § 144.11.

42/   40 CFR § 144.21. SDWA contemplated such temporary authorization only through 1984; see footnote 30 and accompanying text.

43/   40 CFR §§ 144.26 to 144.28.

44/   40 CFR §§ 144.31 to 144.61 and Part 124.

45/   40 CFR § 144.16.

46/   40 CFR § 144.7.

47/   40 CFR § 144.33.

temporary permits may be issued in emergencies, which include the loss or delay in production of oil and gas, and may be continued until a final permit is issued. 48/

4.3 UIC Regulatory Enforcement

Violations of the UIC regulations or permits are enforceable judicially, with civil injunctive relief and civil penalties up to $5,000 per day of violation. Although the UIC enforcement provisions are in a different section 49/ than the primary drinking water standard enforcement sections discussed earlier, 50/ they are substantially similar. Any reasonable state enforcement should block federal enforcement. The same violations are also subject to enforcement by private citizens under the same citizen suit section discussed earlier. 51/

4.4 UIC Permit Substantive Requirements

A UIC permit's substantive requirements depend on the type of injection taking place. The most stringent conditions are for wells injecting wastes classified as hazardous under RCRA. These are called Class I wells.

4.4.1 Class I Wells: Hazardous Wastes

Class I wells may not be located where another known well penetrates the injection zone within the area of the zone expected to be influenced by the Class I well, if the other well could act as a conduit for wastes to escape from the injection zone. 52/ Class I wells must inject below the lowest underground source of drinking water, must be cased and cemented, and must have a packer or approved fluid seal set between the injection tubing and the casing, immediately above the injection zone. 53/ The mechanical integrity

---

48/   40 CFR § 144.34.

49/   SDWA § 1423, 42 U.S.C. § 300 h-2.

50/   See footnote 19 and accompanying text.

51/   See footnote 20 and accompanying text.

52/   40 CFR § 144.55, 146.6 and 144.7.

53/   40 CFR § 146.13.

of the well must be determined from both construction logs and mechanical integrity testing. Also, mechanical integrity demonstrations must be repeated at least once every five years. 54/ The injected wastes must be sampled and analyzed periodically, presumably to determine compatibility with the injection equipment and the injection formation. 55/

The injection rate of the injection fluid and the pressures maintained on both the injection fluid in the injection tubing and the annular fluid between the injection tubing and the well casing must be continuously recorded. 56/ Monitoring wells must be located in underground sources of drinking water to detect fluid movement or pressure from the injection. 57/ A maximum operating pressure for the injection tubing is to be established to prevent fractures of the injection zone or the confirming zone above it. 58/ However, stimulation, e.g., controlled fracturing of the injection zone to increase its injection capacity, is allowed. 59/ Pressure on the annular fluid between the injection tubing and the casing is also to be regulated. 60/ Diesel fuel is often used as an annular fluid, which should be innocuous. Pressure on the annular fluid should be maintained at a higher rate than on the injection fluid so that a leak in the injection tubing will result in a flow of innocuous annular fluid into the tubing rather than possibly hazardous injection fluid leaking out. Injection at a constant rate with constant pressures on both injection and annular fluids is indicative of a properly functioning well. Changes in any one of the three may indicate a malfunction and should be investigated. More than a minimal loss of annular fluid, other than the minimum amount routinely lost through the packer or seal

---

54/   40 CFR §§ 146.13(b)(3) and .8.

55/   40 CFR § 146.13(b)(1).

56/   40 CFR § 146.13(b)(2).

57/   40 CFR §§ 146.6 and .13(b)(4).

58/   40 CFR § 146.13(a)(1).

59/   40 CFR § 146.13(a)(1).

60/   40 CFR § 146.13(a)(2).

assembly, indicates a leak in the tubing or casing. With good equipment, potential leaks of a few gallons a day can be detected, enabling prompt detection and repair of problems with the integrity of injection wells. All of this is not clearly required in the regulations, but should be.

Class I wells must be plugged and abandoned at the end of their useful lives by specified methods to prevent migration of wastes from the injection zone. 61/

Class I wells are hazardous waste disposal facilities and therefore subject to RCRA permitting requirements. For the moment, however, the RCRA program has deferred to the UIC program and exempts UIC permitted Class I wells from RCRA permitting requirements and from interim status regulations. 62/ However, prior to receiving a UIC permit, UIC wells may be subject to some of the RCRA interim status requirements. 63/ Any related surface facilities for storage, treatment or disposal of hazardous waste, however, require RCRA permits and are subject to RCRA interim status regulations. 64/ Moreover, the UIC regulations subject owners and operators of Class I wells to some RCRA regulations. 65/ Through a regulation patterned on the RCRA financial responsibility requirements, owners of Class I wells must establish their financial ability to properly plug and abandon the wells at the end of their useful lives. 66/ The 1984 RCRA Amendments contain a number of provisions directly applicable to Class I wells. They include prohibitions against injection into salt domes, mines and caves and a required review of the safety of injecting RCRA designated hazardous wastes. Possible prohibition against injecting wastes not meeting specified criteria, or potential corrective action may result in the event the review is incomplete within the time

---

61/   40 CFR § 146.10.

62/   40 CFR §§ 264.1(d), 265.1(c)(2), and 265.430.

63/   40 CFR §§ 265.1(c)(2) and 265.430.

64/   See comments to 40 CFR §§ 264.1(d) and 265.1(c)(2).

65/   40 CFR § 144.14.

66/   40 CFR §§ 144.60 to .70.

specified. 67/   These amendments were prompted by Congressional dissatisfaction with the protection afforded by the existing UIC program.

4.4.2 Class II and III Wells
EPA's regulations establish similar requirements for the injection of fluids associated with oil and gas production or oil and gas storage (Class II wells) and for Frasch mining of sulfur, in situ production of uranium and other metals or solution mining of salts or potash (Class III wells). Regulations for Class II and III wells are tailored to the industries to which they apply. 68/

4.4.3 Class IV and V Wells
Wells which inject radioactive wastes or wastes classified as hazardous under RCRA into or above underground sources of drinking water or those which inject such wastes and are not Class I wells (Class IV wells) must be plugged and abandoned within six months after a UIC program is in effect in a state. 69/
Only reporting and notification requirements are in effect for Class V wells at this time. 70/   Because a well injecting a harmful substance, not yet classified as hazardous under RCRA, directly into a public water supply would be a Class V well, this lack of regulation perturbs some. If injection into a Class V well causes a violation of a MCL, EPA or a UIC state may require the owner or operator to obtain a permit or take other corrective action. 71/

5.0 SDWA in Perspective
Although industrial and commercial establishments supplying their own potable water may have to meet primary drinking water standards, those requirements are normally neither onerous nor costly.   Existing aquifer protection requirements apply only to federally-assisted projects above the Edwards aquifer in Texas.

67/   RCRA §§ 3004(b), (f) and (g), 42 U.S.C. §§ 6924(b), (f) and (g), added by § 201 of PL 98–616 (1984).

68/   40 CFR §§ 146.21–146.25 and 146.31–146.35.

69/   40 CFR §§ 146.13 and 146.23.

70/   40 CFR §§ 144.26 and 146.52.

71/   40 CFR § 144.12(d).

SWDA's underground injection program is a comprehensive regulatory program with real impact on those it regulates. The Environmental Protection Agency's tardy, and as some perceive, unaggressive implementation of the UIC program, however, may lead to more stringent statutory requirements in the future.

Chapter 6

AIR POLLUTION CONTROL

G. William Frick 1/
Attorney
Lathrop, Koontz, Righter, Clagett & Norquist
Kansas City, Missouri

Lydia N. Wegman
Attorney
Swidler, Berlin & Strelow
Washington, D.C.

1.0 Introduction

Although generally described as environmental legislation, the Federal Clean Air Act, (42 U.S.C. Section 7401 et seq.) was enacted primarily because of growing recognition, by the Congress as well as the general public, of the serious adverse public health effects that result from air pollution. Certain environmental effects, such as reduced visibility, are readily apparent and, to a certain extent, easy to control; early air pollution control efforts focused on those problems through ordinances against black smoke and open burning. The most serious problems, however, are more insidious and require longer time periods to become apparent, e.g.,

---

1/ Former General Counsel, U.S. Environmental Protection Agency. This chapter is a revision and update of versions written for previous editions of the Environmental Law Handbook by Robert L. Baum, Esq. and Michael A. James, Esq. to whom credit should be given for their contribution.

impaired breathing functions, cancer, lower crop yields, premature deterioration of paint and building materials.

The less immediate, less visible effects of air pollution also make it more difficult to develop public support for the enormous cost associated with air pollution control efforts. As with most "police power" functions, air pollution control was initially left to the states and local governments. However, the political and economic obstacles to controlling sources of air pollution proved too difficult for them to overcome and the need for federal control efforts became apparent. The demand for a comprehensive federal attack on the program also reflected a growing recognition that air pollution does not honor political boundaries and individual members of the public have no way to protect themselves against the hazards in the air they breathe.

The Clean Air Act of 1970 (PL 91-604), along with the major amendments adopted in the Clean Air Act Amendments of 1977 (PL 95-95), constitute a significant step forward in the nation's attack on the emission into the air of harmful pollutants. It creates a wide ranging, coordinated federal/state scheme of regulation that now pervades our social order and national economy, and affects virtually every citizen in the country. Consequently, with its impact on so many commercial and private activities, it is important that persons occupying executive or professional positions in industry and persons responsible for public policy have a basic understanding of its provisions.

2.0 History

The first "Clean Air Act" was passed in 1963. 2/ It provided for grants to air pollution control agencies and contained the first federal regulatory authority. The latter consisted of an abatement conference procedure, to be used in very limited circumstances. Although a number of abatement conferences were held around the country and some control efforts begun as a result of them, the air pollution problem was growing faster than federal, state and local efforts and abilities to control it.

2/   In 1955, the "Air Pollution Control--Research and Technical Assistance Act," PL 84-159, 69 Stat. 322, had been enacted, but it contained no regulatory authority.

In 1965, Congress amended the Act to add Title II, The Motor Vehicle Air Pollution Control Act (PL 89-272, 79 Stat. 991), which authorized federal emission standards for new vehicles. In 1967, Congress considerably broadened the Act with respect to stationary source control. The 1967 Amendments gave the federal government authority to adopt emission control regulations in designated areas which had air pollution problems. It also provided a system of limited federal enforcement.

In late 1970, after extensive hearings and debate, the Congress determined that drastic changes in the governmental response to air pollution were required and a totally restructured federal/ state scheme was adopted in the Clean Air Act Amendments of 1970. While continuing to look to state and local governments as the primary focus of regulatory efforts, Congress provided the newly created United States Environmental Protection Agency (EPA) with authority to establish, in accordance with specific Congressional directives, the minimum air quality and regulatory goals the states and locals were to achieve. Congress also took the unusual step of establishing very stringent, and in many cases unrealistic, deadlines for action by the state and federal government. Where states failed to satisfy the Congressional expectations, EPA was directed to take specific regulatory actions. Furthermore, in addition to a more vigorous new motor vehicle control program with Congressionally adopted emission limitations, the 1970 Act provided for certain national emission standards that would be applicable regardless of air quality or the substantive governmental requirements in the area where the source was located. The Act was substantially amended in 1977, with new provisions added to prevent significant deterioration of air quality, impose stringent requirements in areas that failed to attain national standards, restrict the use of dispersion techniques, and strengthen enforcement of the statutory provisions.

3.0 Establishment of Air Quality Standards

3.1 Air Quality Criteria

Section 108 of the Act requires that the EPA Administrator publish a list of pollutants which he determines have adverse effects on public health or welfare, and which are emitted from numerous and diverse stationary or mobile sources. The "listing" of a pollutant sets in motion the process for establishing ambient air quality standards for such a pollutant. Although the Administrator of the

Environmental Protection Agency considered the determination to list a pollutant to be discretionary, that flexibility was diminished by the court decision in NRDC v. Train, 3/ which required the Administrator to list lead as a pollutant. For each pollutant, a "criteria" document must be compiled and published by the Administrator. The criteria are scientific compendia of the studies documenting adverse effects of specific pollutants at various concentrations in the ambient air. In setting ambient air quality standards for the nation, i.e., prescribing the levels of air quality which the law requires to be attained and which determine the degree of control needed for individual sources, the Administrator is required to base his judgment solely on information in the criteria documents.

Section 108 also requires that, simultaneously with the issuance of criteria, the Administrator issue documents describing techniques for controlling the criteria pollutants. The information in these documents describes the various methods of reducing or eliminating emissions of the pollutant in question, as well as the costs of those methods.

The 1977 Amendments imposed a specific requirement that the Environmental Protection Agency issue a criteria document for nitrogen oxides, covering short term exposure effects of nitrogen dioxide and various suspect carcinogenic derivatives of oxides of nitrogen.

3.2 National Ambient Air Quality Standards

Under Section 109 of the law, the Administrator is required to establish National Ambient Air Quality Standards (NAAQS) for each pollutant for which he issues a criteria document under Section 108. The Administrator must establish a primary and secondary NAAQS for each criteria pollutant. The "primary" NAAQS for a pollutant in Section 109(b)(1) is to be set at the level of air quality which, based on the criteria "and allowing an adequate margin of safety," will protect the public health. The secondary NAAQS in Section 109(b)(2) is that level of air quality which protects the public welfare from any known or anticipated adverse effects.

Two points concerning the primary standards are important. First, the language and history of the Act make it clear that the standards are to be set at levels which protect not only the normal

---

3/   411 F. Supp. 864 (S.D. N.Y.) aff'd 545 F. 2d 320 (2nd Cir. 1976).

healthy majority of the population, but even especially sensitive persons with pre-existing illnesses or conditions which pollution might exacerbate, although not cause. The second, and perhaps more significant point, is that the primary NAAQS are to be established solely on a strictly scientific basis using the data in the criteria documents; cost, technical feasibility or any factor other than public health cannot be considered in setting the standards. Such factors cannot be the basis for either a legal challenge to the standard or an excuse for failure to attain it. Because of the Act's rigid requirements for achievement of the primary NAAQS, there is growing concern that the primary NAAQS should be set only after some consideration of the benefits that would result as compared with the overall cost to society of achieving the standards. This is particularly an issue with respect to pollutants that have significant natural sources, such as particulates and ozone.

The Act defines the components of public welfare that must be considered in setting the secondary standard. "Public welfare" in Section 302(h) encompasses essentially all parts of the environment other than human health that might be affected by an air pollutant, e.g., soil, crops, vegetation, animals, manmade materials, visibility, and personal comfort and well-being. In short, the secondary standard is to protect against any type of adverse effect, even if it could not be scientifically shown to affect man's physiological well-being in any narrow medical sense. The requirement for secondary standards was based on the knowledge that, in some cases, air pollutants had adverse effects on materials, vegetation, or visibility at levels lower than those which could be shown to directly affect human health.

Ambient standards for six pollutants were promulgated by the Environmental Protection Agency on 30 April 1971. 4/ The six were sulfur dioxide (SO_2), particulate matter, carbon monoxide (CO), hydrocarbons (HC), nitrogen dioxide (NO_2), and photochemical oxidants. On 8 February 1979, EPA redesignated the oxidants NAAQS to an ozone standard and increased the level by 50 percent. 5/ In the case of the last four NAAQS, generally associated with emissions

---

4/   40 CFR Part 50.

5/   44 FR 8202 et seq.

from mobile sources, the secondary standards are the same as the primary, because no studies had revealed effects on welfare from these pollutants at levels which did not affect human health. However, for SO_2 and particulate matter, generally associated with emissions from stationary sources, secondary standards were set at more stringent levels than the primary, because effects on vegetation and visibility had been identified at levels which had not been shown to be harmful man.

Hydrocarbons were originally included in the NAAQS because they contribute to the formation of ozone. As a class, hydrocarbons alone do not cause direct health or welfare effects at ambient levels. The hydrocarbon NAAQS was only to be used as a guide for determining achievement of the ozone NAAQS. As part of its review of the hydrocarbon criteria, EPA determined that there was no quantitative relationship between hydrocarbon levels and ozone, and EPA revoked the NAAQS on 5 January 1983. 6/ Hydrocarbon emissions, however, will still be controlled as part of the ozone NAAQS control strategy.

Pursuant to court order, EPA established NAAQS for lead on 5 October 1978. 7/ Although previously regulated only as a fuel additive, regulations on stationary sources are now being imposed.

Despite the importance of the NAAQS in what follows under the Act, only one portion of one standard from the original six NAAQS was challenged in the courts. In the course of a lawsuit by Kennecott Copper Corporation, 8/ EPA withdrew a portion of the secondary standards for sulfur dioxide. Otherwise, the 30 April 1972 NAAQSs remain essentially in effect.

In the 1977 Amendments, Congress directed the Agency to completely review all the criteria documents and NAAQS and to make appropriate revisions to the NAAQS by the end of 1980. Even before this requirement was enacted, EPA had begun a reassessment of the NAAQS for photochemical oxidants which resulted in the 8 February 1979 revision. The 1977 Act also required EPA to develop an NO_2 NAAQS for short-term exposures.

6/   48 FR 628.

7/   43 FR 46258.

8/   Kennecott Copper Corp. v. EPA, 462 F.2d 846 (D.C. Cir. 1972).

Despite their critical importance to the scheme of the Clean Air Act, NAAQS are not directly enforceable. They are the controlling force behind the development and implementation of emission limitations and other controls pursuant to other sections of the statute. It is those requirements that are actually enforced against polluters, rather than the NAAQS itself.

The NAAQS establish ceilings for individual pollutant concentrations that should not be exceeded anywhere in the United States. They, therefore, determine the degree of control that will be imposed on existing sources and the restrictions on location of new sources, depending on whether air quality is better or worse than the NAAQS in the particular area where the source is or will be located.

3.3 Air Quality Control Regions

Prior to the 1970 Clean Air Act, Congress had recognized the difficulties states and their sometimes relatively autonomous political subdivisions had in coordinating efforts to control air pollution. Consequently, in the 1967 Act, the Secretary of Health, Education and Welfare was directed to designate "Air Quality Control Regions" (AQCRs). These are interstate or intrastate areas which, because of common meteorological, industrial and socioeconomic factors, should be treated as a single unit for the purpose of air pollution control. The concept of ignoring jurisdictional boundaries in order to treat regional air pollution problems was preserved in the 1970 law. The 1970 Amendments required the entire country to be divided into AQCRs. 9/

The 1977 Amendments to the Act 10/ reduced the significance of the AQCRs by requiring the states to identify, and EPA to designate formally, areas of the country which meet NAAQS national ambient air quality standards, do not meet NAAQS, or for which there are insufficient data to place them in either of those categories. Many of the areas have been designated on the basis of

---

9/   The 247 AQCRs designated by HEW and EPA are identified in the Code of Federal Regulations (hereafter CFR) in Title 40, Part 81.

10/   PL 95-95, 7 August 1977.

county boundaries. 11/ Some are determined by the area around a single point source that is affected by that source. "Air quality maintenance areas" have also been designated that are not conterminous with AQCRs.

Classification of an area determines what actions the state and EPA will be required to take to regulate air pollution from existing and new emission sources. Areas are classified for each pollutant for which a national ambient air quality standard is in effect, using monitoring data to the extent possible.

4.0 State Implementation Plans (SIPs)

4.1 Content of SIP

The key regulatory section of the Act is Section 110. It implements the Congressional philosophy that "prevention and control of air pollution at its source is the primary responsibility of state and local governments" 12/ and provides a structure under which states are expected to establish the regulatory framework necessary to achieve the NAAQS. However, it also directs the Environmental Protection Agency to impose the necessary regulations if state governments fail to meet the Act's directives.

The structure of Section 110 is as follows. Within nine months of the promulgation of an NAAQS, each state, after public hearings, is to submit to the Administrator of EPA for his approval a plan for implementation of the NAAQS in every AQCR in the state. 13/ Under the timetable in the 1970 Act, State Implementation Plans (SIPs) were due on 30 January 1972. The law gives the Administrator of EPA four months to approve or disapprove the SIP. If a state fails to submit a plan or submits a plan which the Administrator deems to be inadequate, the Administrator must promulgate federal regulations to substitute for or supplement that portion of

---

11/   43 FR 8962, 3 March 1978.

12/   Section 101(a)(3).

13/   EPA's minimum requirements for approvable state plans are set forth in 40 CFR Part 51.

the state's plan. 14/ Approval of a state plan makes its provisions enforceable by the federal government as well as the state. 15/

A SIP is required to include a description of the air quality in each AQCR, an emissions inventory of sources that emit each pollutant covered by an NAAQS, emission limitations and compliance schedules applicable to each source that will reduce pollutant emissions so that the total pollutant contribution is below that necessary to achieve the NAAQS, a permit program for review of new source construction to insure new emissions will not cause a violation of NAAQS, monitoring and reporting requirements, and enforcement procedures. All of those elements comprise the control strategy of the SIP for satisfying the goal of the Act to achieve a level of air quality throughout the country that will protect both public health and welfare.

In the SIPs submitted in 1972 for attainment of the original six NAAQS, states were given substantial flexibility to choose which sources to regulate, and to vary the degree of control among sources; because air quality varied greatly throughout the country, the emission limitations necessarily varied substantially. Some areas already had air quality better than NAAQS, while others have such serious problems that they still have not achieved one or more standards seven years later. In some cases, it is questionable whether certain areas will ever achieve certain standards. While states still have great flexibility, the 1977 Amendments established additional conditions that states must impose, particularly in areas that have not yet achieved the NAAQS. Part D of Title 1 of the Clean Air Act requires states to revise their SIPs, to impose Reasonably Available Control Technology (RACT) on existing sources, and to impose rigorous requirements on new sources in nonattainment areas, including requiring them to obtain offsets from other sources equivalent to the emissions to be added by the new source.

The Act requires that the SIP attain the primary standards "as expeditiously as practicable," but in no event later than three years from the date of plan approval. Section 110(e) permits, if the Governor requests at the time the plan is submitted, up to two additional years for attainment of a primary standard upon a showing

---

14/   Section 110(c).

15/   See 40 CFR Part 52.

that three years is inadequate despite application of all available measures. Since most states in 1972 assumed standards could be met within the three-year period, particularly because of an apparently unlimited, cheap supply of "clean" oil, relatively few states asked for the additional two years.

SIPs are to provide for attainment of the secondary standard within a "reasonable time." The term "reasonable time" is not defined in the Act and states can consider technological and economic problems in deciding on an appropriate date for achievement of the welfare standard. 16/ Although the provisions of Section 110 in the 1970 Act were relatively simple and straightforward, the development and adoption of effective emission controls involved complex technical, economic and political decisions, and many states failed to submit SIPs that could be approved in their entirety. Unfortunately, even when approved, or substitute EPA regulations promulgated, a large number of plans failed to achieve the NAAQS for one or more pollutants in some regions of the state. Consequently, Congress, in its 1977 Amendments, imposed more demanding provisions in Section 110 to reinvigorate the SIP program.

In the 1977 Amendments, Congress retained all of the above requirements and added several others. By 7 August 1978, states were to submit SIP revisions that require each major source to pay fees sufficient to cover the states' cost of handling any construction or operating permit for the source, require state permit and enforcement boards to restructure their memberships and make public disclosures to prevent conflicts of interests, provide for prevention of interference with other states' air quality, require consultation with local governments and federal land managers in carrying out major SIP functions, and provide for notification to the public areas not meeting the NAAQS.

The most significant addition to the SIP process adopted by the 1977 Amendments relates to areas that did not achieve the NAAQS within the statutory deadlines, so called "nonattainment

---

16/ EPA by regulation indicated that, where controls were reasonably available, a "reasonable time" for achievement of the secondary standards for sulfur oxides and particulates would be three years, unless the state could show that good cause exists for choosing a later date. 40 CFR 51.13(b)(1) and (2).

areas." Although much attention has been directed toward the provisions applicable to new sources in nonattainment areas, discussed below, along with the SIP provisions applicable to review new sources in clean air areas to prevent significant deterioration of air quality, the 1977 Amendments also imposed additional SIP requirements on existing sources. Recognizing that many SIPs were inadequate and had not achieved all the NAAQS in all areas of the country, Congress required all SIPs to be reviewed; where standards were still violated, revised SIPs were to be submitted by 1 January 1979. Congress extended the original deadlines to 31 December 1982, with additional time to 31 December 1987, available in certain circumstances to achieve NAAQS for ozone or CO. To gain that additional time, however, the states have to adopt significantly more stringent SIP provisions.

In addition to the significant new source review provisions, Section 172 requires all existing sources to install, at a minimum, "reasonably available control technology." In order to extend the time to 1987 for ozone and CO, which are primarily related to automobiles, states must adopt a vehicle inspection and maintenance program and adopt such other vehicle control measures as may be necessary. States must also show "reasonable further progress" toward achievement of the NAAQS, which is defined in Section 171 as the accomplishment of "annual incremental reductions in emissions." As an "incentive" to states to adopt these more stringent provisions, Congress provided that if revised SIP provisions are not adopted and approved by EPA by 30 June 1979, there was to be no construction of new or modified sources of the air pollutants for which NAAQS are exceeded in the areas where the NAAQS is exceeded. 17/ Although the Environmental Protection Agency has made a number of interpretations of the regulations and the statute to prevent the construction ban from stiffling economic growth, the ban has gone into effect in a number of areas around the country. The difficult decisions involved delayed state action and many SIPs were not revised by the 30 June 1979 deadline. On 31 December 1982, many areas of the country lacked approved SIPs and still violated at least one NAAQS.

17/   Section 110(a)(2)(I).

With the failure of the 98th Congress to amend the Clean Air Act to provide an extension of its 31 December 1982 deadlines, the Environmental Protection Agency faced the prospect of administering the statute with the severe penalties adopted in the Clean Air Act Amendments of 1977. EPA has stated that the failure of states to have adequate plans achieving the standards by 31 December 1982, requires that it impose the construction ban and may require it to take steps to terminate federal highway funds and air grant money for nonattainment areas in the state. The extent to which EPA must immediately impose these sanctions is in sharp dispute, although interpretations of the law may be affected by the political implications of imposition of the sanctions. Extension of the deadlines and adjustments in the method for imposing sanctions will be considered during debate over amendments to the Clean Air Act in 1985.

The Congress did address one deadline problem in the Steel Industry Compliance Extension Act 18/ whereby it provided in an amendment to Section 113(e) that steel production facilities may have their compliance date extended to as late as 31 December 1985. The company must show that the funds to be used for compliance with environmental requirements are needed and will be used for investment in production facilities to improve efficiency and productivity.

4.1.1 Role of Technology and Economics

The principal industry court challenges to the first SIPs involved whether EPA, in determining whether to approve the SIP, must consider the technological and economic feasibility of the measures in the plan. EPA took the position that the statutory requirement that primary NAAQS be achieved within three years overrode any considerations based on cost or availability of technology; sources could always be shut down. Moreover, Section 116 gives a state the right to adopt any requirements it wants, even more stringent than necessary to achieve the NAAQS. Consequently, if the plan when properly enforced would result in achievement of the NAAQS, EPA would approve it regardless of any misgivings it might have regarding the technological or economic feasibility of the particular approach chosen by the state. EPA

18/   PL 97-23, 17 July 1981.

further argued that review of these issues must be accomplished at the state level where the principal responsibility lies or, in a limited fashion, in federal enforcement actions.

Ultimately, the Supreme Court decided unanimously in favor of EPA's position that Section 110 does not require EPA to engage in a review of technological or economic feasibility when considering SIPs for approval. 19/ The Court read the Act to necessitate a review of each SIP only to determine whether it meets the requirements explicit in Section 110, i.e., that it includes specific measures and ensures the attainment and maintenance of the NAAQS. The opinion noted that challenges concerning technological and economic feasibility could be made at the state level through administrative and judicial channels, and suggested that a source might obtain some review on its particular feasibility problems should the SIP be enforced against it in federal district court. The Court chose specifically not to decide what consideration EPA must give to technological or economic feasibility when it promulgates SIP measures.

Union Electric was a particularly important decision because, under the 1977 Amendments, states were required to submit for EPA approval major revisions of many SIPs. While Union Electric should discourage most challenges to EPA's approvals based on economics and technology, arguments are still raised 20/ and court challenges to SIPs at the state level continue.

EPA has attempted to provide states with the ability to choose the most cost effective means to meet emission requirements by authorizing various "emissions trading" approaches. 21/ This policy allows a state and a source to use various techniques to achieve the goals of the statute but in a more cost effective manner. The "bubble" policy allows a source which is subject to several emission limits at the same facility to achieve different reductions at various emission points (higher than required in some cases and lower than required in others) as long as the total emissions from the plant are no higher than would have occurred if the facility met all

---

19/   Union Electric Company v. EPA, 427 U.S. 246 (1976).

20/   See Bunker Hill Co. v. EPA, 572 F. 2d 1286 (9th Cir. 1977).

21/   See 47 FR 15076, et seq., 7 April 1982.

of the requirements as imposed. With respect to new sources, EPA authorizes "netting" whereby intra-plant offsets can be used to avoid new source review; "offsets" where reductions can be obtained from other facilities, which were not otherwise required to achieve those reductions, to offset emissions of another company; and "banking," whereby an accounting system can be developed which will allow a source, which for business reasons reduces emissions to utilize those reductions as offsets for future emissions increases. EPA is considering further refinements in its policy, including the extent to which emission reduction credits by sources should be allowed in areas that have not attained the standards. 22/

4.1.2 Use of Dispersion Techniques

One of the major debates that arose during implementation of the 1970 Act is whether SIPs may rely on techniques other than continuous emission reduction to demonstrate attainment of the NAAQS. To some extent, any air quality management program relies upon the natural dispersion capacities of the meteorology and topography of the area being managed. However, many sources, particularly isolated facilities, proposed to monitor meteorological conditions and curtail operations and emissions intermittently, thereby preventing NAAQS from being exceeded, even where technology or other means of achieving continuous emission control were available. A related approach was to rely upon tall stacks to disperse emissions which might otherwise be controlled by available technology.

These two questions were addressed in three major lawsuits brought by industry and by environmental groups. 23/ The courts uniformly held that dispersion dependent techniques such as intermittent control and tall stacks are permissible to attain NAAQS under Section 110 of the Act only if all available constant emission controls are first applied.

In Section 123 of the 1977 Act, Congress attempted to resolve the tall stack and intermittent controls issues. Continuous

---

22/   48 FR 39580, 31 August 1983.

23/   NRDC v. Train, 489 F.2d 390 (5th Cir. 1974); Big Rivers Electric Cooperative v. Train, 523 F.2d 16 (6th Cir. 1975); Kennecott Copper Corp. v. Train, 526 F.2d 1149 (9th Cir. 1975).

emission controls must be applied, except nonferrous smelters and fuel-burning sources ordered to burn coal instead of oil or gas are allowed on a limited basis to rely on intermittent controls in order to attain NAAQS. The Section allows SIPs to give credit in their control strategies to stack heights representing Good Engineering Practice (GEP), but not for the height of the stack above GEP. EPA published regulations defining "good engineering practice" on 8 February 1982. 24/ The regulations generally provided that a source will be given credit for emissions from a stack 2-1/2 times the height of nearby structures. Those regulations were overturned and remanded in to EPA part by the U.S. Court of Appeals for the District of Columbia Circuit in 1983. 25/ EPA is required to promulgate new regulations in response to the remand by early 1985.

4.1.3 Transportation Control Plans

When SIPs were submitted in January 1972, it was clear that the standards for automobile related pollutants (HC, CO, oxidents, and NO_2) could not always be met through conventional means of control on stationary sources. As newer cars, subject to more stringent emission standards, replaced the older "dirtier" car population, improvements in air quality could be predicted. That improvement, plus control of certain stationary sources would, in many areas, achieve the standards. But, in a significant number of metropolitan areas, such controls were inadequate to correct the problem.

Since neither EPA nor the states had any real experience in coping with this problem, in 1972 the Agency permitted states with problems to submit plans which merely quantified the problems, and permitted them an additional year to submit a plan for solving it. A court eventually held that, although "the Administrator acted in the best of faith in attempting to comply with the difficult responsibilities imposed on him...," the extension was illegal. 26/ As a result, EPA was forced to promulgate requirements that the states impose strategies for lowering concentrations of automobile pollutants by insuring the cars in use are maintained properly and by reducing the

---

24/   47 FR 5864 et seq.

25/   Sierra Club v. EPA 19 ERC 1897 (D.C. Cir.).

26/   NRDC v. EPA, 475 F. 2d 968 (D.C. Cir. 1972).

use of cars. These groups of measures are known as Transportation Control Plans (TCPs). Since the states, almost without exception, did not adopt TCPs, the Administrator was required by the Act to do so and began promulgating TCPs in late 1973.

The TCPs created enormous controversy and, in doing so, dramatized the extent of the mobile source air pollution problem, and the types and extent of the sacrifices which must be made if the health standards are to be achieved. TCPs included the following types of measures: exclusive bus and bicycle lanes; bridge tolls; area-wide computer systems to identify and bring together potential car poolers; surcharges on parking spaces in urban areas to force people for economic reasons to look to alternative means of transportation; state inspection and maintenance systems; requirements that older cars be retrofitted with devices to reduce emissions; requirements for improvements of mass transit systems; and finally, where achievement of the standards could not be reliably predicted, gas rationing to whatever extent necessary to reduce vehicle miles traveled in the problem areas. 27/

It soon became clear that the states and the general public were not ready to support such pervasive measures that intruded into almost all areas of public activity, even though reducing vehicle miles traveled was clearly necessary for reaching air quality goals and also consistent with other national needs during the energy crisis of 1974. The significant public support for air pollution controls quickly faded when it became apparent that improved air quality could only come about with restrictions on automobiles, essential elements of many Americans' lifestyles. Congress reacted to the public mood and, in connection with energy legislation, 28/ adopted provisions of law that deferred any EPA regulations regarding parking management. It also revoked EPA's authority to impose parking surcharges. The need for TCPs to achieve the NAAQS for automobile-generated pollutants in urban areas has not gone away. Although

---

27/   A good example of a comprehensive TCP is the one first proposed for Boston, 38 FR 30960, 8 November 1973. This plan contains virtually every measure which EPA believed feasible to reduce car use. Other TCPs contained these types of measures plus gas rationing.

28/   The "Energy Supply and Environmental Coordination Act of 1974," PL 93-319, 22 June 1974.

the debate on TCPs has been allowed to die down, it will surface again with the revised SIPs for nonattainment areas. Even with a 1987 deadline, some TCP measures are likely to have to be adopted. It remains to be seen whether the public attitude has become more accepting toward restrictions on their freedom to use automobiles.

4.1.4 Maintenance of Ambient Air Quality Standards

The Act requires that SIPs assure maintenance of NAAQSs as well as attainment of them. While EPA's regulations governing SIP content required states to take account of projected growth in developing their plans, most SIPs submitted to EPA in 1972 reflected the lack of time and expertise necessary to include provisions for future growth.

An environmental group challenged EPA's approvals of the plans on this ground and EPA conceded that its one required mechanism for assisting maintenance efforts—preconstruction review of new and modified stationary sources—was not sufficiently comprehensive to enable SIPs to maintain NAAQS after attainment is achieved. In 1974, EPA added requirements that the plans include provisions for long-term maintenance measures and for review of indirect sources. EPA required states to identify those areas which had the potential for exceeding a NAAQS within ten years, called Air Quality Maintenance Areas (AQMAs). Once such AQMAs are designated, states must submit SIP provisions that will maintain the NAAQS for a period of ten years. Ideally, the state would consider the expected and/or desired growth and determine what limitations should be established to ensure the needed air quality. While review of new sources on a case-by-case basis in itself can prevent an ambient standard from being exceeded, without planning it necessarily operates on a first-come, first-served basis. The ten-year maintenance plans were designed to avoid this. As a practical matter, however, such maintenance plans are designed to alert the state to the possibility of violations occurring because of growth in the area and to establish a procedure whereby the state will respond to that threat with appropriate SIP revisions.

While the air quality maintenance plan requirements remain in effect and are specifically referred to in the 1977 Amendments to Section 110(a)(2)(B), state resources in the SIP area will in all likelihood be devoted to the development of plan revisions incorporating measures for prevention of significant deterioration and for attainment in current nonattainment areas, rather than implementing the maintenance requirements.

4.1.5 Indirect Source Review

As part of the settlement of a lawsuit with the Natural Resources Defense Council, EPA extended its new source review requirements to so-called "complex" or "indirect" sources. 29/ Certain sources, such as shopping centers, highways or sports arenas, do not emit pollutants in significant quantities but attract automobiles which can cause high pollutant concentrations. Accordingly, to ensure maintenance of certain standards, e.g., carbon monoxide (CO), it is appropriate to prevent facilities which attract sources of that pollutant from being built in certain areas, or to require them to be designed in such a way that vehicle concentrations will not cause the ambient standard for CO to be violated.

Basically, the regulations required review in larger cities of new facilities that would provide parking for 1000 or more cars, for increases of 500 parking places in existing facilities, and for a new highway that within ten years would be expected to be used by 20,000 vehicles per day. Outside of the larger cities, the triggering numbers were larger. The regulations also covered the construction or modification of new airports.

The reaction was immediate and strong. Commercial interests, primarily developers of large shopping centers, united in an all-out effort to resist this expansion of regulatory authority. Their arguments were strengthened by the fact that the "problem" was created by the automobile, a pollution source over which their new regulators, viz., EPA, had control.

In response to criticism of the indirect source program generated by shopping center and other commercial interests, Congress included in EPA's appropriation bill for several years a restriction on the use of any funds to enforce parking management regulations. In the 1977 Amendments, Congress barred EPA from engaging in any indirect source review, except for federally-funded highways and airports, but reserved to the states the right to have indirect source programs in their SIPs.

4.1.6 Variances

Historically, the chief regulatory means by which states postponed the requirement that a source comply with applicable requirements was by the granting of a variance. One of the first issues

---

29/   40 CFR 52.21, 25 February 1974.

litigated under the 1970 Act was whether and to what extent a state could allow variances to requirements included as part of an approved SIP.

EPA took the position that a variance could be approved so long as it would not interfere with attainment of the NAAQS. If interference with the standards was shown, the source had to proceed under Section 110(f) of the Act, which involved a lengthy formal hearing process.

The Natural Resources Defense Council challenged this approach, claiming that all variances to regulations included in a SIP had to be issued by means of Section 110(f). After seven United States courts of appeals arrived at three different views as to the legality of EPA's interpretation of the Act, the Supreme Court heard the case and decided in favor of EPA's position. 30/

The outcome of the debate is that states may grant a variance which can be approved by EPA as a revision to the SIP if the source's emissions will not interfere with attainment or maintenance of the NAAQS. However, many major sources will not be able to meet this test. The handling of major noncomplying sources is currently through enforcement actions, either federally under Section 113 of the Act, or by the states. The 1977 Amendments placed significant new restraints on EPA's administrative handling of noncomplying sources, but allowed issuance of delayed compliance orders to sources if several requirements were met.

4.2 New Source Review in Nonattainment Areas

Section 110(a)(2)(D) requires SIPs to include a program for preconstruction review of new or modified stationary sources to ensure that such sources will not interfere with attainment or maintenance of NAAQS. After the date for achievement of the ambient standards passed, it became difficult to justify allowing construction of any new facilities in light of this mandate; any new facility emitting a pollutant for which NAAQS were violated would obviously "interfere" with attainment. To prevent a "no growth" situation in such areas, EPA issued the offset ruling on 21 December 1976, indicating how it interpreted this section. 31/ The primary conditions imposed before a new source could be constructed was that a

---

30/   Train v. NRDC, 421 U.S. 60 (1975).

31/   41 FR 55524-30.

reduction in emissions (an offset) be obtained from existing sources, whether owned by the applicant or not, which would not otherwise have occurred and which would provide a more than one-for-one offset to the emissions from the new or modified facility.

This offset policy also required the source to install the Best Available Control Technology (BACT), which was generally new source performance standards, because it was seeking to locate in an area with serious air pollution problems. The policy was controversial because it brought attention to the inherent conflict between achievement of air quality goals and economic growth. Yet, ironically, the offset policy strained the language of the Act and was adopted by EPA in an effort to prevent the Act from imposing more drastic curtailment on growth.

Despite the initial success of the offset policy, EPA felt strongly that Congress needed to address directly the growth issue in the Act. After adopting a very limited scheme for dealing with growth in the 1976 Amendments, which never became law, Congress approached the issue with a comprehensive program in the 1977 Amendments. This program, set forth in Sections 171-178, was the major dividend in the legislative delay from 1976 to 1977.

The 1977 Amendments adopted the EPA offset policy as a starting point, except that the baseline for determining offsets is the applicable SIP rather than the "reasonably available control technology" test in the EPA regulations. EPA was to apply its offset policy until states adopt revised SIP provisions incorporating a preconstruction review program as set forth in Section 172. EPA revised its offset policy on 16 January 1979, 32/ to reflect the changes made by the Congress in the 1977 Amendments. That policy will be effective until 1 July 1979, when state procedures are required to be in place. The policy continues to apply to new sources, or modifications to existing sources, with the potential to emit more than one-hundred tons of a pollutant. The policy also continues to apply in newly-discovered nonattainment areas until a state has submitted a required nonattainment plan or the deadline for submission has passed and a construction ban becomes effective. In another significant change, EPA authorized states to allow the "banking" of emissions offsets; this will allow a source that reduces emissions, beyond that necessary under the SIP, to save the

_____

32/   44 FR 3274, et seq.

emission reductions as offsets against future expansion. Such an approach may give rise to the first marketing of "pollution rights."

The statutory program required by Section 172 to be included in all SIPs for areas not achieving NAAQS must provide for a permit program for all new or modified sources with the potential (design capacity) to emit one hundred tons or more per year of a given pollutant. The preconstruction review is to determine whether the source will be in compliance with applicable SIP requirements and will meet the specific requirements applicable to nonattainment areas.

The definition of "source" for purposes of determining new source review in nonattainment areas was made narrower than the definition for PSD areas due to concern that the Agency should review more sources in areas that were not achieving the standards. EPA, therefore, defined source to include even a single piece of process equipment, which minimized opportunities for intra-source offsets. 33/ In order to allow more flexibility to sources in nonattainment areas to utilize the bubble approach to compliance, EPA, on 14 October 1981, revised the nonattainment requirements to employ the same definition of "source" as in PSD areas in essence defining source as an entire plant. 34/ That decision was overturned in NRDC v. Gorsuch, 35/   The court held that EPA's decision was inconsistent with the nonattainment requirements of the statute and with the court's previous decision in Asarco, Inc. v. EPA 36/ where the court held that a bubble concept is impermissible when the Congressional objective was improvement, rather than simple preservation, of existing air quality. However, the Supreme Court reversed the D.C. Circuit decision and upheld EPA's authority to define source as an entire industrial plant in nonattainment areas. 37/

In addition to the procedural review, these sources must be controlled to a level reflecting the Lowest Achievable Emission

---

33/   45 FR 52746, 7 August 1980.

34/   47 FR 50766.

35/   17 ERC 1825 (D.C. Cir. 1982).

36/   578 F. 2d 319 (D.C. Cir. 1978).

37/   467 U.S. 1984.

Rate (LAER), which is a defined term meaning the most stringent emission standard in any SIP (unless it is shown to be unachievable) or the lowest emissions any source in the same category has achieved in practice. A new source cannot receive a permit unless other sources owned or operated by the applicant in the state are meeting all applicable emission limits or at least meeting all compliance schedule steps. For a source to satisy the statutory requirement that after it starts operation there will be "reasonable further progress" towards achievement of the NAAQS that is being violated, it must obtain permanent enforceable emission reductions at its own facilities or from other sources, or the revised SIP must include provisions that curtail other sources so that allowances for growth have been built into the control strategy.

If a state fails to meet these requirements, there can be serious consequences for growth in nonattainment areas. Section 110 was amended in 1977 to require that unless a SIP meets the nonattainment requirements of the Act, "no major stationary source shall be constructed or modified" in the area if it will emit the non-attaining pollutant. 38/ This provision was meant to spur states toward the kind of planning and strategy development that effective air quality management demands. There is very little time for the planning and regulatory processes to be accomplished, however.

In addition to the prohibition on new facilities, if states do not adopt adequate revisions to SIPs to implement the nonattainment requirements, there are other sanctions built into the nonattainment program. States can lose federal highway funds if transportation control measures would be necessary for attainment. 39/ A state's failure to implement its SIP after the same date will subject it to cutoff of EPA Clean Air Act grants. 40/ Finally, the entire federal government is directed by Section 176(c) not to fund, approve, license or permit any activity that is inconsistent with an applicable SIP.

38/   Section 110(a)(2)(I).

39/   Section 176(a).

40/   Section 176(b).

4.3 Prevention of Significant Deterioration (PSD)

On 5 December 1974, EPA promulgated regulations designed to prevent significant deterioration of air quality in areas of the country where ambient standards are already being met. 41/ The Sierra Club had challenged EPA's determination that it had no authority to regulate in this area on the grounds that the Section 101(b)(1) statement of purpose indicated the Act was to "protect and enhance" the quality of the nation's air resources, and the Act should not allow the air in pristine areas to be polluted, even up to the levels of the relatively stringent secondary standards. In litigation which reached the Supreme Court, Sierra Club won its case when the Court divided 4 to 4. 42/ This had the effect of affirming the lower court decisions, holding not only that EPA had such authority but also was required to issue implementing regulations.

From its proposed regulation on 16 July 1973, through public hearings, reproposals, meetings with states and citizen groups and the expenditure of enormous amounts of internal resources to develop the final regulations, EPA attempted to strike a balance between a sound environmental principle, and the difficulties in its implementation. Without any Congressional guidance, the EPA struggled to develop a system that would satisfy the court yet not stop all growth in clean air areas.

EPA's final regulations were immediately the subject of litigation, both by environmental groups, which considered the regulations inadequate, and by other interests, which considered the regulations more stringent than necessary. EPA's regulations allowed state and local governments to determine what degradation would be "significant" in terms of local conditions. Specifically, the regulations provided for three types of areas with certain "increments" of additional pollution allowed in each. Class I areas were those in which the increments of permissible deterioration were so

---

41/   30 FR 42510.

42/   In Sierra Club v. Ruckelshaus, 344 F. Supp. 253 (D.D.C. 1972), affirmed sub nom. Fri v. Sierra Club, 412 U.S. 541 (1973), the District Court enjoined EPA from approving portions of state implementation plans that did not provide for prevention of any significant deterioration of air quality in those regions that have air cleaner than the secondary ambient air quality standards.

low that they effectively precluded any substantial growth. The increments for Class II areas were designed to allow moderate, controlled growth in these areas; all areas in the country were initially classified as Class II. The Class III areas allowed additional pollution up to the secondary standard. The only pollutants covered by the regulations were SO_2 and particulate matter.

On 2 August 1976, the United States Court of Appeals for the District of Columbia Circuit upheld the regulations in their entirety. 43/ The Supreme Court agreed to review the case but, before briefs were filed, Congress adopted the 1977 Amendments which included a specific national policy to prevent significant deterioration and detailed how that policy is to be implemented.

What Congress did was to expand upon the approach taken in EPA's initial regulations. The classes of areas have now been Congressionally established, with certain national parks categorized as Class I and the rest of the country classified as Class II. The limited amounts of additional pollution that will be allowed in each area are set forth in Section 163, and are more restrictive than EPA's regulations. Although only increments for SO_2 and particulates are established in the statute, EPA was directed to develop increments for other pollutants within two years from the date of enactment of the 1977 Amendments. EPA has not yet taken any action or increments for other pollutants. A preconstruction review is required for any source in one of twenty-eight specified categories with the potential to emit more than 100 tons per year of any pollutant, or any other source that has the potential to emit 250 tons per year. In addition to not exceeding the increments, these new sources must use Best Available Control Technology (BACT), which is to be determined on a case-by-case basis (although nothing less stringent than NSPS will be allowed); BACT must be met for all pollutants regulated by the Act, not just NAAQS pollutants.

Consistency with the increments is predicted by use of diffusion modeling applied to a baseline, which is the concentration of the pollutant at issue on the date of the first application for a PSD permit in the area. Proposed sources are required to conduct monitoring to assist EPA or the state in identifying baseline concentrations.

43/   Sierra Club, et al. v. EPA, 540 F.2d 1114 (D.C. Cir. 1976).

States and Indian governing bodies are permitted to reclassify the Class II areas if they follow detailed procedural requirements which emphasize public involvement, consideration of competing interests, and the approval of local governing bodies. Certain federal lands may not be reclassified to Class III.

EPA promulgated regulations specifying application of the new statutory PSD requirements on 19 June 1978. 44/ EPA's regulations were challenged by environmental groups and various industries. They were upheld in part but remanded in part by the United States Court of Appeals for the District of Columbia Circuit. 45/ EPA then made a substantial change in its regulations and published a new round of final regulations on 7 August 1980. 46/ These regulations were also challenged by various parties and a settlement agreement is in the process of being implemented. 47/

The PSD program is administered primarily through review of new sources and modifications to existing sources. Each state implementation plan is to have provisions that require review of such sources. Where they do not, EPA administers a permit system, established in 40 CFR Section 52.21. A source will have to undergo new source review if it is a major emitting facility and it has the "potential to emit" more than 100 tons of any pollutant regulated by the Clean Air Act, not just SO_2 or particulates. (The amount is 250 tons for sources other than the twenty-eight specific categories, noted above.) "Potential to emit" means the maximum design capacity of the source after application of pollution controls. For a modification to undergo review, it must be a modification of an existing major stationary source which creates a "significant net increase" in emissions of a pollutant regulated under the Clean Air Act. The Alabama Power decision required EPA to define "significant net increase" for each pollutant, which EPA has done. 48/

44/   43 FR 26380, et seq.

45/   Alabama Power Company v. Costle, 13 ERC 1993 (D.C. Cir. 1980); see also, 13 ERC 1225.

46/   45 FR 52676, et seq.

47/   See e.g., proposed revisions at 48 FR 38745, 25 August 1983.

48/   40 CFR Section 52.21(b)(23).

Fugitive emissions will not be calculated in determining potential to emit unless a source category is specifically designated by EPA by regulation. EPA has done so for the twenty-eight listed categories of sources. 49/

In determining the "source" to which the regulations apply, EPA will examine the largest grouping of pollutant-emitting activities located on contiguous or adjacent properties which are under the control of the same person and within the same SIC code major group. 50/ The definition of source is important because new source review applies only to a net increase in emissions from the source. If emissions can be reduced at other locations within the source to levels below 100 tons, new source review may be avoided. Thus, the larger number of emitting activities which constitute the source, the greater the possibilities for offsets.

If a source is subject to new source review, it will have to make several demonstrations before it will be allowed to construct. First, it must show that it will not cause a violation of NAAQS. Second, it must show that any emission of particulates or SO_2 will not cause a violation of the statutory PSD increments. Third, it must show that it will employ Best Available Control Technology (BACT) at the facility. This is defined in Section 165(a)(4) of the Act as a case-by-case determination of the maximum emission reduction achievable by the facility for each pollutant regulated by the Clean Air Act, taking into consideration cost, energy, non-air environmental impacts, and other factors. BACT cannot be less stringent than NSPS. Design, equipment and operational standards or work practices may be mandated as part of BACT. It is important to note that even though the PSD program has focused on particulates and SO_2, it is a much broader program and is designed to minimize increases in pollutant loadings of all pollutants regulated by the Act to preserve air quality as well as provide maximum room for future growth. For this reason, BACT is required for each pollutant emitted by the source in greater than de minimus amounts, (as defined by EPA) once it is determined that BACT applies.

Under the 1977 Amendments' scheme, public hearings are required on applications for permits. An applicant must make a

---

49/   40 CFR Section 52.21(i)(4)(vii).

50/   40 CFR Section 52.21(b)(6).

technical showing on the effect of the proposed source's emissions on visibility and vegetation and describe any general growth in the area which may result from the source's existence. These requirements, and the BACT and air quality monitoring requirements discussed above, are certain to mean that the PSD permit process will be more lengthy now than under EPA's 1974 regulations. Congress recognized this and extended the ninety-day period for permit approval to one year.

The comprehensive preconstruction review programs developed for nonattainment areas and PSD areas mean that all major new source construction, or modifications to existing sources, will undergo careful scrutiny. Because air quality will be either better or worse than NAAQS in all areas, the source will be subject to one or the other of these reviews for every pollutant for which there is an NAAQS, and may be subject to both reviews. In addition to the review for impact on ambient air concentrations, the new or modified source will have to install minimum levels of control equipment based on available technology rather than ambient air considerations. New source performance standards are no longer the most stringent technological standards that may be applied, although they remain the minimum level of control in both situations. Finally, despite EPA's and the states' efforts to administer these programs with flexibility and awareness of the need for economic growth, the opportunities for opponents of projects to delay or thwart construction projects are significant. Moreover, it is the limited "increments" that control allowable growth in PSD areas, not NAAQS, and the air resources available for new construction can be quickly used up. Careful planning for new facilities with a healthy respect for the significance of these provisions is essential for companies planning expansion.

4.4 Energy Related Authority

4.4.1 Conversions to Coal

Due to the problems the country experienced in the 1974 energy crises, amendments to the Clean Air Act were enacted as part of the Energy Supply and Environmental Coordination Act of 1974 (ESECA). 51/ This was part of a Congressional program to

---

51/ PL 93-319, June 22, 1974.

convert major consumers of fuel to burning coal rather than oil or natural gas.

Under Section 119 of the amended Clean Air Act, the Administrator was given authority to extend the date for final compliance in the applicable SIP for sources ordered by the Federal Energy Administration (FEA) to convert to coal on a long-term basis, if the coal available to the source was not of sufficient quality to result in prompt compliance with the SIP. The Administrator was to impose conditions to ensure that the NAAQS would not be violated and to place the source on an enforceable schedule to comply with the applicable emission limitation as soon as possible.

Section 119 of ESECA has now been rescinded and coal conversions are ordered at the direction of the Department of Energy pursuant to the Powerplant and Industrial Fuel Use Act of 1978 (PL 95-260). Exemptions from such conversion orders are available where environmental requirements, including those imposed by the Clean Air Act, would be violated.

The 1977 Amendments transferred the Clean Air Act program for coal conversions to the enforcement provisions of the Act. A new Section 113(d)(5) authorized EPA to issue orders which allow converting sources to delay compliance with applicable SIP emission limits until the end of 1980. The order can be extended for five additional years for a source that cannot comply by 1980.

4.4.2 Energy Emergency Provisions

In the 1977 Amendments, Congress for the first time provided states with a process for suspending SIP requirements when energy is in extremely short supply. This authority, a new Section 110(f), was used in seven states in the winter of 1977-78 when the coal miners' strike caused a virtual halt to supplies of Eastern coal.

To emphasize the gravity it attached to cutbacks in pollution control, the Congress required that the President declare a regional energy emergency before any suspensions of control requirements may be issued to fuel-burning sources. After this declaration, a governor may issue source-by-source suspensions if energy shortages in a source's vicinity are causing serious unemployment or threatening residential heating. These suspensions may last up to four months unless the President sets a shorter term for his declaration or unless the Administrator of EPA determines that the governor's findings were erroneous.

5.0 National Stationary Source Emission Standards

The Clean Air Act provides authority for nationally applicable emission standards that are imposed regardless of the quality of ambient air in the particular location where the source is located. New Source Performance Standards (NSPS) under Section 111 are technology-based while National Emission Standards for Hazardous Air Pollutants (NESHAP) under Section 112 are based on health protection.

5.1 New Source Performance Standards (NSPS)

Section 111 authorizes the Administrator to identify those sources which "...contribute significantly to air pollution which causes or contributes to the endangerment of the public health or welfare." For such sources, he is to set emission standards applicable to the new sources of the types identified, as well as to modifications of existing sources of that type. The standards are to be at levels which the Administrator determines are based on the "degree of emission reduction achievable" through the best technology the Administrator determines has been "adequately demonstrated." In making such a determination, the Administrator is to take into account the cost of meeting the standards and to find that the costs are not unreasonable.

As originally conceived, the NSPS provision had two purposes. First, it reflected the Congressional view that new plants had the greatest flexibility to be designed to incorporate the latest, most effective pollution control technology. Second, it expressed a policy of requiring the same degree of control on all new sources in a particular category regardless of where they are located, thereby preventing states from adopting more lenient air pollution requirements than other states and creating "pollution havens" as a means of attracting industry. The NSPS also conserve air resources for future growth.

With the development of the programs to prevent significant deterioration and for nonattainment areas, the purposes of NSPS have changed substantially. In many cases, NSPS may be only a point of departure for determining BACT or LAER for a new source—although NSPS will always apply as a ceiling on emissions in those determinations.

The importance that Congress continues to attach to NSPS was emphasized by the 1977 Act's requirement that, within one year after enactment, EPA must list all major stationary source categories for which NSPS have not been established and must set NSPS for those categories over the following four years. States were given the right to petition EPA to include additional source categories on the list and to revise NSPS when improved control technologies are developed. The NSPS apply to any new facility or modification of an existing facility that commence construction after the date of <u>proposal</u> of the NSPS.

The most controversial amendment to Section 111 in the 1977 Amendments requires EPA to set NSPS for fossil-fuel burning sources, including electric utility plants, that would require a percentage reduction of the pollutants which would have been emitted had the fuel been burned without emission controls. Precombustion removal of pollutants, mainly sulfur, may be credited toward the reduction requirement. This provision would require flue gas desulfurization (scrubbers) or other technology to be installed in all cases. The requirement is intended to discourage sources from switching to low-sulfur Western coals from high-sulfur Eastern and Midwestern coals and make use of the high-sulfur coal desirable. EPA's NSPS for power plants were revised on 11 June 1979 <u>52</u>/ and challenged by both industry and environmental groups. EPA's implementation of the percentage reduction requirement was upheld, including EPA's decision to establish different percentage reduction requirements depending upon the sulfur content of the fuel being burned. (The required percentage reduction varied between 70 percent and 90 percent.) <u>53</u>/

In response to repeated requests from EPA, Congress included in Section 111 authority for EPA to set NSPS as design, equipment, work practice or operational standards where numerical emission limitations would be infeasible. EPA must allow alternative control methods if they are equally effective, and must revise the NSPS to numerical limits if it becomes feasible to do so.

A little-noticed but increasingly important part of Section 111 is subsection (d), which requires the states to regulate emissions from <u>existing</u> sources in any source category for which EPA sets an NSPS for new and modified sources. This requirement applies only to pollutants not covered by NAAQS, such as sulfuric acid mist and fluorides. States are now in the process of developing standards for

---

<u>52</u>/   44 FR 33580.

<u>53</u>/   See, <u>Sierra Club v. Costle</u>, 15 ERC 2137 (D.C. Cir. 1981).

those pollutants under control technology guidelines established by EPA. EPA must approve each state's standards or establish its own substitute standards—an approach patterned on the SIPs.

5.2   National Emission Standards for Hazardous Air Pollutants (NESHAP)

The problem of particularly dangerous air pollutants which are not emitted by a sufficiently wide range of sources to justify an NAAQS, and establishment of SIPs, is dealt with by emission standards for hazardous pollutants pursuant to Section 112. The pollutants to be covered by Section 112 are those which ". . .may reasonably be anticipated to result in an increase in mortality, or an increase in serious irreversible, or incapaciting reversible illness." In the Senate Report on the 1970 Amendments, a number of such substances were identified as candidates for control under this section. Asbestos, beryllium and mercury standards were promulgated on 6 April 1973 for the most significant source categories. 54/ On 21 October 1976, standards were established for vinyl chloride emissions from plastics industry plants. EPA has also listed benzene, radionuclides and arsenic, and has developed NESHAPs for some sources of these pollutants. Listing of coke oven emissions, cadmium, and acrylonitrite as well as several other pollutants, is under consideration.

The criteria for establishing NESHAPs are that they be set at a level adequate to protect the public health with an ample margin of safety; the Act does not specifically authorize the Administrator to consider costs or availability of control technology.

In reality, EPA does review the costs involved and the availability of technology to control emissions to the desired level. EPA gives less consideration to those factors than in other regulatory decisions under the Act, but absent an overwhelming health hazard, EPA will be reluctant to shut down an industry by requiring zero emissions. In cases of cancer-causing pollutants, only a zero-emissions level would reduce the risk of the pollutant to a level adequate to protect public health with an ample margin of safety. To achieve zero emissions, a plant would have to be closed, a decision that is politically and economically unpalatable, and may not even be justified by the risk to public health.

54/   40 CFR Part 61.

NESHAPs apply to existing as well as new sources. The latter must comply at the time of commencement of operations. Existing sources, however, may delay compliance for a period of up to two years.

Enforcement of the asbestos standard presents a significant problem. Because of the impossibility of measuring asbestos at the site of emissions, the standards for spraying asbestos and for demolition of buildings containing asbestos insulation are written as prohibitions or specifications of work practices rather than numerical emission limits. The standards were challenged in enforcement proceedings on the grounds that only numerical emission standards are authorized by Section 112. The Supreme Court ultimately ruled that work practices were not authorized by Section 112. 55/

Prior to the Supreme Court's decision, the 1977 Amendments revised Section 112 to authorize the EPA to set design, equipment, work practice or operational standards where numerical emission limits would not be practicable, such as in the case of asbestos. Nevertheless, in the Adamo decision, both the majority (five Justices) and minority (four Justices) took the unusual approach of appearing to look ahead to the new amendment and find a technical flaw that may make enforcement under that authority difficult or impossible.

Much of EPA's difficulty in administering Section 112 flows from its inflexible terms. Standards are to be established which provide "an ample margin of safety" and there is no express authority to take into consideration economic and technological feasibility. Many people argue that there is no threshhold level for carcinogens and exposure of any amount could potentially produce cancer. Therefore, as noted above, if implemented literally, Section 112 could require zero emissions of suspect carcinogens. In 1979, EPA floated a proposed policy for regulation of airborne carcinogens which would take into consideration the risk presented in determining whether standards more rigorous than best available technology (which included considerations of economic and technological feasibility) were necessary. 56/ The policy produced substantial comment but no real agreement on the most feasible approach. EPA and

---

55/   Adamo Wrecking Co. v. United States, 98 S. Ct. 566 (1977).

56/   44 FR 58642, 10 October 1979.

the Congress are still searching for a regulatory approach that would protect against the major risks presented by airborne carcinogens, that will not result in unreasonable adverse economic impacts.

Because EPA has promulgated such a limited number of NESHAPs, EPA has received substantial criticism from the environmental community and Congress. Several legislative proposals have been made which would require EPA to make final decisions on approximately forty pollutants, primarily suspect carcinogens, over a several year period. Failure of EPA to act, under some proposals, would result in the pollutant automatically being listed as a matter of law and force EPA to set standards. The 99th Congress will undoubtedly address this issue as part of its consideration of the Clean Air Act.

6.0 Information Gathering Authority

Any agency charged with responsibility for carrying out or overseeing important regulatory programs must have commensurate authority to obtain the information relevant to those programs. In Section 114 of the 1970 Act, Congress gave EPA broad powers to obtain information necessary to the development and enforcement of standards and other regulations for the programs under Title I of the Act, especially Sections 110 through 113 and 120. This authority includes the ability for EPA to require a source owner to test the source's emissions, to enter the premises of the source to emission test, or to inspect aspects of the source's operations relevant to its emissions. EPA may also require source owners to maintain records and submit reports regarding their emissions and controls. EPA's authority to obtain information was upheld as constitutional. 57/

Although the Supreme Court's decision overturning the Occupational Safety and Health Administration's warrantless searches in Marshall v. Barlow's, Inc., 58/ arguably could have affected EPA's authority, the Agency as a general policy has adopted the practice of obtaining search warrants where voluntary inspection is refused.

7.0 Enforcement Authority

The Act sets forth a relatively simple procedure for federal enforcement of applicable implementation plans and other specified

---

57/ U.S. v. Tivian Laboratories, Inc., 12 ERC 1568 (1st Cir. 1978).

58/ 98 S.Ct. 1816 (1978).

requirements of the Act. 59/ Where EPA finds a violation, it issues a "Notice of Violation" through the appropriate EPA regional office. The Notice describes the specific violation and is sent to the alleged violator, as well as to any appropriate state or local control agency. If the violation continues for more than thirty days after the notice issues, EPA may either commence a civil action (for an injunction) or issue an administrative order to the source. Under the 1970 Act, EPA's practice was to issue orders with final compliance dates beyond the date for attainment of the standards, provided the schedule was as expeditious as practicable. EPA's lenient approach led to more stringent requirements for administrative orders in the 1977 Amendments, as discussed below.

Notices of violation are not required where EPA finds violations of NSPS, hazardous emission standards, or certain reporting requirements. In these cases, the Administrator may immediately issue an administrative order or bring an appropriate civil action. The absence of a notice of violation requirement here makes it relatively clear that notice in the SIP context is designed not to assist the violator but to give the state an opportunity to begin the action instead of EPA.

Section 113 also provides that where the Administrator finds that violations in a state are so widespread that it appears the state generally is failing to enforce its plan, he may so notify the state and initiate a period of federally assumed enforcement. This period continues until the Administrator determines that the state has resumed the needed enforcement activities. The EPA has not yet had occasion to implement this portion of the section, but it does enforce the implementation plans which it promulgates.

Paragraph (c) of Section 113 authorizes criminal penalties for "knowing" violations of the law. Violations which (1) occur during a period of federally assumed enforcement, (2) occur more than thirty days after receipt of a Notice of Violation or (3) consist of a failure to comply with an order issued by the Administrator are considered to be "knowing" violations. In addition, persons who knowingly violate the New Source Performance Standards of Section 111 or the Hazardous Emission Standards of Section 112 are subject to the criminal sanction.

59/ Section 113(a).

For the "knowing" offenses, the law authorizes a fine of not more than $25,000 per day and/or imprisonment for up to one year. For subsequent convictions, the sanctions are doubled. In Section 113(c)(2), a $10,000 fine and/or imprisonment for up to six months is authorized for the making of false statements or tampering with monitoring devices required by the Act.

At the request of EPA, Congress included in the 1977 Amendments authority to seek from a court civil penalties up to $25,000 per day of violation. Civil penalties were attractive to the Agency because a court can consider them outside the complexities of a criminal trial.

7.1 Compliance Orders and Noncompliance Penalties

The 1977 Amendments made two major changes in enforcement practices of EPA. Expressing dissatisfaction with EPA's practice of avoiding the strict deadlines of the Act through enforcement orders, Congress provided that the Administrator cannot authorize noncompliance through enforcement orders except pursuant to the Delayed Compliance Order (DCO) procedures of Section 113(d). 60/ Such DCOs may be issued only until 1 July 1979, or three years from the date the SIP requires compliance. In addition, the orders must meet several other requirements, including containing a schedule and time table for compliance. Public participation in the issuance of the DCO is required. Although a DCO will insulate a source from further enforcement actions under the Act, it will not, except in limited circumstances, excuse the source from payment of noncompliance penalties under Section 120, discussed below. Certain sources using innovative technology or subject to coal conversion orders may be given additional time for compliance. This restriction on EPA's authority to issue enforcement orders, coupled with the directive in Section 113(b) requiring the Administrator to bring civil actions against major stationary source violators, means there will be increased emphasis on litigation including consent decrees to enforce the Clean Air Act.

The second major change in enforcement strategy under the Act was the adoption of Section 120 which provides for fines to be paid by noncomplying sources. The fines are designed to eliminate the economic advantage of noncompliance. Section 120 is the first

---

60/   Section 110(i).

attempt by Congress to build into a major regulatory program a scheme wherein economic disincentives are to be used to complement a traditional standards-based regulatory structure. The section's fundamental policy is to recover as a penalty any economic costs a source owner or operator may be avoiding by not making the capital outlays or operation and maintenance expenditures that would be necessary to comply with an SIP or Section 111 or Section 112 standards.

Although the noncompliance penalty program was heralded as being an effective alternative to traditional enforcement systems, interest in the program has slackened considerably. Congress declined to include a similar provision in the Clean Water Act Amendments of 1977. EPA's regulations 61/ became effective on 27 October 1980. Upon notification by EPA that penalties are being assessed under the regulations, the source is to compute its own fine based upon a complex computer analysis which is made part of the regulations. This analysis requires information from the company on approximately fifteen different variables, including capital cost, debt service, and operation and maintenance expenses. The complexity of the process, however, has proved to be a deterrent and EPA has considered using it in only a very limited number of situations. Future use of the procedure also appears limited.

Any major source which in the future is covered by a SIP for the first time, or has a major new requirement imposed, would have three years from the imposition of the requirement before noncompliance penalties would apply.

8.0 Emergency Authority

As is the case with most public health protection statutes, the Clean Air Act recognizes that on occasion the normal regulatory procedures may be inadequate and that extraordinary measures may have to be taken to protect public health. For this purpose, the Act's Section 303 authorizes the Adminstrator to seek a federal court order directing any type of air pollution source to stop emitting, or to take other appropriate action, when he finds that air pollution is "presenting an imminent and substantial endangerment to the health of persons." The 1977 Amendments added authority to issue a short-term administrative order to begin abatement actions while a lawsuit is being prepared.

61/   40 CFR Part 66.

This authority, designed principally to deal with air pollution episodes occurring when stagnant meteorological conditions prevent normal dispersion of pollutants by the wind, has been invoked only once, in Birmingham, Alabama. However, EPA personnel have been ready in several other cities when episodes have occurred to take necessary legal action if the state or local agency response proved inadequate.

9.0 Ozone Protection

In 1975, scientists began to announce the results of studies on depletion of the ozone layer in the stratosphere. Ozone, which is part of the photochemical oxidants complex and injurious to human health when breathed, is essential to screen out harmful ultraviolet radiation that can cause skin cancers and reduced crop yields at excessive exposures.

The chemical agents implicated in the ozone depletion phenomena are the halogenated compounds known as "halocarbons." Though stable in the lower atmosphere, scientists believe they become unstable in sunlight in the atmosphere and react with ozone, forming new compounds, thereby depleting the ozone available for screening. These halocarbons are in widespread use, as aerosol propellants, refrigerants, and foaming agents, and are released in the atmosphere when aerosol-packaged products are used and through leakage or destruction of refrigeration equipment.

Congress became concerned in 1976 that the available data showed that slow but predictable ozone layer depletion was probably occurring. The Toxic Substances Control Act (TSCA), passed that year, included regulatory authority broad enough to allow EPA to deal with halocarbons. Nevertheless, the 1977 Amendments to the Clean Air Act added a new regulatory scheme designed specifically for the regulation of halocarbons, and required numerous federal agencies to participate in a study of the problems, culminating in a report to Congress two years after the enactment of the Amendments.

The regulatory approach prescribed in the new Sections 150-159 is relatively simple, as contrasted with the complex scientific questions involved. The Administrator may issue regulations controlling halocarbons or "any substance, practice, process, or activity" that affects the stratosphere, if the effect "may reasonably be anticipated to endanger public health or welfare." Any regulatory activity is to be deferred until after the report mentioned above is filed, unless EPA obtains information before that time which would be sufficient to make the required findings about effects on the stratosphere and risks to health or welfare.

Before the 1977 Amendments became law, EPA and other federal agencies had already begun regulating halocarbon use as an aerosol propellant. EPA used its authority under TSCA. Congress provided in the Amendments that this activity should go on without interference, but made it clear that future regulation should be under the Clean Air Act scheme.

10.0 Motor Vehicle Emission Control

10.1 Introduction

Since 1965, the federal government has had authority to set emission standards applicable to new motor vehicles and engines. Standards are to be set for pollutants which the Administrator determines ". . .cause, or contribute to, air pollution which may reasonably be anticipated to endanger public health and welfare." Limitations on emissions of hydrocarbons and carbon monoxide were applied to the 1968 model year vehicles and all subsequent model years. An emission standard for oxides of nitrogen went into effect beginning with 1973.

10.2 Statutory Standards and Suspension

With the knowledge that motor vehicle pollutants constituted the single most difficult air pollution problem facing the nation, and noting the limited progress in abating it, Congress in 1970 took the unusual step of actually prescribing the standards to be applied in order to attain and maintain air quality protective of health in urban areas heavily impacted by automobile pollution. The law 62/ required a 90 percent reduction of hydrocarbons and carbon monoxide from allowable emissions in 1970, and a 90 percent reduction in nitrogen oxides emissions from levels measured from 1971 model year vehicles. The 90 percent reductions in HC and CO were to be achieved in 1975, and the NO_x reductions in 1976. In each case, the Administrator was permitted to suspend for one additional year the 90 percent reduction requirements if he found, after public hearing, that the needed technology was not available. In addition, the manufacturer applying for the suspension must have made good faith efforts to meet the standards.

62/ Section 202(a)(1) and (2).

Manufacturers applied for the suspension of the 1975 standards at the first opportunity, viz., January 1972. After evaluation of the extensive written and oral information submitted, EPA determined that the manufacturers had failed to prove that technology was not available, and accordingly denied the one-year suspension. The manufacturers took their case to the United States Court of Appeals. The Court assessed in detail the technical and policy aspects of the problem, 63/ and found that EPA had not adequately supported its conclusion that the standards could be met. Specifically, EPA had not adequately considered whether the available technology, catalytic mufflers, would be available in sufficient quantities to meet market demands.

Subsequent to the decision, EPA held new hearings and granted a suspension. Then, in accordance with the statutory mandate, EPA set interim standards which (although not equal to the 90 percent reduction desired by Congress) were quite stringent.

With the passage of the Energy Supply and Environmental Coordination Act in 1974, Congress re-examined the statutory standards and determined, for fuel conservation purposes, to set back its stringent hydrocarbon and CO standards to model year 1977. Nitrogen oxides standards were also postponed one year. In both cases, an opportunity for a one-year suspension was again provided.

Acting under that authority, in March 1975, the Administrator suspended the standards, based on his determination that the automobile manufacturers' proposed use of catalytic emission controls with air pumps to meet the stringent standards posed a risk of creating high sulfuric acid emissions and that the suspension would provide time to analyze the possible severity of such risk. With the suspension, the Administrator issued interim standards preserving the existing standards for model year 1977.

The biggest controversy that developed during Congress' consideration of the 1977 Amendments was the automobile emission standards and the timetable for implementing them. Congress took up where it had left off in 1970. There was little question that Congress would set the standards and not leave the job to EPA; the debates focused heavily on fuel economy consequences of different sets of standards, particularly standards for oxides of nitrogen.

63/ International Harvester v. Ruckelshaus, 478 F.2d 615 (D.C. Cir. 1973).

What emerged from these often heated discussions was basically another postponement of what were once the 1975 statutory standards. The hydrocarbon standard was set back to model year 1980; the carbon monoxide level deferred to 1981 with the potential of an administrative suspension for two more years. Only for oxides of nitrogen was there a significant loosening of the stringent number originally set for the 1976 models. Section 202 now prescribes a 1.0 grams per vehicle mile standard beginning in model year 1981, although this can be relaxed slightly by EPA for an innovative technology or for diesel-powered automobiles. In 1985, Congress will probably again consider relaxation and postponement of the statutory standards.

In the 1977 Amendments, Congress for the first time took charge of standard setting for heavy duty vehicles, i.e., larger trucks, a field they had previously left to EPA's discretion. EPA was left with the authority to substitute standards reflecting what the best available technology can achieve, if the statutory standards prove infeasible.

Probably the most interesting aspect of the Amendments' treatment of heavy duty vehicles is the provision in Section 206(g) for a "nonconformance penalty." This would allow trucks to be certified and sold if they did not exceed the standard by more than a margin set by EPA, if the manufacturer paid a nonconformance penalty. The penalties would be set by EPA so as to remove any competitive advantage (probably through lower fuel use) that trucks not meeting the standards might have, and EPA would have to increase the penalties "periodically." This scheme is the second instance in the Act where an economic incentive program has been added to complement the traditional regulatory scheme.

10.3 Certification

Under the Clean Air Act, no manufacturer may introduce vehicles subject to emission standards into commerce, unless they have been certified by EPA to conform to the standards. 64/ The certification procedure consists of a lengthy test on prototype vehicles. Most of these tests are conducted by a manufacturer at its own facility, but a few are sent to EPA's laboratory at Ann Arbor,

---

64/   Section 203 sets forth the "prohibited acts" under Title II of the Clean Air Act, Emission Standards for Moving Sources.

Michigan for confirmatory testing. A limited number of cars are run to 50,000 miles and their emissions tested periodically to determine the durability of the vehicles' emission controls. A "deterioration factor" is determined by observation of the increase in emissions from the 4,000 mile test to the 50,000 mile test. This factor is then applied to a single test on a somewhat larger group of the same "family" of cars. This procedure indicates whether or not a prototype vehicle has been designed to meet the standards for the useful life of the vehicle. 65/

If the tests are successful, a certificate of conformity covering that type of engine/vehicle combination is issued. The manufacturer is then free to begin producing cars built the same as the certified prototypes. Certification demonstrates that the manufacturer can build a vehicle capable of meeting the standards, but tests on vehicles in ordinary use have shown that emissions typically do not meet the standards.

10.4 Compliance by Production Vehicles

Certification verifies the capability of prototype to comply with the applicable emission standards, but provides little assurance that production vehicles will comply either at the time of their manufacture or thereafter, when operated and maintained by their owners. At the time Congress was considering the 1970 Act, it was presented with data showing significant failure of compliance by vehicles in use, and decided to adopt measures to enable EPA and the vehicle owners to ensure vehicles' compliance throughout their useful life.

The provisions adopted required compliance by vehicles through a "useful life" of five years or 50,000 miles, required manufacturers to warrant against defects and that vehicles would comply for the useful life period, authorized EPA to require manufacturers to recall vehicles found not to comply for the specified period, and authorized EPA to test production vehicles on the assembly line and to revoke the certificate conformity as to any noncomplying vehicle. Unfortunately, subsequent studies of in use vehicles do not indicate that the durability of the emission controls has significantly increased.

65/   Section 206, 40 CFR Part 86.

10.4.1 Assembly Line Testing

Section 207(b) authorizes the Administrator to conduct assembly line testing of new vehicles. If, based on such tests, he determines that certain vehicles do not conform to the regulations, he can suspend or revoke the certificate of conformity covering the class of vehicles, until such time as the manufacturer has corrected the deficiency. The manufacturer is entitled to a hearing on the determination by the Administrator, and may appeal to the United States Court of Appeals if the final administrative decision goes against him.

The absence of a "short" test for assembly line cars has, until recently, precluded EPA from implementing this section. However, the Agency has developed an assembly line testing program called Selective Enforcement Audit (SEA). 66/ This program uses the lengthy federal test procedure, but only on limited numbers of production vehicles.

Very briefly, SEA functions as follows: EPA orders a manufacturer to conduct tests on a relatively small number of cars chosen at random on the assembly line. If those tests indicate that the cars are meeting standards, the program with respect to that line of vehicles terminates. If, however, the tests indicate that there is a question about compliance, the size of the sample would be increased and testing would continue. A sufficient number of vehicles will be tested to support a valid judgment as to the status of the entire class of cars. If the judgment is that the class is not meeting the standards, the certificate of conformity is revoked, and no vehicles covered by that certificate may be marketed.

10.4.2 Warranties

The Act's imposition of statutory warranties was perhaps a "first" in the history of regulatory legislation. It represents an attempt to make the regulated industry directly responsible to the people who purchase its products.

Section 207(a) requires the manufacturer to warrant to the owner that the vehicle is designed, built, and equipped to conform at the time of sale with applicable standards, and that it is free from

---

66/ The Selective Enforcement Audit Program was promulgated on 28 July 1976, 41 FR 31472.

defects in materials and workmanship which would cause noncompliance. Both of these warranties carry with them rather substantial problems of proof for the owner, and have not proved to be effective remedies.

A potentially more important check on emissions is under Section 207(b), which requires a manufacturer to warrant that the vehicle will perform in compliance with the applicable standards for its useful life. The section predicates implementation of the warranty on the development of a short test which would correlate with the lengthy test used at the certification stage and which could be carried out expeditiously at state, local, or federal testing stations. The certification test covers various modes of operation, and it has only recently been possible to make significant progress toward developing a correlating short test.

When this obstacle is overcome, the performance warranty can be implemented, but even then it is conditioned by the statute to be applicable only if (1) the vehicle was maintained and operated in accordance with the maintenance instructions supplied to the owner by the manufacturer, and (2) the nonconformity resulted in the owner having to bear a penalty or sanction. If these requirements are satisfied, the manufacturer must, at no cost to the purchaser, bring the car back into conformity. What the section means is that even with the short test, manufacturers will not have to fix cars at their expense, until such time as state or local inspection programs are in place. Only a few of these programs are underway.

10.4.3 Recall

Section 207(c) gives the Administrator authority to order manufacturers to recall and repair or modify groups of vehicles which exceed the emission standards when in actual use. The manufacturer has the right to a hearing for the purpose of contesting EPA's finding that his vehicles do not meet standards. These are formal hearings before an Administrative Law Judge.

EPA has required several manufacturers to recall thousands of automobiles for failure to meet the standards to which they were certified. Generally, the needed repair or replacement was readily identifiable. One recall order has been contested through the hearing appeal route.

10.4.4 Vehicle Inspection

The 1970 Act evidenced a great deal of Congressional enthusiasm for motor vehicle inspection and maintenance programs (I + M programs). The Act (Section 210) authorized federal grants to states to encourage their development, required that state implementation plans include them where necessary, and made the Section 207(b) performance warranty dependent on their existence.

This emphasis is understandable, since it is widely believed that a properly designed and operated I & M program, that includes requirements for necessary maintenance on noncomplying cars, is one of the most cost-effective means of holding automobile emissions in check. Development of these programs has been very slow, however, largely because of inadequate funding and lack of public support.

EPA's attempts, as part of the transportation control plans, to require states to adopt and carry out inspection and maintenance programs, were challenged in court by virtually every affected state. The several United States courts of appeals which considered these challenges took different positions on the legality of the requirements, and the Supreme Court refused to issue a decision because of a technical problem with EPA's regulation imposing the requirement.

The 1977 Amendments mandate vehicle inspection and maintenance for areas that cannot meet NAAQS for motor vehicle-related pollutants by the end of 1982. It does not appear that Congress has become less convinced of the merit of this type of program, but it has allowed states the possibility of more time to accept the idea and develop programs suited to their needs. Failure to adopt or implement an I + M program in an area subject to these nonattainment requirements can result in a cutoff of certain federal funds, including highway monies.

10.5 Enforcement

Enforcement of the motor vehicle regulatory program is exclusively through the courts. The Act provides for injunctive relief to stop violations (Section 204) and for civil penalties of up to $10,000 per violation per vehicle (Section 205). A few large civil penalties have been imposed on manufacturers in violation.

11.0 Fuel and Fuel Additive Provisions

11.1 Registration

The Congress expressed its concern about the possible harmful effects of the byproducts of fuel additives, which are so widely used in gasoline, by including in the 1967 Act a requirement that fuel additives be registered with the government for purposes of gathering information about their composition and combinations. This program, which was quite limited and not implemented until regulations were issued in 1970, was broadened considerably in Section 211 of the 1970 Act. The registration requirement was extended to fuels as well as additives, and additional provisions authorized EPA to require information on the products and byproducts of the combustion of fuels and additives, as well as on their effects on health, welfare, and motor vehicle emission control systems. Congress' purpose was to enable EPA to make judgments which might lead to regulation under the Act or point to the need for further legislation.

Regulations implementing the revised registration program were issued in November 1975, 67/ and the registrations are made by the filing of the required information by the manufacturers involved. Largely because of EPA's failure to develop test protocols, however, very little analysis has been done by fuel or additive manufacturers or EPA on the fuel and additives registered, or their combustion byproducts. The 1977 Act includes amendments to Section 211 that attempt to expedite the gathering of information on possible health or welfare effects or effects on emission control systems. Testing was made a prerequisite to registration (and, therefore, marketing), and currently registered products must be tested within four years.

EPA's authority is not without limits, however. The use of additives in motor oil was held to be outside the scope of Section 211. 68/

11.2 Regulatory Authority

The law authorizes two approaches to the control or prohibition of automobile fuels and fuel additives. Under Section 211(c)(1)(B), the Administrator is authorized to regulate the manufacture or sale of motor vehicle fuels or additives, if he finds that products of the additives will impair, to a significant degree, the performance of an existing or proposed emission control device.

67/   40 CFR Part 79, 40 FR 52009.

68/   Lubrizol Corp. v. EPA, 562 F. 2d 807 (D.C. Cir. 1977).

EPA determined that in order to attempt to meet the stringent 1975 standards, automobile manufacturers primarily intended to rely on the catalytic converter—a device which is "poisoned," i.e., rendered ineffective, by lead. As a result of this finding, the Agency promulgated regulations, 69/ which require that there be one grade of unleaded gasoline generally available throughout the country at the larger gasoline stations. 70/

Because lead-free gasoline production uses more crude oil to increase the octane of the fuel to meet minimum car requirements, there was pressure on EPA to defer the 1979 deadline for meeting the 0.5 grams per gallon limit to conserve dwindling supplies of crude oil. EPA's decision to bar use of MMT, a partial substitute for lead as a fuel additive, has also been criticized. Political and practical problems of fuel supply coupled with increasing regulation of stationary sources of lead in SIPs may produce some relaxation on control of fuel additives.

In paragraph (A) of Section 211(c)(1), the Administrator is also given authority to control the use of fuel additives, if he finds they will "endanger the public health or welfare." EPA determined that lead emitted from automobiles as a result of the use of leaded gasoline posed an endangerment to public health, particularly among urban children. On 6 December 1973, 71/ EPA adopted regulations that required the gradual phasing down of the amount of lead used in leaded gasoline. The schedule called for a maximum of 1.7 grams per gallon on 1 January 1975, and then reduced annually the allowable amount to 0.5 grams per gallon by 1979.

The controversy over whether or not lead emitted from motor vehicles affects human health was and is a heated one. The regulations were challenged in the United States Court of Appeals for the District of Columbia, which set aside the regulations. However, upon EPA's motion, the Court of Appeals agreed to have all nine members of the Court consider the case. A final decision upholding

---

69/   40 CFR Part 80.

70/   In addition to various labeling requirements, the Part 80 regulations require that the unleaded gasoline be dispensed from a special nozzle, and that cars with catalytic converters have gasoline inlets designed to mate with the special nozzles.

71/   40 CFR 80.20.

the regulations was issued in March 1976. 72/ Enforcement of the regulations was reinstated after the Supreme Court declined to review the case.

Small refineries (50,000 barrels per day of gasoline or less) owned by small refiners (total capacity of 137,500 barrels per day of gasoline or less) were provided additional time to meet the 0.5 grams per gallon standard. In Section 211(g) of the Act, Congress determined that these smaller firms might have greater difficulty in raising capital or making other necessary capital investments and should be given until 1982, a three-year extension, to meet the standards. Those facilities were required to meet interim levels based upon a statutory scale depending on their size. EPA regulations implementing Section 211(g) were promulgated 7 August 1979. 73/

In response to requests by small refiners and other firms (including lead manufacturers) affected by the lead phasedown regulations, EPA requested comment in early 1982 on whether the final lead phasedown requirement should be retained or other adjustments made in the requirements. A number of firms argued that the natural reduction in leaded gasoline production due to the market demand for unleaded gasoline makes a mandatory restriction on lead usage unnecessary. Small refiners argued that final compliance with the requirement was not necessary for public health reasons and would impose unreasonable adverse economic effects on small refineries. Modifications to the lead phasedown regulations were one of the recommendations of the Vice President's Task Force on Regulatory Reform.

EPA's request for public comment produced a large number of comments from environmental groups, the affected industry, and other interested parties. After considering the comments, EPA withdrew its February proposal and reproposed changes to the regulations. 74/ Based on the earlier comments, EPA determined that there was a continuing need for regulation of lead as a fuel additive on public health grounds. EPA determined that it would make the

---

72/ Ethel Corp. v. EPA, 541 F. 2d 1 (D.C. Cir. 1976), cert. denied, 426 U.S. 941.

73/ 44 FR 53146, 40 CFR Section 80.20(b).

74/ 47 FR 38070, et seq., 27 August 1982.

requirement more stringent by establishing a 1.10 gram per gallon standard for leaded gasoline only. 75/ EPA determined that by 1990 the leaded gasoline restriction would result in approximately 34 percent greater lead reduction than the existing standard. Final regulations were promulgated on 29 October 1982. 76/

With respect to small refineries, although EPA had proposed to allow them an alternative, higher lead standard, EPA determined after considering comments submitted that small refineries should also be required to meet the 1.1 grams per leaded gallon standard. EPA found that concerns for public health and the disruption of competition within the refining industry caused by a dual standard justified its requiring all facilities to meet the same requirement. EPA did grant an approximately eight-month extension of time for compliance. The final regulations became effective 1 November 1982, and were substantially upheld by the D.C. Circuit in 1983, Small Refiner Lead Phase-Down Task Force v. Gorsuch.

12.0 Aircraft Emission Control

Section 231 empowers the Administrator to establish emission standards for aircraft and aircraft engines, following the regulatory pattern set forth in Section 202(a) for motor vehicles. Before setting standards, EPA was required to conduct a study of the effects of aircraft emission on air quality and the technological feasibility of controls.

As a result of the study, EPA concluded that although aircraft emissions did not have major impact throughout AQCRs they were significant contributors to high concentrations in and around airport sites, because of their ground operations as well as takeoffs and landings. Accordingly, EPA established emission standards for most classes of new aircraft and aircraft engines and for the most significant emitters among existing aircraft and engines. 77/

75/ With the 0.5 gpg total gasoline production average, the actual lead content of leaded gasoline would be much higher depending on the percentage of unleaded and leaded gasoline produced by the individual refinery; unleaded gasoline is limited by EPA regulations to .05 grams per gallon.

76/ 47 FR 49322, et seq.

77/ 40 CFR Part 87.

These standards, which can be issued only if the Secretary of Transportation agrees that they do not create safety problems, are required by the Act to be enforced by the Department of Transportation, which has issued regulations for that purpose.

13.0 Citizens Suits

Congress was aware of the immense task of policing regulations applicable to thousands of sources, as well as the historical apparent lack of enthusiasm on the part of the enforcers; in 1970 it offered the public opportunity to assist in the process through citizen suits. Section 304 of the Act authorizes two types of suits by citizens. Under Section 304(a)(1), a person may sue any other person, including the United States government or other political jurisdictions, alleged to be in violation of emission standards or limitations, or enforcement orders issued by the Administrator or a state. In short, Section 304 is designed to make the Act enforceable in federal district courts by anyone with the interest and resources to do so.

Information concerning violations should be readily available to interested citizens. Section 110(a)(2)(f) requires that sources periodically report emission data to the state, and that such reports must be available to the public. Section 114, which authorizes the Administrator to inspect sources and require reports, specifically exempts "emission data" 78/ from information which might be withheld from the public on the grounds that it constitutes a trade secret. Again, in Section 208, emission data on motor vehicles is excluded from restrictions which might otherwise allow it to be withheld from public disclosure.

The 1977 Act expanded the jurisdiction of the federal district courts to hear citizens suits. Citizens can now sue to enforce most of the major requirements imposed under the Act, as opposed to just emission standards and limitations. The Act does not specifically authorize citizens to seek penalties or damages.

While citizen suits against polluters are beginning to be an increasing factor in enforcement of the Act, paragraph (a)(2) of Section 304 has already had an enormous impact. Under this authority, citizens are authorized to bring actions against the Administrator of EPA, ". . . where there is alleged a failure. . . to perform

---

78/   Section 114(c).

any act or duty under this Act which is not discretionary . . ." In those few words, Congress established a mechanism by which the judicial branch of the government would, if asked, oversee a portion of EPA's implementation of the law.

It was a citizen suit in California 79/ which forced EPA to propose a transportation control plan for the South Coast Basin which included a provision requiring in excess of 80 percent gas rationing. It was under the citizen suit provision that the Sierra Club successfully litigated the issue of prevention of significant deterioration. There are other examples where suits under this section have forced the Agency to act at a time, and sometimes in a manner, it would not have chosen of its own accord.

Citizens are required to give sixty days notice, before bringing a Section 304 suit, to the Administrator of EPA, the state and the violator. If EPA or the state is diligently prosecuting an enforcement action against the violator, the citizen may intervene in the litigation.

14.0 Judicial Review

Because of the importance and the controversial nature of most of EPA's regulatory decisions implementing the Clean Air Act, many decisions are challenged in court by environmentalists, by industry or both. Court decisions have played a crucial role in determining the direction of EPA's implementation of the Act as well as ensuring that an adequate technical case has been made by EPA for regulation.

Courts often view their role as one of partnership with EPA in developing the law and procedures implementing this significant legislation and actively grapple with the difficult policy issues EPA faces when attempting to regulate in an area where scientific knowledge is still uncertain. 80/ Consequently, Section 307(b) of the Act is a key element in the overall implementation of the statute. To expedite the reaching of final decisions on EPA's regulations, in view of the short statutory deadlines, Congress provided for direct review of most regulations in the United States courts of appeals and required that challenges be brought within certain time limits.

79/ City of Riverside v. Ruckelshaus, 4 ERC 1728 (C.D. Cal. 1972).

80/ E.g., Ethel Corp. v. EPA, supra.

The 1970 Act required persons who wished to challenge an Agency action to file a petition for review in the appropriate court of appeals within thirty days after the action was taken. The courts have upheld this time limit on judicial review by dismissing late petitions. In the 1977 Amendments, Congress lengthened the deadline to sixty days. Congress also endorsed the absolute cutoff that bars attacks on a regulation as a defense in an enforcement action, if the issue could have been raised in the court of appeals. The 1977 Act also ratified a court's decision that, in order to get judicial review after the deadline, a person must petition the Agency and demonstrate that information is available which was not available when the EPA action was being developed.

In the review by the court, a three judge panel of the court examines the record compiled by the Agency in the course of taking the action, to determine whether the action was arbitrary or capricious. This "arbitrary, capricious" test, experience has shown, can be the basis of an extremely searching inquiry into all facets of an EPA decision; it can be the basis for substitution by the judges of their judgments for those made by the Agency or it can support a quite superficial inquiry into the Agency's rationale. Courts have taken all of these approaches in the many decisions issued since the passage of the 1970 Act.

The court's review also includes a determination about whether the Agency's action exceeded its authority under the Act and whether proper procedures were followed in taking the action.

The Congress provided in the 1977 Amendments that EPA actions of national applicability and effect are to be reviewed in the Court of Appeals for the District of Columbia Circuit. This provision codified a growing body of judicial decisions and is important to EPA because issues often cannot be settled for years if petitioners may obtain review in a number of the twelve courts of appeals. Differences among the circuits are not unusual, and the only solution is United States Supreme Court review, which is always a lengthy process.

15.0 Acid Rain

One of the most controversial issues that is not dealt with directly by the Clean Air Act is the problem of acid deposition or "acid rain." For some time there has been growing evidence that lakes and streams, primarily in the northeast portion of the United States and in Canada are becoming more acidic causing a reduction, or in some cases total elimination, of fish and other life in those bodies of water. Acid deposition is also suspected of reducing forest productivity. Many people believe that the increasing acidity is due to long-range atmospheric transport of sulfur emissions, principally from power plants in the Midwest. The sulfur dioxide is carried by winds until the sulfur precipitates as sulfates in the rain where it causes adverse effects to the land and water. There is, however, intense scientific and political debate over the causes of acid rain, the contribution of power plants, and the appropriate methods for addressing the problem, (e.g., reduction in sulfur emissions or treatment of lakes and land to neutralize the acid). A ten-year study of acid rain was authorized by the Congress under the auspices of the National Academy of Science.

Although the 1977 Amendments to the Clean Air Act do provide for some redress for air pollution caused by out-of-state sources (Section 126), the statute was not drafted with a pollution problem such as acid rain in mind. Rather, the Act is premised on state-by-state control strategies for individual sources and the identification of specific sources which contribute to a particular pollution problem that results in a violation of a NAAQS, a PSD increment or visibility requirements. EPA has generally held that it lacks authority under the Act to address the acid rain problem directly.

The National Commission on Air Quality recommended increased authority for EPA to regulate long-range transport and recommended that there be a significant reduction by 1990 in sulfur dioxide emissions. Canada has also pressed vigorously for control of power plant emissions by the federal government. A number of proposals have been considered by the Congress to address acid rain. These range from stepped-up research to major regulatory programs. One of the most comprehensive statutory proposals would require specific reductions, (e.g., ten million tons of sulfur dioxide) from sources, primarily power plants, within thirty-one eastern states. The exact form of increased authority for EPA to address the problem of acid rain has been and will continue to be hotly contested. Due to the strong political and public pressure for action on this issue, it is quite likely that the next substantive amendments to the Clean Air Act will contain some provision on acid rain.

Chapter 7

WATER POLLUTION CONTROL

J. Gordon Arbuckle and Timothy A. Vanderver, Jr. 1/
Attorneys
Patton, Boggs & Blow
Washington, D.C.

1.0 Introduction—The Historical Perspective

In 1972, Congress put the basic framework for federal water pollution control regulation in place by enacting the Federal Water Pollution Control Act, which was significantly modified in 1977 to deal with toxic water pollutants, and renamed the Clean Water Act.

The Act has five main elements: a permit program, a system of minimum national effluent standards for each industry, water quality standards, provisions for special problems such as toxic chemicals and oil spills, and a construction grant program for publicly-owned treatment works (POTWs).

Some history makes these program elements more understandable, and puts a detailed discussion of pollution control programs into perspective. Prior to 1970, standards were generally set by the states for pollutant parameters for various water bodies. Although this approach was theoretically attractive, it worked badly in most states. Major problems included:

1/ The authors want to thank Russell V. Randle, Esq., for his assistance in making numerous revisions to this edition of the Water Pollution Control chapter.

— Inability to determine with precision when a
discharge violated applicable standards;

— Inapplicability of federal-state water quality
standards to intrastate waters;

— Lack of state initiative in making load allocations
required to set enforceable discharge standards; and

— Cumbersome enforcement mechanisms and the
requirement for state consent for federal
enforcement.

Although a few states made the water quality approach work,
it was clear by 1970 that an effective nationwide approach would
require implementation of a permit program based on federal minimum "end-of-pipe" effluent criteria enforceable directly against the
discharger.

When legislation proposed in 1969 to provide this mechanism
failed to pass, and when courts and citizens groups "discovered" that
the Refuse Act penalized discharges of pollutants which had not
been approved by the Army Corps of Engineers and allowed citizens
to bring actions to enforce those penalties, the Nixon Administration
initiated the Refuse Act permit program in late 1970. 2/

The Refuse Act is an archaic 1899 statute designed to protect
navigation. It does, however, prohibit all discharges into navigable
waters or tributaries thereof unless a permit is obtained from the
Corps of Engineers prior to commencing the discharge. By using this
authority to require all industrial dischargers to apply for and obtain
permits, the granting or denial of which would be based on environmental factors, the administration was able, for the first time, to
pose a credible threat of prosecution. Hundreds of cases were initiated under the Refuse Act.

The Refuse Act was not drafted as a comprehensive water
pollution control statute.   Consequently, the permit program
encountered severe problems:

— The Act provided no standards for the grant or
denial of permits, nor were any regulations
promulgated to provide such standards;

2/   33 U.S.C. § 407.

— As a result of a court decision, <u>Kalur v. Resor</u>, 3/ environmental impact statements had to be prepared for every permit decision, further taxing the inadequate staff in charge of processing the applications;

— Penalties under the Act were thought by many to be inadequate;

— The relationship of the Act to other federal and state water pollution control efforts was unclear, and created considerable confusion.

By late 1971, it was evident that comprehensive water pollution control legislation was a prerequisite for a workable control program.

In late 1972, Congress finally passed, over President Nixon's veto, a comprehensive recodification and revision of federal water pollution control law. The 1972 Act, Public Law 92-500, 4/ made the Environmental Protection Agency (EPA) responsible for setting effluent standards on an industry-by-industry basis and required such standards to be based on the capabilities and costs of pollution control technologies. EPA had to meet a stringent timetable for setting these standards.

The Act continued requirements for water quality standards so that more stringent discharge standards could be imposed where effluent standards were insufficient to assure that the quality of receiving waters did not deteriorate to, or remain at, unacceptable levels. States could take over the administration of the permit program when state control programs met rigorous federal standards.

The basic framework of the 1972 Act—the permit program, national effluent limitations, water quality standards, special provisions for oil spills and toxic substances, and a POTW construction grant program—proved reasonably sound and remains so today. Congress significantly amended the Act in 1977 in an effort to deal more effectively with toxic pollutants, and to resolve numerous definitional and policy issues raised by court and EPA decisions. The Act was revised again in 1978 to deal with spills of hazardous

---

3/   335 F. Supp. 1 (D.D.C. 1971).

4/   33 U.S.C. § 1251 et seq.

substances and in 1980 and 1981 to change certain aspects of the construction grant program for POTWs.

2.0 Federal-State Water Pollution Control Program—Overview

The regulatory program established under the Clean Water Act, as amended, has two basic elements—a statement of goals and objectives and a system of regulatory mechanisms calculated to achieve those goals and objectives.

2.1 Goals and Objectives

The Act's stated objective (Section 101) is to "restore and maintain the chemical, physical and biological integrity of the nation's waters." To achieve that objective, the Act establishes as "national goals":

— Achieving a level of water quality which "provides for the protection and propagation of fish, shellfish, and wildlife" and "for recreation in and on the water" by 1 July 1983; and

— Eliminating the discharge of pollutants into United States waters by 1985.

The "no-discharge" goal was written into early drafts of the 1972 Act in order to encourage the adoption of sewage treatment systems relying on land application of effluent. The "no-discharge" language remained after the legislative emphasis shifted away from land application, in part to encourage the reuse and recycling of industrial process water and chemicals. Even though they are largely unattainable, these national goals are significant factors in determining the stringency of limitations imposed.

2.2 Mechanisms for Achieving These Goals and Objectives

The principal mechanism for achievement of the goals and objectives propounded originally by the 1972 Act is a system for imposing effluent limitations on, or otherwise preventing, discharges of "pollutants" into any "waters of the United States" from any "point source." This system includes five basic elements:

(1) A permit program (the National Pollutant Discharge Elimination System—NPDES) requiring dischargers to disclose the volume and nature of their

discharges, authorizing EPA to specify the limitations to be imposed on such discharges, imposing on dischargers an obligation to monitor and report as to their compliance or non-compliance with the limitations so imposed, and authorizing EPA and citizen enforcement in the event of non-compliance. Citizen enforcement actions have become an important factor in recent years.

(2)   A two-stage system of technology-based effluent limits establishing base-level or minimum treatment required to be achieved by direct industrial dischargers (existing and new sources) and Publicly Owned Treatment Works (POTWs) and a complementary system of pretreatment requirements applicable to dischargers to POTWs. EPA has now set almost all of these standards and the compliance dates for most of them have passed.

(3) A program for imposing more stringent limits in permits where such limits are necessary to achieve water quality standards or objectives.

(4) A set of specific provisions applicable to certain toxic and other pollutant discharges of particular concern or special character (e.g., oil spills, discharges of toxic chemicals, and non-process discharges such as contaminated plant site runoff).

(5) A grant program to fund POTW attainment of the applicable requirements. This grant program has been significantly scaled back as pressures on the federal budget have increased.

The Act is, of course, far more complex than this five-part framework indicates. In order to grasp how the Act applies in concrete situations, it is essential to understand the definitional and policy decisions which translated these broad legislative directives into reality.

3.0   Permitting Under The National Pollutant Discharge Elimination System

The Act's primary mechanism for imposing limitations on pollutant discharges is a nationwide permit program established under Section 402 and referred to as the National Pollutant Discharge Elimination System (NPDES). EPA's present regulations are found at 40 CFR Parts 121-125. This section will consider three basic permit program issues—the program's scope and applicability, the procedures followed in permit issuance, and the nature of the conditions normally included in permits.

3.1 Program Scope and Applicability

Under the NPDES program, any person responsible for the discharge of a pollutant or pollutants into any waters of the United States from any point source must apply for and obtain a permit.

Although the definition of "pollutant" in Section 502(6) of the Act includes only the materials specifically listed in that section 5/ the definition is nevertheless quite broad and has been broadly interpreted to include virtually all waste material, whether or not that material has value at the time it is discharged.

The term "discharge of a pollutant or pollutants" under the Act is defined in Section 502(12) to mean the addition of any pollutant to waters of the United States from any point source. The Act's requirement that there must be an addition of a pollutant in order for an activity to constitute a discharge has been successfully utilized in some situations to preclude the imposition of limitations on the discharge of materials in a waste stream which are present only by reason of presence in intake waters, if the intake water is drawn from the same body of water into which the discharge is made and if the pollutants present in the intake water are not removed by the discharger as part of his usual operations. 6/ The term does not include discharges of water from dams, even if a dam's operations adversely affect the temperature and dissolved oxygen content of the water. 7/

The point source element of the discharge definition has been one of the most difficult aspects of the permit program's implementation process. Section 502(14) of the Act defines the term "point source" to include "any discernible, confined and discrete conveyance, . . . from which pollutants are or may be discharged." The "may be" language is important because it means that permits are

---

5/ Dredged spoil, solid waste, incinerator residue, sewage, garbage, sewage sludge, munitions, chemical wastes, biological materials, radioactive materials, heat, wrecked or discarded equipment, rock, sand, cellar dirt and industrial, municipal, and agricultural waste discharged into water.

6/ See NPDES regulations, § 122.45(h).

7/ National Wildlife Federation v. Gorsuch, 693 F.2d 156 (D.C. Cir. 1982).

required for facilities such as surface waste impoundments from which discharges are not normally anticipated except under unusual but foreseeable conditions such as excessive rainfall. The "discrete conveyance" language of the definition is so comprehensive as to cover a number of types of discharges, such as storm sewers, irrigation flows and the like, which are not really amenable to efficient regulation through the issuance of permits. For this reason, a number of statutory and administrative exemptions from the point source definition or the scope of the permit program have been adopted. These include irrigation return flows, the discharge of sewage from vessels and effluent from properly functioning marine engines, certain agricultural and silvicultural discharges, and certain discharges of dredged or fill material regulated under Section 404 of the Act. Regulations of the Environmental Protection Agency also exclude from the definition of "point source" stormwater discharges which occur outside urbanized areas, provided that the runoff is not from lands or facilities used for industrial or commercial activities.

The term "waters of the United States" is defined by EPA regulations 8/ to include (1) navigable waters; (2) tributaries of navigable waters; (3) interstate waters; and (4) intrastate lakes, rivers and streams (a) used by interstate travelers for recreation and other purposes, or (b) which are a source of fish or shellfish sold in interstate commerce, or (c) which are utilized for industrial purposes by industries engaged in interstate commerce. The intent of this definition is to cover all waters over which the broadest constitutional interpretation would allow the federal government to exercise jurisdiction. 9/ The definition clearly covers wetlands. Few exclusions to the definition have been recognized and those which have been accepted to date seem to be limited to situations where the waterway in question is wholly confined on the property of the discharger, does not result in any flow beyond the property line, and is not available for significant public use.

One remaining major issue is the extent to which discharges to publicly or privately owned sewage systems constitute discharges to waters of the United States so as to be subject to the NPDES permit requirement. It is fairly well accepted that a discharge to a

---

8/   40 CFR § 122.2.

9/   NRDC v. Callaway, 392 F. Supp. 685 (D.D.C. 1975).

sewage system which is not connected to an operable treatment works is a discharge subject to the NPDES program, but that a discharge to a publicly owned treatment works which is capable of meeting its effluent limits is excluded from the NPDES permit requirement. 10/ All industrial dischargers to POTWs are required to comply with general pretreatment standards 11/ and many must also comply with industry-by-industry ("categorical") standards, promulgated together with effluent limitations for each industry. These pretreatment standards, as discussed more fully below, are intended to prevent pollutants produced by industrial dischargers from interfering with POTWs or passing through untreated. There are flexible permit requirements for discharges to privately owned treatment works which give the Environmental Protection Agency substantial discretion to consolidate or issue separate permits as needed to meet effluent standards.

To summarize, though there are important exclusions, the scope of the NPDES permit program is exceedingly broad. The basic intent is to regulate all pollutants discharged from all facilities into virtually all waters in the United States.

3.2   Permitting Procedures

Under Section 402 of the Clean Water Act, the Environmental Protection Agency is the issuing authority for all NPDES permits in a state until such time as the state elects to take over program administration and obtains EPA approval of its program. About three-fourths of the states have approved NPDES programs and function as the issuing authorities for permits in their jurisdictions. Where the state is the issuing authority, permitting procedures are generally comparable to the EPA procedures discussed below, with certain exceptions. For example, the states, unlike EPA, are not required to provide for an evidentiary hearing, though many do. Where the state is the issuing authority, procedures for judicial review of permit issuance are those provided under the state administrative procedure act rather than under the Clean Water Act and the Federal Administrative Procedure Act. State permit issuance is

---

10/   40 CFR § 122.3(c).

11/   40 CFR Part 403.

not a federal action subject to the requirements of the National Environmental Policy Act. 12/

Permits issued by states are subject to review by EPA and a state permit may not be issued if the Administrator of EPA objects within ninety days after the state's proposed issuance. The Administrator must state the reasons in support of his objections and must provide a statement of the limitations and conditions which would be included in the permit if it were to be issued by EPA. States are entitled to a public hearing regarding the Administrator's objections and if the objections are not resolved, at the hearing or otherwise, the Administrator can issue the permit. EPA has the authority to withdraw its approval of a state program and take over the entire program administration if it finds that the state is not carrying out the program in accordance with the requirements of the Act.

Procedures for permit issuance are generally as follows: A permit application, on the appropriate form, must be submitted to the EPA regional administrator (or the state, if it is the issuing authority) at least 180 days in advance of the date on which a proposed discharge is to commence or the expiration of the present permit, as the case may be. Where EPA is the issuing authority, it will require, for new dischargers, submission of a new source questionnaire before it will process the permit application. This questionnaire serves as the basis for an EPA determination as to whether the facility is a "new source." If the facility is determined to be a new source, the applicant will be required to prepare an environmental assessment for EPA's use in determining whether an environmental impact statement is required by the National Environmental Policy Act. 13/

After the application is filed, the district engineer of the Corps of Engineers must be given an opportunity to review the application to evaluate the impact of permit issuance upon anchorage and navigation. Other federal agencies, and specifically the Fish and Wildlife Service of the Department of the Interior and the National Marine Fisheries Service of the Department of Commerce, are provided a similar opportunity to comment on the application.

12/ See Chesapeake Bay Foundation, Inc. v. Virginia State Water Control Bd., 453 F. Supp. 122 (E.D.Va. 1978).

13/ Clean Water Act, § 511(c).

Where EPA is the issuing authority, the state in which the discharge will occur must be provided with an opportunity to review the application. Based on that review, the state is asked to certify, pursuant to Section 401 of the Act, that the permitted discharge will comply with applicable provisions of Sections 301, 302, 303, 306, and 307 of the Act. Since provisions in Sections 301 and 303 deal with the question of compliance with state water quality standards, the state, in effect, is asked to certify that the discharge in question will comply with all limitations necessary to meet water quality standards, treatment standards, or schedules of compliance established pursuant to any state law or regulations.

Although the applicable regulations would appear to require the applicant for an NPDES permit to provide EPA with the required certification, in practice EPA forwards applications received without a certification to the appropriate state and keeps the state advised throughout the permit proceedings. If a state does not either certify or deny certification within a reasonable time after the receipt of the permit application, it will be deemed to have waived the certification requirement. Because this time period starts to run on the state's receipt of an application, it is advisable for the applicant to send a copy of the application to the state rather than waiting for EPA to do so. EPA is barred from issuing any NPDES permit unless the state has either certified the permit or waived its right to certify.

In processing the application, the issuing authority makes tentative determinations as to whether a permit should be issued, and, if so, as to the required effluent limitations, schedules of compliance, monitoring requirements and so forth. These tentative determinations are organized into a draft permit and the discharger is normally given an opportunity to review and comment on this draft. The public is given notice of the permit application proceeding and the issuing authority's preliminary determinations with respect thereto. 14/

The regulations provide for a period of not less than thirty days during which the public may submit written comments and/or

---

14/ If a variance request or other effort to secure relaxation of generally applicable effluent limits is indicated, it is appropriate to submit the request at this point in the proceedings. If this is done, a stay of further action on the permit, pending disposition of the request, would be appropriate.

request that a public hearing be held. The issuing authority is required to hold a public hearing if there is a significant degree of public interest in a proposed permit or group of permits. The public must be notified of such hearings and interested persons must be given at least thirty days in which to prepare for the hearings. Following the public hearing, the issuing authority issues a final determination regarding permit issuance after taking into account the comments received. Where the final determination is substantially unchanged from the tentative determination outlined in the original public notice, the issuing authority must forward a copy of the determination to any person who submitted written comments regarding the permit. Where the issuing authority's decision substantially changes the tentative determinations and draft permit, public notice must be given.

Within thirty days following the date of the notice of final determination, any interested person may request an evidentiary hearing or a legal review to reconsider the determination.

The granting of an evidentiary hearing or legal review stays the effective date of all contested provisions of the permit. 15/ The hearing is an on-the-record quasi-judicial proceeding presided over by an administrative law judge. 16/

The decision reached on the basis of the evidentiary hearing may be appealed to the EPA Administrator. 17/ Where EPA is the issuing authority, the entire permit issuance proceeding, of course, is subject to judicial review under the Administrative Procedure Act. Where the state is the issuing authority, the state administrative procedure act probably governs.

Contested provisions of the permit become effective, and a final permit is issued, upon completion of these review proceedings. The issuance of a permit under the Clean Water Act will be deemed to fulfill the permit requirements of the Refuse Act of 1899, as well as those under the Act itself except for requirements under Section 307(a) covering discharge of toxic pollutants presenting human health risks. It should be noted, however, that issuance of

---

15/ 40 CFR § 124.16(a).

16/ Id., § 124.81.

17/ Id., § 124.91.

a permit does not mean that no further action will be required during the permit term. As the permit makes clear, additional applications must be filed and processed whenever modifications to the facility or method of operation will result in changes to the discharge. Thus, keeping permits up-to-date will often be a continuous endeavor.

3.3   Permit Conditions

An NPDES permit performs two basic functions in the Clean Water Act regulatory process. It establishes with specificity the level of performance which the discharger must maintain and it places on the discharger an affirmative obligation to report to the cognizant authorities when that level of performance is not achieved. Many of the conditions typically included in industrial permits are either negotiable or susceptible to legal attack. Accordingly, proposed permit conditions should not be accepted without question. They should be carefully analyzed and, if inappropriate or unjustified, contested. The more significant permit conditions are discussed below.

Monitoring and Reporting—The monitoring requirements in an NPDES permit are of critical importance. The effectiveness of the permit program in assuring compliance with applicable effluent limitations, water quality standards, pretreatment standards and other requirements established pursuant to the 1972 Act will depend, in major part, on the effectiveness of monitoring and data maintenance requirements included in permits pursuant to Section 308. 18/ Under that section, EPA is authorized to require the owner or operator of any point source to establish and maintain specified records, make specified reports, install, use and maintain monitoring equipment and methods, take specified samples, and provide other information which EPA may reasonably require. As with the permit program in general, the states have the opportunity to administer their own monitoring programs and, upon obtaining EPA's approval of an appropriate monitoring program, the state becomes the monitoring authority for all point sources within its jurisdiction.

18/ POTWs subject to the Act's permit requirements must also impose monitoring requirements on industrial discharges into their facilities.

The enforcing authority will have the right to enter the premises of the discharger at any reasonable time, inspect the records required to be maintained, take test samples and so forth. All data obtained under Section 308 is required to be open to the public except to the extent non-disclosure is necessary to protect trade secrets. This public disclosure requirement is an essential underpinning of the Act's provision for citizen enforcement actions against non-complying dischargers.

The NPDES regulations specify the manner in which effluent limitations are to be included in permits and thus imposed on permittees. 19/ The monitoring requirements in various sections of Part 122 are intended to assure compliance with the limits included in permits. Under these provisions, limits are to be imposed and monitoring is to take place at the point of discharge except in limited situations where monitoring at point of discharge is impracticable or infeasible. The regulations do provide the permit issuer with authority to require monitoring of internal waste streams in certain situations such as where the final discharge point is inaccessible, where wastes at the point of discharge are so diluted as to make monitoring impracticable, or where interference among pollutants at the point of discharge would prevent detection or analysis. A permittee is required to monitor, as specified in his permit, to determine (1) compliance with the limitations on amounts, concentrations or other pollutant measures specified in the permit, (2) the total volume of effluent discharged from each discharge point and (3) otherwise as required by the permit. 20/

The permit must include requirements for maintenance and proper installation of the monitoring equipment, must specify monitoring methods and frequencies adequate to provide reliable data regarding the volume of flow and quantity of pollutants discharged, and must specify the test methodology to be utilized in analyzing the samples taken. The regulations put the burden on the applicant, if he believes that the monitoring requirements specified in a draft permit are inadequate to yield accurate data, to request additional monitoring requirements which are sufficient to achieve an acceptable degree of accuracy. Compliance with the effluent limits set in

---

19/ 40 CFR §§ 122.44, 122.45.

20/ 40 CFR § 122.44(i).

the permit will be assessed through application of the monitoring methods which the permit provides. Thus, unless inadequate monitoring requirements are contested during the permit issuance procedures, it may be difficult to use alleged inadequacy as a defense in any later enforcement action.

Monitoring records, including charts from continuous monitoring devices and calibration and maintenance records, must be maintained for a minimum period of three years, and that period may be extended by request of the permit issuing authority at any time. 21/

The results of monitoring must be reported periodically to the permit issuing authority on forms provided by the authority. Frequency of reporting is governed by the terms of each individual permit and must be at least annual. In addition to the periodic reporting requirement, certain toxic discharges must be reported within twenty-four hours. 22/ Failure to properly monitor and report is a violation of the permit and any person who knowingly makes any false statement in monitoring records, monitoring reports, or compliance or non-compliance notifications is subject upon conviction to substantial fines and criminal penalties, both under the Clean Water Act and under the applicable provisions of the federal criminal code, 18 U.S.C. Section 1001.

It is evident from the foregoing that the monitoring requirements may occupy a considerable amount of employee time, require the installation of sophisticated sampling devices, extensive analysis and testing, and detailed recordkeeping and reporting. Many companies may find it appropriate to develop additional in-house technical capability in order to meet the Section 308 requirements as imposed in the permit.

Schedules of Compliance—Although the Act itself establishes firm deadlines for the achievement of the required levels of treatment, the issuing authority has considerable latitude to require compliance or interim steps towards compliance at earlier dates. The Act also provides mechanisms to extend compliance deadlines in

---

21/ 40 CFR § 122.41(j).

22/ Id., §§ 122.41(e)(6), 122.42(c). The non-compliance reporting requirements are specific and detailed and should be carefully reviewed by all permittees.

limited situations, as where compliance is dependent on connection to a yet-to-be constructed public treatment works or where use of innovative technology is involved. Most of the statutory bases for extensions, however, have now expired.

Effluent Limitations—Where a permit issues prior to the publication of effluent limitations for a particular pollutant or applicable industrial category or subcategory, the determination of the precise effluent limitations to be included in the permit are to be based on "engineering judgment," which is obviously more flexible than published rules. This situation is now most likely to arise as EPA works to promulgate limitations for toxic pollutants, or for facilities for which no specific set of limitations is wholly applicable. Even after promulgation of limitations, the applicant may seek modification of limits in the permit, and there is also considerable opportunity for the permitting authority to impose discharge limitations more stringent than the "base-level" effluent guidelines, where necessary to meet water quality standards, water quality related effluent limitations, the requirements of state planning processes, or other applicable limitations. Thus, there is considerable room for discussion regarding limits to be imposed in permits and a careful engineering analysis of proposed permit limits is a prerequisite to intelligent evaluation and negotiation of permit requirements.

Additional Effluent Limitations—Until recently, NPDES permits normally specified four or five pollutants as being subject to effluent limitations; a far greater number are now included in permits as a result of EPA's toxics strategy, which is discussed below. EPA's NPDES permit application and related regulations (Section 122.21) require extensive waste stream analysis in order to file permit applications, extensive cataloging in the application of virtually all chemicals in the waste stream, and imposition of controls on the discharge of those chemicals. Implementation of these requirements complicates the permit process and requires more extensive monitoring than was true in the past.

Duration and Revocation—Permits may be valid for terms of up to five years, and may be subject to revocation or modification based on a very minimal showing of "cause." A company's interest in connection with the permit process will generally be best served by obtaining a permit with the maximum duration and with as much specificity as is obtainable in regard to the possible grounds of revocation or modification. On the permit's expiration, the permittee, in order to obtain reissuance, must demonstrate compliance with any more stringent criteria which have been promulgated during the term of the original permit. The application for reissuance should be filed well in advance of the existing permit's expiration date.

    Other—Depending on the precise nature of the applicant's operation, consideration might be given to bypass and upset provisions, start-up exclusions and so forth. Those who will be responsible for complying with the permits are well advised to make every reasonable effort to predict potential compliance problems and discuss them fully during the permit issuance process rather than in later enforcement proceedings.

4.0 Establishing the Limitations for Inclusion in the Permit—Technology and Water Quality-Based Limits

    The most difficult questions which EPA has faced in the development of the Clean Water Act program have involved the establishment of limits to be imposed in the permits issued under the NPDES mechanism. As previously noted, the Act contemplates a two-part approach: (1) nationwide base-level treatment to be established through an assessment of what is technologically achievable and (2) more stringent treatment requirements for specific plants where necessary to achieve water quality objectives for the particular body of water into which that plant discharges. While this concept seems simple, its execution requires answers to questions which have proved exceedingly complex:

— What specific pollutants should be addressed in establishing the limitations?

— How can technology-based effluent limits adequately take into account all factors relevant to the question of what is achievable and how can plant-to-plant variability be accommodated?

— What are the mechanics for deciding when more stringent limitations are required to meet water quality objectives and how are the necessary analyses to be performed prior to making permit issuance decisions?

These questions and the process by which they have been answered furnish the subject matter for this section.

4.1 Pollutants to be Addressed

Although the Act broadly defined pollutants subject to regulation and permitting, it furnished little guidance before 1977 with regard to toxic pollutants. For that reason, and because the 1972 Act imposed unrealistic deadlines on EPA's limited staff, EPA focused almost entirely on gross or "conventional" pollutants such as Biochemical Oxygen Demand (BOD), Suspended Solids (SS) and acidity and alkalinity (pH) when it developed the effluent limitations required by the Act. As long as this approach was followed, EPA's basic system of effluent limits and permit requirements failed to deal with the dangers posed by more toxic pollutants such as organic chemicals, heavy metals, pesticides and so forth, and at the same time may have overemphasized removal of solids and oxygen demanding materials contained in conventional wastes. 23/ Regulation of "toxic" pollutants was thought to be the exclusive province of Section 307 (a) of the Act, which authorized EPA to identify and regulate, on a chemical-by-chemical rather than industry-to-industry basis, substances which it could prove to have toxic effects on identified organisms in affected waters.

Because of the stringent burden of proof and extensive procedures which the pre-1977 Section 307 required, EPA failed to establish a workable program to control the discharge of toxic pollutants. Only a limited number of substances were identified as toxic substances; long delays were encountered before final effluent limits were adopted for any of them.

EPA's failure to develop an effective toxics strategy under the 1972 Act led the Natural Resources Defense Council (NRDC), an environmental organization, to sue the Environmental Protection Agency. That litigation was settled, and in the process of settlement, EPA and NRDC developed a policy which focused all of the regulatory mechanisms provided by the 1972 Act upon the effective regulation of toxic or priority pollutant discharges. In developing this policy, the parties identified (1) the pollutants which would be the primary subject of regulation; (2) the industries which would be the primary concern in applying the regulations; and (3) the methods of regulating toxic discharges with the Act's existing legal mechanisms. The agreements reached in these negotiations were embodied

---

23/ It should be noted, however, that conventional treatment frequently, if unintentionally, removes substantial amounts of the more toxic wastes.

in a settlement decree, 24/ and that decree as modified 25/ has become the blueprint for toxics strategy under the Clean Water Act.

The decree mandates full use of all the available regulatory tools under the Act with a specific focus on the identified "priority pollutants." Pursuant to the decree, EPA must develop a program to regulate the discharge of 65 categories of "priority pollutants" (including at least 129 specific chemical substances—see Annex A, at the end of this chapter) by 34 industry categories which include over 700 subcategories. More than 70 percent of the nation's industry are affected by the decree. The 34 industry categories are listed in Annex B.

The consent decree required adoption of best available technology effluent limitations for each priority pollutant in each industrial category by 30 June 1983. These limitations had to be applicable to at least 95 percent of the point sources in each identified industry category or subcategory. Similar technology-oriented requirements had to be adopted for new sources and sources discharging into publicly owned treatment works. The basis for excluding a category of point sources from the toxic-focused system of technology-based effluent limitations is quite limited.

In addition to these stringent new industry-by-industry toxic effluent limits, the consent decree made specific provision for full implementation of the waterway segment-by-segment approach.

The NRDC consent decree provided a judicial mandate for full use of the Water Act's enforcement mechanisms in a carefully tailored effort to reduce discharges of toxic pollutants.

The 1977 Amendments adopted this mandate and enacted it into federal statutory law. The Amendments:

— Adopted the consent decree list of priority pollutants as the list of toxic substances to be given primary emphasis in the implementation of the Water Act (This list of toxic substances is reproduced as Annex A.);

24/   NRDC v. Train, 8 E.R.C. 2120 (D.D.C. 1976).

25/   12 E.R.C. 1833 (D.D.C. 1979).

- Required adoption of best available technology effluent limitations for each listed substance by 1 July 1980, a deadline EPA failed by a substantial margin to meet;

- Required compliance with these BAT effluent limitations by 1 July 1984 (instead of 1 July 1983, as required by the consent decree);

- Permit EPA to add to or remove from the list of "toxic" substances (Although the Act provides no specific criterion for making such additions or deletions, the Conference Committee Report states that a decision by the Administrator to add or remove a substance from the list is final unless it is based on arbitrary and capricious action);

- Require compliance with BAT effluent limitations for toxic pollutants subsequently added to the list within three years of the establishment of the limitations;

- Provide a new system for upgrading and enforcing pretreatment regulations based on both the effluent limitations on the discharge from publicly owned treatment works and the intended use of the sludge from the facilities;

- Authorize EPA to adopt regulations establishing best management practices to control the discharge of the listed pollutants in the form of runoff or other uncontrolled discharges from industrial plant sites, parking lots and so forth;

- Require effluent limitations based on best available technology for other non-conventional pollutants by 1 July 1987; and

- Require the Administrator to publish information related to the factors necessary to maintain fish, shellfish and wildlife in waterway segments.

In short, the 1977 Amendments confirm and institutionalize the consent decree with some modifications.

The 1977 Amendments did not, however, fully replace the consent decree. Instead, that decree has been the primary mechanism by which the toxics program has been modified. The consent decree was amended in 1979 to reflect the changes made by the 1977 Amendments and to respond to the operational problems perceived by EPA since the decree was originally issued in 1976. 26/ The modification also extended the deadlines for the development of technology-based effluent limitations for the thirty-four industrial categories and expanded the permissible bases upon which EPA may exclude substances from regulation pursuant to the consent decree. These deadlines were extended somewhat in May 1982, but the District Court rejected a bid by EPA and various industry groups for extensions of up to thirty months. Pursuant to the deadlines set in the decree, EPA has promulgated final effluent limitations for most of the thirty-four industry categories. Challenges to the consent decree have twice been rejected by the courts. 27/

Under the revised consent decree, the Environmental Protection Agency can exclude industry categories from regulation of certain substances where only "trace amounts" of the substance are found. The Administrator is also authorized to exclude pollutants from coverage under the direct discharge effluent limitations if the amount and toxicity of such pollutants within a category or subcategory does not, in his judgment, justify the development of regulations having nationwide applicability.

The basis for excluding pollutants from the applicability of pretreatment standards was similarly expanded. EPA is authorized to make such exclusions when it finds that the amount and toxicity of all incompatible pollutants discharged by a category or subcategory taken together is so small that regulations of nationwide applicability governing pretreatment of those pollutants is not justified.

In the water quality standards area, the modified consent decree makes more specific the program required for identifying bodies of water which the technology-based effluent limitations are inadequate to protect toxic-related water quality objectives. To date, this portion of the toxics program has had little effect because of EPA's long delays in identifying the affected wastes and developing a control program.

26/ 12 E.R.C. 1833 (D.D.C. 1979).

27/ Environmental Defense Fund v. Costle, 636 F.2d 1229 (D.C. Cir. 1980); Citizens for a Better Environment v. Gorsuch, 718 F.2d 1117 (D.C. Cir. 1983), cert. denied, 104 S. Ct. 2668 (1984).

The consent decree as confirmed by the 1977 Amendments and modified by the court has transformed the entire Clean Water Act program and focused EPA and industry attention on the most dangerous pollutants. The industry-by-industry technology-based effluent limitations have been transformed from limited requirements focused on three or four conventional pollutants to a very specific system of limitations potentially applicable to 129 or more different pollutants for each industry category. Water quality standards will become far more important to industry, although EPA's lengthy delays in this regard have greatly limited the effect of such standards to date.

4.2 Required Level of Treatment—Technology-Based Limits for "Existing" Direct Discharges

Section 301(b) of the 1972 Act provided for the establishment of nationally applicable technology-based effluent limitations on an industry-by-industry basis. These effluent limitations were to establish a nationwide base-level of treatment for existing direct discharge sources in every significant industrial category. This level of treatment was to be achieved in two phases. For "existing" 28/ industrial discharges, Section 301 directs the achievement:

by July 1, 1977, of effluent limitations which will require application of the best practicable control technology currently available, and by July 1, 1983, of effluent limitations which will require application of the best available technology economically achievable.

As the time for achievement of Best Practicable Technology (BPT) is long past, its primary relevance now is as a basis for setting subsequent standards. EPA defined BPT as the "average of the best existing performance by well-operated plants within each industrial category or subcategory." The word "control" in Section 301 emphasized Congress' expectation that, in establishing the 1977 effluent guidelines, EPA would emphasize end-of-pipe treatment

---

28/ The Act's "existing discharge" provisions will in fact apply to some newly constructed facilities since they cover any source for which a new source performance standard (see Part 4.3) has not been proposed.

rather than in-plant control measures. EPA did so. However, Section 304(b)(1) of the Act makes it clear that the alternative of in-plant process changes may be considered, at least for the purpose of determining whether a proposed effluent limitation is "practicable." Under the statute, the word "practicable," was to be read together with the provisions of Section 304(b)(1)(B), and so required that effluent limitations be justifiable in terms of the "total cost of (industry-wide) application of (the required) technology in relation to the effluent reduction benefits to be achieved." This determination was to take into account a number of specific factors such as the age of the equipment and facilities involved, the process employed, and non-water quality environmental impacts. Thus, in developing the BPT limitations, the Environmental Protection Agency was required to make what amounted to a cost-benefit balancing test that took into account a broad range of specific engineering factors relating to the ability of plants within a category or subcategory to achieve the limits. The BPT definition was essentially unchanged by the 1977 Amendments.

EPA defined Best Available Technology (BAT) as the "very best control and treatment measures that have been or are capable of being achieved." The agency can consider in-plant process changes in addition to end-of-pipe treatment measures in establishing these 1983 limitations. Although EPA is required to consider the cost of achieving the required effluent reduction in determining whether a BAT limitation is economically achievable, it is not required to balance cost against effluent reduction benefit as it is in the case of the BPT standards. The engineering factors required to be considered—age of equipment and facility, process employed, process changes, non-water quality environmental impacts and so forth—are the same for BAT as for BPT.

The BAT definition was essentially unchanged by the 1977 Amendments but its scope of applicability was radically altered and its date for attainment was extended until 1984. The BAT effluent limitations now focus primarily on the priority pollutants listed in the NRDC consent decree and on additional toxic pollutants identified pursuant to Section 307(a) of the Act. These new priority and toxic pollutant-oriented best available technology effluent limitations are to be adopted in accordance with a detailed time schedule established by the consent decree as modified and are required to be complied with by 1 July 1984 for the pollutants identified in the consent decree. That date has slipped to as late as 1986 for some industry categories. For pollutants not listed in the consent decree but identified as toxic pollutants under Section 307(a)(1) of the Act, compliance with BAT effluent limits is required no later than three years after the date on which the limitations are established.

The "conventional" pollutant measures, which were the primary focus of EPA's pre-1977 BAT effluent limitations are specifically excluded from the scope of coverage of the BAT limits provided by the 1977 Amendments. Those pollutants are subject to an entirely new treatment standard established for the first time in the 1977 Amendments—Best Conventional Pollutant Control Technology.

The Best Conventional Technology (BCT) effluent limitations are, like the BPT and BAT limitations, to be adopted on an industry-by-industry basis but are to apply for each affected industry only to pollutants which are identified as "conventional." The compliance deadline for the BCT limitations was 1 July 1984. The 1977 Amendments specifically included within the definition of "conventional pollutants" Biological Oxygen Demand (BOD), Suspended Solids (SS), fecal coliform bacteria, and pH. EPA is authorized to include additional pollutants within the conventional pollutants definition, but to date has added only oil and grease to the statutory list of conventional pollutants. The Act specifically excludes heat from the conventional pollutant definition as there are special statutory provisions for thermal discharges. 29/ The BCT limitations were to be adopted by EPA based on a consideration of the reasonableness of the relationship between the cost of attaining a reduction in effluents and the effluent reduction benefits which will result. The cost of providing treatment to comply with these limits was expected by the Congress to be generally comparable to the cost of achieving the secondary treatment limitation for publicly owned treatment works. As with BPT and BAT limits, EPA was required, in adopting Best Conventional Technology effluent limits, to take into consideration factors such as the age of the equipment and facilities involved, the process employed, engineering aspects, process changes and non-water quality environmental impacts (including energy requirements).

The Congress anticipated that EPA, in developing the Best Conventional Technology limits, would conduct a review of the old BAT limits for conventional pollutants and reduce the stringency of

---

29/ Clean Water Act, § 316.

such limits to the extent indicated by the economic justification and cost comparability with secondary treatment requirements of the Best Conventional Technology definition in the 1977 Amendments.

EPA's first effort at developing BCT regulations was reversed because the Agency failed to adequately consider cost-effectiveness in the development of these rules. 30/ EPA then promulgated revised regulations and methodology, which are far less costly than the original rules. In many and perhaps most industry categories, EPA's new methodology resulted in BCT limitations no more stringent than those established for BPT.

The last of the three categories of technology-based effluent limits for existing industry direct discharges which the 1977 Amendments provide is the system of effluent limitations to be adopted for "nonconventional nontoxic" pollutants. This is essentially an "everything else" category which applies to all pollutants other than those identified as priority pollutants, toxic pollutants or conventional pollutants under the preceding sections of Section 301. To date, only about ten substances have been so regulated; most could probably be regulated just as well either as toxic or conventional pollutants. The 1977 Amendments appear to require compliance with best available technology effluent limits to be adopted for these pollutants by 1 July 1984 or three years after the date the limitations are established by EPA regulations, whichever is later, but in no case later than 1 July 1987.

4.3 Required Level of Treatment—Technology-Based Limits for "New Source" Direct Discharges

The establishment of effluent limitations for "new sources" (defined as any facility the construction of which is commenced "after the publication of proposed regulations" prescribing an applicable standard of performance) is separately dealt with in Section 306 of the Act. Although the general approach for establishment of new source performance standards under Section 306 is similar to the approach for the establishment of Section 301 effluent limitations (discussed in the previous section) there are significant differences both as to the level of treatment required and the manner of applying the limitations established. These differences remain important because of EPA's delay in promulgating many BPT and

---

30/ American Paper Institute v. EPA, 660 F.2d 954 (4th Cir. 1981).

BAT limitations, and because the new source standards will govern replacement of certain equipment at an existing discharger. 31/

Section 306(a)(1) of the Act defines the term "standard of performance" as "a standard for the control of the discharge of pollutants which reflects the greatest degree of effluent reduction. . .achievable through application of the best available demonstrated control technology, processes, operating methods, and other alternatives, including, where practicable, standards permitting no discharge of pollutants" (emphasis added). The primary difference between this criteria and the Section 301 criteria is the requirement in Section 306 that EPA consider not only pollution control techniques, but also various alternative production processes, operating methods, in-plant control procedures and so forth. Accordingly, in the establishment of Section 306 New Source Performance Standards (NSPS), alternatives or supplements to end-of-pipe treatment will be emphasized. Production process alternatives, which, though less economic, may have a significantly reduced pollution potential may, as a practical matter, be required.

A second major difference regarding criteria for development of new source performance standards is the absence of the kind of requirements for detailed consideration of economic and technological factors which are established by Section 304 for existing source effluent limitations procedures. The absence of such required considerations reflects a presumption that if a source is yet to be constructed, there is much greater flexibility to alter total facility design so as to be capable of achieving stringent effluent limitations. Thus EPA has far greater discretion in the promulgation of new source performance standards than it does with respect to existing sources.

A third, and major, factor to be taken into account when considering the applicability of new source performance standards is that the Act provides virtually no flexibility for moderating the impact of those standards when applied to specific facilities. The fundamental factors variance and other modification authorities provided by the Act are not applicable in the new source situation and, accordingly, strict conformity with the new source performance standards, where applicable, is essential.

31/ 40 CFR § 122.29(b).

Finally, where EPA is the issuing authority, the issuance of a permit for a new source discharge is a federal action subject to the review requirements of the National Environmental Policy Act. 32/ Thus, where the issuance of a new source discharge permit is found to be a major action with a significant effect on the environment, an environmental impact statement will be required. The result will be both substantial delay in the issuance of the new source permit and the potential inclusion of stringent requirements in permits which are issued, requirements which may address a host of other environmental issues besides water pollution discharges and the quality of receiving waters.

Because the determination as to whether a facility is a new source has such a substantial impact, both in terms of the stringency of the treatment standards applied and the length of time required in order to obtain a permit, the question of precisely when a facility "commences construction" for purposes of determining whether new source performance standards are applicable has been a source of major controversy. This issue is addressed in considerable detail in Section 122.29 of EPA's NPDES regulations and has also been extensively considered in court decisions and in opinions of EPA's General Counsel. The question of when construction is commenced or whether it constitutes a modification as opposed to a new facility are nevertheless difficult factual issues. Companies planning new facilities should carefully review these issues with counsel early in the planning process.

Section 306 does offer both to new sources and to new dischargers which are not new sources one important protection which is not available to existing sources under Section 301. Section 306 specifically provides that any new facility constructed to meet all applicable new source standards of performance in effect as of the time it is constructed, may not be subjected to any more stringent standards for ten years from the date construction is completed or for the period of depreciation under the Internal Revenue Code, whichever is shorter. This protection from more stringent standards of performance, as EPA construes the Act, is not applicable to any more stringent permit conditions which are not technology-based, e.g., it is not applicable to conditions based on water quality standards or toxic pollutant chemical-based prohibitions or on effluent

---

32/ Clean Water Act, § 511.

standards under Section 307(a) or to any new permit conditions which are applicable to pollutants not controlled by the applicable new source performance standards with which the facility complied at the time of construction. It should be noted that, on the expiration of the ten-year protection period, immediate compliance with the standards in effect at the time of such expiration will be required. No implementation period for compliance with those standards will be allowed.

4.4 Required Level of Treatment—Technology-Based Limits for Indirect Dischargers (Pre-Treatment)

Industrial facilities that discharge into Publicly Owned Treatment Works (POTWs) are regulated not by the requirements governing direct discharges, but rather by comparable treatment requirements—pretreatment standards—adopted pursuant to Section 307(b) of the Act. Pretreatment standards are calculated to achieve two basic objectives: (1) to protect the operation of POTWs and (2) to prevent the discharge of pollutants which pass through publicly owned treatment works without receiving adequate treatment. The dual objectives of the pretreatment program result in a two-part system of controls under the applicable EPA regulations. General requirements are imposed under 40 CFR Part 403 and requirements specific to particular industries, so-called categorical standards, are developed and imposed together with other effluent limitations governing each such industry.

The first part of the general pretreatment regulation focuses primarily on preventing the discharge into POTWs of pollutants which will interfere with the proper operation of the receiving treatment works. This "protection" standard 33/ prohibits the introduction into any publicly owned treatment works of:

(i)   Pollutants which create a fire or explosion hazard in the POTW;

(ii)   Discharges with a pH lower than 5.0 unless the works is specifically designed to accommodate such discharges;

(iii)   Solid or viscous pollutants in amounts which obstruct the flow in a sewer system;

33/ 40 CFR § 403.5.

(iv)   Discharges, including discharges of conventional pollutants, of such volume and concentration that they upset the treatment process and cause a permit violation (e.g., oxygen demanding pollutants such as BOD); and

(v)   Heat in amounts which will inhibit biological activity in the POTW resulting in interference, but in no case heat in such quantities that the temperature influent at the treatment works exceeds 40° C (104° F) unless the works are designed to accommodate such heat.

The second major objective of the pretreatment regulations—preventing the discharge in the publicly owned treatment works of pollutants which pass through those treatment works without receiving adequate treatment—is to be achieved by "categorical" pretreatment regulations. These categorical regulations are applicable only to "incompatible" pollutants—e.g., pollutants other than biochemical oxygen demand, suspended solids, pH and fecal coliform bacteria, and which are not adequately treated in the POTW treatment process. 34/ These categorical pretreatment regulations, like the BAT regulations and new source performance standards, focus primarily on the thirty-four industries and sixty-five toxic pollutant categories specified in the NRDC consent decree. For each discharger into a POTW, these categorical standards are intended to result in the same level of treatment prior to discharge from the POTW as that which would have been required had the industrial facility discharged those pollutants directly to the receiving waters. The stringency of these categorical standards can be reduced through the mechanism of removal credits, which takes into account the removal of these pollutants consistently achieved by the POTW in question.

Accordingly, the industrial facility discharging into a POTW will be required to achieve, in meeting the applicable pretreatment limits, a level of treatment performance equivalent to the applicable BAT effluent limitations or new source performance standards

---

34/ Additional pollutants may be identified as "compatible" for a particular treatment works if it can be shown that the facility in question adequately treats those pollutants.

unless the receiving POTW has an approved pretreatment program and requests removal credits against the applicable pretreatment limit based on the POTW's demonstrated capability to consistently remove that pollutant in its treatment process. In order to qualify for a revision, the POTW must provide consistent removal of each pollutant for which a discharge limit revision is sought, and its sludge use or disposal practices must, at the time of the application and thereafter, remain in compliance with all applicable criteria, guidelines and regulations for sludge use and disposal. EPA has modified its regulations in order to account better for normal process variations by POTWs. 35/ The net result of these 1984 changes in the "removal credit" regulation is to make it easier for indirect dischargers to obtain credit against categorical standards imposed on them, thereby decreasing the stringency of the standard, theoretically without materially increasing the pollution discharge.

Pretreatment requirements are directly enforceable by EPA and states with NPDES permit issuance authority, but the EPA regulations contemplate eventual delegation of primary enforcement responsibility to individual POTWs with EPA and the states receding to a backup role.

Under the regulations, any POTW (or combination of POTWs operated by the same authority) having a total design flow greater than five million gallons per day must have developed and implemented a pretreatment program by 1 July 1983, if it receives incompatible industrial waste. A POTW must have an approved pretreatment program in order to grant removal credits although it may grant conditional removal credits while EPA is considering approval of the POTW's pretreatment program. POTW programs must meet funding, personnel, legal, and procedural criteria sufficient to ensure that the POTW's enforcement responsibilities can be carried out. Once the program is developed and approved, the POTW will be responsible for enforcement of the national pretreatment standards. A POTW may exercise enforcement authority through a number of methods including contracts, joint powers agreements, ordinances, or otherwise.

Finally, pretreatment regulations establish extensive reporting requirements for both industrial users and POTWs in order to

35/ 40 CFR § 403.7, 49 FR 31221, 3 August 1984.

monitor and demonstrate compliance with categorical pretreatment standards.

The pretreatment regulations significantly affect industries subject to categorical pretreatment standards, as well as other industrial users of POTWs which will have to comply with general pretreatment requirements.

4.5 Technology–Based Treatment Standards for Industrial Dischargers Dealing with Process Variability

As the technology-based effluent limits address increased numbers of pollutants, setting proper limitations becomes much more difficult. As standards become more complex, valid application of technology-based effluent limits will, in many cases, demand some mechanism by which plant-to-plant variations can be taken into account.

The statutory mechanisms to permit plant-to-plant flexibility are exceedingly limited. Section 301(c) grants the Administrator authority to modify the 1984 BAT requirements or the related pretreatment requirements if it can be shown that the economic capability of the discharger necessitates less stringent limitations. A further prerequisite to such a modification is a showing that it will result in further progress toward elimination of the discharge of pollutants. Though this basis for granting a variance is reasonably broad, the circumstances in which it can be granted are strictly limited. The Section 301(c) variance does not apply to the "Best Conventional Technology" effluent limitations, and Section 301(l) of the Act precludes the modification of any effluent limitation regulating a toxic or priority pollutant. Accordingly, the Section 301(c) variance authority applies only to the "nonconventional nontoxic" pollutants so its utility is minimal.

Section 301(g) is also applicable only to the few nonconventional nontoxic pollutants (excluding heat). It is relevant in only a few cases since a discharger had a very limited period in which to apply for a Section 301(g) variance.

The final statutory basis for modification of BAT effluent limits and pretreatment standards is set forth in Section 301(k). That subsection authorizes the Administrator or state issuing authority to issue a permit providing for compliance by 1 July 1987 rather than 1984 if a source seeks to achieve the applicable limits through the use of innovative technology which has the potential for industry-wide application and has a substantial likelihood of achieving greater effluent reduction than the effluent limitations or will result in significantly lower costs. It is unclear whether this innovative technology variance may be granted for toxic pollutant limits in view of the prohibition against modification of toxic pollutant effluent limitations set forth in Section 301(1).

With respect to the 1977 BPT effluent limits, the Act provided only one now-obsolete basis for extending the time for compliance.

Although the statutory variance authority is of limited utility, EPA has provided, by administrative interpretation, a variance mechanism which is somewhat more helpful. This administrative variance—the "fundamentally different factors" variance—was initially applied to the 1977 BPT effluent limitations through the inclusion in each set of effluent limitations regulations of a variance clause. This clause allowed a discharger to demonstrate that the limitations should not apply to its facility because of the existence of factors which were fundamentally different from those considered by EPA in the process of developing the effluent limitations.

The scope of the required variance clause was expanded in the case of Appalachian Power Company v. Train, 36/ and the necessity of some sort of variance mechanism for "fundamentally different factors" was applauded by the Supreme Court in the Dupont case. 37/ The need for a fundamental factors variance is inherent in the nature of the process for development of effluent limitations under the Clean Water Act and pursuant to the provisions of the Federal Administrative Procedures Act. Since it is virtually impossible to fully consider all of the factors required to be considered by Section 304 of the Act for every plant or type of plant in every industrial category, there must be some mechanism for taking into account factors not fully considered in the regulatory development process at the time the effluent limitations are applied in a permit to a particular facility.

In recognition of this fact, EPA, in the pretreatment regulations and NPDES permit program regulations discussed above, has expanded the circumstances in which the fundamental factors variance is applicable. It is now available with respect to the categorical pretreatment regulations, as well as for all of the technology-based effluent limits for existing sources. It is not available

---

36/ 545 F.2d 1351 (4th Cir. 1976).

37/ 430 U.S. 112 (1977).

for new source performance standards (on the theory that a facility yet to be constructed has considerable design flexibility and is not constrained by the numerous existing factors which may affect attainable treatment levels) or to water quality-related effluent limitations. The Supreme Court recently ruled that the fundamental factors variance is available with respect to toxic pollutants under the Clean Water Act. 38/

In order to obtain a fundamental factors variance, the discharger must bear the burden of showing that factors applicable to this facility are fundamentally different from those considered in the development of the effluent limitations guidelines. Factors which Section 125.31 of the regulations allow to be considered as fundamentally different are:

(1)   The nature or quality of the pollutants contained in the raw waste load of the applicant's process waste water;

(2)   The volume of the discharger's process waste water and effluent discharged;

(3)   Non-water quality environmental impacts of control and treatment of the discharger's raw waste load (are these impacts fundamentally more adverse than those considered during the development of national limits?);

(4)   Energy requirements of the application of control and treatment technology (are they fundamentally greater than those assessed in developing national limits?);

(5)   Age, size, land availability and configuration as they relate to the discharger's equipment or facilities, processes employed; engineering aspects of the application of control technology; and

---

38/ Chemical Manufacturers Association v. Natural Resources Defense Council, U.S. (27 February 1985), overruling National Association of Metal Finishers (NAMF) v. EPA, 719 F. 2d 624, 646 (3d Cir. 1983).

(6)   Cost of compliance with required control tech-
        nology (is it "wholly out of proportion" to the
        removal costs considered in developing national
        limits?).

If it finds that a fundamentally different factor exists, the
Environmental Protection Agency may adopt alternative effluent
limitations for the facility in question. It should be noted that those
limits may be either more or less stringent than the effluent limitations with respect to which the variance is granted.

The fundamental factors variance is not available simply
because the cost of compliance with BPT limitations would force
plant closure. 39/ Instead, the costs of BPT compliance are relevant
in deciding if fundamentally different factors exist at a plant and, if
so, whether the alternate effluent limitations are as cost-effective
as those imposed on the industry in general. 40/

Finally, it should be noted that although the fundamental
factors variance is an important mechanism and will become
increasingly so as effluent limitations become more detailed and
address more pollutants, its potential availability does not reduce
the necessity for careful monitoring of the development process for
applicable effluent limitations to assure that the factors which are
considered during that process are properly assessed and applied.
The fundamental factors variance is available only for factors not
considered in the development process. The only meaningful relief
available for improper application of factors considered during the
development process is an appeal to the courts. Unless this appeal is
taken within ninety days after the applicable effluent limits are
published in final form, the right to raise these issues will be waived.

4.6 Technology-Based Treatment Standards—Publicly Owned Treatment Works

For discharges from publicly owned treatment works (POTWs),
Section 301 directs the achievement: by 1 July 1977, of (1) effluent
limitations based on secondary treatment, as defined by EPA and (2)
any more stringent limitations are necessary to comply with water

---

39/ EPA v. National Crushed Stone Association, 449 U.S. 64 (1980).

40/ Weyerhauser Co. v. Costle, 590 F.2d 1011, 1036 (D.C. Cir. 1978).

quality standards or treatment standards imposed by state law; 41/ by 1 July 1983, the adoption of waste management techniques which provide for the application of best practicable waste treatment technology over the life of the treatment works. 42/

EPA defined "secondary treatment" for purposes of Section 301 in 1973 and modified that definition late in 1984. 43/ The effluent levels prescribed by these regulations are as follows:

	% Removal 30 day average	Concentration (mg/1) Monthly Average	Weekly Average
BOD (5 day)	85	30	45
Suspended Solids (SS)	85	30	45
Coliform		200/100 ml.	400/100 ml.
pH		6.0 to 9.0	

The regulations make special provision for upwards revision of the "secondary treatment" effluent limits (1) where necessary to take into account storm water infiltration into combined sewers

---

41/ The 1977 Amendments provide for extension of the 1977 secondary treatment and other deadlines where, because of lack of federal funding or otherwise, planned facilities have not been completed. The extension shall be to the earliest date on which funding can be provided and construction completed but no later than July 1983. Industrial dischargers whose permits require discharge to a treatment works and who had enforceable contracts for such discharge or who were included in a treatment works facility plan filed with a grant application may be granted an extension on much the same basis as the treatment works itself.

42/ The Best Practicable Waste Treatment Technology requirement has been construed by EPA to mean secondary treatment unless special circumstances applicable to a particular facility indicate that a higher level of treatment is more cost effective or required to meet water quality criteria.

43/ See 40 CFR Part 133.

during wet weather periods; and (2) where necessary to take into account the fact that the Section 301 and Section 306 effluent limitations applicable to major industrial dischargers into the treatment works (those exceeding 10 percent of the design flow) would permit an industrial user to directly discharge greater concentrations than those set forth in the table. In the latter case, the permitted discharge from the POTW which is attributable to the industrial waste received for treatment may be increased to equal, but not exceed, that which would be permitted, under the applicable effluent limitations, if the industrial facility were discharging directly into a waterway.

In the 1981 Amendments, Congress revised the definition of secondary treatment so that such biological treatment facilities as oxidation ponds, lagoons, and ditches and trickling filters are deemed to be the equivalent of secondary treatment. 44/ These modes of treatment are considerably cheaper than other treatment modes, especially for small communities. The changes made pursuant to this standard allow trickling filters and stabilization ponds to meet secondary treatment requirements if the discharge meets the following parameters 45/:

	% Removal	Concentration (mg/1) 30-Day Average	7-Day Average
BOD (5 day)	65	45	65
Suspended Solids	65	45	65
pH		6.0 to 9.0	

The relative stringency of these effluent limitations and the fact that, under the 1972 Act, POTWs were, for the first time, subjected to effective and directly enforceable federal effluent limitations and permit requirements, gave municipal authorities a strong mandate to rigorously enforce flow and concentration limitations on industrial users of their systems. In some cases, the "pretreatment requirements" imposed by municipal authorities pursuant to this mandate have been more stringent than the federal pretreatment

44/ Clean Water Act, § 304(d)(4).

45/ 40 CFR § 133.105.

standards discussed above. In addition, as noted below, the increasing need for high levels of performance by POTWs result in new or upgraded facilities which can drastically increase the cost to industry of waste treatment services.

4.7 More Stringent Treatment Required to Meet Water Quality-Related Effluent Limitations

As has been noted, the technology-based effluent limitations discussed above function as nationwide minimum or base level treatment standards. The Act provides two separate mechanisms for the imposition of more stringent requirements where dictated by the need to protect or maintain water quality in specific bodies of water.

Section 301(b)(1)(C) of the Act requires both industrial dischargers and POTWs to achieve, no later than 1 July 1977, any effluent limitations more stringent than the minimum technology-based standards which may be necessary to meet applicable federal-state water quality standards. This requirement is incorporated into permits issued by EPA through the state certification requirement under Section 401 of the Act. (See Part 3.2 above.)

Section 302 of the Act authorizes EPA directly to establish effluent criteria more stringent than the applicable BAT limits where necessary for the attainment or maintenance in a specific body of water quality which "shall assure protection of public water supplies, agriculture and industrial uses, and the protection and propagation of a balanced population of shellfish, fish and wildlife, and allow recreational activities in and on the water. . ." EPA has interpreted this Section 302 authority as providing a selective tool for the Agency to impose more stringent requirements where necessary to protect important water resources. Although this section has received little if any use to date, it does have great potential impact in that it authorizes EPA to adopt its own effluent limitations for any body of water as to which a state fails or refuses to adopt water quality standards sufficient to maintain fishing and swimming uses.

The water quality standards and water quality-related effluent limitations imposed by these two mechanisms have substantial potential for requiring levels of treatment considerably higher than those required by the technology-related effluent limits in areas of heavy discharge concentration, in waters where very stringent quality standards have been established, and in waters with limited assimilative capacity. This potential impact is exacerbated by the fact that there is no provision for the grant of variances from the Section 301 water quality standards. The requirement for compliance with water quality standards is inflexible and mandatory. The impact of this requirement will depend to a considerable extent on the resolution of a number of major policy questions now being addressed by EPA.

The procedures for setting water quality standards are quite complex. States, acting pursuant to the procedures set out in 40 CFR Section 131.20 hold public hearings every three years for the purpose of revising and reviewing state water quality standards. EPA does not set specific minimums for state standards; instead the rules require that such standards specify and protect appropriate water uses (e.g., water supply, fish, wildlife), 46/ and set specific criteria to attain these ends. 47/ The state standards must attain the Clean Water Act's goal of fishable, swimmable waters wherever attainable, and must, at a minimum, maintain the uses designated in the standards and current uses, 48/, unless the state can demonstrate that the designated use is unattainable or infeasible for one of a short list of reasons, primarily concerning other physical or biological aspects of the water body. 49/ In addition, no degradation of "outstanding national resource" waters, such as those in national and state parks, is to be permitted. 50/

The pollutants required to be addressed by state water quality standards were addressed by criteria for a number of pollutants of specific concern, published in "Quality Criteria for Water," July 1976, the so-called Red Book. These criteria have been rescinded, and not replaced. As a result, most states have placed primary emphasis in their water quality standards programs on conventional measures of pollutants such as dissolved oxygen, pH and fecal coliform bacteria, and very few states have had a substantial program

---

46/ §§ 131.6, 131.10.

47/ § 131.11.

48/ § 131.10(h).

49/ § 131.10(g).

50/ § 35.1550(e).

for the establishment of water quality standards for heavy metals, pesticides and other non-conventional or toxic pollutants.

Pursuant to the NRDC consent decree, EPA adopted criteria for the priority pollutants listed in the consent decree, 51/ in addition to those earlier criteria, the 1976 Red Book.

Adoption of water quality criteria and standards for priority pollutants will have no effect until these standards are translated into end-of-pipe effluent limitations to be imposed on dischargers. Section 303(e) of the Act requires states to inventory all waters within their jurisdictions to identify those waters as to which BAT and other technology-based effluent limits are inadequate to promote and maintain compliance with water quality standards (water quality-limited segments), to establish maximum loadings for water quality limited segments, and to provide a system for allocating those maximum loadings among all dischargers to the affected waters. This requirement has not been fully implemented because of the extreme technical difficulty in performing the necessary mathematical modeling and other studies.

Because of the slow pace of the Section 303 planning process, water quality-related effluent limitations have often not been included in permits when they should have been, a situation which is changing as EPA implements the NRDC consent decree. That decree requires these water quality related effluent limits to be incorporated into discharge permits. 52/ For discharges to water-quality limited segments, the issuing authority cannot issue a permit unless it finds that the facility will not cause or contribute to the violation of water quality standards applicable to the water into which the discharge is made. These requirements can be expected to result in a system similar to that now applicable to the location of new facilities in non-attainment areas under the Clean Air Act, where pressure for new industrial growth results in the imposition of increasingly stringent requirements on existing sources in order to permit new facilities without violation of applicable standards.

EPA has borrowed another concept from the Clean Air Act—the "bubble"—for use in the water pollution context. Under the "bubble" concept, EPA would permit facilities to cumulate the

---

51/ 45 FR 79318 (28 November 1980).

52/ 40 CFR § 122.43(d).

discharges from different outfalls of the plant and meet a single effluent limitation, rather than outfall-by-outfall limitations. So far, the bubble is limited to steel plants, 53/ with the idea being that it will be expanded to other industries if it proves workable. This approach may lead to appreciable cost savings depending on whether it can be used in water-quality limited areas and whether it applies to toxic pollutants. Two subcategories in the steel industry— cokemaking and cold forming—were not permitted to use the bubble, in part because of toxic pollutant concerns. 54/

In summary, it seems clear that, both as to industrial direct discharge and pretreatment requirements, water quality standards on certain bodies of water can be expected, during the next five to ten years, to have a significant impact in increasing the stringency of treatment requirements to be imposed on industrial and other facilities. The toxics orientation of the water quality standards, together with the policy changes and enforcement mechanisms discussed above, merit careful consideration by potentially affected companies. Those companies would be well advised to participate actively in state proceedings related to the review and revision of existing water quality standards and the carrying out of the Section 303 planning process.

5.0 Controlling Non-Process-Related Waste Discharges

Although the system of effluent limits imposed through the NPDES permit program is an effective means of regulating waste discharges which result from normal industrial or municipal processes and which are amenable to treatment prior to discharge, this system is an inappropriate means of regulating and controlling accidental and unanticipated discharges or discharges which, by their nature, are not subject to confinement and treatment (e.g., area-wide or plant site runoff). For this latter class of discharges, the focus of regulation must be on preventing the discharge (in the case of the accidental spill) or on minimizing the volume of pollutants carried (in the case of area-wide and plant site runoff). Since accidental spills and "non-point source" discharges are responsible for a large percentage of the total pollutants introduced into the

---

53/ 40 CFR § 420.03.

54/ 47 FR 23265-66, 23271-74 (21 May 1982), 40 CFR § 420.03(b)(3).

nation's waterways, the Act provides a number of mechanisms, supplemental to the NPDES permit program, to control discharges which are unrelated to industrial process wastes. This system of supplemental regulatory controls is the subject of this section and the next one.

5.1 Controlling Area-Wide Non-Point Source Pollution— Section 208 Planning

The primary mechanism contemplated by the Clean Water Act for controlling area-wide non-point source pollution is the planning and regulatory program created by Section 208. This section would require each state to identify areas of the state which, due to urban industrial concentrations or other factors, have substantial water quality control problems. For each of these designated "waste treatment management areas," a representative of state and local officials would be identified and charged with the responsibility of developing a comprehensive area-wide plan for solving the area's water quality control problems.

After several years, however, Congress stopped funding the development and implementation of 208 plans. As a consequence, little progress has been made under Section 208 since fiscal year 1980. There has been little done since then to address the problem of non-point sources although several EPA task forces have recently begun to consider different regulatory and legislative options.

5.2 Stormwater Discharges and Best Management Practices

EPA's regulations require an NPDES permit for "storm water point sources." 55/ These include any storm water collection system that is either located in an urbanized area or discharges from lands or facilities used for industrial or commercial activities. EPA may also designate additional discharges as storm water point sources on a case-by-case basis. 56/ Where more than one facility discharges to a storm water runoff system, a single permit can be issued, but all dischargers must be covered by individual effluent limitations. 57/ In addition, permitting authorities can issue general permits

---

55/ 40 CFR § 122.26(a).

56/ 40 CFR § 122.26(b)(1).

57/ 40 CFR § 122.26(a).

covering all storm water point sources in a given geographic area or political jurisdiction.

The required contents of an NPDES permit application for a storm water point source vary, depending upon the type of discharge. For those discharges located at an industrial plant or "plant associated areas" or which are subject to specific effluent standards, the NPDES application must contain all of the information required for any other industrial point source. For any other storm water point source, the regulations specify greatly abbreviated application requirements. 58/

This permit system is the primary mechanism for regulating plant site runoff where toxic and hazardous pollutants are not involved. In addition, Section 304(e), which was added by the 1977 Amendments, authorizes EPA to require permittees to adopt "Best Management Practices" to control toxic pollutants resulting from ancillary industrial activities. EPA also is authorized to prescribe regulations to control plant site runoff, spillage or leaks, and sludge or waste disposal. The legislative history of this provision indicates that Congress anticipated that EPA's regulations would specify treatment requirements, operating procedures, and other management practices by classes and categories of point source discharges.

EPA proposed sweeping regulations to implement the best management practices provisions of Section 304(e), 59/ but issued final regulations of more modest scope. 60/ Both the proposed and final regulations, however, attempt to apply the BMP requirements on an across-the-board basis, instead of by categories. This administrative short-cut may lead to difficulties in the operation of the BMP program.

The final regulations emphasize BMPs of a procedural nature (especially preventive maintenance and housekeeping) and BMPs requiring only minor construction. EPA stated that these regulations are the first of two or more steps; Spill Prevention, Control and Countermeasure (SPCC) plans for hazardous substances (which

---

58/ 40 CFR § 122.21(f).

59/ 43 FR 39282 (1 September 1978).

60/ 40 CFR Part 125, Subpart K.

have been proposed but never promulgated) and possibly additional BMP provisions are scheduled as regulatory requirements in the future.

The existing BMP requirements are applicable to all dischargers who use, manufacture, store, handle or discharge any pollutant listed as toxic under Section 307 or as hazardous under Section 311 for all ancillary manufacturing operations which may result in significant amounts of toxic or hazardous pollutants reaching waters of the U.S. Any BMPs required by a Section 304(e) effluent limitations guideline must be expressly incorporated into an NPDES permit and BMPs may be so incorporated if EPA or the State agency determines this to be "necessary to carry out the provisions of the Act. . . ." These requirements appear to have been specifically contemplated by Congress when it added the BMP provisions in 1977.

In addition, the regulations require the permittee to develop a "Best Management Practices program," which must be submitted as part of the permit application and which will be subject to all permit issuance procedures. This program must be written, must establish toxic and hazardous substances control objectives, and must establish specific BMPs to meet these objectives. The program must also address a number of points concerning ancillary activities such as materials inventory and compatibility, employee training, visual inspections, preventive maintenance, housekeeping, and security. It is clear that these requirements will impose considerable administrative burdens on affected permittees.

6.0 Oil and Hazardous Substances

Section 311 of the 1972 Act established an extensive regulatory scheme for dealing with accidental or intentional discharges of oil and hazardous substances. The 1977 Amendments modified Section 311 in several ways, principally with respect to the limits on the liability of a discharger of oil or of hazardous substances. Congress further amended Section 311 in 1978, primarily in order to make the section's provisions with respect to hazardous substances more workable. In 1980, Congress enacted the Comprehensive Environmental Response, Compensation and Liability Act (CERCLA), which has significantly expanded EPA's authority and resources to clean up hazardous wastes listed under Section 311. Spills of petroleum products continue to be regulated solely under Section 311 of the Clean Water Act.

Although oil and hazardous substances are covered by the same Clean Water Act provisions, they have traditionally been treated separately by EPA. The following discussion analyzes each in turn.

6.1 Oil

The Act prohibits the discharge of "harmful quantities" of oil into navigable waters. EPA regulations 61/ have defined the term "harmful quantities" to cover all discharges which "violate applicable water quality standards or cause a film or sheen upon the surface of the water. . ." Thus virtually all discharges of oil are prohibited. 62/

Industry's responsibility under this section has several facets. Owners and operators of large oil (including animal or vegetable oil) storage facilities (1,320 gallons above ground or 42,000 gallons below ground) must comply with EPA regulations 63/ which seek to minimize the probability that an oil spill will occur by requiring the development, implementation and maintenance of Spill Prevention, Control and Countermeasure (SPCC) Plans. Plan implementation is often a matter of considerable expense, since the installation of containment structures, maintenance of inspection procedures, and other preventive measures are often necessary plan elements. Failure to prepare and maintain a plan in accordance with the regulations subjects the violator to civil penalties of up to $5,000 for each day of violation. 64/ Similar, but more stringent, planning and accident avoidance requirements are applicable under Coast Guard regulations governing vessels and oil transfer operations associated therewith. 65/

61/ 40 CFR § 110.3.

62/ It is arguable that the oils and greases contained in an NPDES permitted discharge are not covered by the Section 311 limitations and reporting requirements. However, many NPDES permits contain a condition making it clear that the permit does not in any way excuse Section 311 compliance.

63/ 40 CFR Part 112.

64/ 40 CFR § 112.6.

65/ 33 CFR Parts 154-157.

In addition, vessels must establish evidence of financial responsibility to meet potential liability under Section 311(p)(1) of the Act. The financial responsibility which must be evidenced is the greater of $125 per gross ton or $125,000 for inland oil barges, and $150 per gross ton for other vessels. Financial responsibility may be established by insurance, surety bonds or qualification as a self-insurer.

If, despite compliance with the spill avoidance procedures discussed above, a spill does occur, additional obligations arise. The owner or operator of the source from which the discharge originates must immediately report the discharge to the Coast Guard and/or EPA. 66/ Failure to comply with this requirement results, upon conviction, in a fine of up to $10,000 and/or imprisonment for not more than one year. 67/ It should be kept in mind that this reporting requirement is broadly construed and may apply to oil spills which originate several miles inland (e.g., if the spill goes into a storm sewer which outlets to navigable waters).

In addition to giving notice, the discharger must either contain and clean up the spill or pay the cost of clean up efforts by responsible government agencies. 68/ Section 311(f) limits the discharger's liability for the government's actual removal costs to $50 million unless there is willful negligence or willful misconduct in which case there is no limit on liability. EPA is authorized to establish lower limits of liability for facilities having small storage capacity (1000 barrels or less). 69/ Generally, effective private clean up measures are less costly than similar efforts by the government and, in addition, those efforts are of considerable practical importance in mitigation of civil penalties discussed below.

The discharger's final obligation under the Act is to pay a civil penalty of not more than $5,000 for each spill. 70/ Although the Coast Guard (which is the agency administering the penalties

---

66/ 33 CFR § 153.203; 40 CFR § 110.9.

67/ Clean Water Act, Section 311(b)(5).

68/ Sections 311(c), 311(f).

69/ 40 CFR Part 113.

70/Section 311(b)(6).

section) must assess a penalty, it has considerable discretion to reduce the amount of the penalty based on the size of the business of the discharger, the effect of the penalty on his ability to continue in business, and the gravity of the violation. The Act provides the right to notice and a hearing in connection with civil penalty assessments.

6.2 Hazardous Substances

Although, as noted above, Section 311 governs the discharge of hazardous substances as well as of oil, EPA was much slower in implementing the hazardous substances provision. It finally promulgated hazardous substances regulations in March 1978 and indicated that they would become effective during the summer. Before the regulations became effective, however, a United States district court enjoined significant parts of them so that they could not go into effect. Congress responded to the court's action by amending Section 311 to simplify and clarify its provisions. 71/ The 1978 Amendments were directed toward the two most significant problems identified by the court: the elements necessary to establish what was to be considered a harmful quantity and the relationship of Section 311 to the NPDES program.

Pursuant to these Amendments, EPA has designated approximately 300 substances as hazardous and thus subject to the Section 311 program. 72/ In addition, the Agency has designated quantities of these substances that may be harmful (called a "reportable quantity"). 73/ Hazardous substances are placed in one of five categories: X, A, B, C, D. A harmful quantity of a category X substance is one pound, of a category A substance is 10 pounds, of a category B substance is 100 pounds, of a category C substance is 1000 pounds, and of a category D substance is 5000 pounds. 74/

The second principal feature of EPA's hazardous substance regulations is the exclusion of discharges made in compliance with an NPDES permit. Since a primary purpose of the Amendments was

---

71/ PL 95-576 (2 November 1978).

72/ 40 CFR Part 116.

73/ 40 CFR Part 117.

74/ 40 CFR § 117.3.

to limit Section 311 to "classic" hazardous substance spills, the regulations specify that they are not applicable to chronic discharges of designated substances if the discharge complies with an NPDES permit. 75/ Such discharges, of course, remain subject to regulation under the NPDES program.

Further, if an NPDES facility has intermittent, anticipated spills of hazardous substances (i.e., into plant drainage ditches), it should determine whether these discharges ought to be brought within the terms of its NPDES permit. The regulations give the facility the option of having such discharges regulated through the NPDES program or pursuant to Section 311.

Discharges of hazardous substances may also reach navigable waters through municipal sewers and publicly owned treatment works. Discharges from industrial facilities to a POTW are not covered by the regulations at present. The regulations do apply to all discharges of reportable quantities of hazardous substances to POTWs by a mobile source such as trucks unless the discharger has met certain requirements. 76/

A facility owner or operator who spills a harmful quantity of a hazardous substance must report the spill; failure to do so will subject him to criminal penalties. If there is a spill, the violator is also subject to a fine of up to $5000. In lieu of this fine, EPA can seek a penalty through a civil action in federal courts; this penalty can range up to $50,000 or up to $250,000 if the discharge was the result of willful negligence or willful misconduct within the privity and knowledge of the owner/operator.

Finally, it should be noted that the reporting requirements for spills of hazardous substances (as well as other defined wastes) have been substantially supplemented by the Comprehensive Environmental, Response, Compensation and Liability Act (also known as CERCLA or Superfund). For a fuller description of these requirements, see Chapter 3.

The nature of these regulations and the potential penalties thereunder place a premium on developing compliance procedures before a spill occurs. A facility should first be evaluated to determine whether it discharges, or might discharge, a reportable quantity of any hazardous substance to the waters of the United States.

75/ 40 CFR § 117.12.

76/ 40 CFR § 117.13.

If there is a risk of such a discharge, the exemptions established by the regulations should be considered in order to determine if they will be applicable to the potential discharge. If no exemption is available, it may be advisable to develop a program to prevent such discharges. Further it is essential to implement a contingency plan capable of assuring a prompt and appropriate response in the event of a non-exempt reportable discharge.

7.0 Other Critical Elements of the Water Act Program

In addition to the features of the Water Act program described above, there are several other important elements which must be discussed if the overall program is to be understood as a coherent whole. These elements are described below.

7.1 Abatement Actions and Sanctions

In order to assure compliance with the regulatory program, Congress established extensive provisions to deal with violations of the Act. Dischargers who fail to obtain permits under the Act or who violate the Act's effluent limitations, pretreatment requirements, or monitoring provisions, or any permit conditions required to implement these may be proceeded against under the Refuse Act of 1899, under the Clean Water Act (although there is at least some question as to whether the Section 309 sanctions apply to a failure to obtain a permit), and under the state laws providing for implementation of the NPDES program. All of the foregoing sanctions may be pursued concurrently, although it is likely that EPA will defer to state enforcement action if such actions are expeditiously commenced. As the emphasis of the regulatory program moves from the establishment of standards and the issuance of permits to concerns about compliance with the terms of standards and permits, provisions for dealing with violations will become more and more important.

EPA has a number of enforcement options under the Water Act: (1) issuance of a compliance order; (2) obtaining injunctive relief under Section 309; (3) seeking civil penalties; and (4) initiating criminal prosecution. In addition, Sierra Club v. Train 77/, held that EPA can elect to take no formal enforcement action at all. Should EPA decide not to take any formal action, it can either ignore a

---

77/ 557 F. 2d 485 (5th Cir. 1977).

violation as being de minimis or attempt to resolve the violation by informal procedures.

Compliance orders are administrative orders by which EPA directs the violator to come into compliance with the applicable statutory, regulatory, or permit term. These orders are subject to judicial review.

EPA's second option, obtaining injunctive relief pursuant to Section 504, is applicable to discharges which present an imminent and substantial endangerment to the health, welfare or livelihood of persons. In such circumstances, EPA is empowered to bring suit in a United States district court to immediately stop the discharge of pollutants causing such a situation.

EPA can also seek injunctive relief under Section 309(b). The U.S. district court hearing such an action has jurisdiction to restrain the violation of any condition or limitation which implements Sections 301, 302, 306, 307, 308, 318, and 405 and to require compliance with the condition or limitation.

Violations of these same sections or of permit conditions implementing these sections can also be punished by civil penalties of up to $10,000 for each day of violation. Finally, any person who "wilfully or negligently" violates such provisions or permit conditions (and any person who violates a properly issued administrative order will certainly meet the test) is subject to fines of $2,500 to $25,000 per day of violation or imprisonment of up to a year or both. "Responsible corporate officers" are subject to the same fines and criminal sanctions (including imprisonment) as are their companies. Fines are doubled for second time offenders. The Act also provides fines and imprisonment for willful false statements or incorrect entries in any information required to be filed or maintained under the Act.

In addition to these EPA weapons, those states which have assumed NPDES permit responsibility are also responsible for enforcement. These states have their own enforcement laws, policies and personnel, all of which may be quite different from those of EPA. The situation is further complicated by the fact that EPA does not always agree with state enforcement decisions. If it does not, Section 309(a)(1) permits it to intervene to assure that "appropriate" enforcement action is taken.

From the foregoing, it is evident that there is a great deal of uncertainty about whether and who many bring enforcement actions. Much of this uncertainty springs from EPA's significant discretionary authority concerning enforcement. A discharger who is or may be faced with a potential enforcement action for a violation of the Act or of a permit issued thereunder (and this category includes almost every discharger) must be aware of this discretion and of EPA's efforts to set enforcement guidelines or priorities.

EPA has issued several sets of guidelines concerning the assessment and settlement of civil penalties under the Clean Water Act and other statutes, efforts which have sought to promote uniformity in enforcement and effective deterrence of violations. These guidelines are very complicated, and unrealistically mechanical in the evaluation of subjective factors affecting successful prosecution of a civil penalty action, a prosecution controlled not by EPA but by the Department of Justice. Despite these shortcomings, and changes in emphasis over time, these guidelines are good indications of EPA's enforcement priorities and settlement policy objectives. EPA plainly intends to remove any economic benefit that a violation has conferred on a discharger, both in terms of deferring capital investment in control equipment and in avoiding operation and maintenance costs. EPA has developed considerable sophistication in estimating what these avoided costs are, a sophistication based on expertise developed in setting standards and in refining its non-compliance penalties under Section 120 of the Clean Air Act. It is also clear that EPA will treat violations which cause (or threaten) greater harm to the environment or people's health more seriously than those which do not. Under the penalty policy, self-reporting of violations beyond what is required by law can be a significant mitigating factor. By the same token, actions which threaten the integrity of the self-reporting system, such as tampering with monitors or falsifying data, are viewed as extremely serious violations, appropriate for criminal prosecution.

This civil penalty policy may change substantially in the future, as it is presently focused on dischargers who have not yet installed the appropriate control technology, and not on those dischargers who occasionally violate requirements after installation of appropriate controls.

A second effort to guide EPA's enforcement discretion is a recent EPA memorandum concerning criminal enforcement priorities. This memorandum identifies factors to be considered in deciding whether to bring criminal proceedings, including the intent of the alleged violator, the threat to human health caused by the violation, the effect on EPA's regulatory programs (e.g., falsification of monitoring data), deterrence, and the compliance history of the alleged violator. The memo lists highly specific violations under the Clean Water Act and other statutes in the order of their importance. 78/ EPA has added a significant criminal enforcement staff for the first time although the Agency's criminal enforcement resources seem to be focused more on RCRA and other hazardous waste violations than on Clean Water Act violations.

In addition, these enforcement priorities are not binding on the Department of Justice, the federal agency responsible for these prosecutions. Nonetheless, it may be appropriate to focus compliance efforts on avoiding violations with a higher probability of criminal prosecution.

The broad enforcement discretion enjoyed by EPA and the states, coupled with the requirement of publicly filing monitoring reports, including those showing violations, requires potential violators to take the initiative in dealing with compliance problems. In the event of a possible violation, a discharger must be prepared to spend substantial time and effort with all relevant agencies. When several parts of EPA and several different state agencies are involved, there is no assurance that they are pursuing a coherent strategy or, indeed, are even talking to each other. Thus the discharger must be prepared to keep all federal and state agencies fully informed, preferably in a way that will ensure the most favorable processing of any potential violations. In doing this, the discharger should attempt to accomplish the following three goals:

— Convince the relevant enforcement agencies of its good faith. The EPA civil penalty policy makes it clear that "recalcitrance" is an aggravating factor and cooperation a mitigating one. Since the enforcement agencies will not, for the forseeable future, be able to move against every violation, a discharger's good faith or bad faith will be an important factor in deciding who to move against, and, if so, how severely.

— The discharger must attempt to deal with any major health or environmental problems caused by a potential violation in a manner that is as serious as the manner EPA or the state enforcement agency

---

78/ See the reproduction of this memorandum in the 22 October 1982 "Current Developments" section of the BNA Environment Reporter.

would adopt. Discharges which may create public
health problems, or create unique environmental
impacts, or which are likely to be the subject of
adverse publicity are recognized as aggravating
factors in the EPA's civil penalty policy. To the
degree possible, special efforts should be made to
avoid discharges of such substances and to quickly
control and clean up any spill.

— The discharger must realistically appraise not only
its chances of ultimately prevailing in any enforcement litigation, but the bureaucratic constraints
such as the civil penalty policy on EPA and the
Department of Justice in settlement negotiation. In
any settlement calculus, a discharger must understand that even a successfully defended enforcement action will likely result in substantial adverse
publicity, negative exposure which is not fully overcome by a favorable verdict.

These guidelines are not a panacea to the problems involved in
dealing with potential enforcement actions. However, they can
serve to ameliorate some of the uncertainty surrounding the present
enforcement system.

7.2 Citizen Suits

Section 505 of the Act provides an additional impetus to
vigorous enforcement of the Act's provisions. It authorizes any
person "having an interest which is or may be adversely affected" to
commence civil actions either against a discharger, for violation of
any effluent standard or limitation under the Act, or against EPA
for failure to proceed expeditiously to enforce the Act's provisions.
Experience under the Refuse Act program and the Clean Water Act
indicates that citizen suit provisions are highly effective in increasing the number of enforcement actions brought. While the Clean
Water Act, unlike the Refuse Act, does not make provision for the
payment of a "bounty" to the moving citizen, it does make specific
provision for the payment of attorney and expert witness fees. This
latter provision is probably of more assistance to environmental
action groups than was the bounty provision under the Refuse Act.

Between January 1983 and July 1984, more than 120 notices
of intent to bring citizen suits against dischargers have been filed
with EPA. Giving such notice is the first step in bringing a citizens'

enforcement action, and is frequently the start of settlement negotiations between the discharger and the citizens' group. Normally in
citizens' enforcement actions which are litigated, the plaintiffs use
a discharger's required Daily Monitoring Reports (DMRs) to establish
the discharger's liability. As some courts have held that dischargers
are strictly liable for permit violations, intent is not a good
defense. Most of the recent citizen suits have been settled on the
basis of some combination of:

(1) payment of civil penalties;

(2) adoption of a compliance schedule;

(3) stipulated penalties for failure to meet the schedule; and

(4) attorney's fees and costs to plaintiffs.

Although EPA's minimal enforcement efforts in the early
years of the Reagan Administration were a primary cause of the
recent flurry of citizens' enforcement actions, EPA's view of the
enforcement action can be an important factor in settlement negotiations. In several cases, EPA has refused to agree to settlement
conditions worked out by environmentalist plaintiffs and dischargers,
on the ground that the conditions were too generous to the discharger. EPA's leverage in these negotiations derives from its
statutory right to intervene in any citizen's enforcement action.

7.3. Provisions Having Special Applicability

7.3.1 Discharges to Ground Waters

One byproduct of the Clean Air Act and the Clean Water Act
has been increased pressure to dispose of waste materials on or
below land and the consequential increased threat of groundwater
contamination. However, underground aquifers is one class of water
bodies which is not included in the Act's definition of "waters of the
United States." Thus, although the Act, in Section 402(b)(1)(D),
requires states, as a precondition to approval of their NPDES programs, to "control the discharge of pollutants into wells," it gives
EPA no direct authority to regulate disposal of pollutants by subsurface injection.

Although EPA initially sought to regulate underground discharges pursuant to the Clean Water Act, it met with mixed
results. The courts disagreed as to whether EPA had authority to

regulate disposal into wells under that statute. 79/ EPA is now relying on the authority of the Safe Drinking Water Act (SDWA), 80/ to regulate such discharges and is encouraging the states to develop underground injection control programs pursuant to 40 CFR Part 146.

Part C of the SDWA applies to injection wells. However, well injection is broadly defined as the:

> subsurface implacement of fluids through a bored, drilled or driven well; or through a dug well, where the depth is greater than the largest surface dimension.

Thus, the state underground injection programs will have broad applicability.

Pending adoption by the state of underground injection control programs, EPA is regulating the injection of hazardous wastes under the Resource Conservation and Recovery Act. Waste lagoons and ponds will continue to be regulated by EPA and the states pursuant to the hazardous waste program.

Thus, many companies which had been exempt from wastewater discharge regulation under the Clean Water Act because they did not discharge to navigable waters will now be subjected to requirements governing wastewater discharges pursuant to the Safe Drinking Water Act and the Resource Conservation and Recovery Act.

7.3.2 Dredged or Fill Material

Section 404 of the Clean Water Act substantially affects development in areas adjacent to navigable waters. The section stringently controls dredging activity and the disposal of dredged or fill material into navigable water by granting the Corps of Engineers the authority to designate disposal areas and issue permits to discharge dredged and fill material therein rather than making such discharges subject to the general permit program provided by Sections 301, 304, 402 of the Act. The stringency of these requirements has been reinforced by three factors:

79/ See United States Steel v. Train, 556 F.2d 822 (7th Cir. 1977), and Exxon Corp. v. Train, 554 F.2d 1310 (5th Cir. 1977).

80/ 42 U.S.C. § 300 et seq.

— Section 404 has been construed to extend to all waters of the United States. 81/ Accordingly, the Corps permit program under Section 404 is applicable to many dredge and fill projects which would not have required permits under prior law;

— The Corps has construed Section 404 broadly, so as to cover not only disposal of dredged or fill material, as the section would seem to contemplate, but also the emplacement of dredge or fill material for development purposes and the construction of structures; 82/ and

— Section 511 of the Act, covers only permits issued by the EPA Administrator so that Section 404 permits, unlike most other permits under the Act, are subject to NEPA and possibly to the EIS requirements.

Congress responded to this situation by extensively revising Section 404 in the 1977 Amendments. The principal change was to authorize the states to establish permit programs for dredge and fill activities in non-navigable waters. 83/ In order to establish such a program, a state must comply with extensive requirements prescribed by the Act and must obtain EPA's approval of the program. There are also requirements for the state's operation of its program, including a requirement that a copy of each permit application and each proposed permit be sent to EPA. EPA, the Corps of Engineers, and the United States Fish and Wildlife Service have the right to comment on applications and proposed permits, and provision is made for the situation in which EPA objects to issuance of a permit. (Section 208 was also revised to assure that dredge and fill activities are considered in the water pollution control planning process.)

81/ N.R.D.C. v. Callaway, 392 F. Supp. 685 (D.D.C. 1975).

82/ 33 CFR Part 209.

83/ It is generally thought that, if a state does establish its own program, it will not be subject to NEPA constraints in its permit issuing activities.

A second change authorized the Corps of Engineers (or a state having an approved program) to issue "general" permits for specified categories of activities involving the discharge of dredge and fill materials. To issue such a permit, there must be a finding that the activities in the category are similar in nature and will have minimal adverse effects. Any activity covered by a general permit can be conducted without obtaining an individual Section 404 permit so long as the requirements and standards set forth in the general permit are complied with. The Corps expanded the scope of its general permit program to reduce the regulatory burden on a number of activities which involve incidental dredge or fill work. 84/ As part of a settlement agreement with environmental groups which had challenged these regulations, the Corps has proposed changes in these rules to assure that they are only applied in practice to activities which have a minimal environmental impact. 85/

Finally, Section 404(f) exempts certain dredge and fill discharges from regulation under Section 404 if specified effects on navigable waters are avoided. The activities thus excluded from the scope of Section 404 include maintenance operations, the construction of temporary sedimentation basins, temporary farm, forest and mining roads, and several types of agricultural activities.

7.3.3 Ocean Discharge Criteria

Section 403(c) of the Act directed EPA to promulgate guidelines for determining the effects of pollution discharges on ocean water quality and other aesthetic, recreational, and economic values of the oceans. No permit for an ocean discharge may be issued unless the permit issuing authority determines that the discharge will not cause unreasonable degradation of the environment, and permit conditions may be imposed to insure that such degradation will not occur. 86/

The 1981 Amendments to the Clean Water Act extended the time for municipalities to apply for waivers of secondary treatment

---

84/ 33 CFR Parts 320-330.

85/ 49 FR 12660 (29 March 1984).

86/ 40 CFR Part 125, Subpart M.

requirements for ocean discharges. 87/ In some circumstances, primary treatment may also be waived. EPA has announced that it will process municipal waiver applications in groups from the same geographic areas.

7.3.4 Thermal Discharges

Although heat is defined as a pollutant by the Clean Water Act and thereby is subject to technology-based effluent limitations imposed on industrial dischargers and POTWs, Congress included special provisions for the regulation of thermal discharges, in order to avoid unnecessary control costs. If the discharger can show that the technology based effluent limitations under Section 301 or under a new source performance standard are more stringent than necessary to assure protection and propagation of a balanced, indigenous population of shellfish, fish and wildlife in and on the body of water where the discharge is to occur, the Administrator or state may adjust the effluent limitation to a less stringent level, which will still assure such protection and propagation. This is the only section of the Act where water quality considerations can provide a variance from the otherwise minimum technology-based standards.

This provision—Section 316—is particularly important to power plants because heat is such a significant part of their discharge and because EPA established a "no-discharge" BAT requirement for heat. Even though this effluent limitation was overturned by the courts, 88/ permit issuers most often initially propose no-discharge of heat as an effluent limitation under Section 402(a).

Section 316 proceedings are quite complex; EPA requires substantial amounts of scientific data. There are difficult questions regarding what is the "indigenous" population, when a population is "balanced," and how heat will in fact affect the aquatic organisms. Nonetheless, this provision does excuse thermal dischargers from control requirements to the extent such requirements are unnecessary to protect the environment.

87/ PL 97-117, 95 Stat. 1632.

88/ Appalachian Power Co. v. Train, 545 F.2d 1351 (4th Cir. 1976).

8.0 The EPA Construction Grants Program

The stringent treatment requirements imposed on POTWs by the 1972 Act made a major federal assistance program a necessity if most municipalities were to be able to construct the facilities necessary to comply with the new effluent limitations. The construction grant program which the 1972 Act established in response to this need is one of the largest public works programs now being funded by the federal government.

Under the grant program, the federal share of the cost of approved treatment works was originally 75 percent, but that percentage was decreased to 55 percent in 1981, and may be cut further as budget pressures on the federal government persist. This federal grant is supplemented in many instances by a 15 percent state grant so that, at present, the grantee local government may pay only 30 percent of the eligible costs of the total facility. The Act and EPA's implementing regulations 89/ impose substantial conditions governing factors such as the share of operating costs which industrial users must pay, the eligibility of different parts of the plant and related sewer systems and so forth. The objective is to assure that grants will fund the construction of plants which will meet applicable treatment limits in a cost effective manner. These conditions can substantially affect the costs of POTW treatment to industrial users.

8.1 The Cost Recovery Program and User Charges

When the 1972 Act was enacted, Congress feared that the substantial grant assistance available to municipalities could function as an indirect subsidy to industrial users of the funded treatment works and that this subsidy would give users of POTWs an unfair competitive advantage over direct dischargers. Consequently, the Act required that municipalities provide for repayment of that portion of the construction grant allocable to industrial users.

From the industrial user's viewpoint, the Industrial Cost Recovery (ICR) requirement converted the construction "grant" to the equivalent of a long-term, no-interest loan. However, ICR proved quite difficult to administer and was repealed in 1980 after a legislative moratorium on such projects had expired.

89/ 40 CFR Part 35, Subpart E.

Some local communities continue to assess ICR payments even though they are no longer required by federal law. Such local ICR requirements are often of questionable legality under state law.

As the cost recovery regulations defined industrial users' proportionate share of the capital cost of new, grant funded treatment facilities, the user charge regulations establish requirements to be met by a municipal system for industrial sharing of the annual operating and maintenance charges of such facilities. Section 204 of the Act requires, as a condition of federal construction grant assistance, a finding that the applicant has adopted or will adopt:

> a system of charges to assure that each recipient of waste treatment services within the applicant's jurisdiction . . . will pay its proportional share...of the costs of operation and maintenance (including replacement) 90/ of any waste treatment services provided by the applicant.

The EPA regulations 91/ elaborate on the statutory requirement for proportionate distribution 92/ of O&M costs as follows:

90/ The term "replacement" has been defined by EPA to mean "expenditures for. . .equipment. . .which are necessary to maintain. . .capacity and performance during the service life of the treatment works. . ."

91/ 40 CFR § 35-929-1.

92/ The 1977 Amendments included a provision authorizing applicants which, prior to enactment of the Amendments, used a system of dedicated ad valorem taxes as a basis for funding costs of operation and maintenance of their facilities, to continue such system as the user charge system for their facility, with respect to small residential users as defined by EPA. EPA has defined a small residential user to include industrial users which introduce no more than the equivalent of 25,000 gallons per day of domestic sanitary waste to the treatment works. All industrial users whose flows exceed the 25,000 gallon per day domestic equivalent limit and all users of systems not having in effect an acceptable ad valorem system on the effective date of the 1977 Amendments are required to pay user charges based on actual use. The authorization to use ad valorem tax systems for user charge collection applies only where the system results in a proportionate distribution of costs.

A grantee's user charge system based on actual use (or estimated use) of waste water treatment services may be approved if each user (or user class) pays its proportionate share of operation and maintenance (including replacement) costs of treatment works within the grantee's service area, based on the user's proportionate contribution to the total waste water loading from all users (or user classes).

To insure proportional distribution of operation and maintenance costs to each user (or user class), the user's contribution shall be based on factors such as strength, volume, and delivery flow rate characteristics.

Quantity discounts to large volume users are not acceptable. EPA's philosophy is that savings resulting from economies of scale should be apportioned to all users or user classes. This would not, however, appear to preclude recognition of the fact that some large volume users are able to provide efficiencies to the treatment facility to which they discharge through flow equalization or other measures to control delivery flow rate. User charges may be established based on a percentage of the charge for water usage only in cases where the water charges are based on a constant cost per unit of consumption and thus may be reasonably reflective of the amount of wastewater discharged. The regulations also specifically provide that an industrial user which discharges, to a treatment works, wastewater containing toxic pollutants that cause an increase in the cost of managing the effluent or sludge from the treatment works, must pay for those increased costs. Finally, it should be noted that user charges, unlike cost recovery payments, are to be based on actual use of the facility and not on reserved shares, as is sometimes erroneously asserted by some municipalities.

Appendix B to EPA's regulations sets forth in more detail the guidelines for user charge computations and provides sample formulae for use in that connection. The guidelines are necessarily complex and technical. There is considerable potential for misapplication, particularly by small municipalities. A company which is a substantial contributor to a treatment works would thus be well advised to pay close attention to the municipality's determination of the user charge system which it will adopt.

As indicated above, the treatment works operator is obligated to develop a user charge mechanism, which will require each user to pay its proportionate share of the cost of waste treatment. This obligation is not fulfilled if, due to the selection of an inappropriate or defective formula or improper application of the formula selected, industrial users are required to subsidize waste treatment services performed for other users of the system. EPA approval of any planned federal construction grant application could, if necessary, be contested on that basis.

The basic approach in discussions with the POTW operating entity should be to make certain that the formula adopted (1) gives recognition to economies, other than economies of scale, which may be inherent in the nature of the company's discharge (e.g., the discharge may occur at non-peak periods, it may be low in suspended solids as compared to domestic sewage and so forth) and (2) does not give excessive weight to characteristics of the company's discharge, such as BOD content, which do not result in additional treatment costs. For example, if the treatment works is primarily flow dependent, a high surcharge based on strength of effluent may well be inappropriate. Numerous other technical questions such as the following may arise and should be addressed:

— If the industrial user pretreats its effluent so that its strength is less than that of domestic waste, shouldn't it be entitled to a cheaper rate?

— Shouldn't an industrial user's charge be reduced if it holds its effluent for discharge at non-peak flow periods, thereby contributing to the efficiency of the treatment works?

— If the particular type of industrial effluent makes the treatment works operate more efficiently, shouldn't that factor be recognized? (For example, iron in industrial discharges is used by some municipalities to help remove phosphorous from waste water.)

— If an industrial user's wastes are phosphorous and nitrogen-deficient, isn't it inappropriate to require that user to pay the portion of plant operation and maintenance expense allocable to removal of those pollutants?

— If a substantial portion of the plant capacity is for treatment of water flowing into the system during periods of rainfall due to infiltration and inflow, shouldn't costs allocable to the treatment of this wastewater be primarily allocated to residential connections which are the primary cause of this circumstance?

These and many other similar questions are commonly answered at the local level in connection with the locality's development of the user charge system which will be proposed for EPA acceptance. Since user charges are becoming an increasingly important component of industrial users' total cost of waste treatment services provided by POTWs, the importance of being alert to the proposal of ordinances establishing new user charge systems and of raising questions such as these cannot be over-emphasized.

8.2 Cost Effectiveness and Eligibility

As is evident from the preceding sections, industrial dischargers which use POTWs to treat their wastes have an immediate and substantial interest in minimizing the costs of constructing and operating such works. While the POTW owner-grantee is similarly motivated, these public officials are often unsophisticated in the waste treatment area and need technical and other assistance to assure that their waste treatment program is cost-effective. Although the statute requires that grant-eligible facilities be demonstrated to be the most cost-efficient alternative for compliance with applicable effluent limits over the facility's useful life 93/, there have been numerous cases where plants have been designed to achieve levels of treatment beyond that required by the applicable permit limits, with capacities in excess of that necessary to serve foreseeable needs and so forth. The procedures mandated for the development of Section 201 facilities plans, the preparation of environmental assessments related thereto, and the conduct of value engineering studies provide both industry and concerned citizens with considerable opportunities to help municipalities avoid these wasteful practices.

The final issue which should be considered in any effort to minimize the cost of industrial participation in a grant-funded POTW program is the question of whether all or only some of the elements of the POTW are eligible for federal grant funding. Treatment works costs which are found to be ineligible must be fully funded by the grantee, through a bond issue or otherwise, and industrial users are generally called upon to pay their proportionate share of the cost of amortizing the required bonds. Thus, where a portion

---

93/ Section 212(2)(B).

of the facilities is found to be ineligible, industrial users will be called upon to pay, not only the costs of the treatment works over its useful life, but also their share of the bond interest on that facility.

Consistent with the general objective of minimizing expenditure of federal grant funds, EPA has narrowly interpreted the Act's eligibility provisions as they apply to treatment facilities designed to handle industrial wastes. Thus though the Act's definition of treatment works would appear to apply to facilities which handle industrial wastes, EPA's regulations specify that allowable projects do not include "(1) costs of interceptor or collector lines constructed exclusively or almost exclusively to serve industrial users or (2) costs allocable to the treatment for control or removal of pollutants in wastewater introduced into the treatment works by industrial users, unless the applicant is required to remove such pollutants introduced from non-industrial sources." The scope of this exclusion in individual circumstances is subject to considerable interpretation and there are also considerable legal questions regarding the statutory authorization for this provision. Its application does merit careful attention in a number of situations. 94/

8.3 Construction Grants—Summary

The factors referenced above make it clear that users of POTWs are no longer insulated from the substantial costs of complying with Clean Water Act requirements. In many circumstances, POTWs can be an expensive way for an industrial discharger to meet the Act's requirements. The economics of alternative on-site treatment and direct discharge should be carefully examined before making or continuing commitments to rely on a POTW as a method of compliance.

9.0 Pollution Control Planning in the Current Regulatory Climate

Compliance with the Clean Water Act requirements outlined above would be a difficult and costly proposition under the best of

---

94/ The 1977 Amendments do make provision for funding of privately-owned treatment works serving commercial users where it can be demonstrated that such a facility is the most cost-effective way of providing waste treatment services and governmental entities have certified that the facility will be operated and maintained consistent with the requirements of the Act (Section 202(h)).

circumstances. These difficulties are compounded by inconsistencies in EPA (and state) enforcement policies, EPA's tardiness in developing standards, and the periodic Congressional rewriting of statutory requirements for the construction grant program. Consequently, the questions of how the law will be interpreted and enforced are often not amenable to predictable answers. Participation in the development of standards and continuing contact with officials responsible for permitting and enforcement is necessary if industrial dischargers wish to operate in a more consistent and predictable regulatory environment.

9.1   EPA Standards Development Programs

The suitability and practicability of the standards and regulations which EPA promulgates under the Act are dependent on EPA's thorough understanding of the processes and products to be regulated, the availability of detailed and reliable data on the applicability and limits of available treatment technology, and careful consideration of the economic and environmental impacts involved. Except for industry inputs, most standards (whether done by EPA staff or through outside contractors) tend to be based principally on technical data readily obtainable through review of existing literature. In some cases, these data are outdated, unreliable or inadequate. Thus, absent effective and technically documented participation by industry spokesmen, the standards which EPA promulgates are likely to have unanticipated effects when applied to real world conditions. Particular process or design factors may not have been considered and may be inequitable when applied to a specific plant or product.

Thus, early and active participation in the standards development process, either directly or through appropriate industry organizations, is advisable.   Although EPA has completed the development of most standards, the toxics strategy will continue to require such participation, as will any updating and revision of existing standards. Such participation could properly involve the following steps:

(1)   Assess the probability that standards (or revisions) applicable to your company's operations will be promulgated.

(2)   Determine the procedure which will be followed in developing the standard, the contemplated time schedule, and the areas under consideration where data available to EPA may be deficient.

(3) Assess the standards development procedure to determine whether it provides for taking into account any unusual aspects of your plant process or product design. Make comments to EPA and any private contractor involved as to how the procedure could be improved.

(4) Consider providing EPA and/or the appropriate private contractor any relevant technical data possessed by companies in the industry which is unpublished or otherwise not generally accessible.

(5) If the time schedule permits, consider the desirability of industry sponsored research or analytical projects to fill gaps in existing data on available technology or environmental and economic impact. In this connection, consideration should be given to consulting with EPA on the structuring of the project and exploring the possibility of EPA involvement in the conduct of the project.

(6) After a proposed standard is published in the Federal Register, the company or its spokesmen should participate in the usual comment procedure and consider the possibility of obtaining judicial review if the standard, as finally promulgated, is still unreasonable. In this connection, it should be kept in mind that if objections to standards are not timely asserted in judicial review proceedings, then they are waived. Further, it is generally wiser to litigate a standard at a time when your company does not stand accused of a violation.

9.2 Negotiation of Permit Conditions

Whether a company's authorization to discharge is in the form of an NPDES permit for direct discharge into a waterway or a contract with a municipality for use of its treatment facilities, the terms and conditions of that permit or contract may be every bit as important, in terms of impact on profits, as a major corporate contract. Like such a contract, they can be the subject of negotiations. Accordingly, pollution control managers should determine the areas in which the Act and legislation leave room for negotiation and, based on a careful assessment of the company's long-term interests, should negotiate actively in an effort to obtain favorable permit terms and conditions. These negotiations will be more important and much more complicated if toxic pollutants are involved.

9.3 Discussions With Regional Office and State Officials

No matter how good the standards are or how carefully permits are drawn, there will inevitably be situations where companies are forced to make major investment decisions which are affected by significant uncertainties in determining the applicable environmental control requirements. In these circumstances, serious consideration should be given to obtaining advance guidance from the appropriate EPA regional office and/or state enforcement personnel—whether or not the applicable statute makes provision for obtaining such guidance. A written indication that the cognizant authority has reviewed your proposal and found it acceptable, while perhaps not legally binding, can be of great future benefit. If the proposal is not acceptable to EPA or the state, it may be better to find that out before money has been spent. The chances of acceptance are generally far greater when the company goes to the regulator, rather than the other way around.

9.4 State and Local Planning Activities

Industry would also be well advised to pay considerable attention to the substantial planning requirements which are imposed by the Act on state and local governments. The state and regional water quality implementation plans, continuing planning processes and areawide waste treatment management plans may well be as important as federal rules and regulations in determining a company's future abatement costs. If properly carried out, these planning processes can be of immeasurable aid to business planners in predicting and planning for the future.

10.0 Conclusion

The implementation of and compliance with the Clean Water Act has been and remains complex, difficult, and expensive for all concerned. The increasing focus on toxic pollutants, while environmentally sound, increases the complexity of regulations, the costs of compliance, and the difficulty of monitoring.

Under these circumstances, it is obvious that the development and implementation of a workable and effective program will require the best efforts of regulators, environmentalists, and the regulated community. EPA, for its own part, must establish priorities and allow both industry and its own enforcement personnel to concentrate their attention on resolving the problems which are most significant in terms of impact on human health and the environment. It does little for the environment to spend time, money and effort identifying and monitoring pollutants which are present in inconsequential amounts and to which significant portions of the population are not exposed.

Environmentalists, for their part, must focus their attention on problems which make the most difference in protecting human health and the environment. The NRDC consent decree is a good example of this focus. Environmental progress is better measured by improvements in the quality of life rather than costs inflicted on industry. Industry, for its part, must participate fully in the development of EPA standards, if it is to avoid wasteful and frequently unsuccessful litigation to resolve EPA mistakes and omissions.

Pollution abatement costs can constitute a substantial portion of the total cost of many companies' final product. Consequently, the effectiveness with which a company plans its pollution control program may determine the extent to which the company remains competitive in its industry.

With this kind of cooperative effort there is at least some hope for achieving a regulatory environment in which a company can intelligently plan for compliance with water pollution control requirements—when the requirements established are (1) predictable and understandable; (2) equally applicable to and equitably enforced against all companies; (3) technologically and economically feasible; (4) announced sufficiently in advance of effectiveness to permit lead time for compliance; and (5) constant for a reasonable period of time after final adoption.

Achievement and maintenance of a regulatory climate which facilitates cooperative and intelligent planning is the best, and perhaps the only way of achieving the pollution control objectives announced by Congress when it passed the 1972 Act. These goals will best be met where all parties avoid unnecessary confrontations, focus on the real regulatory issues, and develop a program which reasonably and cost-effectively achieves essential water quality objectives without major economic or social dislocation.

ANNEX A — SECTION 307 — TOXIC POLLUTANTS

Acenaphthene
Acrolein
Acrylonitrile
Aldrin/Dieldrin
Antimony and compounds*
Arsenic and compounds
Asbestos
Benzene
Benzidine
Beryllium and compounds
Cadmium and compounds
Carbon tetrachloride
Chlordane (technical mixture and metabolites)
Chlorinated benzenes (other than dichlorobenzenes)
Chlorinated ethanes (including 1,2-dichloroethane, 1,1,1-ethane and
        hexachloroethane)
Chlorinated naphthalene
Chlorinated phenols (other than those listed elsewhere; includes
        trichlorophenols and chlorinated cresols)
Chloroalkyl ethers (chloromethyl, chloroethyl, and mixed ethers)
Chloroform
2-chlorophenol
Chromium and compounds
Copper and compounds
Cyanides
DDT and metabolites
Dichlorobenzenes (1,2-, 1,3-, and 1,4-dichlorobenzenes)
Dichlorobenzinine
Dichloroethylenes (1,1-and 1,2-dichloroethylene)
2,4-dichlorophenol
Dichloropropane and dichloropropene
2,4-dimethylphenol
Dinitrotoluene
Diphenylhydrazine
Endosulfan and metabolites
Endrin and metabolites
Ethylbenzene
Fluoranthene

---

*   The term "compounds" shall include organic and inorganic
compounds.

ANNEX A (continued)

Haloethers (other than those listed elsewhere; includes chlorophenyl-phenyl ethers, bromophenylphenyl ether, bis (dischloroiso-propyl) ether, bis-(chloroethoxy) methane and polychlorinated diphenyl ethers)

Halomethanes (other than those listed elsewhere; includes methylene chloride methylchloride, methylbromide, bromoform, dichloro-bromomethane, trichlorofluoromethane, dichlorodifluoro-methane)

Heptachlor and metabolites

Hexachlorobutadiene

Hexachlorocyclohexane (all isomers)

Hexachlorocyclopentadiene

Isophorone

Lead and compounds

Mercury and compounds

Naphthalene

Nickel and compounds

Nitrobenzene

Nitrophenols (including 2,4-dinitrophenol, dinitrocresol)

Nitrosamines

Pentachlorophenol

Phenol

Phthalate esters

Polychlorinated biphenyls (PCBs)

Polynuclear aromatic hydrocarbons (including benzanthracenes, benzo-pyrenes, benzofluoranthene, chrysenes, dibenzanthra-cenes, and indenopyrenes)

Selenium and compounds

Silver and compounds

2,3,7,8-Tetrachlorodibenzo-p-dioxin (TCDD)

Tetrachloroethylene

Thallium and compounds

Toluene

Toxaphene

Trichloroethylene

Vinyl chloride

Zinc and compounds

ANNEX B — INDUSTRY CATEGORIES

1. Adhesives and Sealants
2. Aluminum Forming
3. Asbestos Manufacturing
4. Auto and Other Laundries
5. Battery Manufacturing
6. Coal Mining
7. Coil Coating
8. Copper Forming
9. Electric and Electronic Components
10. Electroplating
11. Explosives Manufacturing
12. Ferroalloys
13. Foundries
14. Gum and Wood Chemicals
15. Inorganic Chemicals Manufacturing
16. Iron and Steel Manufacturing
17. Leather Tanning and Finishing
18. Mechanical Products Manufacturing
19. Nonferrous Metals Manufacturing
20. Ore Mining
21. Organic Chemicals Manufacturing
22. Pesticides
23. Petroleum Refining
24. Pharmaceutical Preparations
25. Photographic Equipment and Supplies
26. Plastic and Synthetic Materials Manufacturing
27. Plastic Processing
28. Porcelain Enamelling
29. Printing and Publishing
30. Pulp and Paperboard Mills
31. Soap and Detergent Manufacturing
32. Steam Electric Power Plants
33. Textile Mills
34. Timber Products Processing

Chapter 8

OCCUPATIONAL SAFETY AND HEALTH ACT 1/

Marshall Lee Miller
Attorney
Reid & Priest
Washington, D.C.

1.0 Introduction

The U.S. Occupational Safety and Health Administration
(OSHA) has been called the most unpopular agency in the federal
government. It has justifiably been criticized for its confusing
regulations, chronic mismanagement, and picayune enforcement.
With somewhat less accuracy, some business groups have likened it
to an American gestapo, while labor unions have denounced it as
unresponsive and bureaucratic.

It is not often recognized, however, that OSHA is also perhaps the most important environmental health agency in the government. Even the Environmental Protection Agency (EPA), with far
greater resources and public attention, deals with a smaller range of
much less hazardous exposures than does OSHA. After all, individuals are more likely to be exposed to high concentrations of dangerous chemicals in their workplaces than in their backyards.

2.0 Comparison of OSHA and EPA

There are several distinct differences between OSHA and
EPA, besides the obvious occupational jurisdiction. First, OSHA has

---

1/ A section-by-section outline of the key provisions of the
    statute can be found at the end of this chapter as Appendix A.

major responsibility over workplace safety as well as health. Second, OSHA is essentially an enforcement organization, with a majority of its employees as inspectors, performing fifty thousand or more inspections a year. This "highway patrol" function, inspecting and penalizing thousands of businesses large and small, is the major reason for OSHA's substantial unpopularity. At EPA, on the other hand, inspections and enforcement are a relatively minor part of the operation.

Third, whereas EPA is an independent regulatory agency, albeit headed by presidential appointees, OSHA is a division of the Department of Labor. This organizational arrangement provides not only less prestige and, in theory, less independence for OSHA, but poses an internal conflict whether OSHA should be primarily a health or a labor-oriented agency. Nevertheless, OSHA and EPA regulate different aspects of so many health issues—asbestos, vinyl chloride, carcinogens, hazard labeling, and others—that it is reasonable to regard them both as overlapping environmental organizations.

3.0 Legislative Framework

OSHA was created in December 1970—the same month as EPA—with the enactment of the Occupational Safety and Health Act (OSH Act), 2/ and officially began operation in April 1971. When compared with other environmental acts, the OSH Act is very simple and well drafted. This does not mean that one necessarily agrees with the provisions of every section, but it is clearly and concisely written so that details can be worked out in implementing regulations. And unlike the other environmental laws which have been amended several times, the OSH Act has not been amended or modified since its original passage. 3/

3.1 Purpose of the Act

The Act sets an admirable but impossible goal: to assure that "no employee will suffer material impairment of health or functional

---

2/   Occupational Safety and Health Act of 1970, PL 91-596, 84 Stat. 1590.

3/   Its annual appropriations legislation, however, has been modified several times to restrict OSHA authority over small businesses, farming, hunting, and other subjects.

capacity" from a lifetime of occupational exposure. 4/ It does not require a balancing test nor a risk-benefit determination. The supplementary phrase in the OSH Act, "to the extent feasible," was not meant to alter this. This absolutist position, comparable only to one provision in the Clean Air Act, 5/ reflects Congress' displeasure at previous, flexible state standards which traditionally seemed always to be resolved against workers' health. In fact, the concession to "feasibility" was added almost as an afterthought. 6/

Business groups did obtain two provisions in the law as their price for support. First, industry insisted that states should be encouraged to assume primary responsibility, thereby minimizing the role of the federal OSHA. Second, because of their distrust for the allegedly pro-union bias of the Department of Labor, responsibility for first-level adjudication of violations would be vested in an independent, three-member panel of judges in a separate Occupational Health and Safety Review Commission. Both of these provisions may be mistakes, and (as discussed below) the first has openly been acknowledged as such by many industry leaders.

Congress did reject, however, an industry effort to separate the standard setting authority from the enforcement powers of the new organization. A special role for the National Institute for Occupational Safety and Health (NIOSH) was intended to assure it a primary position in the standard-setting process. Thus, the three main roles of OSHA are (1) setting of safety and health standards, (2) their enforcement through federal and state inspectors, and (3) public education and consultation.

3.2 Coverage of the Act

In general, coverage of the Act extends to all employers and their employees in the fifty states and all territories under federal

---

4/   OSH Act § 6(b)(5), emphasis added.

5/   Clean Air Act § 112, 42 U.S.C. § 1857. There is considerable controversy whether this section, the National Emission Standards for Hazardous Air Pollutants (NESHAPS), was really intended by Congress to have this effect.

6/   The Supreme Court's consideration of this issue will be discussed in a later section.

government jurisdiction. 7/ An employer is defined as any "person engaged in a business affecting commerce who has employees but does not include the United States or any State or political subdivision of a State." 8/ Coverage of the Act was clarified by regulations published in the Federal Register on 21 January 1972. 9/ These regulations interpret the coverage as follows:

(1) The term "employer" excludes the United States and states and political subdivisions.

(2) Any employer employing one or more employees is under its jurisdiction, including professionals, such as physicians and lawyers; agricultural employers; and nonprofit and charitable organizations.

(3) Self-employed persons are not covered.

(4) Family members operating a farm are not regarded as employees.

(5) To the extent that religious groups employ workers for secular purposes, they are included in the coverage.

(6) Domestic household employment activities for private residences are not subject to the requirements of the Act.

(7) Workplaces already protected by other federal agencies under other federal statutes (discussed later) are also excluded.

4.0 Federal and State Employees

The exclusion of federal and state employees 10/ has been the topic of much discussion and debate. Although Section 19 of the Act designates the responsibility for providing safe and healthful working conditions to the head of each agency and implementing regulations have been published according to various Executive Orders, many

---

7/ OSH Act § 4(a)–4(b)(2).

8/ OSH Act § 3(5). The appropriations language, as mentioned, has excluded several "peripheral" categories of employers in the past few years.

9/ Ibid.

10/ Ibid, 37 FR 929, 21 January 1972, 29 CFR § 1975.

commentators feel the individual agencies' programs are inadequate and inconsistent.

In 1980, a new Presidential Executive Order 11/ was issued, which broadened the responsibility of federal agencies for protecting their workers, expanded employee participation in health and safety programs, and designated circumstances under which OSHA will inspect federal facilities. In the operation of their internal OSHA programs, agency heads will have to meet requirements of basic program elements issued by the Department of Labor and will have to comply with OSHA standards for the private sector unless they can justify alternatives.

5.0 Health Standards

Health issues, notably environmental contaminants in the workplace, have increasingly become OSHA'S primary concern over the past few years. Health hazards are much more complex, more difficult to define, and because of the delay in detection, perhaps more dangerous to a larger number of employees. Unlike safety hazards, the effects of health hazards may be slow, cumulative, irreversible, and complicated by non-occupational factors.

If a machine is unequipped with safety devices and maims a worker, the danger is clearly and easily identified and the solution usually obvious. However, if workers are exposed for several years to a chemical that is later found to be carcinogenic, there may be little help for those exposed.

In the nation's workplaces there are tens of thousands of toxic chemicals, many of which are significant enough to warrant regulation. Yet OSHA only has a list of 400 substances with simple threshold limits adopted from the recommended lists of private industrial hygiene organizations.

The promulgation of health standards involves many complex concepts. To be complete, each standard needs medical surveillance requirements, recordkeeping, monitoring, and multiple physical reviews, just to mention a few. At the present rate, promulgation of standards on every existing toxic substance could take centuries. OSHA has explored various generic or categorical approaches to standard setting, but so far these have been poorly organized.

11/   Executive Order 12196, signed 26 February 1980, 45 FR 12769, superseding E.O. 11807 of 28 September 1974.

6.0 Slow Pace of Standards Development: The Noise Example

Many of the criticisms lodged against OSHA stem from the slow standard setting process, and those complaints are generally valid. A good example of footdragging by the agency is its attempt to issue a noise standard. The Labor Department began regulating noise as far back as 1968 under the Walsh-Healy Public Contracts Act of 1936. 12/ With the creation of OSHA, responsibility for noise regulation was transferred to that agency, and in 1972 NOISH submitted a criteria document, which led to an OSHA proposed standard for 85 dB(A) (decibels). 13/ Issuance of the final revised OSHA noise standard has been promised for so long that predictions are no longer taken seriously. For instance, in October 1976, an OSHA official stated that a standard for noise regulation would be published within three months. 14/

In the meantime, labor leaders were complaining about the delay, hinting that political motives were responsible. 15/ In January 1977, a new administration assumed office that was considered to be more friendly to organized labor; but three years later, they still had not released the long-awaited, or long-dreaded, noise standard. The administrator of OSHA indicated in July 1977 that a task force was being established and that the standard would be ready by "early 1978." 16/ It was not, however, and OSHA did not even reopen the rulemaking record to introduce new information and updated cost data until April 1980. 17/ On 16 January 1981, a hearing conservation program was developed, although subsequently stayed by the courts, 18/ but the main noise standard is now not

---

12/   41 U.S.C. §§ 35-45.

13/   NOISH, "Criteria Document on Noise," 18 October 1972.

14/   BNA, Noise Regulations Reporter, no. 64, 25 October 1976, pp. A34-35.

15/   Ibid., no. 63, 11 October 1976, pp. AA-1 et seq.

16/   Ibid., no. 83, 18 July 1977, p. A-25.

17/   45 FR 26366, 18 April 1980.

18/   46 FR 4161, 16 January 1981, amending 29 CFR § 1910.95. This program was overturned by a 1984 decision of the Fourth Circuit, Forging Industry Association v. Secretary of Labor, 12 OSHC 1041 (4th Cir. 1984).

expected in this decade and even the present standard is being reviewed for modifications.

7.0 Standard Setting

To meet the objectives defined in the Act, three different standard setting procedures were established. These three standard setting procedures are:

(1)   Consensus Standards, Section 6(a).
(2)   Permanent Standards, Section 6(b).
(3)   Emergency Temporary Standards, Section 6(c).

We can all recognize the amount of time that could be expended in this process. There are thousands of chemical substances, electrical problems, fire hazards, and many other dangerous situations prevalent in the workplace for which standards needed to be developed.

7.1 Consensus Standards: Section 6(a)

Congress realized that OSHA would need standards to enforce while it was developing its own. Section 6(a) allowed the agency, for a two-year period which ended on 25 April 1973, to adopt standards developed by other federal agencies or to adopt consensus standards of various industry or private associations. This wholesale adoption pleased industry and removed some of the burden from OSHA, at least temporarily. When the agency found a conflict between any existing national consensus standard and an established federal standard, it was to promulgate the standard affording the greater protection to affected employees. This hurried initial standards package was published for the most part in June 1974. 19/ This has resulted in a list of several hundred common toxic chemicals, such as hydrogen cyanide, with maximum permitted air concentrations specified in parts per million (PPM) and in milligrams per cubic meter (mg/M^3).

There are several problems inherent in these standards. First, these threshold values are the only elements to the standard. There are no required warning labels, monitoring, medical recordkeeping, nor do they distinguish between 8-hour, 15-minute, peak, annual average, and other periods of exposure. Second, being thresholds,

---

19/   39 FR 23502, 27 June 1974.

they are based on the implicit assumption that there are universal no-effect levels, below which a worker is safe. This is a controversial subject. There may conceivably be a no-effect level for each individual, with a broad average for a large population, but the scientific data is not able to determine what it might be. Moreover, with carcinogens, the prevailing view is that there may be no threshold: the dose-response curve continues down to zero.

Third, most of the standards were originally established not on the basis of firm scientific evidence but, as the name implies, on the basis of consensus among various industry and governmental hygienists. These various lists had been around for years, with no urgency to keep them current. By the time they were adopted by OSHA, many were out of date. They are now frozen in time, probably for decades, until OSHA goes through the full Section 6(b) process, described below.

Whatever the disadvantages, Congress was undoubtedly correct in requiring the compilation of such a list. Otherwise, there would have been no OSHA health standards at the beginning; there are virtually no others even now.

7.1.1 Standards Completion Process

The Agency has attempted to deal with one of the above objections to the Standards Completion Process for the 6(a) standards. Over a number of years, OSHA has taken a half-dozen or more threshold standards and added various medical, monitoring, and other requirements. The numbers themselves cannot be updated, for legal reasons, 20/ but at least a broader range of protection is offered to exposed workers.

7.2 Permanent Standards: Section 6(b)

Permanent standards must now be developed pursuant to Section 6(b). This is the present standard setting process. Permanent standards may be initiated by a well-publicized tragedy, court action, new scientific studies, or (usually) the receipt of a criteria document from the National Institute of Occupation Safety and

---

20/ Since the 6(a) process ended in April 1972, the standards promulgated thereunder can be revoked, reproposed, or otherwise dealt with afresh, but they cannot be modified or revised without going through the notice and comment administrative procedures under Section 6(b).

Health (NIOSH), an organization described in Section 13.0 of this Chapter. The criteria document is a compilation of all the scientific reports on a particular chemical, including epidemiological and animal studies, along with a recommendation to OSHA for a standard. The recommendation, based supposedly only on scientific health considerations, includes suggested exposure limits (8-hour average, peaks, etc.) and appropriate medical monitoring, labeling, and other prescriptions.

Congress apparently assumed that NIOSH would be the standard-setting arm of OSHA although the two are in different government departments (HHS and Labor, respectively). Theoretically, OSHA would take the recommendations from NIOSH, factor in engineering and technical feasibility, and then promulgate as similar a standard as possible. However, the system has never worked this way. Instead, OSHA's own standards office has regarded NIOSH's contribution as just one step in the process—and not one entitled to a great deal of deference. Criteria documents vary considerably in quality, depending in part on to whom they were subcontracted, but another problem is that too often they are insufficiently discriminating in evaluating questionable studies. That is, one study is regarded as good as any other study, without regard to the quality of the data or the validity of the protocols. Of course, another factor in OSHA's attitude just might be the "not invented here" syndrome.

Following receipt of the criteria document, or some other initiating action, OSHA will study the evidence and, in theory, publish a proposed standard. Most candidate standards never get this far: the hundreds of NIOSH documents, labor union petitions, and other serious recommendations have resulted in (depending on the count) only slightly over a dozen health standards since 1970. 21/

The proposed standard is then subjected to public comment for a sixty or ninety day period, after which the reactions are analyzed and (usually) informal public hearings are scheduled. In a few controversial instances, there may be more than one series of hearings and comments. Then come the post-hearing comments, which are perhaps the most important presentations by the parties.

21/ This meager number does not reflect OSHA's scientific judgment that the other candidates are unworthy or that the Agency has sharply different priorities, although these may be partial factors. More important reasons are: poor leadership, technical inexperience, and a bit of politics.

After considerable further study, a final standard is eventually
promulgated. The entire process could be accomplished in under a
year, but in practice it takes a minimum of several years and
possibly even decades.

Even when issued in "final," the process may not be completed. Some standards are obviously defective. The present
asbestos standard for example, does not even acknowledge that the
substance is a human carcinogen. The standard was reproposed as
such in late 1975, then issued as an emergency standard eight (!)
years later, only to be promptly overturned by a court as a dubious
emergency. A regular 6(b) proposal is still pending. 22/

Under the Reagan Administration, another form of revision
has developed. Standards which have become final and survived
legal challenge all the way up to the Supreme Court, such as cotton
dust and lead standards, have nevertheless been called into question.
23/ With this revision caveat, the following is a list of the ten final
health standards which OSHA has promulgated to date:

(1)   Asbestos 24/
(2)   "14 carcinogens" 25/
            -4-nitrobiphynyl 26/
            -alpha-nephthylamine 27/
            -methyl chloromethyl ether 28/
            -3,3'-dichlorolenzidine 29/

22/   Asbestos Information Association/North America v. OSHA),
      727 F. 2d 415, (5th Cir., 1984).

23/   47 FR 5906, 9 February 1982 - "While the agency has deter-
      mined that the application of cost-benefit analysis to this
      standard is precluded by the Supreme Court's decision, the
      agency has concluded that it is totally appropriate to re-
      examine new health data and alternative compliance ap-
      proaches, as well as matters relevant to the implementation
      and enforcement of the cotton dust standard." 47 FR 26557, 18
      June 1982—"OSHA is currently undertaking a thorough recon-
      sideration of the lead standard...."

24/   29 CFR § 1910.100.
25/   29 CFR § 1910.100.
26/   § 1310.1003.
27/   § 1310.1004.
28/   § 1910.1006.
29/   § 1910.1007.

-bis-chloromethyl ether 30/
-beta-naphthylamine 31/
-benzidine 32/
-4-aminodiphenyl 33/
-ethyleneimine 34/
-beta-propiolactone 35/
-2-acetylaminofluorene 36/
-4-dimethylaminoazobenzene 37/
-N-nitrosodimethylamine 38/
-(MOCA—stayed by court action)

(3) vinyl chloride 39/
(4) inorganic arsenic 40/
(5) lead 41/
(6) coke oven emissions 42/
(7) cotton dust 43/
(8) 1,,2-dibromo-3-chloropropane 44/
(9) acrylonitrile 45/
(10) ethylene oxide 46/

30/ § 1910.1008.
31/ § 1910.1009.
32/ § 1910.1010.
33/ § 1910.1011.
34/ § 1910.1012.
35/ § 1910.1013.
36/ § 1910.1014.
37/ § 1910.1015.
38/ § 1910.1016.
39/ § 1910.1017.
40/ § 1910.1018.
41/ § 1910.1025.
42/ § 1910.1029.
43/ § 1910.104.
44/ § 1910.1044.
45/ § 1910.1045.
46/ § 1910.1047. This is the only OSHA health standard for a specific substance issued in the first four years of the Reagan Administration. 49 CFR 25796, 22 June 1984. A revised asbestos standard was issued in an emergency form, as mentioned, but was overturned by the courts.

7.3 Emergency Temporary Standards

The statute also provides for a third standard–setting approach, specified for emergency circumstances where the normal, ponderous rulemaking procedure would be too slow. Section 6(c) gives the Agency authority to issue an emergency temporary standard (ETS) if necessary to protect workers from exposure to "grave danger" posed by substances "determined to be toxic or physically harmful or from new hazards." [OSHA Act § 6(c)(1)]. Such standards are effective immediately upon publication in the Federal Register. An ETS is only valid, however, for six months. OSHA is thus under considerable pressure to conduct an expedited rulemaking for a permanent standard before the ETS lapses. For this reason, a quest for an emergency standard is the preferred route for labor unions or other groups seeking a new OSHA standard. In fact, most of the existing 6(b) standards began as emergency standards under Section 6(c).

8.0 Safety Standards

This chapter emphasizes the health aspects of OSHA. Most press attention and the Agency's own emphasis since the mid–1970s has been on health standards. Nevertheless, OSHA is also an occupational safety organization. The two parts of the organization are quite distinct: there are separate inspectors and standards offices for each, and the two groups are different in terms of background, education, and age. There are also far more safety than health inspectors.

Safety hazards are those aspects of the work environment which, in general, cause harm of an immediate and sometimes violent nature, such as burns, electrical shock, cuts, broken bones, loss of limbs or eyesight, and even death. The distinction from health hazards is usually obvious, with mechanical and electrical considered as safety problems, while chemicals are considered health problems. Only noise is difficult to categorize; it is classified as a health problem.

The Section 6(a) adoption of national consensus and other federal standards, created chaos in the safety area. It was one thing for companies to follow guidelines that, in many cases, had not been modified in years; it was another thing for those guidelines actually to be written down as law. The Act provided two years for OSHA to produce standards derived from these existing standards. The Agency should have gone through these standards, simplified them, deleted the ridiculous and unnecessary ones, and promulgated final regulations that actually identified and eliminated hazards to workers. But it did not happen that way.

Almost all of these so-called "Mickey Mouse" standards were safety regulations, such as the requirement that fire extinguishers had to be attached to the wall exactly so many inches above the floor. Undertrained OSHA inspectors often failed to recognize major hazards while citing industries for minor violations "which were highly visible, but not necessarily related to serious hazards to workers' safety and health." 47/

At a conference on Occupational Safety and Health Regulations in 1978, then Deputy Director of the Safety Standards Program at OSHA, John Proctor, stated:

> New standards will be needed to fill major gaps and respond to priority needs disclosed by work injury data or safety research into the causes of injury as well as the means of control or elimination of hazards and risks. The ability to anticipate the potential hazards of new technology or to advance the state of the art for engineering controls and means of safeguarding of exposed employees will be a major goal for OSHA's safety standards staff. 48/

Section 6(g) of the OSH Act directs OSHA to establish priorities based on the needs of specific "industries, trades, crafts, occupations, businesses, workplaces, or work environments." The Senate report accompanying the OSH Act stated that the agency's emphasis initially should be put on industries where the need was determined to be most compelling. 49/ "OSHA's early attempts to target inspections, however, were sporadic and, for the most part, unsuccessful." 50/ The situation has improved somewhat in recent years, for both health and safety, in part because of the recent require-

---

47/ Statement of Basil Whiting, Deputy Assistant Secretary of Labor for OSHA, before the Committee on Labor on Human Resources, U.S. Senate, 21 March 1980, pp. 5-6.

48/ Proceedings of the Occupational Health and Safety Regulations Seminar, (Washington, D.C.: Government Institutes, 10-11 April 1978) p. 15.

49/ For the legislative history of the Act, see especially the Conference Report 91-1765 of 16 December 1970, as well as H.R. 91-1291 and S. Rpt. 91-1282.

50/ Basil Whiting Statement, op.cit., p. 4.

ment that some priority scheme be used that could justify search warrants, but that has brought its own problems. 51/

9.0 Areas Covered by the Standards

To give the reader an idea of the areas covered by the standards, the following is a subpart listing from the Code of Federal Regulations, Part 1910, Occupational Safety and Health Standards. The health standards are contained in Subpart Z; the others are safety related, except for Subparts A, B and C which cover both.

Subpart   A -   General (purpose and scope, definitions, applicability of standards, etc.)

Subpart   B -   Adoption and Extension of Established Federal Standards (construction work, ship repairing, longshoring, etc.)

Subpart   C -   General Safety and Health Provisions (preservation of records)

Subpart   D -   Walking-Working Surfaces (guarding floor and wall openings, portable ladders, requirements for scaffolding, etc.)

Subpart   E -   Means of Egress (definitions, specific means by occupancy, sources of standards, etc.)

Subpart   F -   Powered Platforms, Manlifts, and Vehicle-Mounted Work Platforms (elevating and rotating work platforms, standards organizations, etc.)

Subpart   G -   Occupational Health and Environmental Control (ventilation, noise exposure, radiation, etc.)

Subpart   H -   Hazardous Materials (compressed gases, flammables, storage of petroleum gases, effective dates, etc.)

Subpart   I -   Personal Protective Equipment (eye and face, respiratory, electrical devices, etc.)

Subpart   J -   General Environmental Controls (sanitation, labor camps, safety color code for hazards, etc.)

Subpart   K -   Medical and First Aid (medical services, sources of standards)

51/   See Marshall v. Barlow's Inc., 436 U.S. 307 (1978), which will be discussed later in this chapter.

Subpart   L - Fire Protection (fire supression equipment, hose and sprinkler systems, fire brigades, etc.)

Subpart   M - Compressed Gas and Compressed Air Equipment (inspection of gas cylinders, safety relief devices, etc.)

Subpart   N - Materials Handling and Storage (powered industrial trucks, cranes, helicopters, etc.)

Subpart   O - Machinery and Machine Guarding (requirements for all machines, woodworking machinery, wheels, mills, etc.)

Subpart   P - Hand and Portable Powered Tools and Other Hand-Held Equipment (guarding of portable power tools, sources of standards, etc.)

Subpart   Q - Welding, Cutting and Brazing (definitions, sources of standards, etc.)

Subpart   R - Special Industries (pulp, paper and paperboard mills, textiles, laundry machinery, telecommunications, etc.)

Subpart   S- Electrical (application, National Electrical Code)

Subpart   T - Commercial Diving Operations (qualification of team, pre- and post-dive procedures, equipment, etc.)

Subpart   U-Y- [Reserved]

Subpart   Z - Toxic and Hazardous Substances (air contaminants, asbestos, vinyl chloride, lead, benzene, etc.)

10.0 Variances

10.1 Temporary Variances

Section 6(b)(6)(A) of the OSH Act establishes a procedure by which any employer may apply for a "temporary order granting a variance from a standard or any provision thereof." According to the Act, the variance will be approved when OSHA determines that the requirements have been met and establishes that (1) the employer is unable to meet the standard "because of unavailability of professional or technical personnel or of materials and equipment," or because alterations of facilities cannot be completed in time; (2) that he is "taking all available steps to safeguard" his workers against the hazard covered by the standard for which he is applying for a variance; and (3) he has an "effective program for coming into compliance with the standard as quickly as practicable." 52/

This temporary order may be granted only after employees have been notified and, if requested, there has been sufficient opportunity for a hearing. The variance may not remain in effect for more than one year with the possibility of only two six-month renewals. 53/ The overriding factor an employer must demonstrate for a temporary variance is good faith. 54/

10.2 Permanent Variances

Permanent variances can be issued under Sec. 6(d) of the OSH Act. A permanent variance may be granted to an employer who has demonstrated "by a preponderance" of evidence that the "conditions, practices, means, methods, operations or processes used or proposed to be used" will provide a safe and healthful workplace as effectively as would compliance with the standard.

11.0 Compliance and Inspections

11.1 Field Structure

The Department of Labor (DOL) has divided the territory subject to the OSH Act into ten federal regions (EPA also uses the same boundaries), each containing from four to nine area offices. When an area office is not warranted because of a lack of industrial activity, district offices or field stations are established. Each region is headed by a regional administrator; each area by an area director. In the field, compliance officers represent area offices and inspect industrial sites in their vicinity.

11.2 Role of Inspections

The only way to determine compliance by employers is inspections, but inspecting all the workplaces covered by the OSH Act would require decades. Each year there are over fifty-thousand

---

52/ OSH Act § 7(b)(6)(A).

53/ Ibid.

54/ E. Klein, Variances, in Proceedings of the Occupational Health and Safety Regulations Seminar, (Washington D.C.: Government Institutes, 1978) p. 74.

federal inspections, and twice as many state inspections, but there are several million workplaces. Obviously, a priority system for high-hazard occupations is necessary, along with random inspections just to keep everyone "on his toes."

11.3 Training and Competency of Inspectors

There has been a major problem with OSHA inspectors in the past—the training program has not adequately prepared them. In the early days there was tremendous pressure from the unions to get an inspection force on the job as soon as possible, so training was minimal. Inspectors would walk into a plant where kepone dust was so thick workers could not see across the room, and, because there was no standard as such, would not think there was a problem. Yet had there been a fire extinguisher in the wrong place, and had the inspector been able to see it through the haze, he would have cited the plant for safety violation.

> Competency among staff has markedly improved since the early days of the program. Both in-house training efforts by OSHA and increased numbers of professional training programs conducted by colleges and universities have contributed to these improvements. There is also a greater sensitivity towards workers and their representatives. 55/

11.4 Citations

If the inspector discovers a hazard in the workplace, a citation is in order. Citations can be serious, nonserious, willful, or repeated. A serious violation is found if there is "substantial probability that death or serious physical harm could result from a condition which exists, or from one or more practices, means, methods, operations, or processes which have been adopted by or are in use, in such place of employment unless the employer did not, and could not with the exercise of reasonable diligence, know of the presence of the violation." 56/ A penalty is mandatory for a serious violation; a nonserious violation is discretionary. Even several nonserious

---

55/ Statement of Lane Kirkland, President, AFL-CIO, before the Senate Committee on Labor and Human Resources on Oversight of the Occupational Safety and Health Act, 1 April 1980.

56/ OSH Act § 17(k).

violations considered together do not make up a serious violation unless the combination somehow would be likely to lead to death or serious physical harm to an employee.

11.5 Willful Violations

The Administration has a powerful weapon with which to threaten those employers who are careless of, or indifferent to, their obligations under the Act. Any employer who is aware of a hazardous condition in his plant, yet makes no effort to rectify it, may be held to be a willful violator and penalized as such. A "willful" violation is "properly defined as an act or omission which occurs consciously, intentionally, deliberately or voluntarily as distinguished from accidentally." 57/

> The critical element of proof necessary is that of knowledge....OSHA would have to establish that the employer was aware that a hazardous condition existed and then took no reasonable steps to eliminate the condition. 58/

Penalties for willful violations considerably exceed those for serious or nonserious violations; a penalty of $10,000 may be assessed for each violation.

11.6 Repeat Violations

The same penalty may be applied for repeated violations, with each day being in theory a separate violation. A citation for a repeated violation cannot be issued unless the employer has been cited for a violation, has abated the violation, and has thereafter again violated the same standard or permitted the same hazard to exist in his plant. In the case of a company having multiple sites or plants, in different states or OSHA regions, the issue of repeatedness is more complex. OSHA has changed its definitions several times, and the policy is not yet firm.

When enough time has been allowed for the correction of a violation, OSHA may reinspect the plant to verify compliance with the issued citation. If the employer has failed to abate, a penalty of

---

57/ Guidebook to Occupational Safety and Health (Chicago: CCH, 1974) p. 149.

58/ OSH Act § 17(d).

up to $1000 per day will be assessed "for each day during which such failure or violation continues." 59/

12.0 State OSHA Programs

The federal OSHA program was intended by many legislators and businessmen to only fill the gap where state programs were lacking. The latter were to be the primary regulatory control. It has not happened that way, of course, but approximately two dozen state programs, albeit often limping, are still important.

12.1 The Concept

The OSH Act requires OSHA to encourage the states to develop and operate their own job safety and health programs, which must be "at least as effective as" the federal program. 60/ Until effective state programs are approved, federal enforcement of standards promulgated by OSHA preempt state enforcement. 61/ State laws remain in effect when no federal standard exists.

Before approving a submitted state plan, OSHA must make certain that the state can meet criteria established in the Act. 62/ Once a plan is in effect, the secretary may exercise "authority...until he determines, on the basis of actual operations under the State plan, that the criteria set forth are being applied. 63/ But he cannot make such a determination for three years after the plan's approval. OSHA may continue to evaluate the state's performance in carrying out the program even after a state plan has been approved. If a state fails to comply, the approval can be withdrawn, but only after the agency has given due notice and opportunity for a hearing.

12.2 Critiques

The program has not worked as anticipated, although almost half the states have their own system. Industry has cooled to the local concept, which requires multi-state companies to contend with

---

59/   Ibid.

60/   OSH Act §§ 2(b)(11) and 18 (c)(2).

61/   OSH Act § 18(a).

62/   OSH Act § 18(c)(1) - (c)(8).

63/   OSH Act § 18(c).

a variety of state laws and regulations instead of a uniform federal plan. Moreover, state OSHAs are often considerably larger than the local federal force, so there can be more inspections. Organized labor has never liked the state concept, because of its poor experience with the previous local organizations and a realization that its strength could more easily be exercised in one location—Washington, D.C.—than in all fifty states and territorial capitals. This has meant, ironically, that some of the better state programs, in areas where unions had the most influence, were among the first rejected by state legislators under strong union pressure.

Organized labor and industry are not alone in their criticism of the state programs. Health research organizations, OSHA's own national advisory committee (NACOSH), and some of the states themselves have also voiced disapproval of the state program policy. Ineffective operations at the state level, disparity in federal funding, and lack of the necessary research capability are just a few of the criticisms lodged. 64/

> OSHA had not developed articulate, coherent programs for achieving fully effective enforcement. State plans, in other words, are likely to be defective because they have been formed around defective criteria. OSHA must now go back and redo, to a certain extent, those criteria and reevaluate the state plans. 65/

There is some defense of state control, however. "To the extent that local control increases the responsiveness of programs to the specific needs of people in that area, this [a state plan] is a potentially good policy." 66/ But reevaluation and revision will be necessary in the next several years if OSHA's policy for state programs is to be accepted by all the factions involved.

64/   Robert Hayden, "Federal and State Roles" in Proceedings of the Occupational Health and Safety Regulation Seminar, (Washington, D.C.: Government Institutes, 1978) pp. 9-10.

65/   Ibid., p. 11.

66/   Nicholas A. Ashford, Crisis in the Workplace: Occupational Disease and Inquiry, (Boston: MIT Press, 1976) p. 231.

13.0 Consultation

Employers subject to OSHA regulation, particularly small employers, need on-site consultation to determine what must be done to bring their workplaces into compliance with the requirements of the OSH Act. These consultations should be free from citations or penalties. As in so many other areas of OSHA regulation, there has been a great deal of controversy surrounding the consultation process. Union leaders have always feared that OSHA could become merely an educational institution rather than one with effective enforcement. But Section 21(c) of the Act does mandate consultation with employers and employees "as to effective means of preventing occupational injuries and illnesses." 67/

Along with the consultation provisions, the statute provides for "programs for the education and training of employers and employees in the recognition, avoidance, and prevention of unsafe or unhealthful working conditions in employments covered" by the Act. 68/ OSHA produces brochures and films to educate employees about possible hazards in their workplaces. But, there are problems at every stage of the information process, from generation to utilization. It can be an overwhelming task to generate all the information needed for a particular hazard. But even when useful and pertinent information is gathered and disseminated, decision-makers may be slow in using it.

In 1979, OSHA instituted a New Directions Training and Education Program, which made available up to $2.7 million in grants to support the development and strengthening of occupational safety and health competence in business, employee, and educational organizations. This program supported a broad range of activities, such as training in hazard identification and control; workplace risk assessment; medical screening and recordkeeping; and liaison work with OSHA, the National Institute for Occupational Safety and Health, and other agencies. "The goal of the program was to allow unions and other groups to become financially self-sufficient in supporting comprehensive health and safety programs." 69/ This program, criticized by some as a payoff to constituent groups,

---

67/   OSH Act § 21(c)(2).

68/   OSH Act § 21(c)(1).

69/   U.S. Department of Labor, "OSHA News," 12 April 1978.

especially labor unions, has been a natural target of Reagan Administration budget cutters, but the concept of increased consultation has been given even greater emphasis.

There is also a provision that state plans may include on-site consultation with employers and employees to encourage voluntary compliance. 70/ The personnel engaged in these activities must be separate from the inspection personnel and their existence must not detract from the federal enforcement effort. These consultants not only point out violations, but also give abatement advice.

14.0 Overlapping Jurisdiction

There are other agencies involved with statutory responsibilities that affect occupational safety and health. These agencies indirectly regulate safety and health matters in their attempt to protect public safety.

One example of an overlapping agency is the Department of Transportation and its constituent agencies, such as the Federal Railroad Administration and the Federal Aviation Administration. These agencies promulgate rules concerned with the safety of transportation crews and maintenance personnel, as well as the traveling public, and consequently overlap similar responsibilities of OSHA.

Section 4(b)(1) of the OSH Act states that when other federal agencies "exercise statutory authority to prescribe or enforce standards or regulations affecting occupational safety or health," the OSH Act will not apply to the working conditions addressed by those standards. Memorandums of understanding (MOUs) between these agencies and OSHA have eliminated much of the earlier conflict.

The Environmental Protection Agency is the organization that overlaps most frequently with OSHA. When a toxic substance regulation is passed by EPA, OSHA is affected if that substance is one that appears in the workplace. For instance, both agencies are concerned with pesticides, EPA with the general environmental issues surrounding the pesticides and OSHA with some aspects of the agricultural workers who use them. During the first half of 1973, there was a heated interagency conflict over field reentry standards for pesticides (see Chapter 10 on Pesticides), a struggle which

---

70/   29 CFR § 1902.4 (c)(2)(xiii).

spilled over into the courts and eventually had to be settled by the White House in EPA's favor. 71/

Thus, although the health regulatory agencies generally function in a well-defined area, overlap does occur. As another example, there are toxic regulations under Section 307 of the Federal Water Pollution Control Act, Section 112 of the Clean Air Act, and under statutes of the FDA and CPSC. These regulatory agencies realized the need for coordination, particularly when dealing with something as pervasive as toxic substances, and under the Carter Administration combined their efforts into an interagency working group called the Interagency Regulatory Liaison group (IRLG). Although the IRLG was abolished at the beginning of the Reagan Administration, the concept of interagency working groups is a good one. The federal agencies involved in regulation should rid themselves of the antagonism and rivalry of the past and cooperate with one another to meet the needs of the public.

15.0 Occupational Safety and Health Review Commission

The OSH Act established the Occupational Safety and Health Review Commission (OSHRC) as "an independent quasi-judicial review board" 72/ consisting of three members appointed by the President to six year terms. Any enforcement actions of OSHA that are challenged must be reviewed and ruled upon by the Commission. 73/

Any failure to challenge a citation within fifteen days of issuance automatically results in an action of the Review Commission to uphold the citation. This decision by default is not subject to review by any court or agency. When an employer challenges a citation, the abatement period, or the penalty proposed, the Commission

---

71/ Florida Peach Growers Assn. v. Dept. of Labor, 489 F.2d 120 (5th Cir. 1974). To avoid this type of confrontation, in 1976 Congress provided in Section 9 of the Toxic Substances Control Act the detailed coordination procedures to be followed when jurisdictional overlap occurs.

72/ Ashford, Crisis, p. 145.

73/ OSH Act § 12(a)-(b).

then designates a hearing examiner who hears the case; makes a determination to affirm, modify or vacate the citation or penalty; and reports his finding to the Commission. 74/

> The report of the hearing examiner shall become the final order of the Commission within thirty days after such report by the hearing examiner, unless within such period any Commission member has directed that such report shall be reviewed by the Commission. 75/

The employer or Agency may then seek a review of the decision in a federal appeals court.

One of the major problems with the Review Commission is the question of its jurisdiction. "The question has arisen of the extent to which the Commission should conduct itself as though it were a court rather than a more traditional administrative agency." 76/ The Commission cannot look to other independent agencies in the government for a resolution of this problem "because its duties and its legislative history have little in common with the others." 77/ It cannot conduct investigations, initiate suits, or prosecute; therefore, it is best understood as an administrative agency with the limited duty of "adjudicating those cases brought before it by employers and employees who seek review of the enforcement actions taken by OSHA and the Secretary of Labor." 78/

Another problem inherent in the organization of the Commission is the separation from the President's Administration. There has been a question of where the authority of the Administration ends and the authority of the Commission begins. Because of the autonomous nature of the Review Commission, it cannot always count on the support of the Executive agencies. In fact, OSHA has generally ignored Review Commission decisions, and few inspectors are even aware of the Commission interpretations on various regulations.

74/   OSH Act § 12(j).

75/   Ibid.

76/   Ashford, Crisis, p. 145.

77/   Ibid. pp. 281–82.

78/   Ibid.

16.0 National Institute of Occupational Safety and Health

Under the Act, the Bureau of Safety and Health Services in the Health Services and Mental Health Administration was restructured to become the National Institute for Occupational Safety and Health (NIOSH), so as to carry out HEW's responsibilities under the Act. 79/ (HEW—The Department of Health, Education, and Welfare —has since become the Department of Health and Human Services.) Since mid-1971, NIOSH has claimed the training and research functions of the Act, along with its primary function of recommending standards.

For this latter task, NIOSH provides recommended standards to OSHA in the form of criteria documents for particular hazards. These are compilations and evaluations of all available relevant information from scientific, medical, and (occasionally) engineering research.

> The order of hazards selected for criteria development is determined several years in advance by a NIOSH priority system based on severity of response, population at risk, existence of a current standard, and advice from federal agencies (including OSHA) as well as involved professional groups. 80/

The criteria documents may actually have some value apart from their role in standards-making. Even though they do not have the force of law, they are widely distributed to industry, organized labor, universities, and private research groups as a basis to control hazards. The criteria documents also serve as a "basis for setting international permissible limits for occupational exposures." 81/

To the extent that certain criteria documents may be deficient, as discussed earlier, this expansive role for them among laymen poses a real problem. This problem may unfortunately become worse, if NIOSH declines in both funds and morale. Nevertheless, there is some benefit in having the two organizations separate. OSHA has been able to take action on some matters, such as clarify-

---

79/ OSH Act § 22(a).

80/ John F. Finklea, "The Role of NIOSH in the Standards Process," in Proceedings of the Occupational Health and Safety Regulation Seminar, p. 38.

81/ Ibid, p. 39.

ing that carbon black is not a carcinogen, which NIOSH was bureau-cratically unable to resolve. 82/   And NIOSH has not hesitated to criticize OSHA for regulatory decisions, such as issuing no standard on formaldehyde, which the former believed was scientifically untenable. 83/

17.0 Reprisals Against Worker Complaints: Section 11(c)

Congress assumed that the workers in a given workplace would be best aquainted with the hazards there. It therefore statutorily encouraged prompt OSHA response to worker complaints of viola-tions. 84/ And since this system could be undermined if employers penalized complaining employees, the Act in Section 11(c) provides sanctions against such retaliation or discrimination:

> No person shall discharge or in any manner discriminate
> against any employee because such employee has filed
> any complaint or instituted or caused to be instituted
> any proceeding under or related to this Act or has testi-
> fied or is about to testify in any such proceeding or
> because of the exercise by such employee on behalf of
> himself or others of any right afforded by this Act. 85/

If discrimination occurs, particularly if an employee is fired, a special OSHA team intervenes to obtain reinstatement, back wages, or—if return to the company is undesirable—a cash settlement for the worker. If agreement cannot be reached, the Agency resorts to litigation.

This entire system has not worked as expected. First, the worker complaints have suprisingly not been a very fruitful source of health and safety information. Far too many of the complaints came in bunches, coinciding with labor disputes in a particular plant. OSHA has therefore finally abandoned its policy of trying to investi-gate every complaint.

82/   Letter from John Miles, Enforcement Chief, to author, November 1982.

83/   See G. Fishbein, op. cit., 8 June 1982.

84/   OSH Act § 8(f)(1).

85/   OSH Act § 11(c)(1).

Second, the 11(c) process has worked slowly and uncertainly, so even though an employee may receive vindication, the months (or even years) of delay and anguish are a strong disincentive for workers to report hazards. Third, it is often difficult to determine whether a malcontented worker was fired for informing OSHA or for a number of other issues which might cloud the employer-employee relationship. Does the complaint have to be the sole cause of dismissal or discrimination, or can some (fairly arbitrary) allocation be made.

Fourth, there is continuing controversy over whether 11(c) should protect workers complaining of hazards to other than OSHA, even if the direct or indirect result is an OSHA inspection. In the Kepone case of 1975, an employee complained of hazardous chemicals to his supervisor, was fired, and only then went to OSHA. Not only was he declared unprotected by the Act, but his complaint, no longer being a worker complaint, was not even investigated at the time. 86/

A related current issue is whether an employee who reports a hazard to the press, whose ensuing publicity triggers an OSHA investigation, was protected by 11(c). In one notable instance, OSHA regional officials decided in favor of the worker and won the subsequent litigation in federal district court. The Solicitor of Labor, however, disagreed and attempted in late 1982 to withdraw the Agency from a winning position. 87/

For all these reasons, therefore, a worker must still complain at his peril.

18.0 Constitutional Challenges: The Barlow Case

Litigants have challenged OSHA's constitutionality on virtually every conceivable grounds from the First Amendment to the Fourteenth. 88/

86/ See Marshall Lee Miller "Report on OSHA," submitted to Assistant Secretary Bingham, 20 January 1976, pp. 4-5.

87/ Washington Post, "About Face Considered in OSHA Suit," 20 October 1982.

88/ A good, if dated summary of these challenges is found in Volume I of Walter B. Connolly & Donald R. Crowell, II, A Practical Guide to the Occupational Safety and Health Act, (New York: New York Law Journal Press, 1977).

The one case that has succeeded has led to the requirement
of a search warrant, if demanded, for OSHA inspectors. For diverse
reasons, however, this decision has limited impact.

In sustaining the challenge by a businessman from Pocatello,
Idaho, the Supreme Court in Marshall v. Barlow's Inc. 89/ decided
that the Fourth Amendment to the Constitution, providing for
search warrants, was applicable to OSHA. Section 8(a) of the Act,
in which Congress had authorized warrantless searches was held
unconstitutional. There are circumstances in which warrants are not
required, such as federal inspection of liquor dealers, 90/ gun
dealers, 91/ automobiles near international borders, 92/ and in other
matters with a long history of federal involvement. And despite the
political furor over OSHA, even the John Birch Society has not
objected to elevator and food inspectors. Since governmental regulation of working conditions arguably has a firmer historical basis
than those other areas, which also have definitive constitutional
limits, 93/ requiring a search warrant for inspecting working conditions was not an inevitable result for the court to react.

While the court held OSHA inspectors are required to obtain
search warrants if denied entry to inspect, it added that OSHA need
meet only a very minimal "probable cause" requirement under the
Fourth Amendment in order to obtain them. As Justice White
explained,

> Probable cause in the criminal sense is not required.
> For purposes of an administrative search such as this,
> probable cause justifying the issuance of a warrant may
> be based not only on specific evidence of an existing
> violation but also on a showing that "reasonable legisla-
> tive or administrative standards for conducting an . . .
> inspection are satisfied with respect to a particular
> [establishment]. 94/

89/   436 U.S. 307 (1978).

90/   Colonnade Catering Corp. v. U.S., 397 U.S. 72 (1970).

91/   U.S. v. Biswell, 406 U.S. 311 (1972).

92/   U.S. v. Ramsey, 431 U.S. 606 (1977).

93/   U.S. Constitution, Amendments II and XXI.

94/   Marshall v. Barlow's Inc., supra, quoting Camara v. Municipal
      Court, 387 U.S. 523 at 538 (1967).

Moreover, if too many companies demanded warrants, so that the inspection program was seriously impaired, the Court indicated it might reconsider its ruling. This ironically would make enjoyment of a Constitutional right partly contingent on few attempting to exercise it. It is therefore not surprising that commentators, both liberals and conservatives, were critical of the decision. Conservative columnist James J. Kilpatrick declared flatly,

> If the Supreme Court's decision in the Barlow case was a "great victory," as Congressman George Hansen proclaims it, let us ask heaven to protect us from another such victory anytime soon. 95/

19.0 Hazard Communications Regulation

OSHA's output of health standards has never been an impressive volume. In recent years, it has tried two new approaches to get around this bottleneck. The first was the cancer policy designed to create a template for dealing in an expedited fashion with a number of hazardous chemicals. This is described at the end of the chapter on toxic chemicals.

The other, characterized by one OSHA official as the Agency's most important rulemaking ever, is the hazard communication regulation issued in November 1984. 96/

19.1 Reason for the Regulation

This standard, sometimes known as the "worker right to know" rule, provides that hazardous chemicals must be labeled, material safety data sheets on hazards be prepared, and workers and customers should be informed of potential chemical risks.

How could a rule with such far-reaching consequences be issued from an Administration that has stressed deregulation and has deliberately avoided issuing other protective regulations? The answer lies in an almost unprecedented grassroots movement at the state and municipal level to enact their own "worker right to know" laws which, many businessmen feel, could be a considerable burden on interstate commerce.

95/   Washington Star, 2 June 1978.

96/   49 FR 52380, 25 November 1984.

They therefore lent their support to OSHA in its confrontation with the Office of Management and Budget (OMB) at the White House. A federal regulation on this subject would arguably preempt the multiplicity of local laws.

19.2 Controversy and Litigation

However, the scope of the regulation is not nearly so broad as some of the state and municipal laws: it does not cover government employees, farmers, workers in "lower risk" industries, nor consumers. Critics also observed that its provisions are not as protective as many of these other laws. For those reasons, there is legal controversy over whether, or to what extent, the federal hazard communications regulation preempts these other, quite different rules.

OSHA won the first round before a federal court in late 1984, but the litigation and uncertaintly will continue for several years.

APPENDIX A

OUTLINE OF KEY PROVISIONS
OCCUPATIONAL SAFETY AND HEALTH ACT OF 1970

PL 91-596, 84 Stat. 1590, 29 U.S.C.
(29 December 1970)

§ 1 Title: Occupational Safety and Health Act of 1970

§ 2 Findings and Purpose
  (a)   States findings—injuries are "a substantial burden upon...interstate commerce" because of lost wages, medical expenses, and compensation
  (b)   States purpose—"to assure so far as possible every working man or woman in the Nation safe and healthful working conditions"
    (b) (3)   Authorizes Secretary of Labor to set mandatory standards—(also § 2 (b) (9))
    (b) (7)   "By providing medical criteria which will assure insofar as practicable that no employee will suffer diminished health, functional capacity, or life expectancy as a result of his work experience"
    (b) (9)   "By providing for the development and promulgation of occupational safety and health standards"
    (b) (10)   Establishes enforcement program and prohibits advance notice of any inspection
    (b) (11)   Authorizes state programs, provides grants, encourages improvements in administration and experimental projects

§ 3 Definitions
  (1) (5)   "Employer"—anyone, excluding U.S. or local governments, who has employees
  (8)   O.S.&H. "standard"—practices, methods, etc., "reasonably necessary or appropriate" for safe and healthful employment
  (9)   "National consensus standard"—(1) adopted by a "nationally recognized standards-producing organization" under circumstances (2) giving interested persons chance to comment and (3) designated as such by Secretary of Labor
  (10)   "Established Federal standard"—any U.S. agency standard or law, as of enactment date

§ 4 Applicability

(b)	(1)	Excludes AEC authority (42 U.S.C. 2021 under AEC Act § 274)
(b)	(2)	Supersedes Walsh-Healy Act (41 U.S.C. 35 et seq.), Service Contract Act of 1965, etc., but those standards deemed to be issued under this Act
(b)	(4)	"Nothing in this Act shall be construed to supersede or in any manner affect any workmen's compensation law or to enlarge or diminish or affect any manner the common law or statutory rights, duties, or liabilities of employers and employees under any law...."

§ 5 Duties

(a)	(1)	General Duty Clause: "Each employer shall furnish to each of his employees employment...which are free of recognized hazards that are causing or are likely to cause death or serious physical harm to his employees"
(a)	(2)	Employer shall comply with standards issued under the Act
(b)		Employees shall comply with standards applicable to him

§ 6 Standards

(a)		Secretary to promulgate national consensus and established federal standards on occupational safety and health within 2 years of effective date of Act [21 April 1973 cutoff], without regard for APA procedures; if conflict of standards select most protective rule
(b)		Rules may be modified or promulgated as follows—
(b)	(1)	NIOSH recommendation, possible advisory committee recommendation for standard to be published within 90-days (limit extendable to 270 days)
(b)	(2)	Proposal and comment to be published within 30 days, advisory committee 60 days after report
(b)	(3)	Hearing set 30 days after end of comment period, if requested
(b)	(4)	Rule to be issued within 60 days of hearing completion, with effective date not more than 90 days later
(b)	(5)	Secretary shall set standard "which most adequately assures, to the extent feasible, on the basis of the best available evidence, that no employee will suffer material impairment

of health or functional capacity even if such employee has regular exposure to the hazard...for the period of his working life." The primary consideration is the "attainment of the highest degree of health and safety protection for the employee" but other factors include the "feasibility" of the standard. Performance (rather than design) standards preferred, if possible.

(b) (6) Applications for variances from standards (temporary)

(b) (7) Labels, protective equipment, medical examinations and other items to be in standard

(b) (8) Explanation required when standard differs substantially from consensus standard

(c) Emergency standards for "grave danger" available within 6 months after publication of emergency standards but effective until superseded

(d) Applications for variances from standards (permanent)

(f) Provides for legal challenge to a standard to be filed within 60 days. Filing of petition not to operate as a stay of standard unless court so orders. Test for judicial review: "The determination of the Secretary shall be conclusive if supported by substantial evidence in the record considered as a whole." (See also § 11 "Judicial Review" for non-standards.)

§ 7 Advisory Committees

(a) Establishes National Advisory Committee on Occupational Safety and Health (NACOSH)

(b) Appoints special advisory committees of up to 15 members to be chosen for standard-setting

§ 8 Inspections and Recordkeeping

(a) Authorizes Secretary to inspect working places upon presentation of credentials and at reasonable times

(b) Provides for witnesses and evidence in inspections and investigations

(c) Empowers Secretary of Labor or of HEW [now HHS, Health and Human Services] to require records and posting of notices, reports of injuries, exposure to toxic substances, and warnings to employees

(d) Directs authorities to minimize the burden to small businesses

(e) Allows employer and employee representatives to accompany inspector

(f) Allows employees to request inspection of violation or imminent hazard

(g) Authorizes Secretary to respond to § 8 (f) if he believes such danger exists

§ 9 Citations
    (a) Details procedure for OSHA issuing citations for violations and setting abatement procedures; de minimis violations need not be cited
    (b) Requires posting of citation
    (c) Sets limit of 6 months on citations after violation (§ 9 (c))

§ 10 Enforcement Procedures
    (a) Notifies employer he has 15 days to contest citation, otherwise a final order is not reviewable
    (b) Sets procedure if employer fails to correct violation
    (c) Sets procedure for contesting citations with Review Commission (5 U.S.C. 554, excl. (a) (3))

§ 11 Judicial Review
    (a) Allows review of court of appeals within 60 days but no automatic stay (§ 11 (b) gives appeal rights to Secretary of Labor)
    (c) Prohibits discharge or discrimination against complaining worker
    (2) Allows 30 days after violation to file complaint
    (3) Allows DOL response within 90 days

§ 12 Review Commission
    (a) Establishes 3 member commission named by President
    (b) Sets terms to run 6 years
    (f) Sets quorum of 2
    (h) Compels witnesses to appear, testify and produce evidence
    (j) Appoints hearing examiners who are to produce report which will be final within 30 days

§ 13 Counteraction of Imminent Dangers
    (a) Gives jurisdiction to district courts to restrain conditions where a danger could "reasonably be expected to cause death or serious physical harm immediately"
    (d) Gives right of a citizen suit against Secretary of Labor for mandamus

§ 14 Representation in Litigation
    Allows Solicitor of Labor to represent Secretary in civil litigation (cf. 28 U.S.C. 518 (a) exception)

§ 15 <u>Confidentiality of Trade Secrets</u>
    Protects trade secrets (18 U.S.C. § 1905) but allows disclosure to officials and in regulatory proceedings

§ 16 <u>Variances for National Defense</u>
    Provides variances, tolerances, and exemptions "to avoid serious impairment of the national defense" after due process
    Limits effect to 6 months unless notice and hearing opportunity given to affected employees

§ 17 <u>Penalties</u>
    (a) Willful or repeat violations—civil penalty up to $10,000 for each violation
    (b) Serious violation—civil penalty up to $1,000 per violation
    (c) Non-serious—civil penalty up to $1,000
    (d) Failure to correct violation after citation—civil penalty up to $1,000 a day
    (e) Willful violation resulting in death—$10,000 fine and up to 6 months prison; on subsequent convictions, $20,000 and one year, or both
    (f) Tip off of inspectors coming—fine of $1,000 and/or 6 months in prison
    (g) False statements—$10,000 and 6 months prison
    (h) Violation of 18 U.S.C. 1111 or 1114 resulting in death of official—liable for imprisonment up to life
    (i) Violation of posting requirements—$1,000 per violation
    (j) Commission's authority to assess all civil penalties, considering size of business; gravity of violation, good faith of employer; previous violations
    (k) Definition of "serious" violation: "serious probability" of death or serious injury and that employer knew or should have known of the violation
    (l) Specifies civil penalties are to be paid to U.S. Treasury

§ 18 <u>State Plans</u>
    (a) State not preempted where no federal § 6 standard exists
    (b) Gives state authority to develop own OSHA programs
    (c) Provides for procedures and requirements for approving a state plan
    (d) Gives opportunity for state to have notice and hearing if plan rejected
    (e) Allows three-year probation period after state plan approved
    (f) Affirms federal supervision of state's effectiveness and authority to withdraw plan approval

(g)   Gives court of appeals review of OSHA approval or rejection decisions

(h)   Allows federal–state agreements on partial enforcement pending § 18 (b) decision

§ 19 Federal Safety Programs

(a)   Establishes responsibility of federal agencies to maintain effective safety programs

(b)   OSHA report to be submitted annually to President and Congress

(c)   Amendment of 5 U.S.C. § 7902 (c) (1)

(d)   Gives OSHA access to records of federal agencies unless to be kept secret for national interest

§ 20 Research

(a)   (1)   Directs Secretary of HEW, [HHS] after consultation with OSHA, to provide grants, research, and other activities

(a)   (6)   Authorizes HEW [HHS] to develop and update a list of toxic substances

(a)   (7)   Directs Secretary to conduct and publish studies of chronic or low-level exposures

(b)   Authorizes HEW [HHS] to make § 8 inspections

(e)   Delegates functions of Secretary to NIOSH

§ 21 Training and Education

(a)   Directs Secretary to provide educational programs, grants, and contracts by qualified personnel

(c)   Provides for education and consultation programs with employees and employers

§ 22 NIOSH

(a)   Establishes National Institute of Occupational Safety and Health at HEW [HHS]

(b)   Specifies a 6-year term for Director

§ 23 State Grants

(a)   Authorizes funding for § 18 state programs development

(d)   Designates appropriate state agency by governor

(f)   Establishes federal share may not exceed 90 percent of application for approval

(g)   Provides for continuing grants to states approved under § 18 limited to 50 percent

§ 24 Statistics

(a)   Establishes responsibility of Labor Department and HEW [HHS] to develop occupational safety statistics

(b)   authorizes federal grants and contracts

Chapter 9

NATIONAL ENVIRONMENTAL POLICY ACT

Timothy A. Vanderver, Jr.
Attorney
Patton, Boggs & Blow
Washington, D.C.

1.0 Introduction

The National Environmental Policy Act of 1969 1/ commonly
referred to as "NEPA," was signed into law by President Nixon on
New Year's Day, 1970. NEPA is a short, general statute: it declares
a national environmental policy and promotes consideration of environmental concerns by federal agencies. Despite its relative brevity
and generality, however, NEPA is one of only a few statutes that
have had a significant effect on the federal decisionmaking process.

In great measure, NEPA's disproportionate impact has
resulted from the vast amount of litigation it precipitated. Indeed,
NEPA may have led to more lawsuits than all our other environmental laws combined. Consequently, a large body of NEPA case
law has been developed, fleshing out and giving specific force to
NEPA's general provisions. In response, even recalcitrant federal
agencies have incorporated NEPA requirements into their routine
procedures, and the early flurry of NEPA litigation has abated. The

---

1/   PL 91-190, 42 U.S.C. §§ 4321-4347, as amended by PL 95-52
      (3 July 1975) (appropriations) and PL 94-83 (9 August 1975)
      (delegation to States to prepare environmental impact state-
      ments in certain limited cases). For a discussion of the latter
      amendment, see Part 4.4.1 of this chapter.

Reagan Administration, however, has sought to reduce NEPA's importance. Although this appears to have increased the level of NEPA-related litigation, the ultimate effect on the law of NEPA remains to be seen.

2.0 Overview

NEPA is divided into two titles. Title I declares a national environmental policy and goals, provides a method for accomplishing those goals and includes some guidance on the fundamental question of how NEPA relates to other federal law. Title II creates the Council on Environmental Quality (CEQ) and defines its responsibilities.

2.1 Title I—Policy and Goals

The national environmental policy declared in Title I of NEPA is the first ever enacted by Congress. It announces a general commitment to "use all practicable means" to conduct federal activities in a way that will promote "the general welfare" and be in "harmony" with the environment. NEPA's six related goals are set with an eye toward assuring "safe, healthful, productive and esthetically and culturally pleasing surroundings" for all generations of Americans.

2.1.1 Enforceability of Title I Policy and Goals

An important practical question about the policy and goals embodied in NEPA is whether they create any enforceable "substantive rights." Although there was once a split of opinion in the United States Courts of Appeals on this question, two United States Supreme Court decisions resolved that conflict.

In Vermont Yankee Nuclear Power Corp. v. NRDC, 2/ the Court found that although "NEPA does set forth significant substantive goals for the Nation, . . . its mandate to the agencies is essentially procedural." And in Strycker's Bay Neighborhood Council v. Karlen, 3/ the Court reversed a Second Circuit decision that looked to the provisions of NEPA for the substantive standards necessary to

---

2/   435 U.S. 519 (1978).

3/   444 U.S. 223 (1980).

review the merits of agency decisions. In so doing, the Court ruled that:

> [O]nce an agency has made a decision subject to NEPA's procedural requirements, the only role for a court is to insure that the agency has considered the environmental consequences; it cannot "interject itself within the area of discretion of the executive as to the choice of action to be taken." 4/

Thus, the Supreme Court has twice held that the policy and goals set forth in Title I of NEPA create no judicially enforceable substantive rights, but impose only a procedural duty on federal agencies to consider NEPA's aims when making decisions. So, although federal agencies are free to exercise their decisionmaking discretion in ways that are consistent with NEPA's ends, NEPA does not require agencies to make decisions promoting the preservation or protection of the environment.

2.1.2 The Environmental Impact Statement

Because NEPA has been found to create no new substantive rights, NEPA's importance today stems almost entirely from its environmental impact statement (EIS) provisions—procedural provisions designed to insure that agencies do in fact consider the environmental consequences of federal actions before they are taken.

With few exceptions, NEPA requires every federal agency to prepare an EIS detailing the environmental impact of, and alternatives to, every proposal for a major federal action significantly affecting the quality of the human environment. A number of lawsuits have involved questions regarding the precise parameters of this requirement, and federal courts have played a leading role in defining what constitutes compliance with it.

The United States courts of appeals in each circuit have addressed the question of what standard of judicial review should be used to determine whether agencies have met NEPA's requirements. The standard has been stated in various ways, and legalistic differences may exist, but the common thread running through the opinions is this: federal courts will take a "hard look" to determine:

4/   444 U.S. at 227 (citations and footnote omitted).

(1) whether the federal agency reached its decision after giving full, good faith consideration to environmental factors, and (2) whether the agency's decision was arbitrary or gave insufficient weight to those environmental factors. The courts will not, however, simply substitute their own judgment for those of the agencies.

Federal courts have also contributed significantly to striking a balanced relationship between NEPA requirements and those of other federal laws.

2.2 Title II—Council on Environmental Quality (CEQ)

CEQ, established under Title II of NEPA, is charged with monitoring progress toward achieving our national environmental goals as set forth in Section 101 of NEPA. The specific statutory duties of CEQ are set out in Section 204 of NEPA. CEQ is to "assist and advise the President in the preparation of the Environmental Quality Report." Issues as broad as its title implies are addressed in this annual report, and an analysis of the need for any further legislation is specifically required to be included in it by Section 201. It is also the duty of CEQ to gather environmental information and to conduct studies on the conditions and trends in environmental quality. Moreover, CEQ is charged with developing and recommending to the President national policies and legislation to protect the environment.

The various members of the Council have worked diligently since its inception to solidify its role as the first and foremost advisor to the President on environmental policy. Although there are grounds for doubting the degree to which its advice was heeded and, indeed, even sought during the Nixon and Ford Administrations, CEQ played a much more significant role under President Carter. The Reagan Administration, however, through budget and staff cuts, has once again relegated the Council to an advisory role of little significance. Indeed, the Reagan Administration reportedly has considered seeking the Council's abolition.

There has been a wide range of opinion concerning CEQ's performance. It has been lauded for its efforts, derided for being ineffective, chastised for failing to achieve its potential, and praised or criticized for intervening in decisionmaking processes when significant environmental impacts were involved. Although these views are certainly colored by the perspectives of their holders, there is no doubt that CEQ has performed unevenly in its advisory role. It is nevertheless true that CEQ studies of particular environmental problems have sometimes been the forerunners to major changes or developments in policy and legislation.   Good examples are its reports on offshore drilling, toxic substances, and marine pollution.

In addition to its role as advisor to the President on environmental issues, CEQ has also been afforded the duty of providing guidance to other federal agencies on compliance with NEPA. Part 4.1 of this chapter discusses the way in which CEQ has discharged this duty.

3.0 How NEPA Relates to Other Federal Law

One of the most fundamental questions about NEPA concerns its relationship with other federal law. More specifically, the question is this: What effect does NEPA have on other federal laws that govern the way federal agencies operate?

Although the Supreme Court has held that a final EIS need not be prepared until an agency makes a recommendation or report on a proposal, 5/ NEPA requires all federal agencies to consider environmental impacts at every important stage in the decision-making process.   This requirement is not explicitly set forth in NEPA, but it is implicit in its various provisions. It was clearly enunciated in the early, yet still definitive case, Calvert Cliffs' Coordinating Committee v. AEC. 6/

Calvert Cliffs' involved Atomic Energy Commission (AEC) rules implementing NEPA, which, in part, provided that if no party to a proceeding raised any environmental issue, environmental issues would not be considered in the decisionmaking process. In reviewing this rule, the U.S. Court of Appeals for the District of Columbia Circuit Court said, "We believe that the Commission's crabbed interpretation of NEPA makes a mockery of the Act," 7/ and proceeded to wonder out loud what possible purpose there could be in requiring an EIS to "accompany the proposal through the existing

---

5/   Aberdeen & Rockfish RR. Co. v. Students Challenging Regulatory Agency Procedures (SCRAP II), 422 U.S. 289 (1975), reaffirmed in dicta in Kleppe v. Sierra Club, 427 U.S. 390 (1976).

6/   449 F.2d 1109 (D.C. Cir. 1971), cert. denied, 404 U.S. 942 (1972).

7/   449 F. 2d at 1117.

agency review process" or, indeed, in requiring EISs at all, if agencies could simply ignore their contents. The court then found that:

> [NEPA] require[s] the . . . agencies to consider environmental issues just as they consider other matters within their mandate. 8/

Thus, Calvert Cliffs' added NEPA's environmental impact provisions to the decisionmaking criteria set forth in other federal law.

If NEPA requires agencies to consider environmental factors when making decisions, does NEPA then expand the authority of federal agencies beyond what is granted them under other federal law? There is no case holding that NEPA gives an agency any direct authority not otherwise afforded it by other federal law. NEPA, however, was clearly enacted in order to provide federal agencies with a new tool for protecting the environment, and the authority to deny agency approval of actions that would result in unacceptable environmental consequences is implicit in the requirement that agencies consider the environmental consequences of an action before deciding to proceed with it. Thus, an agency's authority does appear to be expanded under NEPA, for an agency might well decide not to proceed with an entire project because of environmental concerns that, but for NEPA, might be found to be beyond the agency's power to consider.

A related question is this: What happens when an agency believes, on the basis of an EIS or otherwise, that on balance it should grant its approval if certain conditions are satisfied, but the agency does not have the regular, i.e., non-NEPA based, statutory authority to impose such conditions. For example, the United States Environmental Protection Agency (EPA) once conditioned a grant to Sussex County, Delaware for the construction of a sewage-treatment facility on the County's agreement to halt all rezoning plans (thus effectively blocking major planned construction) until a comprehensive land-use plan was completed. Did NEPA grant EPA the authority to lawfully withhold its approval until this condition was satisfied? The issue was never litigated. How far an agency can go

---

8/   449 F. 2d at 1112 (emphasis supplied).

in expanding its authority under the aegis of NEPA, then, remains an open question of considerable importance. 9/

The third and final basic question in this regard is this: Does NEPA override another federal law when the two are in irreconcilable conflict? Sections 102(1), 103, 104 and 105 of NEPA all bear on this question. Section 102 "authorizes and directs that, to the fullest extent possible: (1) the policies, regulations, and public laws of the United States shall be interpreted and administered in accordance with the policies set forth in this Act." Section 103 required all federal agencies to recommend to the President by 1 July 1971, the changes necessary to bring their authority and policies into conformity with NEPA. 10/ Section 104 provides that nothing in Sections 102 or 103 changes the specific statutory obligations of any federal agency to comply with other laws protecting the environment, to coordinate or consult with other federal or state agencies, or to act in accordance with the recommendations or certifications of any other federal or state agency. Section 105 simply states that the policies and goals set forth in NEPA are "supplementary" to the existing authorizations of federal agencies. These are the statutory provisions upon which the Supreme Court has twice rested decisions finding that NEPA does not override another federal law when the two conflict.

At issue in United States v. Students Challenging Regulatory Agency Procedures (SCRAP I) 11/ was a District Court decision

---

9/ Similarly, EPA maintains that is has the authority under NEPA to impose non-water quality related conditions in NPDES discharge permits under the Clean Water Act, based upon the findings of the EIS, or even to deny a permit on that basis. The Agency has consistently asserted this authority in administering its permitting regulations under the Clean Water Act, including recent revisions to those regulations. See 49 FR 37998, 38016-38018 (26 September 1984).

10/ The response of the federal agencies as a whole to Section 103 was less than enthusiastic. Indeed, environmentalists have described it as a classic example of bureaucrats exalting form over substance. After July 1971, however, federal courts began to find many necessary changes in agency authority that were not otherwise listed in agency Section 103 recommendations.

11/ 412 U.S. 669 (1973).

concerning the Interstate Commerce Commission's (ICC) authorization, without first preparing an EIS, of a railroad surcharge. The
District Court held that NEPA empowered it to issue an injunction
against the Commission's action, notwithstanding another federal
law vesting sole and exclusive power to temporarily enjoin collection
of rates in the ICC itself and withdrawing such power from the
judiciary. Reversing that decision, the Supreme Court held:

> The statutory language, in fact, indicates that NEPA
> was not intended to repeal by implication any other
> statute. Thus, . . . [Section 105] specifies that "[t]he
> policies and goals set forth in [NEPA] are supplementary
> to those set forth in existing authorizations of Federal
> agencies," and . . . [Section 104] instructs that the Act
> "shall [not] in any way affect the specific statutory
> obligations of any Federal agency . . ." Rather than
> providing for any wholesale overruling of prior law,
> [Section 103 of] NEPA requires all Federal agencies to
> review their "present statutory authority, administra-
> tive regulations, and current policies and procedures for
> the purpose of determining whether there are any defi-
> ciencies or inconsistencies therein which prohibit full
> compliance with the purposes and provisions of [NEPA]
> and shall propose to the President . . . such measures as
> may be necessary to bring their authority and policies
> into conformity with the intent, purposes, and proce-
> dures set forth in [NEPA]. . . . It would be anamolous if
> Congress had provided at one and the same time that
> Federal agencies, which have the primary responsibility
> for the implementation of NEPA, must comply with the
> present law and ask for any necessary new legislation,
> but that courts may simply ignore what we described in
> [the previous] Arrow [case] as "a clear congressional
> purpose to oust judicial power. . . "12/

In Flint Ridge Development Co. v. Scenic Rivers Association,
et al., 13/ the Supreme Court reached the same result on the question of irreconcilable conflict between NEPA and another federal
law, but this time relied entirely on Section 102.

Flint Ridge addressed the claim of environmental organizations that an EIS was required for approval of a land development

12/   412 U.S. at 694-695 (emphasis supplied and footnote omitted).

13/   426 U.S. 776 (1976).

project on which an antifraud disclosure document had been filed with the Department of Housing and Urban Development pursuant to the Interstate Land Sales Full Disclosure Act. That Act provides that disclosure documents automatically become effective thirty days after filing (thus allowing sales in interstate commerce), unless suspended because of inadequate disclosure. The document at issue was not found to be an inadequate disclosure, nor was it disputed that an EIS could not be prepared within the thirty day period. Nevertheless, the environmental groups successfully argued in the lower courts that NEPA empowered, and indeed required, a suspension beyond the statutory thirty day period until an EIS was prepared.

The Supreme Court reversed. Relying upon the principle announced in SCRAP I and the language in Section 102, stating that "to the fullest extent possible" (emphasis supplied) all federal agencies shall comply with NEPA's requirements, the court concluded:

> Section 102 recognizes . . . that where a clear and un-
> avoidable conflict in statutory authority exists, NEPA
> must give way.

Thus, it is clear that NEPA will not prevail when it is in irreconcilable conflict with another federal law.

4.0 Environmental Impact Statements

4.1 Background: CEQ's NEPA Regulations

CEQ originally issued advisory "Guidelines on the Preparation of Environmental Impact Statements" 14/ in order to assist federal agencies with the procedural aspects of NEPA. The various federal agencies then developed their own regulations for the implementation of the EIS requirement. These regulations and agency practice, however, did not necessarily adhere closely to the guidelines.

Pursuant to President Carter's Executive Order No. 11991, CEQ itself promulgated regulations implementing NEPA's procedural provisions on 29 November 1978. 15/ These regulations are binding on all federal agencies, replace over seventy different sets of agency regulations on NEPA, and provide uniform standards applicable throughout the federal government for the conduct of

---

14/   Former 40 CFR Parts 1500 et seq.

15/   43 FR 55978, codified at 40 CFR Parts 1500-1508.

environmental reviews. 16/ In promulgating its NEPA regulations, CEQ announced that it hoped to accomplish three principal aims: to reduce paperwork, to reduce delays, and to produce better decisions in furtherance of the national environmental policy.

Perhaps the most notable effort toward reducing paperwork, in light of the inordinate length and encyclopedic nature of many early EISs, is the regulation limiting an EIS to 150 pages or, for proposals of unusual scope or complexity, 300 pages. 17/ Another important part of the effort to reduce paperwork was the creation of a "scoping" procedure, 18/ which has the objective of assisting agencies in deciding what the central issues are, how long the EIS will be, and how the responsibility for preparation of the EIS will be allocated among the lead agency 19/ and cooperating agencies.

The regulations also establish a number of measures designed to reduce delay. Lead agencies are encouraged to set time limits on the NEPA process and are required to do so when requested to by an applicant. 20/ In addition, the regulations seek to reduce significant time delays by providing for the integration of EIS requirements

---

16/ The importance of the old guidelines is an issue that is open to disagreement. Almost every court that has had an opportunity to do so has said that the guidelines are "entitled to great weight" in interpreting the EIS requirement. The guidelines also were important for collecting in one place much relevant information on how to prepare an EIS, and they helped to bring about much needed standardization in EIS procedures among the federal agencies. On the other hand, the guidelines were often of extremely limited utility in providing sound answers to questions regarding the applicability of EIS requirements to a given case. Indeed, if the guidelines had addressed some categories of close cases, at least a few of the many expensive and delay-producing NEPA lawsuits might have been avoided. Further, as noted above, they were not binding, so agencies could go their own way.

17/ 40 CFR § 1502.7.

18/ 40 CFR § 1501.7.

19/ See Part 4.4.2 of this chapter for a discussion of the lead agency system.

20/ 40 CFR §§ 1501.8(a) and (b).

with other environmental review requirements, by emphasizing inter-agency cooperation, and by avoiding legal delays.

In order to foster agency decisions reflecting an increased sensitivity to environmental concerns, the regulations require the lead agency to produce a concise decisionmaking record, indicating how the EIS was used in arriving at the final decision on agency action. 21/ This provision was designed to ensure that an agency considers the EIS that it is required to prepare.

In August of 1981, CEQ requested public comment on how the various federal agencies are implementing its NEPA regulations. 22/ In general, those comments indicated that the regulations have led to more efficient and effective compliance with NEPA requirements. In certain areas, however, agencies were thought to be in need of further CEQ guidance. As a result, CEQ is considering ways in which to:

    (1)   improve agency management of the scoping process;

    (2)   ensure appropriate analysis of alternatives in permitting situations, as opposed to situations in which the agency is undertaking activity at its own initiative;

    (3)   promote agency adoption of analyses prepared by other federal and state agencies;

    (4)   reduce repetitious analyses in environmental documents by promoting the proper use of tiering; and

    (5)   define the circumstances under which an agency may charge an applicant for EIS preparation.

How, if at all, CEQ will amend its regulations to achieve these ends remains to be seen.

4.2 Proposed Actions Requiring an EIS

Section 102(2)(C) requires that an EIS shall be "include[d] in every recommendation or report on proposals for legislation and other major federal actions significantly affecting the quality of the human environment."

Because NEPA makes no pretense of applying its requirements to other than federal agencies, perhaps the best first step

---

21/   40 CFR § 1505.2.

22/   46 FR 41131 (14 August 1981).

toward deciding whether an EIS is required is to determine whether "federal" action is involved. Federal action obviously includes what is undertaken directly by the federal agencies, including operation of programs, construction of facilities, and the provision of funding to others. 23/ Federal action also clearly includes a federal agency's decision on whether to grant its required permission for activities of others, such as private businesses or state or local governments.

In addition to federal involvement, there must also be a "proposal" for action before preparation of an EIS will be required. The Supreme Court made this clear in Kleppe v. Sierra Club. 24/ The Sierra Club contended that Interior Secretary Kleppe was required to prepare an EIS on coal development in the Northern Great Plains region of the country. The Supreme Court carefully reviewed Interior's past and contemplated actions. It found that there was no proposal for regional action concerning coal development.   All Interior proposals were for actions that were either local or national in scope, even though such actions affected the Northern Great Plains region.   Thus, because there was no proposal for regional action, the Court held no EIS was required on coal development in the Northern Great Plains region.

The Supreme Court has also held that federal agencies are not required by Section 102(2)(C) to prepare an EIS to accompany appropriations requests as such requests do not constitute "proposals" for legislation or for major federal action. 25/ In so ruling, the court noted that the language of Section 102(2)(C) is best interpreted as applying to those recommendations or reports that actually propose programmatic actions, rather than to those that merely suggest how such actions may be funded.

There are a multitude of cases on the question of whether a given federal action is "major" and/or "significantly affects" the quality of the human environment within the meaning of NEPA.

23/ General revenue sharing has been held not to require an EIS because it is not sufficiently federal in nature. Carolina Action v. Simon, 389 F.Supp. 1244 (M.D.N.C. 1975), aff'd, 522 F.2d 295 (4th Cir. 1975). This holding is specifically supported by the CEQ regulations. 40 CFR § 1508.18(a). On the other hand, block grants for more specific projects have been held to require an EIS. See, e.g., Ely v. Velde, 451 F.2d 1130 (4th Cir. 1971).

24/ 427 U.S. 390 (1976).

25/ Andrus v. Sierra Club, 442 U.S. 347 (1979).

Almost all of these cases, as well as the CEQ regulations, however, avoid the futile effort of trying to define the amorphous words "major" and "significantly." 26/ The few cases where definition is attempted shed no more light on the issue than does the dictionary. The usual long analysis of those NEPA cases interpreting the meaning of "major" and "significantly affects" is therefore omitted here. Such an analysis yields no valid criterion for deciding whether any other federal action is "major" or "significantly affects" the environment.

Practically speaking, the initial decision of whether to prepare an EIS for any given proposed project lies within the sound discretion of the various federal agencies. 27/ Accordingly, in the last few years, increasing attention has been given to "findings of no significant impact" or "negative declarations."28/

4.2.1 Findings of No Significant Impact

The CEQ regulations define a "finding of no significant impact" (FONSI) as "a document prepared by a federal agency briefly

---

26/   The regulations do provide some limited guidance as to what is "significant" in this context. 40 CFR § 1508.27.

27/   There has been a split in the circuits of the United States courts of appeals as to the appropriate standard to employ in reviewing an agency's "threshold decision" not to prepare an EIS for a given project. Some circuits have adopted an "arbitrary and capricious" standard, others have employed a "reasonableness" standard. See Aertsen v. Landrieu, 488 F.Supp. 314 (D. Mass. 1980) for a discussion of this difference of opinion. Although the level of judicial scrutiny differs in some measure as a result of choosing one standard rather than the other, it is generally true that reviewing courts will simply look for an administrative record that evidences a rational basis for the agency's determination on the issue of whether or not to prepare an EIS on a particular project.

28/   The CEQ regulations prescribe the use of the term "finding of no significant impact" for such documents. 40 CFR § 1508.13. Before the promulgation of the regulations, these documents were most frequently called "negative declarations." The two terms are used interchangeably in this chapter.

presenting the reasons why an action, not otherwise excluded . . . , 29/ will not have a significant effect on the human environment and for which an environmental impact statement therefore will not be prepared." 30/ The regulations further provide that a FONSI must include an environmental assessment or a summary of one. 31/ Although a federal agency need not itself prepare that environmental assessment, the agency is responsible for its content, for if the environmental assessment prepared in connection with the issuance of a FONSI does not provide sufficient evidence to support the agency's finding of no significant impact, that finding will be overturned by a federal court in which review is sought.

Thus, a FONSI can avoid the lengthy EIS process if properly substantiated. As Professor Rodgers has pointed out, the cases "offer many examples of agency negative declarations being repudiated in the courts after a thorough inquiry into what often turns out to be an embarrassingly thin administrative effort." 32/ This has changed over the last few years as agencies have become more familiar with what is legally required for a FONSI and with the substantiation necessary to support one.

4.2.2 EIS Requirements for Special Types of Federal Action

Some particular types of federal agency actions merit special mention in connection with the EIS requirement. One is the preparation of an EIS in connection with legislation. In view of the unique nature of legislative recommendations and reports, CEQ's regulations provide for certain special features for EISs that accompany

---

29/   There are a few exemptions from the EIS requirement. Most notable are the statutory exemptions for United States Environmental Protection Agency actions under most provisions of the Clean Water Act and under all Clean Air Act provisions. 33 U.S.C. § 1371(c)(1); 15 U.S.C. § 793(c)(1). In addition, special exemptions are occasionally granted by Congress for some federal agency projects and for a few private projects that involve some federal agency action. See, e.g., 15 U.S.C. § 793(d). See also, 40 CFR § 1508.4.

30/   40 CFR § 1508.13.

31/   Id.

32/   W. H. Rodgers, Environmental Law (1977). (Footnote and citations omitted.)

legislative proposals. 33/ First, the statement may be transmitted
to the Congress up to thirty days after submission of the proposal in
order to allow time for the preparation of an accurate and complete
EIS. Second, a legislative EIS is to be prepared in the same manner
as an ordinary draft EIS. 34/ Draft and final statements are
required only in certain limited circumstances. Finally, comments
on a legislative EIS are to be collected by the lead agency and forwarded to the Congress, together with the agency's responses to the
comments.

     A second type of federal agency action that merits special
mention in connection with EIS requirements is the agency "program." Agency programs can be viewed as being of two principal
types: (1) future development oriented, such as the liquid metal fast
breeder reactor demonstration program; and (2) ongoing, such as
natural resources management.

     Although NEPA does not specifically require the preparation
of "programmatic" EIS, the courts have required such EISs in certain
circumstances. Scientists' Institute for Public Information v.
Atomic Energy Commission, 35/ is a leading case dealing with EIS
requirements for agency programs relating to future developments.
In that case, the Commission had concluded that it did not need to
prepare a programmatic EIS before deciding to proceed with its
liquid metal fast breeder reactor demonstration program because
the environmental impact of that program would be evaluated in
EISs on each demonstration plant. The Court, looking to environmental effects that today's decisions on development of technology
may have years hence, held that a programmatic EIS was indeed
required. Although the courts have had considerable difficulty in
deciding issues relating to the proper scope of a programmatic EIS,
one simple way to state the EIS requirements for a program involving future developments is to say that a programmatic EIS must be
prepared if institution of the program will foreclose decisions on
whether to approve individual projects that would in themselves
require EISs.

33/   40 CFR § 1506.08.

34/   For a discussion of draft EIS requirements, see Part 4.3 of this
     chapter.

35/   481 F.2d 1079 (D.C. Cir. 1973).

The applicability of the EIS requirement to ongoing federal agency programs is demonstrated by Minnesota Public Interest Research Group v. Butz, 36/ which held that the cumulative environmental impact of Forest Service decisions on the management of timber in a certain area required a programmatic EIS on what amounted to an ongoing but apparently ad hoc management plan. The applicability of the EIS requirement to ongoing federal agency programs appears to have significant potential for those—both environmentalists and private interests— who seek to change what are to them unacceptable, yet entrenched federal agency policies and practices.

4.3 Procedure and Time of Required Issuance

As noted above, Section 102(2)(C) requires that an EIS be "include[d] in" every recommendation or report on proposals for major federal action significantly affecting the environment. That section also requires an agency, prior to preparing its EIS, to consult with and obtain the comments of any other federal agency that has either jurisdiction by law or special expertise with respect to any environmental impact involved. Further, copies of the EIS, federal agency comments on it, and the views of appropriate state and local agencies must be made available to the President, CEQ, and the public and must accompany the proposal through the existing agency review process. No mention is made of a "draft" EIS.

The concept of preparing and circulating for comment a draft EIS is embodied in the CEQ regulations where EIS preparation procedures are set out: the draft is to be prepared "early enough so that it can serve . . . as an important contribution to the decision-making process" 37/ and circulated as required for comment for not less than forty-five days. 38/ The regulations also provide that, as a general rule, no agency action should occur earlier than ninety days after the draft EIS or thirty days after the final EIS is made available to CEQ and the public. 39/

36/   498 F.2d 1314 (8th Cir. 1974).

37/   40 CFR § 1502.5.

38/   Id., § 1506.10 (c).

39/   Id., § 1506.10(b).

In the SCRAP II case, 40/ the Supreme Court rejected the holding of several Courts of Appeals that a final EIS must be prepared prior to agency hearings on an applicant's request for federal action or at other times before the agency actually takes a position on a proposal. The Supreme Court made it clear that "the time at which the agency must prepare the final [EIS] is the time at which it makes 'recommendation or report' on a proposal." Thus, the holding in SCRAP II is strong precedent for requiring a federal agency to issue a final EIS, if one must be prepared, at the time it proposes regulations by publication in the Federal Register.

4.4 Who Can Prepare the EIS and the Lead Agency System

4.4.1 Delegation

It is strongly implied, but not explicitly stated, in Section 102(2)(C), that the federal agency or the "responsible federal official" proposing to take action is charged with preparing the requisite EIS. Early in NEPA's history, several courts of appeals decisions addressed the question of whether, and, if so, to what extent, a federal agency can lawfully delegate responsibility for preparing an EIS. The issue divided the courts into three camps: (1) those disallowing any delegation of responsibility; 41/ (2) those allowing some delegation, but requiring the responsible federal official to significantly and actively participate in the preparation of the EIS 42/ and (3) those permitting extensive delegation of responsibility, followed only by review and adoption by the agency. 43/ In August of 1975, Congress enacted PL 94-83, adding to Section 102(2) a new subsection that settled the delegation question with respect to state officials and agencies, but left open issues involving delegation to private consultants.

40/   Aberdeen & Rockfish RR. Co. v. Students Challenging Regulatory Agency Procedures (SCRAP II), 422 U.S. 289 (1975), reaffirmed in dicta in Kleppe v. Sierra Club, 427 U.S. 390 (1976).

41/   See, e.g., Green County Planning Board v. Federal Power Commission, 455 F.2d 412 (2d Cir. 1972), cert. denied, 409 U.S. 849 (1972).

42/   See, e.g., Life of the Land v. Brinegar, 485 F.2d 460 (9th Cir. 1973), cert. denied, 416 U.S. 961 (1974).

43/   See, e.g., Citizens Environmental Council v. Volpe, 484 F.2d 870 (10th Cir. 1973), cert. denied, 461 U.S. 936 (1974).

The new subsection, which is designated as Section 102(2)(D), provides that an EIS "for any major federal action funded under a program of grants to States shall not be deemed to be legally insufficient solely by reason of having been prepared by a state agency or official," if (1) the state agency or official has state-wide jurisdiction and is responsible for the action, and (2) the responsible federal official (a) furnishes guidance and participates in the preparation of the EIS, (b) independently evaluates it prior to its approval and adoption, and (c) provides early notice to, and solicits the view of, any other state or any federal land management entity on any action or alternatives thereto which may affect its responsibilities. The responsible federal official must also prepare a written assessment of the impacts on other agencies' responsibilities for incorporation into the EIS if there is any disagreement. Section 102(2)(D) goes on to state it does not relieve the federal official of responsibility for the scope, objectivity and content of an EIS or any other responsibilities under NEPA. The provisions of Section 102(2)(D) have been of primary importance in situations involving federal grants to states for highway construction. 44/

Thus, Congress rejected the per se no delegation rule of Green County in the case of projects involving grants to states and adopted the views expressed by those courts taking the middle course, allowing delegation, but requiring significant, active participation by the responsible federal agency. The law with regard to delegation to private consultants, however, remains unsettled.

4.4.2 The Lead Agency System

Projects requiring "major actions" by more than one federal agency are not uncommon. The concept of a "lead agency" to prepare or to supervise the preparation of an EIS for such an action was developed in order to satisfy the requirements of NEPA in the most efficient manner possible. CEQ's regulations incorporate that concept and require that a "lead agency" be designated to supervise the preparation of an EIS in such circumstances. 45/

44/ Congress enacted a special total delegation of responsibility provision for preparing an EIS to applicants under the Community Development Block Grant Program established by the Housing and Community Development Act of 1974. 42 U.S.C. § 5304(h).

45/ 40 CFR § 1501.5(a).

Involved agencies are to determine which shall be the lead agency on the basis of five enumerated factors (listed in order of descending importance):

(1)   magnitude of agency's involvement;
(2)   project approval/disapproval authority;
(3)   expertise concerning the action's environmental effects;
(4)   duration of agency's involvement; and
(5)   sequence of agency's involvement. 46/

CEQ will designate the lead agency if there is no consensual selection. 47/

4.5 Contents

The broad outline of an EIS is set forth in Section 102(2)(C). The EIS must be a "detailed" statement which is issued only after consultation with other appropriate government agencies and which addresses the environmental impact of the proposed action, unavoidable adverse environmental effects, alternatives, the relationship between local short-term uses of the environment and the maintenance and enhancement of long-term productivity and irreversible and irretrievable commitments of resources. Obviously, what a particular EIS must include depends on the proposal and the facts surrounding it.

The federal courts have supplemented the statutory requirements on a case-by-case basis. Although each of the cases concerns a particular EIS and surrounding facts, an individualized analysis with a composite overview reveals these useful guidelines: (1) the EIS must be a self-contained document written in language that is understandable to the layman yet allows for meaningful consideration by decisionmakers and scientists; and (2) it must also be responsive to opposing opinions, and of sufficient depth to permit a reasoned choice.

A fatally defective EIS is usually characterized by one or more of the following: sweeping conclusions unsupported by the facts; vagueness as to important issues; internal contradiction; disregard for local land use planning requirements; cursory treatment

---

46/   40 CFR § 1501.5(c).

47/   40 CFR § 1501.5(e) and (f).

of secondary and cumulative environmental impacts; a failure to include sufficient information on the environmental impact of realistic and plausible alternatives, and to make an unbiased comparison of them with the proposal. Because the consideration of alternatives is accorded the role of "linchpin" of the EIS, it merits some further mention.

The requirement to consider alternatives embodies the simple principle that a rational decision requires a knowledge of the available choices and their ramifications. The alternative of no action must always be discussed. NEPA does not, however, require that the consideration of alternatives be a "crystal ball" inquiry. 48/ Detailed discussion and consideration of alternatives that are remote or speculative are not required. Yet, an alternative may not be given short shrift because it is outside the jurisdiction of the agency or because it is contrary to existing agency policy. Simply put, the agency's consideration of alternatives must be reasonable. 49/

5.0 "International" Environmental Statements

There is nothing in Section 102(2)(C) to indicate that actions having international ramifications are to be treated any differently than others subject to the EIS requirement. Further, there is precedent for applying the EIS requirement to international programs. 50/ Nevertheless, federal agencies with international responsibilities expressed concern that compliance with EIS requirements could interfere with foreign policy objectives. As a consequence, these

---

48/ Natural Resources Defense Council, Inc. v. Morton, 458 F.2d 827, 837 (D.C. Cir. 1972).

49/ See, Vermont Yankee Nuclear Power Corp. v. NRDC, 435 U.S. 519 (1978).

50/ See, e.g., Sierra Club v. Coleman, 405 F. Supp. 53 (D.D.C. 1975), rev'd and remanded on other grounds, 578 Fed. 384 (D.C. Cir. 1978), in which an EIS was assumed to be required for preliminary construction activities by the Federal Highway Administration in connection with a highway through Panama and Columbia. Cf. Natural Resources Defense Council v. Nuclear Regulatory Commission, 647 Fed. 1345 (D.C. Cir. 1981), in which the court declined to require an EIS for export of a nuclear reactor to the Philippines, holding that NEPA does not impose an EIS obligation with respect to impacts felt solely outside the United States.

agencies and CEQ developed a program designed to accommodate these concerns while meeting the objectives of NEPA. In January of 1979, President Carter approved this program and issued Executive Order No. 12114. 51/

Although Executive Order No. 12114 is not formally based on NEPA, its objective is to further the purposes of the Act. It is designed to insure that federal decisionmakers are informed of pertinent environmental considerations concerning actions having effects outside the geographical boundaries of the United States, and that such considerations are taken into account when decisions are made. The Order prescribes the circumstances under which its requirements are applicable and also specifies a number of procedures that must be followed. Affected agencies are further required to develop their own implementing procedures.

Because it is not feasible, from a foreign policy viewpoint, to perform environmental reviews in connection with every action that has environmental impacts outside the United States, specific types of actions are exempted from the requirements of the Order. Examples are intelligence activities, arms transfers and disaster and emergency relief action. Finally, the order specifically does not create any right of judicial review.

In the few years since its issuance, the Order has had little effect. Its lack of impact has been primarily due to three factors: (1) excepted actions far outnumber the actions to which the Order's prescriptions are applicable; (2) even those agency actions to which the Order does apply are not judicially reviewable; and (3) the Reagan Administration has demonstrated very little interest in enforcing its provisions.

6.0 Applicants' Environmental Reports

In situations where the federal action involved is federal agency approval of a non-federal party's proposal, the agency is virtually certain to require an environmental report. The required contents of such a report prepared by an applicant for a permit or other authorization will vary, but are generally spelled out by the federal agency.

In practice, the agency's environmental assessment on which a FONSI may be based is often a rehash of the applicant's environmental report. And, as a practical matter, an EIS itself is often only

---

51/   44 FR 1957 (9 January 1979).

as good as the applicant's environmental report. Thus, it is apparent that this report is critical to the EIS process and is a document on which the applicant should spend much care and effort.

Despite this, frequent difficulties arise from flawed environmental reports. A variety of problems stem from the frequent failure of such a report to reflect a thorough knowledge and appreciation of the law of NEPA. These problems are avoidable to a great extent. In particular, two potentially serious problems can readily be avoided.

The first problem arises from a failure to write carefully, or to think all the way through the practical or legal ramifications of an issue or position. It should be understood at the outset that an applicant's environmental report must state the relevant information in an honest and straightforward manner. 52/ Too often, though, a careful examination of an applicant's environmental report reveals language that is an overstatement, understatement or mistatement of the facts and conclusions. This is damaging to the applicant, for reviewing courts look to the information that was before the agency when its decisions were made and will not themselves undertake to build a more accurate factual record supporting the agency action. Thus, the agency's decision is apt to stand or fall on the accuracy of the applicant's environmental report.

The second problem that can arise in connection with applicants' environmental reports involves the ability of those who conduct the studies and analyses and prepare parts of the report to also serve as convincing expert witnesses if an agency hearing or court action arises at some point. No attempt will be made here to tell an applicant how to select an environmental consultant. Yet it can be a crucial flaw in some cases to discover too late that you have a barely qualified or an inexperienced expert witness or one who is unconvincing or offensive in oral presentations under pressure. Thus, it may be prudent for an applicant to make a careful assessment of the qualifications and the demeanor of the environmental consultant's personnel, particularly those who will be doing the actual work and thus would be the strongly preferred expert witnesses if the need arose.

52/   There are very few instances of an applicant or an environmental consultant intentionally attempting to deceive.

7.0 The Seven Other "Action-Forcing" Provisions

In addition to NEPA's EIS requirements, there are seven other "action-forcing" provisions in Section 102(2). They require federal agencies to: (A) utilize an interdisciplinary approach to planning and decisionmaking; (B) insure appropriate consideration of unquantified environmental values; (E) study and develop alternatives to proposals involving unresolved conflicts over use of resources; (F) recognize the worldwide and long-range character of environmental problems; (G) make usable environmental information generally available; (H) initiate ecological information for resource-oriented projects; and (I) assist the CEQ. These sections are discussed briefly below with a view to neither ignoring nor overstating their individual and cumulative potential for important practical significance in the years ahead.

The seven "other" provisions of Section 102(2) are often thought of as relatively unimportant appendages to the EIS requirement. There is, however, a body of case law indicating that courts view at least some of these provisions as imposing on federal agencies duties that are both independent of and wider in scope than NEPA's EIS requirement. This view suggests that increased attention to these provisions could cause a significant change in the nature and extent of scientific data and information that must be compiled by the agencies in order to comply with NEPA. For, as the boundaries of environmental science continue to expand, national concern over mitigation measures and post-operational monitoring programs is likely to increase concomitantly. Thus, the extra-EIS provisions of Section 102(2) may come to play an ever more important role in the law of NEPA, serving as the legal basis for requiring agencies to secure more and better scientific data on environmental impacts both before and after federal action is taken, whether or not an EIS is required.

Section 102(2)(A) authorizes and directs all agencies to "utilize a systematic, inter-disciplinary approach" in planning and decisionmaking through an integrated use of natural and social sciences and environmental design arts. This section has been held to apply to all federal decisions that may have an impact on the environment, even those that do not themselves require the preparation of an EIS. 53/ Professor Rodgers has perhaps best stated the requirements of Section 102(2)(A):

53/ McDowell v. Schlesinger, 404 F. Supp. 212 (D.C. Mo. 1975).

Section 102(2)(A) lends strength to the argument that the agency must disclose and consider responsible opposing scientific opinions, coordinate expertise within the agency, expand its staff to accommodate environmental evaluations, respond to concerns raised by experts it retains, sponsor research on important issues either as a precondition or concurrently with implementation of a project, answer or perhaps even defer to expert criticism or recommendations from other agencies, actively seek out (as distinguished from passively absorbing) expert advice on opposing opinions or engage in actual consultation with other agencies. On the other hand, the agency need not be paralyzed by conflicting expert opinions, so long as they are fully disclosed; or undertake long-range research commitments as a precondition of actions; or hire a full stable of experts to consider a project or prepare an environmental impact statement so long as its doors are open to expert advice. 54/

Thus, Section 102(2)(A) has been found to have force independent of NEPA's EIS requirements. Its provisions might also be used in conjunction with the EIS requirement to produce greater court scrutiny of federal agency decisions. A court's "hard look" at the EIS should generally reveal whether Section 102(2)(A) has been complied with, but drawing the court's attention to that section might help to bring the agency's actual approach to planning and decisionmaking into focus. The result could well be judicial opinions compelling a significantly more systematic and integrated disciplinary approach to planning and decisionmaking, an approach that employs "state-of-the-art" scientific techniques.

Section 102(2)(B) directs federal agencies to "identify and develop methods and procedures . . . which will insure that presently unquantified environmental amenities and values may be given appropriate consideration in decisionmaking along with economic and technical considerations." What Section 102(2)(B) does and does not do is described very well in the Tennessee-Tombigbee decision:

54/ W.H. Rodgers, Environmental Law, pp. 719-21 (1977). (Citations to cases omitted.)

[Section 102(2)(B)] cannot be fairly read to command an agency to develop or define any general or specific quantification process . . . [I]t requires no more than that an agency search out, develop and follow procedures reasonably calculated to bring environmental factors to peer status with dollars and technology in their decisionmaking. 55/

Section 102(2)(B) clearly adds to the list of factors that must be considered in the agency decisionmaking process, and thus also provides an additional basis upon which to review agency action.

Section 102(2)(E) 56/ requires all federal agencies to "study, develop, and describe appropriate alternatives to recommended courses of action in any proposal which involves unresolved conflicts concerning alternative uses of available resources." 57/ This section, like Section 102(2)(A), has been held to impose duties on federal agencies that are independent of NEPA's EIS requirements. For example, in Trinity Episcopal School Corp. v. Romney, 58/ the Court of Appeals for the Second Circuit reversed and remanded to HUD an agency decision to proceed with a low income housing project in New York City because HUD had not fully considered alternative sites for the project. The court came to this conclusion despite the fact that HUD's decision not to prepare an EIS for the project went unchallenged. The potential significance of this finding is great indeed, for it is now possible to argue that the provisions of Section

---

55/ Environmental Defense Fund, Inc. v. Corps of Engineers, 429 F.2d 1123, 1133 (5th Cir. 1974); see also, Hanly v. Kliendienst, 471 F.2d 823 (2nd Cir. 1972), cert. denied, 412 U.S. 908 (1973).

56/ This provision was originally Section 102(2)(D). It was redesignated when NEPA was amended by PL 94-83 (1975).

57/ The last part of Section 102(2)(E) appears to limit its application to only those proposals which involve unresolved conflicts concerning alternative uses of available resources. It is difficult, however, to conjure up good examples of choices involving environmental impact that are clearly outside the apparent limitation.

58/ 523 F. 2d 88 (2d Cir. 1975), rev'd on other grounds following remand sub nom. Strycher's Bay Neighborhood Council v. Karlen, 444 U.S. 223 (1980).

102(2)(E) are applicable even to those Environmental Protection Agency actions under the Clean Air Act and the Clean Water Act that are categorically exempted from the EIS requirement.

Section 102(2)(F) requires all federal agencies to "[r]ecognize the worldwide and long-range character of environmental problems" and to lend such support as is consistent with our foreign policy to international efforts to protect the world environment. 59/ This section has received almost no attention from the federal courts. It could in the future, however, provide a basis for claims that agencies must develop and consider more scientific data and information in order to assess "long-range" effects of federal actions. It may also be used to buttress efforts to develop more comprehensive policies on international environmental protection issues.

Section 102(2)(G) requires all federal agencies to "[m]ake available to States, counties, municipalities, institutions, and individuals, advice and information useful in restoring, maintaining and enhancing the quality of the environment." This section has been of extremely limited practical utility with respect to particular projects. It does not require by its own terms disclosure of information different from that obtainable under the provisions of the Freedom of Information Act, nor does it add much, if anything, to the Administrative Procedure Act requirement that an agency be fair with public participants and disclose the basis for its decisions.

Another "action-forcing" provision that has received only limited attention to date, but which has great potential significance, is Section 102(2)(H). This section provides that all federal agencies shall "[i]nitiate and utilize ecological information in the planning and development of resource-oriented projects." The usual agency practice, evidenced in many EISs, is to make decisions simply on the best available information at the time. The requirement to "initiate" ecological information, then, could be used to require agencies themselves to generate additional information on particular projects before reaching a final decision to proceed.

Section 102(2)(I) simply requires federal agencies to assist the Council on Environmental Quality. At most, this section slightly strengthens the hand of CEQ (which has relatively little funding or staff) when it wants the cooperation of other federal agencies in undertaking a major examination of an environmental problem area.

59/ For a discussion of "international" EISs, see Part 5.0 of this chapter.

8.0 Who Can Sue for Alleged Violations of NEPA

The question of who can sue, called "standing" by lawyers, is one that has received a great deal of attention from the United States Supreme Court since 1970. In general, the Court's opinions on the issue are in conflict and a lengthy analysis of them yields little of predictive value. 60/ When environmental interests are at stake, however, the Court has consistently left the door to the courthouse wide open. A brief examination of the two leading Supreme Court decisions on standing in environmental cases reveals the limits to which the Court's liberal stand on this issue goes.

Sierra Club v. Morton 61/ is the only major decision denying standing to a litigant in a case involving environmental interests. It involved a challenge to agency approval of construction of the Mineral King Resort in the Sequoia National Forest. Sierra Club treated the action as a test case, seeking to establish the principle that a membership organization with a "special interest" in the environment has standing to challenge action that would adversely affect the environment. Accordingly, Sierra Club intentionally failed to allege that it or any of its members actually used the Mineral King Valley for recreational purposes. Although the Court held that asthetic or environmental harm could constitute "injury in fact" sufficient to confer standing, it denied standing in this case because the Club had not pleaded facts establishing any such injury. The mere fact that the Club had a "special interest" in protecting the environment was not sufficient to allow the Club to challenge the agency action concerned.

The other leading Supreme Court decision on standing in the environmental area is United States v. Students Challenging Regulatory Agency Procedures (SCRAP I). 62/ SCRAP I is generally considered to be among the most liberal standing cases. There an unincorporated association of law students sued the Interstate Commerce Commission for failing to prepare an EIS before allowing

---

60/ For a less timid criticism of the Supreme Court's opinions on standing, see K.C. Davis, Administrative Law Treatise, 1982 Supplement, 325-370 (1982).

61/ 405 U.S. 727 (1972).

62/ 412 U.S. 669 (1973).

railroads to collect a surcharge on freight. They claimed to be "injured in fact" by the Commission's order because they used national parks and forests, and the order would raise the price of recycled materials thereby discouraging the use of such materials, leading in turn to increased mining operations, which would consequently harm national recreational enclaves. The government claimed that the alleged chain of causation was too attenuated to confer standing on the students. The Court, however, responded in a footnote that a "trifle" of injury in fact is enough. 63/ Although subsequent cases 64/ cast some doubt on whether SCRAP I will be followed in the future, no case has directly reversed that decision, and it remains a leading precedent in the environmental area.

Thus, it is possible to briefly answer the question posed in this Part in this way: When violations of NEPA are alleged, anyone who can claim at least a "trifle" of "injury in fact" has standing to sue.

63/   Id., at 689, n. 14.

64/   See, e.g., Simon v. Eastern Kentucky Welfare Rights Organization, 426 U.S. 26 (1976).

Chapter 10

FEDERAL REGULATION OF PESTICIDES

Marshall Lee Miller
Attorney
Reid & Priest
Washington, D.C.

1.0 Background to the Federal Regulation of Pesticides

The benefits of pesticides, herbicides, rodenticides, and other economic poisons are well known. They have done much to spare us from the ravages of disease, crop infestations, noxious animals, and choking weeds. Over the past two decades, however, beginning with Rachel Carson's Silent Spring, 1/ there has been a growing awareness of the hazards, as well as the benefits of these chemicals, which may be harmful to man and the balance of nature. The ability to balance these often conflicting effects is hampered by our lack of understanding of adverse side effects, a problem which will become even more acute during the next few years as EPA investigations shift from the major pesticides, on which an appreciable amount of research has been conducted, to those for which data is relatively sparse.

1.1 Early Efforts at Pesticide Regulations

Although chemical pesticides have been subject to some degree of federal control since the Insecticide Act of 1910, 2/ the

---

1/   Rachel Carson, Silent Spring (New York, 1962).

2/   36 Stat. 331 (1910).

398

relatively insignificant usage of pesticides before World War II made regulation a matter of low priority. This act was primarily concerned with protecting consumers from ineffective products or deceptive labeling, and contained neither a federal registration requirement nor any significant safety standards.

The war enormously stimulated the development and use of pesticides. The resulting benefits to health and farm production made pesticides a necessity and transformed the agricultural chemical industry into an influential sector of the economy. In 1947 Congress responded to the situation by enacting the more comprehensive Federal Insecticide, Fungicide, and Rodenticide Act (FIFRA), 3/ requiring that pesticides distributed in interstate commerce be registered with the United States Department of Agriculture (USDA) and containing a rudimentary labeling provision. The Act, like its predecessor, was more concerned with product efficacy than with safety, but the statute did declare pesticides "misbranded" if they were necessarily harmful to man, animals, or vegetation (except weeds) even when properly used. 4/

Three major defects in the new law soon became evident. First, the registration process was largely an empty formality since the Secretary of Agriculture could not refuse registration even to a chemical he deemed highly dangerous. He could register "under protest", but this had no legal effect on the registrant's ability to manufacture or distribute the product. Second, there was no regulatory control over the use of a pesticide contrary to its label, as long as the label itself complied with the statutory requirements. Third, the Secretary's only remedy against a hazardous product was a legal action for misbranding or adulteration, and—this was crucial—the difficult burden of proof was on him.

The statute nevertheless remained unchanged for fifteen years. Pesticides were not then a matter of public concern and the USDA was under little pressure to tighten regulatory control. Only

---

3/ 61 Stat. 190 (1947). The present act is still known by this name, although there have been major changes, especially in 1972, in the law since then. For convenience, we will refer to the pre-1972 version as the "Old FIFRA."

4/ Old FIFRA (pre-1972) § 2(z)(2)(d). See H. Rep. 313 (80th Cong., 1st Sess.). 1947 U.S. Code Cong. Serv. 1200, 1201.

a handful of registrations under protest were made during that period, and virtually all these actions involved minor companies with ineffective products. The one notable case in this area involving a fraudulently ineffective product was lost by the USDA at the district court level and mooted by the court of appeals. 5/

In 1964 the USDA persuaded Congress to remedy two of these three defects: the registration system was revised to permit the Secretary to refuse to register a new product or to cancel an existing registration, and the burden of proof for safety and effectiveness was placed on the registrant. 6/ This considerably strengthened the Act but made little difference in practice. The Pesticide Registration Division, a section of USDA's Agricultural Research Service, was understaffed—in 1966 the only toxicologist on the staff was the division's director—and the division was buried deep in a bureaucracy primarily concerned with promoting agriculture and facilitating the registration of pesticides. The cancellation procedure was seldom if ever used, 7/ and there was still no legal sanction against a consumer's applying the chemical for a delisted use.

The growth of the environmental movement in the late 1960s, with its concern about the widespread use of agricultural chemicals, overwhelmed the meager resources of the Pesticide Division. Environmental groups filed a barrage of law suits demanding the cancellation or suspension of a host of major pesticides such as DDT, Aldrin-Dieldrin, and the herbicide 2,4,5-T. This hectic and bewildering situation demanded a new approach to pesticide regulations.

1.2 Creation of the Environmental Protection Agency

On 2 December 1970, President Nixon signed Reorganization Order No. 3 8/ creating the Environmental Protection Agency (EPA),

---

5/   Victrylite Candle Co. v. Brannan, 201 F.2d 206 (D.C. Cir. 1952).

6/   Act of 12 May 1964, PL 88-30S, 78 Stat. 190. There were other, less significant, amendments in 1959 (73 Stat. 286) and 1961 (75 Stat. 18, 42).

7/   Instead, a Pesticide Registration notice would be sent ordering the removal of one or more listed uses from the registration.

8/   Reorganization Order No. 3 of 1970, §2(a)(1), 1970 U.S. Code Cong. Ad. News 2996, 2998, 91st Cong. 2nd Sess.

and assigned to it the functions and many of the personnel previously under Interior, Agriculture, and other government departments. EPA inherited from USDA not only the Pesticides Division but also the environmental law suits against the Secretary of Agriculture. Thus, within the first two or three months the new Agency was compelled to make a number of tough regulatory decisions. The EPA's outlook was considerably influenced by judicial decisions in several of the cases it had inherited from USDA or, concerning pesticide residues, from the Food and Drug Administration (FDA) of the Department of Health, Education, and Welfare (HEW), now the Department of Health and Human Services (HHS). These court decisions consistently held that the responsible federal agencies had not sufficiently examined the health and environmental problems associated with pesticide use. These helped to shape—one might even say force—EPA's pesticide policy during its formative period. 9/

EPA's first policy determination, issued by Administrator William Ruckelshaus in early 1971 in response to a court order, was the "Statement of the Reasons Underlying the Decision on Cancellation and Suspension of DDT 2,4,5-T, and Aldrin-Dieldrin," usually called the 18th of March Statement. This order declared that pesticides would no longer be given only perfunctory review at registration nor be virtually immune from examination thereafter, and reemphasized that the statutory burden of proving a product safe rested with the chemical industry. This meant that EPA and the agricultural chemical industry would henceforth need additional resources for more intensive scientific review.

2.0 Pesticide Statute

2.1   Key Provisions of the Federal Insecticide, Fungicide and Rodenticide Act

The Federal Insecticide, Fungicide, and Rodenticide Act (FIFRA), 10/ as amended by the Federal Environmental Pesticide Control Act (FEPCA) of October 1972 11/ and the FIFRA

9/   These cases will be discussed in a later section, (9.1).

10/   7 U.S.C. § 135, et seq.

11/   PL 92-516, 86 Stat. 973, 21 October 1972.

amendments of 1975, 12/ 1978, 13/ and 1980, 14/ is a complex statute. Terms may have a meaning different from, or even directly contrary to, normal English usage. For example, the term "suspension" really means an immediate ban on a pesticide, while the harsher-sounding term "cancellation" indicates only the initiation of administrative proceedings which can drag on for years. There are five key features of the FIFRA; the other points will be discussed more fully in a subsequent section.

The amendments to FIFRA reflect Congressional, industry, and environmentalist concern about federal control of pesticide distribution, sale, and use. The 1972 amendments amounted to a virtual rewriting of the law. EPA was given expanded authority over field use of pesticides, and several categories of registration were created which give EPA more flexibility in fashioning appropriate control over pesticides. The 1975 amendments are significant not for what they actually changed but because of the motivations that prompted them. These amendments were viewed by many as, at best, unnecessary and, at worst, a further encumbrance upon an already complicated administrative procedure. EPA was required to consult with the Department of Agriculture and Agricultural Committees of Congress before issuing proposed or final standards regarding pesticides. EPA also got the authority to require that farmers take exams before being certified as applicators.

The 1978 amendments reflected the near-collapse of EPA's pesticide registration program. EPA was given the authority to conditionally register a pesticide pending study of the product's safety and was authorized to perform generic reviews without requiring compensation for use of a company's data. The 1980 amendments provided for a two-house veto over EPA rules or regulations and required the Administrator to obtain Scientific Advisory Review (SAR) of suspension actions after they were initiated.

2.2 Registration Procedures

All new pesticide products used in the United States, with minor exceptions, must first be registered with EPA. This involves

---

12/   PL 94-140, 28 November 1975.

13/   PL 95-396, 92 Stat. 819, 30 September 1978.

14/   PL 96-539, 94 Stat. 3194, 17 December 1980.

the submittal of the complete formula, a proposed label, and "full description of the tests made and the results thereof upon which the claims are based." 15/ The Administrator must approve the registration if the following conditions are met:

> (A) its composition is such as to warrant the proposed claim for it;

> (B) its labeling and other materials required to be submitted comply with the requirements of this act;

> (C) it will perform its intended function without unreasonable adverse effects on the environment; and

> (D) when used in accordance with widespread and commonly recognized practice it will not generally cause unreasonable adverse effects on the environment. 16/

The operative phrase in the above criteria is "unreasonable adverse effects on the environment", which was added to the Act in 1972. This phrase is defined elsewhere in FIFRA as meaning "any unreasonable risk to man or the environment, taking into account the economic, social, and environmental costs and benefits of the use of the pesticide." 17/

This controversial expression, which appears also in the cancellation-suspension section of the Act, 18/ disturbed some environmentalists who feared that the word "unreasonable" plus the consideration of social and economic factors would undermine the effectiveness of the cancellation procedure, but experience to date has not indicated a problem.

15/   1 FIFRA § 3(c)(1), 7 U.S.C. § 136(c)(1).

16/   FIFRA § 3(c)(5), 7 U.S.C. § 136a(c)(5).

17/   FIFRA § 2(bb), 7 U.S.C. § 136(bb). The 1975 amendments, as will be discussed, added the specific requirement that decisions also include consideration of their impact on various aspects of the agricultural economy.

18/   FIFRA § 6, 7 U.S.C. § 136d.

The registration is not valid for all uses of a particular chemical. Each registration specifies the crops and insects on which it may be applied, and each use must be supported by research data on safety and efficacy. Registrations are for a five-year period, after which they automatically expire unless an interested party petitions for renewal and, if requested by EPA, provides additional data indicating the safety of the product. 19/ For the past several years, pre-EPA registrations have been coming up for renewal under much stricter standards than when originally issued. The agricultural chemical companies have justifiably complained that the increased burden of registration is discouraging the development of new pesticides, but there seems no responsible alternative.

2.3 Federal Control over Pesticide Use

Until 1972 the government had no control over the actual use of a pesticide once it had left a manufacturer or distributor properly labeled. Thus, for example, a chemical which would be perfectly safe for use on a dry field might be environmentally hazardous if applied in a marshy area, and a chemical acceptable for use on one crop might leave dangerous residues on another. EPA's only recourse (other than occasional subtle hints to the producer) was to cancel the entire registration—obviously too unwieldy a weapon to constitute a normal means of enforcement. A second problem was that a potential chemical might be too dangerous for general use but could be used safely by trained personnel. There was, however, no legal mechanism for limiting its use only to qualified individuals.

Because of these problems, both environmentalists and the industry agreed that EPA should be given more flexibility than merely the choice between cancelling or approving a pesticide. Congress therefore provided for the classification of pesticides into general and restricted categories, 20/ with the latter group available only to Certified Applicators. There are several categories of applicators, including private applicators and commercial applicators who use or supervise the application of pesticides on property other than their own. A pesticide label permitting use only "under the direct supervision of a Certified Applicator" means that the chemical is to

---

19/   FIFRA § 6(a), 7 U.S.C. § 136d(a).

20/   FIFRA § 3(d), 7 U.S.C. § 136a(d).

be applied under the instructions and control of a Certified Applicator who, however, curiously is not required to be physically present when and where the pesticide is applied.

The additional flexibility of the certification program was a principal reason the industry eventually supported the 1972 amendments to FIFRA, but some environmentalists were concerned that the program might become a farce, especially when administered by certain states. Certification standards are prescribed by EPA, as are requirements for periodic reporting to EPA, but any state desiring to establish its own certification program may do so if the Administrator determines that it satisfies the guidelines and statutory criteria. 21/

The efficacy of the entire certification program, however, has become questionable as a result of the 1975 amendments to FIFRA. The amendments considerably loosened the procedures for certification by forbidding EPA to demand any examinations of an applicant's knowledge. 22/ These amendments will be discussed more fully in a separate section. There is a possibility that some states may license anyone who applies, but EPA requirements for periodic reporting and inspection provide some degree of control, and there should be no objection to every farmer becoming a Certified Applicator if he were willing to undergo training.

Finally, since 1972 it has been unlawful either "to make available for use, or to use, any registered pesticide classified for restricted use for some or all purposes other than in accordance with" the registration and applicable regulations. 23/ Stiff penalties for violations of these restrictions include fines up to $25,000 and imprisonment for up to a year. 24/

2.4 Cancellation

While the registration process may be the foundation of the FIFRA, cancellation represents the cutting edge of the law and attracts the most public attention. Cancellation is used to initiate

---

21/   FIFRA § 4, 7 U.S.C. § 136b.

22/   PL 94-140 § 5, amending FIFRA § 4(a)(1).

23/   FIFRA § 12(a)(2)(F), 7 U.S.C. § 136(a)(2)(F).

24/   FIFRA § 14, 7 U.S.C. § 136 1.

review of a substance suspected of being a "substantial question of safety" to man or the environment. 25/ During the pendency of the proceedings the product may be freely manufactured and shipped in commerce.   A cancellation order, although final if not challenged within thirty days, usually leads to a public hearing or scientific review committee, or both, and can be quite protracted—a matter of years rather than months. A recommended decision from the agency hearing examiner (now called the administrative law judge) goes to the Administrator or his delegated representative, the Chief Agency Judicial Officer, for a final determination on the cancellation. If sustained, this would ban the product from shipment or use in the United States. 26/

Even under the old FIFRA 27/ it became clear that there were several quite different types of cancellation. First, there was a cancellation when a substance was, in EPA's opinion, a highly probable threat to man or the environment but for which there was not yet sufficient evidence to warrant immediate suspension. Second, there could be a cancellation when scientific tests indicated some cause for concern and a public hearing or scientific advisory committee was desired to explore the issue more thoroughly. And third, there could be a cancellation issued in response to a citizens' suit when a fact-finding hearing was desired to enable both critics and defenders of the pesticide to present their arguments. These distinctions, although not found in the statute, were nevertheless quite important.   State authorities, for example, would often recommend that farmers cease using a cancelled product which they thought had been declared unsafe, although EPA may have considered the action in category two or three above. Conversely, there were occasions when EPA wanted to communicate its great concern over the continued use of a product without resorting to suspension.

This problem is not resolved completely by the amended FIFRA, but two levels of action are distinguished:

25/   EDF v. Ruckelshaus, 439 F.2d 584, 591-92, 2 ERC 1114, 1119 (D.C. Cir. 1971).

26/   The scientific review committee and other features of this process will be discussed later in more detail.

27/   The cancellation-suspension section of the old Act was § 4(c); it is § 6 of the post-1972 FIFRA.

The Administrator may issue a notice of his intent either (1) to cancel its registration or to change its classification together with the reasons (including the factual basis) for his action, or (2) to hold a hearing to determine whether or not its registration should be cancelled or its classification changed. 28/

This revision of the law may not have solved EPA's communications problem with local officials, but it does provide a statutory basis for a distinction which EPA sometimes needed to make.

2.5 Suspension

A suspension order, despite its misleading name, is an immediate ban on the production and distribution of a pesticide. It is mandated when a product constitutes an "imminent hazard" to man or the environment, 29/ and may be invoked at any stage of the cancellation proceeding or even before a cancellation procedure has been initiated. According to the 18th of March Statement, "an imminent hazard may be declared at any point in the chain of events which may ultimately result in harm to the public." 30/ There are two types of suspension orders: an ordinary suspension order and an emergency suspension order.

2.5.1 Ordinary Suspension

The purpose of an ordinary suspension is to prevent an imminent hazard during the time required for cancellation or change in classification proceedings. An ordinary suspension proceeding is initiated when the Administrator issues notice to the registrant that he is suspending use of the pesticide and includes the requisite findings as to imminent hazard. The registrant may request an expedited

---

28/ FIFRA § 6(b), 7 U.S.C. § 136d(b). Note that the Administrator himself may request a hearing, a power which he did not have under the old FIFRA, although in fact he assumed this authority in his August 1971 cancellation order on 2,4,5-T.

29/ FIFRA § 6(c), 7 U.S.C. § 136d(c).

30/ See 18 March 1971 Statement, p.6. A suspension order must be accompanied by a cancellation order if one is not then outstanding. FIFRA § 6(b), 7 U.S.C. § 136d(b).

hearing within five days of receipt of the Administrator's notice. If no hearing is requested, the suspension order can take effect immediately thereafter and the order is not reviewable by a court. 31/

Suspension procedurally "resembles...the judicial proceedings on a contested motion for a preliminary injuction," 32/ hence the tentative connotation of the term, and remains in effect until the cancellation hearing is completed and a final decision is issued by the Administrator. 33/ This does not actually accord with reality but has been the consistent theme of judicial decisions since the Agency's inception. According to this view, the function of a suspension order is not to reach a definitive decision on the registration of a pesticide but to grant temporary, interim relief. 34/ The Circuit Court of Appeals for the District of Columbia has repeatedly stated this view: "The function of the suspension decision is to make a preliminary assessment of evidence and probabilities, not an ultimate resolution of difficult issues," 35/ and "the suspension order thus operates to afford interim relief during the course of the lengthy administrative proceedings." 36/

The court of appeals has emphasized that "imminent hazard" does not refer only to the danger of immediate disaster: "We must caution against any approach to the term 'imminent hazard' used in the statute, that restricts it to a concept of crises." 37/ In another case, the court declared that the Secretary of Agriculture:

> has concluded that the most important element of an 'imminent hazard to the public' is a serious threat to public health, that a hazard may be 'imminent' even if

---

31/ FIFRA § 6(c), 7 U.S.C. § 136d(c).

32/ EDF v. EPA 465 F. 2d 538, 4 ERC 1523, 1530 (D.C. Cir. 1972).

33/ Nor-Am v. Hardin, 435 F. 2d 1151, 2 ERC 1016 (7th Cir. 1970), cert. denied 402 U.S. 935 (1971).

34/ See, In re Shell Chemical, Opinion of the Administrator, pp. 8-11, 6 ERC 2047 at 2050 (1974).

35/ EDF v. EPA, supra, 465 F. 2d at 537, 4 ERC at 1529.

36/ EDF v. Ruckelshaus, supra, 439 F. 2d at 589, 2 ERC at 1115.

37/ EDF v. EPA, supra, 465 F. 2d at 540, 4 ERC at 1531.

its impact will not be apparent for many years, and that the 'public' protected by the suspension provision includes fish and wildlife. These interpretations all seem consistent with the statutory language and purpose. 38/

2.5.2 Emergency Suspension

An emergency suspension differs from an ordinary suspension in that the registrant is not given notice or the opportunity for an expedited hearing prior to the suspension order taking effect. The registrant is, however, entitled to an expedited hearing to determine the propriety of the emergency suspension. The Administrator can only use this procedure when he determines that an emergency exists which does not allow him to hold a hearing before suspending use of a pesticide. 39/

EPA first used the emergency suspension procedure in 1979 when it suspended the sale and use of 2,4,5-T and Silvex for specified uses. EPA issued the suspension orders based on its judgment that exposure to the pesticides created an immediate and unreasonable risk to human health. EPA's action was reviewed by a Michigan district court in Dow Chemical Co. v. Blum, 40/ where the plaintiffs petitioned for judicial review of EPA's decision and a stay of the emergency suspension orders. In upholding EPA's order, the court analogized the emergency suspension order to a temporary restraining order and defined the term emergency as a "substantial likelihood that serious harm will be experienced during the three or four months required in any realistic projection of the administrative suspension process." 41/

The court held that this standard required the Administrator to examine five factors: (1) the seriousness of the threatened harm; (2) the immediacy of the threatened harm; (3) the probability that the threatened harm would result; (4) the benefits to the public of the continued use of the pesticides in question during the suspension process; and (5) the nature and extent of the information before the Administrator at the time he makes his decision. The court also

---

38/ EDF v. Ruckelshaus, supra, 439 F.2d at 597, 2 ERC at 1121-22.

39/ § 6(c)(3), 7 U.S.C. § 136d(c)(3).

40/ 469 F. Supp. 892, 13 ERC 1129 (E.D. Mich 1979).

41/ Ibid. at 902, 13 ERC at 1135.

held that an emergency suspension order may be overturned only if it was arbitrary, capricious, or an abuse of discretion or if it was not "issued in accordance with the procedures established by law." 42/

2.6 Balancing Test in FIFRA

The balancing of risks versus benefits lies at the heart of the FIFRA, and its importance warrants a separate discussion. There are some who feel that certain types of pesticides, particularly carcinogens, should be forbidden per se as done under the Delaney Amendment to the Food, Drug, and Cosmetics Act. 43/ FIFRA does not require this inflexibility, although the courts have cautioned that the law "places a heavy burden on any administrative officer to explain the basis for his decision to permit the continued use of a chemical known to produce cancer in experimental animals." 44/ EPA Administrator Russell Train in 1974 noted this in his decision regarding Aldrin-Dieldrin:

> Since Aldrin-Dieldrin has been found to be carcinogenic in mice and probably carcinogenic in rats, and to present a high risk of cancer to man, it is arguable that any use of Aldrin-Dieldrin, however significant or beneficial in social or economic terms, cannot be justified, even for the limited period of time until the completion of the cancellation proceedings.
>
> As indicated in Part I of this opinion, however, it is appropriate that the possible benefits of Aldrin-Dieldrin, or the absence of such benefits, be considered in this proceeding. Nevertheless, it is apparent that any benefits attributable to Aldrin-Dieldrin must be of high order to affect the findings on carcinogenicity. 45/

42/ Ibid. The court stated that it arrived at its decision to uphold EPA's order "with great reluctance" and would not have ordered the emergency suspension on the basis of the information before EPA, but was not empowered to substitute its judgment for that of EPA's. 469 F.Supp. at 907, 13 ERC at 1140.

43/ FDCA § 409(c)(3)(A), 21 U.S.C. § 348(c)(3)(A). The relationship between the FIFRA and the FDCA will be discussed later in more detail.

44/ EDF v. Ruckelshaus, supra, 439 F.2d at 596, 2 ERC at 1121.

45/ In re Shell Chemical, supra., p.32, 6 ERC at 2057.

The balancing that is applied during the registration process and, more formally, during the cancellation proceedings is determining whether there are "unreasonable adverse effects on the environment," taking into consideration the "economic, social, and environmental costs and benefits of the use of any pesticide." 46/

In a suspension proceeding, however, the FIFRA does not require a balancing of environmental risks and benefits. It has nevertheless been EPA's policy since its inception to conduct such an analysis, although in practice the benefits would obviously need to be considerable to balance a finding of "imminent hazard." One Administrator noted that "the Agency traditionally has considered benefits as well as risks . . . and, in [his] opinion, should continue to do so." 47/

3.0 Trade Secrets

One issue in FIFRA that has generated considerable controversy involves the treatment of trade secrets. 48/ The judicial protection of commercial trade secrets has gradually eroded during the past few years. Many so-called trade secrets were in fact widely known throughout the industry and did not merit confidential status. 49/ Section 10 of FIFRA, added in the 1972 amendments,

---

46/   FIFRA §§ 2(bb), 3(c)(5), and 6(b), 7 U.S.C. § 136(bb), 136a(c)(5), and 136d.

47/   In re Shell Chemical, supra, p.11, 6 ERC at 2050-51, upheld unanimously by the D.C. Court of Appeals in EDF v. EPA, 510 F.2d 1292, 7 ERC 1689 (4 April 1975). This practice was also judicially approved in an unrelated case with the same name, EDF v. EPA, supra, 465 F.2d at 540, 4 ERC at 1530.

48/   FIFRA § 10, 7 U.S.C. § 136h. Trade secrets are also becoming a source of contention in the implementation of the Toxic Substances Control Act.

49/   This is true not merely in the pesticide area but also, for example, in the Clean Air Act under Section 211 pertaining to gasoline additives, where an EPA review several years ago concluded that most of the hundreds of so-called trade secrets relating to additives in gasoline were in fact either common knowledge in the industry or were easily discoverable by back-engineering.

provides that trade secrets should not be released but, if the Administrator proposes to release them, he should provide notice to the company to enable it to seek a declaratory judgment in the appropriate district court. 50/

It is, of course, desirable that university scientists and others outside industry and government should be able to conduct tests on the effects of various pesticides. In one case debated by the Agency for several years, a professor needed to know the chemical composition of a particular pesticide to conduct certain medical experiments. Should EPA or a court furnish this information to a bonafide researcher, with or without appropriate safeguards to preserve confidentiality? EPA resolved that question in the experimenter's favor after an investigation revealed that the chemical composition in fact was not a trade secret within the industry, but the underlying question has yet to be resolved.

Section 10 provides that "when necessary to carry out the provisions of this Act, information relating to formulas of products acquired by authorization of this Act may be revealed to any federal agency consulted and may be revealed at a public hearing or in findings of fact issued by the Administrator." 51/ Consequently, if the public interest requires, whatever that means, a registrant must assume that the formula for his product can be made available, although in practice this may not occur very often.

Because of the controversy surrounding the disclosure of trade secrets, Congress amended FIFRA in 1975 and 1978. The 1975 amendments 52/ cleaned up an ambiguity created by the 1972 amendments by specifying that the new use restrictions applied only to data submitted on or after 1 January 1970. The definition of trade secrets was left to the Administrator.

EPA took the position that the 1972 and 1975 amendments restricted use and disclosure of only a narrow range of data, such as formulas and manufacturing processes, but not hazard and efficacy data. However, the industry challenged this view with some initial

---

50/   FIFRA § 10 (c), 7 U.S.C. § 136h(c).

51/   FIFRA § 10(b), 7 U.S.C. § 136h(b). Note that state agencies are not mentioned.

52/   PL 94-140, 89 Stat. 75 (1975).

success. 53/ In 1978, Congress again amended Section 10 to limit trade secrets protection to formulas and manufacturing processes, thus reflecting EPA's position. 54/

In Union Carbide Agricultural Products Company v. Costle, 55/ the Second Circuit overturned an injunction that Union Carbide obtained to prevent EPA from disclosing confidential research data under Section 3 of FIFRA. The appeals court held that the lower court applied the wrong legal test in evaluating the plaintiff's request; and that the moving party must show "likelihood of success" on the merits, which Union Carbide did not do. 56/

Union Carbide asserted that disclosure of the data effected a taking of its property, but the Second Circuit expressed doubts that such a taking occurred, noting that a distinction must be made between EPA's use of the data and disclosure to the public. Even if there was a taking, the court stated that Union Carbide must establish that it was without an adequate remedy under the Tucker Act. 57/

In Chevron Chemical Co. v. Costle, 58/ a Delaware district court held that FIFRA authorized EPA's consideration of pre-1970

53/ Mobay Chemical Corp. v. Costle, 447 F.Supp 811, 12 ERC 1228 (W.D. Mo. 1978), appeal dismissed 439 U.S. 320, reh. denied 440 U.S. 940 (1979); Chevron Chemical Co. v. Costle, 443 F.Supp 1024 (N.D. Cal. 1978).

54/ PL 95-396, 92 Stat. 812.

55/ 632 F.2d 1014, 15 ERC 1113 (2nd Cir. 1980) cert. denied 450 U.S. 996.

56/ Ibid. at 1018, 15 ERC at 1115. The 1978 Amendments to FIFRA passed during the pendency of the suit so the plaintiff amended his complaint to attack the new provisions on constitutional grounds.

57/ 28 U.S.C. § 1491. The Tucker Act provides compensation for private property taken for public purposes, thus satisfying the Fifth Amendment requirement that the federal government compensate owners when it takes their property.

58/ 499 F.Supp. 732, injunction denied, 499 F.Supp. 745, affirmed 641 F.2d 104 (3rd Cir. 1981), cert. denied 452 U.S. 961.

data for subsequent registrations. It also held that Congress found the use of the data would be a taking for a public, rather than private, purpose. Since FIFRA did not preclude a Tucker Act remedy, the court found that retroactive application of the 1978 amendments did not violate the plaintiff's due process rights.

On appeal, the Third Circuit upheld the district court's decision and clarified the nature of the plaintiff's property rights in its data. 59/ The appeals court found that Congress rejected the idea that there was a common law property right of exclusive use for materials in the government's files prior to 1 January 1970; according to the court, the 1978 amendments, which did not extend the compensation provision to pre-1970 data, was implicit rejection of the exclusive use doctrine for that data. The Third Circuit also held that Chevron's property right on the pre-1970 data was based on 18 U.S.C. Section 1905 which does not confer a private right of action; it only creates a standard by which to judge the legality of an agency's disclosures. That standard is the right of non-disclosure, not of non-use. 60/

4.0 1972 Amendments to FIFRA

The amendments to FIFRA in 1972 which are known as the Federal Environmental Pesticides Control Act (FEPCA) 61/ and amounted to a virtual rewriting of the law. They were considered necessary to (1) strengthen the enforcement provisions of FIFRA, (2) shift the legal emphasis from labeling and efficacy to health and environment, (3) provide for greater flexibility in controlling dangerous chemicals, (4) extend the scope of federal law to cover intrastate registrations and the specific uses of a given pesticide, and (5) streamline the administrative appeals process. Three of the principal changes made by the new law—EPA's expanded authority over field use, the creation of several categories of registration, and trade secrets—have already been discussed. The following discussion will consider other important features of the 1972 amendments to FIFRA.

59/   641 F.2d 104, 16 ERC 2004 (3rd. Cir. 1981), cert. denied 452 U.S. 961.

60/   Id., at 114, 16 ERC at 2013.

61/   PL 92-516, 86 Stat. 973, 21 October 1972.

4.1 Indemnities

Section 15 provides financial compensation to registrants and applicators owning quantities of pesticides who are unable to use them because of cancellation or suspension. This section, although not often invoked, was the most controversial in the entire Act. The amendment's industry supporters threatened to block passage of the entire 1972 legislation if this section were not attached. Public interest groups complained that it would force taxpayers to indemnify manufacturers for inadequate testing and would encourage the production of unsafe chemicals.

As a partial compromise, a clause was added to bar indemnification to any person who "had knowledge of facts which, in themselves, would have shown that such pesticide did not meet the requirements" for registration and continued thereafter to produce such pesticide without giving notice of such facts to the Administrator. 62/ Even under the most expedited Agency procedures, that saving clause may disqualify registrants and manufacturers in virtually all cancellation and suspension actions.

The real purpose of the indemnity provision, according to agriculture chemical lobbyists, was not to compensate manufacturers or even retailers and farmers, but to deter EPA from cancellation and suspension actions. A wide-spread belief in the farming community was that EPA would be reluctant to act if it were forced to buy up large quantities of a banned chemical, using funds from EPA's general budget to indemnify pesticide companies and users. This is, of course, somewhat naive. Federal agencies do not, and should not, make decisions involving human safety and the environment because of such factors; but to the degree that it provides an incentive to EPA to consider its own budget, rather than the public welfare, it is poor policy.

There is one situation in which the section may influence EPA action. Following a suspension or final cancellation order, the Agency has traditionally not attempted to recall or stop the use of those amounts already in distribution. This tradition, which arose before the passage of the 1972 amendments, stemmed from the hazards of bulk disposal 63/ and the training time needed before alternative pesticides could be used, but it may now have become

---

62/ FIFRA § 15(a), 7 U.S.C. § 136m(a).

63/ Recall and disposal will be discussed later.

standard Agency practice. 64/ It is uncertain how much Section 15 unconsciously encourages this practice of condoning the continued use of a chemical which it has declared an imminent hazard.

4.2 "Featherbedding" or "Me-Too" Registrants

The second most contested provision in the 1972 FEPCA, after the question of indemnities, was the issue of "featherbedding" on registration. The original version in the House stated that "data submitted in support of an application shall not, without permission of the applicant, be considered by the Administrator in the support of any other application for registration." 65/ Supporters of the provision, basically the larger manufacturers, claimed that it prevented one company from "free-loading" on the expensive scientific data produced by another company; environmentalists dubbed this the "mice extermination amendment" for requiring subsequent registrants to needlessly duplicate the laboratory experiments of the first registrant.

The groups finally found an acceptable compromise allowing subsequent registrants to reimburse the initial registrant for reliance on its data, adding to the above language the words: "unless such other applicant shall first offer to pay reasonable compensation for producing the test data to be relied upon." 66/ The section provides that disputes over the amount of compensation should be decided by the Administrator, but the 1975 amendments deleted the unfortunate clause which ensured that the original registrant should have nothing to lose by appealing to a district court since "in no event shall the amount of payment determined by the court be less than that determined by the Administrator." 67/ The 1978 amendments removed the unwelcome task from the Administrator entirely by providing for mediation by the Federal Mediation & Conciliation

---

64/   See In re Shell Chemical, supra, p. 2, 6 ERC at 2061. Note, however that in this case the cutoff date was the issuance of the Notice of Intent to Suspend, not the date of the final suspension several months later.

65/   FIFRA § 3(c)(1)(D), 7 U.S.C. § 136a(c)(1)(D).

66/   Ibid.

67/   Ibid. This portion was deleted by PL 94-140 § 12.

Service. 68/ The 1975 amendments also pushed back the effective date of the compensation provision from October 1972, the date of the enactment of the FEPCA amendments, to 1 January 1970. 69/

The data compensation provision has created many problems in the registration process. Pesticide manufacturers brought several lawsuits to determine the breadth of this provision, the proper use of the data, and the amount of compensation that a manufacturer is entitled for use of its data.

In Amchem Products, Inc. v. GAF Corp., 70/ the primary issue before the U.S. Court of Appeals for the Fifth Circuit was the effective date of the 1972 amendments. The plaintiff, a manufacturer of a plant growth regulator, challenged the subsequent registration of the substance by another manufacturer on the grounds that the plaintiff had not been compensated for use of its data on which the registration was based.

In district court, EPA and the second manufacturer successfully argued that the effective date of the compensation provision was controlled by Section 4(c)(1) of FEPCA 71/ which required EPA to promulgate regulations governing registrations within two years. Since EPA did not promulgate regulations covering compensation until after the second manufacturer filed its application, the second manufacturer argued that the compensation provision did not apply. 72/

The Fifth Circuit reversed the district court's interpretation, holding that Section 4(c)(1) neither deferred the effective date of the FEPCA amendments nor gave EPA any discretion to activate

---

68/   PL 95-396 § 2(2), 92 Stat. 819.

69/   PL 94-140, §12, amending FIFRA §3(c)(1)(D). The 1972 amendments had not actually specified an effective date but most authorities assumed it was the date of enactment.

70/   594 F.2d 470 (5th Cir. 1979), reh. denied, 602 F.2d 724 (5th Cir. 1979).

71/   FEPCA § 4(a), 86 Stat. 998, 999.

72/   Amchem Products, Inc. v. GAF Corp., 391 F.Supp 124, 7 ERC 1877 (N.D. Ga. 1975). The "taking" issue also arises under cases interpreting the 1978 amendments.

provisions of the Act by delaying promulgation of implementing regulations. 73/ The Fifth Circuit also rejected the defendant's argument that the compensation provision applied only to data submitted for the first time by the plaintiff after the FEPCA amendments became law. The court held that construing the provision to apply to data already in EPA's possession would satisfy Congressional intent to "[put] an end to free rides" by subsequent applications. 74/

In Mobay Chemical v. EPA, 75/ Mobay sued EPA claiming that EPA's use of its registration data prior to 1970 which was not compensatable under FIFRA was a "taking" for private use and invalid under the Fifth Amendment. Mobay did not base its claim on FIFRA, but rather the Due Process Clause of the Constitution, claiming that it was deprived of its right to exclusive use of its property. The District Court for the Western District of Missouri upheld the 1972 amendment on the grounds that Section 3 of FIFRA was enacted under the Commerce Clause and that Congress' concern with preventing costly duplicative testing was reasonably related to a legitimate purpose. The court also noted that EPA's use of the data did not create a deprivation of property which rose to the level of a taking.

On appeal, the United States Supreme Court dismissed the case on procedural grounds. The Court held that since FIFRA did not address EPA's use of pre-1970 data, the plaintiff's challenge was to "agency practice, not the statute." 76/ Since the three judge district court panel had been improperly convened, the court held that it did not have jurisdiction to hear the appeal.

In the case In re Ciba-Geigy Corp. v. Farmland Industries, Inc., 77/ EPA set out criteria to be applied in determining what constitutes reasonable compensation under Section 3(c). Plaintiff

---

73/   594 F. 2d at 475.

74/   Ibid., at 482. In 1975, this provision was again amended to provide that only "data submitted on or after Jan. 1970" was covered by the section.

75/   447 F. Supp. 811, 12 ERC 1572 (W. D. Mo. 1975).

76/   439 U.S. 320, 12 ERC 1581 (per curiam) (1979).

77/   Initial Decision, FIFRA Comp. Dockets Nos. 33, 34 and 41 (19 August 1980).

Ciba-Geigy claimed that it was entitled to $8.11 million in compensation from Farmland Industries for the latter's use of test data to register three pesticides. The defendant argued that it should pay only a proportional share of the actual cost of producing the data based on its share of the market for the products, approximately $49,000. The plaintiff contended that reasonable compensation should be based on the standards used in licensing technical knowledge: an amount equal to the cost of reproducing the data plus a royalty on gross sales for three years.

The administrative law judge hearing the case ruled that a cost-royalty formula was closer to Congress's intent to avoid unnecessary testing costs. He concluded that the reasonable compensation provision was not intended to provide reward for research and development as the plaintiff's formula would do. The fairest compensatory formula, according to the judge, was using the data producer's cost adjusted for inflation and the defendant's market share two or three years after initial registration. Although no reward for research and development was created, this compensation formula does create an incentive to research because the benefits gained from decreased costs of subsequent registrants outweighs the disadvantages of decreasing the original data producer's projects.

In 1984, the United States Supreme Court ruled in Ruckelshaus v. Monsanto Co. 78/ that pesticide health and safety data was property under Missouri Law Status and thus was protected under the Fifth Amendment of the Constitution. However, the Court overruled a lower court in finding that data submitted prior to 1972 and after 1978 was not a "taking" since the registrant had no expectation of confidentiality. For the period between the 1972 and 1978 amendments, the Court decided there was sufficient ambiguity to warrant a claim. The remedy was not to find FIFRA unconstitutional, however, as the lower court had done, but under the Tucker Act, 28 U.S.C. Section 1491.

4.3 Essentiality in Registration

Another registration change obtained by the pesticide industry was a prohibition against EPA refusing to register a substance because it served no useful or necessary purpose. This was not a

---

78/   Ruckelshaus v. Monsanto Co., 104 S.Ct. 2862 (1984).

dispute as to whether, under both the old and new FIFRA, a registration application must demonstrate that a product would "perform its intended function." 79/ The agricultural chemical companies, however, were apprehensive that EPA might refuse to register a new product because an old one satisfactorily performed its intended function. These fears were largely groundless. EPA's best interest lay in as much duplication of pesticides as reasonably possible, since the existence of a similar but safer chemical facilitates the removal of a hazardous pesticide from the market. There was therefore little objection to this non-essential amendment on "essentiality."

4.4 Intrastate Registrations

One important difference between the old and new laws is that under the old FIFRA, 80/ federal authority did not extend to intrastate use and shipment of pesticides with state registrations. This meant that federal authority could be avoided simply by having manufacturing plants in the principal agricultural states. The new FIFRA 81/ broadens the registration requirement to include any person in any state who sells or distributes pesticides.

The states do retain some authority under Section 24 "to regulate the sale or use of any pesticide or device in the state, but only if and to the extent the regulation does not permit any sale or use prohibited by this Act." 82/ States, furthermore, cannot have labeling and packaging requirements different from those required by the Act—a measure which was popular among some chemical manufacturers who feared that each state might have different labeling requirements. It also seems to exclude a feature common to several of the other environmental laws whereby states may impose stricter requirements than federal on pesticide use within their jurisdiction.

Finally, the section gives a state the authority, subject to certification by EPA, to register pesticides for limited local use in

---

79/ FIFRA § 3(c)(5)(D), 7 U.S.C. § 136a(c)(5)(D).

80/ Old FIFRA § 4(a).

81/ FIFRA § 3(a), 7 U.S.C. § 136a(a).

82/ FIFRA § 24(a), 7 U.S.C. § 136v(a).

treating sudden and limited pest infestations, without the time and administrative burden required by a full EPA certification. 83/

The fears of pesticide manufacturers that the states would impose more stringent labeling requirements were justified in spite of the 1972 amendments.   California imposed additional data requirements under its restricted-use registration. In National Agricultural Chemicals Association v. Rominger, 84/ a California district court declined to issue a preliminary injunction against the state's regulations on the grounds that there was no Congressional mandate to occupy the field when Section 24 was enacted, thus there was no federal preemption of restricted-use registrations. 85/

4.5 Scientific Advisory Committees

An important issue for EPA in the 1972 legislation was a revision of the role of scientific advisory committees in the cancellation-suspension process. 86/ According to the old FIFRA, a registrant challenging a cancellation order could request either a public hearing or a scientific advisory committee; and in practice, cases involving several registrants usually resulted in both. EPA was also strongly dissatisfied with the vague and often contradictory reports of the advisory committees.

In the 1972 amendments to FIFRA, the advisory committee was transformed into an adjunct of the hearing process, resolving those scientific questions which the administrative law judge or the parties determined were essential to the final decision by the Administrator.   This enables the advisory committee to consider questions of scientific fact while the public hearing is in process,

---

83/   FIFRA § 24(c), 7 U.S.C. § 136m(a).

84/   500 F. Supp 465, 15 ERC 1039 (E.D. Cal. 1980).

85/   The court also dismissed challenges to two other provisions of the California laws for lack of ripeness. These challenges were claims that the statute improperly allowed the state to set residue tolerances different from EPA tolerances and that certain labeling requirements for insecticides were improperly imposed.

86/   See FIFRA § 6(d), 7 U.S.C. § 136d(d).

rather than in a separate proceeding with long delays and divisions of responsibility. By meeting outside of the public hearing, the scientists can also avoid being subject to cross examination and other legal burdens they consider unappealing.

The advisory process, however, was again made more formalistic by the 1975 amendments. The use of a scientific advisory committee is now mandated both for cancellation actions (where they are usually requested anyway) and for any general pesticide regulations; and the composition and selection process for the committee is set forth in considerable detail. 87/

In 1980, Section 25(d) was amended to allow the chairman of a Scientific Advisory Committee to create temporary subpanels on specific projects. 88/ Section 25(d) was also amended to require the Administrator to submit any decision to suspend the registration of a pesticide to a scientific advisory panel (SAP) for its comment. 89/ The amendment does not alter the Administrator's authority to issue a suspension notice prior to SAP review, it only requires him to obtain SAP review after the suspension is initiated. The 1980 amendments also require the Administrator to issue written procedures for independent peer review of the design, protocol and conduct of major studies conducted under FIFRA. The latter two amendments are outgrowths of the General Accounting Office (GAO) study of EPA's controversial decision to suspend 2,4,5-T on an emergency basis. GAO reviewed EPA's decision and concluded that EPA did not have clearly defined peer review procedures. The amendments were enacted to require EPA to proceed on the basis of validated scientific information and to avoid another 2,4,5-T controversy. 90/

4.6 Standing for Registration, Appeals and Subpoenas

The old FIFRA assumed that only registrants would be interested in the continuation of a product's registration or the setting of

---

87/   PL 94-140, §7, amending FIFRA §25. A more detailed analysis of the 1975 changes appears in 5.0.

88/   PL 96-539, 94 Stat. 3195.

89/   Id.

90/   No. 96-1020, 96th Cong., 2d Sess. (1980) p.4.

public hearings and scientific advisory committees. It was increasingly evident, however, that this unintended exclusion of both users and environmentalists needed revision.

A registrant, when faced with cancellation, might prefer not to contest those minor categories of use which it regarded as financially insignificant, but a user might regard them as essential for the protection of his crops. The law was therefore amended by FEPCA to allow not only registrants but any "other interested person with the concurrence of the registrant" to request continuation of the registration. 91/ While this amendment remedies the problem of legal standing, it does not provide the resources and data which a user would need to support his renewal application. 92/

Another problem of standing relates to the right of environmental and consumer groups to utilize the administrative procedures under cancellation-suspension. The old FIFRA did not clearly provide for such groups to request a public hearing or scientific advisory hearing, even though they could obtain judicial review in the court of appeals as a "person who would be adversely affected by such order." 93/ The new Act does not specifically give citizens' groups the right to request a public hearing, but the Administrator himself is now empowered to call a hearing which he might do at the request of such a group. Furthermore, as already discussed, all interested parties may request consent of the administrative law judge to refer scientific questions to a special committee of the

---

91/ FIFRA § 6(a)(1), 7 U.S.C. § 136d(a)(1). See also McGill v. GPA, 593 F. 2d 631, 13 ERC 1156 (5th Cir. 1979).

92/ A good example is the Aldrin-Dieldrin suspension proceeding, in which the registrant was almost solely interested in the use for crops, while the USDA had to join the proceeding to insure that other registrations were properly represented. This USDA action under the new FIFRA, however, was necessary not because the users now lacked legal standing, but presumably because they lacked adequate resources. In re Shell Chemical, supra, 6 ERC 2047.

93/ Old FIFRA § 4(d). The standing environmental groups to contest governmental actions in general is quite complex. See, for example, Sierra Club v. Morton, 405 U.S. 345, 3 ERC 2039 (1972).

National Academy of Sciences for determination, a right which did not exist before.

The administrative law judge plays a key role in these proceedings, for his approval is necessary for advisory committee referrals and for the power of subpoena, which is given not to the parties but to him. 94/ It was Congress' intent to allow the judge just sufficient discretion to eliminate frivolous or irrelevant issues, hence the statutory language that "upon a showing of relevance and reasonable scope of evidence sought by any party to a public hearing, the hearing examiner shall issue a subpoena to compel testimony or production of documents from any person." 95/ Some commentators, however, have expressed concern that a judge may have excessive latitude to deny reasonable requests. 96/

The issue of standing came up in Environmental Defense Fund v. Costle 97/ when the D.C. Circuit upheld EPA's denial of standing for an environmental group which requested a Section 6(d) cancellation hearing for the continued use of chlorobenzilate in four states. The Environmental Defense Fund (EDF) requested the hearing after the Administrator issued a Notice of Intent to Cancel the registration of chlorobenzilate for all uses other than citrus spraying in four states. The Administrator denied the hearing holding that FIFRA was not structured for the purpose of entertaining objections by persons having no real interest in stopping the cancellation from going into effect, but who object to the Agency's refusal to propose actions. 98/

94/   See the EPA Rules of Practice 40 CFR § 164.21, 38 FR 19378 (1973) and U.S. v. Allen, 494 F. Supp. 107 (W.D. Wisc. 1980).

95/   FIFRA § 6(d), 7 U.S.C. § 136d(d).

96/   See, for example, William A. Butler, "Federal Pesticide Law," in Erica L. Dolgin and Thomas G. P. Guilbert, Federal Environmental Law (St. Paul, Minn.: West Publishing Co., 1974), p. 1256.

97/   631 F.2d 922, 15 ERC 1217 (D.C. Cir. 1980), cert. denied 449 U.S. 1112.

98/   Final Decision, FIFRA Docket No. 411 (20 August 1979) at 12-22.

The D.C. Circuit upheld the Administrator's decision that EDF was not an "adversely affected" party under Section 6(d), stating that a 6(d) hearing may be used only to stop a cancellation proceeding, not initiate one. The proper procedure for EDF in seeking review of EPA's decision to retain the registration for citrus users was to challenge the notice provisions permitting the limited use in district court under Section 16(a) of FIFRA. 99/

4.7 Judicial Appeals

Under the old FIFRA, 100/ appeals from decisions of the Administrator went to the United States court of appeals. According to Section 16 of the amended FIFRA, however, appeals under some circumstances may go to a federal district court: agency "refusals to cancel or suspend registrations, or to change classifications not following a hearing, and other final agency actions not committed to agency discretion by law are judicially reviewable in the district courts." 101/ District courts are also given the authority to "enforce and to prevent and restrain violations of, this act." 102/ Other appeals go to the court of appeals.

This change provoked considerable controversy in EPA during the legislative process. The rationale for change was that courts of appeals are not designed to develop a record if none existed from the proceeding below. It thus seemed logical that in those instances where a record was developed, after public hearing or otherwise, the appeal should be to the court of appeals, whereas in cases where there was no record for the court to review the matter should go to a district court for findings of fact.

Unfortunately, this creates a certain ambiguity which a party might utilize to prolong the judicial review process. In one case that predated the amended FIFRA, an aggrieved registrant appealed to a

---

99/   631 F. 2d at 935, 15 ERC at 1229. This case is also noteworthy for its treatment of judicial review under Section 16(b): See discussion of Judicial Review in 4.2.

100/   Old FIFRA § 4(d).

101/   FIFRA § 16(a), 7 U.S.C. § 136n(a).

102/   FIFRA § 16(c), 7 U.S.C. § 136n(c).

district court judge whose record for eccentricity was almost legendary. Although he had no jurisdiction whatsoever over the matter, the judge held up the case for almost two years before an order of the court of appeals could be obtained to overturn an injunction which he had issued against the Agency. 103/ The legal process could have taken even longer if the statutory exclusion of the district court from jurisdiction had been less explicit.

Section 16 has been the focus of two courts of appeals decisions which reached contrary holdings on the issue of whether the federal courts or the courts of appeals have jurisdiction to review the denial of a request for a FIFRA Section 6(d) hearing on a notice of cancellation. In Environmental Defense Fund v. Costle, 104/ the D.C. Circuit Court held that if an administrative record exists in support of a denial of a hearing request, jurisdiction lies exclusively with the courts of appeals. In AMVAC Chemical Corp. v. EPA, 105/ a divided Ninth Circuit rejected the D.C. Circuit's analysis and held that a denial of a hearing was a procedural action and not an "order" following a "public hearing" within the meaning of Section 16(b). Hence, the Court held that judicial review of hearing request denials lies in the district courts.

The Ninth Circuit attempted to distinguish the Environmental Defense Fund case because the petitioners in that case were able to present their arguments to a Scientific Advisory Panel, whereas the petitioner in AMVAC did not have such an opportunity. 106/ This distinction is rather unpersuasive because the record on which the D.C. Circuit relied included only the proceedings and pleadings on the procedural question of judicial review. Consequently, these two cases present conflicting interpretations of Section 16(b) which may cause procedural nightmares for future review of EPA actions.

103/   Pax Co. v. U.S., 454 F. 2d 93, 3 ERC 1591 (10th Cir. 1972).

104/   631 F.2d 922, 15 ERC 1217 (D.C. Cir. 1980) cert. denied 449 U.S. 1112. This case is also important for its treatment of standing, discussed in the previous subsection.

105/   653 F.2d 1260, 15 ERC 1467 (9th Cir. 1980) as amended 5 February 1981, reh. denied, 10 April 1981.

106/   Ibid., at 1265.

4.8 Exports and Imports

The old FIFRA 107/ provided that imports should be subject to the same requirements of testing and registration as American products. Section 17 of the new FIFRA kept this provision 108/ and, at the urging of the chemical industry, also retained the controversial provision excluding U.S. exports from the Act, other than for certain record keeping requirements. 109/

There were two reasons for this. First, the agricultural chemical producers, seeing the market for some of their products such as chlorinated hydrocarbons drying up in this country, wished to continue exporting the products abroad. They argued that foreign producers would not be stopped from manufacturing these chemicals and they wished to continue to compete, as well as to keep in operation profitable product lines.

A secondary but more compelling reason was that cancellation decisions made in the United States are based upon a risk-benefit analysis that might have little relevance to conditions abroad. For example, DDT is neither needed nor, because of insect resistance, very useful for the control of malaria in the United States. However, the situation in, say, Ceylon, may be quite different (although resistance is becoming an increasing problem there as well) and should be considered separately.

One problem with this approach is that persistent pesticides may be distributed by oceans and the atmosphere in a world-wide circulation pattern that does not stop at national boundaries. A second problem is that there is no requirement that foreign purchasers relying on EPA registration as proof of a product's safety be notified of cancellation-suspension proceedings. Only after a final Agency decision—which may take years—is the State Department legally required to inform foreign governments. 110/ The 1978

107/   Old FIFRA § 10.

108/   FIFRA § 17(c), 7 U.S.C. § 136o(c). The old FIFRA provisions on exports is § 3(a)(5)(b).

109/   See FIFRA § 8, 7 U.S.C. § 136f.

110/   FIFRA § 17(b), 7 U.S.C. § 136o(b).

amendments did add a requirement that such exports be labeled that they are "not registered for use in the U.S." 111/

In 1980, EPA issued a final policy statement on labeling requirements. 112/ Under the 1978 amendments, pesticides which are manufactured for export must have bilingual labeling which identify the product and protect persons who come into contact with it. If the pesticide is not registered for use in the United States, the exporter must obtain a statement from the foreign purchaser acknowledging its unregistered status. 113/

The policy statement implements these new requirements by requiring exported products to bear labels containing an EPA establishment number, a use classification statement, the identity of the producer, as well as information about whether the pesticide is registered for use in the United States. In the case of highly toxic pesticides, a skull and crossbones must appear and the word "poison" along with a statement of practical treatment written bilingually. 114/

The policy statement also requires that a foreign purchaser of an unregistered pesticide sign a statement showing that he understands that the pesticide is not registered for use in the United States. The exporter must receive the acknowledgement before the product is released for shipment and submit it to EPA within seven days of receipt. EPA then transmits the acknowledgements to the appropriate foreign officials via the State Department. The acknowledgement procedure applies only to the first annual shipment of an unregistered pesticide to a producer; subsequent shipments of the product to the same producer do not need to comply with the acknowledgement process. 115/

On 15 January 1981, President Carter signed Executive Order 12264 establishing procedures for the export of banned or

---

111/ FIFRA § 17(a)(2), 7 U.S.C. § 136o(e)(f). See also 44 FR 4358, 19 January 1979.

112/ 45 FR 50274, 28 July 1980.

113/ PL 95-396, 92 Stat 833; codified at 7 U.S.C. § 136(o).

114/ 45 FR at 50274, 50278, 28 July 1980.

115/ Ibid., at 50276-77.

significantly restricted substances from the United States. 116/ The comprehensive policy was designed to make present statutory controls over exports more consistent and effective. The cornerstone was a provision requiring that foreign importing countries be notified of the importation of a restricted or banned substance. One of the most restrictive provisions and one that reportedly caused the most disagreement between the federal agencies involved in the policy directed the Department of Commerce to develop regulations for licensing exports of hazardous wastes. The order applied to pesticides, chemicals, drugs, and other products which were restricted in some way by federal statute.

The policy was short-lived because President Reagan rescinded it on 17 February 1981, shortly after he took office. 117/ President Reagan sought instead a review of existing U.S. export controls. The recission resulted in no real changes in the notification requirements under Section 17 of FIFRA.

4.9 Disposal and Recall

An important question following a cancellation or suspension action is whether to recall those products already in commerce. 118/ "Misbranded" pesticides may be confiscated, and on several occasions EPA has ordered manufacturers to recall a pesticide when the hazard so warranted, but for both practical and administrative reasons cancellation-suspension orders have generally provided that banned pesticides may be used until supplies are exhausted, without being subject to recall. 119/ It may seem inconsistent to ban a substance as an imminent hazard and yet allow quantities already on

---

116/   46 FR 4659, 19 January 1981.

117/   46 FR 12943, 19 February 1981.

118/   FIFRA §§ 19 and 25, 7 U.S.C. §§ 136q and 136w. See also the previous discussion of indemnities.

119/   Compare the recall authority of the Consumer Product Safety Commission under Section 15 of its Hazardous Substance Act, 15 U.S.C. §1274, PL 91-113, which makes recall almost mandatory. The Consumer Product Safety Act, Section 15, on the other hand, provides several options, 15 U.S.C. 2064, PL 92-573.

the market to be sold, but repeated challenges by environmentalist groups have been unsuccessful. 120/

   This policy was thought necessary, for example, in the mercury pesticides case when EPA scientists concluded that the recall of certain mercuric compounds would result in a concentration more harmful to the environment than permitting the remaining supplies to be thinly spread around the country. In the DDT case the Administrator decided that his final cancellation order would not go into effect for six months to ensure the availability of adequate supplies of alternative pesticides (namely, organophosphates which can be very hazardous to untrained applicators) and to allow time for training and educational programs to prevent misuse of the new chemicals.

   EPA promulgated regulations for the storage and disposal of pesticides in May 1974, 121/ and proposed others which were never implemented. 122/ These detailed the appropriate conditions for incinerations, soil injection, and other means of disposal, established procedures for shipment back to the manufacturers or to the federal government, directed that transportation costs should be borne by the owner of the pesticide, and provided standards for storage. The regulations devote considerable attention to the disposal problem of pesticide containers, which have caused a significant proportion of accidental poisonings.

4.10 Experimental Use Permits

   FIFRA 123/ provides for experimental use permits for registered pesticides. 124/ The purpose of this seemingly innocuous section is to permit a registration applicant to conduct tests and

---

120/   See, e.g., EDF v. EPA 510 F.2d 1292, 7 ERC 1689 (D.C. Cir. 1975).

121/   39 FR 15236, 1 May 1974, 40 CFR § 165.

122/   39 FR 36874, 15 October 1974.

123/   FIFRA § 5, U.S.C. § 136c.

124/   The 1975 Amendments added a specific provision for agricultural research agencies, public or private.

"accumulate information necessary to register a pesticide under Section 3." 125/ This provision, however, has already been used in at least one successful effort to evade a FIFRA cancellation–suspension order. Under strong political pressure from Western sheep interests and their Congressional spokesmen, EPA granted a Section 5 permit for the limited use of certain banned predacides and devices including the "coyote getter." 126/

In March 1974 EPA proposed regulations for experimental permits, noting that in the one-year period from October 1972 to October 1973 almost one hundred experimental permits were issued authorizing the use of a total of 1.5 million pounds of pesticides, and this figure did not include substantial experimental use of federal and state agencies. 127/ These regulations, which became final on 30 April 1975, provided for tighter control over experimental use, including that by governmental agencies, 128/ but did not close the loophole entirely.

EPA issued final regulations on 18 July 1979 under which a state may develop its own experimental permits program. 129/ A state, by submitting a plan which meets the requirements of EPA's regulations, may receive authorization to issue experimental use permits to potential registrants under 24(c) of FIFRA (restricted use registration), agricultural or educational research agencies, and certified applicators for use of a restricted use pesticide.

Permits cannot be issued by a state for a pesticide containing ingredients subject to an EPA cancellation or suspension order, or a

---

125/   FIFRA § 5(a), 7 U.S.C. § 136c(a).

126/   EPA's pesticide regulatory decisions have generally been little affected by such outside pressures, but this action was one of the three exceptions to the rule. The others were an emergency permit for DDT use in the Pacific Northwest, and the protracted deliberations on the ant-killer Mirex.

127/   39 FR 11306, 27 March 1974, 40 CFR § 172.

128/   Ibid. The regulations point out that, except in limited circumstances, the amended FIFRA "does not grant a blanket exemption to federal or state agencies."

129/   44 FR at 41783, 18 July 1978; 40 CFR § 172.20.

notice of intent to cancel or suspend or which are not found in any EPA registered product. 130/ The regulations also contain strict limitations on the production and use of a pesticide. Periodic reports must be submitted by the permittee to the state detailing the progress of the research or restricted use. In addition, permits cannot be issued for more than three years.

5.0 1975 Amendments to FIFRA

Congress' 1975 amendments to the FIFRA are significant not for what they actually changed but because of the motivations that prompted them. The amendments themselves were viewed by many as, at best, unnecessary and, at worst, a further encumbrance upon an already complicated administrative procedure. They did, however, indicate a strong desire on the part of Congress—or at least the respective agriculture committees—to restrict EPA's authority to regulate pesticides. The situation was summarized by an editorial in a Washington, D.C., newspaper captioned, "Trying to Hogtie the EPA." 131/

5.1 Need For FIFRA Renewal

The authorization for FIFRA under the 1972 Act was limited to three years. 132/ Congress was therefore provided the opportunity in 1975 to review the strengths and shortcomings of the 1972 legislation, even though some portions of that law were not scheduled to go into effect until four years after enactment. 133/ This review, however, also provided a chance for those, both within and

---

130/   44 FR at 41788. States may, however, issue permits for products containing ingredients subject to the Rebuttable Presumption Against Review process (RPAR).

131/   The Washington Star, 8 October 1975.

132/   FIFRA § 27. Actually the term for the Act was less than three years since the Act finally went into effect in October 1972 and the authorization expired 30 June 1975.

133/   One such example is EPA's authority under § 27 to require that a pesticide be registered for use only by a certified applicator.

without Congress who believed that EPA had been given too much authority, to seek to redress the balance.

Some environmentalists feared that the Agriculture Committee would allow the bill to lapse altogether, which would have created some uncertainty as to whether the entire FIFRA would have been abolished or merely the 1972 amendments. Practically speaking, it probably would not have made any difference, as EPA could not have administered any part of the law without Congressional authorization of funds. This eventually, however, probably would have created a backlash in favor of the environmentalists and led to much more stringent laws than the House Agriculture Committee or the agricultural chemical industry desired.

Authorization was therefore granted for FIFRA, but the extension was only for one year (to 30 September 1976) rather than the two-year period which EPA originally sought. The reason for this limitation, according to the official House report, was "to give it [Congress] an opportunity to continue to exercise effective oversight activities over its [EPA's] operations," particularly in view of the controversies that had been generated in many of its activities. 134/

5.2 Controversy over USDA's Veto of EPA

The most spirited debate in the Committee hearings was over an amendment submitted by Representative Bob Poage (D-Tex.), the former Chairman of the House Agriculture Committee. The Poage-Wampler Amendment would have permitted the Secretary of Agriculture to veto EPA actions cancelling or suspending a registration, changing the classification of a pesticide, or issuing regulations. The proposed amendment provided no criteria or legal requirements which the Secretary had to meet for such a veto, nor was it necessary for the Secretary to consider the extensive record developed by EPA for the Administrator's decision. Moreover, although less than half of EPA pesticides relate to Agriculture, 135/ the Secretary

---

134/ House Report No. 94-497, "Extension and Amendment of the FIFRA, as Amended," 19 September 1975, for H.R. 8841, p. 5.

135/ See the statement of Russell E. Train, Administrator, EPA before the Senate Agriculture Committee, reprinted in the Senate Report No. 94-452, "Extension of the FIFRA," 10 November 1975, to accompany H. R. 8841, p. 18.

would have been granted authority to block EPA actions on all of
them. The amendment would have also severely compromised the
administering of the Act by fragmenting the authority over pesticides between the two agencies. 136/ There was some sentiment in
Congress for restoring jurisdiction over pesticides to USDA, but the
Department's poor prior record discouraged serious consideration of
this idea. 137/

5.3 Requirement of Consultation By EPA With USDA

Congress decided instead to require that EPA engage in formal consultation with USDA and with the Agriculture Committees
of the House and Senate before issuing proposals or final standards
regarding pesticides. This amended Section 6(b) of the FIFRA to
provide that EPA should give 60 days' notice to the Secretary of
Agriculture before a notice is made public. The Secretary then must
respond within 30 days, and these comments, along with the response
of the EPA Administrator, are published in the Federal Register.
According to the House report, "this represents a real change from
present procedures . . . it would have much the same effect as the
public exposure of an environmental impact statement. . . ." 138/
These consultations, however, are not required in the event of an
imminent hazard to human health for which a suspension order under
Section 6(c) is warranted. 139/

This amendment makes sense only if one assumes either that
USDA had not been contacted regularly by EPA before making major
decisions in the past, or if it is believed (as the above House report
seems to indicate) that USDA's objections to EPA actions had not
been given sufficient public attention. Neither assumption is really
accurate. The amendment does, however, place USDA in the potentially embarrassing situation of having to respond formally within an

---

136/ This difficult situation also exists between EPA and FAA,
      although in that instance the roles are reversed. See the
      chapter on Noise in this book.

137/ See House Report No. 94-497, p.7.

138/ House Report No. 94-497, p.6. These time deadlines may be
      by agreement between the Administrator and the Secretary,
      PL 94-140, § 1.

139/ FIFRA, § 6(c), 7 U.S.C. § 136d(c).

unreasonably short period to EPA proposals. The Department of Agriculture was previously in the politically desirable position of being able to criticize EPA actions without having to provide detailed explanation or supportable objections. 140/

At the same time that the Administrator provides a copy of any proposed regulations to the Secretary of Agriculture, he is also required to provide copies to the respective House and Senate Agricultural Committees. The practical impact of this requirement is that Congress is provided an opportunity to communicate displeasure to the Administrator before a proposal is issued without necessarily having to subject these comments to scrutiny in the public record. 141/

5.4 Scientific Advisory Committees

One of the reforms of the 1972 amendments had been to streamline the Scientific Advisory Committee process so that Committee deliberations could proceed simultaneously with the administrative hearings, thereby saving time and making them a part of the fact-finding and evaluation system rather than a separate procedure. The 1975 amendments require that the Administrator submit proposed and final regulations to a specially constituted scientific advisory panel, separate from the regular Scientific Advisory Committees, at the same time that he provides copies to the Secretary of Agriculture and to the two agricultural committees of Congress. The advisory committee then has 30 days in which to respond. Membership on this committee is prescribed in unusual detail. The Administrator can select seven members from a group

---

140/   The requirement for EPA to consult with USDA is the reverse of the situation regarding small watersheds under PL 566, whereby EPA can formally object to USDA's approval of small watersheds, although USDA does not have to accept the objections. House Report No. 94-497, p.6. A similar authority is found in EPA's right to object to FAA decisions which might affect emissions into the ambient air.

141/   EPA has often required that Congressional communications after the issuance of a proposal be placed on the public record; and where this was not done, as in the DDT proceedings, environmental groups successfully sued to ensure that these contacts and written comments were made public.

of twelve nominees, six nominated by the National Science Foundation, and six by the National Institutes of Health. 142/

One might question the value of yet another advisory committee when, as Administrator Train pointed out, "EPA is already awash in scientific advisory panels." 143/ After all, the statute already provides for a separate scientific advisory committee under the auspices of the National Academy of Sciences for each pesticide cancellation action. EPA has also had, since its inception, a Science Advisory Board (formerly called the Hazardous Materials Advisory Committee) and the Administrator has recently created a Pesticides Policy Advisory Committee. Furthermore, one might question how effective the new advisory committee will be, given its thirty-day time limit, considering that the present advisory committees at EPA and other agencies have great difficulty in producing creditable reports under schedules permitting four months of review or longer.

5.5 Economic Impact On Agriculture Statement

The 1975 amendments also reflected the increasing trend in government toward requiring impact statements before regulations can be issued. Congress, borrowing from the environmental impact statement process 144/ and the economic impact statement requirements, 145/ mandated in the new amendment that the Administrator, when deciding to issue a proposal, "shall include among those factors to be taken into account the impact of the action proposed in such notice on production and prices of agricultural commodities, retail food prices, and otherwise on the agricultural economy." 146/

142/   PL 94-140, § 7, amending FIFRA § 25(d), 7 U.S.C. § 136w.

143/   Statement of EPA Administrator Russell Train to the Senate Agricultural Committee, reprinted in Senate Report No. 94-452, p. 18. This concern apparently did not prevent Congress from amending FIFRA in 1980 to allow the chairman of a SAP to create subpanels. See discussion of 1980 amendments, infra.

144/   National Environmental Policy Act, § 102(2)(c), U.S.C. §§ 4321 et seq., (1969); see also 36 FR 7724 (1971) and 38 FR 20549 (1973).

145/   Presidential Executive Order No. 11821, 29 November 1974.

146/   PL 94-104, § 1, amending FIFRA § 6(b), 7 U.S.C. § 136d.

The necessity for this new legal provision is questionable since the balancing of risks and benefits is at the heart of FIFRA. No one at EPA or anywhere else has contended that the agricultural benefits of pesticides should not be taken into consideration in this balancing equation. In fact, although the courts have stated that EPA legally need not consider benefits in suspension actions involving an imminent hazard to human health and the environment, EPA from the beginning has always made the agricultural factor an essential element in its determinations. 147/ The committees themselves were vague about the actual need for this legislation. The Senate stated, "The Committee concurs in the House position that EPA has not always given adequate consideration to agriculture in its decisions. This concern was also expressed by many witnesses appearing before the Committee." 148/ However, the House position, at least as indicated in their official committee report, suggests less certainty: "The Committee believes that the [present] statutory test is a sound one and that changes are not needed in the formula. There was, however, a strong belief among many witnesses that the impact on the agrcultural economy of decisions in EPA was not fully developed by EPA and was not given sufficient recognition." 149/

5.6 Self-Certification of Private Applicators
The clearest illustration of Congress' altered view toward FIFRA is their treatment of the certification program which had been a major reason for the enactment of the 1972 amendments. This law provided that the pesticides which might be too harmful to the applicators or to the environment if indiscriminately used could continue to be applied by farmers and pesticide operators who had received special training in avoiding these problems.

The program had run into resistance from the beginning from farmers who resented the requirement that they be trained to use chemicals on their own property. As stated in the House report, "The Committee does not see the need for a farmer who would be treating his own farm as he has done for many years to have to go to the county seat or elsewhere for a special training program to get

---

147/   See the discussion of this in paragraph 2.6 of this chapter.

148/   Senate Report No. 94-452, p.9.

149/   House Report No. 94-497, p.6.

certified." 150/ The changed law does not remove the examination requirement from commercial applicators, who apply pesticides to property other than their own. 151/ It does create an exemption, however, which covers not only the farmer who is applying pesticides to his own land but also his employees. And it must be remembered that the hazards are not necessarily limited to the applicator; organophosphates, which are nerve gases, may be highly toxic to the applicators, but many other substances if improperly used may run off to threaten neighboring farms or the environment in general. The amended law does not seem to recognize this latter problem.

The 1975 amendments also removed the authority of the Administrator to require, under state plans submitted for his approval, that farmers take exams before being certified. In other words, EPA may require a training program but may not require a final examination to determine if the information has been learned. 152/ In the opinion of the House Agriculture Committee, "The farmer would be more aware of the dangers of restricted use pesticides if each time he makes a purchase he is given a self-certification form to read and sign." 153/

The report continues, "at the time of purchase of a pesticide, the dealer goes through the information on the label with the prospective buyer and satisfies himself that the buyer understands the limited uses prescribed by the label. Once the dealer is satisfied that the buyer understands the label clearly, he provides the buyer with a certification form for signature in which the buyer certifies he understands the restricted use of the pesticide and will conduct himself accordingly. The dealer is checked periodically to assure that he is informed on the use of the various pesticides that he is licensed to sell and is properly instructing buyers." 154/

150/   House Report No. 94-497, p. 9.

151/   See the definition of commercial applicator in FIFRA § 2(e).

152/   States may themselves require an examination of certified applicators but, under the amended FIFRA, EPA could not make this a prerequisite for state plan approval. See PL 94-140 § 5, amending FIFRA § 4, 7 U.S.C. 136b. See also Senate Report No. 94-452, pp. 7-8.

153/   House Report No. 94-497, p. 9.

154/   Ibid., at 9-10.

6.0 1978 Amendments to FIFRA

6.1 Conditional Registration

The near-collapse of EPA's pesticide registration process prompted creation of a system of conditional registration or reregistration.   This could be applied when certain data on a product's safety had either not yet been supplied to EPA or had not yet been analyzed to ensure, according to FIFRA § 3(a)(5)(D), that "it will perform its intended function without unreasonable adverse effects on the environment."

Three kinds of conditional registrations are authorized by § 6 of the 1978 law which amends FIFRA § 3(c) with a new section, entitled "Registration Under Special Circumstances": pesticides identical or very similar to currently registered products; new uses to existing pesticide registrations; and pesticides containing active ingredients not contained in any currently registered pesticide for which data need be obtained for registration.   These conditional registrations must be conducted on a case-by-case basis, with the last type of conditional registration further limited both by duration and by the requirement that the "use of the pesticide is in the public interest."   Conditional registration is prohibited if a Notice of Rebuttable Presumption Against Registration (RPAR) has been issued for the pesticide. And the proposed new use involves use on a minor food or feed crop for which there is an effective registered pesticide not subject to a RPAR proceeding.

Cancellation of conditional registrations must be followed by a public hearing, if requested, within seventy-five days of the request, but must be limited to the issue of whether the registrant has fulfilled its conditions for the registration. 155/

EPA published final regulations implementing conditional registration on 11 May 1979. 156/

6.2 Generic Pesticide Review

EPA has long complained that registration, and especially reregistration reviews should be conducted for entire classes of chemicals rather than being limited to examining each particular

---

155/ § 12 of 1978 Act, amending FIFRA § 6.

156/ 44 FR 27932, 11 May 1979.

registration as it comes up for five-year renewal. This authority has always existed under FIFRA, but a district court decision in 1975 157/ on compensation for data made this so complicated that the plan was dropped pending a legislative solution.

The amendment that finally emerged under this label in Section 4 of the 1978 Act, however, is considerably different in scope: "No applicant for registration of a pesticide who proposes to purchase a registered pesticide from another producer in order to formulate such purchased pesticide into an end-use product shall be required to (i) submit or cite data pertaining to the safety of such purchased product; or (ii) offer to pay reasonable compensation . . . for the use of any such data." 158/

In September 1978, EPA listed 40 chemicals contained in 21,000 pesticides to which it intended to apply generic review within the next two years. This included kelthane, azides, warfarin, naphthalene, and boric acid. 159/

6.3 Greater State Authority

Several sections of the 1978 amendments reflect Congress' intent to give the states greater responsibility in regulating pesticides. This includes not only training and cooperative agreements, but also increasing federal delegation over such matters as intrastate registrations and enforcement. 160/ The EPA Administrator, however, retains overall supervisory responsibility and ultimate veto authority.

Because some states, such as California, have promulgated stringent guidelines for pesticide regulations, there has been proposed legislation to limit state authority under Section 24 to gather data about a pesticide for state registration. 161/ Pesticide

---

157/ Mobay Chemical Corp. v. Train, 394 F. Supp. 1342, 8 ERC 1227 (W.D. Mo. 1975).

158/ 1978 Act, amending FIFRA § 3(c)(2).

159/ BNA 2 Chemical Regulation Reporter, 29 September 1978, pp. 1157-1158.

160/ §§ 21-27 of 1978 Act.

161/ See "Hearings Before the House Agricultural Committee, Federal Insecticide, Fungicide, and Rodenticide Act Amendments," H.R. 5203, Serial No. 97-R, (1982).

manufacturers have complained for several years that state registration procedures, which may require additional studies and data gathering, are time-consuming and costly. There have been no changes in Section 24 yet; however, Congress may limit the regulatory authority of the states in future legislation.

6.4 Compensation and Confidentiality

The already overlong FIFRA provisions on the procedures for compensating other firms for their scientific test data are made even more lengthy and complex. One improvement, however, is shifting the arbitrator role from the EPA Administrator to the Federal Mediation and Conciliation Service. 162/ As with TSCA, the controversy over trade secrets will continue to be one of the most troublesome in the law. The new amendments do clarify EPA's authority to disclose ecological and toxicological data to the public. 163/

6.5 Efficacy

The requirements for test data on a pesticide's efficacy are now made discretionary for EPA. This does not change the present practice very much, because efficacy information has been increasingly less important over the past few years. But the provision is interesting because it marks a complete reversal from the original purpose of federal pesticide legislation earlier in this century, which was to protect farmers from "snake oil" pesticide claims. 164/

7.0 1980 Amendments to FIFRA

FIFRA was amended again in 1980, but the amendments make only minor changes in Section 25 of the Act. These changes are briefly described in the following two sections.

7.1 Two-House Congressional Veto Over EPA Regulations

The 1980 amendments amended Section 25(a) to provide a two-house Congressional veto over EPA rules or regulations. 165/

162/ § 2 of 1978 Act, amending FIFRA § 3.

163/ § 15 of 1978 Act, amending FIFRA § 10. The trade secrets provision is discussed in 3.0, infra.

164/ § 5 of 1978 Act, Amending FIFRA § 3 (c)(5).

165/ PL 96-539, 94 Stat. 3194, 3195 amending 7 U.S.C. § 136w(4).

Under the amendments, the Administrator is required to submit to each house of Congress new FIFRA regulations. If Congress adopts a concurrent resolution disapproving the new regulation within ninety days of its promulgation it will not become effective. However, if neither house disapproves the regulation after sixty days and the appropriate committee of neither house has reported out a disapproving regulation, the regulation becomes effective.

The constitutionality of Congressional vetoes of administrative rules is unsettled. The Supreme Court in 1983 held that one-house vetoes are unconstitutional, and since then legislation has had to be revised to conform to the legislative mode: both houses must pass legislature which is then presented to the President for his approval or disapproval. 166/ Two-house vetoes have not been the subject of litigation as of this writing.

7.2 Changes in the Function and Design of the Science Advisory Panel (SAP)

Section 25(d) of FIFRA was amended by the insertion of two provisions. One authorized the chairman of the FIFRA Scientific Advisory Panel (SAP) to create subpanels. 167/ The other provision required the Administrator to submit emergency suspension orders to the SAP for review of the environmental impacts of the suspension. 168/

The 1980 amendments also added Section 25(e) to the Act which requires the Administrator to issue written procedures for independent peer review of the design and conduct of major studies performed by EPA. 169/ This provision was an outgrowth of the General Accounting Office (GAO) study of EPA's decision to issue an emergency suspension for 2,4,5-T. GAO concluded that EPA did not have clearly defined peer review procedures and that such procedures were necessary to bolster public confidence in EPA's decision. 170/

166/   Immigration & Naturalization Service v. Chadha, 103 S. Ct. 2764 (1983), affirming 634 F. 2d 408 (9th Cir. 1980).

167/   PL 96-539, 94 Stat. 3194, amending 7 U.S.C. 136w(a).

168/   Ibid.

169/   PL 96-539, 94 Stat. 3195 adding § 25(e), 7 U.S.C. § 136w(e).

170/   H.R. No. 96-1020, 96th Cong., 2d Sess. (1980), pp. 4, 8.

8.0 Legal Cases

The usual way to understand a legal field is first to read the statute and then to read the cases involved. This is much less helpful in understanding the FIFRA, however, for several reasons. First, the FIFRA, especially the old FIFRA, had a very complicated legal framework in which the practice had for many years necessarily deviated from the apparent scope of the statute. One such instance was the shift from a mere labeling statute, in which harmful substances would be removed as "mislabeled," to one where the health and safety issues were in the forefront. Second, the scientific issues involved in determinations of carcinogenicity, teratogenicity, subacute effects, and the sophisticated chains of causation affecting the environment are understandably not simple matters for a court to follow. Third, as a result, the courts have only hesitantly postulated adjudicatory principles, and some of these if taken literally have been too unrealistic for the Agency to follow. Decisions tend either to be declarations of deference to administrative expertise or remands for further elucidation of a point troubling the court.

8.1 Basic Cases

The early cases, originating in the period before EPA's creation, generally resulted in court determinations that the responsible federal agency had not sufficiently examined the health and environmental problems.

A leading case in this respect is the 1970 court of appeals decision by Judge Bazelon in Environmental Defense Fund v. Hardin, 171/ which not only gave legal standing to environmental groups under the FIFRA but also determined that the Secretary of Agriculture's failure to take prompt action on a request for suspension of the registration of DDT was tantamount to a denial of suspension and therefore was suitable for judicial review. 172/

That same year the Seventh Circuit Court of Appeals held en banc in Nor-Am v. Hardin 173/ that a pesticide registrant could not

---

171/   428 F. 2d 1083, 1 ERC 1347 (D.C. Cir. 1970).

172/   As there was no administrative record underlying the Secretary's inaction, however, the court remanded the issue to the Department of Agriculture "to provide the court with a record necessary for meaningful appellate review."

173/   435 F. 2d 1151, 2 ERC 1016 (7th Cir., en banc, 1970).

enjoin a suspension order by the Secretary of Agriculture, since the administrative remedies, namely the full cancellation proceedings, had not been exhausted: "The emergency suspension becomes final only if unopposed or affirmed in whole or in part, by subsequent decisions based upon a full and formal consideration. 174/ An underlying reason for the court's action, which reversed a three-judge court of appeals panel in the same circuit, 175/ was the realization that the suspension procedure, which had been designed to deal with imminent hazards to the public, could effectively be short-circuited by injunctions. In the court's view, therefore, a suspension decision is only equivalent of a temporary injunction which shall hold until the full cancellation proceedings are completed. 176/

One of the most important of the earlier cases was EDF v. Ruckelshaus. 177/ The court in another opinion by Judge Bazelon found that the Secretary of Agriculture failed to take prompt action on a request for the interim suspension of DDT registration but that the Secretary's findings of fact, such as the risk of cancer and its toxic effect on certain animals, implicitly constituted a finding of "substantial question concerning the safety of DDT" which the court declared warranted a cancellation decision. The suspension issue was remanded once again for further consideration.

The decision is worthy of attention on two additional points. First, Judge Bazelon made the sweeping statement that "the FIFRA requires the Secretary to issue notices and thereby initiate the administrative process whenever there is a substantial question about the safety of the registered pesticide . . . The statutory scheme contemplates that these questions will be explored in the full light of a public hearing and not resolved behind the closed doors

---

174/   Ibid., at 1157, 2 ERC at 1019.

175/   435 F. 2d 1133, 1 ERC 1460 (7th Cir. 1970).

176/   435 F. 2d at 1160-1161.

177/   EDF v. Ruckelshaus, 439 F.2d 584, 2 ERC 1114 (D.C. Cir. 1971). This was a sequel to the earlier EDF v. Hardin case, supra, but the name of the Administrator of EPA was substituted for the Secretary of Agriculture since the authority of USDA had been transferred to the EPA the month before.

of the Secretary." 178/ Second, the court approved the findings of the Secretary that a hazard may be "imminent" even if its effect would not become realized for many years, as is the case with most carcinogens, and that the "public" protected by the suspension provision includes fish and wildlife in the environment as well as narrow threat to human health. 179/

Wellford v. Ruckelshaus, 180/ another case inherited by EPA from USDA, involved a partial remand of the Secretary of Agriculture's decision concerning suspension and cancellation of certain uses of the herbicide 2,4,5-T for use around the home, in aquatic areas, and on food crops. This case is primarily important for its articulation of certain procedural ground. It agreed with the contention that suspension is only "a matter of interim relief," 181/ and stated that the criteria for suspension during an administrative process involved the Secretary's first determining "what harm, if any, is likely to flow from the use of the product during the course of administrative proceedings. He must consider both the magnitude of the anticipated harm and the likelihood that it would occur. On the basis of that factual determination, he must decide whether anticipated harm amounts to an 'imminent hazard to the public.' "182/

8.2 Label Restrictions: Theory and Practice

One of the most interesting pesticide cases, In re Stearns, 183/ raised the question whether a chemical could be banned that was too toxic to be safely used around the home but which nevertheless was labeled properly with cautionary statements and

---

178/ Ibid., at 594, 2 ERC at 1119. Because there may be a "substantial question of safety" about most pesticides, administrative necessity has forced EPA to interpret this as requiring cancellation of only the most harmful chemicals.

179/ Ibid., at 597, 2 ERC at 1121-22.

180/ 439 F. 2d 598, 2 ERC 1123 (D.C. Cir. 1971).

181/ Ibid., at 601, 2 ERC at 1124.

182/ Ibid., at 602, 2 ERC at 1125.

183/ 2 ERC 1364 (Opinion of Judicial Officer, USDA, 1971); Stearns Electric Paste Company v. EPA, 461 F. 2d 293, 4 ERC 1164 (7th Cir. 1972).

symbols such as the skull and crossbones. "Stearn's Electric Paste," a phosphorous rat and roach killer, was so potent that even a small portion of a tube could kill a child and a larger dose would be fatal to an adult. There was no known antidote. An incomplete survey of state health officials indicated several dozen deaths and many serious accidents, most involving young children. Because of this hazard and the existence of safer substitutes, the USDA cancelled the registration of the paste in May 1969, before the creation of EPA, and a USDA Judicial Officer upheld this action in January 1971 by relying on the provision in the old FIFRA that "the term misbranded shall apply...to any economic poison...if the labeling accompanying it does not contain directions for use which are necessary and, if complied with, adequate for the protection of the public." 184/

A year and a half later, however, the Seventh Circuit Court of Appeals concluded that the statutory test for misbranding was whether a product was safe when used in conformity with the label directions, not whether abuse or misuse was inevitable. The court was impressed with the conspicuous "poison" markings and contended that "disregard of such a simple warning would constitute gross negligence." 185/ The hazard of young children left the court unmoved: "such tragedies are a common occurrence in today's complex society and must be appraised as discompassionately as possible." 186/ The cancellation order was set aside.

On the same day, that same panel of the Seventh Circuit also decided Continental Chemiste v. Ruckelshaus, 187/ involving a Lindane (benzene hexachloride) vaporizer, which when lighted emitted a cloud lethal to many insect pests. Studies by USDA demonstrated that these devices in the home produced residues of Lindane on food which "posed a threat to human health." 188/ The vaporizers were registered only for use in commercial and industrial

---

184/   Old FIFRA § 2(z)2(c).

185/   Stearns Electric Paste, supra, 461 F.2d at 310, 4 ERC at 1175.

186/   Ibid., at 308, 4 ERC at 1174.

187/   461 F. 2d 331, 4 ERC 1181 (7th Cir. 1972).

188/   See 461 F. 2d at 333, 4 ERC at 1182.

establishments, not for home use, but the registrant's advertising and marketing techniques were specifically designed to promote sales to private consumers. The court declined to rule this illegal, deciding the case on another issue to be discussed later.

The issue was confronted more decisively by the Eighth Circuit a year later in another Lindane case, Southern National v. EPA. 189/ The registrants challenged a proposed EPA label reading in part "Not for use or sale to drug stores, supermarkets, or hardware stores or other establishments that sell insecticides to consumers. Not for sale to or use in food handling, processing or serving establishments." 190/ In EPA's opinion, acceptance of such a label would avoid the necessity of cancelling the entire registration. The court questioned whether EPA was within the scope of its powers under the (old) FIFRA in placing the burden on the manufacturer to discourage distribution to homes but nevertheless sustained the Agency action in all respects.

EPA's policy position, under both the old and new FIFRA, is that if there are safer alternatives to a product which arguably constitutes a substantial question of safety, the hazardous product should be removed from the market. This attitude was clearly expressed In re King Paint, 191/ concerning a paint additive that was toxic to humans but rather ineffective as a pesticide. The Judicial Officer, after reviewing the benefits and alternatives, concluded, the fact "that many hazardous substances find their way into the homes and all too frequently into the hands of children—is no justification for exposing the consumer to another source of accidents." 192/ Since less toxic and more effective alternatives existed, the registration was cancelled and this decision was not appealed. This Agency position has implicitly been approved by subsequent judicial decisions, except for Stearns, for it is difficult to argue the benefits of retaining a hazardous chemical when preferable alternatives exist.

189/ 470 F. 2d 194, 4 ERC 1881 (8th Cir. 1972). This case was decided about a month after the enactment of the new FIFRA on 21 October 1972, but that law was not applied here.

190/ Ibid., at 196, 4 ERC at 1882.

191/ 2 ERC 1819, (Opinion of EPA Judicial Officer, 1971).

192/ Ibid., at 1824.

8.3 Administrator's Flexibility

The courts have recognized that EPA in many cases is operating on the frontiers of scientific knowledge. One leading decision, EDF V. EPA, 193/ noted that "it is not an agency in the doldrums of the routine or familiar." 194/ The issues are highly technical, the available scientific data may be inadequate, and "the concept of the safety of the products is an evolving one which is constantly being further refined in light of our increasing knowledge." 195/

> Environmental law marks out a domain where knowledge is hard to obtain and appraise, even in the administrative corridors; in the courtrooms, difficulties of understanding are multiplied. But there is a will in the courts to study and understand what the agency puts before us. And there is a will to respect the Agency's choices if it has taken a hard look at its hard problems. We emphasize again the judicial toleration of wide flexibility for response to developing situations. . . . The Court's concern is for elucidation of basis, not for restriction of EPA's latitude. 196/

8.3.1 Concerning The Scientific Advisory Committee

In emphasizing the Administrator's regulatory flexibility, the courts have rejected the contention that he must "rubber stamp" the findings of the Scientific Advisory Committee or the Administrative Law Judge. This is illustrated by Dow Chemical v. Ruckelshaus 197/ concerning the herbicide 2,4,5-T. In 1970 the USDA suspended some uses of the chemical and cancelled others because of the high risk that it, or a dioxin contaminant known as TCDD, had proved a potent teratogen in laboratory tests. Most of these uses were not

---

193/   465 F. 2d 528, 4 ERC 1523 (D.C. Cir. 1972).

194/   Ibid., at 541, 4 ERC at 1531.

195/   Ibid., at 535 n.5, 4 ERC at 1527, quoting with approval EPA's 18th of March Statement.

196/   Ibid., at 541, 4 ERC at 1531-32.

197/   477 F. 2d 1317, 5 ERC 1244 (8th Cir. 1973).

challenged, but Dow did contest the cancellation on rice. A Scientific Advisory Committee convoked by EPA concluded that the "confused aggregate of observations indicated registrations should be maintained" but that there remained serious questions needing further extensive research. The Administrator reviewed the report in considerable detail and concluded that a "substantial question of safety" existed sufficient to justify an administrative hearing; in the meantime, the cancellation was maintained. 198/ Dow appealed, but the Court of Appeals for the Eighth Circuit held that the Administrator was not compelled to follow the recommendations of the advisory committee if he had justifiable basis for doing otherwise. 199/

8.3.2 Concerning the Administrative Law Judge
       The Administrator is also not bound by findings of the Administrative Law Judge. This conclusion follows the general principle of administrative law that a hearing examiner's decision should be accorded only the deference it merits. As the Supreme Court said in Universal Camera, "we do not require that the examiner's findings be given more weight than in reason and in light of judicial experience they deserve." 200/ Only if the decision-maker arbitrarily and

---

198/ The deficiencies in the advisory report, which was poorly reasoned and internally inconsistent, contributed to the Agency's skepticism towards this system of information collection and analysis.   The advisory process was improved considerably, however, by providing better staff support to the committee and making it an adjunct of the hearing process.

199/ This case is better remembered for its unconscionable delay of the administrative process.   Dow appealed first to a district court in Arkansas and obtained an injunction against further EPA action on 2,4,5-T, although the statute explicitly excluded district courts from jurisdiction. The Eighth Circuit reversed, noting that the court below lacked jurisdiction and that in any case Dow was not entitled to an injunction during a period when "the cancellation orders have no effect on Dow's right to ship and market its product until the administration cancellation process has been completed." Ibid., at 1326, 5 ERC at 1250.

200/   Universal Camera Corp. v. NLRB, 340 U.S. 474 (1951).

capriciously ignored the findings of an examiner, or if the credibility of witnesses was crucial to the case—a situation that rarely exists in an administrative hearing—would a different conclusion be indicated. In the "DDT" case, the court noted that demeanor was not particularly important, adding that the "examiner himself had no particular expertise, for he was a coal mine accident specialist" borrowed from the Department of Interior. 201/

8.3.3 National Environmental Policy Act

The EPA is also not bound by the National Environmental Policy Act (NEPA) 202/ to file Environmental Impact Statements on its pesticide decisions, since the procedures under the FIFRA are an adequate substitute. Although the strict language of NEPA states that all agencies of the federal government should file impact statements, this law was enacted before EPA existed, and courts almost unanimously have found that there is little logic in requiring an agency whose sole function is protection of environment to file a statement obliging it to take into consideration environmental factors. 203/ Courts nevertheless hesitated to grant a blanket exemption to EPA, preferring to stress that EPA actions are mandated by a given statute, although this justification has not exempted certain non-environmental agencies; or they have noted that Environmental Protection Agency procedures for articulating its position and providing for public comment were an adequate substitute for the same procedures under NEPA. The court in EDF v. EPA 204/ ("DDT" case) discussed all the factors:

> We conclude that where an agency is engaged primarily in an examination of environmental questions, where substantive and procedural standards ensure full and adequate consideration of environmental issues, then formal compliance with NEPA is not necessary, but functional compliance is suf-

---

201/ EDF v. EPA ("DDT" case), 489 F. 2d 1247, 1253, 6 ERC 1112, 1117 (D.C. Cir. 1973).

202/ 42 U.S.C. § 4331 et seq., 83 Stat. 852.

203/ For example, Essex Chemical Corp. v. Ruckelshaus, 486 F. 2d 427, 5 ERC 1820 (D.C. Cir. 1973), Portland Cement Assn. v. Ruckelshaus, 486 F. 2d at 375, 5 ERC 1593 (D.C. Cir. 1973).

204/ EDF v. EPA, 489 F. 2d at 1257, 6 ERC at 1119.

ficient. We are not formulating a broad exemption from NEPA for all environmental agencies or even for all environmentally protective regulatory actions of such agencies. Instead, we delineate a narrow exemption from the literal requirements for those actions which are undertaken pursuant to sufficient safeguards so that the purpose and policies behind NEPA will necessarily be fulfilled. The EPA action here meets this standard, and hence this challenge to the EPA action is rejected.

9.0 Pesticide Regulation Under Other Federal Statutes

Pesticides are not regulated solely under the FIFRA. They may also involve regulatory authority under the Food, Drug and Cosmetic Act (FDCA), under the statutes of several other federal agencies, and under other environmental laws administered by EPA.

9.1 Pesticides Under the Food, Drug & Cosmetics Act

One important function of EPA regarding pesticides is not derived from the FIFRA—the setting of tolerances for pesticide residues in food. This authority, originally granted to the Food and Drug Administration under the Food, Drug and Cosmetic Act, 205/ was transferred to EPA by the 1970 Reorganization Plan establishing the Agency and, more specifically, by subsequent detailed memos of agreement between EPA and FDA.

The reorganization plan provided that EPA should set tolerances and "monitor compliance," while the Secretary of HEW would continue to enforce compliance. The amendments to FIFRA in 1972 also invested EPA with authority to prevent misuse of registered pesticides. Under Section 408 of the FDCA, the Administrator issues regulations exempting any pesticides for which a tolerance is unnecessary to protect the public health. 206/ Otherwise, he "shall promulgate regulations establishing tolerances with respect to . . . pesticide chemicals which are not generally recognized among experts . . . as safe for use . . . to the extent necessary to protect the public health." 207/

205/   FDCA § 408, 21 U.S.C. § 346a, et seq.

206/   FDCA § 408(c), 21 U.S.C. § 346a(c).

207/   FDCA § 408(b)(c), 21 U.S.C. § 346(b) and (c).

Pesticide residues are present in most meats, fruits, and vegetables whether or not chemicals are applied to them. DDT, for example, is detectable in most foods, even in mothers' milk. Before registration of a pesticide, a residue tolerance must be set for the maximum level at which that chemical can be safely ingested. Tolerances are usually set at two orders of magnitude (one-hundredth) below the level at which the pesticide has demonstrated an effect on experimental animals. 208/ Some particularly hazardous chemicals are set at "zero residue," but this is causing an increasing problem as the detection capability of analytical equipment is improved. 209/

EPA's pesticide jurisdiction is supposed to cover only residues resulting from a chemical's use as a pesticide but not exposure resulting from, say, dust blowing from a factory (this may be covered by EPA's Clean Air Act) or a truck carrying the chemicals. 210/ In two major cases involving HCB (hexachlorobenzene) contamination of cattle in Louisiana and sheep in the Rocky Mountains, the HCB was blown from open trucks onto pasture land while being transported from one point to another. EPA assumed responsibility for these cases because the tolerance problems regarding health are really the same whether the chemical entered the food as a result of agricultural use or for some other reason, and FDA was only too glad to oblige.

Several pesticide tolerance cases involved DDT. The leading pre-EPA case was Environmental Defense Fund v. HEW. 211/ EDF proposed that the Secretary of HEW establish a "zero tolerance" for DDT residues in raw agricultural commodities, as they could potentially cause cancer in human beings. 212/ The D.C. Circuit pointed

---

208/   This is an oversimplification. The tolerance margin depends on the particular effects of the chemical.

209/   This problem of the so-called "zero level" exists in other health laws as well. The recent Department of Labor standard on vinyl chloride, for example, set a "no detectable level" arbitrarily defined as one part per million (ppm), plus or minus one-half of a ppm.

210/   FDCA § 306, 21 U.S.C. § 336.

211/   428 F. 2d 1083, 1 ERC 1341 (D.C. Cir. 1970).

212/   FDCA § 408, 21 U.S.C. 301.

out that the Delaney Amendment, 213/ banning all "additives" found to induce cancer when ingested by man or animal, "did not apply to pesticide chemicals, although it did indicate strong Congressional concern with potential carcinogens.

The question of whether DDT was a food "additive" in fish within the meaning of the FDCA was raised again in U.S. v. Ewing Bros. 214/ The Seventh Circuit explained that prior to the Delaney Amendment the term did not cover substances present in the raw product and unchanged by processing, but after 1958 the definition was expanded so a single tolerance could cover both raw and processed foods. Since DDT was an additive and EPA had not issued a tolerance, DDT was theoretically a food adulterative and contaminated items were liable to seizure. 215/

This could mean, however, that most foods could be seized as adulterated, including the Great Lakes fish at issue in Ewing. Realizing this in 1969, the FDA had established an interim action level of 5 ppm DDT in fish, thereby excluding all but the most contaminated samples. 216/ This procedure was approved by the Seventh Circuit Court of Appeals in U.S. v. Goodman, 217/ which held that the Commissioner of FDA had "specific statutory authority in the Act empowering him to refrain from prosecuting minor

---

213/ FDCA § 409(c)(3)(A), 21 U.S.C. § 348(c)(3)(A), of 1958. See also H.R. Rep. No. 1761, 86th Cong., 2d Sess., Appendix 2 (1960) U.S. Code Cong. & Ad. News 2887, 2936.

214/ 502 F. 2d 715, 6 ERC 2073 (7th Cir. 1974).

215/ Under FDCA § 402(a)(2)(C), 21 U.S.C. § 342(a)(2)(C), this affects only a substance that "is not generally recognized among experts...as having been adequately shown...to be safe under the conditions of its intended use...." See FDCA § 201(s), 21 U.S.C. § 321(s). Without a tolerance, "the presence of the DDT causes fish to be adulterated without any proof that it is actually unfit as food." 6 ERC 2073, 2077.

216/ Action levels and enforcement, unlike tolerance setting, remain a prerogative of FDA under Section 306 of the FDCA, 21 U.S.C. § 336.

217/ 486 F. 2d 847, 5 ERC 1969 (7th Cir. 1973).

violations," 218/ and that this permitted him to set and enforce action levels in lieu of totally prohibiting the distribution of any food containing DDT at any level.

9.2 Clean Air Act of 1970

Pesticides in the air may be regulated under Section 112 of the Clean Air Act pertaining to hazardous air pollutants. A hazardous pollutant is defined as one for which "no ambient air quality standard is applicable and which in the judgment of the Administrator may cause, or contribute to, an increase in mortality or an increase in severe irreversible, or incapacitating reversible illness." 219/ EPA publishes a list of hazardous air pollutants from time to time and, once a pollutant is listed, proposed regulations establishing stationary source emission standards must be issued unless the substance is conclusively shown to be safe. This section has so far not been applied to pesticides but could acquire more significance in the future.

9.3 Federal Water Pollution Control Act of 1972

The Water Act as amended in 1972 220/ has at least three provisions applicable to pesticides. Under Section 301, pesticide manufacturers and formulators, like all other industrial enterprises, must apply for discharge permits if they release effluents into any body of water. These point sources of pollution must apply the "best practicable control technology" by 1977 and by 1983 must use "the best available control technology." 221/

Hazardous and ubiquitous pesticides may be controlled under Section 307 governing "toxic substances." 222/ Within one year of

---

218/   Ibid., at 855, 5 ERC at 1974; FDCA §306, 21 U.S.C. §336, U.S. v. 1500 Cases, 245 F.2d 208, 210-11 (7th Cir. 1956); U.S. v. 484 Bags, 423 F.2d 839, 841 (5th Cir. 1970).

219/   Clean Air Act, § 112(a)(1), 42 U.S.C. § 1857c-7(a)(1) (1970).

220/   Federal Water Pollution Control Act Amendments of 1972 (FWPCA), 33 U.S.C. §1251 et seq., 86 Stat. 816 (1972).

221/   FWPCA § 301, 33 U.S.C. § 1311.

222/   FWPCA § 307, 33 U.S.C. § 1317. The criteria for this list is given in 38 FR 18044 (1973).

the listing of a chemical as a "toxic substance," the special discharge standards set for it must be achieved. There was originally some dispute whether pesticides should properly be regulated under this section because, unless they are part of a discharge from an industrial concern, they generally derive from non-point sources such as runoff from fields and therefore could be controlled under a third provision, Section 208, which is largely under the jurisdiction of the states. 223/

EPA's principal function under Section 208 is to identify and oversee problems of agricultural pollution, regulated at the state and local level. By 1977, according to the Statute, state authorities were to have formulated control programs for the protection of water quality, pesticides and other agricultural pollutants such as feed-lots. 224/

9.4 Solid Waste Disposal Acts

The EPA had very limited authority under Section 204 of the Solid Waste Disposal Act, as amended by the Resource Recovery Act of 1970, 225/ to conduct research, training, demonstrations and other activities regarding pesticide storage and disposal. 226/ Enactment of the Resource Conservation and Recovery Act (RCRA) in October 1976 gave EPA an important tool for controlling the disposal of pesticides, particularly the waste from pesticide manufacture. 227/ The role of RCRA is described in detail in a separate chapter of this Handbook.

223/ EPA, however, has not followed this reasoning. The present § 307 list of 299 toxic pollutants contains many of the major pesticides. See NRDC v. Train (D.C. Cir. 1976) 8 ERC 2120.

224/ FWPCA § 208, 33 U.S.C. § 1288.

225/ 42 U.S.C. § 3251 et seq., 79 Stat. 997 (1965), 84 Stat. 1227 (1970); RCRA § 204, 42 U.S.C. § 3253.

226/ RCRA § 212, 42 U.S.C. 3241. Under the Solid Waste Disposal Act, guidelines applicable only to federal agencies have been issued regarding pesticide storage and disposal pertaining to Sections 19 and 25 of the FIFRA. 39 FR 15236, 1 May 1974, and proposed regs., 39 FR 36847, 15 October 1974. See also RCRA § 209, 42 U.S.C. § 3254c.

227/ PL 94-580, 42 U.S.C. 6801 (21 October 1976).

9.5 Occupational Safety and Health Act

The EPA and the Department of Labor share somewhat over-lapping authority under FIFRA and the Occupational Safety and Health Act (OSHA) 228/ for the protection of agricultural workers from pesticide hazards. This produced a heated inter-agency conflict during the first half of 1973, although the FIFRA and its legislative history clearly indicated that EPA had primary responsibility for promulgating re-entry and other protective standards in this area, and that OSHA specifically yielded to existing standards by other federal agencies. 229/ The question was finally settled by the White House in EPA's favor after a court had enjoined Labor's own proposed standards. 230/ Both agencies now seem relatively satisfied with the arrangement. Some farm worker groups, however, still contend that the protective standards on EPA pesticide labels are weak and seldom enforced, and that only California and a few other states have adequate statutory and enforcement programs. It may be that local standards, with some federal monitoring of their effectiveness, would be the preferable approach, since the safe re-entry period after spraying can vary dramatically depending on humidity and other local conditions.

Because of OSHA's recent lethargy, Congress has pressured EPA to step into the regulatory vacuum by using TSCA and FIFRA. 231/ In 1983, EPA issued its first notice of violation of pesticide worker safety against an Illinois applicator who sprayed farm workers in the field. 232/

9.6 Federal Hazardous Substances Act

The Federal Hazardous Substances Act of 1970 233/ regulates hazardous substances in interstate commerce. However, pesticides

---

228/   29 U.S.C. § 651, et seq., 84 Stat. 1590.

229/   OSHA § 6, 29 U.S.C. § 655.

230/   Florida Peach Growers Assn. v. Dept. of Labor, 489 F. 2d 120, (5th Cir. 1974).

231/   See Chapter 4 on "Toxic Substances" for further discussion of this point.

232/   BNA, Chemical Regulation Reporter, 3 June 1983, p.389.

233/   15 U.S.C. § 1261 et seq., 84 Stat. 1673.

subject to the FIFRA and the FDCA have been specifically exempted by regulation 234/ from the definition of the term "hazardous substance." This statute is administered by the Consumer Product Safety Commission (CPSC) which also administers the Poison Prevention Packaging Control Act of 1970, 235/ designed to protect children from pesticides and other harmful substances. It is not yet clear how EPA and the CPSC will divide their overlapping authority in this area. EPA might welcome the involvement of CPSC in this limited portion of the pesticide area to the extent that its own hands are tied by the Court of Appeals decision in the Stearns Paste case. 236/

9.7 Federal Pesticide Monitoring Programs

The FDA and USDA assist EPA in monitoring pesticide residues in food. The FDA conducts frequent spot checks and an annual Market Basket Survey in which pesticide residues are analyzed in a representative sampling of grocery items. The FDA's Poison Control Center also compiles current statistics on chemical poisoning. The USDA's Animal and Plant Health Inspection Service conducts spot checks on pesticides in meats and poultry based on samples taken at slaughter houses throughout the country.

The Department of Interior samples pesticide residues in fish and performs experiments to determine the effects of pesticides which may be introduced into the aquatic environment. The Geological Survey Division of Interior also conducts periodic nationwide water sampling for pesticides and other contaminants. The National Oceanic Atmospheric Administration (NOAA) under the Department of Commerce monitors aquatic areas for pesticide levels, and the Department of Transportation's Office of Hazardous Substances records accidents involving pesticides in shipment and distribution.

10.0 The RPAR Process

The most important new area in pesticides involves the contested reregistration process, usually termed the Rebuttable Presumption Against Registration (RPAR).

234/ 16 CFR § 1500 3(b)(4)(ii).

235/ 15 U.S.C. § 1471 et seq., 84 Stat. 1670.

236/ U.S. v. Stearns Electric Paste, supra.

Many pesticides are coming up for renewal that were originally registered under the USDA or the early days of EPA when the standards for review were less strict. These will have to be given much closer scrutiny this time. This is mandated by the 1972 amendments to FIFRA, which directed EPA to assess the risks of all pesticides by October 1976. 237/ (This deadline was missed, as was a Congressional extension to October 1977.)

Since there are over thirty thousand registrations, EPA realized early that it could not give adequate individual attention to each one, so it sought a procedural shortcut. The obvious solution was to examine in detail only those for which serious adverse data was alleged. Furthermore, since the law placed the burden of proof on the proponent of registration, this feature was naturally incorporated in the new process. 238/

From this uncontroversial basis developed a most controversial program. As set forth in Section 162.11 of the pesticide regulations, 239/ "a rebuttable presumption shall arise . . . upon a determination by the Administrator that the pesticide meets or exceeds any of the criteria for risk set forth in subparagraph (3)." These criteria are extraordinarily detailed; for example, under acute toxicity they specify "an acute dermal LD_{50} of 6g/kg, 'or' an inhalation LC_{50} of 0.04mg/liter or less as formulated." 240/ Chronic toxic effects, such as oncogenicity (cancer) and mutagenicity, are also listed.

The regulations call for EPA then to notify the registrant that a rebuttable presumption exists against the pesticide and allow 45 days (extendable to 105 days) for him to submit scientific data rebutting the allegations of risk. The burden of proof is on him to demonstrate that the product, if used correctly, is not likely to result in any significant adverse, acute, or chronic effects. 241/ If

---

237/   Section 4(c)(2) of 61 Stat. 163, 7 U.S.C. § 135.

238/   Most of the plan was worked out at an EPA conference in Easton, Maryland, in the summer of 1974.

239/   40 CFR § 162.11; 40 FR 28268, 3 July 1975; as amended by 40 FR 32329 and 42746.

240/   40 CFR § 162.11 (3)(i)(A)(2) and (A)(3).

241/   40 CFR § 162.11 (a)(4).

the question is not resolved at this point, a public hearing may be held to assess the balance of risks and benefits.

In practice, the Agency has established a multistage review process, beginning with the placing of a pesticide on a lengthy suspect list and then a pre-RPAR review of all available scientific literature and test data to determine whether any risk criteria are met. Even this preliminary step can have serious economic consequences, and the chemical industry complains:

> The pesticide suffers in the marketplace because people have a tendency to back away when a possible RPAR is mentioned and is put into "limbo" as far as registration is concerned. Even a label amendment is out of the question as long as RPAR is threatened. 242/

The original RPAR candidate list contained forty-five classes of pesticides, of which twenty-four were still undergoing pre-RPAR review at the end of 1977. 243/   An additional 23 new chemicals were added to the pre-RPAR list on December 1977. 244/   Many more suspect pesticides were scheduled for inclusion on subsequent pre-RPAR.

The Reagan Administration has initiated a new policy with respect to RPAR's which will supposedly streamline the process. 245/   Registrants requested a preliminary initial review process, so that chemicals only entered the formal RPAR process when clear risk problems were established. They also sought expedited decision-making once RPAR was triggered.   As a result, EPA proposed to revise its policy to include more opportunity of negotiations between EPA and a registrant.   EPA also proposed a preliminary risk assessment before the public evaluation process is initiated. No new chemicals have been placed on the RPAR or pre-RPAR review under the

---

242/   "A Trojan Horse Named RPAR," Farm Chemicals, August 1977.

243/   Six others had been voluntarily cancelled by the registrants, 12 had been RPAR'ed, and 2 were returned to the registration process. Letter of EPA Administrator Douglas M. Costle to Sen. Edward M. Kennedy, 4 November 1977, reprinted in BNA, Chemical Regulation Reporter, p. 1277.

244/   BNA, Chemical Regulation Reporter, 23 December 1977, p. 1493.

245/   Ibid. 9 July 1982, pp. 506-510.

Reagan Administration, and EPA indicated it would eliminate its backlog of chemicals under review by the end of 1982. 246/ The important but poorly functioning RPAR process is now officially disfavored.

246/   Ibid., 16 July 1982, p. 500.

Chapter 11

MARINE PROTECTION, RESEARCH AND SANCTUARIES ACT

Jeffrey G. Miller 1/
Attorney
Bergson, Borkland, Margolis & Adler
Washington, D.C.

1.0 Administration and Interpretation of the Statute

The Marine Protection, Research and Sanctuaries Act (MPRSA), 2/ often called the Ocean Dumping Act, was enacted in 1972 to regulate the dumping of materials at sea, preventing or limiting the dumping of materials which would have adverse effects. 3/ Unfortunately, Congress did not clearly indicate whether its intention was to end all ocean dumping or to allow it only where it is the best disposal alternative and will not unduly affect the marine ecosystem. This ambiguity has created a continuing tension in the Act's administration and interpretation. This tension is highlighted by the comparative inexpensiveness of ocean dumping when compared to other waste disposal methods. It is further highlighted by the need of land-starved metropolitan areas on the East Coast to

---

1/ Mr. Miller was an Environmental Protection Agency enforcement official for ten years, finishing his government career as head of EPA's Enforcement Office.

2/ 33 U.S.C. §§ 1401 et seq.

3/ MPRSA § 2(b), 33 U.S.C. § 1401(b).

dispose of sludge from new and expanded sewage treatment plants built to comply with the Clean Water Act (CWA). 4/ Congress has bowed to that pressure in part by allowing the ocean discharge of less than secondarily treated municipal wastes at some locations under the CWA, 5/ but it has not provided comparative relief under MPRSA.

There is a fundamental policy anomaly inherent in MPRSA and its administration. The Act imposes different, and in most cases more stringent, limitations on discharging materials into the open ocean than other statutes impose on discharging materials into surface waters, which ultimately or directly drain to marine estuaries. These non-ocean discharges clearly have a far greater potential adverse human impact than ocean discharges. Moreover, because marine estuaries are hosts to a very large part of the marine ecosystem at critical junctures, such non-ocean discharges also have a greater adverse impact on the marine ecosystem. This anomaly is not a rational management of natural resources. Yet it pervades the Act and its administration. Even in the enforcement sections, Congress provided penalties of $50,000 a day for violation of MPRSA, 6/ while establishing only a $10,000 penalty for violating the CWA. 7/

The administration of the Act by the Environmental Protection Agency (EPA), has compounded the anomaly by creating a disparity between its treatment of government and industry under the Act. While EPA boasts of reducing the ocean discharges of industrial wastes from 5,051 thousand tons in 1973 to 304.5 thousand tons in 1983, and eliminating the ocean discharges of construction debris during that period, it has permitted increasing the ocean discharge of sewage sludge from 4,890 thousand tons in 1973 to 8,312 thousand tons in 1983. 8/ Moreover, while EPA's own studies project a need

---

4/   33 U.S.C. §§ 1251 et seq.

5/   CWA § 301(h), 33 U.S.C. §§ 1311(h).

6/   MPRSA § 105(a), 33 U.S.C. § 1415(a).

7/   CWA § 309(b) and (c), 33 U.S.C. § 1319(b) and (c).

8/   Environmental Protection Agency, Report to Congress, January 1981 to December 1983, "On Administration of the Marine Protection, Research, and Sanctuaries Act, as Amended (PL 92-532), and "Implementing the International London Dumping Convention," Table III, p. 9.

for thirty-three ocean-going incinerator vessels for hazardous waste incineration, 9/ it has yet to issue anything but a short-term permit for "research" purposes for at-sea incineration. 10/

2.0 Regulatory Scheme

2.1 Prohibited Materials and Permits

For some materials—radiological, chemical or biological warfare agents and high-level radioactive wastes—MPRSA flatly prohibits:

(1) transportation from the United States for the purpose of dumping in the ocean; 11/

(2) transportation from outside the United States by any employee or agency of the United States or any vessel or aircraft registered in the United States for the purpose of dumping in the ocean; and

(3) transportation from outside of the United States for the purpose of dumping into the territorial sea 12/ or waters contiguous 13/ to the territorial sea.

For all other materials, such transportation or dumping is prohibited except in conformity with a permit. 14/ CWA completes this

---

9/ "Inside EPA," 21 December 1984, pp. 1-2.

10/ EPA, Report to Congress, supra, pp. 29-30.

11/ "Ocean" is defined as waters beyond the base line from which the territorial sea is measured. MPRSA § 3(b), 33 U.S.C. 1402(b).

12/ "Territorial sea" is not defined in MPRSA or regulations promulgated under it, but see the definition in CWA § 502(8), 33 U.S.C. § 1362(8).

13/ The "contiguous zone" is not defined in MPRSA or regulations promulgated under it, but see the definition in CWA § 502(9), 33 U.S.C. § 1362(8).

14/ MPRSA § 101, 33 U.S.C. § 1411. For transportation by an employee or agency of the United States or by a vessel or aircraft registered in the United States, from a country signatory of the London Dumping Convention, a permit from that signatory will suffice. MPRSA § 112(e), 33 U.S.C. § 1412(e).

regulatory picture by controlling discharge to the territorial sea of materials, whether or not they are transported from outside the United States. 15/ Fish wastes are generally exempt from regulation under MPRSA, 16/ although discharge of fish wastes into the territorial sea or waters contiguous to it is regulated by the Clean Water Act. 17/

2.2 Dredged Materials Permits
The Secretary of the Army, through the Corps of Engineers (COE), is authorized to issue permits for transporting dredged materials for ocean disposal. 18/ The COE has promulgated regulations applicable to such activity, 19/ which is also subject to EPA's substantive review criteria, 20/ unless EPA waives the criteria. 21/ Because the permitting of such activity has apparently ceased, 22/ it will not be discussed further, except to note that no permit is necessary for dumping of dredge material involved in "federal projects," 23/ another sign of discrimination against the private sector.

15/   CWA § 301, 33 U.S.C. § 1331.

16/   MPRSA permits are necessary when fish wastes are transported for dumping into harbors, protected or enclosed coastal waters, or other waters where EPA finds an endangerment to health or the environment may occur, MPRSA § 102(d), 33 U.S.C. § 1411(d).

17/   For an effluent guideline applicable to fish wastes under the CWA, see 40 CFR Part 408.

18/   MPRSA § 103, 33 U.S.C. § 1413.

19/   33 CFR Part 324.

20/   MPRSA § 103(b) and (c), 33 U.S.C. § 1413(b) and (c).

21/   MPRSA § 103(d), 33 U.S.C. § 1413(d), 40 CFR Part 225.

22/   See footnote 7 and accompanying text.

23/   MPRSA § 103(e), 33 U.S.C. § 1413(d).

2.3 EPA and Ocean Dumping Permits

EPA is authorized to issue permits for transportation of other materials for ocean disposal and for disposal of other materials in the territorial sea or water contiguous to the territorial sea. 24/

Congress charged EPA with the responsibility of establishing criteria for reviewing applications for ocean dumping permits issued by EPA and the COE. The criteria must consider:

(1)   the need for dumping, including alternative disposal methods and their impact;

(2)   the impact of the dumping on human health and welfare; and

(3)   the impact of the dumping on the marine ecosystem, including the persistence and permanence of such effects. 25/

In 1977, Congress amended MPRSA to require EPA to "end the dumping of sewage sludge and industrial wastes into ocean waters." 26/ It allowed short-term research permits for industrial wastes, 27/ but left no such open door for sewage sludge. 28/ Despite this seeming drastic move, however, Congress changed nothing, for it defined sewage sludge and industrial wastes as materials which unreasonably degrade or endanger human health or the environment. 29/ This throws permitting decisions back on the original criteria Congress charged EPA with developing.

EPA's criteria start with a determination of whether the materials proposed for ocean disposal will have unacceptable adverse impacts. If they will, ocean disposal is allowed, if at all,

---

24/   MPRSA § 102, 33 U.S.C. § 1412.

25/   MPRSA § 102(a), 33 U.S.C. § 1412(a).

26/   MPRSA § 112a, 33 U.S.C. § 1412a.

27/   MPRSA § 112a(b), 33 U.S.C. § 1412a(b).

28/   MPRSA § 112a(a), 33 U.S.C. § 1412a(a).

29/   City of New York v. EPA, 543 F.Supp. 1084 (S.D. N.Y. 1981).

only for a short period of time to allow for orderly phase out. 30/ If they do not, ocean disposal is allowed only if other conditions are met. 31/ EPA has established that materials which Congress has banned for ocean disposal, which are insufficiently described in a permit application, or which are persistent and float, have a rebuttable presumption of unacceptable adverse impact. 32/ The presumption may be overcome by various showings, 33/ some of which are tailored to "research" permits 34/ or permits for ocean incineration. 35/ It has established a more expansive list of materials whose presence, in more than trace amounts, have a rebuttable presumption of unacceptable adverse impact. 36/ The presumption may be overcome only by an elaborate set of bioassays to determine chronic and long-term effects on the liquid, suspended particulate and solid phases of the waste, and by demonstration that the concentration of the pollutant in question does not exceed applicable marine water quality criteria. 37/ If no such criteria exist, studies may have to be performed, in effect, to establish such criteria. 38/ Additional limitations are established for other materials. 39/

If it is demonstrated that materials proposed for dumping will not have an unacceptably adverse impact, a permit will not be issued, except on a short-term basis, if EPA demonstrates that there is not a need for ocean dumping, or that it will result in unacceptable impacts on esthetic, recreational or economic values or on

---

30/   40 CFR § 227.3, 40 CFR § 220.3(d).

31/   40 CFR § 227.2.

32/   40 CFR § 227.5.

33/   40 CFR § 227.6(f), (g), (h).

34/   40 CFR § 227.6(g).

35/   40 CFR § 227.6(h).

36/   40 CFR § 227.6(a).

37/   40 CFR § 227.6(c) and (d).

38/   40 CFR § 227.6(d).

39/   40 CFR §§ 227.7 through 227.13.

other uses of the ocean. 40/ Of these tests, the need criteria is the most onerous. If EPA establishes that there is a practicable production or disposal alternative, ocean dumping is unavailable, notwithstanding great cost differentials. 41/

2.4 Dump Sites

EPA is also to establish criteria for designating dump sites and then designate sites for dumping and sites where dumping will not be allowed. 42/ Because EPA had not done baseline and other studies necessary to where its criteria could be met, it designated already used sites on an interim basis. The National Wildlife Federation challenged these designations as not meeting the requirements of the Act. EPA's decade long failure to do the necessary studies to support final designations gave some credibility to the challenge. The appeal, however, was unsuccessful. 43/

COE may designate disposal sites for dredged spoils at locations other than designated by EPA for disposal of other materials. 44/ It has been established that EPA may specify different criteria for designating sites for dumping dredged spoils than for dumping other material. 45/

2.5 Marine Sanctuaries

In a complementary part of the Act, the Secretary of Commerce, acting through the National Oceanic and Atmospheric Administration (NOAA), is given authority to designate marine sanctuaries and to regulate activities within them to assure their protection. 46/

40/   40 CFR §§ 227.2 and 227.3.

41/   40 CFR §§ 227.14 through 227.16.

42/   MPRSA § 102(a)(g), 33 U.S.C. § 1412(a)(g).

43/   National Wildlife Federation v. Costle, 629 F.2d 118 (D.C. Cir. 1980).

44/   40 CFR § 228.4(e)(2).

45/   National Wildlife Federation v. Costle, supra.

46/   MPRSA § 301, 16 U.S.C. § 1431 et seq., see 15 CFR Parts 935 through 938.

2.6 Permit Applications

Permit applications must contain general information, as well as information sufficient to demonstrate that the criteria for permit issuance have been met and that no additional factors would require denial of a permit. 47/ This information must include data to support designating the proposed disposal site for ocean dumping, if EPA has not already so designated it. 48/ EPA has established such criteria and has designated a number of interim disposal sites. 49/ Permit application fees may be specified 50/ and there is sentiment at EPA to amend MPRSA to mandate that fees be calculated to recoup the cost of evaluating and processing the application. In the case of controversial permits, this cost could be enormous.

Within thirty days after receiving a permit application, EPA must make a finding on the completeness of the application, although a completeness finding will not preclude EPA from requiring further information. 51/ Thirty days after receipt of a completed application, EPA must make 52/ and give public notice of a tentative determination on the application, although the notice requirements may be ignored in bona fide emergency situations.53/ EPA must consider public comments and hold an informal public hearing if a request for a hearing raises genuine material issues. 54/ Permits are to be issued on the basis of the record before EPA, including, if an informal hearing is held, the recommendations of the hearing officer. 55/

47/   40 CFR Part 221.

48/   40 CFR § 221.1(f).

49/   40 CFR Part 228.

50/   MPRSA § 104(a), 33 U.S.C. § 1414(a). They are currently $1000 or $3000, depending on various factors, 40 CFR § 221.5.

51/   40 CFR § 222.2(a).

52/   40 CFR § 222.2(b).

53/   40 CFR § 222.3.

54/   40 CFR §§ 222.4 through 222.7.

55/   40 CFR § 222.9.

2.7 Permit Appeals

Permitting decisions may be appealed in a formal adjudicatory hearing, 56/ with final decisions based on the record of the hearing, including the hearing officer's findings of fact, conclusions of law, and recommendations. 57/ If such decision is made by the Regional Administrator, it may be appealed to the Administrator. 58/ The final determination of the Administrator may be appealed to the applicable District Courts of the United States under the Administrative Procedures Act, no other appeal jurisdiction having been established. 59/

2.8 General, Special, Research and Interim Permits

General permits may be issued upon application, or by regulation without application, for material having minimal environmental impact and disposed of in small quantities. 60/ EPA has promulgated regulations generally authorizing ocean dumping for the purposes of burial at sea, the sinking of Navy target vessels, and disposal of vessels (subject to specified limitations). 61/ Permits for ocean disposal of materials meeting EPA's discharge criteria are called "special permits" and may be issued for three-year terms. 62/ Research permits can be issued for some materials with a term of eighteen months. 63/

Permits for disposal of materials already being disposed of in the ocean and not meeting EPA's criteria, and materials meeting the criteria for which demonstrations have been made of no need, or of

---

56/   40 CFR §§ 222.9 and 222.10.

57/   40 CFR § 222.11.

58/   40 CFR § 222.12.

59/   National Wildlife Federation v. Benn, 491 F.Supp. 1234 (S.D. N.Y. 1980); Save Our Sound Fisheries Ass'n v. Callaway, 387 F.Supp. 292 (D.R.J. 1974).

60/   40 CFR § 220.3(a).

61/   40 CFR Part 229.

62/   40 CFR § 220.3(b).

63/   40 CFR § 220.3(e).

other unacceptable impact, may be issued on an interim basis. Such permits were supposed to have expired by 31 December 1981. 64/

Permits for incineration at sea are considered to be research or interim permits until criteria are promulgated to govern such disposal. 65/ Proposed criteria for incineration at sea are sufficiently onerous to cast doubt on whether the waste disposal industry can pursue this alternative. 66/

2.9 Court Interpretation of the Law and Regulations

Much of EPA's regulatory scheme and interpretation of MPRSA was questioned in the case, City of New York v. EPA. 67/ The court held that EPA's almost conclusive presumption of unacceptable harm in its criteria violated the Act. The court also held EPA had been unduly restrictive in determining that need did not exist for ocean disposal in the case before it: it had not given sufficient weight to the costs and effects of alternative disposal methods. Most importantly, the court held that the 1977 amendments to MPRSA made little difference—they required the same balancing test as previously required, a balancing test the court had already held unduly restrictive. During the course of its long opinion, the court noted and criticized the manner in which EPA had discriminated in favor of government as opposed to industrial discharges in implementing the Act. Its opinion should give comfort to industry.

3.0 Enforcement

Surveillance to determine or detect violations of the Act is to be conducted by the Coast Guard and other appropriate federal agencies. 68/ Violations of the Act or of permits issued under it are subject to:

64/ 40 CFR § 220.3(d).

65/ 40 CFR § 220.3(f).

66/ "Inside EPA," 30 November 1984, pp. 11-12.

67/ 543 F. Supp. 1084 (S.D. N.Y. 1981).

68/ MPRSA § 107, 33 U.S.C. § 1417.

(1)   an administratively assessed penalty of up to
       $50,000 per day of violation;

(2)   injunctive relief in court;

(3)   criminal penalties of up to $50,000 and/or imprison-
       ment of up to one year;

(4)   seizure of the offending vessel; and

(5)   citizen enforcement for injunctive relief in
       court. 69/

4.0 Ocean Disposal Realities

Ocean disposal is an inexpensive and, at times, an environmentally safe and even preferred method of waste disposal. EPA's
implementation of the Act, however, has made it difficult in the
extreme for industry to secure MPRSA permits. The recent opinion
in City of New York v. EPA should make it much easier for industry
to take advantage of ocean disposal. Even so, securing a permit will
not be easy.

69/   MPRSA § 105, 33 U.S.C. § 1415. For a discussion of citizen
       enforcement, see Miller, "Private Enforcement of Federal Pol-
       lution Control Laws," Parts I, II and III, 13 Environmental Law
       Reporter 14-10063 (February 1984), and 14 Environmental Law
       Reporter.

Chapter 12

NOISE CONTROL

Marshall Lee Miller
Attorney
Reid & Priest
Washington, D.C.

1.0 Introduction

Noise is such an integral part of life that we take for granted all but the harshest abuse of our eardrums. This seemingly simple subject is one we all feel we understand. Where we might be awed by the intricacies of toxic chemicals or the complexity of ambient air equation models, we all feel confident that we understand noise. It is, after all, a loud piece of machinery, or a sonic boom, or a blaring stereo next door. Noise can be a nuisance and for generations the law has treated it as merely that. If the din became too oppressive, one could seek remedy in a court of law to restrain another from violating the right to enjoyment of one's property. 1/

But what once might have been considered merely a nuisance is now seen, with intensive industrialization and the increasing crowding of modern life, to be one of the most pervasive health problems of our society. There has also been a growing awareness of the technical complexity of noise. The scientific debates about the physical effects of noise have become just as controversial and replete with jargon as those concerning teratogenic chemicals or

---

1/   For a fuller discussion, see the sections on "Torts" and
      "Nuisance" in Chapter 1.

472

biological oxygen demand. In fact, a prominent acoustical scientist recently urged his colleagues to use simpler terms so that laymen could continue to follow the debate. Because the traditional common law remedies have proved inadequate to deal with these developments, there has been since 1970 an increasing resort to federal regulation.

Under the deregulatory emphasis of the Reagan Administration, EPA's noise program has been almost completely dismantled. Enforcement continues, however, under OSHA and, especially, the Federal Aviation Administration.

1.1 The Characteristics of Sound

Sound intensity is measured in decibels. The zero on the decibel scale is based on the lowest sound level that the healthy human ear can detect. Decibels are not linear units like miles or pounds; rather, they are representative points on a sharply rising, logarithmic curve. Each ten units represents an increase of tenfold, twenty units means a hundredfold (10 x 10), thirty units a thousandfold (10 x 10 x 10), and so on. Thus, one hundred decibels is 10 billion times as intense as one decibel. This system is used because the human ear can detect such a wide range of acoustical energy that otherwise units in the trillions might be required.

For comparison, the rustle of leaves is rated at 10 decibels, a typical office has about 50 decibels of background noise, moderate traffic noise ranges around 70 decibels, pneumatic drills and heavy trucks at 15 meters range between 80 and 90, and a jet takeoff at 60 meters is 120 or greater. Sound levels are measured at their source, unless otherwise specified, because their intensity is inversely proportional to the square of the distance from that source. 2/

A second important element of noise is frequency or pitch, which is the rate of vibrations of the sound wave. 3/ This is measured in cycles per second and expressed in Hertz (Hz). The audible frequency range of sound is often taken to be between 20 Hz and

---

2/ Certain EPA standards, such as for aircraft and trucks, provide that noise measurements be taken at a specified distance from the source. This will be discussed later in this chapter.

3/ There is technically a slight difference between these two concepts.

20,000 Hz.   The ability to hear frequencies declines with age (presbycusis), 4/ and most adults are limited to the range below 12-15,000 Hz.   Some music experts, however, believe we can still "sense" sounds beyond those we can hear.

Sound perception is affected by such factors as background noise level, distance, repetitiveness, tone components, duration, number of sources, insulation, and subjective receiver factors including both conscious and subconscious responses. For outdoor sound there are variables such as baffles, terrain, wind direction and velocity, atmospheric pressure and temperature. Interior sound, in addition to most of these variables, also involves the reverberative and reflective characteristics of various building materials and fixtures, the size and shape of a room, and the absorptive characteristics of its furnishings.

There have been a number of scientific efforts to combine factors such as loudness and duration in one numerical scale which will indicate the degree of human annoyance. One useful scale, the Effective Perceived Noise Level (EPNL), is based upon the relative curve of human discomfort to high frequency sounds such as aircraft or truck engine changes in acceleration. This is then adjusted for the duration and presence of discrete tones such as the whine or scream of jet operations. 5/

2.0 Biological Effects of Noise

It has long been recognized that painfully loud sound can produce deafness or impaired hearing; the biophysical mechanisms by which this occurs and the conditions under which individuals are susceptible have yet to be fully explained scientifically. We are also

---

4/   Some authorities believe that presbycusis is less a natural concomitant of aging than the result of years of aural abuse. See statement of Jack Westman, Department of Psychiatry, University of Wisconsin Medical School, Madison, Wisconsin, before the Senate Subcommittee on Government Regulations, Small Business Committee, 23 July 1975, p.2.

5/   Noise measurement is a complex subject on which the above provides only some of the basic terminology. See, for example, the basic EPA noise criteria document: "Public Health and Welfare Criteria for Noise," 27 July 1973, EPA document, No. 550/9-73-002.

now beginning to realize that noise can harm body organs other than the ears, as well as produce psychological effects which many have long suspected.

2.1 Physical Effects

There is a continuing controversy over definitions of deafness. First, there is a need to distinguish between temporary effects following loud noise from which the ear can easily recover (Temporary Threshold Shift, TTS), and those effects which involve permanent loss of some degree of hearing (Noise Induced Permanent Threshold Shift, NIPTS).

Second, there is a question as to what degree of hearing loss should be considered a serious impairment. There is some scientific feeling that the general population should be protected against a permanent impairment (NIPTS) of more than five decibels, which represents a considerable decrease in aural perceptiveness. 6/ There are others, however, who believe that substantial impairment does not take place until hearing loss reaches 25 decibel attenuation. 7/ This does not represent the beginning of hearing impairment or a satisfactory policy goal but rather is the point at which a severe, compensable handicap is defined. A person with such a hearing loss would be able to understand only 50 percent of monosyllabic words spoken in a quiet room and only 90 percent of all sentences. 8/

Third, at what frequency should hearing impairment be measured? After all, the ability to hear the higher frequencies is usually

---

6/   See, for example, testimony of Daniel L. Johnson, Aerospace Medical Research Laboratory, Wright-Patterson AFB, Ohio, in OSHA Noise Hearings, Washington, D.C., 27 June 1975, transcript 765.

7/   Some scientists have even argued that a hearing impairment should not be considered serious until the loss is 50 decibels or more. W. Dixon Ward, Department of Otolaryngology, Chief, Hearing Research Laboratory, University of Minnesota, testifying on behalf of the American Iron and Steel Institute, OSHA Noise Hearings, 1 July 1975, transcript 1047.

8/   Statement of Joseph H. Hafkenschiel, Economist, Communication Workers of America, Testimony at the OSHA Noise Hearings, July 1975.

lost first. For a proper appreciation of musical harmonics, it is thought important to hear the frequencies between 10,000 and 15,000 Hz which is within the upper range of most normal individuals. The current debate, however, centers around a far more modest expectation: whether good hearing between 2,000 and 4,000 Hz is essential for proper understanding of spoken words. In some of the OSHA noise hearings, the director of that agency's standards office testified in favor of measurements only up to 2,000 Hz, describing those as the "speech frequencies," and defining impairment as a 25 decibel loss in that frequency range. 9/ Witnesses from EPA and NIOSH, on the other hand, have repeatedly emphasized the measurement of hearing loss "in the critical frequencies above 2,000 Hz, which are the soonest and most severely affected by exposure to noise." These frequencies, according to an EPA analysis of the proposed OSHA standard, "are as important as those below 1,900 Hz for determining the intelligibility of speech." 10/

These distinctions, while seemingly technical or trivial, can have important policy consequences. It will be a balancing of the risks to workers against the equally speculative cost to industry that will determine where OSHA will set its important noise standard and what standards EPA and other federal agencies will promulgate for other segments of the economy.

2.2 Physiological Effects

The harmful effects of noise are not limited to the auditory system. We are all aware that a sharp sudden noise can cause the adrenaline to flow. Modern man is subject not to occasional stresses but to an unrelenting bombardment of noise which keeps his body on alert. This stress is not something that exists only in the mind, a synonym for a "nervous" condition. This assumption has been corrected by Dr. Jean Taché of the University of Montreal who has declared, "Now, to most people, stress is something bearing a psychological connotation. Stress is something in our heads. I would

---

9/ Statement of Dan Boyd, then Director of Standards for OSHA, OSHA Noise Hearings, 23 June 1975, transcript p. 13.

10/ EPA review and report, "Proposed OSHA Occupational Noise Exposure Regulation," 39 FR 43802, 18 December 1974.

like to say that stress is something that happens in our body. During stress, the size of our organs change, they are modified; the adrenal is enlarged, the lymphatic system increases in size. So stress is not something merely in our heads, it is something that happens in our body." 11/

These manifestations can be demonstrated objectively by scientific measurements. A hormone, CRF, is secreted by the hypothalmus which stimulates the production of ACTH by the pituitary. This activates the adrenals producing corticoids which in turn mobilize the entire body for a fight-flight situation. Stress, therefore, is not merely a situation which can be diagnosed only by a psychiatrist; it can also be determined quite objectively by, for example, measuring the corticoid level in the blood or the urine. 12/

The effect of these stress hormones on the cardiovascular system is well known. The arteries constrict, raising the blood pressure and placing greater strain on the heart. It is not possible to determine precisely what percentage of coronaries and strokes, if any, might be due in part to the effects of noise. These effects, according to one authority, "are likely to be distributed over a large number of common individual cardiovascular and other maladies whose causation is complex and attributable to other factors as well. Nonetheless, cardiovascular diseases are such a massive problem in our society that even if noise increases the incidence or severity by only a small percentage in the exposed population this would be a very substantial adverse effect. Major cardiovascular diseases account for well over half the deaths in the United States, currently somewhat over a million people per year." 13/

Continuous noise, by putting the body under stress, can lead to irritation and fatigue. This can be the case even if the noise is not at an uncomfortably high level, provided it is loud and relatively

---

11/ Statement of Jean Taché, Institute of Experimental Medicine and Surgery, University of Montreal, Canada, before the Senate Small Business Committee, op. cit., p.23.

12/ Ibid., pp. 23-24.

13/ Statement of Nicholas A. Ashford, Center for Policy Alternatives, MIT, Cambridge, Mass., before the Senate Small Business Committee, p. 249.

continuous. Some observers believe that these tensions can lead to distractions and a generally higher injury rate, although this point must await further studies for verification. There is more substantial evidence that noise can reduce efficiency and promote absenteeism, either because of its physical symptoms or because it is a distraction factor among workers subjected to excessive noise levels. 14/

Finally, animal tests suggest that noise may cause yet another barely explored medical hazard. Pregnant mice exposed to high noise levels produced offspring whose skeletal systems were incompletely developed and had a greater susceptibility to gastric ulcers and other gastrointestinal diseases. 15/

3.0 OSHA Regulation of Noise

Most of the severe noise problems are encountered in the occupational context. The former head of EPA's Noise Office has acknowledged, "As far as hearing loss or impairment is concerned, there is absolutely no question that the workplace represents the most serious exposure for the largest group." 16/ The leading standards and enforcement responsibility for noise is thus the Occupational Safety and Health Administration (OSHA) in the Department of Labor.

3.1 The Present OSHA Standard

The Labor Department first began regulating noise under statutes of limited applicability, the most noted being the Walsh-Healey Public Contracts Act of 1936, 17/ which affected employees under private supply contracts with the federal government.

14/ This will be discussed in more detail in the section on the Economic Costs and Benefits of Noise Regulation by OSHA.

15/ Statement of Jean Taché, supra, p. 26. Recent studies in California suggest that exactly the same effects—spina bifida, cleft palate, and anencephaly—may be produced in humans, see Washington Post, 20 February 1978.

16/ Statement of Alvin F. Meyer, EPA, Senate Small Business Committee, op. cit., p. 119.

17/ 41 U.S.C. §§ 35-45. Similar noise exposure limits were issued under the (McNamara-O'Hara) Service Contract Act of 1965, 41 U.S.C. § 351 et seq.

Under this statute, on 20 September 1968 the Department proposed for comment an 85 decibel (dB(A)) standard for an eight-hour working day. 18/ This level was adopted as the final standard on 17 January 1969, although companies with an effective hearing conservation program were allowed 92 dB(A) until 1 January 1971. The effective date of the regulation was thirty days from the date of publication. 19/

Just before the effective date, however, on 14 February 1969, the initiation date was postponed three months. 20/ No reason for the delay was given, but the Department later acknowledged that it was due to the advent of the Nixon Administration on 20 January 1969. 21/ When the standard finally appeared on 20 May 1969, it differed considerably from the original version. In particular, it established a maximum permissible eight-hour level of 90 dB(A). 22/

In December 1970, with the creation of OSHA, this protection was extended to cover all nongovernmental employees in the United States. 23/

This standard is the one still being enforced today by OSHA. This standard provides, in addition to a noise exposure limit of 90 decibels, a doubling rate of five decibels. This means that for an increase of every five decibels in the sound level, the exposure time

---

18/   33 FR 14258 (1968). The A-scale attempts to relate loudness in decibels to the varying sensitivity of the human ear at different frequencies.

19/   34 FR 788 (1969), revising 41 CFR 50-204.

20/   34 FR 2207 (1969).

21/   See the preamble to the 20 May 1969 promulgation, infra.

22/   34 FR 7946(1969), esp. 7948-49.

23/   OSH Act § 6(a), 29 U.S.C. § 655(a). The effective date of the Act was April 1971. For two years, OSHA could also adopt other "established federal standards" which might be relevant to safety and health but which had not automatically been adopted under OSHA, and "national consensus standards," set forth by private standard-setting associations. This period ended in April 1973.

must be cut in half. For example, exposure at 90 decibels is permitted for eight hours, at 95 for four hours, and at 100 for two hours.

PERMISSIBLE NOISE EXPOSURE LIMITS 24/

Duration Per Day In Hours	Sound Level 90 dB(A) Standard	Hypothetical 85 dB(A) For Comparison 25/
8	90	85
6	92	87
4	95	90
3	97	92
2	100	95
1 1/2	102	97
1	105	100
1/2	110	102
1/4 or less	115	105

The standard also provides for a maximum sound level for impact or impulsive noise of 140 decibels, 26/ and a limit for continuous noise at 115 decibels for a fifteen minute period. As in other OSHA standards, employers are required first to control noise by engineering changes and administrative controls. Only if these methods prove infeasible should employers resort to the use of personal protective equipment such as earmuffs and earplugs, along with a hearing conservation program. 27/

24/   Table G-16 in 29 CFR 1910.95.

25/   Note that the 85 dB(A) column is hypothetical, prepared by the author, which also assumes a 5 decibel doubling rate. It is not a part of the Table G-16 or the official standard, although it might eventually become OSHA's noise standard.

26/   One hundred such 140 dB(A) impacts a day would be allowed with a tenfold increase number each decrease of ten decibels, and ten thousand at 120 decibels. This level, while startlingly high, is in accord with recommendations by the American Conference of Government Industrial Hygienists (ACGIH) and the American Industrial Hygiene Association (AIHA). See BNA, Noise Reporter, 9 June 1975, A-14.

27/   OSHA, "Guidelines to the Occupational Noise Standard," 1971. See also, 29 CFR 1910.95.

3.2 Enforcement

OSHA's enforcement of the present noise standard, although criticized as less than strict, 28/ has exceeded that of many other OSHA health standards. Generally, OSHA inspectors do not make separate inspections for noise, as they might do for toxic chemicals or particular safety hazards, but the ubiquitous nature of noise and its ease of detectability lead to the high citation rate. In 1975, for example, OSHA inspectors cited over 2,400 violations of the noise standard and imposed over a hundred thousand dollars in penalties. These figures, although still inadequate, constituted 4.3 percent of all health citations. This compares with a total of only fifty-one OSHA citations (0.09 percent) for dangerous carcinogenic chemical hazards. 29/

OSHA can impose both civil and criminal penalties for noise violations. For serious offenses, defined as those liable to cause "death or serious physical harm," the maximum fine is one thousand dollars per incident (the average is approximately half that). Repeated or willful offenses may be punished by fines as high as ten thousand dollars per violation. 30/ Most noise violations, however, are treated as "non-serious", for which the average fine on a first offense is around fifteen dollars.

3.3 OSHA Noise Hearings

OSHA's present standard, adopted from a regulation under a prior statute, is only an interim measure. Congress never intended that the temporary consensus and other federal standards adopted by OSHA in 1970 would remain the standards for the indefinite future.

28/ Testimony of Nicholas Ashford, MIT, Senate Small Business Committee, op. cit., p. 253. He testified then that "I think it would be fair to say that, from looking at the compliance history in the noise area by OSHA that there has not been a strict enforcement of the standard."

29/ OSHA, unpublished computer readout of 1975 inspections, 19 February 1976. See also OSHA Press Release, 25 February 1976. The carcinogen category is defined for these calculations as those standards in 29 CFR 1910.1003-1016.

30/ OSH Act § 17, 29 U.S.C. § 666.

The procedure established under Section 6(b) of the OSHA statute is that the National Institute of Occupational Safety and Health (NIOSH), a branch of the Department of Health, Education, and Welfare (HEW, now the Department of Health and Human Services), prepare criteria documents outlining all the relevant scientific information about the health effects of a particular substance or condition. This document is then forwarded to OSHA which conducts its own analysis of the criteria document and other relevant scientific information, often with the help of a special scientific advisory committee, and considers the technological and economic feasibility factors which are beyond NIOSH's statutory purview. OSHA then proposes a standard as a basis for discussions at subsequent public hearings. The proposal is subsequently modified, if deemed necessary, and the final standard is issued. 31/

NIOSH sent its noise criteria document to OSHA on 14 August 1972. 32/ A Standards Advisory Committee on Noise was appointed. 33/ Sixteen months after receipt of the criteria document, the Advisory Committee transmitted its comments and recommendations to the OSHA Standards office on 20 December 1973. The Standards office, after another ten months of deliberation and preparation, issued on 18 October 1974 a proposed occupational noise exposure standard. 34/

OSHA proposed retention of the 90 dB(A) noise level, a peak impulse exposure at 140 decibels, a five decibel doubling rate, and provisions for employee monitoring and audiometric testing with

---

31/ OSHA's standard setting record is not beyond reproach. Although there are thousands of toxic substances for which no standards exist and NIOSH has submitted a dozen or more criteria documents each year for OSHA consideration, OSHA has averaged less than one final standard a year since its creation, and these generally have been the result of court action or emergency procedures.

32/ This is in accordance with OSH Act § 29(a)(3), 29 U.S.C. § 669.

33/ OSH Act § 76, 29 U.S.C. § 656, requires representation from labor unions, management, government and independent experts.

34/ 39 FR 37773, 24 October 1974.

specific recordkeeping provisions. The limited changes in the proposal prompted some critics to wonder why OSHA had bothered to
initiate the time-consuming rulemaking procedure.

EPA immediately objected to the OSHA proposal. This was
not officiousness by EPA but a duty under Section 4(c)(2) of the
Noise Control Act of 1972, 35/ which gave EPA the chief coordinating responsibility for noise within the Administration. Under this
statute, EPA Administrator Russell Train notified OSHA on 6 December 1974 that EPA "believes that the proposed regulation does
not protect the public health and welfare to the extent required and
feasible." 36/ EPA argued that an eight-hour work day exposure
standard of 85 dB(A) was more consistent with available scientific
evidence. In fact, EPA argued that its scientific data "support a
level of 75 dB(A) for an ultimate health goal; EPA believes that the
reduction to 85 dB(A) is an important step toward this goal." 37/

EPA also contended that the OSHA-proposed doubling rate of
five decibels had no scientific justification; the proper rate, based
on the total amount of acoustic energy, should have been three decibels. In addition, EPA criticized OSHA's reliance on audiometric
monitoring, since individual variations and the crudeness of measurement techniques could allow a threshold shift as great as 35
decibels before a worker was informed of his hearing loss. 38/

The OSHA public hearing on the proposed noise standard
began in June 1975 and continued for several weeks. A team of
representatives from the EPA noise office, headed by Alvin Myer,
testified strongly against the OSHA proposal, but the anticipated
bitter clash between the two agencies never occurred. OSHA's position was not as adamant as it had sometimes been described. OSHA
had never held, as some had portrayed, that a 90 decibel standard
would protect against all adverse health effects. This misconception
arose partially from OSHA's deliberate vagueness, but the proposal
document itself clearly stated the following:

35/ PL 92-574, 86 Stat. 1236, 42 U.S.C. § 4903(c)(2).

36/ EPA, "Proposed OSHA Occupational Noise Exposure Regulation," 39 FR 43802.

37/ Ibid.

38/ Ibid., p. 43808.

With regard to the risk of hearing loss, OSHA recognizes that comparatively more workers would be at lower risk at 85 dB(A) than at 90 dB(A). However, we also recognize the technical feasibility problems and the economic impact associated with an 85 dB(A) requirement as reflected in the Bolt, Beranek and Newman study and in the draft environmental impact statement. Therefore, OSHA proposes to keep the level at 90 dB(A) until empirical data and information on the health risks, feasibility, and economic impact indicate the practicality and necessity of an 85 dB(A) requirement. 39/

3.4 Economic and Technical Feasibility

The major controversy between EPA and OSHA was the medical and technical basis of the proposed 90 dB(A) standard. EPA pointed out that NIOSH, while favoring a standard of 85, had stated it "reluctantly concurs" with the 90 decibel proposal. 40/ EPA pointed out that this concurrence was solely the result of NIOSH deferring to OSHA's judgment on economic and technical feasibility, as set forth in Section 20 of the OSHA statute, 41/ and was not an independent conclusion by NIOSH that attainment of noise levels below 90 decibels was generally technically infeasible. 42/

Neither EPA, OSHA, nor any outside experts were really sure just what was attainable and at what cost. OSHA commissioned a sweeping economic impact study to determine the anticipated cost of complying with both 90 decibel and 85 decibel standards. This study by Bolt, Beranek and Newman (BBN) estimated that the cost for attaining a 90 dB(A) level would be about $13 billion—even though this had been the federal standard for a number of years—and

---

39/   OSHA, "Proposed Occupational Noise Exposure," 39 FR 3773, 24 October 1974.

40/   See NIOSH Criteria Document, "Occupational Exposure to Noise," p. II-3.

41/   OSH Act, § 20(a)(3), 29 U.S.C. § 669(a)(3).

42/   EPA, "Proposed OSHA Occupational Noise Exposure Regulation," 39 FR 43802, 18 December 1974.

that the added cost for reaching the 85 decibel level would be $18 billion. 43/

The benefits of a lower noise standard are even more controversial. The BBN study estimated that a reduction from 90 decibels to 85 decibels would reduce by 770,000 the number of workers who would have extreme hearing loss at retirement age. 44/ The reduction from 90 to 85 decibels would also provide protection to an additional 8.2 million workers who would otherwise face serious but not disabling hearing losses over their working life. 45/

The economic costs of this hearing loss cannot, of course, be estimated precisely, partially because of the difficulty in assigning dollar values to human losses. Attempts to quantify some of the data by using workmen's compensation awards (although they are notoriously low) produced estimates in the billions of dollars. 46/ A more interesting, if more speculative, estimate involves estimating the cost of increased absenteeism as a result of annoying noise. The Frye Report calculated that if absenteeism could be reduced one day per year for those workers exposed to noise levels over 85 decibels, a reasonable assumption, this would add $2 billion a year to the GNP. 47/

There have also been attempts to calculate the social costs of irritation annoyance from noise. It is generally accepted that workers prefer quiet working surroundings to the strain of enduring noise levels of 90 decibels or higher. One study took 10 cents an hour as

---

43/ Bolt, Beranek and Newman, Inc., Cambridge, Mass., "Impact of Noise at the Workplace," Report No. 2671. See also OSHA Noise Hearings, transcript p. 281, et seq.

44/ Bolt, Beranek and Newman Report, p. 37.

45/ See Bolt, Beranek and Newman Report, Tables III and IV.

46/ See statement of Nicholas Ashford, OSHA Noise Hearings, 23 July 1975, transcript, p. 84.

47/ U.S. Department of Health, Education and Welfare (HEW), Public Health Service, Protecting the Health of 80 Million Americans, 1965. The Frye estimate has been recomputed for 1976 figures. See also Ashford statement in OSHA hearings, transcript, p. 85; and Ashford statement before Senate Small Business Committee, op. cit., p. 252.

the minimum differential that a worker would accept and 50 cents as a maximum. These computations produced an annoyance esti-mate ranging from $3 to $14 billion a year. Compliance with a 90 dB(A) standard would produce a yearly benefit of (using the high figure) $3 billion, while attaining an 85 decibel level would yield $4.6 billion. 48/

Another authority has estimated that the benefits to workers from reducing noise-related tension to 85 decibels would be between $5.2 and $13 billion and at least another $11 billion for hearing preservation. 49/

3.5 Hearing Protection Devices

A major issue faced by OSHA is the efficacy of hearing pro-tection devices such as ear plugs and muffs. Industry representatives argued that they should be allowed to meet the OSHA noise stan-dard, whether 85 or 90 decibels, in any way possible. This could mean providing personal protective equipment, rather than reducing the general noise level in an industry. According to one company spokesman, the same or better protection to employees could be provided by ear protectors at a fraction of the cost: "the question must be raised as a matter of public policy whether the benefits to be attained from engineering controls justify the allocation of scarce capital to projects that are non-productive." 50/ Union representatives, on the other hand, point to numerous studies and testimony that this reasonable approach has often not worked well in practice. 51/ This problem has also arisen in enforcement proceed-ings before the Review Commission and the courts.

48/ Ashford, OSHA Noise Hearings, transcript, pp. 87-90.

49/ This, he suggested, however, would still total less than the BBN cost estimates. Robert Stewart Smith, The Occupational Safety and Health Act: Its Goals and Achievements (Washington, D.C.: American Enterprise Institute, 1976), p. 51.

50/ Edwin H. Tootham, Senior Noise Control Engineer, Bethlehem Steel, OSHA Noise Hearings, 1 July 1975, pp. 1117 and 1126.

51/ See, for example, the testimony of David Metz, Chairman, Speech and Hearing Department, Cleveland State University, on behalf of OSHA, OSHA Noise Hearings, 24 June 1975, p. 176, et seq.

3.6 The Feasibility and Balancing Debate

Current OSHA noise enforcement, and the eventual new noise standard, will be largely determined by the outcome of a continuing legal debate over feasibility and balancing. The important issues include the following:

(1)   Can OSHA legally consider economic factors in setting health or safety standards levels?

(2)   If so, is this consideration limited only to extreme circumstances?

(3)   Does the Occupational Safety and Health Act provide for a balancing of costs and benefits in setting standards?

(4)   Can OSHA·mandate engineering controls although they alone would still not attain the standard?

(5)   And, can OSHA require engineering controls even if personal protective equipment (such as ear plugs) could effectively reduce noise to a safe level and at a much lower cost?

Although these questions have been extensively litigated before the Occupational Safety and Health Review Commission (OSHRC) and the courts, no definitive answers have yet emerged, even for issue number one. This is due to a difference of opinion between several circuit courts of appeals over the interpretation of "feasibility" in Section 6(b)(5) of the Act.

One must remember that the OSHA legislation was originally seen by Congress in rather absolutist terms: any standard promulgated should be one "which most adequately assumes . . . that no employee will suffer material impairment of health." Only late in the debate was the Department of Labor able to insert the phrase "to the extent feasible" into the text. This was intended to prevent companies having to close because unattainable standards were imposed on them, but it was not spelled out to what extent economic as well as technical feasibility was included. 52/

52/   This account of the behind-the-scenes machinations is based largely on the views of the late Congressman William Steiger (R-Wisc.), a principal author of the act, and of Lawrence Silberman, then Solicitor of Labor. The legislative history is relatively unhelpful on this subject. See, for example, hearings before the Select Subcommittee on Labor, Committee on Education and Labor, "Occupational Safety and Health Act of 1969," two vols., 1969.

Two federal circuits have held that economic factors are included, but to a limited degree. In <u>Industrial Union Department, AFL v. Hodgson,</u> the D.C. Circuit accepted that economic realities affected the meaning of "feasible," but only to the extent that "a standard that is prohibitively expensive is not 'feasible.' " 53/ It was Congress' intent, the court added, that this term would prevent a standard unreasonably "requiring protective devices unavailable under existing technology or by making financial viability generally impossible." The court warned, however, that this doctrine should not be used by companies to avoid needed improvements in their workplaces:

> Standards may be economically feasible even though, from the standpoint of employers, they are financially burdensome and affect profit margins adversely. Nor does the concept of economic feasibility necessarily guarantee the continued existence of individual employers. 54/

A similar view was adopted by the Second Circuit in <u>The Society of the Plastics Industry v. OSHA,</u> written by Justice Clark, who cited approvingly the case above. 55/ He held that "feasible" meant not only that which is attainable technologically and economically now, but also that which might reasonably be achievable in the future. In this case, which concerned strict emissions controls on vinyl chloride, he declared that OSHA may impose "standards which require improvements in existing technologies or which require the development of new technology, and . . . is not limited to issuing standards based solely on devices already fully developed." 56/

Neither court undertook any risk-benefit analysis, such as attempting to compare the hundreds of millions of dollars needed to control vinyl chloride with the lives lost to angiosarcoma of the

---

53/   499 F.2d 467, 1 OSHC 1631 (D.C. Cir. 1974).

54/   1 OSHC 1631 at 1639.

55/   509 F.2d 1301, 2 OSHC 1496 (2d Circ. 1975), cert. den. 421 U.S. 992.

56/   509 F.2d at 1309, 2 OSHC at 1502 (2d Cir. 1975).

liver.   Those who have attempted to develop such equations have generally concluded the task is undoable, at least for most such chronic health effects. 57/

A third federal appeals court, however, has taken a strongly contrary position in a case specifically involving noise.   In Turner Co. v. Secretary of Labor, the Seventh Circuit Court of Appeals decided that the $30,000 cost of abating a noise hazard should be weighed against the health damage to workers, taking into consideration the availability of personal protective equipment to mitigate the risk. 58/

This holding is not unreasonable, but it is based on a highly tenuous interpretation of the law.   The court, without providing any clear rationale for its view, held that "the word 'feasible' as contained in 29 CFR § 1910.95(6)(1) must be given its ordinary and common sense meaning of 'practicable.' " (This may be so but is of no analytical value.)   From this the court concluded:

> Accordingly, the Commission erred when it failed to consider the relative cost of implementing engineering controls . . . versus the effectiveness of an existing personal protective equipment program utilizing fitted earplugs. 59/

This interpretation does not follow from the analysis.   In fact, since the Turner Company had both the financial resources and the technical capability to abate the noise problem, compliance with the regulation would appear to be "practicable."   The court, however, considered this term to mean that a cost-benefit computation should be made.

57/   See, for example, the conclusions of the National Academy of Sciences report, "Government Regulation of Chemicals in the Environment," 1975.

58/   561 F.2d 82, 5 OSHC 1970. (7th Circ. 1977). The Occupational Safety and Health Review Commission (OSHRC) decisions on Turner and the related Continental Can case can be found at 4 OSHC 1554 (1976) and 4 OSHC 1541 (1976), respectively.

59/   5 OSHC 1790 at 1791.

Because of these differing interpretations of the law, OSHA's enforcement of its noise standard was inevitably affected.   The Supreme Court's decisions on benzene and cotton dust (discussed in the OSHA Chapter) have helped to clarify the parameters of feasibility roughly along the lines OSHA had advocated.

3.7 The Long-Anticipated OSHA Noise Standard

Issuance of the final revised OSHA noise standard has been promised for so long that predictions are no longer taken seriously. In May 1976, for example, a senior OSHA official declared that the standard should be published sometime that year. In October another OSHA spokesman said it would be issued within three months.

Meanwhile, several labor leaders hinted darkly that sinister political motives were responsible for the delay, 60/ and one union brought suit unsuccessfully to require publication of the noise standard within thirty days. In January 1977, a different political party considered friendlier to labor assumed control of OSHA. The head of OSHA promised in July 1977 that it would be ready by "early 1978." It was not, however, and when she left office four years later it too had not released the long-awaited, or long-dreaded, noise standard.

This delay is due partly, of course, to the extraordinary complexity of the subject. But many of the issues for which additional information is sought are also ones for which it is probably unobtainable in the foreseeable future. Thus, it is correct that a standard could be issued within three months of a decision on several important questions.

A more important reason for the delay, therefore, is the hesitation of OSHA's leadership, both past and present, to promulgate a standard with such explosive political consequences for themselves and the Agency.

60/   In 1972, the then-head of OSHA, George Guenther, wrote a memo to the Under Secretary of Labor indicating that the organization would trim its sails during the Presidential election campaign. This memo, uncovered a year later, became a favorite topic for union leaders charging the Agency with crass political sellouts. This criticism was specifically leveled at OSHA on noise by Eric Frumin of the Amalgamated Clothing and Textile Workers Union in October 1976.

3.8 The Hearing Conservation Program

The Agency sought to obtain the benefits of stricter control without the political costs by issuing the hearing conservation regulation. 61/ This "interim" measure set an "action level" of 85 decibels which, if exceeded, would trigger a fairly extensive series of requirements for audiometric testing, worker warnings, and hearing protective devices. 62/

The forging industry complained that the regulation mandated certain additional protection for workers found to have had a "significant threshold shift" (STS), defined as 10 dB(A), although this could be due to factors outside the workplace. This, the court held, was beyond OSHA's authority. The entire regulation was struck down in November 1984. 63/

OSHA has requested a rehearing en banc by the Court. Meanwhile, the Agency has issued a directive to its inspector force that other provisions of the hearing regulation are to be enforced. State hearing conservation programs are not directly affected by the federal court decision. 64/

4.0 Environmental Protection Agency Authority

Although OSHA has the primary responsibility for controlling most noise sources in the environment, the Environmental Protection Agency (EPA) has been given statutory authority to oversee federal actions toward noise pollution in general. EPA also has responsibility for a number of environmental noise pollutant sources, ranging from snowmobiles to aviation (in concert with the Federal Aviation Administration), which are of significant national concern.

61/ 46 FR 4161, 16 January 1981.

62/ 29 CFR § 1910.95(c).

63/ Forging Industry Association v. Secretary of Labor, 12 OSHC 1041 (4th Cir. 1984). The dissent by Judge Sprouse, however, is the better opinion.

64/ "Interim Guidance for the Hearing Conservation Amendment (HCA)," from Field Operations Director John B. Miles to all regional administrators, 5 December 1984.

The Reagan Administration came into office in 1981 determined to eliminate the entire EPA noise program, which then numbered about 110 people. On 17 February 1981, the White House's Office of Management and Budget (OMB) issued a "no appeal" directive to phase out the office; the only choice was the timing, either six or eighteen months. Two years later, the staff numbered 2 1/2 people, and most of the regulatory programs were rescinded. 65/ The Administration was not able to eliminate them entirely, however, because certain strong industry groups and their congressional supporters wanted federal preemption of a multiplicity of inconsistent and possibly stricter standards. The Noise Act itself was left in place.

4.1 The Noise Act of 1970

The 1970 Congress enacted the Noise Pollution and Abatement Act, a short act of two sections which was attached as Title IV to the Clean Air Act enacted in the same year. 66/ It directed EPA to establish an Office of Noise Abatement and Control. This office was not then granted any regulatory authority but was to thoroughly investigate the effects of noise on the public health and welfare, to identify major noise sources, and to determine seven statutorily-specified effects of noise. These include the following:

- effects at various levels;

- projected growth of noise levels in urban areas through the year 2000;

- the psychological and physiological effect on humans;

- effects of sporadic extreme noise (such as jet noise near airports) as compared with constant noise;

- effect on wildlife and property (including values);

- effect of sonic booms on property (including values); and

- such other matters as may be of interest in the public welfare. 67/

65/ Charles Elkins, former director of EPA's Noise Office, 28 January 1983.

66/ PL 91-604, 42 U.S.C. § 1857, et seq.

67/ Clean Air Act of 1970, § 402(a), 42 U.S.C. § 1858(a).

This information was to be used in the preparation of recommendations to Congress within one year for further legislation on the
abatement of noise pollution. 68/

4.2 The Noise Control Act of 1972

The Noise Control Act of 1972 69/ set forth the broad goal of
protecting all Americans from "noise that jeopardizes their health or
welfare." 70/ The bill provides four broad duties for EPA: to serve
as a coordinator within the federal government for noise control
efforts, to establish noise standards based on scientific criteria
documents, to regulate noise emissions from products in commerce,
and to provide general information to the public concerning the
noise emission of such products.

A primary feature of the Act, and probably a reason for its
attracting support from such divergent interests, was that it deline-
ated the bounds between federal and local jurisdiction over noise.
The legislation ostensibly placed principal authority for regulating
noise with the states and local communities to ensure that the
federal government will not become enmeshed in nationwide noise
zoning duties. The practical effect of the 1972 Noise Act, however,
was precisely the opposite. While the preamble to the Act acknowledges the "primary responsibility for control of noise rests with
state and local governments," the major emphasis of the Act is indicated by the phrase that follows: "Federal action is essential to deal
with major noise sources in commerce, control of which requires
national uniformity of treatment." 71/

68/   Clean Air Act § 402(b), 42 U.S.C. § 1858(b). EPA, Report to
      the President and Congress on Noise, 31 December 1971. This
      was sent to the White House along with 15 detailed technical
      reports on noise effects, noise measurement, and other
      problems.

69/   PL 92-842, 42 U.S.C. §§ 4901, et seq.

70/   Noise Act § 2(b), 42 U.S.C. § 4092(b).

71/   Noise Act § 2(a)(3). The language on the primacy of local
      governments is lifted almost literally from the preamble to the
      Clean Air Act, Section 101(a)(3), where it has been retained
      through successive amendments even though the section has
      increasingly become an anachronism.

There is an interesting contrast here, distinguishing ambient noise and noise sources, between the noise and air laws. Ambient noise, the level of noise in the general environment, is essentially a local problem, while the noise-producing products and machinery are generally those which are used and sold nationally. Under the air pollution laws, however, the ambient levels are set nation-wide by the federal government on health bases, but the sources of air pollution (other than mobile sources) are generally regulated through state authorities under Sections 110 and 111 of the Clean Air Act.

The federal supremacy issue may have been swayed by important commercial interests: while they wanted no regulations for new products, they preferred uniform federal rules to a hodge-podge of state and local regulations. These, they feared, might constitute a serious burden on interstate commerce.

Despite contrasting interests, on 8 November 1978 the Quiet Communities Act was approved extending the provisions of the Noise Control Act of 1972 and amending some sections of the Act to put more of the burden on state and local governments. Section 14 was expanded to focus more attention on state and local governments providing them with the funds to develop and disseminate information, to conduct and finance research, to purchase monitoring equipment, and in other ways to facilitate the development and enforcement of noise control standards. Nevertheless, the Quiet Communities Act provides that no actions, plans or programs should be "inconsistent with existing Federal authority . . . to regulate sources of noise in interstate commerce." 72/

4.3 Noise Sources and Criteria

In a procedure also modeled after the Clean Air Act, 73/ EPA was required to publish within nine months, i.e., July 1973, noise criteria identifying the effects on health and welfare of different forms and levels of noise. There was also a requirement in the Act for a second report three months later indicating what levels of ambient noise were adequate "to protect the public health and welfare with an adequate margin of safety." 74/

72/ Quiet Communities Act, PL 95-609, § 2.

73/ See Clean Air Act § 108, 42 U.S.C. 1857c(3).

74/ Noise Act § 5(a)(2). This second report was essentially superfluous.

The next report, due 18 months after the enactment of the Act, i.e., April 1974, called for the identification of those specific products or classes of products which are major noise sources. 75/ This report included information on control techniques, economic and technical feasibility data, and alternative noise control methods. 76/ This list was to be revised and supplemented from time to time and published in the Federal Register along with supporting criteria documents. 77/

4.4 Setting of Noise Emission Standards

Following the identification of the principal noise sources that are "feasible and are requisite to protect the public health and welfare," 78/ the Administrator was directed to take into account in determining both feasibility and advisability, "the magnitude and conditions of use of such products (alone or in combination with other noise sources), the degree of noise reduction achievable through the application of the best available technology, and the cost of compliance." 79/

EPA was required to propose noise emission standards within 18 months of enactment for those products or classes of products identified under Section 5(b) as major noise sources, if EPA found such standards were feasible and if the products fell in one of the following categories:

(i) Construction equipment

(ii) Transportation equipment (including recreational vehicles and related equipment)

75/ This requirement was not in fact met until a further thirteen months later.

76/ Noise Act § 5(b).

77/ Noise Act § 5(c). Regulatory actions taken by EPA under this and other sections of the Act will be discussed later in this chapter.

78/ Noise Act § 6(b).

79/ Noise Act § 6(c)(1).

(iii) Any motor or engine (including any equipment of which an engine or motor is an integral part)

(iv) Electrical or electronic equipment 80/

Once a standard was proposed for a noise source, final regulations were to be issued within six months unless the Administrator determined that noise emission standards were not feasible for such products. 81/ This congressional device to hasten the administrative process by a rigorous burden of proof is found in few other environmental statutes. 82/

In May 1975 EPA identified a number of products for Section 6 standards, including (1) buses, (2) wheel and crawler tractors, (3) motorcycles, (4) solid waste compactor trucks, and (5) truck-mounted refrigerators. 83/

It should be noted that while the standard procedure for developing standards under Section 6 derives from the identification of the product as a major noise source under Section 5, EPA has the authority to impose noise standards on any product, even though it has not been identified as a major noise source and no control techniques have been set forth. 84/ This provision, therefore, provides an alternative to the congressionally-declared categories under Section 6(a). 85/

Several other features of the standards-setting section merit further brief explanations. First "any such noise emission standards shall be a performance standard." This is consistent with congressional determination in other environmental acts that industry

---

80/   Ibid.

81/   Noise Act § 6(a)(3).

82/   The most notable are Section 112(b)(1)(B) of the Clean Air Act regarding hazardous air pollutants and Section 307(a)(2) of the Water Pollution Act covering toxic effluent standards.

83/   40 FR 23105, 28 May 1975.

84/   Noise Act § 6(b).

85/   Noise Act § 6(a)(1)(C).

should not be told how to reduce emissions by design standards but rather should be told only what level should be attained to protect public health and welfare and then be allowed to reach it in any fashion desired. This is a reasonable approach, although it ignores those frequent situations in which industry and government agree on what technology is available but disagree on the levels attainable under varying circumstances. 86/

Second, in standards setting EPA is also required to consider the degree of noise reduction possible using best available technology (BAT), considering the cost of compliance. This can be at odds with the requirement for performance standards. What often occurs in practice is that EPA ascertains what is the best available technology, determines from that what level is achievable under normal circumstances, and then sets a performance standard at that level. Thus, standards are often set on the basis of design criteria but are converted into performance standards.

Third, the requirement to take into consideration the magnitude and use of the product, either by itself or in combination with other noise sources, may result in more severe noise reductions in certain cases because of the likelihood that a number of machines or devices will be operating simultaneously.

4.5 Federal, State and Local Jurisdiction Under Section 6

The noise emission standards under Section 6 affect state and local authority over noise only in one sense: local jurisdictions are preempted from imposing their own noise emission standards on new products for which federal standards apply, unless these standards are identical with federal standards. (The term "new product" means, for practical purposes, virtually any product.) 87/ For those products for which EPA has not yet issued standards, local

---

86/ This was the situation, for example, in EPA air standards involving both mercury and asbestos, and with OSHA standards on the coal tar pitch volatiles (CTPV) from coke ovens.

87/ § 3(5) defines "new product" as "(a) a product the equitable or legal title of which has never been transferred to an ultimate purchaser, or (b) a product which is imported or offered for importation in the United States and which is manufactured after the effective date of regulation under § 6 or § 8 which would have been applicable to such product had it been manufactured in the United States."

standards, if any, would continue to apply without preemption. Moreover, local governments would retain their authority "to regulate use, operation, or movement of products—except aircraft— without regard to preemption." 88/

During the legislative debates prior to enactment of the Noise Bill, the Nixon Administration had favored a complete pre-emption of state authority once a federal emission standard had been set (unless the local standard was identical) to prevent imped-ing the nationwide distribution of products. The House declined to accept total state preemption: while states were preempted from regulating products not yet sold to a consumer, they could control noise from products once they had reached their ultimate user. 89/ In 1978, the Quiet Communities Act amended Section 6 of the original act giving states or political subdivisions thereof the right to petition the Administrator to revise a federal standard on the grounds that a more stringent standard is necessary to protect public health and welfare. 90/

Some consideration was given by Congress to a federal ambi-ent noise standard, similar to the ambient procedure under the Clean Air Act. 91/ This was rejected, however, because such a standard "would, in effect, put the federal government in the position of establishing land use zoning requirements on the basis of noise—i.e., noise levels to be permitted in residential areas, in business areas, in manufacturing and residential areas, and within those areas for different times of the day or night. It is the committee's view that this function is one more properly that of the States and their politi-cal subdivisions. . . ." 92/

88/   House Committee on Interstate and Foreign Commerce, "Legislative History of Noise Control Act of 1972," March 1972 pp. 8-9, interpreting Noise Act § 6(e).

89/   E.L. Dolgin and T.G.P. Guilbert, Editors, Federal Environ-mental Law (St. Paul, Minn.: West Publishing Co., 1974).

90/   PL 95-609, § 5.

91/   Clean Air Act §§ 108-110.

92/   House Commerce Committee, "Legislative History of Noise Control Act of 1972," supra, p.9.

4.6 Warranties

After a standard has been issued, Section 6(d)(1) requires the manufacturer to warrant to the purchaser that the product was designed and built to conform with the noise standard at the time of sale. He does not necessarily warrant that the product will conform to the standard over its useful life, although EPA might so require. This warranty makes available to the producer the normal defenses of wear and tear of the product, misuse, and lack of proper maintenance.

However, where a product is inherently defective, any cost obligation incurred by the dealer to correct the defect must be borne by the manufacturer. The transfer of any such cost obligation from the manufacturer to any dealer through a franchise or other agreement is prohibited. In spite of this prohibition, it would appear that where the responsibility for product performance over a period of time might be involved, this might still fall within the normal arrangements a manufacturer may have with his dealer.

4.7 Advertising Restrictions

In an obvious attempt to keep the manufacturers from exploiting the cost aspects of noise control, Section 6(d)(3) requires that if a manufacturer advertises that his product includes valuable or costly noise emission control devices or systems, such claims are subject to verification by the Bureau of Labor Statistics. Access may be afforded to the manufacturer's books, documents, papers and records. To forestall such investigations, manufacturers' advertising will probably focus on performance, compliance with standards, and other benefits, but not refer to cost or value of the noise emission control devices or systems.

4.8 Labeling

In Section 8 the EPA Administrator is required by regulation to designate any product (or class thereof) which (1) emits noise capable of adversely affecting the public health and welfare or (2) is sold wholly or in part on the basis of its effectiveness in reducing noise. The prospective user must be informed of the level of noise the product emits or its effectiveness in reducing noise.

The labeling approach is based on the premise that it constitutes a partial alternative to setting often-arbitrary numerical standards or the outright banning of harmful products. It assumes that consumers will prefer less hazardous products to those which are more hazardous, if they are properly informed of the facts. Or if they prefer the more hazardous, because of lower cost or for some other reason, at least they will have had the opportunity to exercise an informed choice.

Although an advance notice of proposed rulemaking was published in December 1974, 93/ a general labeling proposal was not signed until 10 June 1977. It sets forth the criteria for eventual selection of candidate products for labeling. They should also be coordinated with other federal agencies, such as the Consumer Product Safety Commission, which also have labeling requirements. 94/

The labeling preemption provision is somewhat vague. 95/ The state or political subdivision is not prevented from regulating product labeling or information in any way which does not conflict with EPA regulations. In other words, the state or political subdivision cannot require information of the type required by EPA to be given in a form different from that prescribed by EPA. The Director of EPA's Noise Office declared then that local jurisdictions would indeed be encouraged to instigate their own labeling programs, even though this could have been a serious burden to trade. 96/

With the virtual demise of EPA's noise program, however, this proposal and other regulatory initiatives have been suspended.

4.9 Development of Low-Noise-Emission Products

Low-noise-emission products (LNEP) are defined in Section 15 as any products which emit noise in amounts significantly below the levels specified in noise emission standards applicable at the time of procurement. EPA is empowered to set up procedures to determine which products qualify and to certify them for use in the federal government, if the General Services Administration finds the cost of

---

93/   BNA, Noise Reporter, 9 December 1974, A-12.

94/   The Department of Commerce adopted in May 1977 an experimental volunteer labeling program and invited companies to participate. See 42 FR 26647. The Home Appliance Manufacturers objected to this plan, claiming it would be costly and would add to already overcrowded labels.

95/   Noise Act § 8(c).

96/   See BNA, Noise Reporter, 27 September 1976, A-1.

the product less than that of one for which it would be substituted. Any statutory price limitations would be waived. 97/

In May 1977, EPA proposed LNEP standards for heavy and medium trucks and for portable air compressors. 98/ A month later, the GSA actually completed an LNEP purchase of quieter push power mowers. 99/

4.10 Prohibitions and Penalties

The Noise Act makes illegal the manufacture, distribution, or importation of any new product produced after the effective date of a regulation under either Section 6 (noise standards) or Section 8 (noise labeling information). The Act also prohibits the removal or rendering inoperative of noise control devices prior to sale of the product to an ultimate purchaser, 100/ or "the use of a product after such device or element of design has been removed or rendered inoperative by any person." 101/

Section 11 of the Act prescribes fines and imprisonment for willful violations of Section 10. In the original Act these sanctions were as high as $25,000 and imprisonment for up to one year, or both, for first violations. The penalty for subsequent violations could reach $50,000 and imprisonment for up to two years. 102/ However, the Quiet Communities Act of 1978 reduced these limits to a maximum of "$10,000 per day of such violation." 103/

97/ Final regulations on procurement were issued in 1974. 39 FR 6670.

98/ 42 FR 27442, 27 May 1977.

99/ Reported in BNA, Noise Reporter, 25 April 1977, A-6.

100/ "Ultimate purchaser" is defined as "the first person who in good faith purchases a product for purposes other than resale." Noise Act § 3(4).

101/ Noise Act § 10(a).

102/ Noise Act § 11(a). As in many other acts, each day of a violation may constitute a separate offense under this section, see § 11(b).

103/ PL 95-609, §4, Amending Noise Act § 11(a)(2).

4.11 Control of Transportation Noise

Congress recognized in the Noise Act that the primary sources of noise, other than machinery, were the vehicles involved in general transportation. Thus, while Congress provided one section (Section 6) covering general machinery and motors, three detailed sections were incorporated into the Act to deal with aircraft noise (Section 7), railroad noise (Section 19), and noise from motor carriers (Section 18). EPA is thus given authority in areas where other federal agencies such as the Federal Aviation Administration (FAA) and the Federal Railroad Administration (FRA) normally exercise sole jurisdiction. Moreover, to the extent that these and other federal agencies have not issued standards and regulations protecting their workers from occupational noise, OSHA has authority under its statute to regulate and enforce its own standards. 104/

4.12 Aviation Noise

Congress' primary concern in the transportation area, as reflected in the legislative history, was with aviation noise. 105/ EPA's regulatory involvement has accordingly been much more extensive in this area, as we shall see in a separate section later. 106/ In 1968 Congress had given the FAA, which is responsible for airline safety, the additional responsibility of regulating aircraft and airport noise. 107/ The 1972 Noise Control Act added

---

104/ OSHA Act § 4(b)(1). This authority has not been without legal challenge; in the railroad area, for example, the highest courts have several times considered cases unsuccessfully brought to deny OSHA's jurisdiction to inspect railroad property. The FRA has general jurisdiction in the area but has not issued comprehensive occupational standards.

105/ House Committee on Interstate and Foreign Commerce, "Legislative History of Noise Control Act of 1972," March 1972.

106/ The 1971 EPA Noise hearings revealed that public complaints about noise from aircraft surpassed those from any other source. EPA estimated in its 1971 report to the President, supra, that over 7 million Americans were burdened with aircraft noise.

107/ 1968 Amendment to the Federal Aviation Act of 1958, § 611, 49 U.S.C. § 1431.

to this authority but also extended EPA's authority into the area. The Administration had recommended that EPA be given veto power over all noise standards and regulations issued by the FAA. Some environmentalists favored giving EPA even fuller power, allowing the EPA Administrator to set aviation noise standards directly. Congress rejected both these positions, because it felt that EPA lacked the requisite technical expertise concerning aircraft and engine design. Instead, the 1972 Act provides for joint regulatory authority for FAA and EPA, although the former retains the leading role. 108/

The basic statutory provision is Section 7 of the Noise Control Act of 1972, along with its Section 7(b) which amends Section 611 of the Federal Aviation Act of 1958. Section 7 provided that within nine months after the enactment of the Noise Act, EPA should conduct a detailed and comprehensive study of the adequacy of FAA standards and controls on flight operations and on aircraft, and the available means of reducing the cumulative noise exposure around airports. This important study was sent to the respective committees of the House and Senate on 31 July 1973. 109/

Section 7(b) of the Act amended Section 611 of the Federal Aviation Act to provide that the Administrator of the FAA "shall prescribe and amend such rules and regulations as he may find necessary to provide for the control and abatement of aircraft noise and sonic boom" and shall consult with others to determine what actions are necessary and whether they are "economically reasonable, technologically practicable, and appropriate for the particular type of aircraft, aircraft engine," etc., for application. 110/ The 1972 Amendments specified that the FAA must consult with EPA before taking any regulatory actions on noise.

A more significant authority for EPA is the right to propose noise regulations which the FAA must consider and within thirty

---

108/ House Commerce Committee, "Legislative History of Noise Control Act of 1972," supra, p.9.

109/ EPA, "Report on Aircraft-Airport Noise," July 1973; this was subsequently published as Senate Committee on Public Works, "Report on Aircraft-Airport Noise," series 93-8, 1973.

110/ FAA § 611(b)(1) and § 611(d)(4), 49 U.S.C. § 1431(b)(1) and § 1431(d)(4).

days publish a notice of proposed rulemaking. Within a further sixty days FAA must hold a public hearing and after a reasonable time and after further consultation with EPA, the FAA must prescribe the regulations in whole or in part or detail its reasons for not doing so. 111/ If EPA believes that the action taken by the FAA "does not protect the public health and welfare from aircraft noise or sonic boom," EPA may request the FAA to reconsider its conclusions and report in writing to EPA in detail as to why the original recommendations were not followed. This already lengthy process may then be followed by publication in the Federal Register, additional consultations, the preparation of a supplemental environmental report, and a list of additional factors for consideration. 112/ The final decision remains with FAA subject to court challenge, but the FAA is given every procedural incentive to heed EPA recommendations.

Another requirement under Section 611 is that the FAA not issue any certificates for previously unmarketed aircraft "for which substantial noise abatement can be achieved by prescribing standards and regulations" unless the FAA has in fact issued regulations which apply to that type of aircraft. 113/

4.13 Railroad and Motor Carrier Noise Standards

These almost identical two sections, Section 17 and Section 18 of the Noise Act, were apparently considered of marginal importance by Congress. This conclusion is suggested by the legislative history, in which the House report dealt at length with aviation noise but neglected even to mention the two sections as key items in the summary of legislation. 114/ Nevertheless, these two sections have been the object of considerable activity by the EPA Noise Office. Both sections provide that within nine months of the enactment of

---

111/ FAA § 611(c)(1).

112/ FAA § 611(c)(2), (3), and § 611(d).

113/ FAA § 611(b)(2). The first certification regulations for aircraft noise were issued in December 1969 as Part 36 of the Federal Aircraft Regulations (FAR 36), see 34 FR 453 (1969).

114/ See House Committee on Interstate Foreign Commerce, "Legislative History of Noise Control Act of 1972," March 1972.

the statute, EPA should propose noise emission regulations with specific emission standards for railway and motor carriers engaged in interstate commerce. After years of delay, at the request of the railroad companies, the United States Court of Appeals of the District of Columbia ordered publication of final regulations by 22 February 1979. 115/ However, EPA only issued the proposed regulations on 17 April 1979. 116/ These regulations, when finally issued, are to be in addition to those issued under Section 6 of the statute, and are based on the best available technology (BAT) considering the cost of compliance. 117/

Legislative history indicates that in enacting these two sections Congress may have been more interested in preempting state and local authority than in establishing a federal program. Both of these industries would have been greatly hampered if local regulations could impede their ability to operate in interstate commerce. 118/ According to Section 17(c)(1) (and its twin Section 18(c)(1)), "no state or political subdivision thereof may adopt or enforce any standard applicable to noise emissions resulting in the operation of the same equipment of facility or such carrier unless such standard is identical to a standard applicable to noise emissions resulting from such operations prescribed by any regulation under this section." 119/

A state may still prescribe noise controls which are incidental to other legitimate functions of local government, such as traffic control and licensing regulations, as long as these do not conflict with federal regulations. Also, if particular local conditions require special regulations by state or community, these may be promulgated with the approval of the EPA Administrator after consultation with the Secretary of Transportation. 120/

115/ Association of American Railroads v. Costle, (D.C. Cir. 1977) 565 F.2d 1310.

116/ 44 FR 22960, proposing amendment of 40 CFR 201.

117/ Noise Act §§ 17(a)(1) and 18(a)(1).

118/ See Senate Report No. 92-1160, 92nd Cong., 2d Sess. (1972), pp. 8 and 19.

119/ Noise Act §§ 17(c)(1) and 18(c)(1).

120/ Noise Act §§ 17(c)(2) and 18(c)(2).

4.14 EPA's Coordination Role Within the Federal Government

EPA's primary role under the Noise Act, other than the setting of standards, is to act as the coordinator of all federal activities relating to noise. This means first of all that EPA oversees federal agencies' compliance with Section 4(a) of the Act, which directs all federal agencies to "carry out the programs within their control in such a manner to further the policy" set forth in Section 2(b) of promoting an environment free from noise hazards to health or welfare. 121/ This procedure and admonition closely resemble that under the National Environmental Policy Act (NEPA) directing all federal agencies to promote that Act's goal of environmental protection. 122/

The EPA Administrator is given direct authority to coordinate the activities of all federal agencies relating to noise research and control, and these agencies are directed to provide him with whatever information he requests. 123/ Moreover, if any federal agency issues a noise regulation or standard which the EPA Administrator feels "does not protect the public health and welfare to the extent he believes to be required and feasible," he may request that agency to review that action and report to him on the "advisability of revising such standard or regulation to provide such protection." These detailed findings may be published in the Federal Register, along with supporting documents and detailed statements of findings. The final authority remains with the proposing agency, but the availability of public analysis and comment gives EPA considerable leverage with a recalcitrant agency.

EPA's most notable use of this authority has been in its disagreement with OSHA over the proposed new occupational noise emission standard, which EPA felt was too high to sufficiently protect workers' health. 124/ A similar provision in Section 7 of the Act makes the Federal Aviation Administration (FAA) even more subject to EPA challenge on aviation noise regulations.

EPA is also required under Section 4 to publish periodic status reports on the progress and activities of other federal agencies in

---

121/   Noise Act § 4(a) and 2(b).

122/   See NEPA § 101, 42 U.S.C. § 4321 (1969).

123/   Noise Act § 4(c)(1).

124/   Noise Act § 4(c)(2).

noise research and control. This gives EPA the additional sanction of subjecting unresponsive agencies to the full glare of public criticism. 125/

5.0 Quiet Communities Act of 1978

The Quiet Communities Act of 1978 126/ extended the Noise Control Act of 1972 for one year and amended some of the sections in order to provide state and local governments with funds to promote the development of noise control programs on a local level as long as no actions or programs are inconsistent with federal regulations. 127/

Other than placing more responsibility on state and local governments, the principal changes made by the Quiet Communities Act were: (1) the penalty for violations of Section 10 was reduced from a maximum of $25,000 to a maximum of $10,000 per day, for the first violation; 128/ and (2) the states or political subdivisions thereof were afforded the right to petition the administrator to revise federal regulations on the grounds that a more rigid standard should be imposed to protect the health and welfare of the public. 129/

6.0 Current Regulatory Actions on Noise

Regulatory agencies, principally EPA and the Department of Transportation, have taken actions which affect important industries. These include aviation (both aircraft and airports), motor carriers, heavy equipment, and new products.

6.1 Regulatory Activity Concerning Noise in the Aviation Industry

FAA and EPA have attempted to lower the noise levels around airports by reducing the emissions level from aircraft through retrofit, by the introduction of quieter aircraft, and by the introduction of new operating procedures such as takeoff and landing regulations at airports.

125/   Noise Act § 4(c)(3).

126/   PL 95-609, 92 Stat. 3079, 42 U.S.C. 4901 (8 November 1978).

127/   Ibid., § 2, amending Noise Act § 14(c).

128/   Ibid., § 4, amending Noise Act § 11(a).

129/   Ibid., § 5, amending Noise Act § 6(f).

Federal Aviation Regulation (FAR) 36 was introduced in 1969 to cover aircraft thought "most likely to raise the aircraft noise levels in airport neighborhoods." This regulation covered most types of aircraft but not those currently in use or for which a certificate had already been issued. 130/

The regulation set noise levels for approach, takeoff, and sideline measurements based on weight, with the larger aircraft allowed higher noise levels. 131/

FAR 36 specifies a measurement system whereby noise levels are monitored one mile from the beginning of the runway on approach, three and one-half miles from the beginning of the runway on takeoff, and approximately 0.3 of a mile to the side of the runway. These measurements can be converted into a special decibel reading designed to approximate the discomfort to which the human observer would be subjected. This Effective Perceived Noise Level (EPNdB) scale includes the noise level, frequency, duration, and the occurrence of strong tones. (In practice, this scale gives a reading 10 to 15 decibels higher than the standard dB(A) measurement used by OSHA.)

In October 1976, EPA proposed that all new aircraft, both subsonic and supersonic, certified after January 1980, would have to be 6 to 18 decibels quieter than present aircraft. The recommended numbers for takeoff, landing, and sideline measurements were derived by simple subtraction from the average of seventeen aircraft sampled. 132/ FAA, however, in June 1978 decided to set different standards for the two types of aircraft. 133/

6.2 Retrofit Of Existing Aircraft

The 1969 FAR 36 noise standards were not designed to result in substantial noise reductions in existing aircraft. After years of

---

130/   34 FR 453. It did not cover supersonic transports, vertical and short takeoff landing aircraft (V/STOL), and non-jet business and pleasure aircraft.

131/   FAR 36, appendix C.

132/   Aviation Week and Space Technology, 11 October 1976, pp. 24-25.

133/   43 FR 28406, 29 June 1978.

debate, on 9 February 1976 the FAA proposed lowering the permissible noise levels from all transport aircraft and all single engine turbo jet aircraft. 134/ The proposed rule would lower the permissible noise levels by up to 10 EPNdB on takeoff, 9 EPNdB on sideline, and 4 EPNdB on landing. 135/

This debate regarding retrofit of existing aircraft, through such means as quieter engines and sound absorbing material, has been one of the most controversial issues at both FAA and the EPA Noise Office. The aviation industry has generally favored the phase-out of older aircraft from U.S. fleets. The shaky financial position of American Airlines in recent years has made them increasingly reluctant to spend the funds necessary for improved, quieter aircraft; but this has also served to reduce the phase-out rate of older aircraft to two percent a year. At this rate, even by 1990 half of the aircraft will fail to meet the modest FAR 36 standards.

For this reason, the former FAA Administrator, John L. McLucas, endorsed retrofit of existing aircraft, along with ongoing replacement, as a necessary and cost effective means of reducing aircraft noise. 136/ The price tag on this proposal was about $1 billion for retrofit of U.S. aircraft and $250 million for retrofit of foreign jets. The benefit-cost ratio, McLucas estimated, would still be over two-to-one, and the cost would amount to less than two-tenths of one percent of the total operating cost during the year the maximum number of planes would be retrofitted.

The Secretary of Transportation announced on 18 November 1976 that existing aircraft would be given until the beginning of 1985 to comply with FAA noise regulations under FAR 36. The issue of financial options for the necessary retrofits, however, was reserved for further study. 137/

134/ The original notice of proposed rulemaking, published on 5 November 1975, was more limited in its scope of application.

135/ FAA, Notice 75-378, Docket No. 15131, as amended 9 February 1976; BNA, Noise Regulation Reporter, 16 February 1976, A-5.

136/ John L. McLucas, FAA Administrator, statement before the House Public Works Aviation Subcommittee, 26 February 1976, reported in BNA, Noise Regulation Reporter, 1 March 1976, A-18.

137/ BNA, Environment Reporter, 26 November 1976, p. 1102.

6.3 Airports and Aircraft Operating Procedures

Airport operators in the United States have been among the strongest proponents of aircraft retrofit, because they have borne much public criticism for excessive aviation noise. In 1962, the United States Supreme Court declared in Griggs v. Allegheny County that the airport operator, usually a local government agency, is responsible for securing sufficient land and easements around the airport to ensure the proper functioning of airport facility. Failure to do so, with resultant noise disruption to the neighboring community, makes the operators of the airport—not the federal government—responsible for any damages. 138/

In September 1975, a California superior court ruled that those subjected to high levels of aircraft noise may sue for mental and emotional distress, and that the same plaintiffs may sue repeatedly if the noise continued. 139/ Some authorities have expressed the fear that this could lead to the closing of the long-embattled Los Angeles Airport and perhaps scores of others around the country.

The position of the airport operators has been particularly confused since 1973 when the Supreme Court held 5 to 4 in City of Burbank v. Lockheed Air Terminal that local communities could not use their general "police" powers to control airport noise. 140/ According to the Court, the comprehensive 1972 Noise Act gave authority over aircraft noise to the FAA and EPA, thereby preempting state and local officials.

In October 1980 the United States Supreme Court declined an appeal of a California State Supreme Court decision, thereby upholding its finding that the federal government's preemption of

---

138/   369 U.S. 84 (1962).   In a dissent, Justices Black and Frankfurter argued that "the United States, not the Greater Pittsburgh Airport, has 'taken' the airspace over Griggs' property necessary for flight." Ibid., at 91.

139/   Greater Westchester Homeowners' Association v. City of Los Angeles, 30 September 1974, report in BNA, Noise Reporter, 13 October 1973, A-29.

140/   411 U.S. 624 (1973). The dissent by Justice Rehnquist is the better legal argument, but the policy issues are much harder to call.

aircraft noise standards nevertheless did not bar suit for nuisance by a property owners' association against a local airport authority. 141/

In February 1974 EPA proposed that airport operators submit noise abatement plans to the FAA. Failure to comply could mean loss of federal financial support and possibly even the airport's operating certificate. 142/ The FAA, however, seriously questioned the desirability of regulating airports, arguing that this was a complex and cumbersome approach to a problem better solved by making quieter aircraft.

In July 1975 the FAA declared its intention of formulating a national airport noise policy and requested comments by 1 January 1976. The Agency outlined four possible policy options: to allow airport operators to develop programs for noise abatement without any constraints from the FAA; to develop a federal airport noise abatement plan, in which the airport operator would play no part and for which he would assume no responsibility; to allow operators to develop abatement plans, with subsequent approval by FAA and possibly EPA; and a continuation of the present policy of reducing aircraft noise at its source—the airplane—and leaving to airport operators the right to take whatever additional measures they felt necessary for operating procedures. Of these choices, the FAA seemed to lean heavily toward the fourth option, but hearings were scheduled for public comment in at least twenty cities around the country. 143/

The FAA has nevertheless proposed a partial noise solution using changes in aircraft takeoff and landing procedures. This would be a further development of the FAA's 1972 recommended "get-em-high earlier" takeoff procedure. So on 20 March 1974 FAA issued an advance notice of proposed rulemaking calling for a change in landing procedures that would incorporate the "two segment" landing method. This plan, which involves a rapid descent from altitude and

---

141/   Los Angeles v. Greater Winchester Homeowners' Association, U.S., 14 ERC 1074 (1980).

142/   39 FR 6142 (1974).

143/   40 FR 28844, 9 July 1975. The hearing announcements are reported in BNA, Noise Reporter, August 1975, A-17; additional hearings were announced. Ibid., 10 November 1975, A-19.

then a gradual landing approach, rather than the more common steady gradual descent, has already been used by Northwest Airlines and Air California with considerable success. Not only has landing noise been reduced by 16 decibels, 144/ but there has been a real fuel saving of approximately four million gallons a year for Northwest. 145/

Some experts, however, have questioned the safety of this two segment approach. 146/ One official of the Air Transport Association (ATA), commenting on the proliferation of noise abatement flight procedures, urged the FAA to standardize the system. "We have been begging them to do it." 147/

In August 1976, the State of Illinois threatened suit against the FAA to compel action one way or the other on EPA's numerous proposals for airport and aircraft noise abatement. Included in the list were recommendations for minimum altitudes (December 1974), fleet noise level requirements (February 1975), two segment approaches (August 1975), aircraft noise requirements for operating to and from U.S. airports (January 1976), and others. The state attorney explained, "We're trying to get them off their hands." 148/ The FAA declined to prescribe the above EPA proposals. 149/

6.4 DOT's Concorde Decision

Supersonic transports (SST) were expressly excluded from coverage under FAR 36 on the grounds that special rules would have

---

144/   Captain J.T. Frederickson, Director, Flying Operations, Northwestern Airlines, reported in BNA, Noise Reporter, 23 June 1975, A-29-30.

145/   Aviation Week and Space Technology, 12 April 1976, pp. 30-31; BNA, Noise Reporter, 10 June 1974.

146/   See statement by H.B. Benninghoff, American Airlines, testifying for the Air Transport Association, FAA Hearings, 5 November 1975, reported in BNA, Noise Reporter, 10 November 1975, A-7-9.

147/   Aviation Week and Space Technology, 12 April 1976, p. 31.

148/   Ibid., 2 August 1976, pp. 28-29.

149/   EPA Noise Control Program—Progress to Date, April 1979.

to be designed to deal with this unusual aircraft. The United States dropped the development of the SST for a variety of economic and environmental reasons, but the Anglo-French Concorde and the Soviet Tu-144 were ready for commercial service in early 1976. 150/ The British and French applied for landing rights in New York and Washington, D.C., on a transatlantic route to London and Paris.

There was considerable local and congressional opposition to the granting of these rights, especially from representatives from those two metropolitan areas who characterized the SST as "the noisiest aircraft in the air today." 151/ (A secondary concern was the increase in air pollutants from the aircraft.) Ground monitoring of SST noise indicated that levels were even higher than had originally been indicated: 119.5 EPNdB on takeoff, 116 EPNdB on landing, and 112 EPNdB on sideline. 152/

The level for the Concorde was 129.3, compared with 118.3 for the Boeing 707. 153/

Congressional attempts to ban the SST outright were narrowly defeated in both houses. In the House, an attempted amendment to the aviation appropriations bill was defeated on 10 July 1975 by a

---

150/ Mechanical problems with the Tu-144 kept the aircraft grounded during most of the following years.

151/ See BNA, Noise Reporter, 28 April 1975, A-2.

152/ Ibid., 18 August 1974, A-16. The figures in the FAA Draft Environmental Impact Statement were, respectively, 117.8, 114.9. Moreover, Australian measurements in August 1975 indicated that the production version of the Concorde was significantly noisier than the prototype had been. According to this report, the Concorde was four times louder than the B-707 and eight times louder than the B-747. BNA, Noise Reporter, 29 September 1975, A-25. A somewhat different figure was given by EPA Administrator Train to a Congressional subcommittee on 9 December 1975; he estimated that the Concorde would be twice as loud as the B-707 and four times as loud as the B-747 and DC-10. Ibid., 22 December 1975, A-2.

153/ Ibid., 12 May 1975, A-17.

vote of 214 to 196. 154/ The Senate, after considerable debate, rejected a similar move sponsored by Senators William Proxmire
(D-Wis.) and Birch Bayh (D-Ind.) on 25 July 1975 by a 46 to 44
vote. 155/

Russell Train, then Administrator of EPA, joined the opposition to the Concorde. Although he stressed that his conclusions
were preliminary pending a final evaluation of the FAA's environmental impact statement, he declared that approval of landing
rights would be inadvisable in New York and "increasingly questionable" in Washington. 156/ Although there were other environmental
problems raised by the SST, Train pointed out that his conclusions
were based on noise alone, as EPA does not have authority under
Section 231 of the Clean Air Act to set air emission standards for
SSTs already in production. 157/

Transportation Secretary William T. Coleman had promised a
decision on the SST controversy by early February 1976. On 13 January, the last day for receipt of formal comments on the issue, EPA
sent him a proposed amendment to FAA noise regulations. EPA
proposed to change FAR 91.57 to prohibit non-military SST flights
into the United States by any aircraft that did not comply with FAR
36 noise standards as of the end of 1974. This would have prevented
all flights to the U.S. by all but three or four existing Concordes. 158/

On 4 February 1976, however, Secretary Coleman overrode
these objections and granted "limited landing rights for a demonstration period not to exceed sixteen months under certain precise

---

154/   Ibid., 21 July 1975, A-10.

155/   Ibid., 4 August 1975, A-35.

156/   Testimony of EPA Administrator Russell E. Train, Govern-
       ment Activities and Transportation Subcommittee of the
       House Government Operations Committee, 9 December 1975,
       Ibid., 22 December 1975, A-2.

157/   Ibid., A-3.

158/   BNA, Noise Reporter, 19 January 1976, A-10. This EPA
       proposal was published by DOT as a Notice of Proposed
       Rulemaking on 12 February 1976. 41 FR 6270, 20 February
       1976.

limitations and restrictions." 159/ The Secretary's decision never-theless contained the following proviso:

> The EIS indicates to me that the marginal impact of six additional flights would be small. Given the subjective nature of human response to noise, however, I must conclude that if any flights at all are justified—that is, if there is sufficient affirmative reason for permitting Concorde flights that we are willing to suffer some environmental effect—those flights should be authorized only on a temporary basis, in order to permit a more intelligent and responsible decision to be made at some point in the future, after we have collected information on the subject response to the Concorde during actual operations. 160/

The matter did not end there. Legal challenges to the decision were brought by environmentalist groups, local governments in the affected states, and by congressmen, who had also introduced legislation to ban the SST. 161/ The most serious threat was posed by the New York Port Authority, which controls Kennedy Airport in New York and which sought to deny SST's access to the airport. 162/

A federal district court in May 1977 found the ban unconstitutional, as contrary to the supremacy clause. This decision was overturned the following month by the Second Circuit, which relied upon the Griggs case mentioned earlier. The Port Authority could set non-discriminatory limits on aircraft noise operations but could not arbitrarily exclude the Concorde. 163/ In October 1977, the Supreme Court denied a stay, thereby allowing flights to commence at Kennedy Airport until or unless the local regulations were prepared.

Meanwhile, also in October, the FAA proposed regulations for supersonic aircraft that would allow the present 16 Concordes to

---

159/ DOT, "The Secretary's Decision on Concorde Supersonic Transport," 4 February 1976, p.3.

160/ Ibid., p. 50.

161/ BNA, Noise Reporter, 1 March 1976, A-22.

162/ BNA, Noise Reporter, 19 January 1976, A-4.

163/ British Airways Board v. Port Authority, 431 F. Supp. 1216 (1977); reversed 558 F.2d 75 (2d Cir. 1977).

operate but would require any beginning operation after January 1980 to meet a limit of 108 EPNdB. 164/

6.5 FAA Noise Certification

The FAA carries out its responsibilities by, in part, certifying various classes of aircraft and providing technical requirements for monitoring.

Under the Reagan Administration the concept of Regulation by Objective (RBO) prompted a review of existing noise standards and the methodology for measuring it. For example, the Aerospace Industries Association (AIA) petitioned for modification of FAR 36 rules on turbojets, set twelve years earlier. It is interesting to note, however, that the request disavowed any intent to weaken the standard. 165/ Citizen suits against airports are themselves a considerable deterrent to drastic changes upward in noise levels.

7.0 Major Sources of Noise

EPA is required under the Noise Control Act to identify the major sources of noise as the first step in the preparation of noise control regulations. 166/

On 19 June 1974 EPA issued its report identifying the major sources of noise, their levels, and the estimated number of people subjected. EPA also acknowledged that this list is "partially subjective," as many factors other than mere loudness are involved. 167/ The report concluded that urban traffic noise subjects the most people to annoying levels of noise, based on a 24-hour calculation, followed by aviation noise and construction equipment noise. 168/

164/   42 FR 55176, 13 October 1977. See also 43 FR 28406, 29 June 1978.

165/   47 FR 47854, 28 October 1982; see Illinois v. Coleman (D.C.D.C., 11 March 1981, No. 76-1961.)

166/   Noise Act § 5(b).

167/   EPA, Identification of Products as Major Sources of Noise, 39 FR 22297 (21 June 1974).

168/   Ibid. EPA uses two calculations: the first is the equivalent sound level (Leq), which is used to indicate long term hearing hazards and day-night sound calculation based on a 24-hour period with a 10 dB(A) penalty for sounds occurring at night because of their greater annoyance.

According to the report, medium and heavy duty trucks, motor-cycles, and snowmobiles were the principal transportation noise sources; and power drivers of rock drills were the most annoying sources of construction noise. Of these listed products, however, only two were officially scheduled for regulation under Section 6 as major sources of noise: medium and heavy duty trucks and portable air compressors. The other listed products remained candidates for possible future regulatory action. 169/

On 20 May 1975 EPA published a second list of products iden-tified as major noise sources under Section 5(b). These included motorcycles, buses, wheel and track loaders and wheel and track dozers, truck transport refrigeration units, and truck-mounted solid waste compactors as special auxiliary equipment on trucks. 170/ Subsequent administrative procedure, as usual, includes the publica-tion before rulemaking of information on control techniques, costs, technology, possible labeling requirements, and alternative methods of noise control. EPA also announced a long list of possible candi-dates for identification as major noise sources in the immediate future. These range from almost all forms of surface transporta-tion, plus tires, to many types of household appliances from electric toothbrushes to movie projectors.

EPA declared its intention to study a number of particular candidates for possible future identification as major noise sources, including the following: light trucks, motor boats, chain saws, tires, pneumatic and hydraulic tools, power drivers, lawn care equipment,

---

169/ EPA has characterized the information gathering and scien-tific analysis background to regulation in a slightly different fashion. The first step, they consider, was the Title IV Report, Report to the President and Congress on Noise, Doc. No. 92-63, 92nd Congress, 2nd Session, February 1962; the second step was the publication of the "Criteria Document," Public Health and Welfare Criteria for Noise, EPA, 27 July 1973, pursuant to Section 5(a)(1) of the Noise Control Act of 1972; and, third, the publication of the "Levels Document," Information on Levels of Environmental Noise Requisite to Protect Public Health and Welfare with an Adequate Margin of Safety, EPA, March 1974, pursuant to Section 5(a)(2) of the Noise Control Act.

170/ 40 FR 23105, 28 May 1975.

and other special auxiliary equipment on trucks. 171/ Relatively little subsequently appeared on these items, however, except for power mowers.

In December 1982 EPA issued a notice of intent to delete from the list of major noise sources the following items: power lawn mowers, pavement breakers, rock drills, wheel and crawler tractors, buses, and truck transport refrigeration units. This reflected the Reagan Administration's determination to eliminate the program entirely, even if it meant not considering the jackhammer a noisy device. 172/

7.1 Air Compressors

Air compressors were one of the two products first identified by EPA as major noise sources in June 1974. EPA acknowledged at the time that the current technology which relied upon acoustic insulation was not capable of substantially more development but contended that future noise reduction should stress noise source elimination in compressors themselves. 173/

The report noted that insulation had already allowed equipment manufacturers to lower noise levels by a significant 10-20 decibels, depending on whether the units were diesel or gasoline driven.

Because the mean noise levels reported for the "quieted" models ranged around 75 dB(A) (a significant decrease from previous levels of 82 to 92 dB(A)), EPA's first candidate for noise regulation under this section was thus a common but relatively quiet machine, quiet at least in comparison with certain heavy metal shaping machines producing noise levels far in excess of 100 dB(A). 174/

Four months later, EPA proposed a noise emissions standard for compressors with a rated capacity of over 75 cfm (2.1 m^3) of 76

171/   EPA, "Report on the Identification of Products as Major Sources of Noise," 20 May 1975.

172/   47 FR 54108, 1 December 1982; see also 46 FR 41104, 14 August 1981.

173/   EPA, "Preliminary Cost and Technology Information on Reduction of Portable Air Compressor Noise," June 1974.

174/   Ibid.

dB(A) measured at 7 meters distance. 175/ This standard was expected to benefit approximately 11 percent of the total one million persons severely impacted by construction noise. The cost of this standard, according to EPA estimates, would be approximately $20 million. (Annual sales of air compressors are about $115 million.) 176/

Smaller companies complained that the proposed testing requirements would be a real hardship for them. 177/ Another company representative, on the other hand, noted that the small portable air compressors often made by small companies would be relatively easy to conform to the proposed standard but that larger equipment would become even bulkier and heavier and still might not attain the standard. 178/

EPA held a public hearing on the proposed standard in February 1975 and on 31 December 1975 issued the final regulation. The 76 dB(A) standard was to become effective on 1 January 1978 for compressors with a rated capacity between 75 cfm and 250 cfm; and six months later, on 1 July 1978, for compressors with a capacity over 250 cfm (approximately 7 cubic meters a minute). This extension of the period for compliance, EPA claimed, should have little effect on public health but would reduce the cost of compliance from 16 percent to 12 percent and would avoid the otherwise anticipated 5 percent drop in sales volume. EPA also deferred the requirement that manufacturers certify that their product would meet noise standards for the useful life of the device, pending testing to determine the extent of degradation over time. 179/

175/ 100 cubic feet per minute (cfm) corresponds to 2.8 m^3/min.

176/ EPA Assistant Administrator Roger Strelow, press conference, 22 October 1974.

177/ George Fabian, Jaeger Co., Columbus, Ohio, BNA, Noise Reporter, 11 November 1974, A-11.

178/ Gardner-Denver Co., Quincy, Illinois, ibid.

179/ EPA, Final Noise Emission Limits for Portable Air Compressors, 31 December 1975, published in the Federal Register 14 January 1976; codified in 40 CFR Part 204.

In a major deregulation, however, the Reagan Administration in August 1981 included portable air compressors (along with trucks, motorcycles, and garbage trucks) in a proposal to revoke the reporting and recordkeeping requirements 180/ promulgated in 1976. 181/ Simultaneously, EPA declared its intention to suspend enforcement of these regulations during the period of consideration. 182/ At the end of December 1982, the Agency declared these rules final. 183/

7.2 Trucks

The other major noise source identified by EPA in June 1974 was new medium and heavy duty trucks, defined as vehicles having a gross weight rating over five tons when loaded. 184/ On 2 July 1974, an organization of professional truck drivers (PROD) filed suit in the D.C. District Court seeking to compel EPA to propose regulations on trucks. 185/

In October 1974 EPA proposed an 83 dB(A) noise standard for speeds below 35 mph for model year 1977. This standard was to drop to 80 dB(A) for model year 1981 and to 75 dB(A) by 1983. (Measurements were to be made 50 feet from the center line of traffic.) EPA decided not to propose a regulation for speeds over 50 mph, although a draft proposal a few months earlier had recommended a truck standard of 86 dB(A) at that speed. Because of the uncertainties about tire noise at higher speeds, further action on truck noise must await a resolution of that problem. 186/

180/   46 FR 41104, 14 August 1981.

181/   40 CFR 205.50, et seq.

182/   46 FR 41057, 14 August 1981.

183/   47 FR 57709, 28 December 1982; 40 CFR 204.

184/   EPA, "Identification of Products as Major Sources of Noise," 19 June 1974, 39 FR 22297 (21 June 1974).

185/   BNA, Noise Reporter, 8 July 1974, A-12.

186/   EPA, Press Release, 13 April 1976. See also EPA, "Proposed Noise Standard for Medium and Heavy Duty Trucks," 22 October 1974, 39 FR 38338, 30 October 1974. Tire and pavement noise could be as significant as the truck noise itself over 40 miles per hour. Crossbar tires were found to be noisier than ribbed treads, and recapped tires ranged 10-15 dB(A) higher.

EPA's final regulation on truck noise emissions was announced on 13 April 1976. This draft final differed in a number of respects from the proposed regulation issued in October 1974. The final version postponed for approximately one-half year the 83 dB(A) standard, effective on 1 January 1978, and the 80 dB(A) standard (slated for 1 January 1982). The draft dropped consideration of a 75 dB(A) standard, which had been originally scheduled for 1983, on the basis that further study and research would be necessary for this later period. As with the air compressor standards, the draft regulation also omitted the useful-life provisions from the October proposal which sought to ensure that noise levels did not increase significantly over time.

Administrator Train pointed out that the new standard, although seemingly less stringent than that of Florida and Illinois, was actually more restrictive, because it required that virtually every vehicle meet the standard. This standard, he stated, would slightly increase the initial price of trucks but would reduce the operating costs. 187/

In February 1982, EPA decided to postpone the effective date of the noise emission standard for three years, from 1 January 1983 to 1 January 1986. The level itself remained at 80 dB(A). The deferral, according to the Agency, was to provide economic relief to the distressed industry and allow fuel economy improvements. 188/

7.3 Power Mowers

EPA and the Consumer Product Safety Commission (CPSC) both became embroiled in attempts to regulate noise emissions from power mowers. The CPSC draft proposal in July 1975 called for a limit of 92 dB(A) for walk-behind mowers and 95 dB(A) for riding mowers. This was expected to add a not insubstantial cost of $40 to $112, respectively, to an average machine. The CPSC's interest in power mowers included problems other than noise, particularly the safety hazards. And the need for additional tests on these questions led to several postponements of the planned proposal. 189/

187/   EPA estimates that this regulation would increase truck prices by about three percent, although this varies with the type and size of the engines. The improved fuel economy, however, was estimated at half a billion a year.

188/   47 FR 7186, 17 February 1982.

189/   See BNA, Noise Reporter, 19 July 1976, A-11.

On 12 January 1977 EPA identified power mowers as a major noise source under Section 5(b) and circulated a draft proposal with a standard identical to that originally recommended by CPSC. The Agency estimated that forty million operators were exposed to noise loud enough to cause hearing damage, and twice that number to annoying noise levels. 190/ The CPSC, faced with the possibility of a jurisdictional dispute with EPA, deleted the noise section from its proposed power mower standard. 191/

The Outdoor Power Equipment Institute challenged EPA's listing of power mowers as major noise sources. District Judge John Sirica dismissed the suit in October 1977 for lack of jurisdiction, pointing out that a Section 5(b) determination was an inseparable part of the Section 6(b) standard–setting process which, under Section 16(a), could only be reviewed by a court of appeals. 192/

The Reagan Administration, however, in December 1982 issued a notice that it did not consider lawn mowers as major noise sources under Section 5, thereby effectively ending plans for regulation in the foreseeable future. 193/

7.4 Garbage Truck Compactors

EPA proposed noise standards on 12 August 1977 for solid waste compactors. This was scheduled to reduce noise by 4 to 8 decibels in 1979, with a standard of 78 dB(A); and the limit would drop to 75 dB(A) on 1 January 1982. The most controversial feature was the requirement that the manufacturers had to certify the equipment would remain in compliance for three years, or 7500 operating hours, after sale to the ultimate purchaser. 194/

The National Solid Waste Management Association claimed EPA lacked the authority to require a three–year assurance period.

190/   Leonard Eiserer, ed., Noise Control Report, 17 January 1977, p. 11 and 14 February 1977, p. 265.

191/   Ibid., 18 April 1977, p. 62.

192/   BNA, Noise Reporter, 10 October 1977, A–9.

193/   47 FR 54108, 1 December 1982.

194/   42 FR 43226, 26 August 1977. This feature had caused the delay in issuance of the proposal, which was originally due in November 1976.

New York City officials, however, pointed out that they already had stricter standards than the EPA proposal, and these would be pre-empted once the federal standard became final. 195/

In February 1982, EPA deferred the effective date of the standard (in concert with extension of the truck noise standard) from 1 January 1983 to 1 January 1986. 196/

7.5 Wheel and Crawler Tractors

Wheel and crawler tractors had been identified as a Section 5(b) major noise source on 28 May 1975. On 23 June 1977, EPA issued a proposed rulemaking on these construction vehicles. This contained the controversial requirement, as above, for an assurance period of five years. 197/ The Construction Industry Manufacturers Association (CIMA) objected to this feature and challenged the justi-fication for tractors' identification as a major noise source. 198/

In December 1982, the Reagan Administration issued a notice of intention to withdraw the proposed regulation. 199/

7.6 Buses

On 29 August 1977 EPA announced a proposed regulation on noise emissions, both interior and exterior, for buses weighing over ten thousand pounds. The limit of 83 dB(A) would take effect for new vehicles on 1 January 1979, then would be reduced to 80 dB(A) in 1983 and 77 dB(A) in 1985. Interior limits for the same period would be 83 dB(A) for 1983 and 80 dB(A) by 1985. School buses are included under this regulation. 200/

7.7 Snowmobiles

A more sensitive issue is the continuing debate over snow-mobiles. These undeniably noisy vehicles have strong political

---

195/   BNA, Noise Reporter, 24 October 1977, A-20.

196/   47 FR 7186, 17 February 1982.

197/   42 FR 35804, 11 July 1977.

198/   A similar legal challenge concerning power mowers is dis-cussed above at 7.3.

199/   47 FR 54108, 1 December 1982.

200/   42 FR 45776, 12 September 1972.

support in the northern states. This has hampered EPA's effort to impose a 78 dB(A) standard at open throttle, measured at 50 feet. At 15 miles per hour, the limit would be 73 dB(A). Snowmobile manufacturers contend that these levels are unnecessarily strict.

On 31 May 1977, EPA's Deputy Administrator Barbara Blum wrote thirty northern governors for advice on whether there should be legal noise regulations on snowmobiles, or merely informational labeling. The latter would have been useful for operators who are subjected to potentially hazardous levels of 90-100 dB(A), but it would not solve the extreme annoyance problem to others. For this reason, such states as New York and Minnesota have stricter standards than the federal proposal. The result of this EPA poll, however, revealed little consensus among "snowbelt" governors. 201/

7.8 Motorcycles

On 28 May 1975, EPA identified motorcycles as a major source of noise in the environment and began preparing noise emission regulations for new motorcycles and new motorcycle replacement exhaust systems distributed in commerce. 202/ On 15 March 1978, EPA proposed regulations which called for "an average 5 decibel reduction in new street motorcycle sound levels by 1985, and a 2 to 9 decibel reduction in sound levels of new offroad motorcycles." 203/ The proposal also included standards for replacement mufflers, which EPA hoped would reduce motorcycle noise "by eliminating the availability of ineffective motorcycle replacement exhaust systems." 204/

EPA also proposed prohibitions against tampering with or reducing the effectiveness of muffler systems. 205/ An amendment to prevent tampering with the noise system, proposed in December 1980, was withdrawn in December 1982. 206/

201/   BNA, Noise Reporter, 6 June 1977, A-19; Ibid., 1 August 1977, A-1.

202/   40 FR 23105, 28 May 1975.

203/   43 FR 10822, 15 March 1978.

204/   Ibid.

205/   Ibid.

206/   45 FR 86694, 31 December 1980; 47 FR 54110, 1 December 1982.

8.0 EPA Motor Carrier Regulations

EPA issued similar noise emission standards for motor carriers in October 1974. These provided that carriers in interstate commerce should be limited to 90 dB(A) over 35 mph, 86 dB(A) under that speed, and 88 dB(A) in a stationary high revving mode. (All these measurements were based on a distance of 50 feet.) This standard became effective, one year from publication, in October 1975. 207/ These regulations were the first issued by EPA under the Noise Act of 1972 to reach final status, enforceable as part of the noise law.

Once these standards had been issued, it was the responsibility under Section 18 of the Act for the Secretary of Transportation to issue regulations ensuring compliance with these standards. DOT proposed regulations at the end of February 1975, 208/ and on 20 September 1975 issued final regulations. 209/

8.1 EPA Noise Standard For Railroads

EPA proposed noise emission standards for railroads in July 1974. The noise limit for individual locomotives was set at 93 decibels and at 96 decibels for any combination of locomotives. The standard for railroad cars over 45 mph was also set at 93 dB(A), while for speeds below that a standard was proposed at 88 dB(A). (These measurements were to be made 100 feet from the center of the track.) The proposal also recommended that four years after the date of the final standard, the permissible noise level should decrease to 87 dB(A) for a single locomotive and 90 dB(A) for any combination of locomotives under moving conditions. The proposal exempted steam locomotives, most gas turbines and certain electric locomotives; but approximately 27,000 diesel, electric, road, and

---

207/   EPA, "Final Interstate Motor Carrier Regulations," 39 FR 38208, 21 October 1974.

208/   DOT, BMCs, "Proposed Regulations on Compliance with EPA Motor Carrier Noise Standards," 40 FR 8658, 28 February 1975.

209/   DOT, BMCs, "Final Regulations on Compliance with EPA Motor Carrier Noise Standards," 40 FR 42432, 20 September 1975.

switcher locomotives were covered. The proposal, furthermore, did not apply to warning devices such as horns or bells or to special purpose equipment such as cranes or mass transit systems. 210/

According to the statute, these proposed regulations by EPA were to be considered and promulgated by DOT within 90 days and would go into effect 270 days after publication. This timetable foundered, however, when the Department of Transportation strongly objected to many features of the EPA proposal. In its official response, DOT contended that the EPA proposal should have included recommendations for active and inert retarders, a limit of 70 dB(A) for mechanical refrigeration cars, and a 75 decibel limit on overall noise emissions during 90 percent of any 24-hour period by October 1978 and 70 decibels by October 1979.

The final rail carrier emission rule did not appear until January 1976, 18 months after the July 1974 proposal. For locomotives manufactured after 31 December 1979, the standard was set at 90 decibels for locomotives in motion and 87 decibels for those under stationary conditions. The requirement for mufflers applied only to these newer vehicles. Locomotives and railcars produced prior to that were required to follow the "best maintenance practice," described as 96 dB(A) for moving locomotives and 93 dB(A) for stationary ones. For railcars, this best maintenance practice meant 93 dB(A) over 45 miles per hour and 88 dB(A) under that speed.

Finally, the new regulation added a series of measurement criteria, such as ambient noise conditions and test specifications, in response to criticism that the measurement parameter in OSHA's July 1974 proposal could be distorted by a number of such extraneous factors. 211/

The EPA standards, however, left significant areas of railroad operation unregulated. Perhaps because of desire for federal preemption, the Association of American Railroads brought suit to require noise standards for these other areas also. On 23 August 1977 the Court of Appeals for the District of Columbia Circuit agreed, and ordered EPA within a year to propose additional railroad

---

210/ EPA, "Proposed Noise Emission Standard for Railroad Locomotives and Cars," 39 FR 24580, 3 July 1974.

211/ EPA, "Final Railroad Noise Emission Standard," 31 December 1975.

standards. 212/ The additional standards were not even proposed, however, until 17 April 1979. These proposed regulations state specific noise emission standards for facilities and equipment of the nation's interstate rail carriers. 213/

After EPA promulgated several standards, the parties agreed to dismiss on 12 November 1981. The Agency had meanwhile proposed other standards, including one for refrigeration cars and one on railroad property line determinations. In December 1982, these were withdrawn. 214/

Also on 23 August 1977 the Federal Railroad Administration (FRA) issued a final noise enforcement rule to implement EPA's existing noise standards on locomotives and railroad cars. 215/ The regulations, which had been proposed in November 1976, provided that locomotives produced after January 1979 should be limited to 90 dB(A) moving and 87 dB(A) stationary. 216/

EPA had proposed rules allowing states to assure certain responsibilities of a local nature. 217/ Only one locality ever requested consideration under these rules, however, and after seven years the Agency formally withdrew the proposal. 218/ A similar determination involving motor carriers was made at the same time. 219/

212/ Association of American Railroads v. Costle (CADC 1977) Docket No. 76-1353.

213/ 44 FR 22960, 17 April 1979.

214/ 47 FR 54107, 1 December 1982.

215/ 42 FR 42342, amending 49 CFR Part 210.

216/ BNA, Noise Reporter, 8 November 1976, A-15.

217/ 41 FR 52317, 29 November 1976.

218/ 47 FR 54313, 2 December 1982.

219/ Ibid.

Chapter 13

LAND USE: MAJOR ISSUES IN THE
CONTROL OF INDUSTRIAL DEVELOPMENT

Timothy A. Vanderver, Jr. and J. Gordon Arbuckle
Attorneys
Patton, Boggs & Blow
Washington, D.C.

1.0 Introduction

The critical questions in major facilities siting issues are
those concerning where a facility is to be located, how the requisite
government approvals are to be obtained, and who has the authority
to issue these approvals. When faced with the question of properly
locating a facility, the industrial planner's response might be that
plants should be built where they are most productive from an indus-
trial/economic point of view. Others, however, might respond that
plants should be built where they are least costly socially, environmentally and aesthetically. The function of land use law is to
provide a mechanism for intelligent resolution of this conflict—
achieving the optimum balance between productivity and environmental protection in its broadest sense. To provide such a mechanism, land use law must identify with specificity the approvals that
must be obtained, the proper authorities for granting these approvals, and the basis for grant or denial.

The framework which exists today is not reasonably calculated to perform these functions. Major facilities siting decisions
are more in the nature of endurance contests than orderly and expeditious administrative procedures. The result is unsatisfactory from
all viewpoints. Facilities will be located where they should not be—
if the opposition tires easily or runs out of resources—and they often

cannot be located where they should be—if local opposition is well funded, aggressive and unwilling to carry its share of the environmental burden.

Obtaining necessary governmental approvals today requires navigating a maze of exceedingly complex and often contradictory local, state and federal directives. The situation can be briefly summarized as follows. The local government ostensibly retains primary responsibility for questions of facility siting. However, local decisionmaking is constrained by a variety of state requirements. These include procedural and substantive legal requirements, and planning programs which may be directed specifically to land use or which may be a part of achieving more general objectives such as air or water pollution control.

The federal government has also intervened in facility siting in a number of ways. Although there are no general federal land use controls or planning, the federal government has encouraged state planning for specified areas (i.e., coastal zone planning) and required state planning and controls concerning land use in order to achieve other environmental objectives. The federal government also impacts on the siting process if specific authorizations, such as dredge and fill permits under Section 404 of the Clean Water Act, are required. Finally, in response to the patchwork situation which has developed, several federal statutes have been enacted during the past ten years to provide procedures for siting particular facilities.

One result of the present situation is that it is almost impossible to ascertain which governmental agency or agencies is responsible for determining whether a given facility should be located at a given site. Instead, the process has become one of seeking an apparently endless series of approvals; failure to obtain even one may jeopardize the project. Careful preparation, perseverance, and luck are necessary for successfully negotiating the numerous pitfalls. This is hardly a satisfactory situation.

The basis for these conclusions and the prospects for correcting present deficiencies are the subjects of this chapter.

2.0 Background and Nature of the Problem

Until quite recently, legal constraints on the use of private property for industrial purposes were relatively minimal. Private rights of action under the common law theories of "private nuisance" or "trespass" (see Chapter 1) have been relatively ineffective due to the difficulty in establishing standing to sue and the severe burden of proof imposed on plaintiffs seeking to demonstrate injury or unreasonable interference with "quiet enjoyment."   Government regulatory activities, in the form of "public nuisance" actions (see Chapter 1) or zoning laws, have been almost exclusively a function of local governmental entities and the emphasis has been on the prevention of public health hazards or property uses so incompatible with the established uses of other properties in the same locality as to adversely affect their <u>economic</u> value.

Thus, until the late fifties, control of land use and facilities siting was a purely local matter focused almost entirely on the maintenance of public health and the preservation and enhancement of economic values. Private rights, also defined almost entirely in terms of eminent hazards or economic values, were narrowly defined and difficult to enforce. An industry which was making, or promised to make, a significant contribution to the local economy normally would not have substantial problems with either the local regulators or private litigants as long as it did not create an imminent and substantial health hazard.

Since the late fifties, however, the dynamics of land use control have undergone a radical change. That change could be said to result from general acceptance of these basic premises:

- Economic development at a particular location is not <u>necessarily</u> beneficial; governmental authorities are therefore entitled to restrict or limit development based on broadly defined "public interests" in environmental and even aesthetic values.

- Localized development is not necessarily a matter of purely local concern, but one which may involve regional, state and national interests.

- A property owner does not have a virtually unlimited right to use his property as he pleases: governments and courts are far more willing to impose and uphold "reasonable" restraints on the use of property than was once the case. Further, the definition of what is a "reasonable" restraint has been broadened considerably.

Given acceptance of this basic attitude towards development, two things immediately occur. First, the number of issues which must be addressed and decided upon in any major facilities siting proposal increases exponentially. (E.g., in addition to simple questions such as, "Will it create a substantial health hazard?" or "Will it help the local economy?" numerous complex questions such as "How will it affect the quality of life?" arise and must be answered.) Second, the number of government agencies which must deal with these numerous issues also radically increases: siting decisions once made by the city council are now made by the council, the county and regional planning authorities, the state department of environmental protection, state wildlife and historic preservation officials, the Corps of Engineers, the Environmental Protection Agency, and others.

What emerges from this interplay between the numerous factual and policy issues and exercise of decisionmaking authority by agencies at all levels of government is not, and perhaps cannot be, a coherent body of substantive "Land Use" law. What we have now is bewildering complexity and confusion—where a multimillion dollar project can be defeated on seemingly inconsequential grounds. What we need, at the very least, is a regularized process or system for dealing with the complex interactions between laws and governmental entities which result in constraints on use and development of private property. To some extent, as we will see, there is hope that the necessary procedures will someday be statutorily provided. At present, however, and for the foreseeable future, the complex and difficult questions which arise in connection with major facilities siting decisions must be answered through the ingenuity of industrial planners and their counsel. In the following pages, we will attempt to outline the typical problems which must be faced in siting a major industrial facility and suggest a general approach for dealing with those problems.

3.0 Siting Problems

Table 13-1 provides a generalized matrix of typical decision points involved in any major new facility development or existing facility expansion. A similar, but more specific and more detailed table should be prepared by the facilities planner at the early stages of any development program and detailed assignments of responsibility for obtaining favorable decisions at each critical point should be made. In developing the approach for obtaining siting approval, and at every step along the way, the following general "maxims" should be given careful attention:

- Project approval is nearly impossible if there is strong opposition from the local governmental unit;

- Final disapproval, at any level of government (federal, state or local) can defeat the project; final approval—from all involved government units—will likely be required before the project may proceed;

- Land use decisions are as much social and political as they are legal—the reasons advanced in opposition to a project may be completely different from the opponent's actual reasons. It is important to identify and deal with the actual reasons whenever possible;

- Finally, and perhaps most important, history demonstrates that major, complex projects are often defeated on relatively inconsequential grounds. Thus the cardinal rule for facility siting is: never ignore any potential criticism, never cut any corner, and never fail to openly discuss the issues with all concerned parties.

With these factors in mind, let us proceed with a more detailed examination of the decision points outlined on the chart.

3.1 Local Issues

Authorizations required from local governmental units are still traditional in form—construction permits, zoning variances, sewer connection permits and so forth. However, there are two basic differences between the local authorization process which exists today and that which existed ten to fifteen years ago. First, decisions by local elected officials can no longer be based solely on the officials' perceptions of the needs of their constituencies, but may be constrained by applicable regional or local land use plans. Second, in view of state and federal involvement in the siting process, the locality's approval of a project will not, as might have been the case ten years ago, be the final word. That decision will be subject to review, scrutiny and possible reversal.

As previously indicated, the major development in the area of regional and local planning has been judicial recognition—in cases like Memphis v. Greene, 1/ Village of Belle Terre v. Boraas, 2/

1/   451 U.S. 100 (1981).

2/   416 U.S. 1 (1974).

Giuliano v. Town of Edgartown, 3/ and Golden v. Town of Ramapo 4/—that localities have great freedom to limit major development within their jurisdiction as long as limitations are imposed pursuant to a comprehensive and rational plan. As will be discussed below, the development of comprehensive planning at the local and regional level has been accelerated by federal planning assistance programs under legislation such as the Coastal Zone Management Act, the Clean Water Act, and the Housing and Community Development Act of 1974. As a result of these factors, local or regional planning can be expected to play an increasing role in foreclosing certain areas from industrial development. Though some efforts have been made to provide for administrative review of adverse local zoning decisions at the state level and there have been some successful challenges of restrictive zoning ordinances in state courts, we seem to be coming to the point where local disapproval of a project, particularly if that disapproval is based on some type of comprehensive plan, is almost invariably fatal to the project. Thus, strong opposition by the local governmental unit should give rise to thoughts of relocating any project which is not totally site dependent. Obtaining the local unit's approval and support should be perhaps the highest priority item in any siting project.

Though the local government's disapproval of a project tends to be irreversible, that rule, as previously indicated, does not hold true where the locality approves the project. Obtaining the requisite permits is only one aspect of the local level efforts in connection with major siting projects. The other task, which is nearly as important and often more difficult, is dealing with the local minority opposition. There likely will be such opposition—whether from oystermen who think their livelihood will be imperiled, the local retirement community which doesn't want the inflation that increased employment will bring, the nearby town that thinks its facilities will be overstressed by a population influx and so forth. When land use was purely a local concern, this kind of opposition would not have mattered as long as the local government issued the required approvals. Now there are so many forums where objections can be raised that any opposition can cause severe problems during

---

3/   531 F.Supp. 1076 (D. Mass. 1982).

4/   30 N.Y. 2d 359 (1972).

state and federal deliberations on the project. Thus, at the local authorization stage it is important not only to get the necessary approvals, but also to identify all of the sources of opposition and the "real" reasons for such opposition. Having identified and categorized the opposition, it is important, through full and meaningful communication, to alleviate their concerns insofar as possible.

Local opposition which cannot be neutralized at the local level will make itself felt in authorization procedures provided by state and federal statutes and it is at this point that the basis for opposition begins to be expressed almost exclusively in environmental terms.

3.2 State Law Requirements

Constraints imposed by state laws on the ability of local governments to authorize construction of facilities are both procedural and substantive in nature.

Procedural constraints are usually in the form of a state law, patterned after the National Environmental Policy Act (NEPA). These statutes typically require that the locality, in granting a construction permit or zoning variance or taking other action to authorize a significant project, prepare and process a detailed "Environmental Impact Report" (similar to an impact statement under NEPA). This report is commonly circulated through a "clearinghouse" procedure among all state and regional agencies which might have jurisdiction over the project. Properly handled, this procedure often becomes a way of coordinating the various exercises of state agency authority which are necessary to authorize the project.

The substantive constraints imposed by state statutes are almost infinitely variable. A few states have adopted major facilities siting laws which provide for permitting procedures based on review and regulation of the location and environmental effects, from air pollution to noise, of proposed new commercial and industrial developments. A larger number of states have adopted wetlands and shoreland protection legislation, which comes into play whenever development in coastal or riverside areas is involved. These statutes vary greatly in their regulatory requirements; it is a safe generalization, however, to note that they effectively prohibit or severely regulate potential projects that would be located in protected areas. Fish and wildlife protection, historic preservation and a broad range of other types of state programs, which may not immediately seem relevant, may also be of critical importance as, of course, will the state "categorical pollution" control laws—air, water and noise pollution. In short, any major project authorization may involve numerous separate authorizations and a detailed NEPA-type procedure at the state level. If the local opposition remains active, or if regional or national opposition materializes, each of these decision points could become a matter of great difficulty. The state legal-administrative framework must be a matter of major concern in analyzing the prospects of successful completion of any new facility development project.

In an effort to rationalize the confused situation at the state and local level, the American Law Institute has prepared a Model Land Development Code, which covers both land use planning and development controls. The MLDC integrates state and local powers with respect to development controls, but in general does not require planning as a prerequisite to controls. The basic thrust of the Code is to have local governments continue to control development with state intervention at selected points. The two categories in which state intervention is contemplated are Areas of Critical State Concern and Developments of Regional Impact (DRI) or Benefit (DRB).

The provisions concerning the Areas of Critical State Concern, which have been adopted by several states, assert a state interest in environmentally sensitive areas and in areas adjacent to major public facilities. The concept is to prevent local governments from permitting development in such areas that could lead to net negative impacts.

The DRI-DRB provisions are an attempt to elevate major decisions to the state level by providing for a state override of local decisions concerning significant developments. As contained in the Code, the DRI-DRB requirements are somewhat akin to those in NEPA since they require consideration of specified criteria in the decisionmaking process. The Code provides an appeals process for decisions with respect to DRI and DRB; basically, the standard is that any such development must be approved if authorized by the local ordinance and if probable net benefits exceed probable net detriments.

The MLDC is an effort to establish uniform land development controls, primarily at the local level. Insofar as major facilities siting is in issue, the importance of the Code lies not in the provisions concerning local controls nor in the number of states that have adopted it. The critical factor lies in the influence of the MLDC's state-level concepts—Areas of Critical State Concern and Developments of Regional Impact or Benefit. The former shows potential for preventing or delaying development in certain specified areas; the latter could be a means of overcoming local opposition to major projects. To the degree that these concepts gain acceptability, they will have a significant impact on major facilities siting. One way in which such acceptability could be achieved is through federal land use planning legislation (discussed below), since previous bills on this topic have relied heavily on these concepts.

3.3 State and Federal-State Planning

Virtually all of the local and state review, authorization and permitting provisions outlined above are overlaid by a variety of state and federal-state planning programs. Thus, the regulatory framework in most states is a combination between a permitting approach for specific facilities and a generalized planning approach for industrial development. Assurance of compliance with any applicable plans is normally a condition to any authorization to proceed with the project. Assessment of applicable plans is therefore important in the early stages of formulating any major project. Truly effective site development planning would entail the further step of actually participating in the development of plans for the area in which it is planned to locate.

As can readily be seen, state and federal-state planning efforts and development controls lack coherence, particularly as a result of attempting to serve varied and occasionally conflicting objectives. In an effort to remedy this defect, Congress has considered enacting a federal land use planning program several times. The most serious consideration was in 1974, when proposed legislation passed the Senate, but died in the House. This legislation would have established a program encouraging states to adopt a statewide or areawide planning process by use of positive and negative federal inducements. Although largely devoted to assuring the establishment of state land use planning processes, the bills would have required the consideration of certain issues in the process and the inclusion of certain items in the state plan.

General land use planning has been a dormant issue since 1974 as Congress has turned its attention to specific siting legislation, which is discussed in Part 5.0 of this chapter. Further, the present inclination against new federal programs involving grants to the states makes it unlikely that such legislation will be considered again in the near future. Thus, existing state and federal state planning programs will continue to be the key areas of focus for some time.

The general nature of existing planning requirements which may be of concern is as follows.

3.3.1 Statewide Land Use Planning

A few states have enacted generalized land use planning laws which provide for the establishment of regional development plans, designating areas of critical environmental concern, identifying areas which are and are not suitable for industrial development in an attempt to assure that facilities will not be located so as to violate applicable categorical pollution control laws and so forth.

3.3.2 Land Use Planning for Specific Areas

A somewhat larger number of states have adopted legislation providing for stringent planning and regulation of development in areas of particular environmental value—such as coastal areas, wetlands, and the Adirondacks region in New York. The planning and regulatory approach followed in these areas is, as might be expected, more rigorous and less hospitable to industry than the generalized plans discussed above.

The most significant and widespread state programs are those developed under the Federal Coastal Zone Management Act of 1972, which authorized a system of federal grants for developing and administering state coastal management programs. The Act established detailed procedures that must be followed in developing the management program: participation by relevant government agencies and interested groups, public hearings, the adoption of the governmental authority necessary to carry out the management program, and so forth. In addition, the Act requires that each management program include a number of specified elements, such as definition of what constitutes permissible land and water uses within the coastal zone.

Once a state's program has been approved, no federal agency may issue a license or a permit for any activity in the coastal zone unless the state acknowledges (or is presumed to acknowledge) that the proposed activity is consistent with its program.   Section 307(c)(3)(A). If a federal license or permit is required for a facility which may be located in the coastal zone, this provision will impose another potential obstacle. Further, the amount of time necessary for obtaining the state's acknowledgement of consistency will have to be factored into the planning for the facility.

One of the most significant issues concerning the coastal zone is the need for locating some types of energy development (e.g., offshore oil drilling) in or near these specially protected areas. The Supreme Court recently held that Department of the Interior sales of oil and gas leases on the outer continental shelf, but outside state waters, need not be certified by the affected state as being consistent with the state's coastal zone program. 5/ Exploration of and development on such leases must be consistent with the state's program however. Thus, although an affected state cannot play a significant role in OCS lease sales, it can affect lease development if such development would directly affect the coastal zone.

Congress also attempted to deal with the energy development issue by adding Section 308 to the Act in 1976. Section 308 established a coastal energy impact program to encourage planning for coastal energy activities. It also authorized a system of grants, loans and loan guarantees to enable states (1) to develop projects and programs which are necessitated by coastal energy activities and (2) to prevent or ameliorate loss of environmental or recreational resources which would be caused by such activities. Since most coastal states have developed the programs encouraged by Section 308, the federal role in the CEIP is being drastically reduced. The states will be required to bear an increasing share of the funding and administration of their programs.

Implementation of the Act is carried out by the coastal states, which include those bordering the Great Lakes. An example of the state legislation which has resulted is the California Coastal Act which has come to be regarded as a model for state implementation of the federal Act.

The California Act establishes a comprehensive scheme of planning and development controls for the coastal zone, which is defined as that area extending from the three-mile limit to a point generally one thousand yards inland of the mean high tide line. The zone may extend much farther inland in some areas and not as far in others. Development is defined quite broadly to include construc-

---

5/   Secretary of the Interior v. California, _U.S._, 104 S.Ct. 656 (1984).

tion, grading, dredging, disposal of any waste, changes in land use, and so forth.

A number of statutory goals govern the implementation of the Act. Perhaps the most important is the principle that conflicts in the planning and permitting process be resolved in a manner which is most protective of significant coastal resources. The Act does recognize that it may be necessary to locate certain industrial and energy facilities in the zone even though they may have adverse impacts on coastal resources. Preferential treatment is to be given to "coastal-dependent" industrial facilities and facility location or expansion at existing sites is encouraged.

Local governments are given primary planning responsibility for the coastal zone, subject to plan review by the regional coastal commissions and certification by the state commission. Once the local coastal program has been certified, the necessary coastal development permits will generally be issued by the local government subject to a limited right of appeal. Coastal development permits can be issued by a different mechanism pending certification of local programs.

The Act appears to have a number of worthwhile features. The statutory provisions which attempt to integrate the coastal zone program with other state and local authorities and, especially, the recognition that other needs may outweigh adverse environmental impacts are important. And the Act appears to take account of the need for development to a far greater extent than the virtual moratorium on major development that preceded its enactment.

3.3.3 Planning for Achievement of Categorical Pollution Control Objectives

In addition to the generalized land planning programs previously outlined, virtually all of the states, at the insistence of federal statutes, have specific programs directed towards achieving objectives of "categorical" pollution control laws like the Clean Air Act and the Clean Water Act. Achieving such objectives through land use controls is complicated by the fact that these objectives are very different from the ordinary objectives of the land use process. The result is that land use planning to attain these objectives, while effective from the narrow perspective of air and/or water quality improvement, does not assure that development occurs in a way that is wise or even environmentally sound.

Section 110(a)(2)(B) of the Clean Air Act originally mandated the use of "land use. . .controls" where necessary to achieve air

quality standards. Although that specific requirement was eliminated by the 1977 Amendments, it is evident that, in many respects,
the State Implementation Plan (SIP) under the Clean Air Act must
be a "land use plan." In particular, siting decisions will be substantially affected by the Act's requirements as to the prevention of
significant deterioration (PSD) and nonattainment areas.

The PSD provisions, which apply to those areas whose air
quality exceeds the national secondary standards, limit the increases
in pollutants in accordance with a statutory scheme for classifying
high air quality areas. In addition, every new "major emitting
facility" in an affected area must go through an extensive permitting process and obtain a permit which imposes a number of stringent conditions on the facility, including the use of best available
control technology and air quality monitoring programs. Finally,
protecting visibility in mandatory Class I federal areas is declared a
national goal. Obviously, these requirements may impose severe
restraints on siting facilities in areas covered by the PSD provisions.

The Act also contains provisions for those areas having air
pollutants which exceed any national ambient air quality standard.
Section 172 requires that SIPs for such nonattainment areas provide
for attainment of each national standard as expeditiously as practicable. In this regard, new facilities in nonattainment areas receive
detailed consideration. The Act provides that those states which
could not meet the primary standards for carbon monoxide or photochemical oxidants by 31 December 1982 would be required to establish a program which requires, prior to the issuance of permits for
new emitting facilities:

> an analysis of alternative sites, sizes, production
> processes and environmental control techniques for such
> proposed [facility] which demonstrates that benefits of
> the proposed [facility] significantly outweigh the envi-
> ronmental and social costs imposed as a result of its
> location, construction or modification.

Congress also mandated that, as of 1 July 1979, construction
of major new facilities which emit nonattainment pollutants be prohibited unless there is an EPA approved plan in place. SIPs for all
nonattainment areas must include a permit program for new facilities which is based on a source-by-source or areawide trade-off
policy. Unless pollution from existing sources is reduced sufficiently
so that total emissions (including emissions from the new facility)

are less than before, the new facility will not be permitted. Additionally, the new source must comply with the lowest achievable emission rate and meet certain other requirements.

Finally, federal agencies are prohibited from issuing permits, licenses or any form of assistance for any activity which does not conform to an approved SIP. For those facilities which fall within the nonattainment provisions—roughly those facilities which emit or have the potential to emit one hundred tons per year or more of any air pollutant—the procedures and strictures of the Act will significantly affect siting questions.

The Clean Water Act also has significant impacts on development decisions at the state and local level. The most important of the Act's planning provisions, at least in theory, is Section 208. As a consequence of a number of criticisms of the 208 program, Congress has not funded the program since fiscal year 1980.

Section 208 provides for the establishment of areawide waste treatment planning agencies for "areas which . . . have substantial water quality control problems." Once established, these areawide planning organizations are charged with broad responsibilities, including:

- Developing a plan for future construction of necessary waste treatment facilities;

- Establishing a program to regulate the location, modification and construction of "any facilities" within the area which may result in waste discharges;

- Developing a process to identify various nonpoint sources of pollution, including "land use requirements" to control such sources to the extent feasible; and

- Developing a process to control underground and on land waste disposal.

At the time the plan is approved by the state governor, he designates a management agency or agencies to be responsible for implementing the plan. Where no planning agency has been designated, the state has the responsibility for developing and implementing plans for the non-designated area.

Section 208 is somewhat unique in that the contemplated result is not only a comprehensive plan, but also an identified method to enforce compliance with the plan and a designated agency responsible for that enforcement.   Nevertheless, the coordinated planning approach of Section 208 has not worked out as anticipated. In the last few years, funding that could have been utilized for 208 planning has been directed to the water quality management plan grants (Section 205) and the pollution control programs of Section 106.   These, together with a number of other planning provisions (Section 303 dealing with Water Quality Implementation Plans, Section 209—Basin Planning, Section 314—Clean Lakes and, indeed, Section 402—the NPDES program itself), will have a substantial impact on planning decisions.

EPA's efforts to prevent the degradation of waters whose quality is better than required by existing standards may also affect industrial facilities siting.   Under EPA's "antidegradation" guidelines, a state must develop an antidegradation policy and methods for implementing the policy.   Some long term degradation of high quality waters, other than those which constitute an "outstanding natural resource," may be permitted; EPA's guidelines would permit a state to allow limited degradation where economically or socially justified.   The policy is being implemented through water quality plans and may also be effectuated through the NPDES program.

Another "categorical" pollution control law which could have some direct impact on land use decisions is the Noise Control Act of 1972.   While there are no specific SIP requirements in that Act, it does provide for the establishment by EPA of criteria on the effects of noise on the public health and welfare and on available noise control techniques.   A few states have adopted laws in the nature of implementation plans, but without any direct EPA involvement, providing for enforcement of ambient noise criteria on an area-by-area basis.   They should be considered at early stages of any major siting project.

3.3.4 Other Planning Requirements

There are, of course, numerous other federal and federal-state planning programs ranging from Uniform Relocation Act requirements to Housing and Community Development Act planning grants to flood plain development restrictions, which could have a significant impact on a particular siting proposal.   Proposals to site projects on federally owned lands must comply with the land use planning requirements of the Federal Land Policy and Management Act of 1976.   Again, it is important in the beginning stages of any

major siting proposal to find out what plans are applicable, determine how they might affect the project, and consider how the project might be structured or pursued to avoid or cope with a major
problem area.

To summarize this discussion of the existing planning programs, it is fair to say that the present situation is one of overlap
and contradiction where it is difficult to determine which plans
might be applicable—much less what they require. The involved
agencies have made some effort to coordinate the planning programs
under their jurisdictions, but there is still a long way to go. In the
continuing absence of any national land use policy, a coordinated
approach to federal planning programs will be a long and arduous
process, but there does seem to be at least some hope for some
future element of rationality arising out of the present state of
confusion.

3.4 Specific Federal Authorizations

The final stage of the siting process is the issuance of any
specific federal authorizations and permits required for construction
and operation of the facility. There will be some projects where no
specific federal permit is required. Other projects may require
eight or ten permits from as many different federal agencies. It is,
of course, important at the very outset of any project to know what
federal permits will be required and whether the issuance of any of
those permits will constitute a "major federal action." Amazingly,
however, many companies attempt to shortcut the painstaking
analysis required to obtain such knowledge and, as a result, either
apply for permits they do not really need or fail to plan for permits
that they really do need. This should not happen with proper management and planning.

Obtaining a federal permit or authorization will require satis-
faction of a number of environmental requirements. The broadest in
scope is NEPA, which is discussed below. The Fish and Wildlife
Coordination Act may require the authorizing agency to coordinate
with the United States Fish and Wildlife Service (USFWS) before
taking action. Although other agencies are not required to adopt
USFWS recommendations that permits or authorizations not be
issued because of potential adverse effects on flora and fauna, such
a recommendation will lead to processing delays at the very minimum. Further, some agencies, such as the Corps of Engineers, are
strongly suggesting that applicants work out any potential problems

with the USFWS before processing begins so that effects on flora and fauna must be taken into account if the Coordination Act is applicable.

The Endangered Species Act of 1973 is having an increasing impact on federal action in this area. In order to implement the Act's goal of protecting and preserving endangered species of animals, birds, fish and plants, the USFWS has promulgated regulations governing any federal action, including permits and authorizations, that have the potential to adversely affect an endangered species or its critical habitat. If the USFWS finds, after consulting with the action agency and conducting biological studies, that such an adverse effect is probable, the proposed federal action will almost certainly be disapproved. Due to widespread dissatisfaction with the operation of the Act, it was amended in 1978 to provide for a procedure for reviewing projects which would otherwise be prohibited because of their adverse effects on an endangered species. If this review reveals that the project meets the rigorous standard for granting an exemption, the project will be permitted in spite of its adverse effects on an endangered species or habitat. The Act was further amended in 1982 to expedite the exemption procedure. Regulatory changes to implement the new exemption have been proposed, 6/ but not finalized. Nevertheless, as a general rule, the creation of an adverse effect on an endangered species or its habitat will probably be fatal to the project. Only if the project can be modified to eliminate the adverse effect or relocated to another site will there be any substantial chance of overcoming a finding of probable adverse effect.

NEPA will be involved if issuance of an authorization or a permit constitutes a major federal action. At present, the federal statutes which seem to be most productive of federal authorization requirements that result in NEPA applicability in the generalized industrial siting context are Section 10 of the Rivers and Harbors Act of 1899, which requires a Corps of Engineers permit for building structures or conducting excavation in "navigable waters of the United States," Section 404 of the Clean Water Act, which gives the Corps and EPA authority over the placement of dredged or fill material in any waters of the United States (see Chapter 10) and the wastewater discharge permit program (the NPDES program) under

---

6/   48 FR 52099 (16 November 1983).

the Clean Water Act, which provides that NEPA is applicable to the issuance of permits for "new sources" as defined in the Act. However, other federal authorizations (e.g., Treasury permits for wineries and breweries) required for specific types of facilities, though seemingly inconsequential, may be sufficient to trigger NEPA and involve all of the environmentally oriented agencies, as well as the general public, in the authorization process.

Once the task of identifying the authorizations required and the federal agencies involved is accomplished, there are a number of options for structuring the review process which deserve careful consideration and which might be suggested to the reviewing agencies. In evaluating these options, it should be recognized that there should be a great deal of room left for the development of creative and innovative procedures to minimize duplication and wasted effort without prejudice to the effectiveness of the review process. The major approaches are as follows.

3.4.1 Lead Agency Proceedings

A well-recognized method of preventing unnecessary duplication in situations involving multiple agencies and multiple instances of NEPA applicability is the procedure prescribed by the Council on Environmental Quality (CEQ) regulations in which one involved agency is designated as the "lead agency" and pulls the laboring oar in a single coordinated review proceeding under NEPA. In lead agency proceedings, it is important to assure that there is early agreement on major issues such as the extent of each agency's involvement, the scope of the required impact statement, the timing of agency inputs and so forth. In projects of major scope and complexity, a memorandum of understanding between the concerned agencies may be an appropriate mechanism for achieving such agreement.

3.4.2 Federal-State Coordination

Though less fully explored, there would seem to be considerable potential for reducing duplication between federal NEPA proceedings and proceedings under state and environmental protection or siting laws. In the past, a few federal-state task forces were established to consider regional impacts of critically needed major facilities. State environmental protection acts sometimes provide for acceptance of federal impact statements in fulfillment of state assessment requirements and, in a few instances, federal agencies

have accepted comprehensive state assessments as a basis for finding that further review at the federal level was not required.

Federal-state coordination in connection with environmental
issues has been given a strong boost by the CEQ regulations. In
40 CFR Section 1506.2(b), federal agencies are directed to cooperate with state and local agencies to the fullest extent possible,
unless specifically barred from doing so by some other law. Such
cooperation is to include joint planning, research, public hearings
and environmental assessments.   In addition, 40 CFR Section
1506.2(c) directs federal agencies—again to the fullest extent possible—to reduce duplication between NEPA and comparable state and
local requirements and to prepare joint environmental impact statements. These directives should reduce duplication of effort in complying with NEPA and state environmental quality review statutes,
and lead to a reduction in time delays.

3.4.3 "Third Party" Contracts

A third innovative approach, which has been utilized by some
of the EPA regional offices, is to have environmental assessments
prepared by totally independent contractors paid by the applicant
but supervised by EPA. This approach, which of course requires the
applicant's agreement, can radically telescope the usual two step
procedure of having an environmental report prepared by the applicant and then having much of that report redone in the preparation
of an independent environmental impact statement by the authorizing agency. In addition to telescoping the time period, this "third
party" approach should offer significant advantages from the viewpoint of sustaining the final statement on judicial review.

3.4.4 Legislated Procedures

In truly major siting questions involving facilities of critical
national concern (e.g., the Alaska Pipeline, offshore oil ports, deep
seabed mining) there may be the possibility of legislative action
(similar to the Deepwater Port Act discussed below) to structure and
control the review procedures on the project. This is, of course, a
difficult and sometimes dangerous approach but one which does
merit consideration where serious problems are anticipated.

4.0 Approach Under Existing Law

Though the decisionmaking process which we have described
is highly complex and exceedingly unpredictable, it is possible to

outline a general approach to siting problems which can work, given extreme care and attention and at least moderately good luck. The basic elements of this approach are as follows.

4.1 Participate in the Land Use Planning Process

As a long range planning and development approach, it <u>does</u> make sense to participate, actively, either directly or through trade or business associations, in states and localities where it may be desirable to locate. Plans being developed today will impact siting decisions for many years in the future and, unless industry participates, the planning function will be done entirely by governments and environmentally concerned citizens.

4.2 Select Sites and Formulate Plans Based on a Detailed Understanding of the Siting Process

The site (or preferably alternative sites) should be selected and development plans formulated based on a detailed analysis and understanding of the legal and, at least to some extent, of the political environment in which important decisions will be made. This requires:

- Thorough analysis of likely local opinion, sources and reasons for opposition and so forth;
- Identification and analysis of all applicable land use plans and zoning requirements based thereon;
- Identification and analysis of all requirements for authorizations at local, state and federal levels and NEPA or SEPA applicability thereto.

4.3 Structure the Procedure and Climate in Which the Siting Decision Will Be Made

The following general guidelines are usually applicable:

- Keep local decisionmaking as separate as possible from procedural strictures which arise at the state and federal levels, and get the necessary local approvals as early in the game as possible. It is possible and necessary at the local level to deal with the real reasons for opposition and that may be difficult in the context of an environmental review proceeding;
- Use lead agency or clearing-house procedures under NEPA, SEPAs or general state siting laws to coordi-

nate the exercise of multiagency jurisdiction and to
insure that, at most, the applicant is faced with one
federal EIS and one state EIR;

- Consider more innovative coordination procedures to
further diminish the problems of duplication of effort
and jurisdiction.

4.4 File the Applications

As noted previously, numerous authorizations may be required
at the federal and state levels. However, given success in structuring the procedures, there should, at least at the federal level, be
only <u>one</u> environmental assessment and that assessment should be
considered in a single coordinated review procedure.

For major projects, the basic rule is:

DO NOT STINT ON THE ENVIRONMENTAL
ASSESSMENT DOCUMENT

It is the applicant's basic weapon and also his basic defense.
Opponents can be counted on to be super critical and if they can find
something significant that the applicant and the responsible agency
did not consider, they will get their injunction and delay the project.
If, on the other hand, the applicant has prepared an adequate assessment and considered all significant potential impacts and alternative
approaches, he should prevail as long as the reviewing agencies do
their job.

4.5 Make the Reviewing Agencies Do It Right

The major reason for successful challenges of facilities
authorization procedures is the failure of the reviewing agency to do
its job. Thus, though there is a major temptation to let the agency
cut corners if it is going to issue the required authorization, that
temptation should be resisted and the following should definitely be
assured:

- The agency must base its draft EIS on its own independent review and there must be a record to show
that it has done so.

- The draft must be adequately circulated and the
public given an adequate opportunity to comment.
The CEQ regulations for processing impact statements <u>must</u> be strictly complied with.

- Issues not addressed in the agency's draft EIS may properly be covered in the public hearings. Comments should be designed to insure that the record is complete.

Through close and careful monitoring of the agency's review process, it should be possible to minimize the risk of bureaucratic oversight and thus assure that the authorization to proceed, once granted, will not be taken away by a court injunction.

4.6 Make Sure That Actual Construction Is in Accordance With Your Authorization and the Final EIS

Despite the fact that the authorization is in hand, there still can be problems if the applicant fails to meet its commitments regarding mitigation of environmental harm or if new grounds for contest are discovered. Thus, the communication, conciliation and general good-neighbor approach should be continued throughout and beyond the construction process and care should be taken to notify and discuss with the cognizant agencies all significant changes in the construction plan.

5.0 Prospects For Change: Specific Siting Legislation

Though the approach outlined above may maximize the chances of success in particular siting propositions, the existing legal framework is inadequate and unnecessarily burdensome and some essential facilities simply cannot be timely authorized within that framework. As noted above, Congress has not seriously considered national land use planning legislation recently. Instead, the focus of Congressional concern with the major facilities siting issue has been process-oriented legislation which establishes detailed procedures for expedited decisions on the siting of a key facility or category of facility.

Examples of process-oriented statutes include the Trans-Alaska Pipeline Authorization Act, the Alaska Natural Gas Transportation Act, the Deepwater Port Act, and the Deep Seabed Hard Mineral Resources Act. Differing situations have led to different legislative approaches: the TAPS Act statutorily mandated the location of the Alyeska pipeline system while most siting legislation focuses on establishing authorization procedures.

5.1 The Deepwater Port Example

The Deepwater Port Act which became law on 3 January 1975 is perhaps the best example of this type of legislation. It is a response to perceived problems in the siting process for a unique and critically needed type of facility—offshore ports capable of handling supertanker oil shipments—and its major focus is on the procedures for authorization of those facilities. Thus, in many respects, the Act is an experiment to determine whether we can develop procedures which provide for adequate consideration of all potential adverse effects of a project while, at the same time, acceptably dealing with the problems of multiple jurisdictions, overlapping authorities, uncertainties and interminable delays which have to date caused difficulties in major facilities siting proceedings. The experiment involves the following elements.

5.1.1 Time Limitation

In perhaps its most direct attack on previous siting problems, the Act imposes a definite time limit for the completion of each step in the review process. Within twenty-one days from the filing of an application under the Act, the Secretary must make a finding as to whether the application is "complete." Five days after that determination, a notice must be published in the Federal Register and the time clock established by the Act starts to run. Theoretically, the required impact statement must be prepared and processed and a final decision on the application reached 330 days after that publication.

5.1.2 Single Coordinated Procedure

Less direct, but perhaps even more revolutionary than the Act's time limit, is its so called "single window" approach for coordinating the federal involvement and, to some extent, the state involvement in the siting and overall review process for deepwater ports. This "single window" approach is basically an elaboration of the "lead agency" approach which has been widely accepted as a way of complying with NEPA requirements in situations where multiple permits or authorizations from several federal agencies are required.

The operative provisions of the Act are Section 5(e)(2), which provides that an application filed thereunder

> shall constitute an application for all federal authorizations required for ownership, construction and operation of a deepwater port,

and Section 4(b), which authorizes the Secretary

> . . .upon application and in accordance with the provisions of this Act, to issue. . .a license for the ownership, construction and operation of a deepwater port.

These provisions appear to make it clear that what goes into the "single-window" is one consolidated application and what comes out 356 days later is all federal authorizations required for construction and operation of the port.

The Act attempts to spell out a detailed system for coordinating the inputs of the concerned federal agencies, the public and the states during that 356-day period. It provides for at least one consolidated informal public hearing in the state or states most directly affected and, if necessary to resolve the issues, for a single formal administrative hearing to be held in Washington. It spells out who can and who cannot veto the project (DOT, EPA and "adjacent coastal states" can; others cannot). It establishes specific consultative functions for some agencies, specifically outlines the factors to be considered and the findings to be made in the issuance of a license and, in general, does much to avoid the seemingly limitless uncertainties as to who has jurisdiction, what procedures must be followed, what authorizations are required and so forth, which have made major facilities siting such a difficult proposition.

5.1.3 One Environmental Impact Statement Based on Identified Criteria

The drafters of the Deepwater Port Act were concerned over the possibility that the involvement of numerous agencies at various stages in the authorization process might be characterized as discrete "major federal actions" giving rise to the need for filing and processing a number of impact statements on a single deepwater port. They sought to eliminate this possibility by providing, in Section 5(f) of the Act, that

> For all timely applications covering a single application area, the Secretary, in cooperation with other involved Federal agencies and departments, shall . . . prepare a single, detailed environmental impact statement, which shall fulfill the requirement of all Federal agencies in carrying out their responsibilities pursuant to this Act to prepare an environmental impact statement.

In addition, the Congress made at least a tentative gesture at resolving one of the major problems of the NEPA impact statement process—the lack of certainty as to the factors which must be "considered" in the review process. It did this by providing, in Section 6 of the Act, for the establishment by the Secretary of "environmental review criteria," consistent with NEPA, to be "used to evaluate a deepwater port" and "considered" in the preparation of the impact statement required by Section 5.

The basic intent of these provisions is to simplify the NEPA process and minimize the threat of litigation based on failure to consider impacts or alternatives by identifying at the outset all factors required to be considered in the NEPA process. This is an exceedingly appealing idea and one which could be very beneficial. Unfortunately, the legislation does not spell it out with the detail and clarity required in order to comfortably rely on these criteria in the preparation of the environmental assessment or impact statement. The Coast Guard, therefore, took a compromise approach. It published general environmental review criteria which do not purport to be an exhaustive catalog of factors to be considered in an EIS and supplemented those criteria with Guidelines for Preparation of Environmental Assessments identifying in exhaustive detail the information to be supplied by applicants to serve as a basis for the Coast Guard's independent preparation of an EIS on the project. Both the environmental review criteria and the guidelines were subjected to extensive public comment procedures, and, as long as the criteria and guidelines are utilized carefully, there should be no surprises on what either is or is not considered in an EIS on a deepwater port. This careful process of identifying in advance the data to be considered and criteria to be applied should do much to convince any reviewer that the agency has properly fulfilled its responsibility under NEPA.

The three major Deepwater Port Act initiatives outlined above seem to offer a way out of the existing "endurance contest" theory of site authorization proceedings without sacrificing the basic objective of insuring that essential facilities will be constructed and located based on full consideration of impacts and alternatives and in the least objectionable way possible. However, lest the reader be left the impression that specific siting legislation like the Deepwater Port Act is clearly the answer, the problems of the deepwater port experiment must be considered.

5.2 Problems With the Deepwater Port Act Approach

5.2.1 Specific Legislation Begets Stringent Criteria

In today's legislative climate, a new law to control the development of particular types of facilities is an invitation for lawmakers to impose requirements on facilities to insure safety, environmental acceptability and other benefits. Thus, the licensing process for deepwater ports entails items such as an antitrust review, obligations to tear the facility up and take it away after operations are terminated, a best available technology demonstration, stringent construction standards and operating procedures and so forth. All these requirements are far more stringent than those which might have been applicable if it had been possible to get a port authorized without specific siting legislation.

The strict legislative criteria have been paralleled by an administrative tendency to look more carefully at and impose stricter requirements on deepwater ports than would probably have been done in the absence of specific legislation. For example, the antitrust review led to ownership and operational limitations that are far more restrictive than those imposed on other transportation facilities. These legislative and administrative tendencies should be carefully analyzed by any industry which is likely to become involved in facilities siting legislation proposals. Indeed, these tendencies, unless checked, may prevent widespread use of such legislation as a means of solving siting issues.

5.2.2 "Time Limits" Can Be Illusory

Laws which establish definite timetables for agency action, though rare at the federal level, are not uncommon in the states, and many have found that those time limits are more apparent than real. There is a definite risk of similar problems under federal laws such as the Deepwater Port Act—for example, the regulations provide for stopping the clock when additional information is requested but not forthcoming—and the question of whether the timetable can be enforced is one which is critical to the success of the deepwater port type procedure. The initial deepwater port licenses were issued on schedule, a fact which bodes well for future "time limited" procedures.

5.2.3 It Is Difficult to Enforce the "One Window" Concept

The job of getting fifteen or twenty federal agencies to follow the lead agency in exercising their jurisdiction is not an easy one and a breakdown of the "One Window" authorization process would effectively eliminate the beneficial aspects of the Act. "One Window" did work for the initial deepwater port licenses but this is not a basis for assuming that, without careful attention, it will work equally well for other projects.

5.2.4 The "One Environmental Impact Statement" Concept Failed

When it enacted Section 5(f) of the Act, the Congress neglected to say that when it said "one impact statement" it meant one impact statement. Thus, in addition to the impact statement which the Department of the Interior filed when the Administration proposed the legislation, there was an impact statement on the DOT regulations and an impact statement on the licensing process.

The "Identified Criteria" aspect of the bill's approach to impact statements worked reasonably well for the first two license applications. It appears to be a promising approach.

5.3 The Future of the Deepwater Port Approach

Though the Deepwater Port Act experiment has to date been at least a qualified success, it is not a panacea. This conclusion is confirmed by the experience of the first two applications processed under the Act. One applicant accepted a license, constructed the port, and commenced operations; the other declined the license and withdrew from the project. The latter result is largely attributable to requirements imposed as a consequence of the specified statutory procedures.

For the sake of the integrity of future siting procedures, it is hoped that the Deepwater Port Act and subsequent legislation patterned on the example of that Act (such as the Deep Seabed Hard Mineral Resources Act) achieve their purpose fully and gain broad acceptance. The present approach to siting major industrial facilities is deficient and alternatives must be developed. Most of the deficiencies in the deepwater port licensing procedures, as well as those which are developing under ANGTA, may well be attributable to poor legislative drafting and might well be avoided in the future. However, there may not be further opportunities to try the legislated procedures approach unless at least qualified success is achieved in these initial efforts. Thus, both environmentalists and industry have a stake in making certain that these particular siting proceedings result in correct decisions arrived at in an orderly manner based on the right reasons.

If these experiments are successful, we may see their example followed in other critical and site dependent areas such as energy facilities siting and minerals extraction. For certain types of facilities, this approach is the most promising way out of the current siting dilemma.

6.0 Conclusion

While there is some hope that things will get slightly better in the future, the job of coordinating the effort to obtain the necessary authorizations for a new facility will continue to be a difficult one. If industry is to improve its success rate in the facilities siting area, it must recognize that the siting approval process requires at least the same level of careful and specific planning, detailed assignments of responsibility and attention to detail which is customary in closing a major merger or orchestrating a take-over bid. It is hoped that the information provided in this chapter will contribute to an understanding of the problems involved and thereby decrease the number of projects which are halted or substantially delayed due to a failure to cope in a timely way with environmentally-based objections.

Table 13-1

Decision Matrix: Environmentally Related Constraints on Construction or Expansion of Major Industrial Facilities

Decision Levels	Decision Points	Factors to be Considered in Risk Analysis	Comments on Strategic Considerations
I. Local Property Owners.	Acquisition of proposed site or firm options thereon.	Resistance to selling and higher prices if proposed use is disclosed. Resentment and possible efforts to set aside sale or option if proposed use is not disclosed.	From the viewpoint of overcoming environmental objections, it is generally best to make full disclosure of intentions at the earliest practicable date. The competing risks of price escalation and resistance to selling may be minimized by preserving site alternatives as long as possible. In circumstances where the proposed use is for a purpose such as power generation, corsideration may be given to enlisting governmental aid in site acquisition process.
II. Local Government.	Permit Issuance (Construction, Conditional Use, Sewer Hookup, etc.).	Any applicable state "little NEPA," coastal zone mangement or land use laws. Any applicable local or regional land use plans.	Local level decisionmaking is, in most instances, still primarily political. However, state NEPA or state land use planning laws may impose constraints on purely political decisions.

Table 13-1 (continued)

Decision Levels	Decision Points	Factors to be Considered in Risk Analysis	Comments on Strategic Considerations
	Zoning or Zoning Variances. Taxation and Infrastructure.	Any federal involvement in funding infrastructure which triggers NEPA. Any local political opposition to project.	Environmental concerns make all potential opposition dangerous both in terms of political impact and potential litigation. Thus, all vocal opposition groups should be identified and, if possible, neutralized. Again, the local climate will likely be enhanced if alternative site options remain viable throughout the decision-making process.
III. State and Regional Bodies.	Any required approvals under coastal zone management or land use legislation or review responsibilities under state "little NEPAs." Any required state permit for construction or operation.	Public hearing procedures at state or regional level may be required in connection with coastal zone or land use approvals. Public hearing procedures are also required in connection with NPDES permit issuance.	Except for truly major projects, state decisions will normally be made by administrative rather than elected officials. Environmentalist opposition, especially from local residents, will nevertheless have a strong influence on this decision-making process. As with the previous decision levels, the presentation of several environmentally justifiable site alternatives will minimize the risk of decisions fatal to the project.

Table 13-1 (continued)

Decision Levels	Decision Points	Factors to be Considered in Risk Analysis	Comments on Strategic Considerations
	Any required state permit certification or approval under NPDES (where the state is the issuing authority) or Clean Air Act implementation plans.	State permits under federal programs may be subject to federal veto, review and/or approval.	
		State decisions may be subject to "little NEPA" requirements.	
	Any assurance of compliance with state noise-control laws.	If federal funding is involved in the project, NEPA itself may apply.	
		Adjacent states may have the right to object if their interests are affected.	
IV. Federal Government.	Any required federal permit or authorization (FERC, ICC, Corps of Engineers, etc.)	NEPA applicability.	With limited exceptions, any federal involvement in the decision-making process will trigger NEPA and the detailed deliberative process which it entails (see Chapter 9).
	Any federal funding participation.	Other precise risks are dependent on the nature of the federal authorization required.	
	Any Clean Air Act review or NPDES permit.		

Table 13-1 (continued)

Decision Levels	Decision Points	Factors to be Considered in Risk Analysis	Comments on Strategic Considerations
V. The Courts.	Common law nuisance or tres- pass litigation.	(See Chapter 1).	The threat of litigation lurks in the background at virtually every decision-making level. Thus, in major site development or facili- ties expansion plans, all strategic decisions should be made based on full understanding of the impli- cations of such decisions if and when the case comes to court.
	NEPA litigation.	(See Chapter 9).	
	Citizen's suits under the Clean Water Act or the Clean Air Act.	(See Chapters 7 and 6).	
	Citizen's suits under state statutes.		

Chapter 14

ENFORCEMENT AND LIABILITIES

Michael A. Brown 1/
Attorney
Schmeltzer, Aptaker & Sheppard
Washington, D.C.

1.0 Realities: Multiple Actions

The purpose of this chapter is to place the enforceable requirements of the many different laws and regulations that have been discussed in the preceding chapters in perspective with the realities of the world in which companies must do business. Rarely do acts by individuals or companies that allegedly violate environmental laws result in reaction by only one governmental body under a single provision of one statute. Today's climate of awareness of problems that may affect the environment has resulted in a cast of actors in environmental enforcement that is far greater than may be visible through merely reading a single applicable statute.

This chapter is divided into sections that discuss the liabilities that may arise from government action and sections that discuss potential liabilities from private action. Those categories are further divided between federal and state action and action by private parties based upon federal or state laws. As will be seen, any or all of these actions in various combinations may result from a single alleged violation.

1/ Former Enforcement Counsel, U.S. Environmental Protection Agency.

2.0 Government Enforcement and Liabilities

Enforcement by governmental bodies may be undertaken by agencies of federal, state, regional or local governments. Federal environmental laws are generally organized around the idea that federal laws and regulations may be delegated to the states or other local bodies for enforcement. In some cases this results in two sets of laws or regulations (federal and state) and in other cases, states or localities may enforce their own laws or regulations. Unlike some other areas of federal law, more stringent state or local requirements are usually allowed by federal environmental laws. This means that a proper awareness of the requirements imposed on any individual or business can be achieved only by ensuring that all levels of governmental regulation have been identified.

2.1 Federal Enforcement Organizations and Strategies

The enforcement scheme for federal laws is set by the United States Environmental Protection Agency (EPA). In cases where the laws must be enforced in a federal court, these matters are usually handled by the United States Department of Justice. This is an important point to remember because the number of parties with whom negotiations must be conducted and the number of clearance levels that are required generally doubles if negotiations with EPA are not successful. Once EPA refers the matter to the Department of Justice, you no longer may deal with EPA alone. Instead you must deal with both EPA and the Department of Justice.

The overall approach to enforcement currently used by EPA is to measure compliance with laws and regulations under each of the laws it administers and determine the instances of "significant noncompliance." Profiles of "significant violators" are developed for use by EPA regional offices. The theory is that when a violation is discovered that fits the profile, action must be taken by the regional office to return that violator to complying status. In determining a "profile" EPA considers such factors as the size of the violator, the duration of the violation, the frequency of violations and severity of exposure from the violation. The regional office must report its progress in returning the violator to compliance. EPA headquarters monitors the progress of achieving compliance and provides assistance, where necessary.

This policy encourages the use of means such as persuasion, administrative action and other alternatives before resorting to a court for formal, judicial action. This is a change from the past when EPA enforcement accomplishments were measured by the number of cases referred by EPA to the Department of Justice for judicial action. The current stated policy is directed at achieving compliance at the lowest possible level and measuring enforcement effectiveness by compliance achieved as opposed to judicial cases referred. This policy is relatively new and it is too early to say that EPA will apply it in a uniform manner, particularly in matters that are the subject of great public concern or Congressional interest.

The ability to measure compliance by means other than counting cases referred by EPA to the Department of Justice for judicial action is complicated and time consuming. Historically, EPA has not been very courageous when demands for quick action are made. An expedient means of demonstrating enforcement action is by counting "beans" such as cases referred to the Department of Justice. This is understandable because this provides a more simplistic measure of progress and does not require the more complicated explanation of other activities that may be at various stages of implementation and may not have achieved compliance at the time a count is made. Unfortunately, despite all its protestations that its current policy will be measured by means other than "bean" counts, the recent press releases and press conferences held by EPA officials to announce an even higher quantity of cases referred to the Department of Justice show actions by EPA that appear to be contrary to its newly-stated policy.

Another problem in dealing with the federal government in enforcement matters is that the EPA is not a monolithic organization with centralized enforcement. Enforcement policy, goals and measurement standards originate in EPA headquarters in the program offices charged with administering the different environmental statutes. Once such goals are established they must be coordinated with the legally-oriented Office of Enforcement and Compliance Monitoring which oversees the general enforcement goals of the agency. In turn, this guidance is distributed to the ten EPA regional offices. These regional offices are organized with enforcement lawyers in a single Office of Regional Counsel but the program-oriented enforcement personnel are in different program specific offices. In most cases, the investigative personnel in a region are under the jurisdiction of a third office. Therefore, to achieve coordinated enforcement in an EPA regional office requires close cooperation between at least three offices. To achieve that same coordination nationally involves all ten EPA regions successfully coordinating between at least three separate offices per region plus close coordination in EPA headquarters.

The foregoing explanation is not provided merely to explain the management problems encountered by EPA in enforcing the laws it administers but to illustrate the problems that companies dealing with EPA can expect to face in attempting to get clear interpretations of their obligations under the law or in settling matters before the agency. It is a problem for businesses operating nationally when similar activities in different parts of the country are treated differently. However, the complex enforcement scheme at EPA can lead to this result.

Another complicating factor in ensuring a uniform national approach to federal enforcement is that the evaluation of the merits of a case or the priorities for action on that case may vary between the Environmental Protection Agency, the Department of Justice and the U.S. Attorney (who is the local representative for the U.S. Department of Justice). The Department of Justice or the local U.S. Attorney are not always involved in a matter when it is being developed at a regional level. Discussions with the company involved and enforcement positions of EPA are not necessarily coordinated with the Department of Justice or the appropriate U. S. Attorney until after a case is referred. This can result in one position on a matter being taken by EPA and another by the Department of Justice. Therefore, dealings with the federal government should always be conducted with the awareness that although published policies may be uniform, their application may not be uniform.

Some of the announced new initiatives for EPA enforcement include enforcement to solve problems in particular geographic areas by using all the environmental statutes administered by EPA to remedy the perceived problem. This approach requires a great deal of coordination but it has been touted by EPA enforcement officials as the best way of addressing certain large environmental problems such as ground water and surface water contamination or hazardous waste sites (i.e., air, land and water). To date, no cases have been brought under this initiative but EPA headquarters and regional officials are continuing to mention the initiative.

Another recent emphasis in federal enforcement is the expanded criminal enforcement program. EPA has added over thirty criminal investigators to its staff and stationed them in the ten EPA regions. Additionally, a memorandum of understanding between EPA and the FBI has been signed that provides FBI time to investigate environmental crimes. Although this program only started in late 1982, already the number of criminal indictments and convictions obtained has increased dramatically. EPA reported that during fiscal year 1984 more indictments and convictions had been obtained than the total of all previous years. This potent enforcement tool is usually applied to egregious cases involving deliberate acts of pollution such as "midnight dumping" of hazardous wastes. However, the potential to use the criminal sanctions against other "knowing" violations of environmental statutes is present.

2.2 State Enforcement 2/

As mentioned before, federal environmental statutes are generally structured to allow delegation of enforcement powers to the state. Further, most environmental statutes also allow states to impose their own requirements so long as they are not less stringent than those imposed by the federal law. Of course, in an area of environmental law in which the federal government has not acted, states are free to pass whatever laws and establish whatever requirements they deem appropriate.

Another manner in which states address environmental problems is to use existing state laws. For example, many states use common law concepts of nuisance, trespass or similar theories to pursue environmental remedies. One extreme example is the use by one midwestern state of traditional murder charges against the owners and operators of a facility that violated toxic substances regulations when such practices allegedly resulted in the death of a worker at the facility.

The general scheme of EPA enforcement has been to delegate enforcement authority to states wherever possible. In some cases states have not sought enforcement authority such as NPDES permitting power. However, most states have enforcement agreements with EPA spelling out the division of enforcement responsibilities. These agreements usually provide some level of federal funding to assist state efforts.

A current concern of many states is that the shrinking federal budget combined with state fiscal constraints will result in less money for environmental enforcement. A lack of federal aid and a shift in state priorities can skew an already complicated state

---

2/   Although this portion of the chapter uses the term "state" it also applies to enforcement actions that may be taken by regional or municipal authorities within a state.

enforcement picture. This means that the difference in enforcement from one state to another can be drastic. This situation complicates matters for businesses that wish to comply with the law but are faced with competition from firms that gain a competitive advantage through avoiding the costs of complying with environmental laws. The reality of the type and level of enforcement that businesses face nationally is a concern to EPA. EPA is taking steps to make enforcement by the states more uniform. These steps include renegotiated enforcement agreements with states, increased monitoring of state efforts and an alleged willingness to take action in situations where states cannot or will not enforce. As laudable as this intent may be, the fiscal and political realities are such that uniform and predictable state enforcement is a goal that will not be reached for a long time.

For example, merely getting states to report environmental actions in a format where these actions can be compared to other states and with federal actions is a project that has been pursued with varying degrees of vigor for over four years. No concrete progress has been made to date. The political concerns of some states that they will lose control over enforcement within their boundaries or that close comparison with EPA or other states will not be favorable does not make progress easy. These pressures, however, are in direct contrast to the pressure from Congress on EPA to demonstrate enforcement results by both EPA and the states. Accordingly, it is too early to say when, if ever, the drive for uniform state enforcement will be declared a success.

The foregoing comments should not be interpreted to mean that states will not take enforcement action. In some states the enforcement posture is more agressive than that of EPA. Some states have more strict laws than EPA, such as the so-called "Superliens" allowed in some states on property to satisfy the costs of hazardous waste clean up. In fact, some states have more enforcement resources to apply within their boundaries than EPA. The point of the foregoing discussion is that enforcement varies considerably from state to state and efforts should be made to determine the enforcement attitude and abilities of a state as well as the written laws on the state's books in evaluating the action likely to be taken by that state.

3.0 Private Enforcement

Private lawsuits can be initiated to require compliance with federal or state environmental laws, to recover damages from alleged injuries or damages suffered because of environmental problems or for both purposes. The initial portion of each discussion under this section of the chapter will be devoted to private actions to enforce compliance with environmental laws and the subsequent discussion will deal with actions seeking damages for personal harm.

3.1 Private Enforcement Under Federal Laws: Citizen Suits

Federal environmental laws are not uniform with respect to allowing private parties to sue to enforce federal requirements. 3/ Each law must be examined to determine the scope of private action allowed.   Generally, most environmental statutes allow private action to require compliance with federal law or regulations after notice is given to EPA, the Department of Justice and the alleged violator. The notice is provided to afford the government an opportunity to take action and to give the alleged violator an opportunity to correct the violative conduct.

Some of the more recent environmental laws have expanded the citizen suit provisions. The Resource Conservation and Recovery Act, for example, now allows citizens to bring suit against an alleged imminent and substantial endangerment, after appropriate notice. Unlike other citizen suit provisions, this type provision does not depend on the issuance of regulations or other criteria against which a violation would be measured. Citizens are allowed to allege the violation and then establish it in court even if EPA does not agree with the reasoning. This is an important point because some citizens may be more strict in their interpretations of the requirements of the law than EPA or the state involved. This type of statutory provision entitles them to take their interpretation directly before a judge and have it approved, rather than having to urge government action or await explanatory regulations that set the criteria under which the citizens would be required to act.

Another of the newer type federal provisions that allows suits by citizens is found in Section 107 of the Comprehensive Environmental Response, Compensation, and Liability Act.   Under this

---

3/ For example, Section 505 of the Federal Water Pollution and Control Act, 33 U.S.C. § 1365; Section 304 of the Clean Air Act, 42 U.S.C. § 7604; Section 7002 of the Resource Conservation and Recovery Act, 42 U.S.C. § 6972; Section 20 of the Toxic Substances Control Act, 15 U.S.C. § 2619; and Section 1449 of the Safe Drinking Water Act, 42 U.S.C. § 300j-8.

provision, citizens who have incurred costs in responding to situations allegedly created by hazardous waste may sue for the recovery of these costs. This is supposed to be a different type of lawsuit than the traditional suit for injuries or damages allegedly suffered. However, although a separate right of action for injuries suffered by private parties was deliberately not included in this law, a broad range of activities in "response" to hazardous waste disposal are allowed. Further, numerous private actions are now being filed that stretch the concept of "costs" to where these costs look very much like traditional damages. It will be up to the courts to finally determine the exact limits of these cost recovery actions.

An additional possibility for private action under federal laws is intervention by private parties in government initiated actions. Although federal environmental laws generally do not allow such intervention as a matter of right, most courts will allow citizens to intervene in environmental actions in which they can demonstrate an interest. This is an important consideration from a litigation standpoint because the presence of more parties can add substantially to the time it takes to reach a settlement or complicate the trial of an enforcement issue.

In many recent cases, a private action under the federal law is added to a more conventional claim for damages in tort under state law to create federal jurisdiction. In some legal actions persons suing believe that there is an advantage to being in a federal, rather than a state court. Several of these claims are now pending in various federal courts and it will take some time before the federal court system provides the answers to what types of claims will be allowed to create federal jurisdiction for otherwise state matters.

3.2 Private Action Under State Laws

Another possibility for private actions is a suit to enforce state environmental laws. Although each state's law is different, some states provide for such "citizen suits" and these are other means by which environmentally related liabilities may be imposed on a business.

Another manner in which private parties "enforce" environmental laws and create liabilities for environmental problems is to sue for damages that they allege they have suffered because of a violation of an environmental law or the alleged failure to act using a proper standard of environmental behavior. These so called "toxic tort" suits are becoming more common. (See Chapter 1.) Their origin is generally attributed to the asbestos suits and the "Agent Orange" litigation. Recent decisions in New Jersey and other of the more liberal states have upheld this type of action involving hazardous waste sites.

The potential problem that these type lawsuits represent is that each hazardous waste site identified by the government will spawn several "toxic tort" suits. Action by governmental bodies will establish the presence of pollutants at a site. Private parties can then take the government's scientific and engineering work and use it to support private suits. Absent the government's involvement at a site, the cost of the scientific and engineering analysis of such problems would be prohibitive for most private parties.

4.0 Individual Liabilities: Your Personal Concerns

A final caution should be supplied with regard to potential liabilities for individuals. Although the bulk of the foregoing discussion addresses concerns of businesses in dealing with environmental requirements, these requirements also have application to individuals. Both federal and state authorities are more frequently bringing charges against individuals as well as businesses. This is occurring in both criminal and civil cases.

There are differing reasons for this increase. In some cases the businesses involved are no longer financially viable so the government is motivated to find someone able to perform the acts sought by the government to solve the environmental problem. In other cases the business structure of an alleged violator is thought to be a device constructed to erroneously shield individuals from personal liability and the government seeks to pierce this "corporate veil." Another reason, although most government agencies will not say so, is that individuals are named in some situations to encourage them to testify as to the acts of the business or others involved in the alleged problem in exchange for better treatment.

Whatever the reason, individuals should be aware of their personal liability in dealing with environmental requirements. In both federal and state cases involving both criminal and civil statutes, individuals are being named with increasing frequency. This means that individuals should take steps to ensure that they are aware of the law's requirements and document their compliance. This is especially important in situations where the question of whether a company did or did not comply with the law turns on an individual's actions. Individuals should also remember that in some cases the defenses for the company and the individual may be at odds.   That is, the business entity may claim that its policies or orders were correct but the individual failed to follow them or that the individual mislead the company.

An individual can take steps to avoid personal liability. Of course, the best steps are to discharge his or her duty so that neither the company nor the individual ever becomes involved in a violation. Because companies run according to many different directions from different sources, a prudent action for an individual is to assure that the individual is aware of company policy and follows it. This at least assures the individual of company protection for his or her acts. However, blind obedience is not protection. An individual must use his or her knowledge and good sense. If an order or policy does not seem to be in conformity with the law, steps should be taken to clarify the situation. In cases of doubt, the best course is to obtain orders in writing and obtain assurances that such orders are in conformity with the law.

Another situation that should be understood by the individual is the company policy on defense of individuals and the extent of the company's insurance coverage for damage actions. Many insurance policies only cover officers and directors of companies but not mid-level managers. The extent to which an individual may want to sign documents certifying compliance or sign reports to government agencies may be dependent on a clear understanding of the company's policies with respect to protection from any liability that may flow from these acts.

This does not mean that every step taken must be documented in writing or that no actions should be taken without a conference. It would be naive to suggest such an approach. Modern corporate structures cannot and should not have to escalate every decision to the highest levels. However, the individual should be aware that in important situations it is best to understand the rules before a problem arises, rather than afterwards. The extent to which an individual may wish to "rock the boat" is a balance between his or her desire to please the employer and his or her desire for peace of mind.

5.0 Recommendations

What does all the foregoing discussion of enforcement mean to most companies? It should demonstrate that actions taken to remedy alleged environmental problems and dealings with federal or state agencies in settling such alleged problems should always be conducted with an awareness of the implications that admissions or actions by the company or findings by the government in such dealings may have for other potential lawsuits or types of environmental liability. No steps should be taken to commit to responsibility for conditions or liability for remedying alleged violations without an awareness of the other potential liabilities that may flow from such actions. This does not mean that responsible environmental conduct is not required. It only means that such conduct should be coordinated throughout any business to ensure that all facets of liability are recognized and prepared for.

In practical terms, this means that those portions of the company that are responsible for compliance with governmental regulations, those portions that are responsible for liability suits and those portions that are responsible for insurance matters must communicate at all times when issues that may be of interest to one another come to their attention. Only through full and informed communication can these portions of a company assure the management of the company that all facets of an action or problem are understood before the company acts upon it.